LIVING HOPE
for the End of Days

365 DAILY DEVOTIONALS
FROM THE BOOK OF REVELATION

DR. JOHN S. BARNETT

FOREWORD BY JOHN MACARTHUR

TULSA

To order a copy of this book write us at:
DTBM
5200 S. YALE SUITE 300
TULSA, OK 74135
or simply email us at:
books@dtbm.org

Living Hope for the End of Days
365 Daily Devotionals from the Book of Revelation | © 2009 by John S. Barnett

Published by Müllerhaus Publishing
5200 South Yale Ave. | Suite 501| Tulsa, OK 74135

All rights reserved. No part of this publication may be reproduced, stored in a retrieval system, or transmitted in any form by any means, electronic, mechanical, photocopy, recording or otherwise, without the prior permission of the publisher, except as provided by USA copyright law.

Cover and Interior Design by
Müllerhaus Publishing Group | **mullerhaus.net**
ISBN 13: 9781933561202
ISBN 10: 1933561203

Second printing, 2009 | Printed in Canada
All Scripture quotations in this book, except those noted otherwise, are from the *New King James Version* of the Bible. Copyright 1979, 1980, 1982, Thomas Nelson, Inc., Publishers.

References marked NASB are from *The New American Standard Bible*, copyright 1960, 1962, 1963, 1968, 1971, 1972, 1973, 1975 and 1977 by the Lockman Foundation and are used by permission.

References marked NIV are from *The Holy Bible: New International Version*, copyright 1973, 1978, 1984 by the International Bible Society. All rights reserved. Used by permission of Zondervan Publishing House. The "NIV" and "New International Version" trademarks are registered in the United States Patent and Trademark Office by International Bible Society. Use of either trademark requires the permission of International Bible Society.

9 8 7 6 5 4 3 2

DEDICATION

This book is gratefully dedicated to:

Melvina Helen Dobias Barnett (my mother)—
who taught me to *read* God's Word;

Robert L. Barnett Sr. (my father)—
who taught me to *study* God's Word;

Dr. Stewart Custer (my seminary professor)—
who taught me to *understand* God's Word;

Dr. Jim Berg (my friend)—
who taught me to *live* God's Word;

Dr. John MacArthur (my mentor)—
who taught me to *preach* God's Word;

Grace Community Church, Quidnessett Baptist Church, Tulsa Bible Church, and Calvary Bible Church (the precious saints of all the congregations we have served)—
who taught me to *communicate* God's Word;

Dr. John Reed (my doctorate sponsor)—
who taught me to *write* about God's Word;

Duke and Ann Weir (our co-laborers in ministry)—
who encouraged me to *publish* this book;

John II, Estelle, James, Julia-Grace, Joseph, Jeremiah, Elisha, and Elisabeth (my precious children)—
who taught me to *explain* God's Word;

Bonnie Marie Brann Barnett (my beloved wife)—
who taught me to *love* God's Word;
And to Him Who alone is worthy of praise,

The Lord Jesus Christ (my Savior)—
Who is teaching me His Word through all of the above and for all my days!

TABLE OF CONTENTS

Foreword, by John MacArthur vii
Overview of the Book of Revelation. xi
Introduction xiii
Week 1: Worship the Christ of Revelation 1
Week 2: Knowing Christ's Presence Today 9
Week 3: Signs That the end of Days Is Near 17
Week 4: Get Ready to Meet Jesus 26
Week 5: Christ Is Our Refuge 33
Week 6: Remember Christ's Blood. 40
Week 7: Find Hope in Christ's Majesty 49
Week 8: Look into Christ's Eyes 59
Week 9: Listen to Christ's Voice 68
Week 10: See Christ's Face and Feel His Touch 77
Week 11: Fear Not! For I Am with You! 86
Week 12: See the Risen Christ at Work 95
Week 13: Hear Christ's Message 104
Week 14: Remember Christ's Jealousy 113
Week 15: Experience Christ's Comfort 123
Week 16: Cling to Christ 132
Week 17: Honor Christ's Holiness 142
Week 18: Know Christ Personally 149
Week 19: Enjoy Christ's Approval 158
Week 20: Heed Christ's Request 167
Week 21: Adore Christ's Loveliness 176
Week 22: See Christ in the Old Testament, Genesis–Daniel 186
Week 23: See Christ in the Old Testament, Hosea–Micah 197
Week 24: See Christ in the Old Testament, Nahum–Malachi 208
Week 25: Admire Christ's Perfect Sacrifice 217
Week 26: Understand Christ's Wrath 226
Week 27: Remember Christ's Love 235
Week 28: See Christ's Patience 244
Week 29: Watch Christ's Judgment 255
Week 30: Behold the Mystery of Jesus 265
Week 31: Remember God's Plan of the Ages 278

Week 32: Keep Christ's Perspective 291
Week 33: Marvel at the Genuine Jesus 301
Week 34: Feel the Compassion of Jesus 314
Week 35: Meditate on the Beauty of Jesus 326
Week 36: Rejoice That You Have Christ 338
Week 37: Understand the True Bride of Jesus 348
Week 38: Live for What Is Eternal 360
Week 39: Give All to God 373
Week 40: Giving God What Is His 382
Week 41: Living Contentedly for Christ 392
Week 42: Look for the Returning Jesus 403
Week 43: Rest in the Vengeance of Jesus 414
Week 44: Look for Paradise on Earth 423
Week 45: Fear the Holiness of Jesus 434
Week 46: Taste the Joys of Heaven 446
Week 47: Discover Our Marriage to Jesus 457
Week 48: Behold the Wonders of Jesus 468
Week 49: Fall in Love with Jesus All Over Again 478
Week 50: Experience Jesus Often 487
Week 51: The First Coming of Jesus 496
Week 52: Wise Men Still Seek the King! 507
Endnotes 519

FOREWORD

No book in Scripture reveals the glory of God and Christ in more splendor than does the Book of Revelation. Yet no book has been more misunderstood, misinterpreted, and neglected than this book. At the end of the book, Revelation 22:10 says, "Do not seal up the words of the prophecy of this book, for the time is near." Clearly, God wants His children to know what this book teaches, so that they can appropriate its truth to their lives.

Those who read Revelation and heed its message will be greatly blessed. In fact, it is the only book in the New Testament that begins and ends with a promise of blessing to its readers. In Revelation 1:3, we find, "Blessed is he who reads and those who hear the words of this prophecy, and keep those things which are written in it." And at the end of the book, a similar promise is given: "Blessed is he who heeds the words of the prophecy of this book" (22:7). Those who ignore Revelation deprive themselves of a rich treasure of divine truth, and the promised blessings that come from understanding that truth.

Far from being the mysterious, incomprehensible book many imagine it to be, Revelation's purpose is to reveal truth, not to obscure it. That fact is evident in its title, "The Revelation of Jesus Christ," which primarily refers to our Lord's second-coming glory. The Greek word for *revelation* could also be translated "an uncovering," "an unveiling," or "a disclosure." It is used in the New Testament to speak of the disclosure of spiritual truth (Romans 16:25; Galatians 1:12; Ephesians 1:17; 3:3), the manifestation of the sons of God (Romans 8:19), and the advent of Christ at both His first (Luke 2:32) and second (2 Thessalonians 1:7; 1 Peter 1:7) comings. In each case, the word *revelation* describes something (or someone) that was formerly hidden, but has now become visible. Thus the Book of Revelation unveils truths about Jesus Christ and His final victory, which were alluded to but not fully disclosed in earlier portions of Scripture.

Because this book is first and foremost about Jesus Christ, its focus is inherently devotional. The book depicts Christ as the risen, glorified Son of God ministering among the churches (1:10ff.) as "the faithful witness, the firstborn from the dead, and the ruler over the kings of the earth" (1:5), as "the Alpha and Omega, the Beginning and the End" (1:8), as the One "who is and who was and who is to come, the Almighty" (1:8), as "the First and the Last" (1:11), as "the Son of Man" (1:13), as the one "who was dead, [but now is . . . alive forevermore" (1:18), as "the Son of God" (2:18), as the One "who is holy [and] . . . true" (3:7), as "the Amen, the Faithful and True Witness, the Beginning of the creation of God" (3:14), as "the Lion of the tribe of Judah" (5:5), as the Lamb in heaven, with authority to open the title deed to the earth (6:1ff.), as the Lamb on the throne (7:17), as the Messiah who will reign forever (11:15), as "The Word of God" (19:13), as the majestic King of kings and Lord of lords, returning in glorious splendor to conquer His foes (19:11ff.), and as "the Root and the Offspring of David, the Bright and Morning Star" (22:16). Because of its Christ-centered focus, the

Book of Revelation fuels worship, motivates holiness, and cultivates hope, which is why its message is so desperately needed today.

In *Living Hope for the End of Days*, John Barnett has made the Book of Revelation accessible to anyone, casting it in a wonderful, manageable set of daily devotions. These devotions will do far more than merely pique your curiosity about the book's remarkable imagery. They will serve to enrich both your worship and your walk by prompting you to focus on the central figure of Revelation, Christ Himself. So dig in on a regular basis to this mighty treasury that exalts the glory of our Lord.

—John MacArthur

SPECIAL THANKS . . .

To my Bonnie who typed day and night, edited countless versions, captured all of my thoughts onto paper, and stayed with me through the long wait to finally get all of this into a book;

To dear Duke and Ann Weir for inspiring and encouraging us to actually sit down and write a book—we could not have done it without them;

To faithful and dedicated Doreen Claggett for working on this with us from the earliest days by all her prayers and countless hours of editing;

To our army of faithful volunteers who edited, typed, transcribed, and helped with this book through all its stages: Phil Smith, Jama Raubach, Phil Martin, Renee Gilligan, Julie Wright, Susan Randall, Doris Clatfelter, Marlene Bolton, Jack Bowman, Janice Connors, Charlotte Driver, Becky Faught, Jeff Ferguson, Gatra Miller, Rebecca Hattaway, Don Laidley, Kathy McLandsborough, Gary Nelson, Marcia Reeves, Dave Scott, Mark Turrell, and Jack Babbitt;

To Jim Kelley for transcribing all of these messages;

And finally, to the precious elders and saints at Tulsa Bible Church who so responsively listened, so fervently prayed, and so graciously received these words as my weekly exhortations from the pulpit.

AN OVERVIEW OF THE BOOK OF REVELATION

In Revelation 1, find living hope for the end of days in the majesty of Jesus as He is today. Feel the Apostle John's lonely, forsaken, and painful exile on Patmos. See how his face-to-face meeting with the risen Christ breathes hope into his life—and ours. What Christ did, He still does. What John needed, we still need. What Jesus said, we still hear. Feel hope in Christ!

In Revelation 2 and 3, find living hope for the end of days in the message Jesus gives to us. Listen across the pages of history as Christ's messages to the seven churches of Asia Minor whisper words of hope as we face similar struggles. Although our struggles may be in different forms, God's words of hope still apply. Listen to His Word!

In Revelation 4 and 5, find living hope for the end of days in the worship of Jesus that we share today. Worship is the atmosphere of heaven. The throne of God is the center of the universe. The saints who step into eternity soon kneel at Christ's feet. Get in step with God; join the saints and angels, and feel the majesty of worshiping the Lamb. Worship as you kneel before him!

In Revelation 6–9, 16, and 19, find living hope for the end of days in the return of the real king, Jesus. Watch as the long-withheld wrath of God breaks out. Sin is judged. Mankind is decimated. Civilizations vanish. Imprisoned monsters run wild. Evil goes unrestrained. And then Christ comes—His eyes ablaze, His Words unleashed, and His feet once again standing on earth. Watch for Christ's return!

In Revelation 10–15, find living hope for the end of days in the mysteries Jesus reveals. Ponder the mysteries of God's plan in conquering evil and taking back the Father's world. Countering every nefarious attack of that old serpent, Satan, Christ's truth is unleashed. Nothing surprises Christ. Nothing impedes Jesus. Nothing limits His perfect plan. Whatever life brings, God is providentially weaving His good handiwork into the fabric of our lives. Ponder God's mysteries!

In Revelation 17, find living hope for the end of days in meeting the true bride Christ calls out. Remember that we who love Jesus are also engaged to be marries to Him. In this chapter we see the stark contrast between the false harlot of religion and the true bride of faith in Christ. As deceptions about, as false teachings multiply, and as religion replaces the revelation from God through His Word, nothing is more vital than the truth. Remember the truth!

In Revelation 18, find living hope for the end of days in the true riches Christ gives. Measure your truth wealth by what you have invested in heaven. As Christ reveals the coming meltdown of human civilization, He shows us that our real worth is found in what remains after losing our health, wealth, prosperity, possessions, and power. We must be sure that we are invested in the "stocks" that we know will survive the collapse. Measure true wealth!

In Revelation 20–22, find living hope for the end of days in the mansions Jesus has prepared for us. Wait until you see what God has planned for us! It is out of this world! The curse is restrained. Sinners are eternally judged. And heaven's gates are finally opened. These concluding chapters in Revelation embody every promise God has made. For the answer to the problems of mankind, the end of suffering, and the joys of heaven, here is God's final Word. Wait with hope!

INTRODUCTION

Almost daily we face the warning signs of sin's rampage through the human race, and there are days when life is indeed gloomy! When Paul foresaw life at the end of time, he warned us that it was going to be bad. Listen to his sobering words across the centuries:

In the last days perilous times will come: for men will be lovers of themselves, lovers of money, boasters, proud, blasphemers, disobedient to parents, unthankful, unholy, unloving, unforgiving, slanderers, without self-control, brutal, despisers of good, traitors, headstrong, haughty, lovers of pleasure rather than lovers of God, having a form of godliness but denying its power. And from such people turn away! (2 Timothy 3:1–5).

Once we get into eschatological things (things related to the end of the world or the events associated with it), we are in the part of the Bible in which we should not be dogmatic. Rather, it should cause us to study even further, and have forbearance with differing opinions. The greatest Christian minds of all time have studied the future. The more I read their commentaries, the less I see of total agreement and the more I see of wondrous diversity.

On this one point, however, we can all agree: the Revelation of Jesus Christ, the very last book of God's Word to mankind, describes the final chapter in human history. It is in that book that we see Christ Jesus as the fulfillment of every promise that God has ever made.

In Revelation, the apostle John has recorded God's message, which is the greatest deposit of hope in the Bible. In the 404 verses of its twenty-two chapter we find

Hope for the end of days.

Strength for when we are weak with fear.

Joy when surrounded by dread.

Purpose in the midst of an aimless culture.

Peace when storms of anxiety roll across our horizons.

Through this book, *Living Hope for the End of Days*, we have fifty-two weeks to learn how to live in hope, strength, joy, purpose, and peace! As you read through this entire book, you will discover the precious topics contained in Revelation, each of them rich in hope. And, as you read every word of God's final book of the Bible, you will reap a harvest of promised blessings!

John Barnett
Tulsa, Oklahoma
October 2006

WEEK 1
Worship the Christ of Revelation

{ Revelation 1:1 }

As the end of days approaches, you can find hope as you continually worship Christ anew and afresh through His wonderful names in Revelation!

SUNDAY: Worship the Ever-Present Christ!

The Revelation of Jesus Christ, which God gave Him to show His servants—things which must shortly take place. And He sent and signified it by His angel to His servant John.
—REVELATION 1:1

In the latter part of the first century, in the azure green of the Aegean Sea off the coast of Turkey was a barren island, a Roman penal colony, a rock quarry that cut stones for imperial temples and buildings. A boat carrying John, the last apostle, made its way to that colony island. John, as the final living member of Christ's inner circle, was considered to be the last of the empire's greatest enemies.

When John reached that prison island, he was perhaps eighty years old. Wizened and stooping, gray and halting, and scarred by the fight, he was still forced to work in the rock quarries. Every day, while he worked in those quarries, he had plenty of opportunities to meditate on what Jesus had done while he walked with Him and during his own sixty years of ministry.

As storms blew in over the Aegean Sea, I am confident that he found great peace remembering Jesus' power to still howling winds as He did when the disciples were in the boat on the stormy Sea of Galilee. Jesus spoke authoritatively to the wind and waves, and both immediately became calm, as did His disciples. Whenever John saw withered vegetation on Patmos, he thought about the time Jesus caused the fig tree to wither. When he saw prisoners die, John meditated on Jesus' power to touch dead bodies and bring them back to life. He recalled personally seeing the widow at Nain sobbing as her son's coffin was being taken out to the burial place. But then Jesus walked out and intercepted the crowd, and when He touched the coffin, the boy sat up. John was also there when Jesus raised Lazarus from the dead. So on and on, the Holy Spirit prompted precious memories of the One who loved him so!

No matter where John was, he was near his beloved and ever-present Lord Jesus Christ. When he "looked full in His wonderful face, the things of earth grew strangely dim in the light of His glory and grace." And John's heart, overwhelmed with joy, worshiped!

You and I have the same opportunity to worship the ever-present Christ, but we get to see more of Him than John saw. Having written just one of the four Gospels, John did not personally witness what Matthew, Mark, and Luke reported. But we have *all the Gospels* through which to see Christ, so we have an abundance of precious moments of Christ's power to meditate upon. This same ever-present Christ is with us at home, at school, at work, at play, or wherever we may be! What a thought! I wonder: *Do you purposefully look for evidence of Christ's presence throughout your day and talk about it over dinner?* I hope so!

Like a landmark, Jesus will never be out of sight for us. Consider this illustration: When I was a child, I went on camping expeditions that my father used to lead. We fished and canoed on the great Canadian lakes. We camped in a wilderness area; there were no homes along the lakeshore, no boathouses, no towers, or other man-made landmarks to help us find our way. So we picked out a particular landmark, such as a rock outcropping or a fallen tree along the shore. Then we always stayed in sight of it so that we could find our way back to camp. Like a physical landmark that helps us keep our bearings, Jesus is always in sight.

The next time you feel alone, abandoned, desolate, or useless, remember that just as Jesus was never out of sight for John, He will never be out of sight for you—ever!

Now please join with me in spirit as you read the following prayer for the week ahead. May its words, as well as the others throughout *Living Hope*, sink deep within your heart and soul so that our spirits blend together as one voice before the throne of God.

My Prayer for You This Week: *Father, we thank You that we can very appropriately end our journey through the Word with this wonderful unveiling of Jesus in Revelation, which is a priceless gift. We can think of no higher honor, no greater privilege, and no more solemn responsibility than to come before Your presence. We come humbly, asking You to clothe us with humility. We come reverently, asking You to cleanse and purge us from any of the leaven of sin that always seeks to attach itself to us. We come rejoicing, for the blood of Jesus Christ, unmerited by us, is Your favor upon us. We thank You for His cleansing. We come worshipfully, asking that You would accept the upraised hearts that we offer to You today. We come overflowing with joy, for we know that we are redeemed, and we are persuaded that You, our Redeemer, can keep us unto that day when we sit at Your table in heaven. We pray that every part of our study of this precious book of Revelation will have Your favor upon it. Meet with us in a very special, transforming, and glorifying way in our lives, so that we will know that surely we have been with Jesus, in whose name we ask all this. Amen.*

MONDAY: Behold Your God!

*"And Thomas answered and said to Him, '**My Lord and my God!**' "*
—JOHN 20:28

William Temple (1881–1944), the Archbishop of Canterbury from 1942 to 1944, defined worship as follows: "To worship is to quicken the conscience by the holiness of God, to feed the mind with the truth of God, to purge the imagination by the beauty of God, to open the heart to the love of God, to devote the will to the purpose of God."[1]

If there is no worship, there is no change in the life. Worship is the submission of all our nature to God. How? **Quickening** of our conscience by His holiness—being renewed through the life and power of our endless life in Christ; **nourishment** of mind by His truth; **purification** of imagination by His beauty; **openness** of our hearts by His love; **submission** of our wills to His purpose. All of this gathered together in adoration is the greatest of all expressions of which we are capable.

One clear way God invites our worship is by revealing Himself through His divine names. Since Revelation is a revelation of Jesus and His person, its twenty-two chapters are a gold mine as the Lord unveils His deity through more than sixty-seven names and titles. The greatest insight into adoring the Lord comes by way of His names and titles in His Word. They are real treasures to find!

Chapter 1: He is the Faithful Witness, the Firstborn from the Dead, Ruler over the Kings of the Earth, the Alpha and the Omega, the Beginning and the End, the Almighty, the First and the Last, the Son of Man, the Living One!

Chapter 2: He is the administrator of the church who has the sharp two-edged sword, eyes like a flame of fire, and feet like fine brass!

Chapter 3: He is the One who has the seven Spirits of God and the seven stars, who is holy and true, who has the key of David, who is the Amen, the Faithful and True Witness, the Beginning of the Creation of God!

Chapter 4: He is the One who sits on the throne in heaven!

Chapter 5: He is the Lion of the tribe of Judah, the Root of David, and the Lamb who was slain—who lives forever and ever!

Chapter 6: He is the wrathful Lamb!

Chapter 7: He is the redeeming Lamb and the providing Lamb!

Chapter 8: He is the patient collector of our prayers!

Chapter 9: He holds back the monsters from the abyss!

Chapter 10: He is the Creator of heaven and earth and sea!

Chapter 11: He is Christ, the Lord God Almighty!

Chapter 12: He is the Christ, the Lamb, Jesus!

Chapter 13: He is the Lamb, whose is the Book of Life!

Chapter 14: He is the Lamb on Mount Zion, Jesus, the Lord, the Son of Man!

Chapter 15: He is again the Lamb, the Lord God Almighty, the King of Saints, the Lord!

Chapter 16: He is the One Who was and is and is to be, the Lord God Almighty!

Chapter 17: He is Jesus, the Lamb—Lord of Lords and King of Kings!

Chapter 18: He is the Lord God!

Chapter 19: He is the Lord our God, the Lord God, the Lamb, Jesus, the Faithful and True, the Word of God, Almighty God, King of Kings and Lord of Lords!

Chapter 20: He is Jesus, the Christ!

Chapter 21: He is the Alpha and Omega, the Lamb, the Lord God Almighty!

Chapter 22: He is the Lamb, the Lord God, the Alpha and Omega, the Beginning and the End, the First and the Last, Jesus, the Root and Offspring of David, the Bright and Morning Star, the Lord Jesus—*our* Lord Jesus!

Worship Christ in His majesty—worship Him in all His glorious names! Nothing can possibly come into your life that the all-powerful, all-knowing, and ever-present Christ didn't know about long before it happened. As Creator, He made you as you are; he picked your family, limitations and all. The Lamb has paid the price for sin. And the Lamb is the only One who has the reservation book, the Book of Life, which is the key to enter into the paradise He has prepared for His bride. Have you made your reservation? Is your name written there? Are you in touch with Him to prepare for what is ahead?

Are you worshiping the manufacturer and owner of your life in grateful awe that He knows and cares for you?

TUESDAY: The Bible—God's Worship Guide

*__Let the word__ of Christ richly **dwell within you**, with all wisdom teaching and admonishing one another with psalms and hymns and spiritual songs, singing with thankfulness in your hearts to God.*

—Colossians 3:16 NASB

Could I challenge you? For a wonderful worship experience in Revelation, search for all the names and titles of God the Father, God the Son, and God the Holy Spirit. Over the next few weeks, begin your search by looking, chapter by chapter, for the names and titles of Christ in Revelation. Use markers, colored pencils, or pens to mark each one in a special way that will help you remember where you found them. As you mark each one, ask yourself the "So what?" question: "So what does Jesus as the _____ (fill in a name or title) mean in my life for today?"

Learn to practice noticing God's presence during each day. Worship ought to become a daily habit: Pray without ceasing (1 Thessalonians 5:17). Punctuate every moment with inward whisperings of adoration, praise, and thanksgiving: "Evening and morning and at noon I will pray, and cry aloud, and He shall hear my voice" (Psalm 55:17).

To heighten your preparation for public worship, be sure to have personal times of inner worship, confession, Bible study, and attentiveness to Christ, your present teacher: "This Book of the Law shall not depart from your mouth, but you shall meditate in it that you may do all that is written in it. For then you will make your way prosperous, and have good success" (Joshua 1:8).

Learn to worship God in many different settings of worship. Worship God when you are alone. Have home groups not only for Bible study but also for the very experience of worship itself. Gather in little groups of two and three to learn to offer up a sacrifice of praise. Many blessings can occur in smaller gatherings that, just by sheer size, cannot happen in the larger experience. These little experiences of worship will empower and impact your larger Sunday gatherings as well.

Determine to prepare for the gathering of the church for worship. On Saturday night, prepare by having an inward examination and confession prior to going to bed early. On Sunday morning, before the actual worship service, go over the hymns and Scripture passages that will be used that day. Then pray that God will fill the sanctuary with His presence.

You can have one of the most vital ministries at your church by arriving ten to fifteen minutes early and sitting, with your Bible open, in the worship center. Pray that the Holy Spirit will empower those who will minister during the service: the instrumentalists, the orchestra, the choir, the soloists, the worship leaders, and the one who ministers the Word. Let go of all inner distractions so that you can really participate in the worship service.

If you do these things faithfully, you will be well on the way to growing in your ability to worship!

WEDNESDAY: Cultivate a Life of Worship

*Having risen a long while before daylight, He went out and **departed to a solitary place**; and there He prayed.*

— MARK 1:35

Listen to what one man who spent years meditating on worship has written: "Worship is something we do. Studying the theology of worship and debating the forms of worship are all good, but by themselves they are inadequate. In the final analysis we learn to worship by worshiping."[2]

Willingly offer yourself to the Lord as an instrument for worship. As an individual, learn to let go of your agenda, your concerns, your being blessed, and your hearing of the Word of God. The language of the gathered fellowship is not "I," but "we." So surrender to the ways of God; submit to others in the Christian fellowship; desire that God's Spirit will rise up in the group, not just within you as an individual. Seek to become of one mind, of one accord. Cultivate a life of complete spiritual dependency. Dependency means that you will be completely dependent upon God for anything significant to happen. The work is God's and not yours. A simple way to start this is to pray before doing anything; invite the Lord's presence, blessing, and guidance. Then give Him all the credit for anything good that happens.

Guard yourself from exposure to harmful influences that will kill worship. Cultivating worship also involves dealing with all the weeds that grow and choke the growth of your crop, as well as the pests that try to steal the harvest. For example, some of us are in the high-risk category for skin cancer. So what should we do? We should stay away from exposure to those deadly UV rays. Since all of us are prone to soul cancer that eats away at our worship, we should avoid having a lot of exposure to TV rays because they distract, deaden, and deflate the welling up of our souls in worship to God! If you cannot fast from TV, newspapers, and magazines for even a week, then you are a very *weak* Christian, and at risk spiritually.

Part of learning to cultivate worship is learning how to drown out distractions through prayers of gratefulness to God. For example, when I am preaching, I love to have babies and little children in the congregation. Rather than feeling that distractions somehow deter us from worshiping God, we should learn to simply receive whatever happens in a gathered worship experience. This applies to whatever happens at home or other places of private worship, as God tests our spirit. Grumbling and complaining cannot be successfully partnered with a spirit of adoration and worship!

THURSDAY: The Fruits of Worship

> *Let us continually offer the sacrifice of praise to God, that is,*
> *the fruit of our lips giving thanks to His name.*
> — Hebrews 13:15

Did you know that there will be many times that you will not "feel" like worshiping? Perhaps you have had so many disappointing experiences in the past that you think it is hardly worth it because there is such a low sense of the power of God. Even so, you still need to offer the sacrifice of worship to God.

The sacrifice of worship gets offered to God himself. It is vital that you join other saints to amplify your worship. When we are gathered for genuine worship, we are like a heap of burning coals encouraging one another to warmth of love and devotion. One log by itself cannot burn for very long, but when many logs are put together, even if they are poor logs, they can make quite a fire. Remember the counsel of Proverbs 27:17 that "iron sharpens iron." Even rather dull lives can help each other if they are willing to try.

Go to church—even if you do not feel like it.
Go to church—even if worship has been discouraging and dry before.
Go to church—praying.
Go to church—expecting.
Go to church—looking for God to do a new and living work among you as His family.

The sacrifice of worship deepens repentance. Resentments cannot be held with the same tenacity when we enter His gracious light. As Jesus says, if we have broken fellowship with another person, we need to leave our gift at the altar and go set the matter straight. Christ is very explicit about this: "If you bring your gift to the altar, and there remember that your brother has something against you, be reconciled to your brother, and then come and offer your gift" (Matthew 5:23–24). In worship, an increased power steals its way into the heart sanctuary and an increased compassion grows in the soul.

The sacrifice of worship bears the fruit of obedience. Just as worship begins in holy expectancy, it ends in holy obedience. If worship does not propel us into greater obedience, it has not been worship. To stand before the Holy One of eternity is to change: "Rejoice in Christ Jesus, and have no confidence in the flesh" (Philippians 3:3).

The sacrifice of worship widens our ministry. Holy Spirit–prompted ministry saves worship from becoming an escape from the pressing needs of the real people around us. Worship enables us to hear the call to service clearly so that we respond like Isaiah. When Isaiah had the vision of our majestic, holy, and righteous God sitting on His throne, full of all His glory, he was instantly brought to his knees with a sense of his total unworthiness (see Isaiah 6:1–8). He was humbled; there was no more room for pride. His worship of the Most High God produced repentance, obedience, and finally, ministry, as he cried out, "Here I am, Lord! Send me!" Though still very conscious of his sin, he had been prepared to serve anywhere, anytime, anyhow, or anyway God directed because he was completely submitted to God's will.

How would you evaluate your worship? Are you sensing that God is preparing you to serve anywhere, anytime, anyhow, or anyway as He directs? Are you willing to submit to that will?

FRIDAY: Worship — Then Serve Christ

> *Then Jesus said to him, "Away with you, Satan! For it is written, 'You **shall worship the Lord your God, and Him only you shall serve.**'"*
>
> — Matthew 4:10

Worship is the most vital and life-changing topic of the whole Bible. When Jesus was alone in the wilderness (except for the Devil's presence), He stated His extremely important mandate for serving God. In Matthew 4:10, Jesus gave this order: "Away with you, Satan!" (10a). Then He quoted a verse from His memory arsenal of the Word of God: " 'You shall **worship** the Lord your God, and Him only you shall **serve**' " (Matthew 4:10b).

Did you fully grasp what is supposed to come *before* service? Worship! This is God's order. All service for Him is to flow out of worship. No worship, no service. As a child, if I did not wash my hands, I did not get to eat. But when I got a little older, my credo became this: "No Bible, no breakfast; no Bible, no bed." The Lord's rule is this: "No worship, no service."

Does ministry ever get dull, tedious, and wearying? If so, that is a warning sign that the oil of worship is running low. Worship must always come before service. When the worship wanes, service becomes a drag because the Holy Spirit does not energize it.

We start worshiping God at the moment of our salvation for "we are the true circumcision" (Philippians 3:3 NASB). In this verse, the apostle Paul is talking about the Judaizers who were not followers of Christ. He described them in Philippians 3:2: "Beware of dogs, beware of evil workers, beware of the mutilation!" These are the people who believed in an external form of salvation, or "salvation by surgery." They believed that if you are circumcised, you are going to heaven. This is the same as believing that if you are baptized or join the church or "walk an aisle" that you will go to heaven.

Baptism, joining a church, or "walking an aisle" are all external things. But God is after an internal heart belief. Therefore, He says that the only people who will go to heaven are those "who worship in the Spirit of God and glory in Christ Jesus and put no confidence in the flesh" (Philippians 3:2–3 NASB).

Do not count on what *you* have done, but on what *Christ* has accomplished. If you are born again, you are One who has been transformed from the inside out. God transforms us to be genuine worshipers when we are saved. We can then worship in the Spirit of God, and glory in Christ Jesus, because of no longer having confidence in our own flesh.

Do you see why worship must come before service? Much service can be done in the power of the flesh, but only the Holy Spirit energizes true worship. Worshiping God is the most marvelous, encouraging, strengthening, and uplifting thing we can do!

SATURDAY: Worship Christ through Your Service

For we are the circumcision, **who worship God** *in the Spirit, rejoice in Christ Jesus, and* **have no confidence in the flesh.**
— PHILIPPIANS 3:3

Even our very acts of ministry should be acts of worship that reveal His "worthship," or just how much Christ is worth to us! Motivation is everything; only what is done out of adoration for Christ and love for others will last. We can have such a ministry, serving Jesus in any place, at any time, in any way, and anyhow we are—no matter what is going on in our lives. That is a wonderful way to live!

We can serve Christ in any place. John was isolated on Patmos, far from his home in Galilee, far from the church, far from anyone but God. And yet where was he when Jesus Christ came to reveal himself to him? Revelation 1:10a says, "I was in the Spirit on the Lord's Day." He was serving God right where he was.

Even though his captors tried to restrict John from witnessing, doing church work, and preaching, he grabbed every opportunity to talk about the Word and all that Christ had done. If we are God's servants we will likewise be talking about the Word, and telling others what Christ is doing in our lives.

We can serve Christ at any time. John was at least eighty years old and near death. He had not seen Jesus for sixty years. Everything had been taken away from him—his scrolls, books, church, freedom, and health—for he had to sleep in a cave. John, however, did not let that defeat him; he still served Christ to the best of his ability.

There are no limits to what God can do through us, no matter what age we happen to be. Even a young child can serve Christ. For example, as a young boy, David served the Lord and meditated on Him. The seeds of all the great psalms were planted back in his boyhood days when he was still a shepherd. God says that we can serve Him at any age in life. That is a comforting thought! There is no mandatory retirement from serving the Lord.

We can serve Christ in any way. We can still serve God regardless of where we are, what is taken away from us, or how hard the times might be. John chose to serve the Lord any way he could, and what he loved to do most was worship Christ.

We can serve Christ no matter how we are. We can serve Christ in any condition in which we find ourselves, even when we are suffering. John was suffering loneliness, pain, discouragement, deprivation, and abuse. Most of all, on this pagan island with the soldiers who worshiped false gods, John was suffering spiritual oppression. Because John was in the forefront in fighting the kingdom of darkness, Satan especially attacked him.

Make a choice to live in hope. You can decide today to emulate John's attitude by asking God to give you this spirit:

> It does not matter where I am: I am going to serve Christ in any place. It does not matter how old I am: I am going to serve Christ at any time of life, even at the very end. It does not matter what my circumstances are: I am going to serve Christ in any way I can, no matter what they take out of my life. It does not matter how I am, even if I am suffering: I am going to serve Christ anyhow. This is my way to worship the glorious ever-present Christ—to show Him just how much He's worth to me!

If your heart's desire is to serve the Lord in this manner, I encourage you to bow your head and humbly ask Him to use you anywhere you go, and at any time He wants to—and He will. Like Isaiah, tell Him, "Here I am, Lord! Send me!"

WEEK 2
Knowing Christ's Presence Today

{ Revelation 1:2 }

As the end of days approaches, you can find genuine and lasting hope by knowing Christ's presence!

SUNDAY: Know That Christ Is Alive

*[John] bore witness to the word of God, and to the testimony of Jesus Christ, and to all things **that he saw**.*
— REVELATION 1:2

John saw Jesus on Patmos—alive and powerful. The book of Revelation introduces us to the risen Christ of the Gospels and shows Him as the real Christ. When Jesus stepped from the tomb on Resurrection morning, God unleashed the greatest power of all. And that is what Jesus Christ is like TODAY!

Often we fail to understand the magnitude of what really happened that morning. After His Resurrection, something had wondrously changed: Jesus *no longer limited himself to one location*. From the manger to the cross, He had been limited for thirty-three years to being *in only one place at a time*. Jesus had humbled himself, emptied himself, and limited himself to being localized. But now He was accessible anywhere, anytime, and to anyone! His power was then available everywhere, and all the time! That is absolutely amazing!

Even in His condition of being localized, Jesus accomplished more than any human ever has or will. He grew up perfectly, mastered God's Word perfectly, and related to His family, friends, and neighbors perfectly for thirty years.

At the dawn of Jesus' public ministry, He perfectly obeyed God at His baptism; He perfectly defeated Satan's advances in the wilderness; and He perfectly began to serve God's will as He set out as an itinerant preacher.

For three and one-half years Jesus awesomely served in the power of God. Wherever He went, Christ's very presence made death flee, disease fade, and despair melt. Broken bodies that came in contact with Jesus were mended; ruined lives were repaired; sightless eyes were restored; deaf ears were filled with sound; missing fingers were returned; and hungering lives were satisfied. And Jesus did all that while being *in one place at a time.*

Christ is alive! After the Resurrection, because Jesus was no longer trapped by time and space, He seemed to be everywhere at once. The New Testament records Jesus crisscrossing the tiny land of Israel from north to south over the next forty days.

We find him on mountaintops, back roads, inside locked rooms, on the shore, and everywhere else that He was looked for or needed. He met with the grieving women at the tomb, comforted the sorrowing Mary, calmed the frightened disciples (inside the locked room without opening the door), showed up at dawn on the shores of the Sea of Galilee, confronted and restored a soaking-wet Peter, assured a doubtful, trembling Thomas, and visited with every one of the five hundred others who had believed on Him.

Jesus accomplished all that in an occupied country crawling with spies, soldiers, and religious leaders filled with hatred. And for forty days after the empty tomb, He was never seen, even once, by any unloving eyes; He was never touched, even once, by unloving hands. Christ's presence was unstoppably available—everywhere. And He's the same today!

For the previous three and one-half years, Jesus' followers could have any need met— *if they could find Him*. But now, because of the cross and empty tomb, He is available anywhere, anytime, and to anyone. Therefore, any sin can be forgiven; any doubt can be overcome; any sadness can be comforted; any disappointment can be stopped; any fearfulness can be arrested; any loneliness can be ended; and any defilement can be cleansed.

Today, know that Christ is alive! So think about Christ being constantly available within you to help your fears, doubts, pains, and temptations. He is only a prayer away—so call upon Him!

My Prayer for You This Week: *Father, I pray that "Christ being constantly available within" will become more than just simple words to us. Today, as we contemplate Resurrection morning—the greatest event of all time—may we know that the One who left the tomb that day is present with us even now. For You are everywhere, all the time, for anyone who wants to know You. For those who do not yet know You personally, we pray that they would cry out to You from their heart of hearts and say, "Oh God, be merciful to me, a sinner!" May they come to know true faith in You, Lord Jesus. We thank You for all that You do because You are no longer limited to being in one place at one time, but are with us everywhere! In the name of Jesus, we thank You. Amen.*

MONDAY: Know What Christ Did

That which we have seen and heard we declare to you, that you also may have fellowship with us; and truly our fellowship is with the Father and with His Son Jesus Christ.
— 1 John 1:3

The greatest power unleashed in Jesus is that He is now available anywhere, anytime, and to anyone. In fact, look at all the chapters in the gospel by John where Jesus was meeting people right where they were—just as He does today:

- Watching Nathaniel sit and think under a tree, Jesus answered his questions (1:46–49). The Lesson: **You can bring your questions to Jesus.**
- Attending a wedding, Jesus rescued the servants when the wine ran out (2:9). The Lesson: **You can bring your emergencies to Jesus.**
- Waiting up, Jesus explained salvation to Nicodemus when he slipped to Christ's side in the dark (3:2). The Lesson: **You can bring your struggles to Jesus.**
- Sitting on the well, Jesus revealed His true identity to a seeking woman overflowing with sins (4:18–19). The Lesson: **You can bring your sins to Jesus.**
- Approaching the paralytic lying on the ground, Jesus healed him when he was hopeless and helpless (5:6). The Lesson: **You can bring your limitations to Jesus.**
- Coming across the waves to a storm-tossed boat, Jesus quieted the fearful disciples (6:17–19). The Lesson: **You can bring your fears to Jesus.**
- Crying out for anyone who thirsts to come to Him, Jesus promised to give "rivers of living water" (7:37–38). The Lesson: **You can bring your longings to Jesus.**
- Looking into the heart of the adulterous woman who stood stained by her sins, Jesus showed her mercy and forgiveness (8:3–11). The Lesson: **You can bring your deepest stains to Jesus.**
- Finding the blind man in his darkness, Jesus opened his eyes (9:6–7). The Lesson: **You can bring your confusing times to Jesus.**
- Opening the door to a safe and secure home for lost sheep, Jesus offered safe pasture (10:9). The Lesson: **You can bring your longing for security to Jesus.**
- Defeating death and its hopelessness at the grave of Lazarus, Jesus offered new life (11:25–27). The Lesson: **You can bring your fears about death to Jesus.**
- Accepting the worship of Mary who loved Him so, Jesus received it as a sweet fragrance (12:3–8). The Lesson: **You can bring your love to Jesus.**
- Confronting His disciples with their dirty feet and hearts filled with pride, Jesus washed away their sin (13:5–15). The Lesson: **You can bring your besetting sins to Jesus.**
- Assuring His disciples when they had troubled hearts, Jesus promised that they had a future mansion with Him in heaven (14:1–6). The Lesson: **You can bring your future to Jesus.**
- Coming close to prune away unprofitable parts when lives were fruitless, Jesus caused that pruning to bear fruit (15:2). The Lesson: **You can bring all of your life to Jesus.**

- Promising to convict when hearts were sinful, Jesus sent the Holy Spirit to keep His children on track spiritually (16:7–9). The Lesson: **You can bring your secrets to Jesus**.
- Praying for sanctification by the truth of His Word, Jesus promised to open His children's understanding of the Scriptures (17:17). The Lesson: **You can bring your Bible-study times to Jesus**.
- Watching over His disciples in their darkest hour, Jesus looked out for them in spite of their weakness in the garden (18:8). The Lesson: **You can bring your weakness to Jesus**.
- Caring for His mother even as He died, Jesus set an example of the importance of family (19:25–27). The Lesson: **You can bring your family to Jesus**.
- Finding Thomas in his doubt and bringing him to faith, Jesus lovingly reassured him (20:25–29). The Lesson: **You can bring your doubts to Jesus**.
- Standing on the shore when Peter needed restoration, Jesus lovingly inspired Peter to greater service for Christ (21:15–18). The Lesson: **You can bring your failures to Jesus**.

I encourage you to go back through the above list and pause on the bold action statement at the end of each point. Think about what Christ wants to do in your life personally. It can help cement these truths in your mind if you say each of them out loud: "I can bring my questions to Jesus; I can bring my emergencies to Jesus; I can bring my struggles to Jesus"; and so forth. Do you see the power of personalizing Christ's presence in your life today? Believe that He is just as near to you, and ask for His help!

TUESDAY: Know That You Believe Christ

*And Thomas answered and said to Him, "My **Lord and my God!**"*
— JOHN 20:28

Thomas was not present on the first occasion when Jesus appeared to His disciples after His Resurrection. The others told him about it afterward, but he replied, "Unless I see the nail marks in his hands and put my finger where the nails were, and put my hand into his side, I will not believe it" (John 20:25 NIV).

Thomas is our pattern; he reflects a part of us because we also struggle and doubt. Yet Christ understands and will meet us at that point of struggle—as He did for Thomas by appearing again a week later when he was present. Although Jesus offered to fulfill the conditions of Thomas' test, the mere sight of Him was enough; he fell at Christ's feet and worshiped.

Is that sight not clear enough for you also? Are Jesus' wounded hands not evidence enough for you of His love? God the Father says that His action in Christ is perfectly clear, so much so that there is no excuse for failure to believe it. In fact, He says that the way of salvation in Christ "has been made known" (Romans 3:21 NIV). The way of salvation has been made as clear as a pristine mountain stream.

Today the hand of a gracious God holds out the way of salvation to you. He asks you to look closely at His hand, for it is a wounded hand, one bearing the print of the nail received by Jesus when He died for your salvation. By faith you may put out your hand and touch that wound, which is irrefutable evidence of God's great love for you.

The One extending that hand died for you. Allow Him to enclose your hand, to enclose you, and to bring you into that great company of those who possess eternal life and who shall never perish.[1]

Bring your lack of faith and your doubts to Him. With the hand of faith, reach out and touch Him *today*! For wherever you are, Jesus is there. Just think of all Christ can do now that He is available anywhere, anytime, and to anyone!

WEDNESDAY: Know That Christ Defeated Death

Through death He . . . destroy[ed] him who had the power of death, that is, the devil, and release[d] those who through fear of death were . . . subject to bondage.
— HEBREWS 2:14–15

Over fifty-five million humans will enter eternity this year. Some will perish through starvation or murder, others through disease and accident. Some will die painlessly while others will die painfully, but *all of them* will die. Is that a result of a catastrophic tragedy? No, it is simply daily life and death on planet Earth. Death itself is not the ultimate tragedy; the ultimate tragedy is being *unprepared* for death. The solution God offers for sin is the gift of His Son, whose death on the cross paid the penalty for man's sin and rebellion. *God went to the limit.*

All humans are helpless: rich or poor, armed or unarmed, weak or powerful, known or faceless. To rescue us from our hopeless sinful state, God has communicated with us, and has taken on humanity by becoming the man, Jesus Christ. His life is recorded in the Bible. Jesus has revealed to us, in a life identifiably human and unmistakably divine, that the true nature of God is love. This is how the Bible states it: "God so loved the world that he gave his one and only Son [Jesus Christ], that whoever believes in him shall not perish but have eternal life" (John 3:16 NIV).

Simple faith in Christ gets us registered in heaven (1 Peter 1:4; see also Hebrews 12:23). Christ gives us a special, private PIN number, which is a secret name that only He knows (Revelation 2:17). We are His. We have access to Him through faith, and that is the greatest treasure on earth.

Now comes your part: Are you willing to admit that God is right when He says you have rebelled? Do you recognize your need of a personal relationship with God? Because Jesus took the penalty for your sins, accept the Bible's invitation: "'Believe on the Lord Jesus Christ, and you will be saved . . . .' [for] if you confess with your mouth the Lord Jesus and believe in your heart that God has raised Him from the dead, you will be saved. . . . For "whoever calls on the name of the LORD shall be saved" (Acts 16:31a; Romans 10:9, 13).

If these verses have spoken to your heart, simply tell God that you want to change the direction of your sinful life by receiving Jesus!

THURSDAY: Know That Christ Knows You

*"My sheep hear My voice, and **I know them**, and they follow Me."*
— JOHN 10:27

There is an unforgettable illustration in the funeral ceremony of Empress Zita, the last Hapsburg Empress:

> Thousands fell in line behind the coffin drawn by six black horses. The procession came to a stop at the Capuchin Church in Vienna, and there, a long-observed tradition was enacted. As a member of the funeral party knocked on the closed door of the church, a voice from within asked, "Who goes there?"
>
> The titles were read aloud: "Queen of Bohemia, Dalmatia, Croatia, Slavonia, Galicia. Queen of Jerusalem, Grand Duchess of Tuscany and Krakow." "I do not know her," came the response from within the church.
>
> A second knock, and the question of "Who goes there?" brought forth the response, "Zita, Empress of Austria and Queen of Hungary." Again the reply, "I do not know her."
>
> When the inevitable question was put the third time, the answer was simply, "Zita, a poor sinner." "Come in," came the welcoming voice, as the doors were slowly opened.[2]

Salvation is the greatest work of God in the universe. The convict who found Christ as he studied a Moody correspondence course would certainly agree with that statement. In answer to one of the questions, which gave him an opportunity to express where he stood in relation to his newfound faith, he wrote down: "I am a new man in an old body." It was a most perceptive remark, for that is exactly what salvation is.

Being "a new man in an old body" will go even further than that saved prisoner realized. One day he will be "a new man in a new body." Listen to this seven-step summary of what happens to all who come by faith to God through Christ:

1. **Regeneration**—when God changes my heart: "'I will **give you a new heart** and put a new spirit within you; . . . and cause you to walk in My statutes'" (Ezekiel 36:26–27).
2. **Conversion**—when God changes my life: "'**Unless you are converted** . . . , you will by no means enter the kingdom of heaven'" (Matthew 18:3).
3. **Repentance**—when God changes my mind: "'Bear **fruits worthy of repentance**'" (Matthew 3:8).
4. **Adoption**—when God changes my family: "**You received the Spirit of adoption** by whom we cry out, 'Abba, Father.' The Spirit Himself bears witness with our spirit that we are children of God, and if children, then heirs—heirs of God and joint heirs with Christ" (Romans 8:15–17).
5. **Sanctification**—when God changes my behavior: "For by one offering He has perfected forever those **who are being sanctified**. . . . 'I will put My laws into their hearts, and in their minds I will write them'" (Hebrews 10:14, 16).

6. **Justification**—when God changes my state: "Having **been justified by faith, we have peace with God** through our Lord Jesus Christ" (Romans 5:1).
7. **Glorification**—when God changes my place: "Father, I desire that they **also whom You gave Me may be with Me** . . . that they may behold My glory which You have given Me" (John 17:24).[3]

Are you a recipient of God's greatest work in the universe? When you know God, and salvation's fruit unfolds in your soul, He does a mighty work that I like to call "The Signature of God." Has "The Signature of God" been written across your life? If not, I urge you to make a conscious choice today to live in such hope!

FRIDAY: Know That You Know Christ

Examine yourselves as to whether you are in the faith. ***Test yourselves*** *. . . that Jesus Christ is in you.*
— 2 Corinthians 13:5

Perhaps your name will be called today, and your life will end here on earth. Are you ready? Do you want to make sure you are going to heaven? Be sure you know that your sins are gone. Be sure you know that God has justified you. What does it mean to be "justified"? In popular everyday language justified can be paraphrased "just as if I'd never sinned." Consider this illustration:

Some years ago a wealthy Englishman bought a Rolls Royce car and took it to France on his vacation. It broke down. At great expense the factory flew out a mechanic and not only repaired the car but entertained the customer in the best available hotel. When he arrived home he expected to receive a large bill but none came. Eventually he wrote, asking for his account to be rendered.

He received this reply: "Dear Sir, We have no record of anything ever having gone wrong with your car."[4]

That is exactly what it means to be justified. It means that God has no record of anything ever having gone wrong in your life. Knowing Christ means knowing that your sins are gone forever. Hallelujah!

The Sinner's Prayer: The following prayer expresses the desire to transfer trust to Christ alone for eternal salvation. If its words speak of your own heart's desire, praying them can be the link that will connect you to God.

Dear God, I know that I am a sinner and there is nothing that I can do to save myself. I confess my complete helplessness to forgive my own sin or to work my way to heaven. At this moment I trust Christ alone as the One who bore my sin when He died on the cross. I believe that He did all that will ever be necessary for me to stand in your holy presence. I thank you that Christ was raised from the dead as a guarantee of my own resurrection. As best as I can, I now transfer my trust to Him. I am grateful that He has promised to receive me despite my many sins and failures. Father, I take you at your word. I thank you that I can face death now that you are my Savior. Thank you for the assurance that you will walk with me through the deep valley. Thank you for hearing this prayer. In Jesus' name. Amen.[5]

If you prayed in faith, God will receive you. He will take your sins and put them away—never to remember them against you forever! Oh, how wonderfully complete is the deliverance our God has provided for sinful man!

Christ removes our sin as far as the East is from the West. Thank you Lord!

SATURDAY: Exposed to Christ

When they saw the boldness of Peter and John, [who] were uneducated and untrained men, . . . they realized that they had been with Jesus.

— ACTS 4:13

The transformation Christ brought about in the apostle John is remarkable. He manifested symptoms of intimate, personal exposure to Jesus, such as the following traits, which reflect the character of Christ. Ponder whether or not these traits are also in your life:

- **Authenticity:** John became honest, genuine, wholesome, and real. From Scripture, it is easy to see that he really loved Jesus. In John 13:25 and 21:20, we see him reclining on Christ's chest and talking with Him. John kept as close as he could to Jesus. **Are you experiencing the reality of knowing Christ with authenticity?**
- **Humility:** John was no longer at the center of his own world; Christ was. That is the essence of humility. Thus, the apostle John became the "disciple whom Jesus loved." That precious description of John is found five times in the New Testament (John 13:23; 19:26; 20:2; 21:7, 20). **Are you enjoying life as God meant it to be by experiencing true Christlike humility?**
- **Loyalty:** John always wanted to be wherever Jesus was. Nothing kept him away. It was a passion he had and kept. John was at the Transfiguration (Matthew 17:1); he witnessed the raising of Jairus's daughter (Mark 5:37); and he was invited into the intimate moments of Gethsemane (Mark 14:33). **Are you experiencing the utter completion offered through loyalty to Christ and His family?**
- **Responsibility:** John earned Christ's trust by his obedience. If Jesus gave him a job, he did it wholeheartedly. He was disciplined to the point of being trustworthy. That is why we see the touching moment at the cross when Christ entrusted his mother, Mary, to John's care (John 19:26–27). **Are you experiencing the joy of living up to your God-given responsibility in this life?**
- **Tenacity:** John was willing to endure to the end. Nothing could deflect him; he clung tenaciously to Christ. In John 21:20–23, Jesus told him that he would have to wait "until I come." And wait John did. Revelation is the record of Christ's coming to him, just as He promised. **Are you tenaciously clinging to Christ?**

Make a choice to live in hope. You have a choice to live in despair or hope, so I pray that you will make the choice to live in hope! Get exposed to Christ today. Then live with the "symptoms of exposure to Him" flowing from your life. Read Revelation 1; look at who Jesus really is! See what John saw. Like John, invite Jesus to be near you. Then, for His glory, He will make you authentic, humble, loyal, responsible, and tenacious!

WEEK 3
Signs That the End of Days Is Near

{ Revelation 1:3 }

As the end of days approaches, you can find hope
as you see the signs of His coming again!

SUNDAY: Prophecy by the Numbers

*Blessed is he who reads and those who hear the words of this prophecy, and keep those things which are written in it; **for the time is near.***
—REVELATION 1:3

When Jesus walked on earth, He announced to His disciples that His coming was near. In fact, the anticipation of His soon return was what motivated the early church. Now, two thousand years later, those who love Him are still looking for the Second Coming of Christ. Is there any way we can know that His coming is actually close at hand? I believe there is.

While studying a series I was preparing ("What's Next for Planet Earth?"), I began examining just how much God has left for us to know about events yet to come, and found J. Barton Payne's series of numbers regarding prophecy to be quite enlightening!

The Bible has a total of 31,103 verses, 8,352 of which are prophetic; they speak of events yet to come. All biblical predictions about the future can be grouped into 737 different predictions. Of the 8,352 verses, 6,312 (or 522 different predictions) have already happened exactly as God's Word said they would. About 2,040 verses, with 215 specific predictions from God about the end of the world, are in process of being fulfilled.[1]

These prophecies can be further divided into **eighteen** chronological categories (by the timing of the events). There are only **five** categories of the eighteen left to be fulfilled. Here are the categories: church prophecies, Second Coming prophecies, Millennial prophecies, Final Judgment prophecies, and New Jerusalem prophecies. Each of the prophetic signs that Christ and His apostles gave is very specific. Jesus explained that as we get closer to the Second Coming, we will witness these events, which will begin at the same time, run concurrently, and crescendo like the pains of a woman giving birth.

The list of the biblical signs of Christ's return will not be full blown until the actual Tribulation, after the Rapture has occurred. Each of these signs, Jesus said, is a trend. These trends are speeding up in our generation; the last seconds of the countdown clock of Christ's return are clicking away. The prophetic picture Christ painted grows clearer daily as signs captured by the apostles and prophets between 2,000 and 3,500 years ago are now happening in our lifetime.

In all history—only our generation has seen *every one of these events* starting to unfold. As Jesus said in Matthew 24, when you see these things happening, know that the end of days is getting near.

If Christ were to come today, are you ready to meet Him face-to-face?

My Prayer for You This Week: *Father in heaven, I pray that no one would evade answering this question: What will you do with Jesus who is called the Christ? For what would it profit a man if he gained the whole world but lost his own soul? Oh Christ, You are the One who fulfills every promise that God ever made. And Lord, You are not willing that any should perish, but that all should come to repentance. For those who do not know You personally, I pray that You would stir their hearts as they think about prophecy, the imminence of Your return, and the horrors that are coming. May they repent and turn in simple faith to You, oh Christ. Thank You for laying down the "Steps to Eternity" that we will be studying this week—events which will soon take place on this planet. Help us to not be ashamed before You at Your coming. May we be able to honestly say, "Lord, we're ready! Come or call for us at any time!" In Your precious name we pray. Amen.*

MONDAY: Signs of Christ's Return

"The sign of the Son of Man will appear . . . and they will see the Son of Man coming on the clouds of heaven with power and great glory."

—Matthew 24:30

All of the yet-to-be-completed prophecies fit within specific major events. Probably the most exciting are the dozens of signs of Christ's Second Coming. Jesus described many of them in incredible detail. But here is what I want you to see: Jesus said these signs will not suddenly appear. Rather, they will become a trend that amplifies and strengthens until they become overwhelming, like a woman about to give birth.

Before I survey the major events of the yet-to-be-completed prophecies (Thursday–Saturday), I will cover ten of Christ's precise, clear, and specific predictions. You may be startled. Every one of the signs that He gave to us are present in our world today. You and I are in the first generation in history to experience these signs all at once!

Ten Signs of Christ's Return

1. **The Sign of Global Travel:** Daniel was overwhelmed when he caught a glimpse of the number of people and the speed with which they would be moving about the planet in the end days. So God told him, "'Daniel, . . . seal the book until the time of the end; **many shall run to and fro**, and knowledge shall increase'" (Daniel 12:4).

    The Bible said that there would be many involved in travel, and today the transportation industry is one of the largest segments of the global economy. Prior to the Industrial Revolution, few individuals traveled beyond their community. Until recently, horse, foot, and boat were the only modes of transportation. Yet, in our day, millions travel "to and fro" great distances every year.

2. **The Sign of a Global Explosion of Knowledge:** God said that "knowledge shall increase"

in the end days (Daniel 12:4). For example, we've recently seen the introduction of a new generation of computer chips. Each generation has basically doubled its processing speed and power. However, the newest chip—the "Cell"—doesn't double; everything that the computer does the "Cell" multiplies by *sixty times*!

We live in a fast-paced world where many "run to and fro," frantically searching for whatever seems to be missing in their lives. Yet nothing satisfies: what is "hot" today is quickly "ho hum" tomorrow! God says that in the last days men will be "lovers of pleasure rather than lovers of God . . . always learning and never able to come to the knowledge of the truth" (2 Timothy 3:4, 7). Do you know some people like that? Have you loved them enough to warn them of the judgment to come and to offer the only hope that can truly satisfy?

TUESDAY: Can You See These Signs of Christ's Return?

*"All these are **the beginning** of sorrows."*
—Matthew 24:8

3. **The Sign of Global Weather Gone Wild:** Jesus predicted that there would be a time when weather would be so bad that not just a few but the whole world would be troubled and fearful as many thousands are killed by the prevalent chaotic weather. Jesus foresaw "the sea and the waves roaring" (Luke 21:25) in the last days, like the 2004 Tsunami and Hurricane Katrina, and likened these trends to birth pangs—"the beginning of sorrows." The Greek word *odin*, often translated as "sorrows" in Matthew 24:8, literally means "birth pangs."

   Paul says that the Creation is under the curse of sin but it "will be delivered from the bondage of corruption" (Romans 8:21). While the Creation likewise awaits the coming of the liberator, Christ the Lord, the universe itself will travail in intensity and frequency as the time of its delivery draws near: "For . . . the whole creation groans and labors with birth pangs" (Romans 8:22). Of course, chaotic weather has always existed, but there are indicators that we are witnessing an unusual surge in strange and devastating weather around the globe.

4. **The Sign of Global Telecommunication and Television:** God's Word explicitly specified that the whole world would simultaneously be able to see and hear globally: "The . . . nations will see their dead bodies three-and-a-half days, and . . . will rejoice over them, . . . because these two prophets tormented those who dwell on the earth" (Revelation 11:9–10). In the Apostle John's day, news traveled at "the speed of horseback." But for the first time ever, due to the invention of television and the deployment of global satellite networks during the twentieth century, news can travel the world at the speed of light.

5. **The Sign of Global Evangelism:** Jesus has told us that before the end of days, the gospel would be preached to all nations. We can now preach the gospel of Christ's sacrifice on the cross anywhere on earth through e-mail, radio or television waves. In fact, my little Web site (www.dtbm.org) alone has visitors from over a hundred different nations on earth! The Christian gospel is now being "preached in all the world as a witness to all the nations, and

then the end will come" (Matthew 24:14). Portions of God's Word or the entire Bible have been translated into over 2,300 languages and dialects, covering more than 90 percent of the world's population.

6. **The Sign of Global Pestilences:** Despite an increase in scientific knowledge, the Bible predicted that deadly diseases would still be prevalent in the end days: "'There will be famines, pestilences [deadly diseases], and earthquakes in various places'" (Matthew 24:7). Emerging diseases such as AIDS, Ebola virus, Hantavirus, West Nile virus, SARS, Avian flu, and so forth, underscore this fact. Ironically, only a few decades ago, some scientists were forecasting that advances in medicine might soon eradicate deadly diseases.

For some dear souls, becoming more aware of the details of the coming judgments can be frightening. If you find yourself struggling with fear, be like David and cry out to God, "When my heart is overwhelmed; lead me to the rock that is higher than I" (Psalm 61:2). God promises to keep you in perfect peace if your mind is trustingly focused on Him (Isaiah 26:3)!

WEDNESDAY: Our World Is Changing Fast

*"There will be signs in the sun, . . . moon, and . . . stars; and . . . **distress of nations, with perplexity**, the sea and the waves roaring."*
—LUKE 21:25

7. **The Sign of Global Tracking and Positioning:** The Bible says there will be technology capable of tracking the world's population and commerce: "He causes all . . . to receive a mark on their right hand or on their foreheads, and that no one may buy or sell except One who has the mark or the name of the beast, or the number of his name" (Revelation 13:16–17). Consider this interesting excerpt from a recent article:

    As an example of sophisticated tracking that has already existed for years, being recognized has never been easier for VIP patrons of the Baja Beach Club in Barcelona, Spain. Like a scene out of a science-fiction movie, all it takes is a syringe-injected microchip implant for the beautiful men and women of the nightclub scene to breeze past a 'reader' that recognizes their identity, credit balance, and even automatically opens doors to exclusive areas of the club for them. Conrad K. Chase, director of the club, explains, "By simply passing by our reader, the Baja Beach Club will know who you are and what your credit balance is. From the moment of their implantation they will also have free entry and access to the VIP area."[2]

8. **The Sign of Weapons of Mass Destruction:** The term "weapons of mass destruction" is commonly used these days, but often without the somberness that it warrants. God has warned us that at the end of the world, mankind would be capable of destroying all life: "'There will be great tribulation, . . . And unless those days were shortened, no flesh would be saved'" (Matthew 24:21–22). When Jesus made this prediction, the armaments of His day were swords and spears. However, with our generation's nuclear, biological,

and chemical weapons, it is not only possible to wipe out all flesh on planet Earth, but it is also plausible!

9. **The Sign of the Return of the Wandering Jews to the Promised Land:** Over twenty-six centuries ago, God promised that at the end of the world, Jews would gather together once again in Israel: " 'Thus says the Lord God: "Surely I will take the children of Israel from among the nations, . . . and will . . . bring them into their own land; and I will make them one nation . . . ; they shall no longer be two nations, nor shall they ever be divided into two kingdoms again" ' " (Ezekiel 37:21–22; see also Ezekiel 38:8 and Jeremiah 31:7–10). Since 1948 the world has witnessed the call of God deep within the hearts of 5.4 million Jews who have done everything they could to emigrate to the Promised Land. More arrive each day!

10. **The Sign of Israel Building a Security Wall:** God told Ezekiel 150 years, after Israel had been captured, its cities destroyed, and the population exiled to Assyria by Sargon, that Israel would build walls for security—even though there had been no "Israel" for 150 years! For 2,520 years after the Assyrian conquest, there was no sovereign nation called Israel until 1948. Israel was an occupied land, captured and recaptured by various conquerors for twenty-five centuries. Listen to what Ezekiel was told to say: There would be a people gathered from across the world to Israel (38:12); they would be called Israel (38:18); they would dwell in a land where the walls have been taken down (38:11). Amazing!

    Until 2002, this has always been spoken of as an allusion to defensive preparations. However, for several years now, in an effort to slow the flow of suicide bombers, Israel has been building the most notorious wall in the world. And that wall *will* be totally completed, because Ezekiel saw it taken down when Israel accepts the European Peace Treaty through the Antichrist's rule during the Tribulation, and thus trusts in a false peace (Daniel 9:27)!

Multitudes are already trusting in a false peace, and don't even know it. So God warns: "There is a way that seems right to a man, but its end is the way of death" (Proverbs 14:12). There is only ONE way to escape "the way of death," and that is to trust in Jesus who declared, "I am the way, the truth, and the life. No one comes to the Father except through Me" (John 14:6). In what or whom are you placing your trust today?

THURSDAY: Steps to Eternity

Seek those things which are above, where Christ is.
—Colossians 3:1

We are now going to begin our three-day look at the clear and well-described major events that lay ahead not only for those who know Jesus but also for planet Earth. I call these the "Steps to Eternity"!

Step One: The Rapture
Be ready—Christ is coming!

The Lord Himself will descend from heaven with a shout, with the voice of an archangel, and with the trumpet of God. And the dead in Christ will rise first. Then we who are alive and remain shall be caught up together with them in the clouds to meet the Lord in the air. And thus we shall always be with the Lord. Therefore comfort one another with these words.

—1 Thessalonians 4:16–18

Step Two: The Judgment Seat of Christ (Bema)
Be holy—Christ will test our lives!

For we know that if our earthly house, this tent, is destroyed, we have a building from God, a house not made with hands, eternal in the heavens.... Therefore we make it our aim ... to be well pleasing to Him. For we must all appear before the judgment seat of Christ, that each one may receive the things done in the body, according to what he has done, whether good or bad.

—2 Corinthians 5:1, 9–10

Step Three: Tribulation
Be thankful—Christ will keep us from the hour!

When the Lamb opened **one of the seals**; ... I looked, and behold, a white horse. He who sat on it had a bow; and a crown was given to him, and he went out conquering and to conquer. When He opened **the second seal**, ... Another horse, fiery red, went out. And it was granted to the One who sat on it to take peace from the earth, and that people should kill one another.... When He opened **the third seal**, ... behold, a black horse, and he who sat on it had a pair of scales in his hand. And I heard a voice in the midst of the four living creatures saying, "A quart of wheat for a denarius, and three quarts of barley for a denarius; and do not harm the oil and the wine." When He opened **the fourth seal**, ... I looked, and behold, a pale horse. And the name of him who sat on it was Death, and Hades followed with him. And power was given to them over a fourth of the earth, to kill with sword, with hunger, with death, and by the beasts of the earth. When He opened **the fifth seal**, I saw under the altar the souls of those who had been slain for the word of God and for the testimony which they held. And they cried with a loud voice, saying, "How long, O Lord, holy and true, until You judge and avenge our blood on those who dwell on the earth?" Then a white robe was given to each of them; and it was said to them that they should rest a little while longer, until both the number of their fellow servants and their brethren, who would be killed as they were, was completed. I looked when He opened **the sixth seal**, and behold, there was a great earthquake; and the sun became black ... and the moon became like blood ... the stars of heaven fell to the earth.... Then the sky receded as a scroll when it is rolled up, and every mountain and island was moved out of its place. And the kings ..., the great men, the rich men, the commanders, the mighty men, every slave and every free man, hid themselves in the caves and in the rocks of the mountains, and said to the mountains and rocks, "Fall on us and hide us from the face of Him who sits on the throne and from the wrath of the Lamb! For the great day of His wrath has come, and who is able to stand?"

—Revelation 6:1–17

The Rapture can occur at any moment! Are you ready? Are you living a holy life in anticipation of appearing before the judgment seat of Christ? Are you thankful that God will keep you from the Great Tribulation that is coming upon planet Earth? May God enable you to live your life daily in light of these truths!

FRIDAY: Be Patient

*"**Vengeance is Mine, I will repay**," says the Lord. And again, "The Lord will judge His people."*
—Hebrews 10:30

Christ's Second Coming is a constant reminder that He is coming to right all wrongs! Therefore, we need not waste our precious time trying to accomplish what He has already promised to do. God has everything under control. Allowing hurts to lead to anger and eventually fester into bitterness and a revenge-seeking spirit is a sinful and foolish pattern. For only God can completely and perfectly right all wrongs. The verses in Step Four below reveal the importance of surrendering to the Lord any desires to get even with others for hurting us.

Step Four: Christ's Second Coming
Be patient—Christ will right all wrongs!

I saw heaven opened, and behold, a white horse. And He who sat on him was called Faithful and True, and in righteousness He judges and makes war. His eyes were like a flame of fire, and on His head were many crowns. He had a name written that no one knew except Himself. He was clothed with a robe dipped in blood, and His name is called The Word of God. And the armies in heaven, clothed in fine linen, white and clean, followed Him on white horses. Now out of His mouth goes a sharp sword, that with it He should strike the nations. And He Himself will rule them with a rod of iron. He Himself treads the winepress of the fierceness and wrath of Almighty God. And He has on His robe and on His thigh a name written: KING OF KINGS AND LORD OF LORDS. Then I saw an angel standing in the sun; . . . saying to all the birds that fly in the midst of heaven, "Come and gather together for the supper of the great God, that you may eat the flesh of kings, . . . captains, . . . mighty men, . . . horses and of those who sit on them, and . . . all people, free and slave, both small and great." And I saw the beast, the kings . . . , and their armies, gathered together to make war against Him . . . and against His army. Then the beast was captured, and with him the false prophet who worked signs in his presence, by which he deceived those who received the mark of the beast and . . . worshiped his image. These two were cast alive into the lake of fire burning with brimstone. And the rest were killed with the sword which proceeded from the mouth of Him who sat on the horse. And all the birds were filled with their flesh.

—Revelation 19:11–21

Step Five: The Millennium
Be focused—Christ will perfect the earth!

Then I saw an angel coming down from heaven, having the key to the bottomless pit and a great chain in his hand. He laid hold of the dragon, that serpent of old, who is the Devil and Satan, and bound him for a thousand years; and he cast him into the bottomless pit, and shut him up, and set a seal on him, so that he should deceive the nations no more till the thousand years were finished. But after these things he must be released for a little while. And I saw thrones, and they sat on them, and judgment was committed to them. Then I saw the souls of those who had been beheaded for their witness to Jesus and for the word of God, who had not worshiped the beast or his image, and had not received his mark on their foreheads or on their hands. And they lived and reigned with Christ for a thousand years. But the rest of the dead did not live again until the thousand years were finished. **This is the first resurrection**. Blessed and holy is he who has part in the first resurrection. Over such the second death has no power, but they shall be priests of God and of Christ, and shall reign with Him a thousand years. Now when the thousand years have expired, Satan will be released . . . to deceive the nations . . . , Gog and Magog, to gather them together to battle, whose number is as the sand of the sea. They . . . surrounded the camp of the saints and the beloved city. And fire came down . . . and devoured them. The devil, who deceived them, was cast into the lake of fire . . . where the beast and the false prophet are. And they will be tormented day and night forever and ever.

—Revelation 20:1–10

Step Six: The Great White Throne
Be faithful—point people to Christ!

Then I saw a great white throne and Him who sat on it, from whose face the earth and the heaven fled away. And there was found no place for them. And I saw the dead, small and great, standing before God, and books were opened. And another book was opened, which is the Book of Life. And the dead were judged according to their works, by the things which were written in the books. The sea gave up the dead who were in it, and Death and Hades delivered up the dead who were in them. And they were judged, each one according to his works. Then Death and Hades were cast into the lake of fire. This is the second death. And anyone not found written in the Book of Life was cast into the lake of fire.

—Revelation 20:11–15

Only our God has impeccable wisdom and perfect justice to know how and when to deal with mankind's sins against others and Himself. Our responsibility is to faithfully live a Christ-centered life that is kind, tenderhearted, and forgiving of those who have offended or hurt us—just as God for Christ's sake has forgiven us (see Ephesians 4:32). Such a consistent testimony is the best way to point others to Christ!

SATURDAY: Wise Investments with God

*"For where **your treasure** is, there **your heart** will be also."*
—Luke 12:34

Are you intensely asking God to do anything in particular through your life that will last forever? What do you think would most please Christ?

Step Seven: Heaven
Be investing—lay up treasures in heaven!

Christ said, "Here is something anyone in My family can do! Here is what you can do that I will love, and I will make your investments in these areas last forever!"

- **Jesus collects all your prayers, so pray to Him:** "Now when He had taken the scroll, the four living creatures and the twenty-four elders fell down before the Lamb, each having a harp, and golden bowls full of incense, which are the prayers of the saints" (Revelation 5:8).
- **Jesus multiplies sacrificial gifts, so give to Him:** "Then one poor widow came and threw in two mites, which make a quadrans [a day's wage]. So He ... said to them, '... This poor widow has put in more than all those who have given to the treasury'" (Mark 12:42–43).
- **Jesus counts souls you lead to Him, so win the lost to Christ:** "For what is our hope, or joy, or crown of rejoicing? Is it not even you in the presence of our Lord Jesus Christ at His coming?" (1 Thessalonians 2:19).
- **Jesus remembers humble service, so serve Him:** "As He sat at the table, a woman came having an alabaster flask of very costly oil of spikenard. Then she broke the flask and poured it on His head ... 'to anoint [His] body for burial. [And] wherever this gospel is preached in the whole world, what this woman has done will also be told as a memorial to her'" (Mark 14:3, 8–9).
- **Jesus loves missionaries who do outreach, so go for Him**: "'Everyone who has left houses or brothers or sisters or father or mother or wife or children or lands, for My name's sake, shall receive a hundredfold, and inherit eternal life'" (Matthew 19:29).

Make a choice to live in hope. Investing in heaven is the secret to having living hope for the end of days! Whenever you give significant, regular, sacrificial time to God, you are making a choice to live in hope. Whenever you share Christ with loved ones, friends, neighbors, and others whom God brings into your path, you are giving them an opportunity to live in hope as well. And whenever you invest financially in heaven instead of laying up treasures on earth that will soon be destroyed, you are once again sending ahead "gold, silver, and precious stones" to build upon in heaven.

Are you diligently preparing for Christ's return—eager to lovingly welcome Jesus, with a clear conscience, as you meet Him in the air at the Rapture, or at the time He escorts you through the "valley of the shadow of death"?

I exhort you to consciously make each moment count for God and eternity! For time is the only thing you cannot recover, earn more of, get from someone else, or do over again. It is an irreversible river that is flowing by ceaselessly at sixty seconds per minute, sixty minutes per hour!

I pray that you are excited about seeing Jesus—it could be today!

WEEK 4
Get Ready to Meet Jesus

{ Revelation 1:4 }

As the end of days approaches, you can find hope as you see Christ's soon return through signs of the end of the world like widespread tribulation, tsunamis, and global travel advances!

SUNDAY: The Greatest Tribulation

*John, to the seven churches which are in Asia: Grace to you and peace from Him who is and who was and **who is to come**, and from the seven Spirits who are before His throne.*
—REVELATION 1:4

This week we are examining the Revelation 1:4 promise that Jesus is the *One "who is to come."* What will His coming be like? Every so often, we witness an event so momentous that it touches the whole planet with a glimpse of the ominous things to come when Christ returns. On December 26, 2004, the eyes of the entire world were drawn to just such an event.

That Sunday after Christmas, life ended abruptly for 150,000-plus souls as a result of the Sumatra-Andaman earthquake, which produced what is now called the Boxing Day Tsunami. So many bodies were swept out to sea in that catastrophic event that an exact number of casualties can never be verified.

It is especially notable that secular writers and news reporters used words like "apocalyptic" and "of biblical proportions" as they struggled to describe the horrific scenes of desolation and death they witnessed in Southeast Asia. Some even began to contemplate: *What if there is a catastrophe so big, so deadly, that it could wipe out life on our planet—an asteroid, a comet, or a complete climactic shift away from a life-sustaining world?* In other words, countless people, all around the globe, were anxiously thinking and talking about the end of the world!

As apocalyptic as the 2004 tsunami might have seemed to some, during the seven-year period known in the Bible as the Great Tribulation there will be at least 20,000 times more deaths. Suffering will be so extensive, and desolation so great, that God says it will be "'such as has not been since the beginning of the world until this time, no, nor ever shall be'" (Matthew 24:21).

Most Bible prophecy scholars believe that the greatest number of deaths will occur in the second half of the Tribulation, which lasts forty-two months, or three and a half years. By the end of the Tribulation, over half the population on earth will have perished. With nearly seven billion people alive today, this means more than three and a half billion will die!

Let's put those astronomical figures into perspective. If an event like the 2004 tsunami occurred daily for three and a half years, at the rate of 150,000 deaths per day, it would still only total 189 million casualties. For half the world's population to die by quake and tsunami in forty-two months, there would have to be one quake and tsunami each hour, sixteen hours per day, for three and one-half years. That would be more bodies to bury than we can possibly imagine!

Those figures are staggering to our human minds! That is why Jesus has said so much about the need to get ready for the end of the world. Is it possible to know **an exact date** as to when the world will end? No, for Jesus tells us, "'But of that day and hour no one knows . . . but My Father only'" (Matthew 24:36). However, Jesus promised to give us signs that would indicate the end is near.

The Bible is so unique because God has already mapped out specific future events. Only the living, faithful, and true God could ever, with 100 percent accuracy, declare: "Let Me tell you the future!" God has said that is the way we can know that He is *real*. Because He *is* real, you and I can confidently make a choice to live in hope because we place our faith and trust in Christ "who works all things according to the counsel of His will" (see Ephesians 1:11–13).

> **My Prayer for You This Week:** *Father in heaven, we bow before You who are God because You have written the future in advance. You can be trusted because everything You've said has come true, as it shall into the future. You offer us Your peace like a river. Lord, I pray for those without such peace, perhaps because they've never met You, or they've gotten out of the river and are standing on the shore—separated from You because of sin and iniquity. I pray that they would flee to You, the river of mercy and peace, and be cleansed. May they let those waves of Your righteousness sweep over their lives so they can experience the newness of You, the God of new beginnings—the One who promised us an endless life of new fresh pages because the blood of Jesus Christ Your Son cleanses us from all iniquity. I pray that we would know Your peace and Your righteousness. May we take heed to watch and pray so we can get ready to stand before You. We pray this in Your precious name and for Your glory. Amen.*

MONDAY: Prophecy — Proof That God Is Real

> *"Show the things that are **to come hereafter**, that we may know that you [idols] are gods; yes, do good or do evil, that we may be dismayed and see it together."*
> —Isaiah 41:23

Why do Bible-believing saints love prophecy? The precise timing and exact fulfillment of prophecy proves that God is the living Faithful and True God. Consider these wonderful proofs from the book of Isaiah alone:

- **Only God accurately knows the future.** In Isaiah 41:23 (see above) God is challenging man-made idols to perform as He has done.
- **Prophecy proves that God is real.** In the following verses, God the Father is prophetically speaking to His Son, Jesus Christ, the Messiah: "'I, the Lord, have called You in righteousness, and will hold Your hand; I will keep You and give You as a covenant to the people, as a light to the Gentiles, to open blind eyes, to bring out prisoners from the prison.... I am the Lord, ... and My glory I will not give to another, nor My praise to carved images. Behold, the former things have come to pass, and new things I declare; **before they spring forth I tell you of them**'" (Isaiah 42:6–9).
- **Prophecy proves that God is reliable.** We see this in His fulfilled prophecies as well as His other mighty works: "Remember the former things of old, for I am God, and there is none like Me, **declaring the end from the beginning, and from ancient times things that are not yet done**, saying, 'My counsel shall stand, and I will do all My pleasure'" (Isaiah 46:9–10).
- **Prophecy reveals the God we can trust.** Everything that our all-powerful, all-knowing, and ever-present God predicted for past history came to pass exactly as He said it would: "**Even from the beginning I have declared it to you; before it came to pass I proclaimed it to you**, lest you should say, 'My idol has done them, and my carved image and my molded image have commanded them'" (Isaiah 48:5; see also Isaiah 48:12–13).
- **Trusting God determines our eternal destiny:** "Thus says the Lord, your Redeemer...: '**I am the LORD your God ... who leads you by the way you should go**. Oh, that you had heeded My commandments! Then your peace would have been like a river, and your righteousness like the waves of the sea.... There is no peace,' says the LORD, 'for the wicked'" (Isaiah 48:17–18, 22).

If you are a believer, are you letting your Redeemer lead you in the way you should go? Are you heeding His commandments? Do you have peace like a river and Christ's abundant righteousness in your life? If you do not yet know Christ as Lord and Savior, I pray that you will make a choice to live in hope. Transfer your trust to Christ alone for your eternal salvation!

TUESDAY: Prophecy — The Key to Understanding the Future

*"I am God, and there is none like Me, **declaring the end from the beginning, ... things that are not yet done**."*

—Isaiah 46:9–10

Almost one-third of the Bible is prophetic. Of the 8,352 verses that J. Barton Payne has identified as being prophetic, is there one that particularly explains the end of the world? Here is a real eye-opener: "Daniel, ... seal the book until the time of the end; **many shall run to and fro**, and **knowledge shall increase**" (Daniel 12:4). Although "The Sign of Global Travel" and "The Sign of a Global Explosion of Knowledge" were both discussed last week, I will be expanding those points a bit further today and tomorrow.

"Many shall run to and fro": Running "to and fro" speaks of traveling. Much of the world remained the same from Daniel's day until our great-grandparents' time, but the pace of change in just the last hundred years is incredible. Consider this timeline:

- **3,000 Years Ago**—David hired wooden boats, powered by wind, to help bring special wood for the temple. His son, Solomon, actually built and operated a fleet of wooden ships that sailed by wind power to carry on extensive trade with Africa, Europe, and parts of Asia. And 2,800 years ago, Jonah walked by foot to a port in Israel to sail to what is today Spain.
- **2,000 Years Ago**—The apostle Paul traveled around the Roman world on mapped-out highways by foot, by horse and chariot, or aboard a wooden ship moved along by wind power caught in the sails.
- **500 Years Ago**—Christopher Columbus embarked on a journey across the Atlantic Ocean in search of a sea route to China. He also probably went to the dock on foot, and boarded a wooden ship, not unlike those used by David, Solomon, Jonah, and Paul.
- **200 Years Ago**—Benjamin Franklin walked to a dock in America to board a wooden sailing vessel for his trip to France.
- **100 Years Ago**—President Theodore Roosevelt traveled by steamship from place to place, often taking a week to get there. With the advent of steam, man was no longer tied to animal power and wind power. The steamship, locomotive, automobile, and airplane changed the entire world in just generations!
- **Today**—Scheduled flights of airliners routinely make the trip from any of the six inhabited continents to another continent in only a few hours. No one in the history of this planet ever traveled like we can today. This is **a sign of end times**—that the end of the world is getting close!

With all the advances in travel, it does not take long to reach any place in the world. Even so, as much as one might want to flee to safety, there is nowhere on earth where a person can hide to escape God's wrath during the Tribulation: "Where can I go from Your Spirit? Or where can I flee from Your presence? If I ascend into heaven, You are there; If I make my bed in hell, behold, You are there. If I take the wings of the morning, and dwell in the uttermost parts of the sea, even there Your hand shall lead me, and Your right hand shall hold me" (Psalm 139:7–10).

For the Christian, that Psalm 139 passage is a comfort because God has promised to both lead and uphold us by His power!

WEDNESDAY: Knowledge Shall Increase

*"Many shall run to and fro, **and knowledge shall increase**."*
—Daniel 12:4

Now let us look at the last half of that phrase in Daniel 12:4, which is almost an understatement when you think about life in the twenty-first century!

Today, we sit atop a database containing what is arguably the sum total of the world's accumulated knowledge every time we sit down to browse the Internet.

From wooden boats with sails to space shuttles and hypersonic orbiters; from clay tablets and a stylus to MP3's and DVD's that I can watch or create on the personal computer that can also be my phone, television, radio, stereo, workstation, word processor, electronic document file, movie studio, sound studio, telephone answering service, fax machine, copy machine and printer. And a million other things.

[Our] generation is unique in all human history. Never has humanity been forced to come to terms with so many issues simultaneously—issues for which we have no historical precedent to use as a guide. The explosive growth of knowledge has us reeling from what humanist writer Alvin Toffler terms "future shock." It is only in this generation that last year's encyclopedia is about as useful as last month's newspaper. It has been said that the sum of human knowledge from the Flood to 1850 doubled once. It doubled again following World War II. The doubling of human knowledge increases exponentially.[1]

In light of the exponential growth of knowledge since World War II especially, let me ask you this question: In comparison, how is your growth in the grace and knowledge of your Lord and Savior? Do you see an ever-increasing difference in your understanding of God and His Word from one year to the next?

One way to evaluate your life to answer that question is to think of Scripture you've learned which has revealed a deeper understanding of God. Or perhaps you can recall a difficult circumstance you've endured, and how such suffering drew you closer to the Lord so that you are now more "able to comfort those who are in any trouble, with the comfort with which [you yourself were] comforted by God" (2 Corinthians 1:4). Praise the Lord for the spiritual growth He's granted so far, and then ask Him to strengthen weak areas so that you can better "pass on the faith" to others.

All believers are to become teachers of others, whether it is in a church setting, in the home, spreading the gospel, or exhorting a friend or neighbor in the Word. The writer of Hebrews tells us that we "ought to be teachers . . . of full age, . . . who by reason of use have their senses exercised to discern both good and evil" (5:12a, 14). But anyone who "partakes only of milk is unskilled in the word of righteousness, for he is a babe" (5:13).

If you have not yet done so, I urge you to get into the Word of God regularly so that you can gain the knowledge and wisdom that are necessary to teach others! For God says that we are to be "redeeming the time, because the days are evil" (Ephesians 5:16)!

THURSDAY: Prophecy — Sorrowful Yet Joyful

*I [John] took the little book out . . . and ate it, and it was as sweet as honey in my mouth. But when I had eaten it, **my stomach became bitter**.*
—Revelation 10:10

When Daniel saw what it would be like in the end times, it was so overwhelming—so absolutely incomprehensible—that, like John, it made him sick. Look at what an author has to say about Daniel 10:14:

While in exile in Babylon, the prophet Daniel was given a vision of the future of Israel, up to the coming of the Messiah. Up to this point in the vision, those things that Daniel saw were relatively familiar cities, events, and people in a context that were not too far removed from his concept of reality. But then he was shown the things to come in the last days. The angel told him in Daniel 10:14, "Now I am come to make them understand what shall befall thy people in the latter days; for yet the vision is for many days."

Daniel was so staggered by what he saw it made him faint, and verse 18 records that "one like the appearance of a man" touched him, and strengthened him, so that he could go on. Daniel tried to describe those things he saw using terminology that made sense to him, but it comes to us as a series of baffling symbols, images and beasts. The things he saw terrified him. Because the visions were so completely removed from his understanding of reality, he was unable to describe them in terms that even he was able to comprehend. And so it remained, for thousands of years.

Great Bible commentators like Calvin and Luther did not even attempt to interpret the books of Daniel, or the Revelation, for that matter, saying they were allegorical or symbolic books. Matthew Henry, writing in the eighteenth century, did not fare much better. Even commentators on these books in the early twentieth century admitted they had trouble fitting the pieces together. After all, they dealt with a restored Israel, a revived Roman empire, and a one world government. Such things were deemed to be impossible, therefore to be interpreted as allegories. The revealing angel understood what Daniel did not.[2]

Even with our limited but more enlightened understanding, the holocaust of the Great Tribulation to come is indeed extremely sorrowful! We therefore need to get ready to meet Jesus, and warn others to do the same. So then, "Let us hold fast the confession of our hope without wavering. . . . And let us . . . stir up love and good works, not forsaking the assembling of ourselves together, . . . but exhorting one another, and **so much the more as you see the Day approaching**" (Hebrews 10:24–25).

FRIDAY: The Shock Wave That Rocked the World

*"Men's hearts failing them from fear and **the expectation of those things which are coming on the earth**, for the powers of the heavens will be shaken."*
—LUKE 21:26

On December 26, 2004, while sitting at my computer waiting for a document to print, steady news bulletins began to hit the Google News screen—

A rare earthquake has just occurred in the Indian Ocean . . .

Some people may have died . . .

Reports of a gigantic tsunami are coming in from all over Southeast Asia . . .

The death toll is rising dramatically . . .

Damage is unbelievable! Catastrophic! . . .

On and on the news bulletins flashed. It quickly became evident that the greatest natural disaster of this generation had just occurred! The enormous power of that event actually made our whole planet vibrate. Later, one commentator reported that the earth even wobbled on its axis and the regional map of south Asia was permanently altered. The island of Sumatra moved 100 feet. It was as if time stood still for three microseconds. The impact of the 500 mile-per-hour waves was equal to one million atom bombs.

As devastating as that earthquake was, it is as nothing compared to the power and judgment God will unleash on earth during the Great Tribulation. It is no wonder that men's hearts will fail them from fear in anticipation of what is yet to come!

If you are a born-again Christian, you can rejoice because you no longer need to fear the future. The writer of Hebrews says that "to those who eagerly wait for Him He will appear a second time, apart from sin, for salvation" (Hebrews 9:28). When Christ returns again, it will be to take His children home with Him. At that point our salvation will be complete because we will be with Him at last!

By the way, did you happen to catch that those who were online that December 26th were able to view the quake and tsunami within minutes of it striking? Seismic stations picked up the magnitude of the event, and news stations spread the word electronically at the speed of light—which is more remarkable evidence that "knowledge shall increase" in the last days.

As fascinating as mankind's rapid increase in knowledge can be, that is not God's priority for His children in end times. Rather, we are to "increase and abound in love to one another . . . so that He may establish [our] hearts blameless in holiness before our God and Father at the coming of our Lord Jesus Christ with all His saints" (1 Thessalonians 3:12–13). We need to continually make sure that our priorities are the same as God's!

Are you ready to meet Jesus Christ? Is He your safe haven from the ominous "things which are coming on the earth"?

SATURDAY: Death Is Inevitable

*It is **appointed for men to die** once, but after this the judgment.*
—Hebrews 9:27

Even though "knowledge shall increase" as the Tribulation fast approaches, the knowledge of the exact moment of our "appointed" time to meet God face-to-face is His alone. And, unless the Rapture occurs first, we each must face the inevitability of our own death.

Jesus has warned us that life is fragile. Thus, He expects us to live every day as if it were our very last. Without even a moment's notice we could be ushered into eternity—like all the souls who perished in the 2004 tsunami.

The energy unleashed in that tsunami was staggering, but even more staggering is the fact that the 150,000-plus souls who unexpectedly entered eternity that day had no more chances to get right with a holy God! Thus, that event can serve as a gracious reminder from the Lord of what we are really here on earth to do—seek God while He may still be found!

Make a choice to live in hope. Do you know, beyond a shadow of a doubt, that you are ready to meet Jesus? If you haven't already done so, I urge you to choose to find hope for the end of days in Christ. Only He is a secure and safe refuge!

WEEK 5
Christ Is Our Refuge

{ Revelation 1:4 }

As the end of days approaches, you can find hope in the safest spot in the universe—Christ, our refuge!

SUNDAY: The Safest Spot

Grace to you and peace *from Him who is and who was and who is to come.*
—Revelation 1:4

As Jesus graphically unfolded the events of the end of days before John's eyes, how did He prepare him for what was to come? He reminded him of His grace and peace. Now, as we see those very days actually unfolding before our own eyes, Christ wants to remind us that we, like John, are securely kept by His grace and peace as well.

Have you ever wondered where the safest spot on earth is *physically*? It is located in Colorado, a little over seven hundred miles from where I live in Tulsa, Oklahoma. There, nestled in the Rockies, under Cheyenne Mountain, a half-mile deep in its granite corridors, is a super-secure missile defense command center called NORAD.

Built at the height of the Cold War, the command center is able to withstand any bomb blast or chemical or biological weapon attack. Anyone residing within can be sustained for two years, but *only if he or she is able to get there in time to avoid the attack.*

The safest spot in the universe, even safer than Cheyenne Mountain, is also the closest. It is closer than any man-made shelter on earth. As we approach the end of days, the safest spot in the universe is in Christ, the perfect refuge only God could design.

Jesus Christ is our hope, our refuge, and our salvation. He is as close as a cry, an outstretched hand, or an upturned heart. He is only one thought or prayer away. From any location, anyone can instantly arrive in that safest of all places. That is our ultimate hope as we approach the end of days.

Christ, our forerunner, has forever anchored our souls safely in heaven, and in coming weeks we will see that Revelation explains what Hebrews 6 promises: "The heirs of promise . . . **have fled for refuge** to lay hold of the hope set before us. This hope we have as an anchor of the soul, both sure and steadfast, and which enters the Presence behind the veil, where the forerunner has entered for us, even Jesus, having become High Priest forever according to the order of Melchizedek" (Hebrews 6:17–20).

When all else is shaken, only Christ is that secure and lasting refuge. But how do we reach that refuge? His Word says we are to "lay hold of the hope set before us" (Hebrews 6:18). What is that hope? It is the Lord Jesus Christ Himself (see 1 Timothy 1:1)! In other words, the safest spot in the universe is in the embrace of Jesus.

Are you resting in His embrace? That spot of safety is only a prayer away!

My Prayer for You This Week: *Father in Heaven, we thank You that You've given us this beautiful book—the Revelation of Your Son, our Savior, Jesus Christ—for this book speaks of Him from cover to cover. It is all about You, our hope, and we desire to lay hold of You. You are set before us in all Your glory, in all Your humility, and in all Your suffering in Your great work on the cross for us. I pray that we who know You will lay firmer hold on the hope set before us. For any who don't have this, may today be the day that they see Your arms open wide as You offer salvation to them. Oh Lord, bless us, strengthen us, encourage us, and draw us even closer to You! In the name of Jesus we pray. Amen.*

MONDAY: Entering the Refuge of Christ

*[He] is able to **keep you from stumbling**, and to **present you faultless** before the presence of His glory with exceeding joy.*
—JUDE 24

To understand one of the clearest explanations of entering into the refuge of Christ, let us look back 3,500 years. When Israel entered the Promised Land, God gave them a constant reminder of His salvation. This reminder was ordered by God to be set up throughout the land as a continual visible symbol of Him as God their Savior.

What was that visible reminder? It was a strategically placed group of six cities called "the cities of refuge": "These were the **cities appointed for all** the children of Israel and for the stranger who dwelt among them, **that whoever** killed a person accidentally **might flee** there, and not die by the hand of **the avenger of blood** until he stood before the congregation" (Joshua 20:9).

The cities of refuge present a clear, but often overlooked, picture of Christ as Savior. In those Old Testament passages describing the cities of refuge, the word for "refuge" used in the Septuagint (LXX, the Greek version of the Old Testament) is the same as the Greek word translated "refuge" in Hebrews 6:18 (KJV, NKJV, and NASB). The writer of Hebrews is telling us that the only way to experience the power of God that saves us is to run to Christ in desperation for refuge—to that safest place.

The cities of refuge were wonderful because:
- **The cities of refuge were easy to reach.** Jewish tradition declares that there were signs at the crossroads: Refuge! Refuge! These signs pointed the way to safety. God expressly commanded that roads be made to these cities to make them highly accessible (Deuteronomy 19:3). Some were even located on hilltops in order to be more prominent.
- **The cities of refuge were open to all.** to the Israelite, the stranger, and the sojourner among them (Numbers 35:15). Joshua 20:9 uses this phrase: "that whoever killed a person." What New Testament verse does "that whoever" remind us of? Right! "For God so loved the world that He gave his only begotten Son, that whoever believes in Him should not perish but have everlasting life" (John 3:16.)
- **The cities of refuge were always open.** If that were not the case, a man might be killed while beating on a door to get someone to let him in.
- **The cities of refuge were a completely sufficient refuge.** They not only provided legal protection but also completely met an endangered person's needs once inside. As long as the slayer remained in the city, he was safe, and could look forward to being freed after the high priest died.
- **The cities of refuge were the only hope.** The slayer was told to *flee* to the city; such a person could not afford to delay.

Christ himself is your only hope and refuge! Can you afford to delay fleeing to Him for eternal safety?

TUESDAY: The Cities of Refuge—A Portrait of Christ

We might have strong consolation, ***who have fled for refuge*** *to lay hold of the hope set before us.*
—Hebrews 6:18b

The similarities between the cities of refuge and Christ our refuge are striking when compared point for point. Anyone can come to Christ because:
- **Christ is easy to reach.** We may cast ourselves upon Christ at any time, in any place. His church is to be the teller of this good news that cries "Refuge! Refuge!" to the lost world. This emphasis is made at the very end of Revelation: *Let him who thirsts come* (Revelation 22:17b). The Savior is within the reach of all, even to those who are in the utmost peril of His wrath.
- **Christ is open to all people.** Anyone who wants to may come to Him: "Come to Me, all you who labor and are heavy laden, and I will give you rest" (Matthew 11:28; see also Genesis 3:9 and Isaiah 45:22).
- **Christ's arms are always open—He never locks His gates.** Jesus is "the door" (John 10:7, 9), and that door is never shut. Many have stood by a deathbed and seen sinners come to belief in the last moments of life. There is no gate to unlock, and men can enter quickly. The way to the heavenly city of refuge is clear, and Christ will never turn any sinner away (John 6:37). Just as

prominent roads led to each city of refuge, and their gates were always open, so Christ's gate is always open to whoever will come to Him.

- **Christ is a completely sufficient refuge.** "Christ's death in space-time history is completely adequate to meet our need for refuge from the true moral guilt that we have. It is final because of who He is. He is the infinite second person of the Trinity; therefore, His death has infinite value. Just as the suburbs or borders of the city [of refuge] were a sufficient security to the offender (Numbers 35:26–27)—so there is virtue even in the hem of Christ's garment for the healing and saving of poor sinners. If we cannot reach to a full assurance, we may comfort ourselves in a good hope through grace."[1]

- **Christ is our only hope**. If we do not flee to the refuge, which God has given to us at such a great price, there is no other hope for us. Hebrews relates this negative emphasis to the Old Testament: *Anyone who has rejected Moses' law dies without mercy on the testimony of two or three witnesses. Of how much worse punishment . . . will he be thought worthy who has trampled the Son of God underfoot, counted the blood of the covenant by which he was sanctified a common thing, and insulted the Spirit of grace?* (Hebrews 10:28–29).

  The IVP Bible Commentary puts it well:

  > There isn't one of us who does not stand in that situation. We have heard the gospel, so if in the Old Testament ignoring God's law brought death, what about us if we despise the work of Christ and the grace which He showers upon us? Nor can lost sinners today afford to delay in fleeing to the only refuge, Jesus Christ.[2]

Today, meditate upon these soul-gripping truths: Christ is easy to reach; His arms are open to all; His entrance is never locked; He is a completely sufficient refuge; and He is the only hope! How wonderful!

WEDNESDAY: Christ—Better Than Any City of Refuge

"Come to Me, all you who labor and are heavy laden, and ***I will give you rest***."
—MATTHEW 11:28

Why is Christ better than any earthly city of refuge? While those cities were only for temporary refuge, Christ offers only permanent refuge. Even though the cities of refuge were strategically placed to be easy to reach, because of angry relatives, they could still only be reached after a hard and dangerous journey. Christ, however, can only be reached through simple, childlike faith in His sacrifice on the cross, which makes Him forever closer than any man-made refuge.

Christ is *so much* better because He died only for the guilty, but the cities of refuge protected only the innocent. They were reserved for the man who killed by mistake. When the slayer came to the city, he was admitted and then tried, for the elders of the city only protected someone who was innocent of murder. With us, there is no trial. We are already condemned in our sins, but Christ welcomes and receives guilty sinners. What grace!

Christ died for the deliberate sinner. Who is that? Every one of us can say, "It is I!" How can a holy and righteous God accept those who are guilty? It is not by giving up His holiness; He does not devalue that, or we would have no moral absolute in the universe. Rather, the reason Christ is able to be our Redeemer is that He is the High Priest, and the sacrifice He gave was His own death. Now, think about your life today in these terms: Christ is my refuge—Jesus found me guilty in God's court and convicted me of first-degree sin. Because I am a sinner, God's penalty (or wages) for my sin is death. But instead of forgetting my debt to God's holiness, it was paid in full by another. Jesus died in my place, bearing my sin. That payment made me free.

Because of Christ's death in my place, I will never face God's wrath. Now I can boldly come before God's throne and, surrounded by His mercy and grace, find all that I need to live life and serve Him. When I sin, I have a Savior who is also my High Priest who actually lives to speak to God on my behalf. It is this powerful picture of Christ that Paul taught the Corinthians: "Now all these things happened to them as examples, and they were written for our admonition, upon whom the ends of the ages have come" (1 Corinthians 10:11).

Christ, our High Priest, died once for all, and lives forever. Although we are legally guilty before God, when we cast ourselves upon Christ we are free forever. (Hebrews 7:23–27 says this strongly.) When you humbly come to Christ with a repentant heart, His arms will open wide! If you have not already done so, I urge you to accept His embrace and start living for Him today!

THURSDAY: Christ—Our Permanent Refuge

*This hope we have as an anchor of the soul, **both sure and steadfast**, and which enters the Presence behind the veil.*
—Hebrews 6:19

Hebrews also speaks of Christ as the forerunner who has entered for us (Hebrews 6:20). Christ has entered into God's presence so that we can enter too. When do we enter this refuge?

We enter in **once for all** at the moment we cast ourselves upon Christ and accept Him as our Savior. At that moment we are declared justified by God who judges us on the basis of Christ's finished work at Calvary: "We also rejoice in God through our Lord Jesus Christ, through whom **we have now received the reconciliation**" (Romans 5:11). In that verse, Paul uses the Greek aorist tense, which indicates that our justification is a past thing, completed forever. If we were saved, we are saved. Justification (and its subset, reconciliation) means that God has no record that we ever sinned. Our sins are paid for, put on Christ's account, and are gone forever!

We enter **every daily moment** into this refuge as Christians when we claim the blood of Christ to cover specific sin that has broken fellowship with God: "The blood of Jesus Christ His Son **cleanses us from all sin**. . . . If we confess our sins, He is faithful and just to forgive us our sins and to cleanse us from all unrighteousness" (1 John 1:7, 9).

We will enter in **perfectly and completely** at that great moment when we die, or when the Lord returns: "He is also able to **save to the uttermost** those who come to God through Him" (Hebrews 7:25).

Christ is better than any city of refuge because He is nearer. A man from the city who ran out to help a weary refugee to the gate could fall and not be able to shelter him within the walls of safety before the avenger overtook the fugitive. But a man who looks to Christ to reach safety can never fail. The Bible makes a specific promise: "The one who comes to Me I will by no means cast out" (John 6:37). In fact, Jesus says, "I stand at the door and knock" (Rev. 3:20). He Himself seeks us.[3]

Have you come to Jesus Christ by faith and allowed Him to save you once for all? If so, you can rest in Christ, for He is your permanent and only refuge!

FRIDAY: Are You in Christ?

*"And **this is eternal life**, that they may know You, the only true God, and Jesus Christ whom You have sent."*
—JOHN 17:3

How near is Christ? To answer that, let me share the following story that was told by Harry A. Ironside (1876–1951), who traveled for more than fifty years as a home missionary, evangelist, and Bible teacher. He was pastor of Moody Memorial Church, a visiting professor at Dallas Theological Seminary, and the author of more than sixty books and pamphlets. The following is drawn from a tract he wrote called "The Way of Peace." The essence of the story is that a pastor named Dr. Charles Berry served a congregation in Boston. He was part of the movement that denied the deity of Christ, His substitutionary death on the cross and the need of personal salvation. But he was immensely popular to the people of Boston. He could hold vast audiences with his story telling abilities, and everyone always felt better when they left the service.

Those who knew him well noted that at the height of his ministry there was a dramatic change in his life. When asked to explain the amazing changes he had experienced he told them the story. It started on a rainy Saturday night. Dr. Berry was in his study at home just finishing up a moving message for the next morning when the doorbell rang. Opening the door, he found a poor and hungry teen. She asked for the minister. Dr. Berry tried to send her to the local relief agencies and rescue missions—but she insisted that a minister needed to come with her.

Finally, at the point of embarrassment, Dr. Berry agreed to go out into the stormy night following this young lady, totally against his better judgment. It was the event that followed that the Lord used to change his life forever.

The young lady kept repeating over and over as they walked that she needed a minister to, "get her mother in." Not sure exactly what she meant, Dr. Berry followed. He wondered if she was sick or fallen or even worse in some state of intoxication that she had to be carried. When suggesting that maybe a policeman would be better to help the young lady again repeated, "No, I need a minister to get my mother in!"

At last Dr. Berry began to understand as the young lady continued by explaining that her mother was not drunk but afraid to die. She then explained that she had assured her mother that she would find a minister, and the minister would explain to her how to get in—to Heaven! At that point Dr. Berry slowed down. He asked if he could send a local inner city missionary or someone from the rescue mission. The trembling daughter looked at him so intently and begged him to wait no longer. She said again, "Do come, sir. I want you to get my mother in before it's too late. Please, sir, do come with me."

At last he consented to go, and the girl led the way to one of the worst sections of the city. In this miserable neighborhood she took him into a tenement house and up a rickety flight of stairs to a poverty-stricken room. Downstairs many men and women were drinking and carousing, and the air resounded with horrid oaths and vile language. The minister found the poor woman lying on a miserable makeshift of a bed, evidently near to death.

"I've brought him!" exclaimed the daughter. "I've got the minister from the big church where the swells go. He'll get you in, Mother. Just do what he says."

"What can I do for you, my poor woman?" he inquired as kindly as he could.

"Why, sir, I'm dying, and I want you to get me into heaven. I've been a great sinner, and I don't know how to get in."

The minister began to speak of the necessity of a good life, of building a noble character, and how goodness always paid in the end.

"You don't understand, sir!" she cried. "That won't do! I'm dying and I've lived a bad life. It's too late for me. Oh, can't you get me in?"

He tried again and gave some good advice and endeavored to comfort her by expressing the hope that all would be well if she would only seek to lead a Christian life.

"That won't do!" she exclaimed. "I'm a poor sinner! I've no time to lead a Christian life. I'm dying and I want to go in. Oh, can't you tell me how I may get into heaven?"

Dr. Berry did not know what to say or how to comfort her. At last he thought, "Why not tell her what my mother used to tell me? Why not give her some of the simple texts and Gospel stories I learned as a child?"

With this in mind he began to repeat some of the precious Gospel verses telling of God's love for sinners and of the Savior who had died to redeem. The woman listened eagerly. "That's it! That ought to get me in, shouldn't it! Did he die for sinners? Then that should get me in."

Stirred to the depths of his own being he told the story of the cross as he had not preached it for years. Like a thirsty soul, she drank in the living water. Finally, he knelt and prayed with her.

She trusted Christ for herself. Her fears were allayed and she entered into peace.

"Jowett," said Dr. Berry years afterward, "I helped get her in that night, and while I was helping to get her in, I got myself in also!"[4]

Are you in? If not, I exhort you to bow before Him this moment; believe on Jesus and freely receive His salvation!

SATURDAY: Christ's Wonderful Benefits

"Take My yoke upon you and learn from Me, for I am gentle and lowly in heart, and **you will find rest for your souls.**"

—Matthew 11:29

Once you are in the safe arms of Jesus, what will you find? You will find the perfect refuge, the One who has so much to offer all of us. The six cities of refuge named in Joshua 20:7–9 are representative of six truths for those who flee to Christ, the safest place in the universe. Each of the following Hebrew words that name the cities of refuge speak of one powerful facet of Christ's present ministry to us:

- **Kedesh** means a "holy place" or "righteousness." Christ is our "holy place" and our "righteousness." He is the only refuge for us when we feel unclean, defiled, or guilty (1 Corinthians 1:30).
- **Shechem** means "shoulder." Christ is our safe and strong "shoulder." He is the only refuge for us when we feel weary, exhausted, or stressed (Matthew 11:28–30).
- **Hebron** means "fellowship." Christ is the only refuge for the lonely who feel left out, left behind, homeless, or forsaken (John 14:21).
- **Bezer** means a "stronghold" or "fortress." Christ is our "stronghold," or "fortress." He is the only refuge for us when we feel helpless, fearful, and powerless (Matthew 28:18).
- **Ramoth** means "exalted" or "heights." Christ is the only refuge for us when our hearts darken and we feel hopeless (Ephesians 2:6).
- **Golan** means "separated." Christ is the only refuge for us when we struggle and feel weak when we are tempted (Hebrews 4:16).

Make a choice to live in hope. Each of these city names portray details of the refuge Christ offers for us to lay hold of every day, every hour, and every moment of our lives. Jesus is the closest, safest, and only refuge we can turn to when we are unclean, weary, homeless, helpless, hopeless, tempted, and fearful.

WEEK 6
Remember Christ's Blood

{ Revelation 1:5–8 }

As the end of days approaches, you can find hope as you remember Christ's blood that has washed away your sins!

SUNDAY: The Cleansing Power of Christ's Blood

Jesus Christ...loved us and washed us from our sins in His own blood, . . . to Him be glory and dominion forever and ever. Amen.
—Revelation 1:5–6

The blood of Christ has loosed us from our sins. Why do we need that power? From the dark hour of the Fall in the splendors of the Garden of Eden, every man, woman, and child has since been chained by the bondage of sin—stained by an indelible mark that grips our very souls. All pain, decay, fear, sorrow, death, and evil in our world traces its origins back to that very moment.

In the Bible, one of the pictures or metaphors for sin is found in the oldest and most feared of all diseases in history—leprosy. My first exposure to this feared disease occurred in a third-world country while riding a city bus through the squalor of the slum dwellers. In a billowing cloud of high-sulfur diesel, smoldering garbage, and filthy, dirt-laden air, we jerked to a stop as an oxcart lumbered across the road. Out of the corner of my eye a movement toward the bus caught my attention. A beggar pulled back the rag shawl that draped his shoulders and, in desperation, ran up to my slightly open window. Flinging his frail body at the bus, now just starting up again, he thrust a hand into the window. At least it used to be a hand: an oozing, ulcerated, gangrenous stump was all that remained. It was in the window but for a moment, yet its image is indelibly burned into my mind.

Leprosy is the first disease recorded in the Bible. It is found in the mummified bodies of Egypt's tombs. It was a horror in Israel, as Luke records: "And many lepers were in Israel in the time of Elisha the prophet, and none of them was cleansed except Naaman the Syrian" (Luke 4:27).

What we know today as Hansen's Disease is terrible as it ravages the human body. A natural response to leprosy is revulsion. Lepers were ostracized and feared. They were under penalty of death, kept outside of the camp or city, and avoided as unclean. God then used the disease's physical disfigurement, and the resulting ceremonial uncleanness, as a spiritual illustration. Leprosy is a vivid and graphic physical picture of the spiritual defilement of sin.

It is in this context that the power of Jesus is so beautifully seen: "Now a leper came to Him, imploring Him . . . , 'If You are willing, You can make me clean'" (Mark 1:40). Just as Christ's power could heal that leper physically, so His power can wash us and loose us from our sin. All we will ever need was accomplished by the inestimable, infinite, power of the blood of Christ.

The New Testament details these powerful truths of salvation that are directly tied to the blood of Christ: His blood, which is our **forgiveness**, powerfully paid the penalty of our **past sin**; His blood, which is our **victory**, absolutely defeats the power of our **present sin**; and His blood, which is our **security**, totally secures us from the presence of our **future sin**.

There is power in the blood of Christ: power to cleanse, change, and keep us—power to redeem, restore, and renew us. It is all the power of God's amazing grace in the sacrifice of our Lord Jesus as He poured out His blood on the cross.

Jesus has taken care of our **past lives**. Christ has the power to purchase us (Acts 20:28), to remove God's wrath from us (Romans 3:25), to justify us (Romans 5:9), and to scrub our minds clean (Hebrews 9:14).

Jesus is taking care of our **present lives**. Christ has the power to liberate us (Ephesians 1:7), to cleanse our sins (1 John 1:7), and to loose us from sin's grip (Revelation 1:5).

Jesus will also take care of our **future lives**. Christ has given us the power to experience fellowship with Him (1 Corinthians 10:16), to know His intimacy (Ephesians 2:13), to have His peace (Colossians 1:20), to enter God's presence (Hebrews 10:19), to live His life (Hebrews 13:20–21), and to live obediently (1 Peter 1:2).

Jesus is a wonderful Savior! For truly, there is power in the blood of Christ!

My Prayer for You This Week: *Oh Lord, we pray that You will open this precious portion of Your Word to us! May the blood of Jesus Christ Your Son, shed to take away our sin, and to loose us from the bondage of sin, be the focus of our worship to You throughout this week. In His precious name, the lovely name of Jesus, we pray. Amen.*

MONDAY: The Saving Power of Christ's Blood

The blood of Jesus Christ His Son cleanses us from all sin.

—1 JOHN 1:7

Jesus is the refuge for the unclean. There is no sin He cannot forgive; there is no stain He cannot remove; there is no failure He cannot forget. The leper in Mark 1:40–42 understood this well when he implored Jesus, "If You are willing, You can make me clean." Jesus, moved with compassion, touched him, and immediately he was cleansed. Jesus was the perfect refuge for this unclean leper!

Physically, leprosy is awful. Leprosy was the scourge of the ancient world. Nothing evoked more fear, more dread, or more revulsion than the sight of these "walking dead."

Spiritually, leprosy is a vivid and graphic picture of the dreadful power of sin. The instructions given to the priests in Leviticus 13 help us better understand the true nature of sin:

Sin, like leprosy, is inside us, deeper than the skin (Lev. 13:3) and cannot be helped by mere "surface" measures (see Jer. 6:14). Sin also spreads just like leprosy (Lev. 13:8). Sin always defiles (Lev. 13:45–46). People with leprosy were looked on as "dead" (Num. 12:12). Because of his defilement, a leprous person had to be isolated outside the camp (Lev. 13:46), so lost sinners one day will be isolated in hell. And just as leprous garments are fit only for the fire (Lev. 13:52, 57), so those who die while clothed in sin will burn forever. How important it is for lost sinners to trust Jesus Christ and get rid of their "leprosy"![1]

We are all born infected with the sin virus that remains in our system. Like leprosy, sin becomes a part of every fiber of our life. It infects our every thought, motivation, word, and deed. Sin cannot be removed on our own; only Jesus Christ can loose us from its infection by thoroughly washing us in His blood.

WEEK 6: REMEMBER CHRIST'S BLOOD

The blood of Jesus Christ took a "leprous" man like John Newton and transformed him into one of the most respected men of his generation in eighteenth-century England. History notes that he had Alzheimer's disease before he died. In the last two years of his life, as he lay in bed, many of the notable people of England would come to visit him. Newton had lost his ability to remember except for one thing. He would tell his visitors, "My memory is nearly gone; but I remember two things: that I am a great sinner, and that Christ is a great Savior."

Christ's blood has the same power to cleanse and transform "leprous" men and women in our twenty-first-century world. Jesus Christ, through His blood, has paid the *penalty* of sin, has broken the *power* of sin, and will eliminate the *presence* of sin. What a wonderful Savior!

TUESDAY: The Liberating Power of Christ's Blood

*Jesus Christ...loves us and **has freed us from our sins by his blood**.*
—Revelation 1:5 NIV

Sin is like barnacles that stick to your soul unless it is removed by one element in the universe: the blood of Jesus Christ, God's Son. Listen to the testimony of One who experienced the amazing cleansing power of Christ's blood that liberated him from a life of sin:

Who am I? My godly mother died when I was a young child. Reared by a sea-captain father, taken to sea at age eleven, I soon forgot the Scriptures she had taught me.

Several years later, I was pressed into the British navy and became a midshipman. By then I had earned the reputation of being able to curse for two hours straight without repeating a word. Restless and wild, I tried to desert, was caught, stripped, whipped severely, and degraded to the ranks. I eventually ran away to Africa, but only so "I might sin my fill." And I did.

Debauched and distant from God, I fell into the hands of a Portuguese slave trader. For months the chief woman of the trader's harem treated me like an animal, beating me and forcing me to grovel in the dirt for my food.

Reduced to a mangy cur of a man, I finally escaped and made my way to the shores of Africa. Picked up by a passing ship I earned the position of first mate because I was a skilled navigator. But while the captain was ashore one day, I broke out the ship's rum and got the entire crew drunk. When the captain came back, he was so furious he hit me, knocking me overboard.

I would have drowned were it not for a sailor who pulled me back on board by spearing my thigh with a boat hook. The wound was so large that it left a scar big enough to put my fist in. Some weeks later, when the ship neared the coast of Scotland, it sailed into a storm and almost sank. For days I manned the pumps below deck in what seemed a hopeless nightmare.

It was then that I desperately called out to God. He answered my helpless cry, and I emerged from the hold of that ship to later become the chaplain of England's Parliament and even to preach before the king. I am the vile blasphemer whom many would subsequently refer to as the second founder of the Church of England. And it was I who wrote:

> Amazing grace! how sweet the sound,
> That saved a wretch like me!
> I once was lost, but now am found,
> Was blind, but now I see.

These were the lyrics born out of my wayward, free-versed life. And to my ears, there is no sweeter sound than grace in all the world. Who am I? John Newton.[2]

"Amazing Grace" has become a beloved part of American culture. The song speaks of the amazing grace of God the Father who sent God the Son down to earth to become a sacrifice, to actually shed His own blood for each of us. I hope that you are clinging to the blood of Jesus as your only hope and assurance for the cleansing of your sin!

WEDNESDAY: The Deleting Power of Christ's Blood

> *In Him we have **redemption through His blood**, the forgiveness of sins, according to the riches of His grace.*
> —Ephesians 1:7

Because I want you to really understand how wonderfully Jesus' blood has met our deepest need, today we will study the theology of the blood of Christ. Consider again just what it is that He has done for us: "I will be merciful to their unrighteousness, and their sins and their lawless deeds I will remember no more" (Hebrews 8:12).

Christ's blood has the power to purchase us. "[Overseers], shepherd the church of God which He purchased with His own blood" (Acts 20:28). In Greek, that word "purchased" is *peripoieo*, which means "obtained for himself." Jesus bought us for himself and has taken care of our past lives—defective, defiled, and stained as they were. He bought us just like we were. That is incredible love and mercy!

Christ's blood has the power to remove God's wrath from us. "God set forth [Jesus] as a propitiation by His blood, through faith, to demonstrate His righteousness, because in His forbearance God had passed over the sins that were previously committed" (Romans 3:25). "Propitiation is all that the Old Testament expiation [covering and putting away of sin] was, and very importantly, 'The Pacifying of the Wrath of God Thereby.' It is the quenching of God's wrath against us by obliterating our sins from His Holy sight."[3] In the Old Testament, God passed over all the endless sacrifices that never took away sins because He knew that Jesus would one day pay the ultimate price with His blood.

Christ's blood has the power to justify us. "Having now been justified by His blood, we shall be saved from wrath through Him" (Romans 5:9). In justification, a sinner stands before God as the accused and is declared free (Romans 8:33). It is like standing accused at a tribunal before the judge of the universe and being declared not guilty. We *are* guilty; we committed those sins, but Jesus steps up and says, "Not guilty! I took the penalty." God the Father then imputes His Son's righteousness to the sinner's account (Romans 4:11b).

Justification is an outside or external event that changes our standing before God: "Having been justified by faith, we have peace with God through our Lord Jesus Christ" (Romans 5:1). Justification does not make us personally righteous; sanctification does that (Romans 3:28). The end result of justification is that we have eternal peace with God and endless life with Him that can never be taken away from or lost by us.

Christ's blood has the power to scrub our minds clean. "How much more shall the blood of Christ . . . cleanse your conscience from dead works to serve the living God?" (Hebrews 9:14). He will cleanse us of memories of sins that we have committed, pictures of things we should not have seen, feelings that we should not have felt, and all those things that were leading us to death and drying up the vitality of our lives. In other words, God has the power to scrub our consciences clean so that we do not persist in a self-defeating guilt life in which so many Christians live (also see Hebrews 10:22).

Every time Satan comes with his two-edged sword of doubt and discouragement, and you feel helpless and guilty (thinking you've done something one too many times and God is not going to forgive you), you can resist Satan by reciting these truths: *Jesus has already died for my sins; they are paid for; I am forgiven; God has forever accepted me in Christ—and my earthly life is daily catching up, bit by bit, to that eternally settled reality!* (See Galatians 2:20.)

Jesus has removed guilt—the curse and sting of sin. However, when we sin and offend God, He wants us to acknowledge that sin so He can cleanse us. We are to confess it to God, and not try to "work it off" by flailing ourselves with guilt. According to 1 John 1:9, it is as simple as saying: "I confess; I agree with You that I committed that sin, and thank You that Your blood cleanses me."

God wants to clean out everything that fuels defeat in your life. For sin to defeat you, you have to keep feeding those memories by remembering them. It is not that the memories will be totally forgotten, but that through Christ's blood their power to disable, discourage, and defeat you will be broken. If you are struggling with guilt feelings, I exhort you to ask God to scrub your mind clean!

THURSDAY: The Securing Power of Christ's Blood

*He is . . . able to **save to the uttermost** those who come to God through Him, since He always lives to make intercession for them. . . . Having a High Priest over the house of God, let us draw near with a true heart in full assurance of faith.*

—Hebrews 7:25; 10:21

What security it is to be owned by Christ! In the Levitical system, people were kept outside of God's presence, but believers can now boldly draw near to God! Because we have a High Priest who intercedes for us before the Father's throne, we are wonderfully saved "to the uttermost" and are eternally secure through the power of Christ's blood.

Christ's blood has the power to liberate us: "In Him we have redemption through His blood, the forgiveness of sins, according to the riches of His grace" (Ephesians 1:7). *Redemption* could be described as "when I stood before God as a slave and He bought me from the slave market of sin." This is present power to liberate us from our sins. Have you experienced this today?

Christ's blood has the power to allow us to experience Him daily. "The cup of blessing which we bless, is it not the communion of the blood of Christ? The bread which we break, is it not the communion of the body of Christ?" (1 Corinthians 10:16). In the Greek, the word "communion" is *koinonia*, or fellowship. "It is the blood that unites us into perfect fellowship. In the book of Acts, this is seen by the use of the term 'brethren' over forty times. 'It describes those who share a common heritage, like citizens of the same country, though it carries the additional force of brethren born of the same Spirit, when applied to Christians.' [Acts 1:16; 6:3; 9:17; etc.] In brief, disciples must have devoted Christian friends to follow, and this can only be facilitated by being together over a period of time."[4]

Christ's blood has the power to draw us near. "In Christ Jesus you who once were far off have been brought near by the blood of Christ" (Ephesians 2:13). Christ's blood has the power to let us experience intimacy with God—to *know Him* personally. Do you know Him so well that any lack of fellowship with Him grieves your heart? Do you know Him so well that you look forward to meeting with Him daily? People are creatures of habit: many get up early, have a cup of coffee, and read the news to see what is going on in the world. But if we love Jesus, we should begin our day by reading God's Word and seeking intimate fellowship with Him—the One who so greatly loves us and wants to spend time with us!

Christ's blood has the power to give His peace. "For it pleased the Father . . . by Him to reconcile all things to Himself, . . . having made peace through the blood of His cross" (Colossians 1:19–20). When we are still in our sin, God is at war with us. So the Father wants to reconcile us to himself by giving us peace *with* God (no guilt over the past) and *of* God (no anxiety for the future). When we accept the sacrifice of Christ, His justice is satisfied, and we become at peace with Him. The more we get to know God intimately, the more we can then experience the peace of Jesus, "which surpasses all understanding" (Philippians 4:7)!

As you meditate upon today's verses, Christ will open God's presence to you so that you may live in the power of His blood!

FRIDAY: The Providing Power of Christ's Blood

Elect according to the foreknowledge of God the Father, in sanctification of the Spirit, **for obedience** *and sprinkling of the blood of Jesus Christ.*

—1 Peter 1:2

Have you ever considered that the blood of Jesus Christ provides the power to live obediently? If you are a genuine, born-again saint of God, according to 1 Peter 1:2, you can live obediently because God provides the way to do so. Every time you disobey Him, He won't strike you in punishment, and you don't have to somehow *earn* His forgiveness. God bought you in Christ in spite of knowing your liabilities. He knows not only what you have done in the past but also everything you will do in the future. God loves you *unconditionally*!

Christ's blood has the power to cleanse you and loose you from sin's grip. "The blood of Jesus Christ His Son cleanses us from all sin" (1 John 1:7). Jesus can cleanse every sin in the past, present, or future because of His once-and-for-all sacrifice on the cross. "For He loved us and washed us from our sins in His own blood" (Revelation 1:5). His blood sacrifice provided the power to break the hold of any sin!

Christ's blood has the power to elicit our proper response. "God be merciful to me, a sinner!" (Luke 18:13). The loveliest picture I know of Christ's forgiveness is the story of the woman who was caught in the act of adultery, deserted by her companion in sin, and dragged before Jesus. John 8:3 tells us that "the scribes and Pharisees brought to Him a woman caught in adultery. And . . . **set her in the midst**." The word "set" connotes "throwing down or dumping." This woman was literally dumped in front of Jesus!

Next, they said to Jesus, "Teacher, this woman was caught in adultery, in the very act. Now Moses, in the law, commanded us that such should be stoned. But what do You say?" (John 8:4–5). Apart from Christ, this is how all of us are in God's presence. We are guilty, vile, helpless, and hopeless. We are crumpled before Him, unable to look up because the Law points out every sin we have committed, and our accusers scream that we deserve death.

Jesus insightfully told the accusers that whoever was without sin should throw the first stone at the woman. After they departed, one by one, with no one left to condemn her, Jesus compassionately said, "Neither do I condemn you; go and sin no more" (see John 8:6–11).

This incident clearly reveals the difference between how Satan and Jesus want to treat us: Satan's goal is "to steal, and to kill, and to destroy" (John 10:10a), while Jesus, who forgives and does not condemn, desires that we "may have life, and . . . have it more abundantly" (John 10:10b). Our proper response to Jesus Christ is to thus cry out: What a Savior—"To Him be glory and dominion forever and ever" (Revelation 1:6b)!

SATURDAY: New Beginnings by Christ's Blood

Behold, He is coming with clouds, and every eye will see Him. . . . And all . . . will mourn because of Him. . . . "I am the Alpha and the Omega, the Beginning and the End," says the Lord, "who is and who was and who is to come, the Almighty."

—Revelation 1:7–8

Are you ready to meet this Jesus—the almighty God who is coming soon? You will be if you let Him "give you **a new heart** and put **a new spirit** within you; . . . and cause you to walk in [His] statutes" (Ezekiel 36:26–27).

God's Word offers a life of new beginnings. The ultimate new beginning is called the new birth, or being born again by God's Word. Being born a second time is the ultimate new beginning because you get to start life completely over again—like the woman caught in adultery.

Christ's blood gives us a new beginning in our assurance of God's complete forgiveness. In Christ, rather than crumpling before Him with the law pointing out all our sins, the law becomes our delight: "Let Your tender mercies come to me . . . for Your law is my delight" (Psalm 119:77). The words "tender mercies" remind us that none of us get what we deserve. That is what mercy is all about. Grace is getting the undeserved favor of God; mercy is not getting the rightly deserved punishment of God. When God is merciful, He is withholding what we deserve. "For Your law is my delight" translates into "As I read Your Book, I realize that You have made provision for my sins."

Here is the good news of salvation: *The only thing that you and I have to give to God is our sins*. We don't have anything good enough to give to God. So He says to us, "Do you know that you are a guilty sinner? Then give Me your sins, and let Me put them upon Christ!" He became sin for us, so we can now say: "I have a new beginning in my assurance of God. Because of Your tender mercies, You are withholding Your wrath from me. That has revived me that I may live, for Your law is my delight!"

Christ's blood gives us a new beginning in praise. "Let my soul live, and it shall praise You" (Psalm 119:175). "Let my soul live" simply means "Let my soul be energized to worship You!" Instead of being dead in our sins, like the "walking dead" of the leper colonies, we are alive in Christ who gives us new life. He revives us so that we can praise Him!

Can you, with all your being, worship, magnify, and praise the Lord? If not, you need a new beginning. The good news is that the Lord Jesus Christ says to you, "You don't have to live with a hard heart. You don't have to live with a sin-stained heart. You don't have to live in despair—feeling hopeless, helpless, and having no purpose in life. My power is ever-present to provide a new beginning for you!"

Make a choice to live in hope. When you are born again, you become a new creation; old things have passed away; behold, all things have become new (2 Corinthians 5:17). And through the power of Christ's blood, God wants to give you:

A new beginning in the Word.
A new beginning in love.
A new beginning in obedience.
A new beginning in repentance.
A new beginning in spiritual renewal.
A new beginning in the assurance of God.
A new beginning in trusting the Lord.
A new beginning in boldness.
A new beginning in understanding God's plan.
A new beginning in the only lasting help.
A new beginning in hope for your troubles.
A new beginning in strength.
A new beginning in patience.
A new beginning in praise.
A new beginning in what is truly worth living for!

Not only do we have a new beginning in this lifetime—one of hope as we face the end days—but also soon, very soon, we will experience the ultimate new beginning! For Jesus tells us that "'God will wipe away every tear from [our] eyes; there shall be no more death, nor sorrow, nor crying [or] pain, for the former things have passed away.' Then He who [sits] on the throne [will say], 'Behold, I make all things new'" (Revelation 21:4–5a).

Are you ready to meet Him? Are you safely "under the blood of Christ"? There is wonder-working power in the precious blood of the Lamb!

WEEK 7
Find Hope in Christ's Majesty

{ Revelation 1:9 }

As the end of days approaches, you can find hope as you discover Christ's majesty!

SUNDAY: When You Feel Abandoned

*I, John, . . . **was on the island** . . . called Patmos for the word of God and for the testimony of Jesus Christ.*
—REVELATION 1:9

John felt alone when he was exiled to Patmos, but Christ became nearer to him then than he had ever experienced before. The more of Christ's majesty that we too experience, the nearer He will become to us so that we can walk securely in hope at the end of days.

John was not the first of God's servants to feel alone and in need of Christ's majestic presence. Three thousand years ago, another of God's faithful servants had that same hope. His name was David, and his life is the single most-recorded life (over 140 chapters) in God's Word. As we look at David's life, we will discover how to find living hope for anything we may face ourselves.

Everything was going so well for David for a long time: after defeating Goliath, he became worship leader for the king, a great warrior, a member of the king's cabinet, and the king's son-in-law. But then everything fell apart.

In the lives of believers, there can come a point so low that we actually feel that everyone, even God, has abandoned us. That is how David felt in Psalm 13. In Psalm 13 we see that Christ cannot be our refuge if we do not hear His invitation to flee to Him, or if we do not even remember He is there. Sometimes we have to hit bottom, go through dark waters, or face incredible convulsions in our lives to see Him, even though He's been with us all the time.

I learned that lesson well at 27,000 feet. While flying home from a Shepherds Conference in Los Angeles, I received an insight I will never forget. Having flown enough to have heard the pre-flight safety lecture dozens of times, I usually read and ignore the lecture completely, never thinking about anything other than what I need to do before we land.

This particular flight was uneventful. I had an empty seat beside me that became my desk, and as the world slowly drifted by outside my window, I worked. After a bit, clouds began to darken the sky, and I had to turn on the light to see, but I kept on studying.

Suddenly a reminder to fasten seatbelts caught my attention. I began to listen intently when the plane did its first roller-coaster move. Soon we were dropping, and then we were going straight up like an elevator. After that, a very hard jolt knocked open a few overhead compartments and things fell out. Throughout the plane, there were some scattered cries of fear.

From that moment on, all I thought about was this: *Who exactly is up front flying this plane? How much experience does he have? How skilled is he in thunderstorm management?*

What tremendous lesson did I learn about flying? That we don't pay much attention if all goes smoothly. After all, who gives the pilot a thought unless the weather gets rough? But when the world around us jolts, jumps, rocks, and swerves unexpectedly, all we can think about then is this: *Who is steering this careening machine?* We are forced to realize how important the pilot really is, and that our lives are in his hands.

The same is true in our spiritual lives: the fewer bumps, the more we ignore the pilot, our Lord. The smoother the ride, the more we forget the One whose hands hold our lives. But let the rough family times come, the roller-coaster ride of our emotions, the crash of our finances, or the sudden plummet of our health, and then we think about the pilot.

David experienced many a bumpy ride in his lifetime, and at times even became fearful, but consistently he chose to put his trust in the pilot of his life. As we continue to focus on how to find living hope for the end of days, we can learn a lot from how David handled his tribulation periods, especially during times of great loneliness.

After the Lord rescued him from Gath (1 Samuel 21:10–15), David fled to the wilderness and lived in a cave. (Compare 1 Samuel 22:1–5 with Psalm 57 and 142.) During his cave time, David went through a period of feeling abandoned by God. But in that dark hour he found hope. How did he do that? Troubles, trials, tests, and temptations always pushed David toward the Lord. God was his choice; God was his habit; God was his desire because David supremely loved the Lord with all his heart. Those dark times simply exposed the reality, deep down in his soul, that David had entrusted his life to the Lord.

Throughout the Psalms, David made confessions about the Pilot who was flying his plane during the turbulent and stormy skies of his life. As you go through this week, I pray that you will discover, like David, that even if you happen to feel abandoned right now—God is still there flying you safely through!

My Prayer for You This Week: *Father in Heaven, I pray that we would cultivate those holy habits energized by Your Holy Spirit that make us useful. Make us those who want to give our lives back to*

You. May even our habits revolve around You so that we are disciplined, trustworthy, responsible, and obedient. We want to be energized by Your Spirit to honestly say, "Lord, I'm Your servant." Anything that is out of control—be it our tongue, our finances, or our calendar—is just a testimony that You are not in control of that part of our lives. Help us to not think so highly of ourselves that we do not put everything under Your Lordship. May every part of our lives honor You, and testify that we are Your servants. For that is what we want to be. Lord Jesus, be our Master; hear our hearts as we whisper back to You. For we give ourselves to You in the name of Jesus. Amen.

MONDAY: Common Causes for Cave Times

*We are **hard-pressed on every side**, yet not crushed; we are perplexed, but not in despair.*
—2 CORINTHIANS 4:8

As a pastor, biblical counselor, and a follower of Christ for over forty years, I am convinced that feelings of abandonment are very common among believers, no matter how mature they might be in the Lord. Both the apostles John and David knew what it was like to feel alone and in desperate need of Christ's presence. Look at David's opening words in Psalm 13:1–2: "How long, O LORD? Will You forget me forever? How long will You hide Your face from me? How long shall I take counsel in my soul, having sorrow in my heart daily? How long will my enemy be exalted over me?"

David experienced many such cave times, and it is likely that we will also. What are some common causes of cave times—those periods in life when we feel utterly abandoned by others as well as God?

Cave times may start through a protracted illness that seems to never end, when strength never comes, when future plans fade, and so does hope. If hope is lost, uncontrolled emotions can wreak havoc not only in the ill person's life but also in the lives of his or her family.

Another common cause for feeling abandoned is a sudden loss of income, when financial needs become difficult, and eventually seem overwhelming. This type of trial can place a great deal of stress on a marriage and family. So can a demanding and unreasonable boss, a grueling and unending schedule, or a jealous, spiteful, and injurious coworker. Wayward children also cause immeasurable pain to believing parents, as does an alcoholic or abusive spouse, or unsaved family members.

Usually, times like these make us feel that no one really cares about us. So more and more we start to feel rejected by others, which then starts the downward spiral into thinking that God has abandoned us as well. David experienced such a depth of feeling abandoned that in Psalm 13 he cried out to God as if he could no longer hang on.

Amazingly, there is little said or written in Christian literature about helping believers who feel abandoned by God. Even D. Martyn Lloyd-Jones didn't cover this topic in his classic work entitled *Spiritual Depression: Its Causes and Cures*.[1]

Why do you suppose this is? I think it is because we have been taught that Christians are not to experience such things, that we are only to have "life more abundantly" or to "live victoriously." . . . The dying French atheist Voltaire . . . said, "I am abandoned by God and man."

We are not surprised to hear an unbeliever say that. But if any of us should admit to such feelings, many of our friends would look askance [disapprovingly] at us, shake their heads, and wonder whether we are Christians. Isn't that true? Isn't that the chief reason why you do not talk to other Christians about this or about many other problems?"[2]

Aren't you glad that a spiritual giant like David did not hide his negative feelings? He did not mind being thought of as weak, failing, or troubled; he just unashamedly cried out to God for help.

This David—the psalmist, the king God chose, the man God said was after His own heart—was not embarrassed to bare his dark struggles of the soul for all to see! In fact, he wrote more psalms during his cave times than at any other period in his life (Psalms 4, 13, 40, 57, 70, 141, 142). All were lessons on how to overcome feelings of loneliness and abandonment when far from help or away from home.

If you feel unable to go on, like David did in Psalm 13, I encourage you to read through his cave-time psalms. Meditate on how he responded to God in his difficult times! If you do, you'll not only be blessed but also better understand what made David "a man after God's own heart."

TUESDAY: Where Are You, God?

> ***How long**, O LORD? Will You forget me forever? **How long** will You hide Your face from me? **How long** shall I take counsel in my soul, having sorrow in my heart daily? **How long** will my enemy be exalted over me?*
> —PSALM 13:1–2

At the beginning of Psalm 13, David was feeling abandoned and dejected. The first two verses express the depths of his soul in four cries of anguish. Each cry is a figure of speech called erotesis, which is asking questions without waiting for or even expecting an answer. These cries also represent a second form of speech called anaphora—when the same word is repeated at the beginning of successive sentences.

David's repetitive cries pleaded with God for an answer: "How long . . . ?" He didn't even pause because he was so overcome with sorrow, grief, and a feeling of being totally alone and abandoned. By repeating himself four times, David revealed how deep this feeling ran as he cried out to God: "I just can't go on any longer!" As we consider his confessions carefully, some may strike a chord in your own heart.

My life feels like an endless struggle. "How long, O LORD? Will You forget me **forever**?" (v. 1a). Everyone had left David. He was hunted by his own family, his own fellow people of God, and was being threatened by his enemies. And now, on top of all that, he had stepped into a bleak desert region. With every fiber of his being, David felt humanly dejected and abandoned. One commentator writes:

> Well must David have understood what this was, when, hunted by Saul, he knew not where to betake himself, at one time seeking refuge among the Moabites, at another in the wilderness of

Ziph; now an outlaw hiding himself in the cave of Adullam, and anon a captain in the service of the King of the Philistines; and amid all his projects haunted by the mournful conviction, "I shall now one day perish by the hand of Saul."³

My life seems to have lost God's blessing. "How long will You **hide Your face** from me" (v. 1b). David was saying, "Nothing is like it used to be. Every part of my life is troubled and seems to lack Your blessing." So he cried out to God: "I don't see *You* anymore in my home, my work, or my life!" Think about how that might feel:

- **My family doesn't seem blessed anymore:** "The early joys of being a newlywed have long since faded as the reality of personality differences stress our relationship. And now, our formerly quiet, content children are growing into selfish and rebellious youths. The joy of home life has been replaced with the tension of confrontation, correction, and sorrow. Has God ceased to bless our family?"
- **My work doesn't seem blessed anymore:** "The early days of idealism, creativity, and boundless energy leading to growth and success in my career have been replaced with constant obstacles and personal stagnation. Has God ceased to bless my work?"
- **My ministry doesn't seem blessed anymore:** "The spring in my step is gone; my feet have felt like lead as I've crossed the parking lot to serve in my ministry at church! I have lost all my former joy and purpose! Has God ceased to bless my ministry?"
- **My spiritual life doesn't seem blessed anymore:** "The Word seems stale; my singing is lifeless; coming to worship is drudgery. My sins feel unforgiven, and my past is coming back to haunt me. I can't escape feeling so stained . . . so distant from the Lord . . . I feel like no one—not even *God*—cares about my soul! Has God ceased to bless me?"

Should any of these feelings reflect your own life, remind Jesus of His promise: "Come to Me, all you who labor and are heavy laden, and I will give you rest" (Matthew 11:28)! Ask Him to speak His sweet peace to your heart, and then cling to Him in hope, trusting that He who cares so deeply for you will lead you safely through the difficult challenges you face. He is only a prayer away!

WEDNESDAY: Feeling Dejected and Abandoned?

*For we . . . are **always delivered to death** for Jesus' sake, that the life of Jesus also may be manifested in our mortal flesh.*
—2 Corinthians 4:11

David had dark thoughts and uncontrolled emotions. He loved the Lord, but all the stress of his terrible plight had drained him of peace and joy. As we continue to study David's Psalm 13 confessions, perhaps you can identify with how deeply wounded he felt.

My mind seems so troubled. "How long shall I take counsel in my soul, **Having sorrow in my heart daily?**" (v. 2a). David was swept away by his emotions, which is a common experience. He couldn't calmly reflect on God's faithful hand in the past so that he could be comforted by trusting the future to Him. David had ruminated so long on disaster after disaster that he was feeding on the dark thoughts of hopelessness. So he cried out in anguish again, "God, I can't stop these feelings of dejection and abandonment!"

Usually, there are some clear causes for these feelings David confessed: emotional temperament, physical weakness, and "let down" are often at the root of discouragement. David was probably of the temperament that is more prone to discouragement. As Lloyd-Jones writes in the opening pages of his monumental book, "foremost among all causes of spiritual depression is temperament."[4]

James Boice says that "A plunge into disquieting thoughts and emotions can be caused by physical factors—illness, for example. Charles Haddon Spurgeon was one of the greatest evangelical leaders of the [nineteenth] century, but he suffered from severe bouts of depression. Why? The main reason is that he suffered from gout, marked by painful inflammation of the joints and an excess of uric acid in the blood. It was common in the [nineteenth] century, and it drained Spurgeon's energies."[5] At times of illness or extreme fatigue, we are more vulnerable to the Devil or our flesh trying to push us down.

A weak time called "let down" often follows great events. For example, after Elijah's great mountaintop experience, he felt so low that he was ready to die. But God took him away to a quiet place to feed him, refresh him, and meet with him (1 Kings 18–19). It is helpful to remember that "Elijah was a man with a nature like ours" (James 5:17a). Even Jesus retreated from the crowds after big events like the feeding of the 5,000 and preaching campaigns because He needed extra time alone with God to refresh and renew His life. Since Elijah, Jesus, and David all needed to exercise care to protect themselves from let downs, we should not be taken by surprise when we face similar experiences in our own lives.

My life seems to have lost God's victory. "How long will my **enemy be exalted** over me?" (v. 2b). David soulfully concluded, "It's no use. Saul is going to win. He has all the troops, resources, and time he needs. He will end up destroying me!" So, once again, David cried out in anguish, "God, I am constantly defeated!"

Most of us probably do not have literal human enemies, at least not serious enemies. But if you are a Christian, you do have one great spiritual enemy who is worse than any human enemy imaginable. This is the devil, whom the apostle Peter compared to "a roaring lion looking for someone to devour" (1 Peter 5:8).[6]

The devil [is] the adversary of our souls. He can use our temperaments and our physical conditions. He so deals with us that we allow our temperament to control and govern us, instead of keeping temperament where it should be kept. There is no end to the ways the devil produces spiritual depression. We must always bear him in mind.[7]

David survived his cave times by choosing to live in hope, and not the pits. In verses 3–6 of Psalm 13, he looked to the Lord, who alone could rescue him: "**Consider** and **hear me**, O Lord my God; **Enlighten my eyes**, lest I sleep the sleep of death; lest my enemy say, 'I have prevailed against him;' lest those who trouble me rejoice when I am moved. But I have trusted in Your mercy; my heart shall rejoice in Your salvation. I will sing to the Lord, because He has dealt bountifully with me."

David prayed, **"Look at me!"** (v. 3a). He felt that God had turned His back on him, so He asked the Lord to turn around and **consider him** by paying attention to how much he was hurting. When I am overwhelmed, my sweet wife Bonnie will come and sit down to talk with me. If I do not respond, she says, "Look at me, Honey." She then gently puts her hand under my chin and lifts my face up to look at her eyes of love and smile of comfort. That is how God wants to encourage us as well. He says, "Look up at Me, My child!"—and when we do, His eyes of love and smile of comfort beautifully minister to our wounded spirit.

David prayed, **"Answer me!"** (v. 3b). He felt that God had stopped talking to him, and he wanted God to **hear him**. This Hebrew word for "hear" literally means "answer." David was asking the Lord to let him hear His voice just as he did in former days. When we face times like that, we need to take God's Word and say to Him, "Open Your Word to my heart again. Let me cling to Your truth. Help my unbelief!"

David prayed, **"Restore me!"** (v. 3c). David needed God to **enlighten him** because he believed that he was going to die, and never be king. Thus he asked God to do what He had promised. When we are discouraged, we should boldly say to the Lord, "You promised to never leave me, so I need to sense Your presence again! You told me that You loved me to the uttermost, so I need to sense Your power again! You said that You would comfort me, so I need to sense Your peace again!"

Think on this:

To be abandoned means that once you were not. For the true child of God, there is always some awareness of this truth, regardless of how deep his or her depression may be. We may be depressed even to the point of feeling utterly abandoned, but the fact that we even feel abandoned means that we really know God is there. To be abandoned, somebody actually needs to abandon you. Because we are Christians and have been taught by God in Scripture, we know that God still loves us and will be faithful to us, regardless of our feelings.[8]

THURSDAY: The Most Incredible Treasure of All

*"Did not our heart burn within us while . . . **He opened the Scriptures** to us?" . . . And He opened their understanding, **that they might comprehend the Scriptures**.*
—Luke 24:32, 45

The owner of the universe has given something priceless to us. First, God let Jesus reveal himself personally to the apostle John. Then God the Father gave a gift—The Revelation of Jesus Christ—to the Son. Next, God the Son shared that gift with the Apostle John, the last living apostle. Finally, John wrote it down and shared it with us. And that is the truest of treasures!

I remember a time when I thought I had a treasure. Shortly after my family moved to New England, every resident received a lottery ticket certificate in the mail. When I was growing up, swearing, smoking, chewing, drinking, and the lottery were all sins. With trepidation I therefore opened up the envelope and read: "You're a winner!" I rushed to the nearby gas station where there were banners proclaiming a multi-million dollar jackpot. After the ticket printed out, I checked the numbers. The first matched, then the second, third, and fourth—all the way to the $1,000,000 level. I had won the grand jackpot! The attendant was so excited that he was getting ready to call the radio, the newspaper, and the TV station, but then we looked at the bottom of the ticket. It was just a demonstration copy. That was as close as I ever got to an earthly treasure.

Even if I had actually won that jackpot, it could never compare to my delight in God's heavenly treasure: "I . . . count all things loss for the excellence of the knowledge of Christ Jesus my Lord" (Philippians 3:8). Seeing the glorious majesty of Jesus Christ in the Scriptures is the most incredible treasure we could ever possess!

The Apostle John's Cave Time. Have you ever thought about what disturbing days John was going through when he received the Revelation? Near the end of the first century, he lived alone in a world violently hostile to Christians.

The Roman emperor was personally committed to finding Christians and erasing their influence. He had captured and killed Paul and the other apostles, and now he was hunting John, the last living apostle. Twenty-five years before John wrote out the Revelation, the emperor dipped Christians in tar. Then he tied them to posts, and lit them on fire to light his gardens at night. That is how bad the world was in John's time!

The Roman world sent infiltrators into the church. In Acts 20:29 KJV, Paul called them "grievous wolves" because they secretly reported what was said at the intimate church fellowship meetings. Some Christians even defected to the world—false doctrine, materialism, and immorality. The Roman government also allowed its citizens to break in and rob believers' homes. In fact, this was so common that the writer of Hebrews spoke of Christians who "joyfully accepted the plundering of [their] goods" (Hebrews 10:34).

As the only surviving apostle, think of how discouraged John must have felt. For he had heard about or seen all his dearest friends savagely murdered. According to traditional church history, Peter had been crucified in Rome with his head upside down because he felt he was unworthy to die in the same manner as Christ; Andrew had been crucified at Edessa near modern Russia; James, brother of John, had been slain by Herod's sword; Matthew had been beheaded in Ethiopia; Thomas had been thrust through with a spear in India; Simon the Zealot had been crucified in Briton; Thaddeus had been crucified at Edessa; Bartholomew had been beaten and crucified in India; Philip had been crucified at Heliopolis in Phrygia; and James the Less had been clubbed to death in Jerusalem.

Although John was not under an immediate threat of death when he was first sent to Patmos, he knew that his turn would be coming soon. (Some records indicate that he was horribly martyred by being cast into boiling oil, but no reliable account of his death has survived.) What a nightmare to be living through!

Jesus is with us always. The promise Jesus gave to His disciples at the Great Commission never changed. Jesus accompanied each of His beloved apostles as they entered the fiery furnace of troubles. He stayed beside them "to the end" (Matthew 28:20). When it was their "appointed" time to die, the Good Shepherd walked each disciple through the valley of death's shadow. As promised, Christ took them all home safely.

Do you also know that Jesus is with you? Are you able to trust Him to see you through—even to the end of the age?

FRIDAY: Christ's Majesty—God's Answer for Bad Times

"Let not your heart be troubled; you believe in God, believe also in Me."
—JOHN 14:1

Although those were very dark and disturbing days for John, they were also very dangerous times for Christ's church. This period in time was the closest, I believe, to the church ever becoming extinct.

Paul had founded the church at Ephesus, but Timothy pastored it until he was brutally martyred by a mob. After that, until he was taken prisoner by the emperor and banished to Patmos, the Apostle John shepherded that great Ephesian church, which had become the largest in Asia Minor (about 5,000 saints!).

How painful it must have been for John when it appeared that his family, the church, was falling apart under the vicious attack from without, and rotting from the decay of false teaching within! Knowing that he was the last living witness of Christ—the last link to His earthly life—must have given him cause for great concern. For he was the only one left who had actually seen Jesus walk on the water, feed thousands, and raise dead corpses to life by a word!

What was God's answer for this aged, weary, distressed, saddened, frightened, and troubled servant? God made him take a long look to discover anew and afresh the most beautiful picture there is in all the Scriptures—Jesus Christ. Revelation is all about teaching us to do just that.

There is no more beautiful or more clearly painted portrait of Jesus in the whole Bible than the first chapter of Revelation. It is here that we discover Jesus revealing His glorious majesty so that we can see Him as He is (1:1–20)! If you want to discover the magnificent sovereign majesty of Jesus Christ, you need to get into the habit of looking for Him throughout the Scriptures. Make that your heart's desire, for He can be seen all the way through the Bible.

One night, I came into the church building where my wife was attending a ladies' salad supper. I needed to talk with her for a moment. Scores of women were milling around, so I just stood there in the doorway looking across the room. I kept looking until I saw my Bonnie, and my eyes locked on her. Later, someone said to her, "That was so sweet! I saw the look on your husband's face when he finally saw you." And that is the kind of look you should have in your heart when you read the Scriptures. You should not be content until you see Jesus every time you get into His Word. Every time!

If you are going through disturbing, dangerous, despairing days in your life, *look for Christ.* His purpose is not that we should primarily fear Him, but that we should *trust* Him. For **Christ is in control.** That is why we believe that His church will not be subjected to all the turmoil and death of the Great Tribulation: "For God did not appoint us to wrath, but to obtain salvation through our Lord Jesus Christ" (1 Thessalonians 5:9).

Hope for the End of Days: Revelation is a book that offers a hope that is the answer to all fears: thinking the world is "going down the drain"; economic instability and future economic upheavals; friends turning their backs on Christ; potential terrorist acts and global plagues; and any other trouble, trial, or upset we may face.

Are all the closest people in your life dying, getting weak, or going through terrible times of physical, emotional, or spiritual oppression like the Apostle John experienced? Instead of weakening in those times, that is a call of God for you to take a careful look at Jesus. Ask Him to allow you to see Jesus like never before (Psalm 119:18).

Are you trusting Jesus? As the hoof beats of the horsemen of the end are heard louder each day, I pray that your heart will rest in the One who holds you securely!

SATURDAY: Find Hope in Christ's Reign of Majesty

And when I saw Him, I fell at His feet as dead. But **He laid His right hand on me, saying to me, "Do not be afraid; I am the First and the Last."**
—REVELATION 1:17

Chapter after chapter of Revelation, God's final book, is one of the amazing discoveries about the Christ who is beyond the capacity of human minds to fully comprehend! The first chapter alone far exceeds any ideas we may have previously formed of this One we call Jesus. For it is here that we discover Christ revealing His glorious majesty so that the scales fall off our eyes, and we are able to see Him as He truly is: "the Alpha and Omega, the Beginning and the End," the One "who is and who was and who is to come"—the Almighty God (1:8)!

In chapters 2:1–3:22, we see Christ's glorious majesty challenging His church universal through special messages to the seven churches of Asia Minor. And the Lord says, "He who has an ear, let him hear what the Spirit says to the churches" (2:7, 11, 17, 29; 3:6, 13, 22). His admonitions to each church also have a direct application to our generation as we face the soon return of Christ.

In chapters 4:1–16:21, we learn that Christ's majesty is controlling His cosmos. Suddenly John is caught up into heaven where he sees a vision of God Almighty on His throne being worshiped by all of Christ's followers and the heavenly angels (4:1–11). But then John sees God give a scroll with seven seals to the worthy Lamb, Jesus (5:1–14). As the Lamb begins to open the seals one by one, a new vision appears, and God's wrath and judgment associated with each seal is unleashed upon the earth's inhabitants (6:1–16:21).

In Revelation 17:1–20:15, we see Christ's majesty conquering the rebellion on earth. During this period He unmasks the apostasy and reveals His own saints.

In Revelation 21:1–22:5, Christ's majesty unveils His paradise. As we discover the husbandly love of Jesus and the wonders of what He has prepared for His bride, the church, we can find hope in all His plans and adore Him as our future husband!

In Revelation 22:6–21, Christ's majesty is again seen in the extravagance of His salvation offer to all who come to Him: "Let him who thirsts come. Whoever desires, let him take the water of life freely" (22:17).

But Christ also gives this ominous warning to those who read Revelation: "If anyone adds to these things, God will add to him the plagues that are written in this book; and if anyone takes away from the words of . . . this prophecy, God shall take away his part from the Book of Life, from the holy city, and from the things . . . written in this book" (22:18–19).

In light of all these wonders of Christ's majesty, may you be able to genuinely pray, like John: "Amen. Even so, come, Lord Jesus" (22:20).

Make a choice to live in hope. Worship Jesus in the splendor of His redeeming love, His perfect patience, His perfect holiness, His perfect redemption, His perfect justice, and His perfect wrath! Ask God to open your eyes to see Jesus in all His glorious majesty! Adore Him for who He really is, *For of Him and through Him and to Him are all things, to whom be glory forever. Amen* (Romans 11:36). Like David, cry out, *I will bless the LORD at all times; His praise shall continually be in my mouth. . . . Oh, magnify the LORD with me, and let us exalt His name together* (Psalm 34:1–3).

WEEK 8
Look into Christ's Eyes

{ Revelation 1:14 }

As the end of days approaches, you can find hope as you look into the amazing eyes of Jesus Christ!

SUNDAY: The Amazing Eyes of Jesus Christ

His head and hair were white like wool, as white as snow, and **His eyes like a flame of fire.**
—Revelation 1:14

Have you ever wondered what it would be like to personally look into the eyes of Jesus Christ? When most people think of Jesus, they immediately picture His eyes of compassion—perhaps as the Good Shepherd carrying a lamb, or of Jesus tenderly cradling a little child on His lap. There's no doubt about it: Jesus cares deeply about His children!

Consider these different ways that the eyes of the Lord so lovingly watched out for His children: Hagar experienced Christ's **eyes of compassion** (Genesis 16:1–13); Joseph experienced Christ's purifying **eyes of consecration** (Genesis 39:1–9); David experienced Christ's ever-present **eyes of comfort** and confidence when he felt alone and fearful (Psalm 139); the disciples experienced Christ's calming **eyes of rescue** (Matthew 14:22–33); and Peter experienced Christ's sad **eyes of chastening** when he tried to live in his own strength (Luke 22:54–62).

When we are troubled, Jesus says, "Look up! See My eyes of compassion and concern for you." He longs for His children to keep on looking into His eyes so that He can guide and care for us.

All of us, adults and children alike, are easily drawn to Christ's eyes of compassion, but we should never forget that He also has **eyes of fiery judgment**. When Jesus stood before the Apostle John, John was so afraid that he "fell at His feet as dead" (Revelation 1:17). What he saw revealed that the eyes of Jesus were ablaze with an otherworldly glow, a fire that nothing can stand before. For just a moment, consider what it means to have laser-like eyes:

> A laser is a beam of coherent or focused light. Sunlight is incoherent and unfocused light of many wavelengths, and going in every direction. A laser is light of one wavelength and direction. Thus a laser can focus the energy of light to a point bright enough to melt and vaporize steel, rock, or any other material we know of on earth. A laser works a million times faster and more powerfully than a nuclear explosion. A concentrated point of light all going in one direction and at the same wavelength can heat material at a rate of *one trillion degrees per second*.[1]

Applying that knowledge to the eyes of Jesus, imagine what it would be like to personally look into His eyes—*the amazing eyes of God!*

The eyes of Jesus inspect and refine our lives. He can see right through us. He can see people in the dark, far away, and even in the future. Jesus sees into the very core of our being as His "eyes like a flame of fire" penetratingly scrutinize us. He "is the God of gods, the Lord of kings, and a revealer of secrets" (Daniel 2:47). Do you remember the comment of the woman at the well who fell under Jesus' gaze? He told her the secrets of her past, things that she thought were long forgotten: "The woman said to Him, 'Sir, I perceive that You are a prophet'" (John 4:19a). Incredibly, God Almighty "knows the secrets of the heart" (Psalm 44:21b)!

Christ always sees us and wants to help. Pastor Kent Hughes reports what the College Church of Wheaton has observed:

> For the Christian, the most chilling fact is this: there is little statistical difference between the ethical practices of the religious and the non-religious. Sadly, Christians are almost as likely as non-Christians to: surf through polluted waters on the internet, misreport their income on tax returns, commit acts of plagiarism (teachers especially witness this), ignore proper building permits and say "but that's the way business is done," use an illegal copy of a computer program, steal time from their jobs, use the company phone for personal toll-calls, oversell a product to the point of untruthfulness, tell people just what they want to hear, or be selective in obeying various laws.[2]

With that in mind, since Jesus continually looks through you with His laser-like eyes, ask yourself: *Do I like what He sees? Does Jesus like what He sees?* While in your sin, you need to look up and see the sad eyes of Jesus. But when you do, remember that He always offers forgiveness and a way out that leads to victory. Through Christ's power, you *can* please the Lord with what He sees in you!

My Prayer for You This Week: *Oh Father, through Your Spirit, open our hearts to Your Son: that we, through Your Word, might behold the wonder of the eyes of Jesus; that we are never out of sight; that we are never far from His compassionate, comforting, and convicting gaze. I pray that we would know the wonder of ever-being before Your eyes, oh God, with whom we have to do. May the reality that we live every moment in the sight of God impact us in a positive way that will direct our hearts to make choices to choose to please You with what You see. We thank You, for in Jesus' precious name we pray. Amen.*

MONDAY: The Watchful Eyes of Jesus

"The **eyes of the Lord are on the righteous**, and His ears are open to their prayers; but the face of the Lord is against those who do evil."

—1 Peter 3:12

We can experience the amazing, watchful eyes of Jesus wherever we are in life! Here are some more instances where the eyes of our Lord Jesus had a very powerful ministry to those who acknowledged that He was looking at them:

- As the Creator, Jesus walked through the Garden of Eden with Adam and Eve. God the Son created the universe: "For by Him all things were created. . . . All things were created through Him and for Him. And He is before all things, and in Him all things consist" (Colossians 1:16–17).
- Jesus said, "Abraham rejoiced to see My day: and he saw it and was glad" (John 8:56). The Old Testament doesn't say that Abraham actually saw Jesus; he saw the Lord. But the only Lord we see is God the Son, Jesus Christ, who came and manifested himself throughout the Old Testament.
- When Hagar saw the Angel of the LORD—that was Jesus! (Genesis 16:6–9).
- When the children of Israel went through the Red Sea, Jesus Christ was leading them. Even though the Old Testament says that the Angel of the LORD led them, from the New Testament we know that this was Jesus Christ. (Compare 1 Corinthians 10 with Exodus 14, 16–17.)

As Jesus stands in the midst of the church, His laser-like eyes look with a penetrating gaze into the core of your being. Those eyes are like a refining fire, and "the God who sees you" wants to help you, just as He did the saints in Bible times. You are never out of His sight— never far from His compassionate, comforting, and convicting gaze.

May the reality that you live every moment in His sight impact you in a positive way that will direct your heart to make choices to please Him!

TUESDAY: The Compassionate Eyes of Jesus

*Then [Hagar] called the name of the L*ORD *who spoke to her,* **You-Are-the-God-Who-Sees**; *for she said, "Have I also here seen Him who sees me?"*

—GENESIS 16:13

In the verse above, we see the compassionate eyes of Christ on a downcast, forsaken, homeless woman with child who had fled to the desert. What happened that caused Hagar to flee? Let's look at God's Genesis 16 account of her plight and find out.

Sarai suffered decades of shame by having no children. Even after God's promise to Abraham, they still had no child; so she took matters into her own hands. Although it was important to have an heir, Sarai calculatingly took it upon herself to try to work out God's will for Him. She thus said to Abram, "'See now, the LORD has restrained me from bearing children. Please, go in to my maid; perhaps I shall obtain children by her.' And Abram heeded the voice of Sarai. . . . So he went in to Hagar and she conceived" (Genesis 16:2, 4).

When Hagar discovered that she was going to have Abram's child, she thought she would now be his favored wife. Hence, a rivalry developed between her and Sarai. To keep peace, Abram gave Sarai permission to do with Hagar as she pleased. After being treated harshly by Sarai, Hagar ran away (Genesis 16:5–6).

The Angel of the LORD (Jesus) found her by a spring of water in the wilderness and said, "'Hagar, Sarai's maid, where have you come from, and where are you going?' She said, 'I am fleeing from the presence of my mistress Sarai.' The Angel of the LORD said to her, 'Return to your mistress, and submit yourself under her hand'" (Genesis 16:7–9).

In spite of Hagar's difficulties, Jesus told her, "Return, even if Sarai despises you and treats you wrongly." In other words, He is telling us that we should not run from our problems—He wants to give us His grace to go *through* them victoriously.

Jesus then said to her, "I will multiply your descendants exceedingly. . . . Behold, you are with child, and you shall bear a son. You shall call his name Ishmael, because the LORD has heard your affliction" (Genesis 16:10–11).

It is interesting that this is very similar to the announcement in Matthew: "Behold, the virgin shall be with child, and bear a Son, and they shall call His name Immanuel" (Matthew 1:23). This is the Lord foretelling someone's name and his or her destiny.

But Ishmael had quite a different destiny than Christ: "'He shall be a wild man; his hand shall be against every man, and every man's hand against him. And he shall dwell in the presence of all his brethren.' Then she called the name of the LORD who spoke to her, **You-Are-the-God-Who-Sees**; for she said, 'Have I also here seen Him who sees me?'" (Genesis 16:12–13).

Since God paid attention to someone like Hagar, how much more will He diligently pay attention to those who bear the name of Christ? Hagar did not choose Abraham as her husband; she did not want trouble. She was only trying to be a mother and a wife. God understood Hagar's dilemma: right from the beginning, she did not have a choice in Sarai's plan; Hagar was a servant who should never have been purchased in Egypt in the first place. He therefore understands when you are thrust into situations that you did not plan on either. No matter how difficult your life may be, Jesus' compassionate eyes see you in your troubles, and He is waiting for you to look up to Him for help!

WEDNESDAY: The Purifying Eyes of Jesus

Search me, O God, and know my heart; try me, and know my anxieties; and **see if there is any wicked way in me**, *and lead me in the way everlasting.*
—Psalm 139:23–24

When we are tempted, we need to discover Christ's purifying eyes. He looks at us in our temptation much like a parent looks at a child. Jesus foresees what choice we are going to make, and wants us to seek His help to avoid sinking into that temptation. At such times, He will give us the needed consecration and purity.

Let's consider how God helped Joseph in this respect as we examine portions of the account of his life in Genesis 37–50. Joseph is a wonderful example that true success comes from the Lord being with us: "The LORD was with Joseph, and he was a successful man" (Genesis 39:2a). Every other success is merely temporal.

I once read in the *Jerusalem Post* that many Jewish people think that because Bill Gates is so wealthy, he is the most amazing man in the world. You see, they equate success with wealth. Yet, with all his billions, Bill Gates can have no greater happiness or joy in life (less in fact) than a believer who has Jesus Christ and no money. Do you understand that to be true? Jesus is the only One who can possibly bring true success.

If the Lord is seen in your work, like Joseph, you should be blessed in everything that you do: "The LORD made all he did to prosper in his hand" (Genesis 39:3). As you give your life totally to the Lord, He will make you prosperous also. Although I am talking here about evident blessing, and not monetary prosperity, sometimes God grants that as well.

God will even bless those for whom you work if they honor your convictions: "From the time that he had made him overseer of his house and all that he had, . . . **the LORD blessed the Egyptian's house for Joseph's sake"** (Genesis 39:4–5).

I remember telling a former employer that I would not do certain things because it would be dishonest to do so. That company released me from those requirements, but the rest of the sales people followed them. I honored God, and my sales went up. This testifies to the fact that God will honor honesty and bless your employer as well.

If you put a Christian and a non-Christian on an equal playing field, the Christian should always do better in everything because the God of the universe indwells him or her. We have hope, joy, and peace; we live in reality, but the people of the world do not.

Here is a classic case of the purifying eyes of Jesus when we are tempted: "Joseph was handsome in form and appearance. And it came to pass . . . that his master's wife cast longing eyes on Joseph, and she said, 'Lie with me.' But he refused and said to his master's wife, 'Look, my master . . . has committed all that he has to my hand. There is no one greater in this house than I, nor has he kept back anything from me but you, because you are his wife. How then can I do this great wickedness, and sin against God?'" (Genesis 39:6–9).

Joseph was always aware of Jesus' eyes upon him—His purifying eyes that lead to consecration. Jesus continually sees our business, social, romantic, private, and public lives. If we, like Joseph, acknowledge that He is watching us, there will be a very strong consecrating effect on us as well.

I can personally testify that being aware that Jesus is watching works anywhere. The first time I traveled overseas I was all alone, thousands of miles from home, with every conceivable temptation confronting me. Whether it was literature, people, or things, I was so aware that God was watching that I would sometimes even talk out loud and say, "Lord, help me." It is always possible for you to know the purifying power of seeing the eyes of Jesus watching you everywhere, every time.

Jesus can keep you pure in temptation. Joseph was kept pure when he faced being disloyal to his employer and sinning against God. He could not have had a more direct attack on his personal holiness than this, so he exercised his will and ran. Keeping pure involves far more than standing in the midst of temptation and saying, "Lord, save me." God has not promised to remove you bodily from temptation. Rather, He expects you to choose to flee evil (2 Timothy 2:22). So turn off the television, throw away the literature, or stop being around that person who drags you down spiritually.

At the instant of any temptation, Jesus' purifying eyes are watching you so that all you have to do is look up and say, "Lord, help me!" If you just ask Him, He will give you the grace to resist: "God is faithful, who will not allow you to be tempted beyond what you are able, but . . . will also make the way of escape, that you may be able to bear it" (1 Corinthians 10:13).

THURSDAY: The Comforting Eyes of Jesus

*The **eyes of the LORD** run to and fro throughout the whole earth, to show Himself strong in behalf of those whose heart is loyal to Him.*

—2 Chronicles 16:9

David certainly experienced "the eyes of the Lord" that continually watched over him! His life tells us much about the ever-present comforting eyes of the Lord when we feel alone and afraid. It seems that everywhere David turned there was trouble. His brothers did not like him; his father, Jesse, did not think much of him either. When the prophet Samuel came and asked to see his sons, his father did not even consider David to be one of them—he had left David out in the field with the sheep!

After God anointed David, he still had to take care of the animals; he was not honored at all. When he became king, he continued to have a multitude of problems; enemies everywhere were trying to kill him. Trouble was around every bend in his life. In light of all David's imperfections, failures, and blatant sins, why did God call him "a man after My own heart" (Acts 13:22)? We find the secret in Psalm 139. David lived in constant awareness that God was watching him.

Look at the eyes of Jesus that were on David: "O LORD, **You have searched me and known me**.... You understand my thought afar off. You comprehend my path and my lying down, and are acquainted with all my ways.... You have hedged me behind and before, and laid Your hand upon me" (Psalm 139:1–5).

Do you understand what that passage means? God says that He is right there with you, and that He surrounds you! He already knows about all the days of your life: "**Your eyes saw my substance**, being yet unformed, and in Your book they all were written, **the days fashioned for me**, when as yet there were none of them" (Psalm 139:16). What a comfort!

That is why God says in Hebrews 9:27 that it is *appointed* unto us once to die. Because of that, we can rest in the fact that we will not die accidentally or before our time! Why? Unless the Rapture occurs first, we each have a God-appointed time for Jesus to meet us and take us home. That is both a wonder and a comfort!

You can find confidence in Christ. In Psalm 139:23–24, David asked the Lord to show him why he felt anxious. Basically, this is what he said: "What do I fear when You have told me not to fear? What am I focusing on that I should not be? Turn me from any wicked way, Lord, and help me to follow Your way alone!"

Since God knows how we are made, He knows both our changeable and unchangeable features. He is thus never caught off guard by our weaknesses, anxieties, and fears. As we open up to Him, like David, we will realize that God sees us, and that He will help us walk confidently in the everlasting way. The Bible says, "The wicked flee when no one pursues but the righteous are bold as a lion" (Proverbs 28:1). God wants us to be boldly confident, and not fearful. He is watching over us to give comfort and confidence, and He knows every step of our way!

FRIDAY: The Calming Eyes of Jesus

He saw them straining at rowing, for the wind was against them. Now about the fourth watch of the night He came to them, walking on the sea.
—MARK 6:48

The disciples saw the calm rescuing eyes of Jesus when they were sinking in the storm. The account in Matthew 14:22–33 is one of the most precious and insightful portions of God's Word, dealing with His tender love and care for us as His children. As I was writing this, a group of us were reflecting on these truths while taking a devotional walk through the land of the Book. The image of this scene from high atop the Arbel Cliffs is still etched upon my soul!

- **Jesus made His disciples get into the boat.** When their lives were in danger, it was out of obedience to Him. If they had not obeyed Jesus, they would not have learned what He wanted to teach them. The Lesson: **Obey Jesus!**
- **Jesus left them all night.** He waited until 3:00 A.M.— when the disciples were at the extremity of their trial. Remember Mary, Martha, and Lazarus? Jesus did not hurry to them. He let Lazarus get sicker and sicker and actually die (John 11). Jesus does not run to us to

prevent the trial. In this instance, His purpose was to demonstrate to His disciples, in an unforgettable way, that He would do whatever was necessary to rescue them. He wants to do the same for us as well. The Lesson: **Trust Jesus!**

- **Jesus went to them, walking on the sea.** Jesus' pathway was the very object that was testing their faith. He knew exactly where they were the whole time. They were never out of His sight. They might have forgotten all His promises, but Jesus did not forget. We will never find ourselves anywhere the Lord cannot find us. That is comforting! There are no storms in life that Jesus cannot subdue *in His time*. There is never a valid reason to fear, nor to be anxious. We are to trust in the One who will never leave us nor forsake us (Hebrews 13:5b). So through the storm, on the pathway, and in whatever it is that is giving you a hard time, know that He is coming to your aid. The Lesson: **Keep looking for Jesus!**
- **Jesus brought calm in their boat.** When we are obedient to the Lord, we are in the safest place in the universe. No matter how frightening the circumstances may be around us, Jesus is there; He will calm the seas of trouble *in His time*. The most secure place to be is in God's will. Peter sank because he did not understand that the lesson was to love the Lord Jesus enough to trust Him. Peter did love Him: did anyone else say, "Command me to come to You on the water; I will obey whatever You say; Your Word is my command!"? We should not think badly of Peter for sinking; we should love Jesus as he did, and do whatever He says. The Lesson: **Love Jesus!**

When you invite Jesus into the boat of your stormy life, your life will become calm. (Anything that is "out of control" has not been fully surrendered to God.) Even though you may be tossed all about, if the Lord is in your boat, all is well!

SATURDAY: The Chastening Eyes of Jesus

The Lord ... looked at Peter. Then Peter remembered the word of the Lord, how He had said to him, "Before the rooster crows, you will deny Me three times."
—LUKE 22:61

In Luke 22:54–62, God gives us the account of when Peter saw the sad and chastening eyes of Jesus because he was living in his own strength. Peter first walked with the sinners, then he stood with them, and finally he sat with them around the fire. It was a progression—the more Peter sat with those who were a part of Jesus' condemnation, the farther away he was getting from Christ. God tells us: "Blessed is the man who **walks not** in the counsel of the ungodly, **nor stands** in the path of sinners, **nor sits** in the seat of the scornful" (Psalm 1:1).

That is one of the reasons why Peter fell into this situation that the Lord had warned him about: But Peter said, "'Man, I do not know what you are saying!' Immediately, while he was still speaking, the rooster crowed. And **the Lord** turned and **looked at Peter.** Then Peter remembered the word of the Lord.... So Peter went out and wept bitterly" (Luke 22:60–62).

Sometimes the eyes of Jesus are not just the eyes that are giving compassion, comfort, and confidence; they must also be chastening eyes. With His chastening eyes, He looks at us when we give in to our sins. The laser-like eyes of Jesus are continually inspecting and refining our lives. If we give in to temptations, we will receive the chastening look of sadness as Jesus looks on us and says, "Oh, My child, I *warned* you to not do that!"

Make a choice to live in hope. Sometimes you will need to look up in your sin and see those grieved eyes of Jesus. When you do, remember that He always offers a way out; He always offers a way through; and He always offers you victory. I exhort you to choose His victory today by making the following promise to Him:

- **When troubled**—I will look up for Jesus' loving eyes of compassion. I will remember Hagar's experience of His compassionate eyes! (Genesis 16:1–13)
- **When tempted**—I will look up for Jesus' purifying eyes of consecration. I will remember Joseph's experience of His purifying eyes when tempted! (Genesis 39:1–9)
- **When watched**—I will look up for Jesus' refining eyes like laser beams. I will remember the Israelites' experience of His refining eyes as He led them through the Red Sea and in the wilderness! (Exodus 14, 16–17)
- **When lonely or afraid**—I will look up for Jesus' comforting eyes of confidence. I will remember David's experience of His ever-present eyes of comfort when feeling alone and afraid! (Psalm 139)
- **When scrutinized**—I will look up for Jesus' caring eyes of concern. I will remember the woman at the well and her experience of Jesus' caring eyes as He revealed the secrets of her past! (John 4:1–26)
- **When sinking in despair**—I will look up for Jesus' calming eyes of rescue. I will remember the disciples' experience of His calm rescuing eyes when sinking! (Matthew 14:22–33)
- **When sinning**—I will look up for Jesus' chastening eyes of sadness and come back to Him. I will remember Peter's experience and Christ's sad eyes of chastening when living in my own strength! (Luke 22:54–62)

I encourage you to make a choice even today to live in hope by experiencing the eyes of Christ—*the amazing eyes of God!* If Jesus has touched your heart in a special way this week, you can affirm your promise to Him by offering a prayer of renewed dedication of your love for Him!

WEEK 9
Listen to Christ's Voice

{ Revelation 1:15 }

As the end of days approaches, you can find hope as you listen to the awesome voice of Christ!

SUNDAY: Listen to Your Creator

His feet were like fine brass, as if refined in a furnace, and **His voice as the sound of many waters.**
—Revelation 1:15

Have you heard the almighty and powerful voice of Jesus? He is speaking every day! As the Creator, Jesus' voice resounds throughout planet Earth! Have you heard Jesus' voice speaking in nature?

The apostle John writes that His voice is "as the sound of many waters" (Revelation 1:15b). In that verse, John used the metaphor of a thunderous waterfall. Have you ever stood at the crest of the impressive Niagara Falls? My family and I have, and it is an incredible combination of sight and sound as the avalanche of rushing water vibrates the ground as it thunders downward and then bursts upward in mist. It is magnificent to behold!

Since most of us do not live by a mighty waterfall, Psalm 29 uses another metaphor for the voice of the Lord—the deep rumble and loud roar of thunder. I, therefore, happen to like Oklahoma's severe thunderstorms that make our windows shake and rattle! Why? They always focus my thoughts on Psalm 29. Jesus wants us to *listen* for His voice in the storms. So the next time you experience a bad thunderstorm, instead of worrying about it, worship Him through it!

All Creation declares God's glory! As you listen for His voice in the storms, ponder these interesting scientific facts about thunder and lightning:

Thunder is merely a byproduct of lightning which is a river of electricity careening at 100,000 miles per second, down a twisting canyon of air. About 400 people per year are killed by lightning, [normally] more than any other natural disaster. Yet, without lightning, life as we know it could not exist.

Air molecules are heated to about the temperature of the Sun's surface by that electricity. They are white hot at 30,000 degrees Celsius when the bolt of lightning passes through them. Around the planet 100 times each second, lightning strikes the earth with its intense, hot strokes. In a very real sense, it is feeding the plants as the nitrous oxide distills in the rains and goes to the roots of plants. Almost all plants need nitrogen as their basic food. Although 22 million tons of nitrogen hangs in the air over every square mile of the planet, it is unusable without the effects of lightning.

WEEK 9: LISTEN TO CHRIST'S VOICE

Lightning that we see is actually traveling upward. It is the meeting of a "leader" coming down from the negatively charged base of a thundercloud, meeting a "streamer" coming up from the positively charged earth beneath that cloud. In the one second long duration of the lightning, as many as 40 pulses of energy have occurred. Heat rising so rapidly out of this super hot path breaks the sound barrier and "thunder" is produced.[1] Each stroke contains hundreds of thousands of amperes, and hundreds of millions of volts. All told a single storm produces more electricity than all of America's generators combined.[2] A single stroke lasting one second could power a city.[3] And with over 600 storms at any given moment on the earth, God's power dwarfs all of man's efforts!

The sound of the Lord as He shakes the earth is a call to reverence Him. God uses thunder and lightning for many things. For example, He used it in the seventh plague against the Egyptians: "The LORD sent thunder and hail, and fire darted to the ground" (Exodus 9:23). Another wonderful example is when Samuel cried out to God in behalf of Israel, and the Lord answered him in a miraculous way: "The LORD thundered with a loud thunder upon the Philistines that day, and so confused them that they were overcome before Israel" (1 Samuel 7:10).

Those two examples alone are enough to cause us to be awed by the Lord God Almighty's powerful and thunderous voice! Will you listen to God's voice today as He speaks to you through His Word?

My Prayer for You This Week: *Oh Father, I pray that we would each hear the voice of Jesus, that we would respond to His voice, and that we might live ever-mindful that You wish to commune with us. Ever since the first time You spoke to Your creatures in the Garden of Eden, to the moment when we enter glory and forever shall be with You, how we long to hear and respond to Your voice! We love You, and ask that You would open our hearts, illumine our minds, quicken our spirits, motivate our wills, and engage us to be Your pleasing servants through exposure to Your Word. We pray that Christ will get all the glory, and that we be purified that we may offer exceedingly precious and fragrant worship to You. In the blessed name of Jesus we pray. Amen.*

MONDAY: Listen to Your Redeemer

I was in the Spirit on the Lord's Day, and **I heard** *behind me* **a loud voice, as of a trumpet**, *saying, "I am the Alpha and the Omega, the First and the Last," and "What you see, write in a book and send it to the seven churches which are in Asia."*

—REVELATION 1:10–11A

God created us to hear the voice of Jesus. So it is not strange that, when the Creator met with John on Patmos, John heard His voice. As we listen to those words captured by John, every one of these facets of Christ's beauty calls us to the same response: worship.

Can you imagine how John felt when he first heard the voice like a trumpet? Or what it might have been like for him to see Jesus in the beauty of His deity, and the wonder of who He is? To then be chosen to write down what he saw, and what was yet to come, must have been awe-inspiring to this lonely exile!

In Revelation 1–3, Jesus' voice is calling the church throughout the ages to worship Him! In Revelation 1, there are nine reasons why we must listen to and worship our divine Redeemer:

1. **Jesus is the Conqueror of Adam's fallen race**—One like the Son of Man, robed to His feet. (1:13)
2. **Jesus is the Perfect Priest**—with hair as white as snow. (1:14a)
3. **Jesus is the Ancient of Days**—with eyes like a flame of fire. (1:14b)
4. **Jesus is the Seer of All Secrets**—with feet like fine brass. (1:15a)
5. **Jesus is the Ultimate Judge**—crushing all foes with a voice as thunderous as the twelve million cubic feet of water crashing at Niagara's base! (1:15b)
6. **Jesus is the Voice of God**—commanding all to pay attention. (1:15b) Even the deaf and the dead can hear it, and so should we!
7. **Jesus is the Possessor of All Secrets of the Universe**—holding the stars in His hand, which He spoke into existence by His Word. (1:16a)
8. **Jesus is the Creator of All Things**—with the face of incomprehensible countenance, blazing with the power of the sun. (1:16b)
9. **Jesus is the All-Powerful Lord of Glory**—who says to us, "Will you worship Me?" (1:17–18)

As you reflect upon the nine signs of Christ's divinity listed above, listen for Jesus' voice—and worship Him! One way to worship the Lord is to dwell on the truth that Jesus came and rescued you. Another is to meditate upon how thankful you are that He is your perfect priest. Or you can praise Him for being the eternal One you can trust! Another example of fragrant worship is to express adoration that His all-seeing eyes always know where you are and what you need! On and on the list can go. Now take a moment and offer thanksgiving for all the other things He brings to mind!

TUESDAY: The Voice of Jesus in Eden

*The LORD **God called to Adam** and said to him, "Where are you?"*
—Genesis 3:9

The final book of God's Word is The Revelation of Jesus Christ. Within the chapters of that book are reflections from every part of the Scriptures. It is amazing that each element of God's revelation starts in Genesis and finds completion in Revelation. In other words, answers to the age-old questions that began in the book of Genesis are found in Revelation.

Let's go back and meet the first two humans on earth. Listen to the inspired, accurate, and divine recounting of their experience of hearing the voice of Jesus in the Garden of Eden.

Think with me of life as a perfect human. Picture yourself at the dawn of creation as Adam or Eve, perfect and sinless. Your first memory is that of waking up in God's garden, Eden. You live in a comfortable world with no extremes of hot and cold, no storms, no disasters to fear. Your home is secure; there are no pestering bugs, poisonous snakes, or deadly spiders. There is just the continual beauty of fragrant and color-filled flowering orchids hanging from the verdant green trees and blooms that never fall off, never yellow, or wilt. Full, juicy fruit hang ripe on the branches, but never fall off and rot.

Even more, you have a body that never aches, a digestive system that never rebels, eyesight that needs no correction, and ears that hear the sweet sounds of life all around. No pains; never a sorrow; no weariness; not even a fear—just peace-filled living.

God's perfect garden is a paradise. Every day is an adventure of new colors, new fragrances, and new symmetry in flowers, butterflies, and all the wonders of a perfect animal world. There are no predators, no scavengers, and no carnivores. Only placid and magnificent creatures reflecting the majesty of God live in the garden. And around every corner of towering and graceful trees, each perfectly planted by God, are flocks, herds, and gatherings of exquisite living animals that God has created and brought to life.

But the best of everything is the sweet sound of the voice of your Creator, God the Son, Jesus Christ. About suppertime each day a gentle breeze whispers by, and then you hear His voice. The Gardener and Planner of the universe soon walks with you in the cool of the day. He seeks fellowship with you, His best friend, whom He has made to look just like Him. And your ears hear the sweetest sound of all—the voice of Jesus who created you!

But soon your paradise will be lost. The "bad guy" has entered into God's perfect garden, and nothing will ever be the same again!

WEDNESDAY: Satan Hates the Voice of God

*Then **Jesus said** to him, "**Away with you, Satan!** For it is written, 'You shall worship the Lord your God, and Him only you shall serve.'" Then the devil left Him, and behold, angels came and ministered to Him.*
—MATTHEW 4:10–11

The "bad guy" in paradise—that old serpent, Satan—planned a masterful scheme for mankind! More than anything, he has wanted to make us doubt, reject, and become deafened to the voice of God! And had you and I been in the Garden of Eden instead of Adam and Eve, we would have made the same fatal choice. Instead of listening to God, they listened to Satan, who took God's Word and twisted it. Satan must have thought that he'd scored a final coup with his plan to cut off the voice of Jesus from His children:

> Now the serpent was more cunning than any beast of the field, which the Lord God had made. And he said to the woman, "Has God indeed said, 'You shall not eat of every tree of the garden'?" And the woman said to the serpent, "We may eat the fruit of the trees of the garden; but of the fruit of the tree which is in the midst of the garden, God has said, 'You shall not eat it, nor shall you touch it, lest you die.'" Then the serpent said to the woman, "You will not surely die. For God knows that in the day you eat of it your eyes will be opened, and you will be like God, knowing good and evil" (Genesis 3:1–5).

Satan's plan, even to this day, involves four elements from Genesis 3 that are the main threads that weave together through all the false religions of the world. All false religions are derived from these lies of Satan that seek to keep mankind from listening to the voice of their Creator. We will cover three of them now, and then go over the fourth in tomorrow's devotional.

Satan's first lie: doubt God's Word. When young people are first exposed to secular scientific theories (with the God of Scripture left out), Satan always plants this seed of doubt in their minds: "Has God indeed said...?" (3:1b). Since listening to the voice of Jesus always involves the Bible, Satan tries to persuade us that God's Word is just like any other book. "Oh," he says, "The Bible is nice, perhaps helpful, but it is not absolute." His ultimate plan is to keep us from regular contact with the Lord by questioning, avoiding, or neglecting the Word. The Lesson: **You doubt God when you doubt His Word.**

Satan's second lie: doubt God's goodness. Satan planted seeds of doubt in Eve when he said, "Did God really say, 'You shall not eat of every tree of the garden'?" (3:1b). He wanted her to doubt God and His goodness. He likewise bombards each of us by whispering lies such as: *God is trying to hold out on you ... He is robbing you of some good times ... He is out of touch with your needs ... He missed that disaster you just went through ... He messed up on how He made you ... God means well, but since He doesn't quite have everything under control, that makes Him not good.*

Satan's fiery darts of lies are reserved for our most vulnerable moments. For instance, when a baby is born who is not fully functioning, or a young person's life is cut off in what seems to be a tragic and untimely death, a normal reaction is to cry out, "Why, Lord?" Things like this simply make no sense to our finite minds, so we may be tempted to doubt God's goodness.

Another example is when teens idolize those who grace magazine covers or are otherwise in the social spotlight. At some point, however, they have to come to grips with the fact that they will never look like those people. So they may begin to despise their own features and question God's goodness by thinking, *Why did God make me this way?*

When the storms of life are at their fiercest, don't give in to thoughts like this that challenge your faith: *Is God really in control? Why is He letting this happen to me? Where is He? Is He really good?* At such times, watch out because Satan acts like a prowling lion (1 Peter 5:8), and you must not give the devil a place to land in your life (Ephesians 4:27). In Ephesians 4:25–31, Paul lists sins that can open you up to Satan's influence in ways that will hinder your walk in Christ. Satan lurks at the door of your mind, so do not let him in! The Lesson: **You doubt God when you doubt God's goodness.**

Satan's third lie: doubt God's authority. In Satan's next all-out attack to deceive Eve, he says pointblank: "You will not surely die" (3:4). Satan loves it when we doubt God! He wants us to believe that God is not in charge, that God is not interested in our choices, and that God will not hold us accountable for our deeds. When that happens, every man or woman does whatever seems right in his or her own eyes. That is the hallmark of our world—take charge of your own life, and be all you can or want to be! The Lesson: **You doubt God when you doubt God's authority.**

Never forget that Satan's masterful scheme is to make you doubt, reject, and become deafened to the voice of Jesus. Because you are not listening to the voice of Jesus when you think wrongly about God, daily ask yourself, *Whose voice am I listening to?*

THURSDAY: Satan Wants to Silence God's Voice

*"The thief [Satan] does not come except **to steal, and to kill, and to destroy.**"*
—John 10:10

Yesterday we learned that Satan has four spiritual flaws that he uses to try to silence God's voice in our lives. We have discussed the first three in which Satan tempts us to doubt God's Word, doubt God's goodness, and doubt God's authority. Here is his fourth spiritual flaw:

Satan's fourth lie: doubt God's plan. In Genesis 3:5 Satan blocked the Creator's voice when he said, "Your eyes will be opened, and you will be like God, knowing good and evil." From the very beginning, Satan has sought to convince mankind that his way is better than God's. Thus he tries to entice us with his own plan for how we can achieve immortality, glory, and happiness. How does Satan do that? He tries to solidly plant this thought in our minds: *Abandon all those restraints—just let go and work out your own plan for pleasure!* The Lesson: **You doubt God when you doubt His plan for you.**

Satan loves it when he gets us to doubt God and His plan! The devil's scheme is to plant thoughts that God's way is too restrictive, but his way allows freedom to pursue whatever lusts will bring the greatest pleasure. In fact, if Satan were to summarize his plan for us as a billboard ad, it would probably read: "Go for the gusto! You only go around once! Get your gratification *now*."

Satan delights in whispering to us: *Lust won't wait, so lust for what you want—and take it every chance you get!* That is exactly what Adam and Eve did when they gave in to their desire for pleasure (Genesis 3:6). Thus the horrible precipitous slide down into sin began, as these verses reveal: "Then the eyes of both of them were opened, and they knew that they were naked. . . . And **they heard the sound of the LORD God** walking in the garden . . . , and Adam and his wife hid themselves from the presence of the LORD God" (Genesis 3:7–8).

Before this awful day, Adam and Eve had been drawn to the voice of the Lord, and responded to Him. They both had longed to talk with their Creator and tell Him of their discoveries. They loved to ask Him questions about His universe and the garden they lived in. But now they discovered that His voice repelled them, so they hid among the trees of the garden. Then God—this Jesus who came "to seek and to save that which was lost"—had to become the seeking One (Luke 19:10).

The Creator Himself is the One who seeks out His fallen creatures: "Then the LORD God **called to Adam** . . . , 'Where are you?'" (Genesis 3:9). When the Lord confronted Adam concerning his sin, he abdicated his leadership role and blamed it on his wife, saying: "The woman whom You gave to be with me, she gave me of the tree, and I ate" (Genesis 3:12). Eve then blamed her sin on the serpent: "The serpent deceived me, and I ate" (Genesis 3:13).

Satan inhabited the serpent, which was upright, and the most beautiful of all the created animals as it glistened with all the lovely colors. But Satan's use of the serpent brought God's curse to crawl in the dust and become a sign of evil: "'Because you have done this,' God said to the serpent, 'You are cursed . . . ; on your belly you shall go, and you shall eat dust all the days of your life. And **I will put enmity** between you and the woman, and **between your seed and her Seed**; He shall bruise your head, and you shall bruise His heel'" (Genesis 3:14–15).

Every time a new child is conceived in this world, he or she, as a descendant of Adam, is already a sinner because of divine decree. But as soon as the child is old enough to make conscious choices, proof of being a sinner is soon evident through wrong actions.

As for the term "her Seed," women don't have seed. This is a very strange idea until you understand the virgin birth of Christ—that the virgin Mary would bear a child without the seed of a man (Isaiah 7:14). The Seed of the woman is Jesus Christ. Jesus' body was buffeted and broken because of sin. But on the cross, He crushed the head of Satan "that through death He might destroy him that had the power of death, that is, the devil" (Hebrews 2:14b).

Because Satan is not omniscient (all-knowing), he thought that he was scoring a major coup in the Garden of Eden! But God was actually in control—as always—working out His masterful plan for the ages so that you and I can have enduring hope for the future!

FRIDAY: Listen to Jesus' Voice in His Word

How shall we escape if we neglect so great a salvation, which at the first began to be spoken by the Lord, and was **confirmed** *to us* **by those who heard Him***?*
—Hebrews 2:3

For every one of Satan's spiritual flaws, God counters with a positive and powerful law. Therefore, He has *four spiritual laws* that destroy Satan's *four spiritual flaws*.

God's Four Spiritual Laws:

1. **Trust God's Word:** "Forever, O Lord, Your word is settled in heaven" (Psalm 119:89). God's Word has never been proven to be in error scientifically, morally, or historically. God's Word is the only thing that you can stake your life on!
2. **Rest in God's goodness:** "Truly God is good . . . to such as are pure in heart" (Psalm 73:1). God is indeed good, and He has revealed himself to be so. He always makes good decisions! He made you well; you are a beautiful work of art, created in Christ Jesus for good works (Ephesians 2:10). He made you for His glory, so never wonder why He has allowed something to happen in your life; trust His goodness and rest in that truth.
3. **Submit to God's authority:** "Submit to God. Resist the devil and he will flee from you" (James 4:7). Resist Satan's lies; resist his desire to make you rebel, and he will flee from you.
4. **Follow God's plan:** "Trust in the LORD with all your heart, and lean not on your own understanding; in all your ways acknowledge Him, and He shall direct your paths" (Proverbs 3:5–6). As soon as we head *away* from the Lord to follow after our own understanding, we are heading *toward* Satan's path. Satan always moves us away from God's Word, so we need to listen to the voice of Jesus in His Word!

Christ's voice in Revelation calls for action. The voice of Jesus calls out to His church for utter devotion. For example, the observance of the Lord's Table is an act of utter devotion to Christ. There we say, "We are partaking of Your body and Your blood. We are communing with You, and we are unable to live apart from You. We love You and we worship You!"

Look at Christ's indictment of the church at Ephesus: "I have this against you, that you have left your first love" (Revelation 2:4). Jesus is telling us to examine ourselves to determine whether He is the most important person in our lives, like He once was. Are you still drawing near to Him as you first did? If not, He says, "Remember . . . from where you have fallen; repent and do the first works" (Revelation 2:5).

Jesus wants us to continually seek Him like we did at the beginning. I always tell married couples: "Work as hard to keep your beloved as you did to win him or her." The key to a strong marriage is to never stop dating. That is an even bigger key to worship: love Christ like you did the first day you knew that your sins were washed away, and that your destiny was secure in Him.

The voice of Jesus also calls out to the lost for salvation. Any time there is a gathering with the preaching of God's Word, there should always be an acknowledgement of anyone who has not yet heard the voice of Jesus. An invitation ought to be extended to him or her to come to Christ: "Let him who thirsts come. And whoever desires, let him take the water of life freely" (Revelation 22:17).

Up to the very end of God's Revelation, He is still offering salvation to all who will respond to Him. In the privacy of your will, you may say yes to Jesus Christ: Yes, He died in my place! Yes, He is the One who came to seek and save me, a lost sheep! Yes, He is my only hope and my sin is taken care of by His sacrifice. That is how simple salvation is.

Have you responded to Christ in faith yet?

SATURDAY: Jesus Waits for Us to Hear His Voice

*The **voice of the LORD** is powerful; the **voice of the LORD** is full of majesty.*
—Psalm 29:4

In Psalm 29 we hear His voice in the earth, and it is calling us to worship Him! In that psalm, the Lord reveals five elements of His eternal greatness that we are to reverence as we hear Him. Hear the powerful and majestic voice of the Lord:

Through thunder God is declaring His ownership. "O you mighty ones, Give unto the LORD glory and strength. Give unto the LORD the glory due to His name; worship the LORD in the beauty of holiness" (Psalm 29:1–2). We cannot make the sky thunder; neither can we make it stop thundering. God owns and controls the physical universe.

Through thunder God is declaring His majesty. "The voice of the LORD is over the waters; The God of glory thunders; The LORD is over many waters" (Psalm 29:3). I can easily envision David high on a hillside overlooking one of those massive storms that blows in from the Mediterranean Sea. As the anvil-shaped thundercloud begins to rise, he knows he has to comfort his sheep, and get them safely into the fold before they become frightened and scatter. As he is out there with nowhere else to go, he soon hears the rumble in the distance come ever closer, and watches the frequent bolts of lightning. And then David listens in awe as the voice of the Lord thunders again and again—and he worships! If thunder is just the power of God's voice, imagine what kind of total power He has!

Through thunder, God is declaring His power. "The voice of the LORD breaks the cedars, Yes, the LORD splinters the cedars of Lebanon. He makes them also skip like a calf, Lebanon and Sirion like a young wild ox. The voice of the LORD divides the flames of fire" (Psalm 29:5–7). What manner of God is He that at the very sound of His voice the earth rumbles and shakes and quakes and burns before Him?

Have you ever seen a tree that was hit by lightning? It is literally splintered. Lightning contains hundreds of millions of volts! I had a friend who used to be a park ranger. He told me about times when he sat in the tower watching for forest fires during thunderstorms. Because the towers were grounded, he was safe. So when he saw lightning hit the rock wall around the tower, and the balls of fire tumbling along the ground, he always opened his Bible to Psalm 29:7: "The voice of the LORD divides the flames of fire." Amazing!

Through thunder God is declaring His worship. "The voice of the LORD shakes the wilderness; the LORD shakes the Wilderness of Kadesh. The voice of the LORD makes the deer give birth, and strips the forests bare; and in His temple everyone says, 'Glory!'" (Psalm 29:8–9).

This is not people who are saying "Glory!" It is all of Creation that is in the temple of God. Remember: Jesus "came to His own, and His own did not receive Him" (John 1:11). The first "His own" is neuter gender in the Greek, which means that He came into His own world. Creation always received Him. For example, trees would bow in front of Him when He spoke to them, and the sea would calm when He spoke to it. Jesus controlled the natural world, and it worshiped Him.

Although God does not get much glory from His creatures who are created in His image, at the sound of His voice all the earth shouts "Glory!" Should not we? The next time you are in a thunderstorm, shout "Glory!" to declare your worship of the Lord from your heart!

Through thunder God is declaring His judgment. "The LORD sat enthroned at the Flood, and the LORD sits as King forever. The LORD will give strength to His people; the LORD will bless His people with peace" (Psalm 29:10–11). God is the judge, and He is in control. When you hear the thunder and see the lightning, declare His judgment. God is going to right all wrongs. Do not try to get revenge on people. At the Flood, He destroyed those who pushed Him out of their lives, and He is going to do the same when He comes back again. That is why Psalm 29 is so very important!

Make a choice to live in hope. As we approach the end of days, I encourage you to find hope as you listen to the awesome voice of Christ, your Creator and Redeemer! Remember that the sound of the Lord as He shakes the earth is a call to reverence Him! So wholeheartedly join David in praise and worship as he says:

> *I will extol You, my God, O King; and I will bless Your name forever and ever.... Great is the LORD, and greatly to be praised; and His greatness is unsearchable.... All Your works shall praise You, O LORD.... They shall speak of the glory of Your kingdom, and talk of Your power.... Your kingdom is an everlasting kingdom, and your dominion endures throughout all generations.*
>
> —PSALM 145:1, 3, 10–11, 13

WEEK 10
See Christ's Face and Feel His Touch

{ Revelation 1:16–17 }

As the end of days approaches, you can find hope as you see Christ's glorious face and feel His powerful touch!

SUNDAY: Face-to-face with Jesus

His countenance was like the sun shining in its strength.
—REVELATION 1:16

There are so many pictures of Jesus in our minds. From Sunday school lessons to the *Jesus* movie, we have countless images that float by us in life. Yet God's Word gives us the only exact picture of Christ's face in the entire universe.

As the apostle John prayed and adored God through His Son, Jesus Christ, he heard a sound and turned—it was *Jesus!* But it was not the Jesus he was used to seeing, or that we think of in pictures and movies. It was the *real Lord Jesus Christ.*

First, John saw Jesus' eyes, which were as flaming fires penetrating like laser beams. Then he heard the voice of Jesus, thunderous and big, bigger than anything on earth. After that he saw His face of glory shining "like the sun"—and it changed John's life!

Something fascinating about Jesus and the sun is revealed in the first chapter of Genesis. On the fourth day of creation, God said, "'Let there be lights . . . in the firmament of the heavens to give light on the earth'; and it was so. Then God made two great lights; the greater light to rule the day, and the lesser light to rule the night: he made the stars also" (Genesis 1:14–16).

Just by Jesus speaking a few words, the sun suddenly appeared ninety-three million miles out from earth! Isn't that absolutely amazing? It just flamed to life. Traveling at the speed of light, it may have taken about eight minutes for the first warmth and light from the sun to get to the earth. Then the moon started reflecting that light on the backside of the planet. That is phenomenal!

One of the most amazing statements in the Bible is the last five words of verse 16: "He made the stars also." In that short sentence God describes what scientists cannot comprehend—the limitless expanse of the rest of the universe. Jesus put some of those stars in spiral galaxies, some of them in beautiful filmy nebulae, and others of them in clusters of galaxies. Then he made one hundred billion stars just in our own Milky Way Galaxy. "He made the stars also" reads almost like a postscript.

As you read the following description of the sun, think of what it must have been like for John to see Jesus' face shining "like the sun":

At the center, or core of our sun, things are incredibly hot. The atoms stripped of their outer electrons are so densely packed it is absolutely dark and intensely hot. In fact, it is 16 million degrees centigrade.[1]

How hot is "16 million degrees centigrade"? A piece of the sun the size of a pinhead would kill you one hundred miles away because of the heat radiating from it! The energy radiated from the sun in one second is more than all the energy used on the earth since Creation!

So, on a Sunday, over 1,900 years ago on Patmos—a barren speck of rock just sixteen miles square and fifteen miles from nowhere in the Mediterranean Sea—John heard a voice and turned and saw the face of Jesus shining like the sun! And what did that do to him? It flattened him: "When I saw him, I fell at His feet as dead" (Revelation 1:17).

What happens when a person comes face-to-face with Christ in all His power and glory? It smites us with an overwhelming sense of our humanity: our fallen nature and our weakness. Do you remember Isaiah's response when he saw the Lord sitting on a throne, high and lifted up, and heard the seraphim crying out: "Holy, holy, holy is the LORD of hosts; the whole earth is full of His glory!" (Isaiah 6:3)? He said: "Woe is me, for I am undone! . . . for my eyes have seen the King, the LORD of hosts" (Isaiah 6:5).

A face-to-face encounter with Jesus Christ cannot help but strike us with His majesty and His glory. As His creatures, we would want to respond by worshiping Him, and that is exactly what John does. Have you met Jesus face to face? Have you responded in heartfelt worship? A genuine encounter with Jesus Christ is life changing!

My Prayer for You This Week: *Father in Heaven, we want to be found worthy when we stand before You face-to-face; we want to be there clothed in Your righteousness. We don't know when You are going to come or call us home. It could be that the days written in Your book for us end this week. We pray that we would therefore be those who live for You, Lord Jesus, a life that is true and right. I pray that You, Holy Spirit, will put Your finger into the hearts of each one of us and point out those untoppled idols, those unforsaken sins, those unrestrained areas of flesh in our lives, and that we would say, "Lord, I don't want to be found living, talking, acting, or doing that in my last moments when You come or call for me." We love You, Lord! Captivate our hearts we pray! In the name of Jesus. Amen.*

MONDAY: John Felt the Touch of Christ

And when I saw Him, I fell at His feet as dead. **But He laid His right hand on me**, *saying to me, "Do not be afraid."*
—Revelation 1:17

Have you ever considered the power of touch? At this very instant, as you use your senses to read this page, there are five trillion chemical operations occurring each second in your brain. The brain has no contact with the outside world. It is inside a box of bone connected through cables coming up through the spinal column, and from the optical nerve, the auditory nerves, and all the central nervous system—from our touch to our taste. All of these come in and converge in the brain.

Inside our heads all roads lead in from our senses, five gates through which we comprehend the world about us. The capabilities of our senses are impressive! Animals and insects might outdo us in hearing (dog, bat, horse), seeing (eagle), or smelling (moth and salmon), but when our five senses are combined, we are unmatched in our sensory powers.

Our Sense of Hearing: How do we distinguish the myriad of sounds we hear? Every distinct sound has a signature of vibrations per second. Our ears can pick out 300,000 different sounds and distinguish between them.

Our Sense of Smell: It is with the second sense that we touch our world. Our noses are primitive compared to a salmon's or a moth's, but we can smell one garlic molecule in 50,000 molecules of air and our minds instantly identify it. We can discern between 10,000 different odors. And, because God made our sense of smell and sense of taste to work together, our ability to smell is what enables us to more fully enjoy the taste of different foods!

Our Sense of Sight: It is staggering that God made us with 127 million cells in each eye. Together they could detect a single candle's light at fifteen miles; that is one photon of light to activate our eyes!

Our Sense of Touch: This is the strongest of our senses. Touch is the sense most alert when we sleep. Is there any human activity that does not vitally rely on touch?

Although scientists cannot agree on how touch works in humans, they can measure it. For instance, one tap of your fingernail can discern between paper, fabric, wood, plastic, or steel. A finger can detect lines etched 1/2500 of an inch deep. It can feel even the slightest breeze that is 1/1000 of an ounce at the tip of a one-half inch hair. But those sensitivities in us, His creatures, pale in comparison with our Creator's power to sense and feel our touch.

The touch of Jesus is likewise the strongest sense we get of His power. Have you ever pondered the wonderful joy of being touched by Jesus? He reached out and touched the sinners and the sick, the demonized and the defiled, the young and the old, the living and the dead, and the hopeless and the helpless. And all were changed marvelously!

The Gospels record no less than forty times when Jesus touched individuals in His ministry. Some of the most well-known are the **touch of cleansing** a leper (Matthew 8:1–4); the **touch of liberation** for Peter's mother-in-law (Matthew 8:14–15); the **touch of completion** as multitudes pressed to touch Him (Matthew 14:36); the **touch of encouragement** for the astonished disciples (Matthew 17:7); and the **touch of sight** for Bartimaeus and his friend (Matthew 20:34).

Over sixty years after Christ's ascension, as John worshiped Christ that Sunday, he gratefully received Jesus' **touch of perfect love** in His resurrection glory. For "there is no fear in love; but perfect love casts out fear" (1 John 4:18).

Have you experienced the touch of Jesus? His nail-scarred hands are reaching out to touch those who will let Him! Do you *need* the touch of Jesus? He is extending His hand to you, if you will seek Him. **Reach out by faith.** Acknowledge that God senses every fiber of your life. He can feel your needs, and by faith you can touch God. **Ask for His touch.** Only Jesus Christ can fully meet your needs, so you must go to Him. **Confess His work in you.** If He has touched you, you should admit it publicly. Have you touched God today? Has He touched you? Do you need to tell someone?

For more on the wonder of being touched by Jesus, read Mark 5:21–43. Being touched by Him is shown beautifully in that passage. It should encourage you to desire to draw ever nearer to Him through His precious Word!

TUESDAY: The Wonder of Being Touched by Jesus

*Jesus, **moved with compassion**, stretched out His hand and **touched him**, and said to him, "I am willing; be cleansed."*
—MARK 1:41

The wonder of being touched by Jesus is clearly seen in Mark where some, like the grateful leper in 1:41, were touched by God in a mighty way. Ponder this familiar setting in Mark: "When Jesus had crossed over again by boat to the other side, a great multitude gathered to Him; and He was by the sea" (5:21). Now use your senses to relive the scene:

- **Feel** the rough-hewn, handmade boat, as it lay weathered on the shore.
- **See** the sun glinting off the blue-green waters of the Sea of Galilee.
- **Smell** the thick smells of fish, weeds, and wetness blended with the odors of a time when people seldom bathed.
- **Hear** the presence of numberless multitudes that swarmed around Christ like flies.
- **Taste** the excitement as they pressed upon Him so much that He couldn't get through them; so He stayed on the shore.

Jairus, a ruler of the synagogue at Capernaum, crashed through the crowd that had been pressing upon Jesus. As he caught sight of Christ, he "fell at His feet" (Mark 5:22)! Oh, to have that great a desire to meet with Jesus! Have you ever felt like crashing through the crowd at your church to dive at the feet of Christ—to delight in looking for Him in His Word? That is why these people experienced Him so deeply.

With complete faith, the ruler earnestly begged Jesus to come and heal his daughter: "'My little daughter lies at the point of death. Come and lay Your hands on her, that she may be healed, and she will live'" (Mark 5:23b). So "Jesus went with him, and a great multitude followed Him and thronged Him" (Mark 5:24).

During this time, everyone was still trying to touch Jesus, even if it was just the bottom of His robe. At this point an unknown, withered woman who had been aged by a horrible uncleanness "came behind Him in the crowd and touched His garment." For she knew that Jesus alone was her hope: "'If only I may touch His clothes, I shall be made well'" (Mark 5:27–28).

Her "flow of blood for twelve years" made her unclean in the eyes of Levitical law. She "had suffered many things from many physicians and had spent all that she had and was no better, but rather grew worse" (Mark 5:25–26). This woman was ashamed of her uncleanness. The bleeding woman knew, as do Christians today, that Jesus alone can meet our deepest needs.

The dying woman was motivated by faith; she touched Christ, and instantly was healed of her affliction. Do you remember the sensitivity of the five senses? She *intuitively* knew that her affliction was gone. Then Jesus, "immediately knowing in Himself that power had gone out of Him, turned around in the crowd and said, '**Who touched My clothes?**'" (see Mark 5:30).

What would that moment have been like? Picture being at the Rose Bowl in California for the Olympic Games, with all 100,000 people leaving at once after the games. You would be in an ocean of bodies! Can you imagine one person in that crowd saying, "Who just touched me?" It would have been a joke!

Jesus Christ is the only One who could feel the trembling, withered hand of a dying woman's touch upon the tassel of His coat. He alone can truly feel your heart's cry right now, and He has the power to make you whole! If you or a loved one fear death, or are desperate, helpless, sick, or feel unable to go any further, come to Jesus for help!

You have seen two people who had needs: Jairus, who came to Jesus for the healing of his daughter, and the aged woman, who came to Jesus to be healed of her disease. They came in two ways, but both had to confess Jesus publicly. Perhaps you need to be honest before others as well. Have you ever confessed to the church that God has touched you and made you whole? If not, you should do so through baptism, which is public confession—it will change your spiritual life!

WEDNESDAY: Jesus' Greatest Touch

*She said, "No one, Lord." And Jesus said to her, "**Neither do I condemn you**; go and sin no more."*
—John 8:11

The loveliest picture I know of Christ's forgiveness is the story of the woman caught in the act of adultery. Her story, recorded for us in John 8:1–11, represents one of the most beautiful portraits of the greatest touch of Jesus, His complete cleansing and forgiveness.

As you read this retelling of that incredible moment in Christ's ministry, watch for the contrasts between man's touch and Jesus' touch; man's countenance and Jesus' countenance; man's tone of voice and Jesus' tone of voice; man's lack of mercy and Jesus' mercy. Whom would you rather face?

John 8 opens early in the morning in the wide spaces of the Temple courtyard where Jesus often taught, and crowds often gathered to hear Him. As the sun rose higher and coolness of the dawn began to melt away Jesus was seated and holding the complete attention of a growing crowd. Suddenly the sound of an angry mob shatters the quietness of Christ's message.

Surging forward are well-known religious leaders, both scribes and Pharisees. They push their way roughly through those who listened to Christ and drag a woman forward. She is dazed, unkempt, weeping, and limp as they cast her in a heap at Christ's feet.

With voices of hatred, eyes of contempt, and faces hard as stone the accusation they brought is hurled at Christ like a spear. This woman was guilty of adultery; they were the witnesses—and she should be stoned. Silently Jesus took in the situation. The sobbing woman lay in a heap at His feet, like a garbage bag on the curb. The accusers were so much like their father the Devil, who is an accuser and destroyer, just like them. Then Jesus looked at the crowd. How they needed to understand the depth of redeeming love and forgiving grace!

Jesus began to look around the circle of the accusing religious leaders, His eyes began to pierce their souls. The hatred boiling over in their souls began to burn them within. It seemed as if Jesus were looking into their minds and hearts, and they felt instantly undone before Him. The accusers felt accused, and the accused felt protected.

Then suddenly the silence was broken. Christ's admirers and haters all were now captivated by the One who spoke and acted like no one ever had done. He got down in front of the cast-off bit of humanity that had been tossed at His feet. On her level he knelt and began to slowly trace letters in the dust of the marble floors. This is the only time the Gospels record Jesus writing anything—but those who watched will never forget what they felt. Starting at the oldest Jesus wrote a word, and then gazed into each of their eyes. Perhaps it was the word *lust* or *pride* or *greed* or *liar*, but no matter what He wrote the effect was the same. The touch of Jesus' eyes made them blanch with a shudder of unearthly fear, they dropped the rock they had clutched and with downcast eyes fled Christ's presence. The other accusers couldn't stop watching and trembling as they each faced a personal judgment day before the Judge of All.

There is the thud of stone after stone falling on the pavement. Not many of the Pharisees are left. One by one, they creep away—like animals slinking into the shadows . . . shuffling off into the crowded streets to lose themselves in the multitudes.

"He that is without sin among you, let him first cast a stone at her." But no stones have been thrown. They lie around the woman on the pavement. They have dropped them where they stood, and now she is left alone at the feet of Christ.

Only her sobbing breaks the stillness. She still has not lifted her head . . . And now Christ looks at her. He does not speak for a long moment. Then, with eyes full of understanding, He says softly: "Woman, where are those thine accusers? Hath no man condemned thee?" (John 8:10) And she answers, "No man, Lord."

That is all the woman says from beginning to end. She has no excuse for her conduct. She makes no attempt to justify what she has done.

And Christ, looking at her, seeing the tear-stained cheeks and her eyes red with weeping, seeing further into her heart, seeing the contrition there, says to her: "**Neither do I condemn you**; go and sin no more" (John 8:11).

What He says here is—Not that He acquits the woman, but that He forgives her. Not that He absolves her from blame, but that He absolves her from guilt. Not that He condones the act, but that He does not condemn her for it—He forgives her instead.

Perhaps He smiles upon her, as she slowly raises her eyes, a slow, sad smile of One who knew that He himself has to pay the price of that absolution. And it may be that His finger writes again in the dust, tracing this time the outline of a cross or the shape of a hill—a hill shaped like a skull.

No, we do not know her name, or where she lived, or who she was. But of this we can be sure—she was never the same again. She was a changed woman from that moment. Of that we can be sure."[2]

God is willing to forgive us, and to cleanse us from all unrighteousness, because the blood of Jesus Christ, His Son, cleanses us from all sin! The woman caught in adultery was never the same after she experienced Jesus' touch in her life! Have you received His touch—His greatest gift ever?

THURSDAY: Life in the Minor Key

*We were **troubled on every side**. Outside were conflicts, inside were fears. Nevertheless God, who comforts the downcast, comforted us.*
—2 Corinthians 7:5–6

Most of the Bible is in the major key in which saints are fearlessly witnessing and churches are valiantly serving against all odds. As much as those portions bring great joy to our souls, side-by-side with all that wonderful testimony is the minor key of Scripture.

In the minor key accounts, God provides true glimpses into His children's weaknesses and frailties by showing how some of His greatest saints struggled with being sad, discouraged, and depressed. Yet the Lord did not correct them and tell them they were in sin. So, as we study Revelation's unveiling of the Great Tribulation coming upon this world, know that He understands if at times you struggle with anticipation of what is to come. He wants you to give your fears to Him and find living hope for the end of days!

I believe that having a better understanding of God's view of depression can encourage your heart. Think about these questions: Is it always sin that *makes* us depressed? Is it always a sin to be depressed? It may surprise you that God's answer to both questions is no. What do Moses, Elijah, Hezekiah, Job, Ezra, David, Jeremiah, Jonah, and Paul share in common with us today? They were all Spirit-filled servants of the Lord, and they all struggled with negative emotions.

I looked up *depression* in the *Webster's Dictionary* and found the descriptions fascinating: "(1) A state of feeling sad; a disorder marked especially by sadness, inactivity, difficulty in thinking and concentration, a significant increase or decrease in appetite and time spent sleeping, feelings of dejection and hopelessness, and sometimes suicidal tendencies; and (2) A reduction in activity, amount, quality, or force; a lowering of vitality or functional activity."

We must be careful to not say that anxiety, depression, discouragement, and other negative emotions are in themselves sinful. Why? God's servants have experienced these same emotions, and in Christ we see sinless anger, deep emotional distress, grief, and anguish—all of which were perfectly displayed. For example, in the Garden of Gethsemane, Jesus "began to be very distressed and troubled" and His soul was "deeply grieved to the point of death" (see Mark 14:33–34 NASB). In coming to earth, He took upon himself the form of a human with all its frailties, yet He did not sin.

We should not call each occurrence of a negative emotion sin, but neither should we stay "in the pits." The following servants of the Lord all suffered from crippling, and sometimes even paralyzing, depression:

- **Moses:** "I am not able to bear all these people alone, because the burden is too heavy for me. If You treat me like this, please kill me here and now!" (Numbers 11:14–15).
- **Elijah:** "But he. . . prayed that he might die, and said, 'It is enough! Now, Lord, take my life, for I am no better than my fathers!'" (1 Kings 19:4).
- **Hezekiah:** "Then he turned his face toward the wall, and prayed to the LORD. . . . And Hezekiah wept bitterly" (2 Kings 20:2–3).
- **Job:** "Why did I not die at birth? Why did I not perish when I came from the womb?" (Job 3:11).
- **Ezra:** "My soul clings to the dust; revive me according to Your word" (Psalm 119:25).
- **David:** "Bring my soul out of prison, that I may praise Your name" (Psalm 142:7).
- **Jeremiah:** "See, O LORD, that I am in distress; my soul is troubled; my heart is overturned within me, for I have been very rebellious" (Lamentations 1:20).
- **Jonah:** "God prepared a vehement east wind; and the sun beat on Jonah's head, so that he grew faint. Then he . . . said, 'It is better for me to die than to live'" (Jonah 4:8).
- **Paul:** "Our flesh had no rest, but we were afflicted on every side: conflicts without, fears within. But God, who comforts the depressed, comforted us" (2 Corinthians 7:5–6, NASB).

When caught up in the throes of depression, emotions can run so rampant that it is difficult to think clearly. If that happens to you, like David, remember to cry out to the Lord: "O God, be merciful to me! For my soul trusts in You; and in the shadow of Your wings I will make my refuge; until these calamities have passed by" (Psalm 57:1). Jesus is the safest refuge in the universe!

FRIDAY: Temptation and Struggles Are Not Sin

> *[Paul and Barnabas]* **strengthen[ed] the souls** *of the disciples, exhorting them to continue in the faith, and saying, "We must through many tribulations enter the kingdom of God."*
> —Acts 14:22

Yesterday we looked at various notable saints in the Bible who suffered from crippling, and sometimes paralyzing, depression. Now we're going to look at a few examples of God's choice servants who have likewise suffered in this manner. It may surprise you to learn that Martin Luther was among those who've struggled with depression.

The great hymn we all love to sing, *A Mighty Fortress Is Our God*, was penned by the great sixteenth-century reformer, Martin Luther (1483–1546)—during his darkest days of depression. It was a testimony to God's power to lift him out of the prison of his soul, back to hope and strength.

As a devoted pastor, he sought to bring spiritual counsel to struggling souls. His compassion for those souls shines in numerous places, including his sermons, lectures, Bible commentaries and table talks.[3]

Besides observing mental difficulties in others, Luther had a greater reason to affirm their reality—he also endured many periods of depression. He described his personal experience in varied terms: melancholy, heaviness, and depression, dejection of spirit, downcast, sad, and downhearted. He suffered this way for much of his life and often revealed these struggles in his works. Luther evidently did not think it a shameful problem to be hidden.

Charles Spurgeon (1834–1892), who lit the fires of the nineteenth-century revival movement, struggled so severely with depression that he was forced to be absent from his pulpit for two to three months a year. In 1866 he told his congregation: "I am the subject of depressions of spirit so fearful that I hope none of you ever get to such extremes of wretchedness as I go to." Those words were spoken in a sermon by Spurgeon whose marvelous ministry in London made him perhaps the greatest preacher England ever produced.

John Henry Jowett (1864–1923) pastored leading churches, preached to huge congregations, and wrote books that were best-sellers. In a message he confessed: "You seem to imagine that I have no ups and downs, but just a level and lofty stretch of spiritual attainment with unbroken joy and equanimity. By no means! I am often perfectly wretched and everything appears most murky." Yet Dr. Jowett was often called in his day the "Greatest Preacher in the English-speaking World!"

I could go on and on through the "Who's Who" of ministry and find countless other testimonies that say the same. The point is this: Spirit-filled Christians can experience emotional problems. Some godly believers, especially those of certain temperaments, will always struggle with feeling "down."

As we look back on history, we can conclude that many of these saints suffered because of physical conditions that prompted depression. One Christian medical doctor, who has spent his lifetime helping people, writes this:

> Consider this thought experiment. Give me the most saintly person you know. If I were to administer certain medications of the right dosage, such as thyroid hormone, or insulin, I could virtually guarantee that I could make this saint anxious with at least one of these agents. Would such chemically induced anxiety be explained as a spiritual sin? What if the person's own body had an abnormal amount of thyroid hormone or insulin and produced nervousness?[4]

We as believers should never condone willful sin, but we must learn to accept that some fellow believers may suffer from emotional symptoms that are not the result of unconfessed sin. It is possible to feel horrible, and be in great emotional anguish, and still be obedient to the Lord.

Consider what godly Job cried out in the midst of his suffering: "For sighing comes to me instead of food; my groans pour out like water. . . . My days are swifter than a weaver's shuttle, and they come to an end without hope. . . . I despise my life. . . . Surely, O God, you have worn me out; you have devastated my entire household. . . . But if I go to the east, he is not there; if I go to the west, I do not find him. . . . And now my life ebbs away; days of suffering grip me. Night pierces my bones; my gnawing pains never rest. . . . I cry out to you, O God, but you do not answer" (Job 3:24; 7:6, 16; 16:7; 23:8; 30:16–17, 20 NIV).

Notice that in spite of Job's depression, the Bible says, "In all this Job did not sin" (1:22 NIV). Moreover, God reproved his friends for accusing him of sin and for their failure to speak rightly concerning His servant (see 42:7–8). We must never forget: "Death and life are in the power of the tongue" (Proverbs 18:21). So when we notice that a sister or brother in Christ is struggling with depression, we must be careful to not be judgmental but to be an encourager instead!

SATURDAY: Share Struggles—Share Prayers

*You also **helping together** in prayer for us, that thanks may be given by many persons on our behalf for the gift granted to us through many.*

—2 Corinthians 1:11

The word *sunopourgeo*, translated "helping together," is used only here in the Greek New Testament and is composed of three words: "with, under, work." It is a picture of laborers under the burden, working together to get the job accomplished. Paul enlists the help of other believers to hold him up in his emotional, physical, and spiritual struggles. (This was in addition to the Holy Spirit's promise in Romans 8:26 to assist us in our praying and help carry our load.)

Difficulties, especially in these end days, should draw us closer to other Christians as we share our burdens and prayer needs. When experiencing the trials of life, we need to remember what God has promised us, and what He has commanded us to do.

In 1 Thessalonians 5, there are more commands than in any other paragraph in God's Word. It is one of the clearest descriptions of the basic duties of a believer in Christ's church. Read verses 11–26, and note all the many commands. In other words, we must take seriously Paul's command to "comfort the fainthearted, uphold the weak, be patient with all" (1 Thessalonians 5:14).

Make a choice to live in hope. What can depression, discouragement, and faintheartedness do for us? If we choose to live in hope, as we regularly cry out to the Lord, it can inspire us to some of the deepest and greatest discoveries about God we can ever make!

WEEK 11
Fear Not! For I Am with You!

{ Revelation 1:17–18 }

As the end of days approaches, you can find hope in the Revelation of Jesus Christ, for the ultimate victory is Christ's, and He will never leave or forsake you!

SUNDAY: Troublesome Times Are Here

And when I saw Him, I fell at His feet as dead. But He laid His right hand on me, saying to me, "**Do not be afraid**; *I am the First and the Last. I am He who lives, and was dead, and behold, I am alive forevermore. Amen. And I have the keys of Hades and of Death."*
—Revelation 1:17–18

While on Patmos, John felt Christ's comforting touch, which is exactly what Jesus offers to each of us. At the end of His ministry, He promised to be with us always, even to the very end of days. Since we may be living in those actual days right now, we need to feel His calming presence—His comforting touch that removes all fear.

There are fearful times coming to this planet, but if you compare our American news with that of the national papers of the industrialized nations of the world, you can easily see that our news lacks foresight and discernment. Why is that? News reporters in other nations look at the entire world while we Americans usually focus on ourselves. Unless the news is of a catastrophic nature, like the 2004 tsunami, our major American news sources do not generally report on global events other than the usual happenings in the Middle East. But sticking one's head in the sand when it comes to discerning the signs of the times globally will not hold back God's ultimate plan for mankind. All the events He has foretold in His Word will happen exactly as predicted, and precisely on schedule.

Every time something that was predicted in Luke 21 happens, Jesus said it should cause us to lift up our heads. Actually, the Greek words mean "to turn your body; to cause your whole body to focus upward." Jesus said that we are headed toward such trying days that people will "expire" due to fear of things to come: "Men's **hearts [will be] failing them from fear . . . of those things which are coming** on the earth, for the powers of the heavens will be shaken" (Luke 21:26).

In verse 26, the Greek word *apopsucho* means that their "breath or soul pops out" or "expires" because of complete fear. Isn't that a graphic word? It is not that some fearful disaster happens, and then people react by becoming afraid. No, they see it coming toward them and just die at the very *thought* of what is going to happen. Jesus is not referring to just the elderly, or a person who already has a bad heart. He is talking about healthy people who see the Tribulation events coming—and it literally scares them to death!

The overwhelming tribulations on the horizon will cause a "panic attack" in many healthy humans who will then expire in fear. Events like scientists' flurry of concern over the solar explosion on October 28, 2003 (reported only in overseas papers) are but a small taste of things to come.

For seven days, scientists all over the world were glued to their seats watching the space weather. Then, that Tuesday, they sat up in their chairs, rubbed their eyes, and started to sweat because of anticipation of what might happen. They watched the sun bulge, the buildup of the energy, and then saw the sun explode a cloud of superheated gas equivalent to a million hydrogen bombs! It all exploded at once in one small area, then went out from the surface of the sun, and headed across the solar system away from the earth.

That explosion was the greatest solar event ever measured. It was so big that scientists didn't have descriptions that could explain its magnitude. And they didn't even get to see the fullness of the explosion because, as the sun turned, it just floated off in the opposite direction—almost as if the Lord did not want it to be seen!

God is in control. What a wonderful comfort to know that our Creator is in charge of the entire universe! Not even a tiny sparrow falls to the ground apart from the Father's will (Matthew 10:29b). If it were possible for any person or thing to possess even a tiny modicum of power greater than God's, then He would cease to be our sovereign King of Kings and Lord of Lords! So rejoice in the fact that all authority has been given to Jesus in heaven and on earth, and in Him we live and move and have our being (Matthew 28:20; Acts 17:28)!

We need never fear because God *is* in absolute control—not only of the past and present, but also of the future!

My Prayer for You This Week: *Father in heaven, this is Your message: we are to have a Word-filled life in fearful times. We are not to fear terrorists, bioterrorism, economic terrorism, cancer, stalkers, somebody in the dark around our house, the future, a new job, or whatever it is. I pray that we would see that Your prescription for not fearing is meditation—a Word-filled life. For when we meditate on Your Word, we know that You are with us always to the end. So help us to have a Word-filled life even in fearful times. Help us to truly understand and grab hold of that reality! In the name of Jesus we pray. Amen.*

MONDAY: Signs in the Sun

*"And there will be **signs in the sun**."*
—Luke 21:25a

What did Jesus mean by "signs in the sun"? I believe that the marked increase in sunspot activity and solar flares is the beginning of the horrors to come. Paal Brekke, Deputy Project Manager of the SOHO spacecraft, a solar orbiting heliosphere study observatory which looks at the sun, had this to say about those solar explosions that occurred on October 28, 2003: "I think the last week will go into the history books as one of the most dramatic periods of solar activity we have seen in modern time."[1] He, an unbeliever, was trying to come to grips with the significance of three additional bursts on top of the two back-to-back monster flares.

Scientists now know that all of this is a cycle. There is an eleven-year cycle of events on the sun, such as sunspot activity and solar flares. Since 1755, twenty-three eleven-year cycles have been recorded by solar observatories. The sun has observable patterns; it will have numerous solar flares and then be very quiet for a season. At this moment (2006), we are four years into the quiet side, but, according to Mr. Brekke, there are signs that the sun is revving up like it never has before in history.

On March 6, 2003, the largest sunspot ever observed developed. The unusual spot created a new, giant flare almost daily, saturating the space between the sun and earth with solar x-rays, gamma rays, and protons, and creating surging waves in the solar wind that disturbed the earth's magnetic field with unprecedented regularity. Scientists say the sunspot activity is harmless to human beings and that we are protected from radiation by the atmosphere. The only effects most of us will notice will be sporadic problems with cell phones, TV reception, and a bumpier Internet than usual. In practical terms, it is an interesting non-story. It was a non-event until the morning of Tuesday, October 28, 2003. In spiritual terms, I believe that we now face "a whole different ballgame." Fascinating, isn't it?

Where to find hope in troublesome times. "May the God of hope fill you with all joy and peace in believing, that you may abound in hope by the power of the Holy Spirit" (Romans 15:13). Hope comes from the living and written Word of God; as you read and meditate upon the Scriptures, the Holy Spirit will apply His truths to your heart, filling you with joy and peace. For example, as you read Psalm 121 below, God will encourage you to know that He is your helper, keeper, protector, and preserver. So whenever fear attacks, be comforted by meditating on these wonderful truths:

> I will lift up my eyes to the hills—From whence comes my help? My help comes from the Lord, Who made heaven and earth. He will not allow your foot to be moved; He who keeps you will not slumber. . . . The LORD is your keeper; The LORD is your shade at your right hand. The sun shall not strike you by day, nor the moon by night. The Lord shall preserve you from all evil; He shall preserve your soul. The LORD shall preserve your going out and your coming in from this time forth, and even forevermore.
>
> —Psalm 121:1–3, 5–8

TUESDAY: We Live in Fearful Times

> "When you see Jerusalem surrounded by armies, then know that its desolation is near. . . . And **Jerusalem will be trampled** by Gentiles until the times of the Gentiles are fulfilled."
>
> —Luke 21:20, 24b

Jesus has said that Jerusalem will be a focal point globally in the end times. At the end of Luke 21:24, He was referring to where we are right now in history. After A.D. 70, Jerusalem ceased to exist as it had previously. No longer could the Jews worship God as they once had because Jerusalem had been trampled by the Gentiles. In fact, Revelation reports that there would be an abomination up on the Temple Mount, and it is there today—the Dome of the Rock!

Jesus spoke of wars and rumors of wars, famines, earthquakes, pestilences (deadly diseases), and changes in climate. He spoke of Israel as a literal place in the last days, and of Jerusalem's rise to global prominence. Have you ever considered that Jerusalem has the third largest press corps in the world? Why is that? After all, Jerusalem has less than one million people, so why do they have more reporters there than anywhere, except for New York City and Washington, D.C.? The only possible explanation is that the whole world is fascinated with Israel! Other nations do not like Israel being there; they are afraid of Israel because it is so disproportionate in its influence and attention.

To a science fiction enthusiast, a paraphrase of Luke 21:25–26 might read like news reports in a futuristic episode or miniseries: "The end of the world is upon us! There are troubles with the sun, moon, and stars! On earth there is distress of nations, with mass confusion, and the waves are roaring! All over the planet men and women are dying from fear!" From a Christian perspective, however, look at what Jesus says when all that happens: "When these things begin to happen, look up and lift up your heads, because your redemption draws near" (Luke 21:28).

There are two separate Greek verbs in verse 28. Not only are we to lift up our eyes, but we are also to turn our whole bodies toward Christ because His coming is near! Every time I hear of a major solar event, a huge earthquake, a catastrophic hurricane, or an unprecedented tidal wave, I am grieved for all those who have been snatched into eternity without knowing Christ. Yet my heart is also thrilled because such events remind me that our redemption is getting nearer!

Whenever there are signs in the sun, moon, and stars; signs on earth when the nations are in distress; and signs when fear and deadly "panic attacks" hit the planet, we should *"look up"* because Jesus said our redemption is close at hand. In Luke 21:31–33, Jesus says the generation that is alive when these things begin will be the final generation, and will see His coming—if they survive!

Where to find hope in fearful times. More and more we see the reflection of society's fears in apocalyptic-themed films. From some of the early global disaster movies in the 1980s and 1990s, such as *Apocalypse Now*, to more recent ones like *The Day After Tomorrow*, people are watching and thinking about fearful themes on this doomed planet. Sometimes just reading those titles is enough to scare anyone who is not grounded in the Word of God!

God has an offer for those who live in fearful times. More than any other prohibition in Scripture, He repeatedly calls out to us, "Fear not!" To conquer fear, a truly wise person will earnestly pray, "Let the words of my mouth and the meditation of my heart be acceptable in Your sight, O LORD, my strength and my Redeemer" (Psalm 19:14; see also Proverbs 3:21–26).

WEDNESDAY: The Antidote for Fearfulness

*Whenever I am afraid, I will trust in You. In God (**I will praise His word**), In God I have put my trust; **I will not fear**.*
—PSALM 56:3–4

We live in a world that is possessed by fear. The "spirit of fear" is all around us—even in unexpected places. For example, once I was standing in line next to someone and was about to give my order when the clerk looked me right in the eye and said, "I know what you want." She then proceeded to tell me what I wanted to order. I asked her, "How did you know that?" She replied, "I am a psychic." "If that is really true," I told her, "I am sorry for you. You are going to have a bad ending."

That clerk didn't understand where I was coming from, so I continued, "The psychic realm is from the devil, and if that is who you are associated with, God says you are going to have a very bad ending." As she was confronted with the Word of God, her eyes widened and got hard as she exclaimed, "You are wrong!" A pastor from that town, in line behind me, whispered in my ear, "Don't you know that woman is a practicing witch?" And I said, "Well, I found out, didn't I?"

We live in a world filled with darkness. Therefore, God repeatedly tells us, "Fear not!" We are to live in constant touch with the God of heaven so that no matter what happens we can walk in boldness. I therefore challenge you, from the Word of the living God, to live what I call "the Word-filled life." This is what Paul described in Ephesians 5 as a Spirit-filled life, and in Colossians 3:16 he said to "let the word of Christ dwell in you richly in all wisdom."

God offers His presence and influence to permeate each of us, for that is what the Word-filled life is all about. It means letting God take total control of us, much like that psychic has let the devil control her. To use biblical words, in a positive supernatural sense, God wants to utterly possess our reins, the very center of our feelings and passions. This applies even in fearful times, for that is when we should be most confident that we know Him. The Word-filled life is an anchor during those distracting times when the whole world seems to be falling apart around us.

Joshua is a wonderful example of how to conquer fear by living the Word-filled life. In Joshua 1:1–3, God himself commissioned Joshua to be the head of His army on earth—Israel. Then God promised: "Every place that the sole of your foot will tread upon I have given you, as I said to Moses. . . . No man shall be able to stand before you all the days of your life; as I was with Moses, so I will be with you. **I will not leave you nor forsake you**" (vv. 3, 5).

Because it is natural to be afraid when facing what Joshua was facing, God reminded him: "**Be strong and of good courage**, for to this people you shall divide as an inheritance the land which I swore to their fathers to give them. **Only be strong and very courageous**" (Joshua 1:6–7).

God not only commanded Joshua to not fear, but He also told him what to do to be successful: *"This Book of the Law shall not depart from your mouth, but you shall* **meditate in it day and night**, *that you may . . . do . . . all that is written in it. For then you will make your way prosperous,* **and . . . have good success**" (Joshua 1:8).

In light of the fact that Joshua was a soldier, how could God command him to meditate on the Scriptures day and night? Was he supposed to carry a scroll along with his sword and shield? Can you imagine trying to lug one of those things around while trying to fight at the same time? No, God intended that Joshua *meditate* on His Word. The Lord expected him to absorb His words into his mind, into his heart, and be saying or thinking upon them constantly. In other words, he was commanded to be involved in Scripture memory and meditation. Why was that so important?

Meditation is the key to success. Whether it is business, the arts, homemaking, relationships, a military campaign, or anything else, meditation is God's prescription for success in any endeavor. If you want to succeed, you need not pay for a seminar to inspire you—just learn to meditate faithfully on the Scriptures. You will always succeed if God is with you and your mind and heart are filled with His Word.

Living a Word-filled life will conquer any fears you might have. Meditating on God's precious Word will provide the needed assurance that Jesus is with you always, even to the very end of life!

THURSDAY: Joshua's Plan

*"This Book of the Law **shall not depart from your mouth**,*
but you shall meditate in it day and night."

—Joshua 1:8a

Joshua's hectic schedule and constant life on the road, heading to and from battles, never stopped him from spending time with the Lord twice daily. How did General Joshua Ben-Nun keep this up when he became a career military and political leader?

Joshua started a lifelong habit when he was a young man. "[Moses'] servant Joshua the son of Nun, a young man, did not depart from the tabernacle" (Exodus 33:11). What was that habit? He loved to spend time at the Tent of Meeting (similar to church and Sunday school), which was the representation of God's presence. In today's vernacular, you could say that Joshua formed a habit in his youth of hanging around church and the fellowship of God's saints. He was different from the typical young person of today. He did not hang around with the crowd; he preferred to hang around with his Creator, the Lord God of the universe. When he was older, the habit of investing time for God to the exclusion of other activities never left him.

Joshua obeyed God's command. "This Book of the Law shall not depart from your mouth, but you shall meditate in it" (Joshua 1:8a). Having made a habit as a young man to love God's presence, he immediately followed the Lord's command when He said, "I want you to let My Word be in you so full that it overflows!" In other words, Joshua obediently cultivated the Word-filled life by meditating upon and loving God's Word.

Joshua stayed with it to the end. "Choose for yourselves this day whom you will serve. . . . **But as for me and my house, we will serve the LORD**" (Joshua 24:15). Do you know why Joshua could make such a majestic statement—one that we love to hang on our walls? Because, in his youth, he purposed that he would always love God and linger in His presence, even to the neglect of the crowd. He continually kept God's Word in his heart and mind, and that is why he could stay with it to the end. Thus, no matter what any other family did, Joshua and his family determined to stay faithful to the Lord.

Whom do you serve? Ask yourself these questions: Am I lingering in God's presence? Am I writing His Word on my heart so that I don't fear? Am I committed to saying, "But as for me and my house, we will serve the Lord"?

The most powerful form of leadership is not the leadership of position: *I am the manager.* It is not the leadership of expertise: *I know more than everybody else.* It is the leadership that is impossible to be challenged: the leadership of character, living a life that people *want* to follow. That is what Joshua had.

Are God's words stuck to your heart, your mind, your mouth? That is what the Lord wants. Then you can lead your family God's way. Fearful times are coming, but don't get swept up by the spirit of fear all around us because "fear is not from God" (2 Timothy 1:7)! So remember to meditate upon the promises the Lord has made!

FRIDAY: Joshua's Command

*"Have I not commanded you? Be strong and of good courage; do not be afraid, nor be dismayed, for the LORD your **God is with you wherever you go**."*

—JOSHUA 1:9

When Moses died, and Joshua was commissioned to be the head of God's army on earth, it must have seemed like a formidable task to him! Of this challenge, John MacArthur writes:

> Joshua was approaching 90 years of age when called on by God to lead a seven plus year war against entrenched enemies. At age 90, Joshua had graduated from prep school. He had followed Moses for 40 years, everywhere he went. He had learned to obey and see God at work in protecting the nation of Israel, providing for their daily needs. But now the legendary presence of that monumental man from Egypt is gone.
>
> There were giants, there were huge walled cities and vast armies, and there was this group of people that hadn't been exactly cooperative with Moses. And what would be a normal human response? FEAR. And that is exactly what the Lord confronts and comforts Joshua about—be courageous, don't fear since I am with you.
>
> God speaks to Joshua, and gives him a promise—Joshua 1:9. "Have I not commanded you? Be strong and of good courage; do not be afraid, nor be dismayed, for the Lord your God is with you wherever you go."[2]

When the Lord God the Son, the Commander of the hosts of the Lord, came and spoke to Joshua, He called him to lead the nation and to perform all the conquests ahead. Think about what a monumental task that involved: Joshua was to lead an untrained army of three million into a hostile territory and do frontal attacks on established armies, cities, and walled towns. Imagine coming up to a forty-foot-high wall with your bow and arrow and saying, "All right you guys, you might as well surrender now. We're here to take over your city!"

Joshua's army didn't have aerial bombardment drones or M-16s; these farmers and herdsmen had only arrows, slingshots, and spears. So this was a fearful prospect indeed—for *all* Israelites! Therefore, God told Joshua in verse 9: "I don't want you to be dismayed or afraid. I want you to know that I, the Lord, am with you. And the way you will experience My presence is by meditating on My Word. Let it fill and overflow your heart!"

Fearfulness is a common malady. I meet people all the time who are terribly afraid. In fact, a while ago, one young man ran up to me and announced, "I heard a sound in the closet!" Of course, since he was only six years old at the time, his being afraid came as no surprise. (The sound was his sister playing with her toys, but he thought it was a monster.) Now then, if you are six, afraid of the dark, and you suddenly hear strange sounds in the closet, a fear response is normal. But should you still be that fearful in a few more years, that is bad news. Therefore, the Lord says to be progressively letting His Word richly dwell in you. Being a Word-filled believer will keep you from fearing terrorist attacks, ill health, lack of security, and an unknown future. God does not want us living in constant fear, so He tells us plainly, "Fear not!"

There is one solution for facing trouble: take God with you. There is one antidote for fearfulness: experience God's presence as you live out the Word-filled life!

SATURDAY: Fear Not!

> "**Fear not**, for I have redeemed you; I have called you by your name; **You are Mine**. When you pass through the waters, **I will be with you**; . . . When you walk through the fire, you shall not be burned, nor shall the flame scorch you. For I am the Lord your God."
>
> —Isaiah 43:1b-3a

It is just like our Lord to speak to us when we need Him the most. His tender "Fear not!" can calm the storm in our hearts regardless of the circumstances around us. Consider how He assured these great saints:

- **Abraham:** "The word of the LORD came to Abram in a vision, saying, '**Do not be afraid**, Abram. I am your shield, your exceedingly great reward'" (Genesis 15:1).
- **Isaac:** "And the LORD . . . said, 'I am the God of your father Abraham; **do not fear**, for I am with you'" (Genesis 26:24).
- **Jacob:** "So He said, 'I am God, the God of your father; **do not fear** to go down to Egypt, for I will make of you a great nation there'" (Genesis 46:3). In other words, God said to Jacob, "Don't worry! I am running this."
- **Daniel:** "O man greatly beloved, **fear not!** Peace be to you; be strong, yes, be strong!" (Daniel 10:19).
- **Mary:** "Then the angel said to her, '**Do not be afraid**, Mary, for you have found favor with God'" (Luke 1:30). Do you know what that word "favor" is? It is grace. If you are saved, you have been graced with grace! Thus, there is no need to fear.
- **Peter:** "And Jesus said to Simon, '**Do not be afraid**. From now on you will catch men'" (Luke 5:10).
- **Paul:** "**Do not be afraid**, Paul; you must be brought before Caesar; and indeed God has granted you all those who sail with you" (Acts 27:24). That was when he was in the storm.

I love highlighting verses like these in my Bible so that when fearful times come, whatever shape they take, I have an instant source to remind me of God's promises! The next time you are afraid, and fear comes over you as you feel alone and defeated, claim by faith the presence of the Lord, for He truly is with you.

Do you recall that Hebrews 13:5—**"I will never leave you nor forsake you"**—is from Joshua 1:5? God never changes: "Jesus Christ is the same yesterday, today, and forever" (Hebrews 13:8). God said to Joshua, "I have been with you in the past, and I will never leave you. I am right by you, and I want you to experience My presence. When you feel My presence you will not fear." He says the same to us today!

Isaiah 41:10 is a wonderful promise: "Fear not, for I am with you; be not dismayed, for I am your God. I will strengthen you, yes, I will help you, I will uphold you with My righteous right hand." Have you caught the connection that "fear not" always comes with an "I am with you"? As parents, we like to say that to our children, don't we? During storms in the night when my little ones have felt insecure, I have comforted them by saying, "Daddy's here!" Oh, it has been so sweet! I remember a precious time when my youngest, Elizabeth, was troubled about something, so I went into her room and said, "I am here, Elizabeth!" I loved it when I saw her relax, crawl back in that tiny little bed, and snuggle up to her blanket once more. She felt as secure as if she was in Fort Knox. She simply had forgotten for a moment that Daddy was there, but once she was reassured, she could rest once more.

As a beloved child of God, when you are afraid, cry out to Him, "Abba, Father!" (Romans 8:15). Since "Abba" is the equivalent of the English words "Daddy" or "Papa," listen for His comforting voice as He says to you, "Fear not! Daddy's here!"

Make a choice to live in hope. "Fear not!" is the most repeated negative prohibition in the Bible, used no fewer than seventy-two times. Fear is not from God, for He "has not given us a spirit of fear, but of power and of love and of a sound mind" (2 Timothy 1:7). Fear comes from our flesh; it surrounds us in the world, and it is the realm of the devil. So when the signs of end times multiply, and you are feeling anxious or fearful, ask God for His peace "which surpasses all understanding" (Philippians 4:7).

Jesus says to you: "Do you want to live in hope during fearful times? Have a Word-filled life, and you will experience My presence as never before—for I am your eternal refuge and hope."

WEEK 12
See the Risen Christ at Work

{ Revelation 1:9–20 }

As the end of days approaches, you can find hope as you see the risen Christ at work in your life!

SUNDAY: What Is Jesus Doing Today?

I, John, . . . on the island . . . called Patmos . . . was in the Spirit on the Lord's Day, and I heard behind me a loud voice, as of a trumpet, saying, "I am the Alpha and the Omega, the First and the Last," and, "What you see, write in a book and send it to the seven churches which are in Asia: to Ephesus, to Smyrna, to Pergamos, to Thyatira, to Sardis, to Philadelphia, and to Laodicea."

*Then I turned to see the voice that spoke with me. And having turned I saw seven golden lampstands, and in the midst of the seven lampstands: One **like the Son of Man**; clothed with a* *garment down to the feet* and *girded* about the chest **with a golden band**. His head and **hair were white like wool, as white as snow**, and; His **eyes like a flame of fire**; His *feet* were **like fine brass**, as if refined in a furnace, and; His **voice as the sound of many waters**; He had in His right hand seven stars, out of His mouth went a sharp two-edged sword, and His **countenance** was **like the sun shining in its strength**.

And when I saw Him, I fell at His feet as dead. But He laid His right hand on me, saying to me, "Do not be afraid; I am the First and the Last. I am He who lives, and was dead, and behold, I am alive forevermore. Amen. And I have the keys of Hades and of Death. Write the things which you have seen, . . . which are, and . . . which will take place after this. The mystery of the seven stars . . . and the seven golden lampstands: The seven stars are the angels of the seven churches, and the seven lampstands which you saw are the seven churches."

—REVELATION 1:9–20

In this week's devotionals, I invite you to see Jesus anew with me—as John did that Lord's Day when he came face-to-face with the risen and glorified Christ! We, too, can be comforted by knowing that Jesus identified himself as "I am He who lives, and was dead, and . . . am alive forevermore" (Revelation 1:18a).

Think about it: Jesus is *alive*! And since He is alive, He is doing the same things now as He did when He was with the disciples physically, for He is the same yesterday, today, and forever. Oh, how John needed that reminder!

To best understand what Jesus is doing now, let us look at the only eyewitness account that describes the ascended and glorified Christ of heaven. Over sixty years after Resurrection Sunday, a meeting took place. From God's flawless record of that Lord's Day meeting, we can derive seven perfect descriptions of what Jesus looks like. From those seven descriptions we discover exactly what He was doing then as well as now. Notice that each of these seven glorified descriptions matches a ministry of Christ's while He was on earth:

1. **"like the Son of Man"** (v. 13a): This describes Christ's *humanity*—so He can truly have compassion upon us.
2. **"garment down to the feet, girded. . . with a golden band, hair white as wool and snow"** (vv. 13b-14b): This describes Christ's *priesthood*—so He can truly forgive us.
3. **"eyes like a flame of fire"** (v. 14c): This describes Christ's *omniscience*—so He can truly see us where we are.
4. **"feet like fine brass"** (v. 15a): This describes Christ's *omnipotence*—so He can truly protect us.
5. **"voice as the sound of many waters"** (v. 15b): This describes Christ's *omnipresence*—so He can truly encourage us.
6. **"countenance like the sun shining in its strength"** (vv. 16b): This describes Christ's *majesty*—so He can truly be worshiped by us.
7. **"hand on me"** (vv. 17b-20): This describes Christ's *touch*—so He can truly help us.

What did Jesus do on earth? As we see Christ's risen and glorified humanity, it is a reminder of what He did on earth (Revelation 1:13a)—"the Son of Man" had compassion for us weak and wandering humans!

Anyone felt they could come to Him because He was approachable: the woman with the blood disorder; the leper; the father with the dying daughter; the centurion with the sick servant; the two blind men sitting by the road; the great multitude who were like sheep without a shepherd; and many, many more. Of the twelve times "compassion" is used in the New Testament, it always speaks of Jesus.

What is Jesus doing now? He is having compassion upon us in all our needs! For in His humanity, He experienced what it is like to be us (but without sin): "In that He Himself has suffered, being tempted, He is able to aid those who are tempted" (Hebrews 2:18).

This same Son of Man who stood "in the midst of the seven lampstands"—which speak of His church—visits us today. When we gather together in His name, He checks our hearts to see if we come to worship Him as our "first love," or if we have a spiritually cold heart. When we come into His house with clean hearts and prepared to seek Him, this God of all comfort reaches out to encourage His needy children so that we can also comfort others who are in trouble (2 Corinthians 1:3–4).

Are you weak? Jesus understands. Are you afraid? Jesus is acquainted with all that you face. Are you alone? Jesus experienced the long loneliness of the Garden of Gethsemane, the wilderness temptation, and those horrific hours of darkness on the cross. He knows what it is like to be alone.

I could go on and on with examples of the risen and glorified Christ's compassion! But my point is this: Jesus knows how to identify with your humanity, and He wants you to experience the power of His victory—if you will just invite Jesus to be at work in you!

My Prayer for You This Week: *Father in heaven, I pray that this beautiful, glorious picture that John saw of You, oh Christ, would be burned into our hearts and that we would choose to meet with You, the risen Christ, every day, all through each day, until You come or call for us. I pray that Your Spirit will draw and move and work in our hearts today. May those who don't know You humbly say, "God be merciful to me, a sinner. Cleanse me! I turn in faith from my sins to you, oh Christ!" For those who do know You, may we realize that You are compassionate, honest, and come to us in our time of need. May this be a wonderfully encouraging study as we meet the risen Christ this week. We love You and worship You! In the name of Jesus we pray. Amen.*

MONDAY: Christ's Risen and Glorified Priesthood

*But He . . . has **an unchangeable priesthood**. Therefore He is . . . able to save to the uttermost those who come to God through Him, since He always lives to make intercession for them.*
—Hebrews 7:24–25

As we see Christ's risen and glorified priesthood, we are reminded that He truly can forgive us (Revelation 1:13b-14b)!

What did Jesus do on earth? He forgave sins as pictured in the healing of the leper who knelt before Him saying that, if He wanted to, He could cleanse him. And Jesus, full of compassion, said to him, "I am *willing*; be cleansed" (see Mark 1:40–45; emphasis added).

To the paralytic who was lowered on his bed into that crowded house in Capernaum, Jesus said, "Son, your sins are forgiven you" (see Mark 2:1–5).

To the woman caught in adultery, when her accusers left, Jesus said to her, "Neither do I condemn you; go and sin no more" (see John 8:1–11).

That same Jesus, the Son of Man and Son of God, has promised to be with us always, even to the end of the age (Matthew 28:20). He is not a distant, unknowable, infinite Creator God. No, He is with us always!

Because the Jesus who is with us is the risen and glorified Son of Man, He can truly have compassion on us because He knows our frame, "that we are dust" (Psalm 103:14). Because He knows our weaknesses so well, His most frequent emotion is compassion. He is literally "moved within." The Bible says that Jesus was moved both physically and emotionally when He saw people.

Do you truly understand the depth of love that Jesus Christ has for us? God himself is moved with compassion for you and me, and He longs for us to realize that He is with us as the Son of Man!

What is Jesus doing now? He is still forgiving sins: "We have a great High Priest who has passed through the heavens, Jesus the Son of God, [so] let us hold fast our confession. For we do not have a High Priest who cannot sympathize with our weaknesses, but was in all points tempted as we are, yet without sin" (Hebrews 4:14–15).

As we saw in Hebrews 7:24–25 at the beginning of this devotional, because Jesus has "an unchangeable priesthood" He is able to "save to the uttermost" those who come to Him in faith because He "always lives to make intercession" for us!

Do you feel defiled? He alone can forgive and cleanse. Do you feel the fear of future judgment? He can forever take away that penalty you deserve. So trust in Him, and then rejoice in your risen and glorified High Priest!

TUESDAY: Christ's Risen and Glorified Omniscience

When evening came, the boat was in the middle of the sea; and He was alone on the land. Then **He saw them straining at rowing**, *for the wind was against them. Now about the fourth watch of the night He came to them, walking on the sea.*

—Mark 6:47–48

As we see Christ's risen and glorified omniscience—His infinite understanding and insight with his "eyes like a flame of fire"—it is a reminder that He can truly see us wherever we are (Revelation 1:14c)!

What did Jesus do on earth? In His omniscience, He always knew where His disciples were and what they needed. (See also Matthew 14:22–33 and John 6:15–21.) Jesus Christ's laser-like eyes penetrated through the storms of His disciples' lives that threatened them with darkness, clouds, and overwhelming difficulties. His eyes saw right into the depths of their souls, and all that they were thinking and feeling. But He did not stop there; He faithfully and lovingly met with them in their times of need.

What is Jesus doing now? Jesus is still meeting His children in their storms and weaknesses—when they are feeling "at the end of themselves." Do you realize that such dark periods can actually be our best times? How is that possible? That is not only when He is the closest, but it is also when we get to experience *Him*. Although He couldn't get any closer than He already is, we become more aware of His presence when we are in trouble and struggling.

This glorified and risen Christ, with His eyes of fire, knows our every fear, every weakness, and every detail of our lives so that He can truly help us. So we should "come boldly to the throne of grace, that we may obtain mercy and find grace to help in time of need" (Hebrews 4:16).

A little later in our study of Revelation, we will see Jesus talking to the church in Laodicea, saying, "Behold, I stand at the door and knock. If anyone hears My voice and opens the door, I will come in to him and dine with him, and he with Me" (Revelation 3:20). Holman Hunt's famous painting of Jesus rapping against a door is still in the British Art Gallery; it is one of the most beautiful paintings of a biblical scene. His picture portrays only Jesus' head with Him listening and knocking on the door. The curious thing about that picture is that there is no handle on the *outside*. Why? Because Jesus wants us to open the door of our hearts and let Him in!

Hebrews 4:16 tells us that He offers mercy and grace in time of need. Sometimes God comes to our rescue without being asked, but He usually waits until we call out to Him for help. Jesus wants to commune with us in our stormy periods so that He can give us His wisdom, strength, and insight. He wants us to understand "the big picture" of His plan for our lives so that we are not just down here operating on our own. His ultimate plan is to work freely in us "both to will and to do for His good pleasure" (Philippians 2:13).

Through His "eyes like a flame of fire," Jesus knows your every detail, every fear, and every weakness—and longs to help you. Will you let Him in today?

WEDNESDAY: Christ's Risen and Glorified Omnipotence

No temptation has overtaken you except such as is common to man; but **God** *is faithful, who* **will not allow you to be tempted beyond what you are able**, *but with the temptation will also make the way of escape, that you may be able to bear it.*
—1 Corinthians 10:13

As we see Christ's risen and glorified omnipotence—His infinite power and strength with "feet like fine brass"—it is a reminder that He can truly protect us in every situation (Revelation 1:15a).

What did Jesus do on earth? He was always protecting His own by delivering them from danger, and stilling their storms (see Matthew 8:23–27; Mark 4:35–41; Luke 8:22–25). When His disciples were afraid in their "rocking boat," He came to them *walking* on the sea. Isn't that interesting? He showed His strength and power through His *feet!*

When John saw Christ like "the Son of Man," he saw His High Priestly garment and then His "eyes like a flame of fire." Those eyes must have been so awesome to him that he had to avert his gaze, so he looked down and saw Christ's feet—His "feet like fine brass." That strength and power came to His disciples across the storm, across their problem, and demonstrated Christ's omnipotence!

What is Jesus doing now? He ever lives to intercede for us to protect and help us in every danger we face! He is omnipotently "able to save to the uttermost"!

Have you ever really thought about the fact that Jesus Christ, the God of the universe, is praying for *you*? What an incredible ministry! What Christ did in Bible times, He does now: He prays that our faith will not fail. Christ our refuge has the power to deliver you and me from danger, and to still the storms in our lives. There is no temptation or trial that is beyond His strength and power to conquer.

In 1 Corinthians 10:13 the words "overtaken you" are very interesting. They mean that temptation is chasing us until we are in the grave. Our flesh is continually trying to come up behind us and trip us up: "But each one is tempted when he is carried away and enticed by his own lust. Then when lust has conceived, it gives birth to sin; and when sin is accomplished, it brings forth death" (James 1:14-15 NASB).

When the flesh and the lust keep talking to our will until we say, "All right—just this once I am going to give in," lust conceives and brings forth sin; for sin is when we yield willfully to the temptation.

We will be tempted in proportion to how much we are feeding our lusts. For example, every time we get angry, that lust is fed and will only grow stronger. Whenever we give in to impatience, that, too, feeds the lust, and it will grow as well. Each time we give in to materialism, that lust will all the more tighten its tenacious hold on us. The only way to break free is to quit feeding whatever it is that is dragging us down. If we starve whatever lust plagues us, we will have fewer and fewer temptations, and thus grow stronger in Christ instead.

Remember this: temptation itself is not sin—it is merely a reflection of the strength of our lust and how much we have fed it. That is why mature Christians mortify their lusts by constantly saying no, thereby starving and putting to death all of that struggle.

To form the habit of mortifying lusts, we must stay alert to the devil's schemes to entice us. Temptation will always come through one of these three channels of temptation in the spiritual world: **(1) lust of the flesh**—fulfilling a legitimate desire (like sexual desires) in an illegitimate way (like fornication); **(2) lust of the eyes**—the constant desire for more and more of the finer things of life; and **(3) pride of life**—the hunger for applause or the accolades of others—the arrogance of an independent spirit that competes with God for control and glory.

God is faithful: the Son of Man feels compassion; the Great High Priest, wearing that priestly robe, is ready to forgive our sins and cleanse us; Christ's penetrating eyes always know where we are, and exactly what we need; His omnipotent feet like brass will powerfully provide a way for us to escape whatever temptation or trial in which we find ourselves.

"A way of escape" is the omniscient One Who says, "You don't have to commit to that sin. You don't have to yield to that temptation. You don't have to give in to that trial. You don't have to feed your lusts because I am here for you to give you all the power you need to resist the Devil, and flee from him."

Martin Luther used to say: "When the Devil knocks with temptation, I send Jesus to answer the door. And Jesus says: 'Yes?' The devil says 'I'm coming for Martin Luther,' to which Jesus says, 'Martin doesn't live here any more—I do.'"

My Heart—Christ's Home, by Robert Boyd Munger, is a book about giving up every room in our lives so that there are no locked doors that we don't open up to Jesus.[1] As you completely yield yourself to Him, you will find hope that whatever you've been struggling with can become a sweet memory of triumph! Have you given up every room to Christ yet—or are you still reserving a nook or two for yourself? If you will yield to Jesus, you'll gain the precious fulfillment of His promise to be with you, to provide a way to experience triumph, and not defeat.

THURSDAY: Christ's Risen and Glorified Omnipresence

"I am with you always, even to the end of the age."
—Matthew 28:20

As we see Christ's risen and glorified omnipresence—His presence in all places at all times with a "voice as the sound of many waters"—it is a reminder that He is always speaking to people at their time of greatest need (Revelation 1:15b). His voice can be heard anywhere, for He is everywhere present, and can thus truly encourage us.

What did Jesus do on earth? He was always meeting people's most desperate needs. Consider Mary who went to the empty tomb as sorrow and confusion flooded her mind with all the memories of Jesus. He had loved her, forgiven her, and made her many promises. But now He seemed to be so far away, and all those things seemed distant to Mary. Mary *needed* to see Jesus. That is why she was last at the cross and first at the tomb. Mary came needing Him, and now she would be the first to see the risen Christ!

What strength did Mary need? She needed to believe what she knew. She *knew* He promised that He would rise again, but she just didn't believe it. But when she heard the One whom she thought was the gardener call her name, she instantly recognized Him! For Jesus says, "My sheep hear My voice, and I know them, and they follow Me" (John 10:27). Then Mary *believed*, and had a wonderful time of worship! (See John 20:13–16.)

Now let's look at another person who had a great need—Peter. Peter also longed to hear the voice of the Lord. He, too, needed to hear that risen and glorified voice "as the sound of many waters"!

So when they had eaten breakfast, Jesus said to Simon Peter, "Simon, son of Jonah, do you love Me more than these?" He said to Him, "Yes, Lord; You know that I love You." He said to him, "Feed My lambs." He said to him again a second time, "Simon, son of Jonah, do you love Me?" He said to Him, "Yes, Lord; You know that I love You." He said to him, "Tend My sheep." He said to him the third time, "Simon, son of Jonah, do you love Me?" Peter was grieved because He said to him the third time, "Do you love Me?" And He said to Him,

"Lord, You know all things; You know that I love You." Jesus said to him, "Feed My sheep" (John 21:15–17).

Peter was grieved because Jesus asked three times. (Everything in threes might have bothered him because he could not forget his thrice betrayal of Jesus—it was such a deep wound!)

Jesus knew that Peter needed His special touch that day. If Jesus had only asked him once if he loved Him, Peter might have thought: *Did He really mean that everything is all right?* If He asked just twice, again Peter might think: *He says all is well, but I'm not sure . . .* But Peter sensed that Jesus was tracking with him: "Peter, I knew that you denied Me three times, so I want you to tell Me you love Me three times so that you will have peace that this thing is all taken care of and that you will now be that one to strengthen the brethren." Oh, how the grieving Peter *needed* to hear that reassurance of Christ's love and forgiveness, and that he was *not* being set aside in his ministry!

What is Jesus doing now? Jesus, with His omnipresent voice "as the sound of many waters," always comes to those who need Him. No matter where you are in life, Jesus says to you, "I am with you always! I am there; and you will hear My voice as I speak to you!"

He will never leave your side so that He can encourage and help you at any place and at any time. All you have to do is to invite Him to come to your rescue!

FRIDAY: Christ's Risen and Glorified Majesty

[After Jesus calmed the sea] those who were in the boat came and worshiped Him, saying, **"Truly You are the Son of God."**

—Matthew 14:33

As we see Christ's risen and glorified majesty—with His "countenance like the sun shining in its strength"—it is a reminder that He desires our reverence and worship (Revelation 1:16b–17a).

What did Jesus do on earth? He was always inviting the worship of those who loved Him. He performed miracles (that which only God can do) to cause those who witnessed them to be overwhelmed with wonder. Christ is glorious in His majesty and power, and He reminds us of that truth so we can truly worship Him.

Christ's majesty produces a sense of awe: "[Jesus] went up into the boat to them, and the wind ceased. And they were greatly amazed in themselves beyond measure, and marveled" (Mark 6:51). When Simon Peter saw the abundance of fish, where there had been none before, "he fell down at Jesus' knees, saying, 'Depart from me, for I am a sinful man, O Lord!'" (Luke 5:8). From this, we can see that Christ's majesty brings conviction. On the Isle of Patmos, after only one look at Jesus, John simply crumbled in awe and wonder-filled worship at His feet (Revelation 1:17a)! Christ's majesty commands worship.

When Jesus performed miracles such as healing the sick, raising the dead, cleansing lepers, or restoring eyesight, people responded in wonder and worshiped Him. The majestic Son of Man and Son of God is always waiting for His children to lavish their love upon Him and worship Him! (See Matthew 28:9; Luke 24:52; and Philippians 3:3.)

What is Jesus doing now? He continues to remind us of His glory so that we will be inspired to worship Him with all our heart, strength, mind, and soul! Jesus wants us, like the psalmist, to spontaneously and joyously exclaim: *Oh, give thanks to the Lord! Call upon His name; make known His deeds among the peoples! Sing . . . psalms to Him; talk of all His wondrous works! Glory in His holy name; let the hearts of those rejoice who seek the Lord!* (Psalm 105:1–3).

Are you honoring the risen and glorious Jesus in all His majesty and power? Pause now to worship Him in adoration!

SATURDAY: Christ's Risen and Glorified Touch

When Jesus departed . . . two blind men followed Him, crying out and saying, "Son of David, have mercy on us!" . . . Then **He touched their eyes, . . . And their eyes were opened.**
—Matthew 9:27, 29–30a

As we see Christ's risen and glorified touch, it is a reminder that He holds His church and guards its message and its messengers (Revelation 1:16a; 17b-20). He is always there to provide help in the time of need—as He did with the two blind men who needed His healing touch!

What did Jesus do on earth? He was always touching those He loves at their point of need: Jesus touched Peter when he was sinking on the sea and cried out, "Lord, save me!" (Matthew 14:30); He touched the leper by cleansing him at his direst moment of decay (Luke 5:12); He touched Thomas when he was filled with doubt (John 20:28); and He touched John when he was overwhelmed with fear (Revelation 1:17–18).

That was 2,000 years ago, which seems so long ago and so far away. But we need not live so distant from the quietness of that garden on Resurrection morning, because the truth of the Resurrection is that Jesus is alive! And since He is alive, He is doing the same things as He did then.

Did you catch that? Jesus wants us to know that He is still doing just what He did that morning, and in the days that followed. So much of His ministry involved assuring the disciples of what they already knew, and encouraging them to do what He left them here to do. Have you met again the risen Christ?

What is Jesus doing now? Jesus wants us to see Him, to believe Him, and then respond to His work in us through His Word. Are you willing to see Jesus anew? You can experience all that He wants to do in your life if you will invite Him to be at work in you. He is always there to touch you, lift you, encourage you, restore you, and remind you that all that He promised is true.

Jesus, who was always inviting worship from those who loved Him back then, who was inviting it on the Isle of Patmos around sixty years after His resurrection, is still waiting for us to crumble in reverent worship before Him.

As Jesus left the earth, the last thing His beloved disciples saw was His exit as He went up out of sight with outstretched hands lifted up in blessing. In that gesture, He was trying to convey this message: "I just want to pour out My blessing on you! I want to give you everything you need, and that is the last thing I want you to think about when you remember Me going back to My Father!"

What was their response? They worshiped Him and then went back to Jerusalem (see Luke 24:50–52)! They didn't go to some distant place; they went home. That is what worship does; it doesn't take us off to mountaintops where we live an unreal life, like in a monastery somewhere. No, we go back into our real world with great joy. Luke 24:53 says that they were continually in the temple, praising and blessing God. That is what worship does: "You shall worship the LORD your God, and Him only you shall serve" (Matthew 4:10b).

We have it all mixed up in the twenty-first century: we serve God and hope we get around to worship, but most of the time we don't. But Jesus said, "Worship Me before you do that ministry. Then, as you serve, you will be full of joy and thanksgiving!" Jesus is waiting for you and me to lavish our loving worship on Him!

As a father, I love to give my children what they want. I ask them, "What can I do for you? How can I help you? What would you like?" I also love to do things that please my wife, Bonnie! If I, a frail, sinful, fallen human, long to do these things for those I love—how much more will our heavenly Father give us good gifts? (See Matthew 7:7–11.)

Make a choice to live in hope. Have you met the risen Christ? Do you see Him as the compassionate "Son of Man"? Do you understand that He is the High Priest who forgives, cleanses, and doesn't condemn you? Do you recognize Him as the One with penetrating "eyes like a flame of fire" Who always sees you, and omnisciently knows everything about you? Do you see those "feet like fine brass" as He omnipotently comes in power to meet you in your storms? Do you hear His omnipresent "voice as the sound of many waters" that is always able to talk to you in any situation? Do you see His "countenance like the sun shining in its strength" that is so full of majesty that you crumble before Him in worship? Can you say, like John, "I feel the gentle touch of His 'hand on me'"?

The risen and glorified Christ wants to be all that to you. So He is telling you, this very day, "Just like I was in Bible times, I still am today. And I want to always be with you!"

I hope that you will invite Jesus Christ into every part of your life and say, "Risen Christ, see me; come to me! I bow before You. Touch me! I need You!"

WEEK 13
Hear Christ's Message

{ Revelation 2–3 }

As the end of days approaches, you can find hope as you hear Christ's message in Revelation!

WEEK 13: HEAR CHRIST'S MESSAGE

SUNDAY: Hearing God's Voice

God, who . . . spoke in time past to the fathers by the prophets, **has in these last days spoken** *to us* **by His Son**, *whom He has appointed heir of all things.*
—HEBREWS 1:1–2

When Congress "pulled the plug on NASA's elaborate search for radio signals from alien life," a newspaper reported: "The American scientific community is mourning the loss of NASA's elaborate search for radio signals from alien life. Some speculate that alien intelligence might beam vast streams of coded information, a virtual encyclopedia galactica, with insights into *the origin of the universe and immortality.*"[1] The Search for Extra Terrestrial Intelligence (SETI) project had been priority in the American scientific community for many years. Because of the evolutionary belief system so prominent in our culture, there is a desire to find more highly evolved life forms. Some even hope that such aliens can provide solutions to help solve the ever-increasing problem of violence in our society.

The violence issue is unsolvable, however, unless people turn their lives over to their Creator. What our culture is experiencing is exactly what the apostle Paul predicted: in the last days people will be "without self-control, brutal" (2 Timothy 3:3).

Whether it is in the scientific or the social realm, our world is desperately searching for answers. Yet they continue to show an absolute disregard for the indisputable fact that there is already a stream of infinite knowledge available. You see, God has coded all the answers to man's questions in His Book—a virtual stream of encyclopedic galactica for which we do not even need to spend hundreds of millions of dollars for radar dishes to receive. The highest intelligence of the universe has already beamed us about our origin, and He's freely offered immortality to all!

God's Word has the answer to all of life's struggles. Did you know that 2,000 years ago Jesus wrote some letters to you as a member of His beloved church? He sent them by way of the last living apostle, John. These letters were a group message, customized for seven churches that represented all the churches then as well as now.

If you were to ask any Bible student how many epistles (letters) are in the New Testament, the answer would probably be twenty-one: thirteen authored by Paul, plus Hebrews, which appears anonymous; and the seven "general epistles" by Peter, James, John, and Jude.

The seven most important letters in the Bible are usually overlooked—the seven authored by Jesus personally and sent to us individually. For many reasons, those seven letters, comprising chapters 2 and 3 of Revelation, are probably the most important part of the Bible for you and me. For in them, and in chapters like the following, Jesus has written the secrets of how we can live forever (John 17:3), how we can have a joy-filled life (John 10), how we can experience real love (1 Corinthians 13), how we can be prosperous no matter what the economic, social, or political climate (Joshua 1:8–9), and how we never need fear the future (John 14).

My Prayer for You This Week: *Oh Lord, I pray that by Your grace and for Your glory, You will help every one of us to have an ear to hear Your message. I pray that we would look at this Book* *differently. The world around us is waiting for some alien intelligence to tell them what to do. But we have You, the Creator of the universe, who has already told us what to do, and we want to obey You. In Jesus' name we pray. Amen.*

MONDAY: God Speaks through His Word

*"You search **the Scriptures**, for in them you think you have eternal life; and these are they which **testify of Me**."*

—JOHN 5:39

The Bible is like many textbooks in school: all the answers are found at the end of the book. The end of the Bible is, of course, the Revelation of Jesus Christ that John recorded for us.

The Bible is composed of sixty-six books, written by forty authors over fifteen centuries, yet it possesses a supernaturally engineered message. The guiding hand of God, through the Holy Spirit inspiring each human author, placed every word, letter, name, place, and number there. Thus every detail of God's Word was orchestrated by God to reveal himself and His plan.

Nowhere is this more clearly demonstrated than in Revelation. Its 404 verses, which hold allusions to over 800 Old Testament verses and passages, tie the entire Bible together in a grand finale. In fact, if you understand the Old Testament, you will understand Revelation.

Jesus wrote messages to the seven churches that we all need to hear. There were many other churches at that time which would seem to be more historically significant than the seven that Jesus addressed, such as the churches at Jerusalem, Rome, Galatia, Corinth, Antioch, Colossae, Iconium, Lystra, Derbe, and Miletus. So why did Jesus select just these seven: Ephesus, Smyrna, Pergamos, Thyatira, Sardis, Philadelphia, and Laodicea? The reason is that they represent all of us today. Seven is always God's "number of completion." He picked seven local, individual congregations to write to, using some very interesting words. His message was not only to them there and then but also to us here and now. Jesus actually gives us at least a four-level message in each of these letters.

Jesus gives a specific message. "To. . . the church in . . . " (Revelation 2:1 NASB). He spoke to the local churches that were in those geographic places then. Jesus is likewise interested in today's churches. God's Word speaks to individuals in the twenty-first century because God knows what they are doing at church, at work, and at home. He knows what is going on in private and public lives. He says, "I know what your church is doing; I know where you are headed." When we offer worship to God, if it is cold, it is because we came in cold; if it is fervent, it is because we came in fervent.

Jesus gives a universal message. "Hear what the Spirit says to the churches" (2:7). This is plural and speaks of an admonition to all churches throughout all the history of the church. Here Jesus addresses His divine expectation that He wants our devotion to Him.

Jesus gives a prophetic message. This is perhaps the most fascinating part of Revelation, as Jesus describes, with divine precision, the seven successive eras the church would pass through from Pentecost to the last days of apostasy. Jesus was also describing the seven types of Christians who would make up the visible church throughout the church age.

Jesus gives a spiritual message. "He who has an ear let him hear what the Spirit says to the churches" (2:7). To Him, the one with the "ear" is the individual "who overcomes." This is the most valuable part of these letters. Jesus goes from speaking to the local church to all the local churches throughout the ages, and then He zeros in on the individual. At the tail end of all seven of these letters is the greatest set of promises in the Bible. Because it is a spiritual message, the most valuable part of this book is probably to individuals who listen to these practical, personal messages and respond in faith and obedience to the Lord—and actually live the lives Jesus calls them to live.

Jesus' seven letters describe the unfolding of all subsequent church history. In any other order, this prophetic panorama would not be true. Just as the book of Acts covers about thirty years of the growth and ministry of the church, the second and third chapters of Revelation cover the next 1,900 years and seem to be the explanation for the interval between the sixty-ninth and seventieth "weeks" of Daniel 9. (For a full explanation of Daniel's seventy weeks, see Week 31: "Remember the Plan of the Ages.")

I pray that you are among those who will listen to Christ's practical, personal messages and respond in faith and obedience to the Lord by actually *living* the life Jesus calls you to live!

TUESDAY: God Speaks to Us

*"He who has an ear, let him **hear what the Spirit says to the churches**. To him who overcomes I will give to eat from the tree of life, which is in the midst of the Paradise of God."*
—REVELATION 2:7

The specific message: Christ is speaking to His church. Each letter to the churches has all or part of these seven components:
1. Jesus addresses each **assembly:** "To the angel of the church in . . . " (2:1a NASB).
2. Jesus also addresses specific **individuals.** Jesus knows all about the problems of the local church—He is not out of touch.
3. Jesus addresses each church with **authority:** "[He] walks in the midst of the seven golden lampstands" (2:1b).
4. Jesus addresses each church with an **approval:** "I know your works, your labor" (2:2–3).
5. Jesus addresses each church with an **admonition:** "I have this against you . . . " (2:4).
6. Jesus addresses each church with an **appeal:** "Repent and do the first works" (2:5).
7. Jesus addresses each church with an **assurance:** "To him who overcomes . . . " (2:7).

Jesus knows what is going on in both your local assembly and your life. This is His message to each of His local churches!

The universal message: Christ is waiting for His church. To all churches throughout history Jesus says, "I always expect your *devotion* to me!" That is phenomenal!

The seven churches in every age represent seven varieties of Christians—true *and* false. Everyone who professes Christianity is like one or more of these seven.

The Church at Ephesus: These Christians had a great start but left their first love, their all-consuming passion for Christ. Jesus told them, "You started out so well—you could not get enough of My Word; you could not get enough of fellowshiping with My people; you could not get enough of worshiping Me; and you could not get enough of doing everything for Me!"

That is Christ's universal message throughout the church age: some will start great, but sooner or later their devotion will wane. So Jesus says, "Listen to what I have to say, for I am all you need! Be an overcomer and come back to Me!" Overcomers know that Jesus is all they need, so they will repent and return to their first love!

The Church at Smyrna: The Smyrnean Christians stood fast during great persecution. No matter what the Devil threw at them, they became even more purified. Christ's universal message to the churches is this: saints should expect to suffer and, as a result, be purified. Are you suffering in your family? Are you suffering through spiritual warfare in your private communion with the Lord? Are you suffering at your job or at school? Wherever you are suffering, Jesus says, "I know that you are being purified by persecution. Be faithful!" Overcomers know that Jesus is all they need, so they will remain faithful to Him at all costs.

The Church at Pergamos: These Pergamite Christians were drowning in worldliness. Some were wed to the world like "country club Christians" with no standards. Do you have a focus and grip on your money, your car, and your job? Have you decided that you will do what is socially acceptable—even if it compromises Scripture's absolutes? Are you more concerned with fashion than with holiness? In every church there are "country club Christians." There are always those who try to reconcile Christ to the world. They try to make Him palatable so that no one is offended. Overcomers know that Jesus is all they need, so they will resist worldliness and keep their eyes on the Lord.

The Church at Thyatira: The false teacher, Jezebel, seduced the Thyatiran Christians. Some believed her and started following a false doctrine, which had a social gospel rather than a divine call to the new birth. They thought that God just wanted to clean up the *world*, but not the individual. To them, the gospel was a call to society, and not the sinner. Overcomers know that Jesus is all they need, so they will resist all such evil teaching and lifestyles.

The Church at Sardis: These Christians had a big name, but no life. Throughout the centuries, the persecuted in Christ's church have sat right next to the cold and lifeless. Jesus said that His message universally goes to all; He calls us where we are, and asks us to come to Him! Sardian Christians are as dead as last week's cut flowers—cold and lifeless—in a spiritual stupor. Overcomers know that Jesus is all they need, so they will not defile themselves with the "corpses."

The Church at Philadelphia: Jesus gave these believers no condemnation or blame. Philadelphian Christians of today are sound in doctrine and zealous in ministry, and are reaching out to the world with their deep love for the Lord Jesus Christ! Overcomers know that Jesus is all they need, so their heart beats for Christ alone.

The Church at Laodicea: These individuals are apostate, counterfeit, and sickening to Christ—members of the Christless church that will thrive in the Tribulation under Satan's leadership. They are part of the visible church in name only. Jesus therefore told them that He would spit them out of His mouth!

This is Jesus' universal message: the whole church is comprised of these seven types of Christians—there are some of each in every age. So, in a most emphatic way, if you are a born-again Christian, this letter is addressed to you. If you are among the persecuted, remain faithful! But if you have left your first love, *remember* what Jesus did for you. *Repent! Repeat* those things you did at first for Christ! Go back to Him with your whole heart!

WEDNESDAY: God Speaks about the Future

*"**Declaring** the end from the beginning, and from ancient times **things that are not yet done**, saying, 'My counsel shall stand, and I will do all My pleasure.' "*
—Isaiah 46:10

The prophetic message: Christ is being faded away by His church. The church throughout the ages has gone through seven successive stages. There are seven letters in Revelation 2 and 3 that show us the church from God's prophetic perspective. The seven churches represent seven phases or periods in church history, stretching from the time of the apostles to the coming again of Christ. Each has a characteristic that is set forth within the letter and, interestingly enough, within the name of the church. Each name of these churches represents the age in which they lived.

The Ephesian Period (A.D. 30–60): This apostolic era was a time of warmth, love, and labor for Christ. However, defection began by the gradual cooling of the love of some, the false professions of others, and the incoming of undue exaltations of the clergy and church offices. The church mushroomed and grew rampantly through the Roman Empire. But as it grew, it gradually cooled.

The Smyrnean Period (A.D. 60–313): This was a time of martyrdom. It was a sweet savor to God when His children showed "faithfulness unto death," but this period was also marked with further developments of defection through the establishment of castes and orders, the license of Judaizing inclinations, and consequent departures from the true simplicities of the gospel. However, the church was purified in this era because of the persecution. History records that in Bythinia, in Asia Minor, the Roman governor marched all the inhabitants of one city out to a cliff. He ordered them to deny Christ and say "Caesar is lord," or the soldiers would throw them off the cliff. Ten thousand were executed in that manner.

The Pergamite Period (A.D. 313–500): True faith more and more disappeared from view. Clericalism gradually formed itself into a system: the church united with the world, and Babylon began to rear itself aloft. When Constantine legalized Christianity in A.D. 313, he put a whole group of pagan priests into the church. Robes, beads, candles, headdresses, mass, and purgatory came from paganism *into* the church—*not* from the Bible. This was the time the church became wed to the world.

The Thyatiran Period (A.D. 500–1500): This was the era of Romanism with its purple and glory for the corrupt priesthood and darkness of truth. It was the age of clerical domination in which the church usurped the place of Christ, but His witnesses were given dungeons, stakes, and inquisitions. It was the age of the enthronement of the false prophetess, Mother Mary, reaching to the days of Luther and the Reformation.

The Sardian Period (A.D. 1500–1800): This period represents the separation of the church from the world and the return of Christ's rule. There were many great revivals and many worthy names, but this time was still marked with deadness overall, and having great need of repentance. This was an age covering the spiritual lethargy of Protestantism, which was centuries before the great evangelical movements began.

The Philadelphian Period (A.D. 1800–1948): During this time, there was great missionary fervor, evangelistic outreach, and devotional godliness. The world was penetrated with the gospel during these years like no time since Pentecost. The British Empire was worldwide, and its monarchy wanted Christ exalted!

The Laodicean Period (A.D. 1948—): This speaks of the time from 1948 until the end of the age. Why 1948? Because the steps to globalism were started that year more than any other year in history. What steps? The birth of the United Nations (so we can have Revelation 13), the birth of the World Council of Churches (so we can have Revelation 17), the birth of the computer/transistor (so we can have Revelation 18), and the rebirth of the State of Israel (so we can have Revelation 12–19). In our western culture, churches are full of lukewarmness, self-sufficiency, empty professions, and false peace. Judgment day will reveal the unthinking multitudes who have supposed that they were Christians, but were not.[2]

Jesus maps out the course of history for the church, and He says, "I am in every age!" I wonder: have you been able to discern which church period most describes your own life at the moment?

THURSDAY: God Tells Us His Plan

*You will show me **the path of life**; in Your presence is fullness of joy; at Your right hand are **pleasures forevermore**.*
—PSALM 16:11

The spiritual message: Christ is seeking out His church. The last message Jesus has for us is His wonderful plan! He has spelled out what He wants us to be like, and He has detailed how He, by His grace, will enable us to live such a wonderful life!

Christ offers an abundant life: "He who has an ear, let him hear what the Spirit says to the churches. To him who overcomes I will give to eat from the tree of life, which is in the midst of the Paradise of God" (Revelation 2:7). This means that true believers have abundant lives in paradise regained. Jesus described what we have in Him as an overflowing life: "He who believes in Me, . . . out of his heart will flow rivers of living water" (John 7:38).

There is no life like Christ's in us! It is an extraordinary life: He came "that [we] may have life, and that [we] may have it more abundantly" (John 10:10). The word "abundant," *perissos*, means "over and above, more than is necessary, exceeding abundantly, supremely."

This is what grips the world. This is why, when you are going through a prophetic study, you must come to terms with this question: If you lost all your physical assets—real estate, stocks, bonds and retirement accounts—what would you have left? Your *real* treasure—Jesus Christ! Think about it: while your things still have value, give them to the Lord instead of regretting it later when their value is gone. God says, "What you keep you lose, but what you give lasts forever!"

Christ offers an indestructible life: "He who has an ear, let him hear what the Spirit says to the churches. He who overcomes shall not be hurt by the second death" (Revelation 2:11).

There are two very powerful truths that are assuring to us. Jesus promised that we will be secure from any physical adversary: "And I give them eternal life, and they shall never perish.... My Father, who has given them to Me, is greater than all; and no one is able to snatch them out of my Father's hand" (John 10:28–29).

Paul reminds us that we are also secure from any spiritual adversary: "Neither death nor life, nor angels nor principalities nor powers, nor things present nor things to come, nor height nor depth, nor any other created thing, shall be able to separate us from the love of God which is in Christ Jesus our Lord" (Romans 8:38–39).

Christ offers an inexhaustible supply: "To him who overcomes I will give some of the hidden manna to eat. And I will give him a white stone, and on the stone a new name written which no one knows except him who receives it" (Revelation 2:17).

Jesus promises that all our spiritual needs will be met: "I am the bread of life. He who comes to Me shall never hunger, and He who believes in Me shall never thirst" (John 6:35).

Non-Christians look at us and, on the surface, they may see only our suffering. Yet a Christian, even one in the hospital suffering from cancer or another deadly disease, can still encourage fellow believers when they visit or phone the patient. This is God's inexhaustible supply!

Jesus also assures us that all our spiritual desires, those prompted by the Holy Spirit, will be fulfilled: "And I will do whatever you ask in my name, so that the Son may bring glory to the Father. You may ask me for anything in my name, and I will do it" (John 14:13–14 NIV). Wherever you are—hospital bed, retirement home, on the job, or on the road—you can have His *inexhaustible supply* and, through prayer, see God acting to take His glorious power to the ends of the earth. The checkbook of faith is backed by an *inexhaustible* account. All the power of the Godhead is operational by faith through our prayers.

Christ offers an inexpressible future: "And he who overcomes, and keeps My works until the end, to him I will give power over the nations" (Revelation 2:26). God will reward us with immeasurable treasures: "There is no One who has left house or brothers or sisters or father or mother or wife or children or lands, for My sake and the gospel's, who shall not receive a hundredfold now in this time ... and in the age to come, eternal life" (Mark 10:29–30).

As you follow Jesus, you should be willing to leave all behind for the sake of the gospel. If you do, God will one day overwhelm you with unbelievable pleasures! The apostle Paul, after he had been "caught up into Paradise," would have excitedly shared what he saw and heard, but he was not permitted to do so. For God said that it was "not lawful for a man to utter" (2 Corinthians 12:4). But this we do know: Paul experienced a remarkable foretaste of what Christ has in store for those who love Him! Are you excited about all that He has planned for you?

FRIDAY: Christ Speaks Your Name
*"He who overcomes shall be clothed in white garments, and . . . **I will confess his name** before My Father, and before His angels."*
—REVELATION 3:5

Christ has something far better than insurance coverage: He has promised that He will never forget us, and will someday confess our name before His Father in heaven. Could there be anything greater than that?

Many would like to be related to wealthy people because they hope to inherit a fortune some day. But *we* have something far more precious—Christ as our garment, our Advocate, and our relative.

- **Christ is our garment:** "But put on the Lord Jesus Christ, and make no provision for the flesh, to fulfill its lusts" (Romans 13:14).
- **Christ is our Advocate:** "He . . . has an unchangeable priesthood. Therefore He is . . . able to save to the uttermost . . . , since He always lives to make intercession for [us]" (Hebrews 7:24–25).
- **Christ is our Relative:** "And if children, then . . . joint heirs with Christ, if indeed we suffer with Him, that we may also be glorified together" (Romans 8:17).

True believers have an inescapable destination: "He who overcomes, I will make him a pillar in the temple of My God, and he shall go out no more. I will write on him the name of My God and the name of the city of My God, the New Jerusalem, which comes down out of heaven from My God. And I will write on him My new name" (Revelation 3:12).

We are a pillar because we are secure: "Let not your heart be troubled. . . . In My Father's house are many mansions. . . . I go to prepare a place for you. And . . . will come again and receive you to Myself; that where I am, there you may be also" (John 14:1–3).

We have a new name because we are a love gift from the Father to the Son: "Father, I desire that they also whom You gave Me may be with Me where I am, that they may behold My glory" (John 17:24).

In light of all He's done, and is doing for you, what have you done for Jesus?

SATURDAY: God Wants to Talk to You
*"Oh, that you had **heeded My commandments!** Then your peace would have been like a river, and your righteousness like the waves of the sea."*
—ISAIAH 48:18

We commonly struggle daily: we get up in the morning, bleary and tired, and we read our Bibles. We then try to read again when our minds are clearer. Then at night we remind ourselves to study and pray. There are many distractions that come and go, and we have to focus our minds on so many things. We struggle with the flesh, spiritual warfare, and all the disappointments of life. But God promises *intimacy* to those who will rise above their distractions in life and truly seek Him: "He who has My commandments and keeps them, it is he who loves Me. And he who loves Me will be loved by My Father, and I will love him and manifest Myself to him" (John 14:21).

- **Intimacy is a Person:** "And this is eternal life, that they may know You, the only true God, and Jesus Christ whom You have sent" (John 17:3).
- **Intimacy is permanent:** "He who overcomes shall inherit all things, and I will be his God and he shall be My son" (Revelation 21:7).

Make a choice to live in hope. In every one of Christ's letters to the churches, Jesus says, "He who has an ear." Do you have "an ear" to hear Him? Jesus always gives an invitation. Do you hear His voice? Have you received what He offers today?

If you have not yet heeded His call, find hope in Christ by hearing Christ's message and becoming an overcomer (Revelation 3:20)! Admit that you are lost; open your eyes to behold Jesus in all His beauty; turn from darkness to the Light, and from the power of Satan (Acts 26:18). Then believe that only Christ saves, and receive forgiveness for sin through the saving faith of Christ. And finally, confess Jesus Christ with your mouth (Romans 10:9–10).

WEEK 14
Remember Christ's Jealousy

{ Revelation 2:1–7 }

This week as we approach the end of days, you can find hope as you remember Christ's jealousy!

SUNDAY: The First-Century Church

*I write so that you may know **how you ought to conduct yourself** in the house of God, which is the church of the living God, the pillar and ground of the truth.*
—1 Timothy 3:15

Jesus jealously longs for us to love Him supremely—like His faithful saints did in the early church!

From the depths of the catacombs, by dim and flickering light, the upturned sea of faces sang praises to the Lamb that was slain. Above ground, just thirty feet over their heads, a chariot clattered along the Roman road heading to the Coliseum. Inside that magnificent structure, nearly 80,000 spectators already strained to get a good view. The preliminary activities of fighting beasts drew only partial approval from the crowd. Soon blood would be seen, and that was what they came to see. Human blood from helpless Christians herded into the red-stained sand always drew rapt attention. As gladiators jabbed the unarmed participants, rounded up from various raids on the fledgling church, hunger-crazed predators circled in their cages awaiting a meal of those being pushed into the pit. Then the trumpet sounded! The crowd roared as defenseless men, women, and children faced the attacking wave of claws, fangs, and roars. Soon it was over. Blood and some bones were all that remained. As the mesmerized crowds departed, they were eagerly anticipating yet another exhibition on the morrow.

The next attraction for the day was in the torch-lit gardens of the Forum. At dusk the emperor would raise tied-and-pitch-covered human torches on wooden poles—Christians being martyred. They suffered greatly as they were burned alive to light the path of the citizens of the persecuting empire!

As night mercifully fell, the worshipers who lived in the catacombs crept up the city storm sewers to risk their lives in search of bones from the arena's blood-soaked sands and body parts from the smoldering stakes. They reverently carried them down into the catacombs and buried them with tear-filled songs of praise to the God of Hope and Comfort who alone could give them courage to go on. This was life for the followers of the Lord Jesus Christ during the latter part of the first century in the Roman Empire.

What was it that made them behave so bravely in such trying times? They were godly saints who followed the narrow path, the cross of Jesus—"the Way" (John 14:6; Acts 24:14–15). In Acts 19:11–20, Luke described many extraordinary and miraculous events with amazing conversions and life transformations. These saints believed the truth about God. Because they believed rightly, they behaved rightly.

Jesus would love for us to daily affirm that we love Him, and want to serve Him with their same depth of devotion! We thus need to cultivate and embrace the truths that made these early saints so faithful: they were assured that Christ had saved them; they lived each day like they belonged to Him; and they really believed that they were headed to heaven to live forever with Him. Those who embrace these truths will have powerful effectiveness in their lives, and that is what our jealous Lord wants to see in each of us.

> **My Prayer for You This Week:** *Oh Lord, as we hear Your letter to the church at Ephesus, and listen to Your words to us, I pray that You would help us to have ears to hear. Help us to have spiritual understanding so that Your message might be personal and very practical. We want to love You as at the first all the way to the end. We want to hold You in first place in our lives. We pray that as we look through this letter, and as Your Spirit illumines us, that we will see those keys You have given us to loving You most and first, because You are a jealous God. You long for us to love You and not just to serve You. I pray that such love would be evident in our lives and in our church lest you remove our lamp stand, and we are no longer effective for You. We thank You in the name of Jesus. Amen.*

MONDAY: Ephesus in the First Century

> **Paul**, *having passed through the upper regions*, **came to Ephesus**. *And* **finding some disciples** *he said to them, "Did you receive the Holy Spirit when you believed?" So they said to him, "We have not so much as heard whether there is a Holy Spirit." . . . They were baptized in the name of the Lord Jesus. And when Paul had* **laid hands on them**, *the Holy Spirit came upon them. . . . Now the men were* **about twelve in all**.
>
> —Acts 19:1–3, 5–7

Ephesus was second among the cities of the empire; only Rome exceeded her in wealth and power. If you were arriving in Ephesus, the center of Greek mythological worship, there was only one sight that would catch your eyes. It would not be the bustling harbor teeming with boats, nor the roads lined with the exotic spices and goods from the East. It would be the lustrous golden gleam of the Seventh Wonder of the Ancient World: the Temple of Diana (Artemis to the Greeks). It was the largest building of that period—four times the size of the Parthenon in Athens—the size of a city block, ten stories high, and covered with gold. Cities that wanted to be "rained on" with prosperity sent a gold-covered column for this temple.

Gross immorality existed in Ephesus due to the temple's presence. All day long, in the confines of this magnificent golden palace, thousands of male and female prostitutes gave themselves in the sordid worship of the pagan fertility deities. At dusk, they would then go into the city to earn a living in the bustling atmosphere of travelers from both land and sea.

In the midst of all this debauchery, Jesus Christ had a church planted at Ephesus, one that was well-pleasing to God. In fact, they were honored by receiving the first of Christ's personal letters to His seven churches (Revelation 2:1–7). The church at Ephesus was the most important church in the de facto capital, the landing-place for a messenger from Patmos, and at the head of a circular road joining the seven cities in order.

Here is the best part of that city: Jesus was shining through the saints at Ephesus! The church at Ephesus was a vibrant church. Jesus Christ was preeminent: *"Fear fell on them all, and the name of the Lord Jesus was magnified"* (Acts 19:17). It wasn't the denomination, the buildings, or the leaders that drew the attention of these saints—it was the presence of the Lord!

The Ephesian church was repentant: "Many who had believed came confessing and telling their deeds. Also, many of those who had practiced magic brought their books together and burned them" (Acts 19:18–19). The Ephesian Christians made public renunciation of their old lives because God's Word was prominent in their church: "So the word of the Lord grew mightily and prevailed" (Acts 19:20).

The Ephesian saints were heirs to the greatest and longest days of Paul's earthly ministry—his three years at Ephesus (Acts 20:31). Having been privileged to see Paul in his finest hours of ministry, they became a dynamic church that was pleasing to the Lord.

You, too, can please God by making Christ and His Word pre-eminent, thereby renouncing your old life. To grow in the Lord, ask Him to give you spiritual understanding so that His message to the church at Ephesus might become personal and practical. And, above all, pray that He will empower you to love Him as much at the end of your life as you did when you were first saved!

TUESDAY: The Loyalty Christ Seeks

*"I know your works, your labor, your patience, and that you cannot bear those who are evil. And you have tested those who say they are apostles and are not, and have found them liars; and **you have persevered** and have patience, **and have labored for My name's sake** and have not become weary.... But this you have, that you hate the deeds of the Nicolaitans, which I also hate."*
—Revelation 2:2–3, 6

The Ephesian church was tremendously nurtured by Paul, Timothy, and John. Paul wrote 1 and 2 Timothy while Timothy was the pastor at Ephesus. Paul had sent him to that church and, as church history records, Timothy stayed until a mob brutally murdered him for his strong preaching against sin. After that, until the apostle John was taken prisoner by the emperor and banished to Patmos, he shepherded that great Ephesian church, which had become the largest in Asia Minor (about 5,000 saints!).

The saints in Ephesus were loyal to Christ's church, and this particular assembly had a tremendous history. Church history also indicates that Mary, the mother of our Lord, moved from Jerusalem with John, and later died there. This city had an honor no other knew: Ephesus was the only church that had two apostles, Paul and John, who wrote them inspired letters—Paul's Epistle to the Ephesians and John's writing down of Christ's personal letter to this assembly.

A generation from its founding, the church and the Ephesian Christians were mature. Two generations from Pentecost, the church at Ephesus had perhaps the richest history of any church in the ancient world. They were loyal to God's standards. Jesus approved their purity in the midst of a wicked culture.

In our own culture, just a generation ago people had to search to find anything that was off-color or pornographic. But today you have to work to not find that wickedness. Yet we are not that much different from the society in which the Ephesians lived. Ephesus was a city much like Las Vegas or Atlantic City, and when you entered it, they might as well have had a sign saying WELCOME TO SIN CITY! What I want you to see is this: their purity in the midst of a wicked culture is the reason Jesus approved of the Ephesian church.

It is also notable that the saints at Ephesus were not followers of Nicolas—a deacon (Acts 6) who later became an apostate and led the church astray into immorality and wickedness. Instead, the Ephesians were doing what Christ wanted them to do: they were toiling to exhaustion, pouring themselves into the work for Christ. They refused to even eat with someone who was living in immorality and disobedience. When things got tough, they did not let go of Christ, they kept going. They had patience even in persecution, and there was plenty of it!

How can gross immorality, such as existed at Ephesus, be overcome? The Ephesian Christians learned how to be overcomers through Paul's letter to them forty years earlier. Let's look at the principles he taught so that we can apply them to our own lives.

Repent of your past. "We all once conducted ourselves in the lusts of our flesh, fulfilling the desires of the flesh and of the mind. . . . But fornication and all uncleanness or covetousness, let it not even be named among you, as is fitting for saints; neither filthiness, nor foolish talking, nor coarse jesting, which are not fitting, but rather giving of thanks" (Ephesians 2:3; 5:3–4).

Having renounced all connection with their old ways (Ephesians 5:12), they would not even talk about them, or remind others of what they used to do. (That principle is something to bear in mind when giving a "before and after" testimony of salvation.) A simple application is this: do not let your mouth go back to the old ways of telling or laughing at off-color stories, double meanings, or the innuendo. Do not quote the TV shows. Instead, use your mouth to give thanks to God. Have you fully renounced your old ways and repented of your past?

Learn that your calling is different. "We are His workmanship, created in Christ Jesus for good works, which God prepared beforehand that we should walk in them" (Ephesians 2:10). Have you truly comprehended what a special calling God has given to you?

Learn the spiritual secret of putting off and putting on. "Put off . . . your former conduct [lifestyle], . . . be renewed in the spirit of your mind, and . . . put on the new man which was created according to God, in true righteousness and holiness" (Ephesians 4:22–24). In the streets of Ephesus, Christians were exposed daily to carved symbols of various immoral deviations that were to be followed to the place where those lusts could be fulfilled. But they "put off" those lusts by the grace of God. Have you learned their spiritual secret of putting off the old habits and putting on the new in Christ? Are you being renewed by getting God's Word deep within your heart?

Resist evil influences. "Have no fellowship with the unfruitful works of darkness, but rather expose them" (Ephesians 5:11). Because the Temple of Diana was the most revered site in the ancient world to literally millions of worshipers, a custom had arisen that anyone, regardless of their status, was "free" within a 200-yard security zone. Thus, criminals came from far and wide to find a haven, and their presence permeated the city with evil. Do you resist all evil influences?

Commit to truth and kindness. "Putting away lying, 'Let each one of you speak truth with his neighbor.' . . . Be kind to one another, tenderhearted, forgiving one another, even as God in Christ forgave you" (Ephesians 4:25, 32). Are you committed to honesty and kindness? Are you willing to humbly forgive—even when ill treated?

Release anger and pride to God. "Be angry, and do not sin . . . , nor give place to the devil. Let him who stole steal no longer, but rather let him labor . . . that he may have something to give him who has need. Let no corrupt word proceed out of your mouth, but what is good. . . . And do not grieve the Holy Spirit of God. . . . Let all bitterness, wrath, anger, clamor, and evil speaking be put away from you, with all malice" (Ephesians 4:26–31). Have you released your anger and pride to God?

Jesus addresses His people with authority. He says, "I have the message—the eternal gospel. I am the One who holds the message in My right hand, and I walk in the midst of the church; I am examining what you are doing with it. I am looking at how you are living in light of the message you have received." Are you, like the saints at Ephesus, loyal to God and His Word?

WEDNESDAY: The Love Christ Seeks

*"I have this against you, that **you have left your first love**."*
—REVELATION 2:4

"For over 40 years, since its founding," writes John MacArthur, "this church had remained faithful to the Word and the Lord. Through difficulty and persecution, the members had endured, always driven by the right motive, i.e., for Christ's name and reputation. . . . But the Ephesian's passion and fervor for Christ had become cold, mechanical orthodoxy. Their doctrinal and moral purity, their undiminished zeal for the truth, and their disciplined service were no substitute for the love for Christ they had forsaken."[1]

Jesus therefore gave them an admonition in Revelation 2:4: "You have left (quit or forsaken) your first love." In other words, it is not *what* you are doing; it is *why* you are doing it. You are not serving in this church for the right reasons, and that is not pleasing to Me. I am pleased that you are saved and living a pure life, but you are not pleasing to Me when you are motivated by yourself and not by pure love for Me."

When life is only orthodox, routine, smoothly running, and the inner springs of life are running dry, that is not the spiritual life that God intends for you. The abundant life that Jesus offers is one filled with His love that conquers, captures, and crowns every part of your life. It is 1 Corinthians 13 love that can only be described, because it is so impossible to define. John spoke much of love and Christ (twenty-nine times in the synoptic gospels; forty-five times in John; fifty-one times in the epistles). Christ is present with you right now, and waiting for you!

What is First Love?

- **First love prompts us to patience**—like the love experienced by Jacob. Laboring and waiting seven years for his bride, Rachel, "seemed only a few days to him" (Genesis 29:20). Yet for some in today's church, praying for just seven *minutes* seems like an eternity.
- **First love prompts us to worship**—like David's love that overflowed from the shepherd boy's heart into worshipful psalms. He never complained about having to sit out in the weather watching the sheep while his seven older brothers got to stay home. Instead, he loved his Savior so much that he saw Him in the mighty power of the wind and thunder, the brooks, the animals, and the stars. David worshiped the Lord wherever he was (Psalm 19).
- **First love prompts us to give our treasures**—like Mary of Bethany who broke the alabaster box of ointment and poured it out for Christ (Matthew 26:7). She could have kept her treasure, but she lavished it on the Lord! A martyred saint, Jim Elliot, once said, "He is no fool who gives what he cannot keep to gain what he cannot lose."
- **First love prompts us to thanksgiving**—like the woman who wept at Christ's feet, washed them with her tears, and wiped them with her hair (Luke 7:37). First love loves much, for much has been forgiven.
- **First love prompts us to sit at Jesus' feet and just love Him**— like Mary of Bethany when she worshiped at Christ's feet while Martha was busy about the house serving. Martha

failed to perceive that her most important priority was to *adore* Christ, not serve Him. (See Luke 10:38–41.)
- **First love prompts us to love His coming**—like Paul who longed for Christ's return! Yet he faithfully did what Christ wanted him to accomplish (Philippians 1:21–26).
- **First love prompts us to love His Word**—like the Berean Christians demonstrated by their insatiable desire to read and know God's Word (Acts 17:11). They also understood the importance of having a passion to be with God's people when they met.

How is your spiritual temperature today? Has your passion for Christ cooled, and are you now laboring without love? Has your spiritual life become so mechanical that the inner springs have run dry? Do you have a love that conquers, captures, and crowns every part of your life? Is your love like that in 1 Corinthians 13 that can only be described because it is so impossible to define? Giving Christ the love and attention He desires is not only possible, but it is also essential if you are to avoid grieving His Holy Spirit!

THURSDAY: The Worship Christ Seeks

> "**No one can serve two masters**; *for either he will hate the one and love the other, or else he will be loyal to the one and despise the other.* **You cannot serve God and mammon** *[material possessions]*."
> —MATTHEW 6:24

The church at Ephesus had been loyal to God and His Word in spite of being surrounded by strong materialism in their city. Because of the nearly universal worship of Diana, no one would dare to rob her; thus, behind the altar was the World Bank. One might say that Ephesus was the New York City of the ancient world. Perhaps the evil influence of this materialistic environment may have gradually weakened the first love of some of the Ephesian Christians. For lusting after money and possessions is certain to cool a believer's love for Christ.

How did the devoted Christians at Ephesus resist Satan's stronghold of materialism? As Paul said in Colossians 3, they set their affections on things above, not on things on the earth. As specific biblical principles were followed, they broke free of the lust for money and possessions. These same principles apply to us today as well.

Live for your new inheritance reserved in heaven. "In Him also we have obtained an inheritance, being predestined according to the purpose of Him who works all things according to the counsel of His will" (Ephesians 1:11).

Rejoice in your secure inheritance. "[The Holy Spirit] is the guarantee of our inheritance until the redemption of the purchased possession, to the praise of His glory" (Ephesians 1:14). God is safeguarding our inheritance! After the Resurrection, Jesus went back to prepare a place for us. In light of the fact that it took Jesus only six days to make the whole universe, the heavenly mansions He is preparing must be *spectacular* (John 14:2).

Rejoice in your magnificent inheritance. "The eyes of your understanding being enlightened; that you may know what is the hope of His calling, what are the riches of the glory of His inheritance in the saints" (Ephesians 1:18). What Christ has in store for us is far greater than we could possibly ever imagine, for His riches are unsearchable (Ephesians 3:8)!

Rejoice that your wealth in Christ is more than can be counted. "In the ages to come He [will] show the exceeding riches of His grace in His kindness toward us in Christ Jesus" (Ephesians 2:7). The only way to get victory over the lust of materialism is to rejoice wholeheartedly in Jesus himself—and the richness of what Christ has in store for you. "For where your treasure is, there your heart will be also" (Matthew 6:21).

Our greatest treasure is to be *Jesus*—Whom we are to worship with our whole heart, mind, and soul. In contrast, the full worship of Diana involved silver "letters" (the images made and sold there), which led to very alluring, sordid, and ecstatic worship. How did the Ephesian Christians keep from getting caught up in such false worship? They saw that their access in Christ was instant and universal through prayer, and not localized to a pagan temple. They understood that true worship is spiritual: "God is Spirit, and those who worship Him must worship in spirit and truth" (John 4:24; see also Ephesians 5:18–21). Diana's temple fell into ruins, but Christ's church can never be destroyed: "The whole building, being fitted together, grows into a holy temple in the Lord" (Ephesians 2:21).

Now then, what seems to be the root cause behind the Ephesians' loss of their first love? Although materialism may have cooled the passion of some for Christ, I believe the root cause is that they stopped worshiping because they were so busy. Regardless of what competes for our affections to rob us of our first love—even service for Christ himself—we need to repent and return to the way things were at first with the Lord (Revelation 2:5).

Jesus says, "Worship *before* You serve Me! You can't worship Me 'in spirit and in truth' if you have left your first love! And see to it that you maintain your passion to be with My people every time they meet!"

Do you have "an ear to hear" His voice speaking to you? I pray so!

FRIDAY: Beware of Jesus' Jealousy

*"Do you not know that **friendship with the world is enmity with God**? Whoever therefore wants to be a friend of the world makes himself an enemy of God."*
—JAMES 4:4

In yesterday's devotional, we saw that no one can serve two masters. In James, God strongly tells us that Jesus is so jealous of us that He does not want us to have friendship with the world. I am not talking about having friends that are unsaved, but loving the world system. In other words, Jesus does not want us to get involved in things that make us forget Him. He does not want the world to be on our minds all the time. He does not want us to be willing to sacrifice for it. He does not want the world, and all that is in it, to block Him out.

Before marriage, in order to have a relationship, you must be selective: you cannot have a relationship with just anyone—only one person. You aggressively pursue the one you love, and this is to continue on into marriage. Thus, God is saying, "You are married to Me, so you cannot be out dating anymore."

Did you know that one of the prime characteristics of God is jealousy? We humans believe that jealousy is bad and, from a human standpoint, it indeed can be. But because God is perfect, His jealousy is also perfect. Exodus 20:5 says that "you shall not bow down to them nor serve them [the gods of this world]. For I . . . am a jealous God." (See also Exodus 34:14 and Deuteronomy 4:24.)

God truly wants us to listen to Jesus (Matthew 22:37–38). We should therefore regularly examine our focus by asking these questions: *Who or what is my God? What is the center of my life? What do I rely on?*

Worldliness is not so much a matter of activity, but of attitude. A Christian can stay away from questionable amusements and places and still love the world, for worldliness is a matter of the heart. Worldliness not only affects our response to the love of God, but also affects our response to the will of God: "If anyone loves the world, the love of the Father is not in him" (1 John 2:15; see also 2:17). Doing the will of God is a joy for those living in the love of God (John 15:14), but when a believer loses his or her enjoyment of the Father's love, it will be hard to obey His will. Combining those two factors leads to this practical definition of worldliness: **Worldliness is anything in a Christian's life that causes him to lose his enjoyment of the Father's love or his desire to do the Father's will.**

The extent to which we fail to respond to the Father's love (our personal devotional life), and fail to do the Father's will (our daily conduct), is the degree of worldliness that has entrapped us. Always remember: if we fraternize with the world, we become enemies with God.

At the end of an incredible life, the apostle John wrote some interesting words. He had met and followed Jesus as a very young man. After those climactic days of the Crucifixion, Resurrection, and birth of the church, John had outlived all the apostles. The very last thing that he wrote to us was this warning: *Little children, keep yourselves from idols* (1 John 5:21). We don't have Ashteroths and Baals, but we do have plenty of modern-day idols that God has always condemned.

Our careers, jobs, occupations, or even today's technology can become idols. You might ask, "The Bible talks about that?" Yes, God is vitally interested in all that we fill our brief lives with as we journey heavenward: "They take up all of them with a hook, they catch them in their net, and gather them in their dragnet. Therefore they rejoice and are glad. Therefore they sacrifice to their net, and burn incense to their dragnet; because by them their share is sumptuous and their food plentiful" (Habakkuk 1:15–16).

That passage refers to worship of the occupation that brings work, the job that brings the income, the career that brings success, and the technology that brings pleasure. Worship is thinking about something or someone all the time. You shouldn't know the stock market, sports statistics, or the latest hit tune better than you know God's Word. Habakkuk 1:15 says that it is idolatry to sacrifice to our net. The net is just a tool, but we will lose our first love if we start worshiping that tool.

Our appetites and desires can become idols. Some people live to satiate themselves, like the rich fool of Luke 12:19 whose motto was to "eat, drink, and be merry." Philippians 3:18–19 says that many live as enemies of the cross of Christ. Therefore, their destiny is destruction; their god is their stomach (a reference to all physical desires, not just to food); and their glory is in their shame because their mind is on earthly things.

Money can become an idol. The book of Job, written sometime after the Flood, is the oldest book in the Bible. Job said that if he put his security in money (or even nature), instead of the Creator, he could not worship the Most High God: "If I have . . . said to pure gold, 'You are my security,' if I have rejoiced over my great wealth . . . , if I have regarded the sun . . . or the moon . . . so that my heart was secretly enticed and my hand offered them a kiss of homage, then these also would be sins to be judged, for I would have been unfaithful to God on high" (Job 31:24–28 NIV).

At the Transfiguration, "suddenly a voice came out of the cloud saying, '**This is My beloved Son**, in whom I am well pleased. **Hear Him!**'" (Matthew 17:5–6). Because God never changes, that command still stands. God the Father, who is a jealous God, expects us to heed whatever His Son says to us, and in James 4:4 Jesus has told us that "Whoever . . . wants to be a friend of the world makes himself an enemy of God." Whom do *you* worship? The modern idols of this world—or God? Remember: no man can serve two masters.

SATURDAY: Christ's Offer of Victory

*Now thanks be to **God** who always **leads us in triumph** in Christ, and through us diffuses the fragrance of His knowledge in every place.*
—2 Corinthians 2:14

Not only did the church at Ephesus struggle with worldliness all around them, but they also had to be on constant alert to strong satanic influence. As Acts 19 records, there were many who used and followed occultist books and their witchcraft powers of Satan—just as is occurring more and more in our age. Maybe your weakness is not immorality or materialism; maybe you are spiritually sensitive and are oppressed by demonic powers. How do you handle that? The letter of Jesus to Ephesus (Revelation 2:1–7) is best understood when you read Paul's epistle to the Ephesians.

How did the Ephesian saints resist strong Satanism? They saw that their victory was in Christ. We can learn much from these principles Paul taught about being an overcomer. First, know that **Jesus is above all others:** "He worked in Christ when He raised Him from the dead and seated Him at His right hand in the heavenly places, far above all principality and power and might and dominion, and every name that is named. . . . And He put all things under His feet, and gave Him to be head over all things to the church" (Ephesians 1:20–22).

Next, acknowledge that **Satan was our old master:** "You once walked according to the course of this world, according to the prince of the power of the air, the spirit who now works in the sons of disobedience" (Ephesians 2:2). That was in the past; Satan and his demons do not have a hold on us anymore. We must destroy the things of the past so that they do not tempt us to fall back into sin.

Resist Satan: **don't let Satan have a foothold.** Ephesians 4:27 tells us to not "give place to the devil." Take a moment to look at the more than a dozen sins that surround that verse. Paul seems to imply that any of those sins left unattended can grow into a beachhead for the world, the flesh, and the devil to get a place to defeat us.

Finally, **don't relax around Satan's cronies:** "Have no fellowship with the unfruitful works of darkness, but rather expose them" (Ephesians 5:11). Do not let Satan expose you to his trash through the pipeline of entertainment: TV, movies, inappropriate material on the Internet, music, the arts, and so forth. Do not let Satan's lusts get into your mind. If you listen to music simply because it is beautiful, but its words are ungodly, then you are allowing Satan to fellowship with you. Reprove him instead; keep a guard on your ear gate, eye gate, and other senses.

Never forget: "The thief [Satan] does not come except to steal, and to kill, and to destroy," but Jesus came that you might have life—and "have it more abundantly" (John 10:10)!

Make a choice to live in hope. Jesus jealously longs for you to love Him supremely—like His faithful saints did in the early church. If you have left your *first* love, I exhort you to go back to where you departed. Repent; change your will. Simply tell Jesus: "I know that I have left that fervency, warmth, and longing for You. I'm starting to worship my 'net' and get my security in something other than You. Help me to repent, and remember where I came from. Help me to again do those works I did in the beginning for You."

By His grace, choose to then repeat those things you did at the first, when you were so in love with your Lord. But be aware that when you got away from the Word of God, and stopped fellowshiping with His people, your heart grew cold, and it will seem hard to restore what you once had. However, if you daily get back into the Word and fellowship with the saints, your heart will soon warm up again. So Jesus lovingly says to you: "Come back to Me! I miss you!"

As a worshiper of the true God, you need to come into His presence alone as well as in a group. God wants you to gather together with other believers to magnify Him as His family. Although this will cost you time and resources, He will draw you so close that at times the things of earth will grow strangely dim. As you become very involved in such worship, you will receive joy unspeakable and full of glory!

WEEK 15
Experience Christ's Comfort

{ Revelation 2:8–11 }

This week as we approach the end of days, you can find hope as you experience Christ's comfort!

SUNDAY: Be Ready to Listen

"He who has an ear, let him hear what the Spirit says to the churches. He who overcomes shall not be hurt by the second death."

—Revelation 2:11

In our journey through the Book of Books we have seen Jesus in so many wondrous ways! For instance, we've seen that Jesus has a voice "as the sound of many waters" (Revelation 1:15). But did you know that He also speaks in a "still small voice" (1 Kings 19:12b)? Have you heard Him as He has spoken from the pages of His Book? Through His Word, He speaks to all who have the spiritual ears to hear Him. Are your ears tuned in to Jesus?

Last week we saw that the Ephesian period, dating directly from the apostles (A.D. 30–60), was a time of warmth and love and labor for Christ. In Ephesus the true believers had an abundant life (Revelation 2:7), an overflowing life (John 7:38), and an extraordinary life (John 10:10). Defection, however, began by the gradual cooling of the love of some, the false professions of others, and the incoming of undue exaltations of the clergy and church offices.

This week we will now study the second period of church history, the Smyrna period (A.D. 60–303). These saints lived during an era of martyrdom, which kept them basically pure due to the persecution they suffered. As true believers they had an indestructible life (Revelation 2:11).

The saints in Smyrna were faithful unto death, which was a sweet savor unto God. Unless Christ returns soon, we all must face the inevitability of our own death. We can learn how to die in a godly manner from these models: Jacob died trusting the promises of God (Genesis 47:29); Joseph died pointing to the faithfulness of God (Genesis 50:24); David died exhorting his family to follow God (1 Kings 2:1–4); Stephen died praising God (Acts 7:59–60); Peter died reminding the saints about the Word of God (2 Peter 1:12–15); Paul died finishing the plan of God (2 Timothy 4:6–8); and our Lord Jesus Christ died pointing the way for another to come to God (Luke 23:43).

Have you planned for the spiritual aspects of your death? So many only get the funeral arrangements and their life insurance in order, yet there is so much more to plan and prepare for as a Christian. Are you ready to honor Him in life as well as in death? Are you hoping in Jesus?

My Prayer for You This Week: *We bow before You, Lord Jesus, our Savior. We want to discover the hope that You offer. The only thing that your children actually possess is our hope of everlasting life. Everything else can be stripped away from us—our possessions, all the prizes we have won in life, even those dearest to us. Oh Jesus, what we really possess is our hope in You! Open our eyes and hearts as You speak to us through this special letter that You wrote to the church at Smyrna. Help us to embrace You as the hope to which we cling, the hope toward which we press, and the hope which can never be taken away from us. And then, with that precious and very blessed hope in mind, help us to face the inevitability of our own death in a way that will glorify You. For we recognize that unless You come for us in the Rapture, we will all die. Oh, how we hope for Your return—come quickly, Lord Jesus! In Jesus' precious name we pray. Amen.*

MONDAY: Be Ready to Trust Christ

*"**Do not fear** any of those things which you are about to suffer. . . . **Be faithful until death**, and I will give you the crown of life."*

—REVELATION 2:10

"Smyrna" is a very interesting word because it is derived from the Greek word *smurna*, which is translated "myrrh." Myrrh is an aromatic resin taken from a thorny tree, and was the chief product of this city, the seaport of Myrrh. It was taken by hacking the tree with a machete. Wherever the tree was cut, it would exude the resin. The more it was cut the more this very expensive resin would flow out. Myrrh thus became associated with suffering because this beautiful tree would be attacked and cut and scarred.

In this town where myrrh was gathered, we think of the church that was going to face the cutting edge of persecution. In fact, Jesus essentially told them, "Some of you who receive My letter are going to be put into jail. Some of you are going to be persecuted. Some of you are going to die." Each one of these declarations was like a cut on the tree of the church there.

Today's true church is not exempt from persecution either, because Christ has said that all who live godly will suffer persecution (2 Timothy 3:12). The more we are cut, the more we are persecuted, and the more we are facing hard times, the more Christ wants the sweet-smelling fragrance of faithfulness to exude out of our lives.

What happens when we get tested? A friend of mine says that all of us are spiritual teabags: when we get dunked up and down in hot water, whatever is inside of us comes out. This past week, if things got hot, tense, tight, and hard, what came out of your life? Was it the aroma of Christlike myrrh? Or was it something less than that?

This Smyrnean church, which represents the suffering period of church history, had a sweet-smelling fragrance unto the Lord. As we just saw, the name "Smyrna" was derived from a Greek word translated "myrrh." Myrrh was always associated with the sufferings of Jesus' life. At Christ's birth, the Magi gave gold, frankincense, and myrrh to Jesus, who was crushed for our sins. We see a notable example of that in Mark 15:23. While Christ hung on the cross He was offered a sponge filled with wine mixed with myrrh. Because myrrh also served as an anesthetic, His crucifiers were trying to dull His senses to lessen the intense pain He was experiencing. Jesus refused it, however, because He wanted to have full sensation of the pain He suffered for us.

Suffering is an opportunity to choose whether we believe that serving Christ is far better than anything we could ever have. Are you willing to suffer for Christ? Paul said, "The sufferings of this present time are not worthy to be compared with the glory which shall be revealed in us" (Romans 8:18). "If we suffer with Christ, we will also be glorified with Him" (Romans 8:17b).

TUESDAY: Be Ready to Suffer

*All who desire to **live godly** in Christ Jesus will **suffer persecution**.*
—2 Timothy 3:12

Jesus wrote a letter through the apostle John who was exiled on the Isle of Patmos, just a short distance from Ephesus. He wrote the seven letters Jesus dictated to him, and then sent them by boat to Ephesus where there was a world-renowned library and book distribution center. Those letters were copied down and distributed around the postal route (the geographical circle of the locations of the seven churches). Smyrna was the first city, about forty miles from Ephesus. Can you imagine their reaction when they read Jesus' letter telling them that someone was coming to kill them? That would have been quite a shock!

How did Smyrna get under such a wave of persecution? The problem of that day was called "Emperor Worship." In A.D. 26, during the life of Jesus Christ, an altar was built to Emperor Tiberius. He was on the throne of the Roman Empire that controlled the entire western world at that time. In the center of Smyrna a temple to Tiberius was built. On it was an inscription that said: "This is dedicated to the glorious Emperor God Tiberius."

To remain an accepted part of the Empire, each person had to declare his or her loyalty to the emperor by visiting the temple, scooping a pinch of incense, and putting it on the fire. Afterward, a certificate was given to certify that you passed. That was the one act that unified the masses of people in the Roman Empire. However, most Christians would not do this because it required them to say, "Caesar is Lord." This ritual was not enforced upon Christians until A.D. 94, when the letter to the church at Smyrna was written.

Meet the villains. The first was just three years old when his father died. It was little loss to the boy, for his father had been a killer, a bully, and a cheat. His mother took over the family trade and continued the boy's education. She murdered his stepfather with a dish of poisoned mushrooms. Reared in squalor, the son was molded into his parents' image. While still young, he committed his first murder—a teenaged boy who stood in his way; with callous indifference, he watched him die. He married at fifteen, had his wife killed, married again, and slew her also. To marry a third time, he murdered the husband of the woman he wanted. Because his mother annoyed him, he arranged her murder as well—at first by guile, but when that was unsuccessful, without pretense. He was an ugly man with a bull neck, beetle brows, a flat nose, and a tough mouth. He had a potbelly, spindly legs, bad skin, and an offensive odor. At age thirty-one he was sentenced to death by flogging. He fled to a dingy basement, and cut his own throat while in the house of a slave. He gave the infant church its first taste of things to come. Who was he? His name was Nero. He was the first of the persecuting Caesars of Rome.

Nero's successor, Domitian, was on the throne thirty years later. It was A.D. 94 when he said, "If you will not take that incense and throw it on the fire, in honor of me as god, then you will be killed because all the Empire will worship me!" When Domitian commanded even the Christians to confess, "Caesar is Lord," or pay the price of death, Jesus wrote them the letter recorded in Revelation 2:8–11.

The church at Smyrna was about to face the ultimate test of their lives: "You shall worship the LORD your God, and Him only you shall serve" (Matthew 4:10b). The choice before them was this: Deny Christ, and live; worship Christ—and die! If you were to face that edict today, do you know how you would respond?

WEDNESDAY: Be Ready to Die

I [Paul] am already being poured out as a drink offering,
and **the time of my departure is at hand***.*
—2 Timothy 4:6

The church at Smyrna had one of the more famous people in history at this time. He knew that the most important decision you will ever make in life is how you want to die. Under his leadership, the saints at Smyrna made a choice that they wanted to die in Jesus.

During the persecutions that followed Christ's letter, Polycarp, the last living person led to Christ by the apostle John, was martyred. "Because he preached Jesus Christ, whom the Jews had crucified, he offended the Jews in Smyrna who were blaspheming and persecuting the Christians. In Revelation 2:9, Jesus referred to these Jews as being "a synagogue of Satan." That is not mere speculation because history has left us with an account of the death of Polycarp, the pastor of the church in Smyrna."[1] The account follows:

> It was the time of the public games; the city was crowded; and the Jews excited the crowds and suddenly the shout went up throughout the Jewish community: "Away with the atheist; let Polycarp be searched for." They came to arrest him and not even the police captain wished to see Polycarp die. On the brief journey to the city he pled with the old man: What harm is it to say, "Caesar is Lord" and to offer sacrifice to be saved? But Polycarp was adamant that for him only Jesus Christ was Lord. When he entered the arena . . . [the] proconsul gave him the choice of cursing the name of Christ and making sacrifice to Caesar or death. Polycarp said, "Eighty and six years have I served Him, and He has done me no wrong. How can I blaspheme my King who saved me?" So the crowds came flocking with burning faggots from the workshops and from the baths, and the Jews, even though they were breaking the Sabbath law by carrying such burdens, were foremost in bringing wood for the fire. They were going to bind him to the stake. "Leave me as I am," he said, "for He who gives me power to endure the fire, will grant me to remain in the flames unmoved even without the security you will give by the nails." So they left him loosely bound in the flames. Think about watching your pastor being burned at the stake.

Polycarp dying for Christ was just one incident in the life of the suffering Smyrnean church.[2]

Hope in Jesus when life is painful. The message Christ gave in Revelation 2:10 is simple: "Do not fear any of those things which you are about to suffer. . . . Be faithful until death, and I will give you the crown of life."

It is interesting the way this is written: "Either be faithful when you are killed for your faith, or remain faithful all the way until death comes. But don't fear; be faithful and I will crown you!"

Every word of Christ's brief letter to the church at Smyrna was so vital to those saints, but because of the urgency of the times there was an economy of words. It was the shortest of the seven letters to the churches, having only four verses and 127 words compared to the twelve verses written to Thyatira.

Because all the letters to the churches tie together with this description of Christ, look at what Jesus said to John earlier: "Do not be afraid; I am the First and the Last. I am He who lives, and was dead, and behold, I am alive forevermore. Amen. And I have the keys of Hades and of Death" (Revelation 1:17 18).

Now look at Revelation 2:8: "These things says the First and the Last, who was dead, and came to life." Do you see how Jesus identifies himself as the author? He says that He identifies with them as they go through this persecution unto death!

Jesus thus reveals himself to them as the One who is best suited to comfort them in their sorrow and to encourage them in their sufferings: "[I] was dead, and behold, I am alive forevermore." He consoled them by reminding them that He also had passed through suffering and death, and triumphed over it.

Do you see why Jesus is the author of eternal life? He is the One who was dead, who died in our place "that through death He might destroy him who had the power of death, that is, the devil" (Hebrews 2:14). Throughout human history the power of death has gripped people with fear. Jesus destroyed the devil to "release those who through fear of death were all their lifetime subject to bondage" (Hebrews 2:15). Jesus gave us hope!"

After Jesus wrote to Smyrna, He identified Himself as the Lord of Life who conquered death. Now He gave them an approval: "I know your works, tribulation, and poverty (but you are rich); and I know the blasphemy of those who say they are Jews and are not, but are a synagogue of Satan" (Revelation 2:9).

The martyred Christians were able to die faithfully because they lived faithfully for Christ. They were triumphant in death because they were triumphant in life. And He says to us likewise: "Be faithful unto death, and I will approve of you!"

THURSDAY: Be Ready for Troubles

*"**You will have tribulation ten days**. Be faithful until death, and I will give you the crown of life."*
—Revelation 2:10c

Look out saints at Smyrna—trouble is coming! Christ's warning to them is interesting. It could be that they had persecution for ten calendar days. Or it could refer to ten periods of time, or that there were ten Roman emperors who persecuted the church. Personally, I believe that all three apply.

The early church did indeed have ten great persecutions under the Roman emperors. It all began with Nero and ended with Diocletian, whose ten-year-long persecution was probably the most terrible of all. Nero, Domitian, Trajan, Marcus Aurelius, Severus, Maximus, Decius, Valerian, Aurelian, and Diocletian were the ten principal pagan persecutors. However, there was constant, though not always general, trouble until Constantine's edict of toleration in A.D. 313.

To the Smyrnean church, and His children in every church age, Jesus exhorted: "Be faithful!" Why? Because Christ is the One who will award the prized crowns. The faithful will be specially crowned if they are saved by grace and are triumphant in life. Here are the five prized crowns that Christ will present to His faithful ones:

1. **The crown of righteousness** is reserved for the victorious warriors who said no to sin throughout their lives (2 Timothy 4:8).
2. **The unfading crown** is reserved for the steadfast racers who disciplined their body for Christ (1 Corinthians 9:25–27).
3. **The crown of life** is reserved for those who were faithful unto death (Revelation 2:10; James 1:12).
4. **The crown of honor** is reserved for those who were unselfish soul winners in life (1 Thessalonians 2:9; cf. 3–6; Philippians 4:1).
5. **The crown of glory** is reserved for those who were examples to the flock (1 Peter 5: 3–4).

G. Campbell Morgan has noted that "faithful" means "be convinced." In Revelation 1:5 Christ refers to Himself as "the faithful witness." Because He is always so faithful, His children are convinced they must rest in Him, and depend on what He says. So "be convinced" of Him, and He will be your constant strength and courage!

FRIDAY: Seven Godly Ways to Die

*These all **died in faith**, not having received the promises, but having seen them afar off were assured of them, embraced them and confessed that they were strangers and pilgrims on the earth.*
—HEBREWS 11:13

This week we have been learning about the church at Smyrna—the saints who experienced martyrdom for Christ's sake. Their faithfulness unto death was such a sweet-smelling savor unto God. Unless Christ returns soon, all of us face the inevitability of death. Are you ready? Have you planned for the testimony you'd like your funeral to be?

By a few simple preparations, you can really bless your family and friends who stay behind after you've gone home to be with Jesus. If you have never done this, I encourage you to take out a sheet of paper and label it: "My Home Going Celebration." Write out a brief description of how you came to Christ, and of your hope in His salvation. Then share some of your favorite verses, songs, and hymns—and even a word to bless those you leave behind. Do this and, like Abel, you will "speak" even after you've died (Hebrews 11:4). To further prepare, consider once more the seven godly examples in Scripture of how to die with grace.

Jacob looked for the Land of Promise to the end of his life. When he was close to death, Jacob called Joseph to his side and said, "Now if I have found favor in your sight, . . . deal kindly and truly with me. Please do not bury me in Egypt, but let me lie with my fathers" (Genesis 47:29–30). When

Jacob was a young man, God had promised that his people would someday have a Land of Promise, but Egypt was not that land. Jacob therefore asked to be laid to rest in the actual land God was giving to his descendants. He had followed his Shepherd all the way, and trusted his Redeemer to save him from his sins (Genesis 48:15–16). Have you thanked the Lord lately for His grace that is greater than all your sins?

Joseph died pointing to the faithfulness of God. He told his brethren, "I am dying; but God will surely visit you, and bring you out of this land to the land of which He swore to Abraham, to Isaac, and to Jacob" (Genesis 50:24). In the ancient world, when someone was failing in health and was coming to the end of life, the family would gather around and listen to their last words. Inheritances were then divided up. Joseph died pointing his family to the Lord's promises: "God will surely come to your aid, for He is faithful and will do what He said."

David died exhorting his family to follow God. When he was about to die, David charged Solomon his son, saying, "'I am about to go the way of all the earth,' he said. 'So be strong, show yourself a man, and observe what the LORD your God requires: Walk in his ways, and keep his decrees and commands, his laws and requirements, as written in the Law of Moses, so that you may prosper in all you do and wherever you go'" (1 Kings 2:2–3 NIV). David earned the right to exhort his family spiritually because he had lived a godly life. Lot, however, did not. His family laughed and mocked him, saying that he was scoffing (Genesis 19:14). To make our last moments on earth really count, it is so important that we get ready to die by *first* living for Christ.

Stephen died praising God. While he was being stoned, he prayed, "'Lord Jesus, receive my spirit.' Then he fell on his knees and cried out, 'Lord, do not hold this sin against them.'" When he had said this, he fell asleep (Acts 7:59–60 NIV). What an incredible testimony of dying faith! Stephen was radiant, worshiping, and offering his spirit into the presence of the Lord!

Peter died reminding the saints about the Word of God. He said, "I will always remind you of these things, even though you . . . are firmly established in the truth you now have. . . . It is right to refresh your memory as long as I live in the tent of this body, because I know that I will soon put it aside" (2 Peter 1:12–14 NIV). Jesus had told Peter that some day his hands would be stretched out, and he would be crucified (John 21:18). History tells us that he was crucified upside down because Peter had declared that he was not worthy to die like Jesus did.

Paul died finishing the plan laid out for Him by God. When death was near, he said, "I have fought the good fight, I have finished the race, I have kept the faith. Now there is in store for me the crown of righteousness, which the Lord . . . will award to me on that day—and . . . to all who have longed for his appearing" (2 Timothy 4:6–8, NIV). Paul faithfully followed the course that God had laid out for him. His last days were spent in the maximum security Mamertine Prison in Rome. He did not protest or try to get out; he placidly sat there and wrote letters, knowing that he had faithfully completed what God asked him to do, and was prepared to go to heaven.

Christ died pointing the way for another to come to God. Jesus told one of the criminals being crucified, "Today you will be with Me in Paradise" (Luke 23:43). Is Jesus *your* hope? If you died today, would you be with Him in paradise? Are you ready to die?

I frequently hear people regretfully say, "I wish I could do that over." In Philippians 3:13–14, Paul said to forget what is behind and live for the Lord from today on. If you have not been as faithful as you need to be, start *now*. Finish the course Christ has laid out for you, and you will experience a great calm as you follow God's will daily. This is the very best approach to being ready to go "home" any day—and not just when your "to do" list is complete. Consistently living like this is a wonderful way to die!

SATURDAY: Be Looking Forward to Heaven

*It is **appointed** . . . to die once, but after this the judgment.*
—Hebrews 9:27

None of us knows the exact date of our appointment with Jesus Christ to take us home to heaven, but we do know that what lies ahead is far superior to anything we could ever envision. Even now Jesus is preparing a mansion for us so that we can be with Him (John 14:2). What will it be like there?

Heaven will be a joyous and satisfying place! The joy of heaven's inhabitants is pictured by the scenes of praise in the book of Revelation, the white-robed conquerors waving palm branches (Revelation 7:9), and the guests at a wedding supper (Revelation 19:1–9). This is buttressed by the imagery of some of Jesus' parables where attaining heaven was compared to attending a banquet (Luke 14:15–24) or entering into the joy of one's Master (Matthew 25:21, 23).

From the perspective of life in this world, heaven is the object of human longing and the goal of human existence. The book of Hebrews employs the imagery of quest to express this reality: "These all died in faith, not having received what was promised. . . . For people who speak thus make it clear that they are seeking a homeland" (see Hebrews 11:13–14).

In addition to being the goal of a quest, heaven is the reward for earthly toil, as in Paul's picture of himself as having "finished the race" and looking forward to "the crown of righteousness" (2 Timothy 4:7–8). We see this imagery again in Peter's vision of "the chief Shepherd" conferring "the unfading crown of glory" on those who have served faithfully (1 Peter 5:4). There is also the glorious picture of believers having come to "Mount Zion, to the heavenly Jerusalem, the city of the living God" where thousands upon thousands of angels are in joyful assembly (Hebrews 12:22 NIV).

Images of satisfaction emerge from the pictures in Revelation of saints being guided by a divine Shepherd to springs of living water (Revelation 7:17), and having access to "the tree of life with its twelve kinds of fruit, yielding its fruit each month" (see Revelation 22:2).

Heaven is also portrayed as a rest after labor: those who die in the Lord "rest from their labors, for their deeds follow them" (see Revelation 14:13). Similarly, "there remains a sabbath rest for the people of God," which believers strive to enter (see Hebrews 4:9–11)

WEEK 16
Cling to Christ

{ Revelation 2:12–17 }

This week as we approach the end of days, you
can find hope as you cling to Christ!

SUNDAY: The Security of Christ's Plan

[We] are kept by the power of God through faith for salvation ready to be revealed in the last time.
—1 Peter 1:5

This week we will tackle one of the hardest parts of Christian living—being *in* the world, but not *of* the world; loving the *lost*, but not loving the world system. That is the message that Christ's challenge brought to the church at Pergamos.

Geographically, Pergamos was a city eighty miles north of Smyrna, fifteen miles inland from the Aegean Sea, on a hill 1,000 feet above the fertile valleys. Historically, when John wrote in A.D. 95, it was an old city that had been the capital of Asia Minor (modern day Turkey) for 300 years. Culturally, it was a university town, having the largest library in the ancient world, rivaling that of Alexandria. With 200,000 volumes, Pergamos was noted for producing the parchment (boiled animal skins) on which books were written.

Theologically, it may be that Satan himself had a personal throne in Pergamos as headquarters for his global rebellion during that period of time (Revelation 2:13). Satan, "the ruler of this world" (John 12:31), was served by his hierarchy of servants that followed him: "For we do not wrestle against flesh and blood, but against principalities, against powers, against the rulers of the darkness of this age, against spiritual hosts of wickedness in the heavenly places" (Ephesians 6:12).

Pergamos, the focal point of Satan's kingdom, was a sacred city to the pagans. Worship of the king of the gods of the Graeco-Roman religion of Zeus (Jupiter) was headquartered there. Pagans also worshiped Aesculapius, the false god of healing. False healing has always been a tool of Satan to persuade people that there is divine power coming upon them, for he consistently imitates God. Because all parts of life had a god attached in that city, a pantheon of gods was worshiped there.

Practically, Pergamos was an awful place to try to live for Jesus because it was the immorality center of the ancient world. Can you imagine being in a composite of the glitz of Las Vegas, the immoral filth of Mardi Gras, and the ease of access to evil on the Internet—all in one place? Pergamos was just like that due to the worship of Dionysus (Bacchus), the gods of orgies, wine, and debauchery.

And in that place was a church—the assembly at Pergamos—which testifies that God can grow His church anywhere, even in one of the most desperate places. Many Pergamite saints had been converted from Satanism, idolatry, false healing, and immorality. Because they became very secure in Christ, they flourished for Him right where He planted them, even sitting under the throne of Satan: "I know your works, and where you dwell, where Satan's throne is. And you hold fast to My name, and did not deny My faith" (Revelation 2:13).

The church at Pergamos, however, had a problem. Some had lost their vital joys of being born again; they no longer had purity of life, intimacy with God, and nourishment from His Word. How did that happen? They had gotten too close to the world by mixing with it, marrying it, or loving the system. But Jesus lovingly offered a solution to their woeful problems, and ours: Repent of worldliness; do not be conformed to the world like unbelievers who are driven by earthly goals, desires, and values!

If you have lost your purity, Christ says, "Come back, and I'll give you My white stone" (Revelation 2:17c). He wants to wash and cleanse you, and make you as pure and white as snow! If you have lost your intimacy, Christ says, "Come back, and I'll give you My new name—a name which 'no one knows except him who receives it'" (Revelation 2:17d). He wants to draw you to spend precious and intimate time alone with Him! If you have lost your nourishment, Christ says, "Come back, and I'll feed you with My hidden manna" (Revelation 2:17b; see also Jeremiah 15:16). He wants to nourish you in His Word!

How inescapable is the Lord of the Church, Jesus Christ, as He penetrates every heart, searching for each person's condition. There is no sin too dark, no stain too deep, and no life too defiled that the blood of Jesus Christ cannot cleanse. The ultimate lesson from this church is that Jesus Christ wants us to cling to Him—and not to the world!

My Prayer for You This Week: *We bow before You, Lord Jesus, our Savior. We want to discover the hope that You offer today. I pray that we will listen as You speak to us through this special letter to the church at Pergamos. Help us to find You as the hope to which we cling, the hope toward which we press, the hope which we truly possess as that which can never be taken away from us. And then, with that hope in mind, help us to prepare for the time when You will call us home. For You have told us that as Christians we can get ready so that we can die in a way that will glorify You. Help us to learn that precious and very blessed message of hope! Open our eyes and hearts we pray! In Jesus' precious name. Amen.*

MONDAY: The Security of Christ's Purity

"Blessed are the **pure in heart**, for they shall see God."
—Matthew 5:8

Beware of the new paganism in the twenty-first-century church. The majority of those who call themselves Christians follow a way of worship that would have offended the apostles and early saints. What do I mean? Would they not see the statues of Christ and saints as idols? Would they not equate the candles and incense burning with that of pagan temple worship? Would they not have trouble with the separation into orders of priests and monks, and taking on the titles of pontiff, vicar, and "most excellent," very offensive and contradictory to Christlike humility? The calendar of observances, holy water, purgatory, and so much more would not have been accepted because it all came directly from the pagans—whom the early saints tried to convert.

Christ's letter to the church at Pergamos warns of the deadly sin of loving and being communion with that which God has condemned and will destroy. There is only one action to take when confronted with worldliness and apostasy: *separate from it!*

God says, "Do not be unequally yoked together with unbelievers. For what fellowship has righteousness [believers] with lawlessness [unbelievers]? For you are the temple of the living God. . . . Therefore 'Come out from among them and be separate, says the Lord. Do not touch what is unclean, and I will receive you'" (2 Corinthians 6:14–17).

The proper thing to do when involved in something that is apostate is to get out of it. Where Christ's name is dishonored, and there is false teaching and idolatry, leave. Separate from it physically; do not participate, for whoever "wants to be a friend of the world makes himself an enemy of God. Or do you think that the Scripture says in vain, 'The Spirit who dwells in us yearns jealously'?" (James 4:4–5).

Those are very sobering words. The Holy Spirit is inside of us, and is jealous for us. We are espoused to Christ as His pure bride. We are not to get our clothes soiled needlessly with the love of the world. Look at James 4:7–8: "Submit to God. Resist the devil and he will flee from you. Draw near to God and He will draw near to you. Cleanse your hands, you sinners; and purify your hearts, you double-minded."

If we choose to go along with the flow of the world, there is something wrong (1 John 2:15). Because the Holy Spirit lives within us, we should not purposefully want to offend His holiness. Though we slip at times, and are weak, we will not wed ourselves to the world. Why? God will not let us. He will chasten us: "For all that is in the world—the lust of the flesh [chasing after pleasure], the lust of the eyes [chasing after stuff], and the pride of life [chasing after status]—is not of the Father but is of the world" (1 John 2:16–17).

This is a prophetic message for us today: God will destroy commercial and religious Babylon. This message is also to people of all ages who think they can reform an apostate religion by staying in it. In Revelation 18:4 Christ says, "Come out of her, my people, lest you share in her sins, and lest you receive of her plagues."

Visiting the Great Physician may be painful, but you can trust His diagnosis. For only Jesus can see exactly what is good, bad, and dangerous. When He ran a diagnostic test on the saints at Pergamos, this was His analysis of their needs: "But I have a few things against you, because you have there those who hold the doctrine of Balaam, who taught Balak to put a stumbling block before the children of Israel, to eat things sacrificed to idols, and to commit sexual immorality" (Revelation 2:14).

The Pergamite saints were saved—they claimed the true name, and they didn't deny Christ in fierce trials. For that, they were to be commended. Nevertheless, Christ said, "You are in sin, and I have a few things against you . . . " His rebuke was related to "the doctrine of Balaam" which represents compromise. In Numbers 22–24, Balaam taught the Moabites that the way to defeat God's people was through leading them to compromise their obedience to God's Word. Hence the old adage: "If you can't defeat them, join them; defile them so that God will judge them." Christ therefore warned the church at Pergamos: "Repent, or else I will come to you quickly" (Revelation 2:16a). What Christ said to the church then, He also says to the twenty-first-century church.

Many begin well in Christ, but then gradually slip away and lose their first love. Over the next few days, by observing the life of Samson, we will see a powerful scriptural example of the dangers of not staying alert to the wiles of the devil (Ephesians 6:11–13).

Do you feel yourself slipping back into sin? Then Christ lovingly says to you, "Repent, and come back to Me today!"

TUESDAY: Samson Began Well

*So the woman **bore a son** and called his name **Samson**;*
and the child grew, and the LORD blessed him.
—JUDGES 13:24

God recorded Samson's life as an example of both the destructive power of sin and the restoring power of grace. His life is a testament to the fact that if you sow to the flesh, you will reap corruption; if you sow to the Spirit, you will reap life everlasting (Galatians 6:7–8).

Samson was one of the most amazing Old Testament personages. So many details in his life are unique, and thus profound in their meaning. For example, God's angels announced his birth. He was one of only three people whose births were announced by angels (Jesus and Isaac are the other two). So Samson started in the top one-tenth of 1 percent of all the 3,000 people named in the Bible.

Amazing as it might seem, because they sought God's help raising him, Samson's parents rank up there with the fewest of the few. Only Joseph and Mary, Job, Abraham, Hannah, and Samson's dad, Manoah, are recorded in the Bible as asking for and receiving wisdom from God on how to raise their children. Samson's parents feared the Lord, and they wanted to instill that same awesome reverence in their son.

Although God has a special purpose for all His saints, only a few people in the Old Testament (Jeremiah, Samuel, and Samson) are identified as being chosen from birth for a particular purpose. (In the New Testament, John the Baptist and Paul were selected for that same distinction.) Before Samson was born, God declared that he was to be a Nazirite (Judges 13:5). Such a "God's man" was to be outwardly committed to total abstinence from wine, avoidance of dead bodies, and never cutting his hair. The inward response to this special calling was to be a chosen life; everything he did was to point to the Lord through obedience. God, coupled with the Nazirite vow, gave Samson a special supernatural strength.

Physically, Samson was only an ordinary Israelite, about 5' 2" to 5' 4" tall, with no outward sign of strength, just the mark of his consecration. Now picture that size man picking up the gates to a city, ripping them off their hinges, setting them on his shoulders, and walking away with them! The archaeological reports of the digs of the city of Gaza and all the Philistine encampments revealed that the city gates were twelve feet wide, set down into solid stone, and built into solid walls. They were massive wooden gates, often covered with iron that easily weighed tons. Ancient Jewish tradition says Samson left the gates on a hilltop, just outside of town, as a mockery to the city. He definitely had supernatural strength!

To have grown up with Samson must have been a remarkable experience. His neighborhood pals would certainly have been awed at his immense strength, and his enemies must have fled quickly. Having him around would have been like having a one-man army. Yet he often lived in the lust of the flesh, the lust of the eyes, and the pride of life.

Surprisingly, in the final analysis, God viewed Samson as a man of faith. What a picture of grace! At his darkest hour, in one moment of godly sorrow that led to a repentant prayer of faith, God brought him back to the place of blessing. Oh, what a wonderful truth! Our God is the God of the second chance! When I think of that fact, it makes me burst forth into singing, "Marvelous grace of our loving Lord, Grace that exceeds our sin and our guilt!" I always like to say: "If Samson made it—anybody can." He was about as far defiled as one can get, yet through grace, he became one of God's dear heroes of the faith (Hebrews 11:32).

Have you experienced the miraculous grace of the God of the second chance?

WEDNESDAY: Sin Blinds, Binds, and Grinds

*These . . . became **our examples** . . . that we should not lust . . . as they . . . lusted.*
—1 Corinthians 10:6

As a young man, probably in his teens, we get the first indicator that Samson greatly needed God's grace. When he began to live by his own desires instead of God's, and serve his own lusts instead of God's Words, Samson was no longer heading in the direction in which the Lord had pointed him.

A string of women began to parade through his life. In fact, seven times Samson was guided by the lust of his eyes when he "saw a woman that pleased him." Each was a dangerous choice. The final, and deadliest woman, was Delilah. She was so deadly that even today her name has become synonymous with lust, deceit, betrayal, and ruin. C. H. Spurgeon's summary says it all:

> At last he falls into the hands of Delilah. She is bribed with an enormous sum, and she endeavors to get from him the secret of his strength. He foolishly plays with his own destruction. At last he lets out the secret, his strength lay in his locks. Not that his hair made him strong; but that his hair was the symbol of his consecration, and was the pledge of God's favor to him.
>
> While his hair was untouched he was a consecrated man; as soon as that was cut away, he was no longer perfectly consecrated, and then his strength departed from him. His hair is cut away; the Philistines begin to oppress him, and his eyes are burned out with hot iron. How are the mighty fallen!
>
> And now he comes to the very city out of which he had walked in all his pride with the gates and bolts upon his shoulders; and the little children come out, the lower orders of the people

come round about him, and point at him—"Samson, the great hero, hath fallen! Let us make sport of him!" What a spectacle!

Why, he must be the sport and jest of every passerby, and of every fool who shall step in to see this great wonder—the destroyer of the Philistines made to toil at the mill. That he should have lost his eyes was terrible; that he should have lost his strength was worse; but that he should have lost the favor of God for a while; that he should become the sport of God's enemies, was the worst of all.[1]

Though Samson descended into the depths of a lust-filled life, and wandered far from his calling and consecration, the Lord never let go of him. (That should give us great hope for those we know who are born again, yet are wandering far from Christ.) His soiled life is recorded; his defeats are unvarnished and clear for all to see. But against the backdrop of Samson's sin is a reminder of the powerful beauty of God's grace.

Practicing sin blinds us, then slowly binds us with its fetters, and then, finally blinded and bound, we begin to grind through life. Talk to anybody who has come to Christ out of an immoral life, the drug culture, or the world of alcohol and bars, and you will find that it is not the exciting life that the media claims it to be. Living in that manner can never satisfy because it is always a passing pleasure. Only God can break the fetters that blind and bind us to grind out an existence totally captive to sin! God forgives—and He beautifully restores!

THURSDAY: The Consequence Engine in Action

I discipline my body . . . , *lest, when I have preached to others, I myself should become disqualified.*
—1 Corinthians 9:27

The life of Samson depicts the awful consequences of living a life of compromise with the world and the flesh. Judges 13 records one of the most incredible accounts in the Bible; few are as tragic as this one. God had given Samson twenty years to begin to overcome the enemy, the Philistines. However, in the end, Samson was overcome by the greatest enemy of all—himself. Samson's history is an illustration of Paul's warning in 1 Corinthians 9:27. Heaven remembers Samson as a man of faith, but earth remembers him as a man who was *disqualified.* Although Hebrews 11:32 cites him for his faith, apart from this, very little can be said in his defense. The lesson to each of us is this: "Let him who thinks he stands take heed lest he fall" (1 Corinthians 10:12).

What steps led to Samson's sin and tragic end?

Samson wandered from his heritage. He was born into a godly home. The Angel of the LORD (Jesus Christ pre-incarnate) appeared to Manoah's wife and said, "You shall conceive and bear a son. . . . Please be careful [before his birth] not to drink wine or similar drink, and not to eat anything unclean. . . . And no razor shall come upon his head, for the child shall be a Nazirite to God from the womb; and he shall begin to deliver Israel out of the hand of the Philistines" (Judges 13:3–5).

Samson had a godly giftedness and calling. God gave him a special endowment of the Holy Spirit that made him a conqueror (Judges 13:25). When he was old enough to understand, his parents informed him that God had called him to be a Nazirite, a "separated one" wholly surrendered to the Lord. When grown, however, Samson despised his wonderful heritage. Instead of putting himself in God's hands to accomplish his God-given task, he tragically chose to live to please himself.

Samson disobeyed his parents. His disobedience gave clear evidence of his spiritual decline. He knew that the God given Jewish laws of separation meant marrying only within the covenant people, but that didn't matter to him. Samson went into enemy territory and fell in love with a heathen woman. He told (not asked) his father: "Get her for me, for she pleases me well" (Judges 14:3). Samson's focus was totally outward: he only viewed the woman's body, but never saw her inner spirit, soul, or character. He was living for the moment, for the lusts of his flesh (see Genesis 24:1–4; Exodus 34:16; Deuteronomy 7:3; and 2 Corinthians 6:14–18).

By disobeying his parents, Samson was choosing to be his own authority. He therefore ignored their admonition: "Don't do that, Samson!" It did not bother him that his desires displeased his parents. God overruled in this circumstance, however, because He knew Samson's propensity for sin, and was going to use his lust as a vehicle of His judgment on the Philistines (Judges 14:4). However, I can imagine God holding Samson accountable for his actions, saying, "Be not deceived, for I will not be mocked. What Samson sowed, he is going to reap."

What valuable lesson can we learn from this? Christian young people need to stop and consider carefully when they find themselves defying godly parents who know God's Word. It is a fearsome matter when God is against someone who refuses to repent.

FRIDAY: When God Is Against Us

> *"Whoever . . . wants to be **a friend of the world** makes himself **an enemy of God**."*
> —JAMES 4:4

Yesterday we looked at two steps Samson took that eventually led to his sin and tragic end: he wandered from his heritage (Judges 13), and he disobeyed his parents (Judges 14:1–4). Now let us look at some other steps that led to Samson's total downfall.

Samson compromised his life. He was supposed to be a man of the Word, to be a mighty judge, but he sought to be unequally yoked instead. So the Lord sent Samson some ominous warnings. The first was a big one. On his way to visit his bride-to-be, a young lion came roaring against him. The lion was representative of the devil who "walks around like a roaring lion, seeking whom he may devour" (1 Peter 5:8b). What a picture! The devil wanted to use him for his purposes, for he knew that Samson was going in his direction by following his lust.

As the lion attacked him, look what happened: "And the Spirit of the LORD came mightily upon him, and he tore the lion apart as one would have torn apart a young goat, though he had nothing in his hand" (Judges 14:6). Talk about an amazing super-human strength! Even though Samson was not walking completely in God's will, He provided the power to overcome the lion—but he did not get the Lord's message.

When Samson went back later to complete the marriage, he was tested again. Although Nazirites were never to touch a dead body, for the sake of a little honey in the lion's carcass, Samson defiled himself. (Many Christians today likewise defile themselves just to enjoy "a little honey in the carcass of a lion"—perhaps with a questionable book, movie, or friendship.) Sad to say, Samson passed that sinfully gained honey along to his parents, and then made a joke about it to entertain his friends!

Samson ignored God's warnings. When Samson burned the fields of the Philistines, they retaliated by burning the woman he had loved, her father, and their house (Judges 15:6 and 14:15). After he avenged their deaths, his own people turned against him and delivered him to the enemy (Judges 15:11–13). Although Samson was rescued by God, this test had been another warning to show how weak he really was.

Judges 15 is a chapter of seeming victories, yet it ends with the "strong man" utterly exhausted for lack of water. That need prompted one of the two prayers Scripture records Samson made: for water (Judges 15:18–20) and for strength to destroy the Philistines (Judges 16:28). Samson's parents had been prayerful people, but he never followed their example. Thus, he still would not heed God.

Samson played with sin. (See Judges 16.) His heart was far from the God he should have known, and loved, and served. Even though he'd already gotten into trouble with one woman, he now tried again. This time his lusts took him deep into enemy territory to Gaza. Pride had taken hold of him; after all, he was "Superman," so he marched right into the epicenter of the Philistine army to pursue another woman.

This time, God warned him by allowing the enemy to almost catch him, but Samson would not repent. Then Delilah came into his life and led him to his doom. Three times she enticed Samson, and three times he lied to her. Each lie he told took him one step closer to having the truth about his strength revealed. When the enemy attacked him afterward each time, he should have realized he was in danger. (Read Proverbs 7:21–27 to see why Samson yielded.) He was asleep when he should have been awake. How dangerous it is to play with sin!

What was Samson's problem? He was *dominated by lust*. That passion led Samson to desire a Philistine woman as a wife, which was strictly forbidden by God's Law. That passion also led him to liaisons with prostitutes like Delilah (who betrayed him for money). Many times men will say, "I'm doing that because I love her." But that is not really true: love can wait; lust can't. Do you know the difference between love and lust? Can you wait? If you can't, it's lust. Love waits.[2]

Samson was also *driven by pride and revenge*. He was more moved by anger at personal affronts—which caused him to strike out at the Philistines—than by the suffering of the people he was supposed to lead (cf. 14:19–20; 15:7–8; 16:28).

In the end, Samson was *defeated by himself*. Imagine what Samson might have been if, with his great strength and godly heritage, he had daily lived out the formal commitment to God expressed in that Nazirite vow!

The tragic end of disobedience. The rest of the story shows the disastrous end of the believer who will not let God have His way with his or her life. From Judges 16:20 on, Samson does nothing but lose: he lost his full usefulness to the Lord, his testimony, and ultimately his life. And all this started when Samson despised his blessings and defied his parents!

Samson ended up as a castaway: he had committed the sin unto death, so God had to take him off the scene. But before he died, God allowed Samson one last act of faith—and a huge victory over the Philistines. (Although his usefulness had been diminished, it had not been completely lost.) That victory was a great triumph in a life littered with tragedy.

What can we learn from Samson's tragic life? There is no such thing as being able to safely play around with a little bit of sin. Remember: sin first blinds, then binds, and finally grinds. No matter how alluring it may seem, habitual sin grinds away at the soul, like gravel in the mouth (Proverbs 20:17).

If you willfully choose to operate in your own strength, and fail to heed God's warnings, He will let you operate without walking in the Spirit, and you will reap what you have sown.

SATURDAY: A Day of Reckoning

*We must all **appear before the judgment seat** of Christ, that each one may receive the things done in the body, . . . whether good or bad.*

—2 Corinthians 5:10

Just as the assembly at Pergamos faced the judgment of God for sin that was never dealt with in their lives, so will we if we don't repent. Because God *hates* sin, we need to flee from it and fear the holiness of God.

As a warning to everyone called to lifelong consecration to the Lord, let's look at what happened to Samson in New Testament terms. Here are some passages, which explain that there are "sins unto death."

All New Testament believers are consecrated to the Lord, like Samson was. "Do you not know that you are the temple of God and that the Spirit of God dwells in you?" (1 Corinthians 3:16). The Spirit is so specific. There were two words in the ancient world for "temple": we are not the *hieron*, which means "the whole temple building"; we are *naos*, which means "the most protected part," the sacred chamber where God dwelt, or "the Holy of Holies." Glorify God in your body and in your spirit, which are God's. Don't offer excuses or try to justify your sin, because God says you and I are to be consecrated.

We will each answer to God for what we did with our bodies. "Each one's work will become clear; for the Day will declare it, because . . . the fire will test each one's work. . . . If anyone's work . . . endures, he will receive a reward. If anyone's work is burned, he will suffer loss; but he himself will be saved, yet so as through fire" (1 Corinthians 3:13–15).

Have you ever heard the term of getting into heaven "by the skin of your teeth"? There are people who are going to be in heaven, but that is all. They are going to suffer the loss of their earthly life because they were "Samsons" who lived for the lust of their eyes, the lust of their flesh, and the pride of life. The sins that God has forgiven will burn away, and anything not for God's glory, in obedience to God, will also be burned away in God's refining fire. God, therefore, wants us to redeem our time as carefully as possible. Although life is more than Bible reading and prayer, everything we do should still be done for the glory of God (1 Corinthians 10:31).

God will not stand by as we sin. "For this reason many are weak and sick among you, and many sleep. For if we would judge ourselves, we would not be judged" (1 Corinthians 11:30–31). What is "sleep"? Biblically, "sleep" refers to the death of the body, but the spirit is with Christ. Some believers get weak, sick, and die—not because they're at that age when it is time for it to happen (and it is a glorious home going), but because they did not deal with their pride, lust, and fleshly appetites.

God gives us warnings and chastens us to prove His love. "Whom the LORD loves He chastens, and scourges every son whom He receives" (Hebrews 12:6). Those who will not separate from the love of the world will be chastened. One might say, "Well, I'm living it up and doing what I want and nothing is happening." Hebrews 12:8 should speak to you then: if you are without chastening, then you are illegitimate and not a child of God. God says that all His sons and daughters will be disciplined if they continue to live in sin.

Going too far in sin can be deadly for believers. "There is sin leading to death. . . . All unrighteousness is sin, and there is sin not leading to death" (1 John 5:16b–17). What that unusual language means is this: if you go too far, too long, God will say, "That is enough!" He will then take you out of the world. What happened to Samson? He went too far, too long, and God took him out. He tragically sinned to the point that God felt his ministry must end, even though he had repented.

God kills believers who won't repent in time. "Unless they repent of their deeds. . . . I will kill her children with death" (Revelation 2:22–23). God has a time period. He waits, chastens, weakens, and sickens His continually disobedient children. And when that does not bring about godly sorrow that leads to repentance, then God kills believers who will not repent: "All the churches shall know that I am He who searches the minds and hearts. And I will give to each one of you according to your works" (Revelation 2:23).

Apparently, during the grinding at the mill, Samson repented of his sin. The Philistines had made this sightless former hero their center of attraction, like an amusement park. But while that was going on, God offered him one more merciful chance to act by faith. His hair had begun to grow, Samson remembered his calling, and he asked God for strength to win one more victory over the enemy (Judges 16:28–30). He accomplished more in that one prayer than he did in twenty years of fighting. He defeated the Philistines, but in defeating others, he lost his own life.

Samson illustrates people who have power to conquer others, but who cannot conquer themselves. He could set the Philistine fields on fire, but could not control the fires of his own lust. He could kill an attacking lion, but could not put to death the passions of his own flesh. He could easily break the bonds that men put on him, but the shackles of his own sin gradually grew stronger on his soul. And He could have led the nation, but he preferred to work independently and, as a result, left no permanent victory behind.

Samson could have been remembered for what he built up, but instead everyone except God only remembers what he destroyed—lions, foxes, fields, gates, soldiers, women's purity, thousands of God's enemies, and his own life and ministry.

Make a choice to live in hope. Samson's life is a powerful reminder of God's grace. Even if you have lived like Samson, it is not too late to turn in faith, repent, and look to God. If you are a lost person, turn to Christ while you can still hear His voice, and then cling to Him. If you are a believer, you have not gone too far yet to miss God's grace; respond and cling to Him while there is still time. But if you willfully choose to continue in your sin, you *can* go too far; there is indeed a sin that leads to death. Sin destroys, but God beautifully restores!

WEEK 17
Honor Christ's Holiness

{ Revelation 2:18–29 }

This week as we approach the end of days, you can find hope as you honor Christ's holiness!

SUNDAY: Holiness Is Fearing Sin

*The solid foundation of God stands, having this seal: "The Lord knows those who are His," and, "Let everyone who names the name of Christ **depart from iniquity**."*
—2 Timothy 2:19

The letter to Thyatira is the longest of the seven letters Christ wrote to His church. Yet Thyatira, located thirty miles from Pergamos and Sardis, is the least described of all the seven churches in Revelation. In fact, the only thing we know is the name of the first Christian from Thyatira. On Paul's second journey, as he stopped in Philippi, he led a seeking woman to Jesus, a "seller of purple [scarlet fabrics]" (Acts 16:14). Lydia, a merchant from Thyatira, was his first European convert.

Thyatira was renowned for its trade guilds. Much like our unions of today, the guilds set prices for labor, sales areas, and so forth. Potters, dyers, tanners, bakers, metal workers, textile makers, bronze smiths, slave dealers, leather workers, and the rest all had their guilds in this town.

Trade guilds were compulsory; only people in a guild could be employed in a trade. It was a closed shop. Every guild in Thyatira had a patron god or goddess, and every guild function began with paying homage to that deity by an obligatory offering; business followed, and then the customary banquets known for their sexual freedom.

Sir William Ramsay, the famed nineteenth-century archaeologist, described the scene of what he had excavated as being a place where intoxicated partygoers indulged themselves in immorality as the standard conduct of these pagan trade guilds. Clearly, lounging at a meal surrounded by strippers is not where any believer would want Christ to find him asking for deliverance from temptation. In short, a guild was no place for Christians, but quitting the union was economic suicide.

Thyatira was the church of the Dark Ages (A.D. 600–1500); this period covered from the time of the first pope, Gregory the Great, to the Reformation. If Pergamos was the church that was first wed to the world, then Thyatira was the dead church that had been living a long time in that condition.

Have you, like the wayward Thyratirans, been "dead' inside for a long time? If you have not said no to all sin in your life, and said yes to Christ by asking Him to give you clean hands and a pure heart, that neglect can trigger the chastening hand of God. Our Scripture meditation this week, Revelation 2:18–29, reminds us that Jesus Christ is "He who searches the minds and hearts." He very explicitly speaks of what happens to those who refuse to come before Him in purity. The chastening hand of God is real, and it will reach out and touch you if you do not choose to fear the Lord.

Fearing the Lord (appearing over 100 times in God's Word) is a huge scriptural concept—for God commands reverential awe that leads to loving obedience. Have you learned to fear the dreadful consequences of sin? I exhort you to listen this week to Christ's call to holiness!

My Prayer for You This Week: *Lord Jesus, You have written this letter to the church at Thyatira, and we believe in the inerrant, inspired, supernatural revelation of Your Book; it is the very Word of You, the living God; and You, the living Word. Lord Jesus, we ask that Your Spirit would communicate Your words to our hearts with conviction and piercing sharpness that we might fear Your chastisement. And that in fearing You we might say no to sin and yes to Your sanctifying process in our lives. Search our hearts and know our innermost thoughts. May we at all times abhor, turn from, flee, and disregard the allurements of the lust of the flesh, the lust of the eyes, and the horrible pride of life. Illumine us; touch our hearts with clarity, understanding, and insight into Your Word as we come before You seeking. In the lovely name of Jesus we pray. Amen.*

MONDAY: Holiness Is Wanting to Grow

Grow in the grace and knowledge of our Lord and Savior Jesus Christ. To Him be the glory both now and forever.
—2 Peter 3:18

The fear of the Lord is a reverential, awesome awareness of how holy God is, and how unholy we are. The phrase "the fear of the Lord" is repeated often in the Bible, but it does not tell us that we are to live in an attitude of terror, "for God has not given us a spirit of fear" (2 Timothy 1:7). As God's children we are to reverence the Lord so much that we will not deliberately disobey Him or try His patience. We must have a holy respect for God.

Consider this illustration: When I was a little boy, one of my friends was mowing the lawn barefooted. He was pushing the mower up the side of a drainage ditch and got distracted. The mower rolled back down and cut off his toes. It is hard to walk without toes because they help us balance. For the rest of my time growing up, I remembered the great difficulty that boy had, so I learned to fear the lawn mower. No, I don't lie awake at night thinking it was going to come out of the garage and get me, but when I start the mower, I have my children stand back out of the way. And when I push it, I always remember how quickly that spinning blade can do great damage. My fear of the lawn mower caused me to be respectful of its power, and to do nothing that could lead to harm in my life.

Our fear of God should likewise cause us to respect His power, and do nothing that could lead to His displeasure and consequent chastisement. While it is true that we can now boldly come to Christ, we must always remember *who* He is: He is always God. If we cultivate this kind of fear, we will realize that there is great benefit in fearing Him. Here are some of the benefits that are ours through fearing the Lord.

- **Fearing the Lord shows us what can last forever:** "The fear of the Lord is clean, enduring forever" (Psalm 19:9). If you will attach your life and all your desires to Him, what you do, what you are, and what you have will last for eternity.
- **Fearing the Lord gives eternal wisdom:** "The fear of the Lord is the beginning of wisdom; a good understanding have all those who do His commandments" (Psalm 111:10). Fearing God and obedience always go together. If you fear God, you will obey Him.
- **Fearing the Lord reflects the eternal character of Christ:** "The Spirit of the Lord shall rest upon Him [the promised Christ], the Spirit of wisdom and understanding, the Spirit of counsel and might, the Spirit of knowledge and of the fear of the Lord. His delight is in the fear of the LORD" (Isaiah 11:2–3). This is a prophecy of Christ, like the one in Isaiah: the seven-fold Spirit of God—the complete ministry of the Holy Spirit through Jesus Christ. When we fear Him, as we yield to His Spirit, we will reflect the holy character of our triune God and be walking in Christlikeness.
- **Fearing the Lord produces eternal riches:** "Wisdom and knowledge will be the stability of your times, and the strength of salvation; the fear of the Lord is His treasure" (Isaiah 33:6). Our real treasure is found in fearing the Lord; even things like economic upheavals cannot take that treasure away.

This is the wonder of Christ: you can make a decision right now that will totally transform how you experience Him. Remove the idea that you are just a spectator and engage yourself by participating fully in worship and service to Him, whether at church or in daily life. As you ponder what has been said—all that lines up with the Word of God—respond wholeheartedly by saying "Yes!" to the Lord.

TUESDAY: Holiness Is Staying Pure

*We should **live soberly, righteously, and godly** in the present age, looking for the blessed hope and glorious appearing of our great God and Savior Jesus Christ.*
—Titus 2:12–13

The fear of the Lord prompts us to seek to be as pure as possible on this sin-cursed earth, and that leads to personal holiness. If you want to advance your walk with the Lord, this exhortation is critical: "Having these promises [the Word of God], beloved, let us cleanse ourselves from all filthiness of the flesh" (2 Corinthians 7:1a).

The apostle Paul said that he was as susceptible to picking up the filth of the flesh as we are. He abhorred it, so he purposefully closed the door to it. Every time we leave the door open through anger, an unforgiving and bitter spirit, lust, or an insubordinate and rebellious attitude toward authorities, it is like letting wild animals come into our house. If a tiger had escaped from your local zoo and was prowling your neighborhood, would you go to bed that night and leave your door open?

Shut the door to temptations. Listen to how Peter encouraged those early saints of Roman Asia in his first letter: "Be sober, be vigilant; because your adversary the devil walks about like a roaring lion, seeking whom he may devour" (1 Peter 5:8).

The devil wants to discourage us and make us doubt God's power and promises. That is what Paul warned us about. We must not give the devil a foothold in our lives through sin (see Ephesians 4:25–32). The instant we are aware of any wrong decision and filthiness of the flesh, we should seek Jesus Christ's cleansing. But there is also filthiness of the spirit, which is coming to God unprepared. Again look at what Paul said to cleanse: "filthiness of the flesh **and spirit**" (2 Corinthians 7:1b).

God wants us to have cleanness of the flesh and of the spirit. If you were invited to an event honoring a dignitary, but it required formal dress, would you attend in old ragged clothes and dirty tennis shoes? If so, you would not be allowed in. Why? Dignitaries deserve respect; they demand respect. Therefore, you must come before God with the right attitude and make sure you are not holding on to sin. You must cleanse yourself from all filthiness of the flesh and spirit in order to be "perfecting holiness in the fear of God" (2 Corinthians 7:1c).

This touching story reflects the lifestyle we are to cultivate: A teen once demonstrated this heart attitude when his friends suggested that they go to a certain restaurant for a good time. "I'd rather go home; my parents don't approve of that place." "Afraid your father will hurt you?" one of the girls asked sarcastically. "No," he replied, "I'm not afraid my father will hurt me, but I am afraid I might hurt him."

Young people: love your parents' desires so much that you don't want to go against them. A true child of God, who has experienced the love of God, has no desire to sin against that love. That is how you will know when you have reached adulthood. Be motivated by love. Obey God, not because you are afraid that He will punish you, but because you love Him so much that you don't want to ruin your relationship with Him—you don't want His Spirit to be grieved and quenched.

WEDNESDAY: Holiness Is Making Right Choices

*"****Choose*** *. . . this day* ***whom you will serve****. . . . But as for me and my house, we will serve the* L̲O̲R̲D̲*."*

—Joshua 24:15

Clearly, having a reverential fear of God is not optional: "Be zealous for the fear of the LORD all the day; for surely there is a hereafter, and your hope will not be cut off" (Proverbs 23:17–18). We are to "fear Him who is able to destroy both soul and body in hell" (Matthew 10:28).

We do not have to fear that our soul is going to go to hell, but we do need to fear that God will destroy our body if we do not repent of sin. The chastisement of Jesus Christ goes from conviction of sin, to the grieving of the Holy Spirit, to the quenching of the Holy Spirit, to weakness of the body, to sickness of the body, then to death. This is clearly taught in 1 Corinthians 11, 1 John 5, and Revelation 2–3.

Fearing God has both positive and negative elements: "Obey in all things . . . , fearing God" (Colossians 3:22). In a positive way, every true believer has reverential fear of God—an awesome awareness of His power, His holiness, and His glory. Proper worship always includes that kind of fear of the Lord.

"The negative aspect," writes John MacArthur,

has to do with dread and terror. Even believers should have a measure of that kind of fear, which acts as a protection from sinning. The writer of Proverbs observed, 'By the fear of the Lord one keeps away from evil' (16:6). For the very reason they are God's children, believers are subject to His chastisement (see Heb. 12:5–11). Sometimes His dealing with disobedient believers can be severe, as with Ananias and Sapphira, who lost their lives for lying to the Holy Spirit. God used that punishment to produce godly fear and obedience within the early church (see Acts 5:1–11). Some of the believers in the church at Corinth also died or became ill by the direct infliction of God's chastisement for their sin (1Corinthains 11:30).[1]

Every day we face this choice: serve Christ or the world. The letters in Revelation have a timely application for our lives. They each emphasize why and how we must fear Jesus.

- **Ephesus (2:1–7):** Remember that Jesus is jealous of your love, so lay hold of your first love for Christ.
- **Smyrna (2:8–11):** Hope in Jesus through life until the end and trust Christ through your suffering.
- **Pergamos (2:12–17):** Rest in the security that comes from clinging only to Jesus, and conform to Christ, not the world.
- **Thyatira (2:18–29):** Fear the chastening love of Jesus so He will not have to discipline sin in the church.

As it was in Thyatira, so it is in your life today. Daily you have opportunities to either please God or please self. But for a devoted believer, there is only one right choice: honor the holiness of Jesus by purposing in your heart to respond in obedience to Him regardless of the cost.

THURSDAY: Holiness Is Pleasing Jesus

*We urge . . . that you should abound more and more, just as you received from us how **you ought** to walk and **to please God**.*
—1 Thessalonians 4:1

In the first chapter of Revelation, John captures several characteristics of Christ that point to fearing the Lord. Each characteristic is a wonderful lesson to meditate on throughout the day.

Jesus is God the Son. The "Son of God" in Revelation 2:18 is not the same as the "Son of Man" in Revelation 1:13. "Son of God" signifies the fullness of His divine power. Why does He introduce himself as the Son of God? He is warning His church not to compromise nor tolerate evil.

Jesus is all-seeing, all-knowing, and always present. He has "eyes like flames of fire" (1:14). Why does He say that? Because Christ is always penetrating, discerning, seeing, and assessing the thoughts and actions of man: "I, the LORD, search the heart, I test the mind, even to give every man according to his ways." And, "there is no creature hidden from His sight, but all things are . . . open to the eyes of Him to whom we must give account"(Jeremiah 17:10; Hebrews 4:13).

Jesus is the Judge of the entire universe, and of my sin. He has feet like "burnished bronze" (1:15a). Bronze almost always pictures judgment upon sin: "For the Father judges no one, but has committed all judgment to the Son" (John 5:22).

The author of Revelation is the Son of God, the Lord Jesus Christ, with fullness of divine power, with searching eyes, who alone knows our hearts and will mete out judgment accordingly. Always remember that Jesus Christ knows your heart perfectly well today, and is ready to judge if necessary.

Before Jesus addressed the corruption in the church at Thyatira, He acknowledged these good things about its saints: "I know your works, love, service, faith, and your patience; and as for your works, the last are more than the first" (Revelation 2:19).

Jesus commended the Thyatirans for these qualities: Christ saw what they did for Him; He saw their love (this is the only church with love noted); their ministry as servants to others; their faithfulness, loyalty, and fidelity; their steadfast endurance; and that they were growing because their latter deeds were greater than those at the beginning.

Here is a lesson to meditate upon: The Christian life is a life of works, love, service, faith, and patience. Christ commended the saints at Thyatira because they did not pull back in their service. Paul gave the Thessalonians a similar commendation: "We . . . thank God always for you . . . because your faith grows exceedingly, and the love of every one of you all abounds toward each other" (2 Thessalonians 1:3). The spiritual lives of these Thessalonians did not hit a peak and then decline. If Christ is alive in you, there will be growth. No growth indicates that you are sick, and that you need to honor Christ's holiness by returning to Him.

If you can remember a time when you served and loved the Lord more than now, you need to repent, or end up like the Thyatirans who failed to receive the approval of Christ. The Lord wants you to ever-increasingly love, seek, and worship Him!

FRIDAY: Holiness Is Staying Scriptural

"He who has My commandments and keeps them . . . loves Me. And he who loves Me will be loved by My Father, and I will love him and manifest Myself to him."

—John 14:21

What did the visiting Christ say that He had against the church at Thyatira? He said that there was toleration of evil in the assembly. Does that mean we shouldn't bring the lost to church? No, bring them—just don't start parading them as saints, redeemed ones, and part of the body of Christ. What was the evil? They allowed a disobedient and sinful woman to teach them: "I have a few things against you, because you allow that woman Jezebel, who calls herself a prophetess, to teach and [seduce] My servants" (Revelation 2:20). Who was Jezebel? She may have been the wife of a pastor or a powerful false teacher who was leading the church astray.

There is a heritage of women who have educated generations of young people. They have a gender specific role in the church, as they have in the family. However, they are not to be the primary teacher or leader of a church. This is normal; the world is abnormal. God said women are not to teach *the* church (1 Timothy 2:12), but they may teach *in* the church. Women are not less or inferior; God simply gave women a specific role that is subordinate. Jesus is subordinate to God the Father; the church is subordinate to Jesus Christ; men are subordinate to the church; and women are subordinate to men. Jesus is not less than God. This is how God ordained things. But the Thyatirans decided not to obey that divine order.

Women being in submission to men in the home and the church has its roots in Creation, not the Fall. This is mandatory in Christ's church: women are not to lead the assembly (1 Timothy 2:12–14; 1 Corinthians 14). But this Jezebel defied God's order and was leading Christ's bondservants astray. However, that was not new. In 1 Kings 18, Ahab's Jezebel led Israel into gross idolatry and introduced male and female sex perverts into the priesthood of Baal worship. The falsehoods of Christian Science were started by Mary Baker Eddy. Theosophy's errors were propounded by Annie Besant and Madame Blavatsky. Seventh Day Adventism was led astray in the teachings of Ellen White, and so forth. Beware of women who go against God's Word and lead churches, for they will face judgment.

What can we learn from today's lesson? Be scriptural and be balanced. We should not be hardhearted, legalistic, Ephesus-like Christians who harshly judge others and punish with loveless indifference. Neither should we be weak and limp, tolerating all in love, with no rules and no offense. Both legalism and undue tolerance lead to error and judgment. Be scriptural: know it and do it. Be balanced: love with a pure heart, and hate sin.

SATURDAY: Holiness Is Trusting Christ's Promises

"And he who overcomes, and keeps My works until the end, to him I will give power over the nations—'He shall rule them with a rod of iron; they shall be dashed to pieces like the potter's vessels'—I also have received from My Father; and I will give him the morning star. "He who has an ear, let him hear what the Spirit says to the churches."

—Revelation 2:26–29

In Revelation 2:25, when Jesus says, "Hold fast what you have till I come," He is making the first mention of His return in the seven letters. There are many precious promises concerning Christ's coming to remember. I'll share some of them with you now.

God will reward us with immeasurable treasures. This is an investment that will reap blessings which will never pass away: "There is no One who has left house or brothers or sisters or father or mother or wife or children or lands, for My sake and the gospel's, who shall not receive a hundredfold now in this time— . . . and in the age to come, eternal life" (Mark 10:29–30).

God will overwhelm us with unbelievable pleasures. When we reach heaven, we will finally become all that God created us to be: "He was caught up into Paradise and heard inexpressible words, which it is not lawful for a man to utter" (2 Corinthians 12:4).

God will give true believers an important future. We will reign with Christ over the earth. I do not know what each of our specific duties will be, but we will have authority: "To him I will give power over the nations—'He shall rule them with a rod of iron; They shall be dashed to pieces like the potter's vessels'—as I also have received from My Father" (Revelation 2:26b-27).

God will give true believers a bright and glorious future. We can never lose Jesus' light, life, and hope in the dark and gloom, so we are on the winning team with Christ! Consider these precious promises: Jesus is "the Dayspring from on high" and salvation is described as when "the day dawns and the morning star rises in [our] hearts" (Luke 1:78; 2 Peter 1:19). What glory lies ahead for us! For "there shall be no night there: they need no lamp nor light of the sun, for the Lord God gives them light. And they shall reign forever and ever" (Revelation 22:5). All true believers will make it safely to the end. Hallelujah!

Make a choice to live in hope. You cannot experience these pleasures if you come before God with unclean hands and filthiness of heart and spirit. Are you tolerating evil? Stop. Are you growing in Christ? If not, start. Are you pressing on to the end? Good—you're an overcomer!

WEEK 18
Know Christ Personally

{ Revelation 3:1–6 }

This week as we approach the end of days, you can find hope as you make sure that you know Christ personally!

SUNDAY: Professing without Possessing

*"Not everyone who says to Me, 'Lord, Lord,' shall enter the kingdom of heaven, but he who does the will of My Father in heaven. Many will say to Me in that day, 'Lord, Lord, have we not prophesied in Your name, cast out demons in Your name, and done many wonders in Your name?' And then I will declare to them, '**I never knew you**; depart from Me, you who practice lawlessness!'"*

—Matthew 7:21–23

Sardis was a church planted in a very famous city of the ancient world—the home of Aesop and his fables. Situated at the junction of five roads, commanding the Hermus Valley, thirty miles northwest of Philadelphia, Sardis was a very wealthy commercial city. It had been the capital of King Croesus, who was proverbial for his riches. The city's easy wealth apparently made them lax when it came to being alert to possible dangers.

Because Sardis lacked preparedness, it was conquered twice: by Cyrus the Persian (549 B.C.) and by Antiochus (218 B.C.). The city was built on a hill so steep that its defenses seemed impregnable. Yet on both occasions, enemy troops scaled the precipice by night and found that the overconfident Sardians had set no guard.

John does not mention anything like the persecutions at Smyrna and Pergamos, or the heresies of the Nicolaitans. It is worth noting, however, that this church differs from those at Pergamos and Thyatira, which also had mixed memberships. In those churches the unsaved members were in a minority, but at Sardis they were predominate. In Christ's letter to the Sardian assembly, He stated that only a few of them had not defiled their garments and thus were worthy to walk with Him (Revelation 3:4).

When Christ visited the church body at Sardis, He said to them, "I know your works, that you have a name that you are alive, but you are dead" (Revelation 3:1c). He reached out to check their vital signs and, as the great Bible teacher Dr. Lehman Strauss once put it, "The Great Physician felt their pulse [and] pronounced them dead." They had degenerated from holiness to phoniness.

Oh, the dreadful condition of being artificial! Many people know only the appearance and not the reality of Jesus Christ. Do *you* know the difference between appearance and reality? God does! In every generation He has had to pronounce this woe against certain ones: "These people draw near Me with their mouths, and honor Me with their lips, but have removed their hearts far from Me" (Isaiah 29:13).

Think of the excruciating eternal impact of being busy and active in the church—but ending up unknown by Jesus Christ! Is your heart in the same place that your mouth is saying you are? You talk and sing about the Lord, and perhaps even teach a class, but does your *heart* belong to Him?

My Prayer for You This Week: *Dear Lord Jesus, as You wrote this letter to the church at Sardis, You warned about the danger of those who professed something they never possessed. And while You were here on earth, one of Your constant emphases was dislodging people from a false sense of security—those who thought they were in the kingdom because they were Abraham's seed, circumcised, going to the temple, sacrificing, giving, and serving—but had no heart for change.*

We pray that You would show us that the only true riches are in possessing Jesus Christ. To profess a knowledge of You, and yet to not possess that life-giving, life-changing, born-again relationship with You, is the most horrible deadly condition we could be in. Oh Lord, open our eyes to behold Your wonderful truths! Thank You for the blessing of Your Word! Let Your Spirit pierce our hearts with the assurance of true riches in Christ. We pray in the lovely name of Jesus, and for His glory. Amen.

MONDAY: Professors Not Possessors

"Remember . . . how you have received and heard; **hold fast and repent***."*
—Revelation 3:3a

Jesus spared no words to convey His utter contempt for religious charlatans producing only the false fruits of self-righteousness. Perhaps the strongest warnings ever uttered in His earthly ministry came from the heart of the loving Savior whenever He came across phonies—the religious fakes, the "stuffed shirts," the con-men and women with false pretenses who only appeared to be His. Some of His most graphic illustrations were about these Christian look-alikes.

Jesus warned: "Beware of false prophets, who come to you in sheep's clothing, but inwardly they are ravenous wolves" (Matthew 7:15). Such people live for their own desires—like animals. Instead of loving and serving others, they "use them," like objects, for their own gain. Jesus called them fruitless trees that were to be "cut down and thrown into the fire" (Matthew 7:19).

Jesus said that it does not matter whether you have made a profession, been circumcised, joined a church, or been baptized. None of those things really matter if you aren't a genuine fruit-bearer for Christ. Are you bearing fruit? The evidence of salvation is not reassurance from your parents that you prayed for salvation as a little child, or someone else saying, "I remember when you went forward at that crusade, and you wrote it in your Bible." You are a Christian and will go to heaven if the Spirit of God is bearing fruit in your life. When Jesus came and knelt beside the still and cold body of the church at Sardis and felt their pulse, He pronounced it dead.

Jesus pointed to the shocked church workers who never really knew Him personally: "Not everyone who says to Me, 'Lord, Lord,' shall enter the kingdom of heaven, but he who does the will of My Father" (Matthew 7:21). Fruit bearing is a result of a transformed heart, an internal prompting that longs to do the will of God. Though no child of God can perfectly or always do His will, there is an ever-growing desire that says: "No longer I, but Christ—not my will, but Yours be done."

At the beginning of Matthew 13, through the story of the sower and the seed, Jesus compared the church to a grain field. The seed falling on the first three types of soil represents people who are not truly born again. Only the seed in the fourth type of soil represents One who will go to heaven. Some people bring forth a little fruit, some more; however, everyone who is born again produces fruit. You cannot get to heaven without salvation; this involves a true saving faith that changes your life and results in godly fruit.

When we lead people to Christ, we will know that they are really saved if they start bearing fruit. A lot of people *profess* Christ but do not *possess* Him. So in Matthew 13:30, Jesus tells us, "Let those who profess to love Me stay in the church. At the harvest, the judgment, they will be gathered up and burned." His verdict: fire, judgment, and hell for those in the visible church who do not bear fruit.

Jesus says that those who profess Christ but do not possess Him, are like fancy cups fouled with filth on the insides: "Woe to you . . . hypocrites! For you cleanse the outside of the cup and dish, but inside . . . are full of extortion and self-indulgence" (Matthew 23:25–26).

This is a damning sin. This is the person who measures everything by what it will do for himself—whether a job, relationship, or service. Jesus was talking about people who tithed and went to the temple every day. But He saw through their hypocrisy.

Jesus described such people as "whitewashed tombs which indeed appear beautiful outwardly, but inside are full of dead men's bones and all uncleanness" (Matthew 23:27). Believers are filled with life that is endless, but lost people are walking coffins filled with death.

The wages of sin is death. There is a barrier between man and God—man's refusal to acknowledge God's prior claim to his life. Mankind is self-centered instead of God-centered. The Bible identifies this as rebellion, and calls it sin. Furthermore, the Bible declares that "the wages of sin is death," but God offers a solution: "The gift of God is eternal life in Christ Jesus our Lord" (Romans 6:23). Through the gift of His only Son, whose death on the cross paid the penalty for man's sin and rebellion, *God went the limit.* Now comes your part.

Are you willing to admit that God is right when He says you have rebelled? Do you recognize your need of a personal relationship with God? Because Jesus took the penalty for your sins, trust God that He will forgive you and give you eternal life. Accept the Bible's invitation: "Believe on the Lord Jesus Christ, and you will be saved" (Acts 16:31). The Bible also says that "if you confess with your mouth the Lord Jesus and believe in your heart that God has raised Him from the dead, you will be saved" (Romans 10:9). Simply speak to God and tell Him you want to change the direction of your sinful life by receiving Jesus. That is the repentance God wants to work in your life. Then confess Jesus as your Lord, and you will find true living hope for the end of days as He produces the fruit of His salvation in your life—His love, His joy, and His peace.

TUESDAY: Some Horrible Biographies

> *"If you will not watch, I will come upon you as a thief*, and you will not know what hour I will come upon you."
> —Revelation 3:3b

These Sardians professed the truth without possessing Christ personally. God says that such hypocrites will face this final end: "His winnowing fan is in His hand, and He will thoroughly clean out His threshing floor, and gather His wheat [the fruit-bearing ones] into the barn [heaven]; but He will burn up the chaff [unsaved ones] with unquenchable fire [hell]" (Matthew 3:12).

There are many Scripture writers who record horror stories of **false believers** who are called dogs, pigs, wolves, thistles, fire, and rotten fruit. All of these are destined for destruction:

- **The Cains** grow up near paradise, hearing about God from faithful parents, but do not choose to know the true God. They depart, and never look back at Jesus Christ (Genesis 4).
- **The Esaus** sell an eternally valuable spiritual inheritance for a moment of fleshly desire. They find no place of repentance, and thus miss the heavenly city (Genesis 25–38).
- **The Balaams** want to die the death of the righteous, but live the life of rebellion and greed. They, too, will be going to hell (Numbers 22–24).
- **The Pharisees** face damnation because they live hygienically sterile lives, having an exterior holiness but corrupted and rotting hearts (Matthew 23).
- **The Judases** live around Jesus for years, hearing and seeing Him daily, but inwardly they only grow colder and harder by the year (John 19).
- **The modern-day liberal churches** are the dead, liberal, cold, and lifeless churches that keep the gospel in a coffin. The Great Physician pronounces *them* dead!

Is it possible in this great era of the church that your heart is also cold, dark, and empty? In the cathedral of Lubeck, Germany, there is an engraving from the Middle Ages entitled "The Lament of Jesus Christ Against the Ungrateful World." The engraving from that church wall, copied below, beautifully reflects our Lord's teaching on this subject:

Thus speaketh Christ our Lord to us,
You call Me master and obey Me not,
You call Me light and see Me not,
You call Me the way and walk Me not,
You call Me life and live Me not,
You call Me wise and follow Me not,
You call Me fair and love Me not,
You call Me rich and ask Me not,
You call Me eternal and seek Me not,
If I condemn thee, blame Me not.

Ponder this message today: God *hates* profession without possession. Beware if you are merely a pretender. The only one being fooled is you, not God. Stop and do what Paul advises in 2 Corinthians 13:5—examine yourself. Look for evidence that the Holy Spirit lives within your life. His presence brings love for God, spiritual hunger for the Word, a desire to repent from sin, a longing for holiness, and a genuine desire to serve and sacrifice for others.

WEDNESDAY: When Jesus Visits

*"His head and hair were white like wool, as white as snow, and **His eyes like a flame of fire.**"*
—REVELATION 1:14

What did Jesus say to the assembly at Sardis? He told them, "I want you to meet with Me again. I am the Lord Jesus Christ, and I know everything about you." Jesus stood by them, waiting for a pulse, saying, "You are in church, and appear to be alive, but when I check your pulse, there is no life."

Jesus is all-knowing, all-powerful, and ever-present. He is the One who sees and knows all as He speaks to the churches; He is the One who holds their message, their witness, and their existence; and He is the One who stands by their lampstand.

Look again at verse 1 of Revelation 3: "I know your works, that you have a name that you are alive, but you are dead." Note that Christ gives no approval to the Sardians. God won't tolerate phonies; nor will He tolerate mere caretaker-Christianity. His way is life, growth, and fruit—or nothing. They were dead; their deeds were incomplete. They were still reciting the creed, saying their prayers, but the fire was absent. Remember: "Man looks at the outward appearance, but the LORD looks at the heart" (1 Samuel 16:7c)!

Their deeds had not come to maturity; there was no fully formed fruit. They were dying in the bud, an unformed fruit dropping that was worm-eaten, stunted, and dying.

Jesus appealed: "Be **watchful**, and **strengthen** the things which remain, that are ready to die, for I have not found your works perfect before God. **Remember** therefore how you have received and heard; **hold fast** and **repent**" (Revelation 3:2–3).

Consider these five imperatives from the Lord of the Church:

1. **Be watchful.** The word "watchful" (*agrupneo* in Greek) that Jesus uses in Revelation 3:2 expresses the idea of "being wakeful, sleepless, as the watchfulness of One who is intent upon a thing." It comes from two Greek words meaning "to chase sleep."
2. **Strengthen that which remains.** The word "strengthen" is often in Paul's writing. It means "buttress, build a strong support, get grounded."
3. **Remember.** "Remember" (a present imperative) means "keep on remembering the Word of God."
4. **Hold fast.** This basically means to "keep on, never stop, be not wavering, do not be on again and then off again."
5. **Repent.** Repentance is the answer—the hope not only for the Sardians, but also for us today. Make a conscious choice to say no to sin by definitive action once and for all.

Our Lord called upon the few faithful at Sardis to be vigilant. He urged them to strive to strengthen and revive what remained but was at the point of death. Sardis was conquered twice, which should serve as a warning to us to not be overconfident as Christians. No commandment appears more frequently in the New Testament than this: "Watch." We must therefore be watchful, continually on guard, so that we don't lose our first love.

THURSDAY: How to Defeat the Devil Daily

He who sins is of the devil. . . . For this purpose the Son of God was manifested, that He might destroy the works of the devil.

—1 JOHN 3:8

It has been said that "eternal vigilance is the price of liberty"; similarly, it could be said that "eternal watchfulness is the price of salvation." Watchfulness should be the constant attitude of the Christian life. "It is high time," said Paul, "to awake out of sleep" (Romans 13:11). He exhorts, "Watch, stand fast in your faith, be brave, be strong" (1 Corinthians 16:13).

Watch out for the prowling lion—Satan. "The devil walks about like a roaring lion, seeking whom he may devour" (1 Peter 5:8). The Christian must constantly be on the watch against the wiles of the devil (Ephesians 6:10–13). The history of Sardis had its vivid examples of what happens to the garrison whose watch is slack. As Christians, we likewise face continual attack by the powers that seek to seduce us from our loyalty to Christ. Often these attacks are subtle; therefore, we must be ever on guard. God expects us to resist or fight Satan. We are never to turn our backs on our battles; there is no defensive gear in the armor of God to cover our backsides. Face the Devil; resist him using the shield of faith, the helmet of salvation, the sword of the Spirit, the armor, and prepared feet (Ephesians 6:14–18).

Watch out for the crouching monster of sin. In the Christian life there must be unceasing vigilance: "Watch and pray," said Jesus, "lest you enter into temptation" (Matthew 26:41). Temptation waits for our unguarded moments and then attacks. Sin, however, is even worse than Satan. Satan is defeated, so all we have to do is this: (1) speak the Word of God, (2) resist, and (3) stand our ground. (See James 4:6–7.) But God says that sin is *so bad* that we must run or flee from it (2 Timothy 2:22), and then He will deliver you.

Watch out for the unexpected coming of Jesus. The New Testament repeatedly urges Christians to be on the watch for the coming of our Lord: "You do not know on what hour your Lord is coming.... What I say to you, I say to all: 'Watch!'" (Matthew 24:42–43; Mark 13:37; 2 Thessalonians 5:6). In my own life, the greatest deterrent to sin is that I do not know when Jesus is coming. I stay watchful because I do not want Him to come and find me doing something that dishonors or displeases Him.

Watch out for your "last day." No man knows the day and the hour when eternity will invade time for him. "The last day is a secret," says Augustine, "that every day may be watched." A man should live every day as if it were his last.

We must also avoid the permeating evil of false doctrine. The Christian must be on the watch against false teaching. In Paul's last address to the elders of Ephesus he warned them that grievous wolves would invade the flock from without and within, and men would arise to speak perverse things. "Therefore," said Paul, "watch!" (See Acts 20:29–31.)

Respond to the tireless eyes of Jesus. Never forget that even as we must watch for Jesus Christ, so Jesus Christ is watching us! "I have not found your works perfect," said the risen Christ, "in the sight of my God" (Revelation 3:2). Christ is looking for something from us. We so often regard Him as the One to whom we look for things: His strength, His help, His support, His comfort. But we must never forget that He is looking for our love, our loyalty, and our service.

The things a man must do lie in his hand. This old saying is true: "Fate is what we must do; destiny is what we are meant to do." The Christian does not believe in an inescapable fate, but he does believe in a destiny that he can accept or refuse.

Jesus Christ is looking for something *from* each of us, and there is something He wants done *by* each of us. Is there an area in your life that the Lord wants you to surrender? Is He leading you to give something of worth to someone else? Could He be leading you to spend more time with Him in prayer? Pray about the possibilities, and then make yourself readily available to however He leads.

FRIDAY: Living in Assurance

*"You have **a few** names even in Sardis **who have not defiled their garments**; and they shall walk with Me in white, for they are worthy."*

—Revelation 3:4

Do you realize that we are to put on and wear Christ as our garment? For Christ said, "He who overcomes shall be clothed in white garments" (Revelation 3:5a). In Romans 13:14 we are told: "Put on the Lord Jesus Christ, and make no provision for the flesh, to fulfill its lusts." So whenever you get dressed, ask yourself: *Would Jesus approve of what I am wearing?*

Evaluating in this manner should change the way some of us dress. Jesus does not want us to wear anything that would draw attention away from the holiness of God. Yet our culture does that all the time. The more you are conformed to today's immodest culture, the more you will allow your body to dishonor God. As the beautiful hymn expresses below, every day we are wearing Christ, so we should consciously consider whether our clothing reflects all that He is to us as our righteous and holy Redeemer. As one great reformer wrote in his hymn, "Jesus, Thy Blood and Righteousness":

Jesus, thy blood and righteousness
My beauty are, my glorious dress;
'Midst flaming worlds, in these arrayed,
With joy shall I lift up my head.
Bold shall I stand in thy great day,
For who aught to my charge shall lay?
Fully absolved through these I am—
From sin and fear, from guilt and shame.
Lord, I believe were sinners more
Than sands upon the ocean shore,
Thou hast for all, a ransom paid,
For all a full atonement made.

—Nicolaus L. von Zinzendorf (1700–1760)
Translated by John Wesley (1703–1791)

SATURDAY: Embrace Christ

***He who has the Son has life**; he who does not have the Son of God does not have life.*

—1 John 5:12

WEEK 18: KNOW CHRIST PERSONALLY

Know that Christ holds you: *"He who overcomes . . . I will not blot out his name from the Book of Life"* (Revelation 3:5b). This does not indicate that we can lose our salvation. To have your name kept in the Book of Life means that you are saved. Can you lose your salvation? Scripture clearly says no! In Sardis, the king could blot you out if he did not like you, but not in the kingdom of God. True believers will never have their names blotted out.

A true believer does not practice sin; a counterfeit believer cannot help but practice sin, because he does not have God's new nature within him. But these words were not written so that you and I might judge other people. The words were inspired so that we may examine ourselves. I exhort you to answer these questions honestly before God:

- Do I have the Holy Spirit within me, or am I merely pretending to be a Christian? In other words, am I merely professing rather than possessing new life in Christ?
- Do I cultivate my walk in the Spirit by daily Bible reading and prayer?
- Has any unconfessed sin defiled my inner person? Am I willing to confess and forsake it?
- Do I allow my old nature to control my thoughts and desires, or does the divine nature rule me? When temptation comes, do I "play with it" or flee from it? Do I immediately yield to the Spirit of God within me?
- Is there life and growth and fruit in my life—or nothing?

Warren Wiersbe once told a great story about a Sunday school teacher who was explaining the Christian's old and new natures to a class of teenagers:

"Our old nature came from Adam," he explained, "and our new nature comes from Christ, who is called 'the Last Adam.'" He had the class read 1 Corinthians 15:45: So also it is written, "The first man, Adam, became a living soul." The Last Adam became a life-giving spirit (NASB). "This means there are two 'Adams' living in me," said one of the teenagers. "That's right," the teacher replied. "And what is the practical value of this truth?" The class was silent for a moment, and then a student spoke up. "This idea of the 'two Adams' really helps me in fighting temptation," he said. "When temptation comes knocking at my door, if I send the first Adam to answer, I'll sin. But if I send the Last Adam, I'll get victory."[1]

The life that is real is honest with God about these vital issues.

Make a choice to live in hope. Here is what living in hope is all about: "I will confess [your] name before My Father and before His angels" (Revelation 3:5c). If you are a true believer, one day you will "be taken by the hand by the Lord Jesus, to be led up past the marshaled ranks of the angels, up along the golden boulevards of glory, up past the cherubim and the seraphim, up, up, to the Throne of God Himself and . . . hear the Lord Jesus call you by your name and present you in person as His well beloved!"[2] Next, you will hear the Father saying, "Bring the best robe and put it on My child." Picture it: a robe of white, bright as the day, and pure as the light!

When the Lord Jesus was transfigured on the mount, something happened not only to His countenance but also to His clothes. His raiment became white as the light. What a reward for faithfulness—to have a robe like that draped around your shoulders and to be invited to walk the shining ways of glory in light-transfigured clothes! Even Solomon in all his glory was never arrayed like one of these!

This week you have seen the way to know Christ more personally. Does He know your name? Are you robed in white? Wake up and be watchful! If you think that perhaps you have only been professing Christ, and not possessing Him, ask Him to convict your heart right now, and, as your holy Advocate, to argue for your righteousness by pleading His blood shed for you. If you have truly prayed in faith, thank Him that now He will be able to confess your name before His Father in heaven. Then, in these closing precious moments, let the Son of God enfold you with His Spirit and His love.

WEEK 19
Enjoy Christ's Approval

{ Revelation 3:7–13 }

This week as we approach the end of days, you can find hope as you enjoy Christ's approval!

SUNDAY: Flight 961 to Eternity

You do not know what will happen tomorrow. For what is your life? It is even a vapor that appears for a little time and then vanishes away.
—JAMES 4:14

Thanksgiving Day, 1996: It was a typical flight—one that occurs thousands of times every day around the world. Ethiopian Air Flight 961 took off November 23, 1996, from Addis Ababa. Onboard were 163 passengers and twelve crewmembers. Among those flying that day were Mr. and Mrs. Andy Meakins. Andy, an elder at the International Evangelical Church of Addis, at one time pastored that large Bible-believing church. In less than two hours, more than 120 people died, including five from that church. Andy, a good friend of mine, did not survive the crash.

Somewhere near Kenya, the horrifying hijack began. Escaped convicts, brandishing an ax and a supposed bomb, stormed the flight deck, savagely beating the copilot and throwing him down. They then ordered the pilot to turn the plane eastward. In spite of the plane's dangerously low fuel tank, he was forced to submit to their demands. The pilot kept pleading for a refueling stop, but to no avail. The hijackers threatened to blow up the plane if he didn't comply. After trying to hug the coast of Africa, the pilot attempted to make it to the Indian Ocean island of Comoros. When it became evident they would not make it, the captain announced to the cabin passengers: "Listen, guys, we're all dead people. There is no argument now." "People began to scream," one witness said, "and others began to pray."

The crash is now well known: a Japanese honeymooning couple filmed the descent, dip of a wing, the flip, the crash, and the disintegration of the 767 over the water. News reports, however, never contained what was in a fax to me from Andy Meakin's wife. This is what she told her church: "As soon as the captain told us we were going to crash I heard the distinct snap of my husband's seat belt. He was up and out of his chair. Going down the aisle row by row he earnestly shared the gospel of Christ with any who would listen. Before the sickening screech of twisting metal and the 110 mph crash of our plane into the water, Andy had signaled me that 20 passengers had trusted in Jesus for their salvation. Andy never made it back to the safety of his seat belt. But he took twenty souls with him to paradise."

You see, there was a safe spot in that plane—a shelter where no twisted wreckage could permanently harm—a haven that no crushing impact could erase. Andy knew and shared the divine directions with those souls being rushed into eternity: "God's directions are the only way to make it to happiness now and forever!" He knew how to escape the plane before it was too late for eternity. Do you know those directions? Are you following them? Are you sharing them with those whom God has placed around you?

My Prayer for You This Week: *Thank You, dear Father, for our wonderful Lord Jesus Christ who has written a letter to both the church at Philadelphia and us. This is perhaps the most important letter we could ever read in the world—for it expresses what those who will be good and faithful servants are doing during their earthly lives. How we long for Your approval! Do we have Your approval? If not, what can we do? How can we live? What can we invest our life's breath in that will lead to Your saying, "Well done, good and faithful servant!"? That is what we long to be. We want to have Your spiritual ears today to hear what You have to say. We want to be doers of Your Word, like Andy Meakins, and not just hearers. To that end we commit ourselves and pray with expectancy for You to illumine our hearts and quicken our wills that we might have Your approval. In the lovely name of Jesus we pray. Amen.*

MONDAY: Seeking Christ's Approval

"**Well done**, good and faithful servant; **you were faithful** over a few things, I will make you ruler over many things. Enter into the joy of your lord."
—MATTHEW 25:21

The approval of those we love means so much, but there is an approval that far surpasses what anyone on earth can offer us. When our lives are over, our last breaths have been taken, and time has ceased to exist for us, all things on earth fade away quickly. In fact, as we weaken and approach death, the fading starts even before we die. At such a time, our thoughts ought to center more and more on the joy of seeing our beloved Lord and Savior, Jesus Christ, and hearing Him say, "Well done!" Is that what you are living for?

We have come to Revelation 3:7–13, the sixth of seven letters our Lord Jesus wrote to seven literal, historic churches. Each church was given a powerful message from Christ. Each letter closes with an application to all to "hear what the Spirit says to the churches" (2:7, 11, 17, 29; 3:6, 13, 22).

Before we begin our study of this sixth letter, ask yourself: *Why did Christ not admonish this church for any error?* There are only two churches out of the seven that received the approval of Jesus—the assemblies at Smyrna and Philadelphia.

The reason for Christ's approval of those two churches is this: Smyrna was purified by obediently suffering persecution; Philadelphia was purified by obediently fulfilling God's commission and winning souls. Smyrna was triumphing through adversity; Philadelphia was ministering through opportunity. Smyrna was a suffering church; Philadelphia was a serving church. Smyrna was a church that stood alone; Philadelphia was a church that spoke out.

Like the Smyrnians, are you being purified as you obediently suffer persecution? Is God enabling you to triumph through adversity? Are you willing to stand alone for Christ in any situation? And are you, like the Philadelphians, obediently and joyfully telling people about Christ's offer of salvation? Are you ministering Christ to others in need? Do you speak out for Christ every chance you get?

Which of the six churches we've studied so far most represents your life right now? The two who received Christ's approval or the others who were subject to hearing His "I have this against you . . . "?

I pray that you are longing for His approval—to hear His "Well done, good and faithful servant!"

TUESDAY: Real People in a Real Place

*"To the angel of **the church in Philadelphia** write, 'These things says He who is holy, He who is true.'"*
—REVELATION 3:7A

Jesus wrote to the church at Philadelphia—a real place, with real people, experiencing real problems—to whom He offered real answers. Revelation 3:7 is the seventh time that the word "Philadelphia" is used in the New Testament. *Philadelphia* literally means "brotherly love." Hebrews 13:1 says, "Let brotherly love [Philadelphia] continue." What a name! What a church that must have been back in the first century! And we are to be the same kind of church today—a church for God's glory!

Philadelphia was located thirty miles southeast of Sardis, on the road to Laodicea. The most striking historical note about the city was the very frequent tremors and earthquakes that were characteristic of its area. It had been destroyed by earthquakes several times. Fissures, ground cracks, volcanic activity in thermal pools, hot mud, and regular tremors were common. In fact, at times (sometimes even weekly) the Philadelphians would have to grab their tents and go live outside of the city to be safe from shocks, aftershocks, and bigger quakes.

The frequent tremors and quakes in Philadelphia help us to better understand Christ's words in Revelation 3:12: "He who overcomes, I will make him a [stable] pillar in the temple of My God, and he shall go out no more." The saints at Philadelphia had seen everything dear to them devastated many times, but they had enduring safety in following Christ. For Jesus gave them a precious promise: "Live out My love in you, and someday you'll be safe with Me forever!"

The people of the assembly at Philadelphia realized, like those souls on Flight 961, that "the plane was about to crash"—the plane of this world, that is. Later on we will see just how bad the crash is going to be; but for now, we need to understand that at the end of the world one out of every two people will die a gruesome, unnatural death. There is no doubt about it: the world is headed for a devastating and deadly crash.

Before you are taken out of this world, you have the privilege of going up and down the aisles of this life to tell those who are afraid and lost how to find a permanent place of safety in Christ, our refuge. Are you willing to do that for them? For Jesus?

WEDNESDAY: Jesus Is Holy

> "I am the LORD your God. You shall therefore consecrate yourselves, and you shall **be holy; for I am holy**. Neither shall you defile yourselves with any creeping thing that creeps on earth."
> —LEVITICUS 11:44

What the Lord said in Leviticus has never changed. In fact, in Revelation 3:7 Jesus identified and introduced Himself as "He who is holy." There is no doubt about it: Jesus wants to remind us that He, as God the Son, is the holy, eternal God of the universe—"the High and Lofty One who inhabits eternity, **whose name is Holy**" (Isaiah 57:15).

Although God is referring to dietary laws at the end of Leviticus 11:44, there are worse things than that which "creeps on the earth." Many things on this earth defile us. In stark contrast, however, the preeminent feature of the character of God is holiness. Holiness is utter other-worldliness, a complete detachment from anything that is impure or unclean. There is a great gulf between what we are as fallen, defiled creatures and who God is in His eternal godhood. He is separate from all He has created, which is deteriorating. But God Himself is eternally self-existent; everything else derives its existence from Him.

Nothing will last forever that is not attached to God. When the tornado comes, the earthquake comes, or the plane is crashing, grab hold of that which will last forever: "I dwell in the high and holy place, with him who has a contrite and humble spirit, to revive the spirit of the humble, and to revive the heart of the contrite ones" (Isaiah 57:15). God says that He is holy, but we can dwell with Him. However, "the wicked are like the troubled sea, when it cannot rest, whose waters cast up mire and dirt. 'There is no peace,'" says my God, "for the wicked'" (Isaiah 57:20–21).

The wicked are like the sea churning up mire and dirt, or an overflowing sewer ditch. But the holy infinite God of the universe says that if you are contrite, and humble yourself, He will bring you out of that ditch by His grace (Psalm 40:2) so that you can dwell with Him. That is the wonderful gospel! A miraculous gift!

THURSDAY: Jesus Is the Truth

*The Son of God has ... given us an understanding, that we may **know Him who is true**; and we are in Him who is true, in His Son Jesus Christ. This is the **true God and eternal life**.*
—1 John 5:20

There is a lot of doctrine in that verse. Jesus is God, and our source of eternal life. John is particularly fond of that word "true." Paul describes the end of the age as a time of lawlessness and deception, but Jesus Christ is declared to be holy and true. When lawlessness surrounds us, He who is holy keeps His children safe; when deception abounds, there is One who is Truth.

Look at how Jesus introduced himself to the church at Philadelphia: "He who is holy, **He who is true**, 'He who has the key of David, He who opens and no one shuts, and shuts and no one opens'" (Revelation 3:7). The word for "true" in that verse is very specific. In Greek there are two words for true: *alethes* and *alethinos*. *Alethes* denotes the reality of the thing; that which is "true to fact." For example, "Hitler led Germany" is true to fact, but the *truth* is that he led them in error. *Alethinos* denotes "true" in the sense of "real, ideal, genuine."[1] The Greek word for "true" in Revelation 3:7 thus means "genuine truth"; Jesus Christ *is* Truth. When you confront Him face-to-face, you are facing Truth himself, and not merely true statements. As John MacArthur has said, "There is no substitute for God, and Jesus Christ is the genuine reality of God."

Jesus has the key of David. Except for Revelation 3:7, the only other place "the key of David" appears in the Word of God is in Isaiah 22. At that time, King Hezekiah was on the throne of Israel, and 185,000 Assyrian enemy soldiers were on their way. These fierce warriors had their tents, chariots, and all their battle gear with them; they covered a vast territory, which greatly intimidated the Israelites. But Hezekiah came out on the wall of the city, looked at all those Assyrian warriors, got down on his knees, and asked God to defeat them. That night, God sent one angel and killed them all!

What is this "key of David"? In Isaiah 22, the city of Jerusalem was weak; its walls were broken down, but its people had not even looked to their Maker for help. God said that He would therefore find a faithful servant through whom He would work. Shebna, the unfaithful steward of the king, had an unrepentant heart and was judged; but God found Eliakim to be a faithful servant, so he was entrusted with the royal authority of God to speak. In other words, God said, "I will give My authority to Eliakim." In Revelation 3:7 Jesus was saying, "That is what I am like. I am the faithful Son of God who has been entrusted with the authority of God." He continued, "If I open a door of ministry for you, no one can shut it. If I close a part of your life, no one can open it. You should trust My authority."

The "key of David" is all about Christ's authority. After Jesus healed the crippled man at the pool of Bethesda, people were so excited about His authority to heal that they gathered around Jesus and were willing to listen to Him speak: "He who hears My word and believes in Him who sent Me [Jesus has the key of authority] has everlasting life, and shall not come into judgment, but has passed from death into life.... The hour is coming ... when the dead will hear the voice of the Son of God; and those who hear will live" (John 5:24–25).

In that passage, Jesus is saying that all of us are dead, but if we can hear His voice, we can come alive. We are born spiritually dead and spiritually blind: "For as the Father has life in Himself, so He has granted the Son to have life in Himself, and has given Him authority to execute judgment also, because He is the Son of Man. Do not marvel at this; for the hour is coming in which all who are in the graves will hear His voice and come forth—those who have done good, to the resurrection of life, and those who have done evil, to the resurrection of condemnation" (John 5:26–29).

That resurrection has many parts. In 1 Corinthians 15:20–24, Paul speaks of multiple resurrections. There are resurrections that we will also be a part of in which the dead in Christ will rise first, and get their celestial bodies; those who are still alive will be caught up together with them, so both groups go up together. Jesus has all authority and judgment given to Him; this is the *"key of David"*—the authority of Christ; His voice can thus speak and the dead will rise.

What the people were when they went in the grave will reveal what they will be forever. If they went into the grave clothed with sin, they will be condemned to hell. Every time I think of that dreadful sentencing, I am so grateful that, though I am a sinner, I shall not die in my sins! My sins are gone and will never be remembered by God because Jesus, in His mercy, tenderly forgave me. I hope you know that to be true in your own life as well! For Jesus has said, *"I am He who lives, and was dead, and behold, I am alive forevermore. Amen. And I have the keys of Hades and of Death"* (Revelation 1:18).

FRIDAY: Doing What Jesus Wants

*"I know your works. See, I have set before you an open door, and no one can shut it; for **you** have a little strength, **have kept My word, and have not denied My name**."*
—Revelation 3:8

What did Jesus approve of in the church at Philadelphia? In Revelation 3:8 Christ shows us what He commends.

Holiness. "He Who is holy" said to them, "I am intimately acquainted with your deeds, and they are pleasing to Me." How can God be pleased with what we do? By our being holy, as He is holy. That means agreeing with God, being clothed with the righteousness of Christ, and responding to the Holy Spirit by saying yes to Jesus Christ. It is a wonderful thing to walk in holiness, in the power and energy of His Spirit, accomplishing the life of Jesus Christ here on earth.

Disciple-Making and evangelism. Jesus commended the Philadelphians, "I have given you great opportunities that you have taken and fulfilled. I have put before you an open door, and no one can shut it." This is disciple-making and evangelism. All of us are supposed to be doing that. Like my friend, Andy Meakin, we are on a plane that is crashing, so it is time to undo our seat belts and share the gospel with as many as we can.

Do you know what today's church does? The captain has announced over His intercom that our plane is crashing! Instead of undoing our seat belts, and jumping up to rescue people for eternity, we are pulling out our personal DVDs and playing a movie because "we are going to heaven." Everybody else can go to hell. Do you get the metaphor? It is very dangerous to think that if we send our money for someone else to evangelize, we are all right because we did our part. No, God says that we are all to be disciple-makers. We need to get out of our seats and start walking the aisles of life urgently telling people about Jesus. Jesus praised the Philadelphians for going through that open door.

Dependence. Jesus told them, "I know you are weak and leaning on My power because you have little strength." This is dependence. We are all supposed to be weak in this manner—knowing that we are ineffective apart from God's power. For Jesus has said, "Without Me you can do nothing" (John 15:5).

I often hear excuses for not witnessing, such as: "I'm too afraid to share the gospel"; "People might laugh at me"; or "I might be asked a question I don't know the answer to." When ideas like that pop into your head, resist them and tell Jesus, "I don't want to be apart from You. I want to depend on You and Your power." If you are asked a question you do not know how to answer, be honest, and say, "I don't know the answer to that question, but I do know this: I am going to heaven; are you?" You do not have to be a great Bible scholar to witness. Just let people know that when the plane crashes they are going to die. Did you know that Jesus talked more about hell than He did about heaven? Are you ready? Are you willing to find out if others you come in contact with are ready?

Obedience. Jesus told the saints at Philadelphia, "I know you are devoting yourselves to My Word, and have kept it." This is obedience, which gives proof of our love for Christ, for He has said, "If you love Me, you will keep My commandments" (John 14:15).

Commitment. Jesus said to the Philadelphians, "I know you love Me so much that you magnify My name unashamedly, and have not denied My name." This is commitment. There is passive and active denial. Active denial is like getting up and flat out saying, "I don't believe in Christ"; passive denial is simply remaining quiet about Jesus and any relationship with Him.

When I was a student at Michigan State University, a professor walked into the class of about 500, looked us over, and smiled as he said: "This semester we are going to talk about the mythology of the Bible. Some of you have been taught to believe that thing. I am going to teach you it is not true. You don't have to be bound by that weakness." He was very effective, and then he asked if we had any questions about the mythology of the Bible. Since I did not know any better, I raised my hand and stated: "I believe the Bible is true—and it is not mythology." He just pointed at me, and everyone started laughing and snickering. He made his point silently: "There! Look at the dinosaur. A relic from the past sits among you!"

That professor never did answer me; he only said, "We will talk about the mythology of the Bible this semester." Afterward, fifty students who said they were Christians came up to me and asked if I would help them start a campus Bible study that semester. Be committed! Raise your flag at work, at home, at school. Even if you are scared to death, speak out! When you are weak, the Lord promises to make you strong (2 Corinthians 12:10).

If speaking out for Christ is what He likes in someone, shouldn't we be seeking those pursuits in place of others that crowd Him out? God gives the same promises to us as He did the Philadelphian assembly.

Victory over God's enemies. "Indeed I will make those of the synagogue of Satan, who say they are Jews and are not, but lie—indeed I will make them come and worship before your feet, and to know that I have loved you" (Revelation 3:9). Not even the gates of hell can withstand the attack. This is representative of the historic Philadelphian church of great outreach (approximately A.D. 1800–1950) when the gospel went all over the world through men like William Carey, Hudson Taylor, Jonathan Goforth, C. T. Studd, and D. L. Moody. Although that zeal for spreading the gospel seems to now be a relic in a museum, Jesus still promises: "I will give you victory over your enemies—if you will just *go*."

Deliverance from the Tribulation. "Because you have kept My command to persevere, I also will keep you from the hour of trial which shall come upon the whole world, to test those who dwell on the earth" (Revelation 3:10). This is referring to the Great Tribulation, and is a promise that the church will be delivered out of the world.

In Luke 18:8, Jesus says, "When the Son of Man comes, will He really find faith on the earth?" He wonders: "There are so many people caught up with chasing after stuff that I am not sure they are really in My kingdom!" Are you chasing after the pleasures that this world brings—or after Christ, who is to be your greatest joy?

SATURDAY: Approved!

*"He who overcomes, I will make him a pillar in the temple of My God, and he shall go out no more. I will write on him the name of My God and the name of the city of My God, the New Jerusalem, which comes down out of heaven from My God. And **I will write on him My new name**."*
—Revelation 3:12

Like Smyrna, the church at Philadelphia received no criticism from Christ due to laxity or disobedience. Smyrna was the suffering church; Philadelphia was the soul-winning church.

As vital as these words to the churches must have been 2,000 years ago, so they are to us today. Thus, we need to listen to what Christ has to say in these powerful appeals.

Be watchful—no quitting is allowed. "Behold, I come quickly!" (Revelation 3:11a). We need to heed Paul's call to finish the race to the very end: "I have fought the good fight, I have finished the race, I have kept the faith" (2 Timothy 4:7). God intends that we race all the way to the end of life, and not simply walk the last lap. There is no such thing as retirement from serving the kingdom of God. From all the New Testament metaphors of races, finish lines, rewards, and crowns, it appears that how you *end* is how you will be rewarded!

Be diligent—no coasting is allowed. "Hold fast what you have" (Revelation 3:11b). Paul gives a call to life-long spiritual growth: "Be diligent to present yourself approved to God, a worker who does not need to be ashamed, rightly dividing the word of truth" (2 Timothy 2:15). No coasting is allowed in life; we ought to be found doing what we were left here to do.

Be cautious—no self-indulgence is allowed. "That no one may take your crown" (Revelation 3:11c). How can we lose our crown? By becoming disqualified. Self-discipline is a fruit of God's

Spirit; we must not give in to laxity and self-indulgence. It used to be in Israel that they had boundary stones that marked off inheritances. God always condemned moving the ancient boundary stones. Do you know what the church has started to do? We don't set boundaries by saying we will not participate in anything that God hates (like watching bloodshed, iniquity, nudity, immorality, and witchcraft). Instead we say that we are careful not to see *too much* of what God hates, or stay *too close* to what He has condemned. Beware of becoming conformed to the ways of this falling world.

One of the most glaring Christian sins today is self-indulgence. We live in a world where people are suffering horribly, and yet we indulge ourselves. We spend too much of our time being beautiful and pampered. Paul, who was probably the greatest born-again Christian who ever walked the face of the earth, said, "I discipline my body and bring it into subjection, lest, when I have preached to others, I myself should become disqualified" (1 Corinthians 9:27). Paul did not want to "step out of his lane" in the race and get disqualified. He was intent on finishing the course well. God always counts how we finish—not just how we start!

Christ offers true believers an inescapable destination with wonderful promises. Look at Revelation 3:12 again: "He who overcomes, I will make him a pillar in the temple of My God [**security**], and he shall go out no more [**stability**]. And I will write on him the name of My God [**eternal life**] and the name of the city of My God, the New Jerusalem, which comes down out of heaven from My God [**purity**]. And I will write on him My new name [**intimacy**]."

To the earthquake-weary citizens of Philadelphia, weak and insecure, Christ gave permanence. As for us, we can be *pillars* in the end of days because we are *secure* in Him. Have you lost your treasures on earth to disasters? Have you lost your loved ones to death? Have you lost your dreams to unexpected changes? If so, then you know there is nothing better than stability: "Let not your heart be troubled; you believe in God, believe also in Me. . . . I go to prepare a place for you. And . . . I will come again and receive you to Myself; that where I am, there you may be also" (John 14:1–3).

We are given an intimate name because we are a love gift from the Father to the Son (John 17:24). That means we are adopted: "And if children, then . . . heirs of God and joint heirs with Christ" (Romans 8:17). To those who have confessed Christ, Jesus promises: "He who overcomes shall be clothed in white garments, and I will not blot out his name from the Book of Life; but I will confess his name before My Father and before His angels" (Revelation 3:5).

Make a choice to live in hope. We need to listen to Jesus *today*. For He has said, *"He who has an ear, let him hear what the Spirit says to the churches"* (Revelation 3:13). Do you have hearing ears? Are you saved and listening to Jesus?

- A cold wave cooled the loving passion of the **Ephesians**. Watch out! Don't catch cold.
- Tribulation and poverty tempted and tried to discourage the **Smyrnians**. Watch out! Don't be discouraged.
- False doctrine and impurity tripped up some **Pergamites**. Watch out for imitations and immorality.
- False teachers and wickedness killed the **Thyatirans**. Watch out for truth and purity—not lies and deceit.

- Lifelessness robbed the **Sardians** of the Name. Watch out! Be sure you are clothed with Christ. Born-again believers will listen to Jesus, overcome, and be crowned.
- An open door stood before the **Philadelphians**, and they stepped through by faith. Watch for open doors of ministry. Serve Christ for eternal rather than temporal gain.

I wonder: Do you know that the plane is crashing? This world is headed to a very abrupt conclusion. Think about the people you love: your family, friends, coworkers, classmates, and neighbors. If they don't know Jesus Christ, do you mind that they are going to a place of blackness of darkness where worms do not die and there will be endless fire? Does it matter to you? Jesus wants you to unashamedly go forth and tell them about Him!

Oh, how I pray that you earnestly desire the blessing of Christ's approval, and therefore covet hearing His "Well done!"

WEEK 20
Heed Christ's Request

{ Revelation 3:14–22 }

This week as we approach the end of days, you can find hope as you heed Christ's request!

SUNDAY: Welcome to Laodicea

*"I know your works, that **you are neither cold nor hot**. I could wish you were cold or hot."*
—REVELATION 3:15

Laodicea has the grim distinction of being the only assembly of the seven that the Lord of the church did not commend in some way. It is the only church Christ warned: He said He would take away their lampstand and snuff them out if they did not repent and follow Him. This is the seventh historic church, and the seventh type of Christian. It also represents the final era of Christ's church (from about 1950 onward), and is perhaps today's most prevalent church type—contented here and not looking for the heavenly city there.

Let's look again at the facts about Revelation, which is divided into three parts by the author (1:19): Christ is gloriously unveiled (Chapter 1); Christ confronts His church (Chapters 2–3); and Christ conquers the world (Chapters 4–22).

If you recall, in the curse at the fall of Satan, Adam relinquished his dominion in this world, but when Jesus Christ came, He took back what the "prince of the power of the air" had usurped. Our sovereign and omnipotent God has always been in control, but to suit His own perfect purposes, He has permitted sin to run rampant throughout the centuries. However, starting in chapter four of Revelation, Christ will conquer evil and take it all back forever.

Now let's focus again on the letters to the churches. Each letter has six parts:

1. **Assembly**—seven separate and distinct churches (Laodicea, in this week's lesson).
2. **Author**—Jesus Christ, who identified himself in a unique way through His names.
3. **Approval**—what the assembly was doing right (except for Laodicea).
4. **Admonition**—what they were doing wrong.
5. **Appeal**—to follow Christ faithfully.
6. **Assurance**—granted if they responded rightly to Christ.

Revelation 2–3 reveals what Christ said to the seven churches, a select group in a circular loop. His message to them speaks across the centuries to us today.

- **Ephesus**, the careless church, left their first love. Christ said to them, "Come back to Me!"
- **Smyrna**, the crowned church, suffered persecution. Christ said to them, "Be faithful to the end!"
- **Pergamos**, the compromising church, tolerated evil. Christ said to them, "Separate yourselves!"
- **Thyatira**, the corrupted church, joined the world. Christ said to them, "Divorce yourself from the world!"
- **Sardis**, the feeble church, wasn't on guard. Christ said to them, "Wake up before it is too late!"
- **Philadelphia**, the faithful church, was pleasing to God. Christ said to them, "Keep on keeping on!"
- **Laodicea**, the foolish church, needed nothing. Christ said to them, "Find what you need in Me!"

Note that what He said to the seven churches also applies to individual Christians. Therefore, I exhort you to ask the Lord Jesus to apply His letter to the seventh church to your own heart!

My Prayer for You This Week: *Father, I pray that You would open, illumine, and powerfully minister Your Word to our hearts. If there is any coldness, blindness, nakedness, or spiritual poverty in our lives that is unnoticed, or that we are not concerned about, may You, Lord Jesus, make it so evident to us that we will be as sickened about it as You are. Before You vomit in Your displeasure, help us to repent and get rid of those things that grieve You. Oh Lord Jesus, thank You for this last letter to the church at Laodicea as well as Your other six glorious letters to the churches. Thank You for the privilege of immersing ourselves in Your Word! May we never grow tired or indifferent to the privilege of being in Your Word, but always come expectant of the blessing that You promised would come from the reading and hearing of the Scriptures. We pray in Your precious name, Lord Jesus. Amen.*

MONDAY: Sounds Like Life in the U.S.A.

*Let him who thinks he stands **take heed** lest he fall.*

—1 Corinthians 10:12

WEEK 20: HEED CHRIST'S REQUEST

When you step back and look at where the church of Laodicea was geographically, culturally, and historically, it sounds ominously like American life in the twenty-first century. There are some powerful insights we can draw from this ancient city. As you read through each of the following points, think about the similarities to our society, and perhaps even to your own life.

The Laodiceans were wealthy. Laodicea was the wealthiest of all the cities—a very rich banking and commercial center located thirty miles southeast of Philadelphia. Her great wealth produced an independent spirit; even Christ's church boasted of having no needs, not even for God. Jesus therefore said that He would vomit them out of His mouth "Because [they] say, 'I am rich, have become wealthy, and have need of nothing.'" (Revelation 3:17a). Christians always get drawn into the culture around them, yet Jesus wants us to be separate from it. We are to be *in* the world, but not *of* it. We must not allow ourselves to be squashed into the world's mold. Because the Laodicean church was conformed to the world, they felt they did not need God. *Beware of the subtle dangers of wealth.*

The Laodiceans were self-sufficient. They thought they needed only themselves, like the kings of Israel who trusted in their armies, neglected to call on God, and were sadly defeated. God stirred up enemies from all directions to march on Jerusalem; then He would wait to see what Israel would do. God does not want us to neglect coming to Him for our needs. In less wealthy parts of the world, the Christians pray that God will move in their lives, and do great and mighty things. However, in more affluent areas, some believers get conformed by the world to plan everything themselves. *Beware of trusting in riches—lest you neglect God.*

The Laodiceans were fashionable. The city was a renowned center for clothing. They raised sheep that produced glossy jet-black wool that was woven into a garment called a "trimita." These garments were much in demand, and a source of great income. They were so proud of their clothing! But Jesus said, "[You] do not know that you are wretched, miserable, poor, blind, and naked" (Revelation 3:17b). For that reason Jesus said to them, "I counsel you that you are so proud of your clothes, but you need to come to Me and get real clothing." *Beware of staying in step with everyone but God.*

The Laodiceans were worldly. By following the fashion trends of this world, many Christians have forgotten that God's primary calling is for us to be a walking temple of God. When entering a shrine or a temple in the Middle East, visitors are required to wear the proper covering. You see, even the pagans, the apostates, and the godless realize that a temple is to be kept reverently holy. Yet the walking temples of the infinite God of the universe, whose name is holy, are often defiled—all in the name of what is "fashionable."

Women, especially, need to be aware that the eyes of men are never satisfied. In 2 Peter 2:14 men are described as "having eyes full of adultery." Ladies, you should never want to be in any man's adulterous imagination. *Beware of focusing on externals and keeping up with the culture—lest you forget God.*

The Laodiceans were insecure. The city was truly indefensible and vulnerable because it had no water supply; thus, just to keep the peace, it sought to never offend anyone. In the ancient world, there were only three things necessary for an inhabitable city: dependable water, food supplies, and security. The Laodiceans' hearts toward God were like their water supply from an aqueduct that brought water in from the city of Colosse: not hot or cold—merely lukewarm (Revelation 3:15–16). *Beware of finding security in anything but God.*

The Laodiceans were compromisers. They were non-confrontational; they always looked for the middle ground. This is what is happening in our religious world today. People are seeking to build a visible unity in the church of Jesus Christ, but that will never happen. Jesus said this type of unity can only take place spiritually among those who are blood-bought. Many long to have the biggest gathering and political clout because they desire to change the morals of the world. But Christendom has largely forgotten that this only transpires through right doctrine. Thus, to avoid divisiveness, holding fast to right doctrine has been replaced by stressing love, joy, and external things. That is what ecumenism is all about. Almost every major constituent group of Christianity is caving in and signing peace agreements with heretical and apostate groups. Who will we evangelize then? *Beware of seeking peace to the point of compromise—lest it be God who is offended.*

The Laodiceans were health conscious. Laodicea was a center for medical discoveries and advancements, especially in the temple of Carian. They developed a special antiseptic eye salve called kollurion that could heal infections and was highly sought after. The salve was not exported; people came from far and wide to get it, and as a result, Laodicea became a resort city. People would spend a fortune for the privilege of using the salve to cure their eye problems. But Jesus told them, "You do not know that you are blind!" They were so trusting in their medicine that they felt perfectly able to care for their sight. Spiritually, however, they were totally blind.

How long has it been since you have personally seen Jesus in His Word? You cannot depend on great preachers on radio and television, the latest Christian books, or Christian videos or CDs. How long has it been since you have personally opened His Word and seen the glory of God on every page? Many men cannot spiritually lead their families because they cannot open the Bible and see anything in it. Men, you just need to come to the Lord and ask for His eye salve: "Open my eyes, that I may see wondrous things from Your law" (Psalm 119:18). *Beware of keeping only your body healthy, and not your soul.*

The Laodiceans were spiritually insensitive. Today's church by and large is in the same condition. Friends I went to college with have told me that they don't have Sunday evening church services anymore because our world is running too fast, and they cannot generate enough excitement to get people to come. We cannot generate excitement—but God can. We need to get people excited about reading and studying God's Word! *Beware of depending on human progress—lest it be God's hand that is ignored.*

So then, a wealthy, commercial, peace-seeking, medically advanced city called Laodicea was the home of the assembly that received Christ's seventh letter to the churches. Did its lack of character remind you of what is happening in America in the twenty-first century? How about in your own life? Is all well between you and the Lord? If you are a born-again Christian, and you can't see something of value in God's Word, then you need to look at what is ruining your eyesight. If that is your situation, I exhort you to get right with Him today!

WEEK 20: HEED CHRIST'S REQUEST

TUESDAY: Jesus Is the Greatest!

"And to the angel of the church of the Laodiceans write, 'These things says **the Amen, the Faithful and True Witness, the Beginning of the creation of God**.*' "*
—REVELATION 3:14

Laodicea was the foolish church. They needed nothing, not even God. Therefore, Christ said to them, "Find what you need in *Me!*" As we look at what we find in Christ, we will see that He reveals himself in three ways. As you study them with me, I hope that you will conclude, as I have, that *Jesus is the greatest!* Now discover what we can learn about Christ in Revelation 3:14.

Jesus is the Amen. "Amen" is a word put at the end of a solemn statement affirming its truth. Jesus himself *is* Truth; thus, He is God's last word to man. Therefore, we ought to listen to Him. This is what the writer of Hebrews says so beautifully: "Who being in the brightness of His glory and the express image of His person, and upholding all things by the word of His power, when He had by Himself purged our sins, **sat down** at the right hand of the Majesty on high" (Hebrews 1:3).

In the tabernacle and the temple there were no chairs or benches. The priests were constantly on the move making sacrifices, lighting and maintaining lamps, and shuffling the showbread. They were never done, and could never sit down. But Jesus, our High Priest, offered himself only once, and then sat down. He is "the Amen"—God's last word!

Jesus is the Faithful and True Witness. Only Jesus explains God, for "no one has seen God at any time. The only begotten Son, who is in the bosom of the Father, He has declared Him" (John 1:18). Because only Jesus explains God, we must believe in Him. Many of today's preachers and theologians no longer believe that Jesus is the only way to God. We should not be alarmed, though. The apostle Paul warned his apprentice in the faith, young Timothy the pastor, about this danger: "Now the Spirit expressly says that in latter times some will depart from the faith, giving heed to deceiving spirits and doctrines of demons" (1 Timothy 4:1). We must not leave the Word of God for the sake of compromise and peace: Jesus is the only way to God.

Jesus is the "Beginning of the creation of God." This does not mean that Jesus was God's first creation. Rather, it means that He is the Creator, the origin, the source. He is the Creator God who began all other creations: "All things were made through Him, and without Him nothing was made that was made" (John 1:3). Now look at this wonderful description of Christ, which I dearly love: "He is the image of the invisible God, the firstborn over all creation. For by Him all things were created that are in heaven and that are on earth, visible and invisible, whether thrones or dominions or principalities or powers. All things were created through Him and for Him" (Colossians 1:15–16).

When the ancients used to do mathematics, they did it opposite of us. We write down numbers in a column, and put the answer at the bottom. The ancients put the answer at the top because it was thought to be better than all the combined elements. They called this the *prototokos*—"the thing above all the rest." That is the name Jesus was given: Creator, God the Son. I hope you agree with me that *Jesus is the greatest!*

WEDNESDAY: They Didn't See Christ

But the natural man does not receive the things of the Spirit of God, for they are foolishness to him; **nor can he know them,** *because they are spiritually discerned.*

—1 CORINTHIANS 2:14

Did you notice Christ's commendation to this church? There is none! Any good word is grimly missing in His letter to the Laodiceans. They were tepid, thoroughly evangelical, but not *evangelistic*. Tepid is the condition where conviction does not touch one's conduct, heart, or decisions. Tepid is when the cross brings delight as an ornament but not as a grisly, painful reminder of how we must die to our self, flesh, and pleasures daily. Jesus said, "If any man would come after me, let him deny himself and take up his cross daily and follow me" (Luke 9:23 RSV). That was His call to those following Him faithfully as His disciple.

The church at Laodicea had facilities (probably paid for), programs, budgets that were filled, and respect in the community. However, they lacked humility, contrition, depth of prayer, and passion for the lost. Worship to them was simply another service rather than a personal longing poured out to God.

In Isaiah there is a passage written like a miniature portrait of the whole Bible: "But we are all like an unclean thing, and all our righteousnesses are like filthy rags; we all fade as a leaf, and our iniquities, like the wind, have taken us away. And there is no One who calls on Your name, who stirs himself up to take hold of You; For You have hidden Your face from us, and have consumed us because of our iniquities. But now, O Lord, You are our Father; we are the clay, and You our potter; and all we are the work of Your hand" (Isaiah 64:6–8).

That is an indictment of us today. In my ministry experience, the number-one sin that saints struggle with is getting anything out of the Word of God. We need to cultivate a burning passion for the Word, and cool our passion for the world (entertainment, health, exercise, finances, hobbies, and our children's advancement).

The Laodicean church didn't see Christ, and He is also hiding His face a great deal today because of our misplaced values. We ought to value knowing God, and leading our families to know and seek Him, rather than fashion, success, sports, and riches. Many parents want their children to attend the top schools to become professionals, but that is a worldly desire. What if, as they go to that high-status school, they lose their faith and never return to God's church? I would rather have a poor, but righteous, eighth-grade graduate than a graduate from a prestigious university who mocks God.

Do you see Christ moving in your life? Or is He hiding His face from you because of misplaced values? Have you examined your priorities in light of God's Word? To whom have you given first place in your life? If any of this hits home with you, ask the Lord to give you a burning passion for His Word—and to cool your passion for the world!

THURSDAY: A Geography Lesson

"I know your works, that you are neither cold nor hot. I could wish you were cold or hot. So then, **because you are lukewarm, and neither cold nor hot, I will vomit you out of My mouth.** *Because*

you say, 'I am rich, have become wealthy, and have need of nothing'—and do not know that you are wretched, miserable, poor, blind, and naked—I counsel you to buy from Me gold refined in the fire, that you may be rich; and white garments, that you may be clothed, that the shame of your nakedness may not be revealed; and anoint your eyes with eye salve, that you may see."
—Revelation 3:15–18

This is the heartbeat of the letter to the Laodicean assembly—Christ's admonition, or accusation: "You are lukewarm; you needed nothing, so I will spit you out!" What an incredible contrast to His "Well done!"

A spiritual lesson from geography. The setting was graphic. Colosse (the destination of the letter to the Colossians), which was known for pure, cold, crystal clear waters that spring up, was six miles away. Hierapolis, with its hot springs steaming up from the ground, was also close at hand. Because there was no water available in Laodicea, they built an aqueduct from Colosse, but by the time their water traveled six miles it was never cold, only lukewarm. Hence the apt description Jesus gave to this church in Revelation 3:15–18 above.

Christ wanted the Laodiceans to either be like a cold drink that refreshes or like a hot bath that cleanses and renews. But they were not to compromise by striving to live between both worlds—and hence become uselessly lukewarm.

A spiritual warning from Jesus. Here is an insight to ponder: perhaps the borrowed, lukewarm, secondhand water was a portrait of borrowed, secondhand Christianity. They were not getting the water themselves out of the Rock; they relied on others. *Secondhand Christianity is a curse.*

Do you drink daily of Christ's living water? Or does someone have to give you a bottle? Do you feed on the manna of God's Word? Or does someone have to spoon-feed you? Is your experience of the transforming divine power in salvation secondhand or personal? Watch out if your salvation is not zestfully and hotly and personally yours. If you do not repent, Christ will have to chasten you even to the point of weakness, sickness, or death (see 1 Corinthians 11:30).

That was Christ's appeal to the Laodiceans, which showed the heartbeat of His love. The lesson: He does not immediately write us off; He always pleads with us. Note what He has to say in Revelation 3:18.

- **Revelation 3:18a:** "I counsel you to buy from Me gold refined in the fire, that you may be rich." How do rich people buy gold from Christ? In two ways: suffering and giving. Jesus loves our suffering and giving. Exchange the treasures of this world for heavenly treasures. Jesus exhorts us: "He who finds his life will lose it, and he who loses his life for My sake will find it" (Matthew 10:39). If you want to lose something, hold on to it. If you want to gain something, give it away. Have open hands for Christ.
- **Revelation 3:18b:** "I counsel you to [get] white garments, that you may be clothed." Seek Christ. Remember those black garments called "trimitas"? Get rid of those things. Jesus wants us to get white garments from Him: "Put on [the Lord Jesus Christ—His] tender mercies, kindness, humility, meekness, longsuffering" . . . "and make no provision for the flesh, to fulfill its lusts" (Colossians 3:12; Romans 13:14).

- **Revelation 3:18c:** "That the shame of your nakedness may not be revealed." What is this? What we are going to wear in eternity is what we wear on earth: "Those who are wise shall shine like the brightness of the firmament, and those who turn many to righteousness like the stars forever and ever" (Daniel 12:3). Every saint will be happy and rejoice in heaven, but there will be levels of rewards; we will not all be equal there. So we need to seek Christ with all our hearts here. It is not the length of time we serve that matters, but the depth of our passion for Him. Start living today for how you want to end the race!
- **Revelation 3:18d:** "And anoint your eyes with eye salve, that you may see." Simply put: study God's Word!

How incredibly Christ loves! In spite of their unbelief and unconcern, even to them He made these appeals. If you are a Laodicean Christian, He is calling out to you as well: "Come back to Me. I love you!"

FRIDAY: Six Steps to True Joy

*"I counsel you to buy from Me gold refined in the fire, **that you may be rich**.*
—REVELATION 3:18

Jesus says, "Give Me your treasures—I advise you to buy from Me." Scripture tells us that "all who desire to live godly in Christ Jesus will suffer persecution. . . . That the genuineness of [our] faith, being much more precious than gold that perishes, though it is tested by fire, may be found to praise, honor, and glory at the revelation of Jesus Christ. . . . [For] when [we are] tried and purified, [we] will come forth [as] gold" (2 Timothy 3:12; 1 Peter 1:7; Job 23:10). What is all this about? It is Christ saying: "Remember Laodicea's riches. Without enduring suffering there is no possession of lasting riches." What is the gold? It is faith refined by suffering.

Jesus sets forth six steps to true joy.

1. **Seek real clothing from Christ:** He counsels us to put on His "white garments" (3:18a). We are to "pursue holiness, without which no one will see the Lord" (Hebrews 12:14b). We are to "be clothed with humility [the root of all virtues] . . . for 'God resists the proud, but gives grace to the humble'" (1 Peter 5:5). Christ is saying that whoever pursues holiness possesses eternal life.
2. **Plan for the ultimate day** "that the shame of your nakedness may not be revealed" (3:18b). As Paul says, "Each of us shall give account of himself to God . . . For we must all appear before the judgment seat of Christ, that each one may receive the things done in the body, . . . whether good or bad" (Romans 14:12; 2 Corinthians 5:10). Start thinking today about the final moment of your earthly life when you will explain to Jesus what you did with your days.
3. **Study to know Christ:** "Anoint your eyes with eye salve, that you may see" (3:18c). Paul was sent to open the eyes of those who were still in darkness (Acts 26:18). Jesus said that men who love darkness hate the light because their deeds are evil (John 3:19). Without needed awakening there is no entrance into spiritual sight.

4. **Learn where Christ is taking you:** "As many as I love, I rebuke and chasten" (3:19a). Yield to Him. See how much He loves even His wayward children: "For whom the Lord loves He chastens, and scourges every son whom He receives" (Hebrews 12:6).
5. **Return to Christ from wandering:** "Be zealous and repent" (3:19b). Return to Christ! Like the prodigal's father, Jesus waits to receive us, forgive us, welcome us, clothe us anew, and feast with us. He only waits for us to look up from the "pigpen of life" and think of Him!
6. **Commune with Christ daily.** He beckons: "I stand at the door and knock. If anyone hears My voice and opens the door, I will come in to him and dine with him, and he with Me" (3:20). What a precious invitation!

Those who lived in the ancient world usually had three meals. In the morning, they had *akratisara*—bread dipped in wine; at noonday, they had *ariston*—a snack eaten at work, or on the roadside; the word *deipnon*, used for "dine" in verse 20, refers to the evening meal, the main meal of the day—a time for lingering over the meal after a long day's work.

Jesus is standing at the door of your heart, waiting for you to invite Him in to linger in fellowship as your Lord and Savior throughout your life. Remember Holman Hunt's famous picture of Christ standing at the door knocking: the handle of salvation is on *your* side, lost friend; the handle of fellowship is on *your* side, Christian.

SATURDAY: Intimacy Assures

*"**He who has the Son has life**; he who does not have the Son of God does not have life."*
—1 John 5:12

Amazingly, true believers can actually have intimacy with God: "To him who overcomes [a true believer] I will grant to sit with Me on My throne, as I also overcame and sat down with my Father on His throne" (Revelation 3:21). Wow! Did you really catch what He was saying? And look at what He offers:

- **Intimacy is a promise:** "He who has My commandments and keeps them, it is he who loves Me. And he who loves Me will be loved by My Father, and I will love him and manifest Myself to him" (John 14:21).
- **Intimacy is a Person:** "This is eternal life, that they may know You, the only true God, and Jesus Christ whom You have sent" (John 17:3)
- **Intimacy is permanent:** "He who overcomes shall inherit all things, and I will be his God and he shall be My son" (Revelation 21:7).

Make a choice to live in hope. What impression are you leaving with others? Jesus' appeal to each of us is to heed His request for intimacy by turning our eyes upon Him to linger long in His presence! Oh, look full in His wonderful face! Looking at and longing for the world will only make you His enemy; but intimacy with Christ is the greatest treasure you can ever have on this earth!

WEEK 21
Adore Christ's Loveliness

{ Revelation 4 }

As the end of days approaches, you can find hope as you adore Christ's loveliness!

SUNDAY: Adoring the Loveliness of Jesus

*Your eyes will **see the King in His beauty**; they will see the land that is very far off.*
—Isaiah 33:17

Revelation is one of the few books that has a divinely inspired outline. Look at God's outline in 1:19: "Write the things which you have seen [chapter 1], and the things which are [chapters 2–3], and the things which will take place after this [chapters 4–22]."

Revelation 4 marks the beginning of our Lord Jesus Christ's re-conquest of the cosmos. As this chapter opens, we step into the worship center of the universe. By faith, gaze at the One seated on the eternal throne. Exalt God in your spirit for the endless praise ascending around His throne. Be still and know who it is before whom you stand. Adore the loveliness of Jesus as the center and focus of your worship. See Christ in all His resplendent beauty, for He alone is worthy of all worship and all praise!

To worship Jesus is our duty and purpose for existence. In fact, the amount of time we spend worshiping Christ reveals His true "worthship" to us. True worship is to ascribe to Him the honor, praise, glory, and majesty of which He is worthy. This day, stand with me in the vestibule and peer through the door into the chambers of the Most High God!

Adoring the loveliness of Jesus fills the entire fourth chapter of Revelation in which we see the awesome Sovereign Lord on the throne (vv. 1–3, 5); the awesome scene around the throne (vv. 4, 6–7); and the awesome song before the throne (vv. 8–11).

That faithful and true disciple of love, the lone heir of the apostolic band, tried to voice with his pen that which, when Paul saw it, was inexpressible. Listen to the choirs of angels in numberless circles about the glassy sea and its throne as they speak His worthy praise. Listen to those eternal creatures chant, "Holy, holy, holy, Lord God Almighty, Who was and is and is to come!" (v. 8b). Let us see with John that band which no man could number and listen to their songs of adoration and praise. Do you know Him, Christ the Lord, Who merits such praise? See Him now as the Lamb that was slain! For He is to be praised by we who owe Him our all!

My Prayer for You This Week: *Oh Father, we thank You for Your Word that transports us to our eternal refuge! Yet, Lord, we are reminded of what is ahead in the book of the Revelation. How our* hearts break when we think about the carnage, the bloodshed, the din of warfare, the dreadfulness of the pestilence, the scorching sun, the demonic hoards screeching from the pit causing havoc and horror upon the earth, and the malignant sores of oozing blackness that will destroy half the population of our planet. Nevertheless, we praise You that while all that is going on, above it all You are seated upon the throne. And before You rises endless adoration. Before You the breathtaking scene of thunder, lightning, and the colors of the rainbow mingle with the brilliantly awesome song of the redeemed before Your throne as the bowls of prayer are poured out as the voices of the saints rise before You. We long to join that day, that scene, that moment, that wonder. Sometimes it seems so far away . . . I pray that Your Spirit would minister to our hearts; help us to realize that we are only a heartbeat away from eternity, and we should get ready. Perhaps today You may gloriously come for Your saints, or call for us through the door of death. We pray that this moment would be a time of preparation. Stir our hearts to worship; prepare our souls for that awesome scene before Your throne. Oh, worthy Lamb, Creator, and Redeemer, fill our hearts with praise and adoration that overflows for You! In the precious name of Jesus we pray. Amen.

MONDAY: The Awesome Sovereign on the Throne

*After these things I looked, and behold, a door standing open in heaven. And the first voice . . . was like a trumpet . . . saying, "Come up here, and I will show you things which must take place **after this**."*
—REVELATION 4:1

The phrase "after these things" is a key: by the inspiration of God's Spirit, you are now looking into the future. All that God says is going to happen in chapters 4–22 of Revelation will come to pass exactly as predicted. Now step with me into the worship center of the universe to hear heaven rejoicing in our Lord Jesus Christ as He prepares to take back what Satan has usurped.

Worship of God and His loveliness is at His invitation. Because God is the One who invites us into His presence, worship is not to be taken lightly. Worship is not a right—it is a privilege. God will invite us to worship when we are going through cave times (like David); He will also invite us when we are enraptured with joy (perhaps by inspirational music). No matter where we are on the spectrum, God invites us to come into His presence. We can thus worship the Lord anywhere, anytime, and anyhow—just as the apostle John did while imprisoned on Patmos.

In his classic booklet, *My Heart—Christ's Home*, Robert Boyd Munger compares being saved to Jesus taking over our "body house" by moving in and systematically cleaning out each room. My favorite chapter is the "Dining Room" where Jesus sits every morning, noon, and night inviting us to come and eat with Him (Revelation 3:20). He wants us to dine with Him daily, and linger lovingly in His presence.[1]

Worship of God must acknowledge that He is in charge. "Immediately I was in the Spirit; and behold, a throne set in heaven, and One sat on the throne" (Revelation 4:2). Worship is Spirit-energized; it is a spiritual activity. It is not carnal, or something we can pump up. All true worship will focus on God, not on the human level. Worship lifts us out of the mundane and into God's presence.

We cannot fully worship God, however, if we are trying to run our own lives. Anything that is out of control is not under His control. All the areas of our lives must be under God's control: emotions, appetites, family, and finances. Jesus Christ, the Son of God and Son of Man, sits on the throne, and He wants us to acknowledge that truth anywhere, anytime, and anyhow.

Worship of God is utterly beautiful. "He who sat there was like a jasper and a sardius stone in appearance; and there was a rainbow around the throne, in appearance like an emerald" (Revelation 4:3). Jasper is a clear gem, and sardius is red. Like Saturn, the throne of God is ringed: vertically, like a 360-degree arch, a rainbow surrounds God's throne; horizontally, like a vast plain, the saints gather at the foot of God's throne.

Do you want to see the emerald rainbow, the jasper, and the sardius Ancient of Days sitting on His throne? Then "pursue peace with all people, and holiness, without which no one will see the Lord" (Hebrews 12:14; see also Matthew 5:8).

Worship of God unites the redeemed of all the ages at the feet of Jesus. "Around the throne were twenty-four thrones, and on the thrones I saw twenty-four elders sitting, clothed in white robes; and they had crowns of gold on their heads" (Revelation 4:4). The number 24 suggests many biblical ideas. There were twenty-four courses of priests in the service of the tabernacle and temple (1 Chronicles 24:3–5). There were also two groups of twelve that represent God's saints: the twelve tribes of Israel and the twelve apostles of Christ's church. God says, "I want an everlasting constant priesthood before My worship in the tabernacle." The number twenty-four also speaks of priests offering ceaseless worship; the gates and the foundation stones of heaven; the old and new people of God, the redeemed of all time; and the Old and New Testament saints merging together into the people of God who offer worship to Him.

Will you be among these worshiping saints? I hear a lot of people say they are going to heaven. In some locales, it seems that everyone is a Christian, or at least they think they are. So I ask them, "Have you made your reservations? Are you 'registered in heaven'?" (See Hebrews 12:23a.) Have you ever gone to a hotel and been told that your reservation had been lost, that no one knew you were coming, and that all the rooms were full? A lot of people who are in churches every Sunday are going to have that horrible experience when they face Jesus (Matthew 7:21–23). I therefore exhort you to "serve God acceptably with reverence and godly fear. For our God is a consuming fire" (Hebrews 12:28–29).

TUESDAY: The Awesome Scene around the Throne

*And from the throne proceeded **lightnings, thunderings, and voices**.*
—Revelation 4:5

The writers of Scripture, seeking to describe the indescribable, have portrayed the presence of God as an unbelievable display of power filled with thunder and lightning, blinding light, and a sparkling, dazzling array of colors and rainbows. That very thought of Him should make you want to burst forth in worship exclaiming: "Give unto the LORD the glory due His name: Worship the LORD in the beauty of holiness" (Psalm 29:2)!

Worship of God flows when we heed His holiness. In his visions, Ezekiel saw what Moses saw at Mount Sinai (Ezekiel 1–2); when God came down to give the law, thunder and lightning accompanied Him (Exodus 19:16; see also Hebrews 12:18–23). God's voice was so powerful that it frightened them; they thought that they were going to disintegrate! God told them, "I am so holy and you are so unholy that if even your animals get near Me, kill them." His theme of all the Old Testament legislation was thus: "Stay away from Me; you are unholy!"

Worship of God is unceasingly offered in His presence. "Before the throne there was a sea of glass, like crystal. And in the midst of the throne, and around the throne, were four living creatures full of eyes in front and in back" (Revelation 4:6). This verse hearkens back to Ezekiel and what he saw. The "four living creatures" seem to be a hybrid of the cherubim (living ones) of Ezekiel and the seraphim (burning ones) of Isaiah. In verse 7, below, they are the living-burning ones with four faces. Note that even though Scripture writers usually used terms that no human fully understands, they always did so with a view of magnifying the Lord.

Worship of God is to reflect Jesus' attributes of kingship, servanthood, humanity, and deity. "The first living creature was like a lion [royalty], the second living creature like a calf [servanthood], the third living creature had a face like a man [image of God], and the fourth living creature was like a flying eagle [divinity]" (Revelation 4:7). True worship will always reflect God's attributes.

When God came down and expressed himself in an image, what did He look like? *Jesus Christ.* He looked like us because we are created in the image of God. In the Old Testament there are four prophecies of Christ called the Branch Prophecies. Jesus was prophesied to be: King—the Root of David (Isaiah 11:1); My Servant—denoted by the calf (Zechariah 3:8); my perfect man (Zechariah 6:12); and God—the eagle (Isaiah 4:2).

The New Testament begins with the four Gospels which have corresponding themes: Matthew—the Perfect King; Mark—the Perfect Servant; Luke—the Perfect Man; and John—the Divine One, God in human flesh.

These "four living creatures" in 4:7 seem to be connected with the whole revelation of God, and thus reflect His attributes. As a child of the King, what attributes of His life do *you* reflect?

WEDNESDAY: The Awesome Song before the Throne

*The four living creatures, each having six wings, were full of eyes around and within. And they do not rest day or night, saying: "**Holy, holy, holy, Lord God Almighty**, Who was and is and is to come!"*
—Revelation 4:8

Night and day "the four living creatures" focus solely on God's holiness. In Hebrew, when something is repeated three times (as in "Holy, holy, holy!") it indicates an utter and complete emphasis. "Almighty" is used nine times in Revelation; the only other time in the New Testament is in 2

Corinthians 6:17–18 where our utterly holy "LORD God Almighty" tells us that if we will separate ourselves from false religion and sinful practices, He promises: "I will be a Father to you, and you shall be My sons and daughters." Oh, how getting to experience the full richness of being His child should prompt us to worship and adore our almighty God!

Worship of God is to be centered on Him. Isaiah told us that with two wings the living creatures covered their feet, with two they covered their face, and with two they flew. This speaks of total submission before God—utter humility seeking holiness and utmost service to God.

If you want to enjoy God's presence by lifting your heart and voice in worship to Him, avoid anything that will detract from your relationship with Him and His holiness. Instead, expose yourself daily to His Word. For if you hunger and thirst for God and His righteousness, and separate yourself from the world, "He shall give you the desires of your heart" (Psalm 37:4b). If you do not want God's presence on earth, however, you will not have it in eternity. The Lord will give you what you want.

Worship of God is to always honor and glorify Him. "Whenever the living creatures give glory and honor and thanks to Him who sits on the throne, . . . the twenty-four elders fall down before Him . . . and worship Him . . . , and cast their crowns before the throne" (4:9–10). In verse 10, the twenty-four elders are saying to the Lord, "I don't want the crowns; I am not in charge of my life any more. God, You are the One who deserves all that I have!"

A popular notion is that "cast their crowns" refers to giving our rewards to the Lord, but that is not all that the Apostle John meant. To understand that verse, we need to apply the first law of interpretation: What did the author mean, and what did the primary audience understand it to mean?

In the first century, the Roman Empire was approaching its zenith. When a kingdom was conquered, the Romans had triumphal processions that began with all the conquered citizens, soldiers, and the spoils; then the conquering general followed in his chariot. When the Roman general got to the center of the Forum before the emperor, the conquered king was brought in and, on his knees, would cast his crown at the feet of the general, who then put his hobnail-sandaled foot on the defeated king's neck. Afterward, the king was executed.

It will be a far different scene for us when we appear before the Lord God Almighty. We won't be marched in with chains; we will come before Him saying, "You don't have to put Your chastening foot on our necks or drag us with chains. We willingly and lovingly want to serve You!" Worship demands our total submission to God, which says to Him: "King of my life I crown Thee now / Thine shall the glory be; / Lest I forget Thy thorn-crowned brow, / Lead me to Calvary."

THURSDAY: Worship Fills Revelation

*"**You are worthy, O Lord**, to receive glory and honor and power; for You created all things, and by Your will they exist and were created."*

—Revelation 4:11

At this point in God's plan for the ages, we will have already arrived in heaven by way of "the snatching away," the Rapture. Thus, we will be part of the redeemed of all the ages who will worship in this celestial atmosphere around the throne.

Worship—to glorify God and enjoy Him forever—is our main purpose for existence. And true worship will always center totally on God, as is seen in the fourth stanza of this glorifying old hymn: "Holy, holy, holy, Lord God Almighty! / All Thy works shall praise Thy name in earth, and sky, and sea. / Holy, holy, holy! merciful and mighty! / God in Three persons, blessed Trinity!"

Let us now look in chronological order at chapters 4–22 and see Christ, the Lamb, being exalted by the faithful angelic hosts and the redeemed saints. You see, worship is the background music of God's kingdom. Songs of worship and triumph, which occur in eleven chapters of Revelation (4, 5, 7, 11, 12, 15, 16, 17, 19, 21, and 22), make up the background music to the story.

Chapter 4—Jesus is worthy of worship as the Creator. God, as Creator, is on the throne. Salvation starts with the acknowledgment of Jesus as Creator: "For by Him all things were created that are in heaven and that are on earth, visible and invisible, whether thrones or dominions or principalities or powers. All things were created through Him and for Him" (Colossians 1:16; see also Acts 14:15; 17:24).

Jesus is worthy of worship because He "is the God who commanded light to shine out of darkness, who has shone in our hearts to give the light of the knowledge of the glory of God in the face of Jesus Christ" (2 Corinthians 4:6).

All the angelic hosts worship Him: "Holy, holy, holy, Lord God Almighty, who was and is and is to come!" (Revelation 4:8). By this point we will get to join in the worship of heaven! At last, we will blend our voices with all of the angels and all of Creation and start our eternal, sacrificial service to our King.

The twenty-four elders worship Him: *"You are worthy, O Lord, to receive glory and honor and power; for You created all things, and by Your will they exist and were created"* (Revelation 4:11; see also Ezekiel 36:26; 2 Corinthians 4:6).

Chapter 5—Jesus is worthy of worship as the Redeeming Savior. In this chapter, the focus turns to Jesus the Redeemer, God's Son, who is before the throne. And the twenty-four elders worship Him: "You are worthy to take the scroll, and to open its seals; for You were slain, and have redeemed us to God by Your blood out of every tribe and tongue and people and nation, and have made us kings and priests to our God; and we shall reign on the earth" (Revelation 5:9–10; see also Titus 2:14).

In Revelation 5:13 the worship goes to Father and Son, which affirms Christ's deity: "Worthy is the Lamb who was slain to receive power and riches and wisdom, and strength and honor and glory and blessing! . . . Blessing and honor and glory and power be to Him who sits on the throne, and to the Lamb, forever and ever!" (5:12, 14). The innumerable angelic hosts and all Creation worship Him, for He is our blessed Savior for all eternity!

Chapter 7—Jesus is worthy of worship as the Giver of Life. The innumerable multitude cries out in worship: "Salvation belongs to our God who sits on the throne, and to the Lamb!" (Revelation 7:10). This is salvation from death's power. Eternal life liberates us to see that we are only temporarily in this body. All the angels and creatures fall and say, "Amen! Blessing and glory and wisdom, thanksgiving and honor and power and might, be to our God forever and ever. Amen" (Revelation 7:12). He is worthy of all praise, for He is the giver of life (John 14:6; Acts 5:20)!

The heartbeat of God's Word is worship. In fact, Jesus defines believers as *worshipers* because the driving message of salvation is to worship the God of heaven. The Scriptures open in Genesis with God walking and talking with Adam and Eve, His worshipers. Exodus contains elaborate plans for a tent—its sole purpose being to bring worshipers to God. Psalms, the longest book at the heart of God's Word, is a manual on ways to worship the God of the universe. The rest of the Old Testament is a series of prophets lamenting the neglect and abandonment of worship by God's people who were to be a kingdom of worshipers (priests).

The New Testament opens with the introduction in the Gospels of the God of heaven, on earth, seeking creatures who would be willing to be worshipers. The Book of Acts records what happens when average people from every walk of life, every strata of society, and every depth of sin, are bound together with a common passion for being lifelong worshipers. The Epistles are a manual on how to grow as worshipers. God's Word then closes in Revelation with all of God's worshipers home at last with their Creator—and joyfully worshiping Him!

Is your heart the heart of a worshiper? The word "worship" is full of meaning; it expresses the idea of "falling down, prostrating oneself, and kissing the feet or the hem of the garment of the one honored." We should ponder William Temple's wonderful definition of worship, which is "to quicken the conscience by the holiness of God, to feed the mind with the truth of God, to purge the imagination by the beauty of God, to open up the heart to the love of God, to devote the will to the purpose of God."[2]

FRIDAY: The Essence of True Worship

> *For we . . .* **worship God in the Spirit**, *rejoice in Christ Jesus, and have no confidence in the flesh.*
> —Philippians 3:3

Worship that focuses on God and God alone is true spiritual worship—worship that is energized by the Spirit of God. How do we know when we are operating in the power of the Holy Spirit? Here is a test: where God's Spirit reigns, believers relate to the Word—this is Spirit-filled teaching; where God's Spirit reigns, believers relate to each other—this is Spirit-filled fellowship; where God's Spirit reigns, believers relate to the Lord—this is Spirit-filled worship; where God's Spirit reigns, believers relate to the world—this is Spirit-filled evangelism.[3]

God is the cause of all things, the fountain of all perfection, without parts or dimensions, for He is eternal. He is an infinite Spirit—filling the heavens and the earth—pervading, governing, and upholding all things!

God is pleased only with that which resembles Himself. Therefore, He hates sin and sinfulness; He delights only in those who are made partakers of His own divine nature. Since all creatures were made by Him, all owe Him obedience and reverence; but, to be acceptable to this infinite Spirit, the

WEEK 21: ADORE CHRIST'S LOVELINESS

worship must be of a spiritual nature—springing from the heart, through the influence of the Holy Ghost. It must be in truth, not only in sincerity, but performed according to that divine revelation which He has given men of himself.

God is worshiped in spirit when, under the influence of the Holy Spirit, "believers bring all their affections, appetites, and desires to the throne of God; and God is worshiped in truth, when God's Word guides every purpose and passion of a believer's heart, and regulates every act of a believer's worship."[4]

The essence of worship is spiritual. In John 4, Jesus told the woman at the well, "The location of worship is no longer the main concern. The issue is not where you worship, but rather whom you worship and how you worship." God is an immortal, invisible, and omnipresent Spirit. He cannot be seen or touched, and He cannot be represented by an idol or any kind of likeness. Yet, just as an earthly son looks like his dad, so Jesus came to give us the image of the invisible God. And so *Father* was Jesus' favorite title for God.

The Gospels record about seventy times when Jesus spoke to God, and every time He called Him Father, except when He was on the cross bearing the judgment for man's sin. Then He said, "My God, My God, why have You forsaken Me?" (Matthew 27:46).

Jesus spoke three times in John 4 of worshiping "the Father." But only once does Jesus refer to God as "our Father," and that was not a direct address to God. It was a sample prayer, as the content shows, for Jesus would not have asked for forgiveness (Matthew 6:9).

The woman at the well needed a lesson in what real worship was all about. She was looking for the proper method of worship, but saw only two options—the Samaritan method and the Jewish method. Look at how John MacArthur compares the differences between man's worship and God's:

Samaritan worship	Jewish Worship	True Worship
Done in ignorance.	Done strictly.	Flows from God's Spirit within us.
Samaritan spiritual knowledge was limited because they rejected all of the Old Testament except the Pentateuch.	Jews were full of knowledge and accepted all the books of the Old Testament.	When God's Word is honored, and God's Spirit is honored, God is pleased with the worship.
Warm heresy is enthusiastic worship without proper information.	Cold orthodoxy is dead worship with the right information.	Eager, excited, enthusiastic heartfelt devotion to the truth of God is worship that flows from the inside out.
They worshiped in spirit, but not in truth. That is why Jesus said, "You worship that which you do not know" (v. 22).	They worshiped in truth but lacked the spirit.	God seeks those who will worship in spirit and in truth.

Enthusiastic heresy is heat without light.	Barren orthodoxy is light without heat.	Worship is not an external activity for which an environment must be created.
Sincerity, enthusiasm, and aggressiveness are important, but they must be based on truth.	Truth is foundational, but if it doesn't result in an eager, excited, enthusiastic heart, it is deficient.	It takes place on the inside, in the spirit. Psalm 45:1 is the expression of David's worshiping heart: "My heart overflows with a good theme."
Worship that occurred on Mount Gerazim was enthusiastic heresy.	Worship offered at Jerusalem was barren, lifeless orthodoxy.	The same two extremes are still with us today.
Gerazim had the spirit but not the truth.	Jerusalem had the truth but not the spirit.	Jesus rebuked both styles of worship when He said, "God is spirit, and those who worship Him must worship in spirit and in truth" (John 4:24).[5]

Spiritual worship is an evidence of salvation. One who is not saved cannot truly worship; One who is truly saved will be motivated by the indwelling Holy Spirit to worship. It is fair, then, to examine ourselves on the basis of our worship. If you have trouble worshiping, maybe you are not saved. If you get bored in church, or if you do not mind missing church altogether, it may be because the Holy Spirit is not in you prompting your heart. If He is there, you must yield your will to His power.

SATURDAY: Adoring Your King

*"The kingdoms of this world [will] become the kingdoms of our Lord and His Christ, and **He shall reign forever and ever!**"*
—Revelation 11:15

In Wednesday's devotional, we saw that in the first century the Roman Empire held triumphal processions and victory ceremonies to honor conquering generals. The apostle Paul had that imagery in mind when he wrote: "God . . . always leads us in triumph in Christ" (2 Corinthians 2:14). Jesus is the conqueror of all kingdoms!

Chapter 11—Jesus is worthy of worship as the conquering warrior. When it is announced in heaven that "the kingdoms of this world have become the kingdoms of our Lord and of His Christ" (Revelation 11:15), the twenty-four elders "fell on their faces and worshiped God, saying: 'We give You thanks, O Lord God Almighty, the One who is and who was and who is to come, because You have taken Your great power and reigned" (11:17). At this point, Jesus is reigning over all!

Chapters 12, 15, 16, 17—Jesus is worthy of worship as the crusher of Satan. First John 3:8 tells us that the person who practices sin is "of the devil, for the devil has sinned from the beginning," but

Jesus came to "destroy the works of the devil." Because Satan was defeated by Christ at Calvary, we can have victory over our adversary's attempts "to steal, and to kill, and to destroy" (John 10:10) us here, and in heaven we will never face his hatred again.

In Revelation 12:10–12, Satan and his angels are cast out of heaven—to nevermore have access to God. That is cause for great rejoicing and worship—forever and ever!

In Revelation 15:3–4, the victorious Tribulation warriors "sing the song of Moses . . . and the song of the Lamb, saying, 'Great and marvelous are Your works, Lord God Almighty! Just and true are Your ways, O King of the saints! Who shall not fear You, O Lord, and glorify Your name? for You alone are holy. For all nations shall come and worship before You, for Your judgments have been manifested.'" His saints sing songs of victory!

In chapters 16 and 17, the angels of the altar, the waters, and the earth all say, "You are righteous, O Lord, the One who is and who was and who is to be, because You have judged these things. For they have shed the blood of saints and prophets, and You have given them blood to drink. For it is their just due. . . . These will make war with the Lamb, and the Lamb will overcome them, for He is Lord of lords, and King of kings; and those who are with Him are called chosen, and faithful" (16:5–6; 17:14).

Chapter 19—Jesus is worthy of worship as our just judge. Creation echoes the majesty of His worthy judgment and sacrifice! In Revelation 19:1–5, the redeemed multitude and the twenty-four elders proclaim: "'Allelujah! Salvation and glory and power belong to the Lord our God! For true and righteous are His judgments, because He has judged the great harlot who corrupted the earth with her fornication; and He has avenged on her the blood of His servants shed by her.' Again they said, 'Alleluia! Her smoke rises up forever and ever!' And the twenty-four elders and the four living creatures fell down and worshiped God who sat on the throne, saying, 'Amen! Alleluia!' Then a voice came from the throne, saying, 'Praise our God, all you His servants and those who fear Him, both small and great!'"

They then fall before their just judge, to whom they submit. In unison, the multitude cries out to the Lord in exultation: "Alleluia! For the Lord God Omnipotent reigns! Let us be glad and rejoice and give Him glory, for the marriage of the Lamb has come" (19:6–7). This is the shout of anticipation for unbroken union with the King of the universe!

Chapters 21–22—Jesus is worthy of worship for coming as the Bridegroom, our Emmanuel. All praise Emmanuel! God is now with us as He promised (Matthew 1:22). Look at what is in store for His children: "Behold, the tabernacle of God is with men, and He will dwell with them, and they shall be His people. God Himself will be with them and be their God. And God will wipe away every tear from their eyes; there shall be no more death, nor sorrow, nor crying. There shall be no more pain, for the former things have passed away" (21:3–4).

At the end of Revelation, the voice of Jesus is calling all who are thirsty to come to Him: "I, Jesus, have sent My angel to testify to you these things in the churches. I am the Root and the Offspring of David, the Bright and Morning Star." And the Spirit and the bride say, "Come!" And let him who hears say, Come!" And let him who thirsts come. Whoever desires, let him take the water of life freely (22:16–17).

Make a choice to live in hope. To live in hope, it is vital that you understand three aspects of the nature of true worship: (1) true worship of God must be founded on God's Word (Colossians 3:15–17); (2) true worship of God must be clear of sin (Psalm 66:18); and (3) true worship of God must be Spirit-energized.

All true worship is a spiritual activity that centers on God, not on the human level. As you yield to Him, the Holy Spirit will energize you to adore Christ in all His loveliness—the One who is a multi-faceted diamond in eternal cascading glory. Jesus Christ is our eternal Creator, our Redeeming Savior, our giver of life, our conquering warrior, our crusher of Satan, our just judge, and our Bridegroom, Emmanuel.

WEEK 22
See Christ in the Old Testament

{ Genesis—Daniel }

As the end of days approaches, you can find hope as you see Christ in the Old Testament-from Genesis to Daniel!

SUNDAY: See Christ in the Entire Old Testament

Beginning at Moses *and all the Prophets,* ***[Jesus]*** ***expounded*** *to them in all the Scriptures the things* ***concerning Himself.***
—LUKE 24:27

Last week we were transported in time to the worship center of the universe to adore the loveliness of our awesome Sovereign, Jesus Christ, who sits on the throne in Revelation 4. Now hold onto your seat, because we are about to depart on a "Jet Tour" of the Old Testament prophets. Many of the 404 verses of Revelation are quotations and allusions to these prophets, but most believers have trouble understanding the Old Testament in general, let alone the seventeen prophetic books of Isaiah to Malachi.

If you will stay on board with me over the next three weeks, you should grasp the simple message and direction of each Old Testament book, and especially the seventeen prophetic books. As you see the whole scope and plan of God in these books reflected in Revelation, they will become even clearer.

The Scriptures are all about God revealing himself to His human creatures. The ultimate expression of God's nature and character is Christ. Note the words of Hebrews 1:3: "Who being the brightness of

WEEK 22: SEE CHRIST IN THE OLD TESTAMENT

His glory and the express image of His person, and upholding all things by the word of His power, when He had by Himself purged our sins, sat down at the right hand of the Majesty on high."

W. A. Criswell liked to say that the only God we will ever see is Jesus Christ. There is one God in three persons: God the Father, God the Son, and God the Holy Spirit. God the Father and God the Holy Spirit are invisible. They have representations such as a dove and a glowing light, but they are not corporeal. However, God the Father did take on some kind of form at times; it was called a theophany, which is a *visible* but not necessarily *material* manifestation of deity to a human person. Christ, however, will eternally exist in His resurrection body.

Since the Word of God reveals God, and Jesus is the image of the invisible God, then we can find and worship our Lord Jesus Christ in every part of the Bible. Each book reveals some truths about our beautiful Lord Jesus! (To see the central theme of Christ in all the Scriptures, look at Revelation 19:10, John 5:39, and Luke 24:27.)

The Scriptures are Christ-Centered. They are unique, powerful, and divine! Note the symmetrical pattern God presents in the Old Testament:

- **Books of history—17:** Five are major (Genesis to Deuteronomy); twelve are historical (Joshua to Esther).
- **Books of poetry—5:** Job to the Song of Solomon (located in the middle of the Old Testament).
- **Books of prophecy—17:** Five are the Major Prophets (Isaiah to Daniel); twelve are the Minor Prophets (Hosea to Malachi). Of these twelve, nine are pre-Exilic and three are post-Exilic.

Today is an overview of seeing Christ in the books of history; the books of poetry will be covered on Monday; and on Tuesday we will begin our tour of the seventeen prophetic books.

The five major books of history. The Pentateuch is the designation for the first five Old Testament books that were authored by Moses. We are sure of that because Jesus said so in His ministry while here on earth. In the books of History we see God's servants following the Lord Jesus Christ. He was the Creator in the garden, the Rock in the wilderness, the Angel of the Lord, and so on. These five books are crucial because they lay a foundation for the rest of God's Word; note their unifying themes:

1. **Genesis** pictures Christ as **"calling all things into being"** by creating the universe. The Scriptures are the only reliable source of information on the origin and purpose of the universe, man, sin, nations, the Covenant, and the Curse. Key word: *generations* (used ten times as an outline).
2. **Exodus** pictures Christ as **"calling Israel out of bondage"** by delivering His people. He is "the Way" out of Egypt, out of sin, out of earth. Key word: *deliverance*.
3. **Leviticus** pictures Christ as **"calling Israel unto consecration"** by opening the approach to a holy God. He is present with His people (*"before the Lord"* appears sixty times), and He demands holiness of them (11:44; 19:2; 20:7). Key word: *holiness* (occurs ninety-three times).
4. **Numbers** pictures Christ as **"calling Israel from confusion"** by dealing with His unfaithful people. Christ is the Faithful One. Key word: *chastening*.

5. **Deuteronomy** pictures Christ as **"calling Israel back to the covenant"** by seeking loyalty from His chosen people. He is the Promise Keeper. Key word: *covenant* (occurs twenty-seven times).

The twelve historical books.
1. **Joshua** pictures Christ as **Commander of the Lord's Army.** He is leading His people in conquest. Key idea: *obedience*.
2. **Judges** pictures Christ as the **Chastener of His Wayward People.** There are seven specific sin-salvation cycles in this book. Key idea: *disobedience*.
3. **Ruth** pictures Christ as the **Kinsman to His Needy People.** Key word: *loyalty*.
4-9. **First Samuel–Second Chronicles** pictures Christ as the **Perfect King.** In Samuel, God seeks for a man; in Kings, God sees all; in Chronicles, God saves, preserves, and rewards His own. Key words: *eyes of the Lord* (used thirteen times).
10. **Ezra** pictures Christ as our **Peg** (this was a figure of speech that indicated permanence and prominence) **in the Holy Place** (9:8). Key word: *returning*.
11. **Nehemiah** pictures Christ as our **Sure Foundation.** Key word: *restoring*.
12. **Esther** pictures Christ as our **Unseen Defender.** Key word: *protecting*.

The whole Bible is unlike any other book in the universe! And with that truth deeply upon your heart, in the days ahead, shouldn't you treat His Word differently, read it diligently, wait before it expectantly, and from it learn to live triumphantly? Remember: Jesus shines from every book of the Bible!

My Prayer for You This Week: *Lord Jesus, thank You for letting us see a little bit of what You must have taught on the road to Emmaus—beginning with Moses and pointing out to those disciples how You are in every part of the Bible. There's no greater study than to find that one thread links together every part of Your Word, and that thread is finding Christ in all the Scriptures. Thank You for letting us go on this journey together. Strengthen our hearts, and attune our minds, to the treasures of Your Word. We want to see, to find, to believe, and to feast upon those treasures! Oh Christ, thank You for making us conquerors, satisfying us, giving us hope in all our days. We thank You in the name of Jesus, and for His glory we pray. Amen.*

MONDAY: See Christ in the Books of Poetry

*They **divide My garments** among them, and for My clothing they **cast lots**.*
—PSALM 22:18

The Five Poetic Books. These five books, in the middle of the Old Testament, deal with the heart of Jewish life: pain, worship, living, life, and love.
1. **Job** pictures Christ as our **sure Redeemer**. This book gives the truth from God that "Christ is our sufficiency" in pain and suffering.
2. **Psalms** pictures Christ as our **Good Shepherd**. This book gives the truth from God that "Christ is our worship."

3. **Proverbs** pictures Christ as our **wisdom**. This book gives the truth from God that "Christ is our wisdom"—He is wisdom incarnate. Proverbs teaches us how to live by principles, not promises.
4. **Ecclesiastes** pictures Christ as our **hope of contentment**. This book gives the truth from God that "Christ is our way of life."
5. **The Song of Solomon** pictures Christ as our **beloved**. This book gives the truth from God that "Christ is our altogether lovely one."

The Scriptures are all about God revealing himself to His creatures. The ultimate expression of God's nature and character is Christ. In the Books of Poetry we see God's servants worshiping the Lord Jesus Christ. He is the suffering One, the Good Shepherd, the Redeemer!

We can learn from a seasoned sufferer—Job. High on the list of what Job's perseverance taught is this: even when suffering, pleasing God should be our goal in life—not happiness, comfort, or satisfaction. For "happy is the man whom God corrects; therefore do not despise the chastening of the Almighty.... Whatever you do, do all to the glory of God.... Make it [your] aim ... to be well pleasing to Him" (Job 5:17; 1 Corinthians 10:31; 2 Corinthians 5:9).

Following God often entails losing precious possessions and suffering pain for His sake: "Look, I go forward, but He is not there, and backward, but I cannot perceive Him; when He works on the left hand, I cannot behold Him; when He turns to the right hand, I cannot see Him" (Job 23:8–9). Tests like this are meant to be faith builders. When we need God most, yet He seems silent, it is time to stretch our faith and, like Job, say "He knows the way that I take; when He has tested me, I shall come forth as gold" (Job 23:10). What a precious and proven truth!

Trusting God turns present losses into future gains: "And the LORD restored Job's losses when he prayed for his friends. Indeed the LORD gave Job twice as much as he had before. Then all his brothers, all his sisters, and all those who had been his acquaintances before, came to him and ate food with him in his house; and they consoled him and comforted him for all the adversity that the LORD had brought upon him.... After this Job lived one hundred and forty years, and saw his children and grandchildren for four generations. So Job died, old and full of days" (Job 42:10–11, 16–17).

Ecclesiastes 9 contains some valuable life principles. For example, by the fruit of the Spirit called joy, we can rise above our circumstances by choosing to be contagiously happy: "Go, eat your bread with joy, and drink your wine with a merry heart; for God has already accepted your works" (Ecclesiastes 9:7). As God's children, through Christ's forgiveness and approval, we can be continually free of guilt and its bondage: "Let your garments always be white, and let your head lack no oil" (Ecclesiastes 9:8).

Ecclesiastes 9:9 tells us of the importance of being constantly committed to God in every area of life: "Live joyfully with the wife whom you love all the days of your vain life which He has given you under the sun, all your days of vanity; for that is your portion in life, and in the labor which you perform under the sun" (Ecclesiastes 9:9). God desires that we live life to the maximum by the power of the Holy Spirit: "Whatever your hand finds to do, do it with your might; for there is no work or device or knowledge or wisdom in the grave where you are going" (Ecclesiastes 9:10). In other words, live life zestfully!

Now that we have had an overview of seeing Christ in the Old Testament books of history and books of poetry, tomorrow we will begin focusing on the theme of these three weeks—seeing Christ in the seventeen prophetic books. Remember: many of the 404 verses in Revelation are quotations and allusions to these prophets. By understanding Isaiah to Malachi, we can better appreciate the richness of Revelation and more fully worship the One Whom the book exalts. Are you worshiping Christ as He deserves?

TUESDAY: Isaiah Says to Worship Our God of Salvation[1]

> "But He was wounded for our transgressions, He was bruised for our iniquities; the chastisement for our peace was upon Him, and by His stripes we are healed. All we like sheep have gone astray; we have turned, every one, to his own way; **and the LORD has laid on Him the iniquity of us all**.
> —Isaiah 53:5–6

Isaiah (740–681 B.C.) was a contemporary with Hosea (753–715 B.C.) and Micah (742–687 B.C.). From the revolt of Satan to the rule of the Savior, all is told by this most eloquent prophet, Isaiah. He was the "Shakespeare of the prophets" and the "Paul of the Old Testament." Isaiah has more to say about the greatness of God (Isaiah 40, 43), the horrors of the Tribulation (Isaiah 24), the wonders of the Millennium (Isaiah 35), and the ministry of Christ (Isaiah 53) than any other book in the Bible. Isaiah 53 is probably the most important and far-reaching chapter in the Old Testament, as it is quoted from or alluded to eighty-five times in the New Testament. Jesus said that Isaiah saw His glory and spoke of Him (John 12:41).

The book of Isaiah is an extended commentary on Jonah 2:9, where that prophet exclaimed from the fish's belly, "Salvation is of the Lord!" The word "salvation" appears thirty-three times in the writing of the prophets and, of these, twenty-six instances occur in Isaiah. Isaiah is divided into two sections: chapters 1–39 and chapters 40–66.

The first thirty-nine chapters describe the judgment by the Lord. (This seems to almost parallel the Old Testament's thirty-nine books that declare the holiness, righteousness, and justice of God.) The next twenty-seven chapters describe the comfort in redemption and restoration. (This seems to almost parallel the New Testament's twenty-seven books that declare the grace, compassion, and glory of God.)

The book of Isaiah has three major themes that may be summarized in personal choices similar to those made by Isaiah.

First Theme—The overwhelming sense of sin and the wrath of God against it. This is clearly seen in the twenty-one times that Isaiah uses the word "woe." In God's sight, "We are all like an unclean thing, and all our righteousnesses [good deeds] are like filthy rags; . . . And there is no One who calls on Your name, who stirs himself up to take hold of You; for You have hidden Your face from us, and have consumed us because of our iniquities" (Isaiah 64:6–7). **Personal choice:** I will become a person of conviction.

Second Theme—The all-pervading awareness of the power, majesty, and holiness of God. Twenty-three times Isaiah uses the divine name of "The Holy One of God," a name nearly unique to Isaiah (except for five other passages). "The work of righteousness will be peace, and the effect of righteousness, quietness and assurance forever" (Isaiah 32:17). **Personal choice:** I will confess that You, oh God, are holy.

Third Theme—The crystal clear sight of the salvation and coming victory of Christ: "Your eyes will see the King in His beauty; they will see the land that is very far off" (Isaiah 33:17). **Personal choice:** I will live with confidence.

I pray that you will choose to become a person of conviction: acknowledge that God is holy, and is therefore One in whom you can place your total confidence. Oh worship your King in all His beauty, and bow before Him!

WEDNESDAY: Jeremiah Says to Worship Our God of Repentance

"Your own wickedness will correct you, and your backslidings will rebuke you. . . . It is an evil and bitter thing that you have forsaken the LORD your God, and **the fear of Me is not in you**," says the LORD God of hosts.

—JEREMIAH 2:19

Some contemporaries of Jeremiah (627–586 B.C.) were Habakkuk (612–588 B.C.) and Zephaniah (640–621 B.C.). The Scriptures tell us: "Before I formed you [Jeremiah] in the womb I knew you; before you were born I sanctified you; I ordained you a prophet to the nations" (Jeremiah 1:5). This is a great scripture for those who say that human life begins at conception. God communicated with a human in the womb; Jeremiah was there as a person, and God chose him there. Jeremiah must have had an incredible childhood!

Jeremiah's woes were unimaginable to our relatively peaceful lives. He lived through the death throes of the nation of Judah. From an earthly perspective, his life was a failure. During his lifetime he watched the decay of God's chosen people, the horrible destruction of Jerusalem, and the deportation of the nation to Babylon. **The lesson:** We can hope in Christ even when we feel like our lives are failures.

Jeremiah preached for forty years and saw no visible result among those he served. Instead, those countrymen sought to kill him if he wouldn't stop preaching doom (11:19–23). He had virtually no converts to show for a lifetime of ministry. **The lesson:** We can hope in Christ even when we see no results from all we try to do for God.

This suffering and lonely prophet had no one in whom to find joy and comfort; his own family and friends were involved in plots against him (12:6). He never had the joy of a godly home because God never allowed him to marry, and thus he suffered incredibly agonizing loneliness (16:2). **The lesson:** We can hope in Christ even when we are alone.

Jeremiah lived under a constant threat of death; there were plots to kill him in secret so no one would find him (18:20–23). **The lesson:** We can hope in Christ even when we are close to death.

He lived with physical pain; he was beaten severely and then bound in wooden stocks (20:1–2). **The lesson:** We can hope in Christ even when we are filled with pain.

He lived with emotional pain; his friends spied on him deceitfully and for revenge (20:10). **The lesson:** We can hope in Christ even when we are sad and disheartened and feel betrayed.

He was consumed with sorrow and shame; Jeremiah even cursed the day he was born (20:14–18). His life ended with no relief; he was falsely accused of being a traitor to his own country (37:13–14). **The lesson:** We can hope in Christ even when we are sorrowing.

He was arrested, beaten, thrown into a dungeon, and starved many days (37:15–21). If an Ethiopian Gentile had not interceded on his behalf, he would have died there (38:7–13). **The lesson:** We can hope in Christ even when we find no relief from trials.

Perhaps the most striking feature of the book of Jeremiah is the fact that despite the terrible woes in his life (1:5), he saw that it was from the master potter's hand (18:1–6). At the point of near despair over his failed ministry, God asked him to go to the potter's house, and there he would get a message from the Lord (18:2). Although Israel had failed so grievously, the heavenly potter was willing to bless His people again if they would repent and yield to His perfect touch.

In the end, tradition tells us that Jeremiah was exiled to Egypt. While faithfully preaching God's Word to the exiles, he was stoned to death by his own people. In spite of everything, he found hope in worshiping our God of repentance. And you, too, can find living hope in Christ even when supposedly bad things happen to good people. Here is how: Through the LORD's mercies we are not consumed, because His compassions fail not. They are new every morning; Great is Your faithfulness. 'The LORD is my portion,' says my soul, 'Therefore **I hope in Him**!' The LORD is good to those who **wait for Him**, to the soul who seeks Him" (Lamentations 3:22–25).

When troubles come, knowing that God is good to all who turn to Him for help, the person who is genuine trusts in Christ and finds hope to "keep on keeping on"!

THURSDAY: Lamentations Says to Worship Our God of Hope

*"**The LORD is my portion**," says my soul, "therefore I hope in Him!"*
—Lamentations 3:24

Lamentations was written by Jeremiah. As he sat down and looked over the smoldering ruins of his beloved Jerusalem, his voice rose to the wail of sorrow, a lament. That is why the book is called Lamentations, which was a funeral dirge over the City of God. Inspired by the Spirit of God, this serves as a message of encouragement that the next time things crash and burn in your life and your whole world is falling apart—family, health, finances, emotions—look to God as the God of hope!

Lamentations is a beautiful master-crafted poem with five stanzas. Chapters 1–2 and 4–5 each start with a successive letter of the Hebrew alphabet (twenty-two in all). This form of poetry, called an acrostic, is lovely in form and powerful in communication. Chapter 3, the poem's centerpiece, has three acrostics, or a total of sixty-six verses. The theme of Lamentations and this middle chapter agree: "Great is Your faithfulness, almighty God!" The Lord taught Jeremiah that no matter how the world was falling apart, personally or nationally, he could still hope in God. And that is why we can find living hope for the end of days!

For an even clearer picture, let's go back to where we started in Lamentations. Meet Jeremiah. With his life in shambles—his friends all dead, and the smoke and stench of destruction all around everything he had ever held dear—Jeremiah wrote the poem that explains the pathway of hope.

The pathway of hope. Have you ever felt that life was too painful to even go on? Jeremiah did, and without the benefits and blessings we have in this church age. He persevered with living hope in the midst of that pain. In Lamentations 3, we can see the pains God uses, manages, allows, and, most of all, handles for us. Note how Jeremiah trusted and endured through the pain of these stresses.

- **Broken physical health:** "He has aged my flesh and my skin, and broken my bones" (v. 4).
- **Deep emotional strain:** "He has besieged me and surrounded me with bitterness and woe" (v. 5).
- **Periods of dark depression:** "He has set me in dark places like the dead of long ago" (v. 6).
- **Desperation and the burden of being trapped:** "He has hedged me in so that I cannot get out; He has made my chain heavy" (v. 7).
- **Feeling out of touch and distant from God:** "Even when I cry and shout, He shuts out my prayer" (v. 8).
- **Frustration and confusion:** "He has blocked my ways with hewn stone; He has made my paths crooked" (v. 9).
- **Anxiety and sadness:** "You have moved my soul far from peace; I have forgotten prosperity" (v. 17).
- **Physical weakness and hopelessness:** "And I said, 'My strength and my hope have perished from the LORD'" (v. 18).
- **Bitter affliction and aimlessness:** "Remember my affliction and roaming, the wormwood and the gall" (v. 19).

If Jeremiah were to stop with verse 19, we might feel discouraged as we face our own trials. But his list of woes actually crescendoed until it broke forth into overflowing hope in verses 21–26. After praising God for His daily compassions and great faithfulness, Jeremiah testified: "The LORD is good to those who **wait for Him**, to the soul who seeks Him. It is good that one should **hope and wait quietly** for the salvation of the Lord" (vv. 25–26).

What a God we serve! Just as He offers *hope* in Lamentations, allow Him to be what you need to make it through life on a *hopeless* earth. As we speed toward the end of days, God offers living hope to each of His children. Let Him weave your weaknesses, like fragile fibers, in with the countless strands of His promises. Let Him stretch and twist you into waiting hope. And then, when troubles increase, let Him bring you a fresh portion of His hope and goodness as you wait enduringly with hope in Christ.

FRIDAY: Ezekiel Says to Worship Our God of the New Heart

"I will give you a new heart and put a new spirit within you; . . . I will put My Spirit within you and cause you to walk in My statutes, and you will keep My judgments and do them."
—Ezekiel 36:26-27

Some contemporaries of Ezekiel (593-571 B.C.) were Daniel (605-536 B.C.), Habakkuk (612-588 B.C.), and Jeremiah (627-586 B.C.). While Jeremiah (forty-one years of ministry, 627-586 B.C.) played the funeral dirge of doom over Jerusalem, a lonely exiled prophet named Ezekiel (twenty years of ministry, 592-572 B.C.) was watching the gathering storm God would use to sweep Judah into captivity. In 598 B.C., Nebuchadnezzar captured Ezekiel along with 10,000 other fellow Judeans. Ezekiel arrived in Babylon at the age of twenty-five (2 Kings 24:8-16; Ezekiel 1:1-2). Deported to 200 miles north of Babylon, Ezekiel was 600 miles from Jeremiah in Jerusalem for the last twelve years of Jeremiah's ministry. And for twenty-six years Ezekiel was 200 miles north of Daniel (606-533 B.C.) who was in Babylon for his seventy-three years of ministry. These three prophets overlapped parts of their prophetic ministries. As Ezekiel lived away from his home and his people, he learned that he was never far from his God. God taught him that His presence was not limited to the temple in Jerusalem.

During the exile, Ezekiel lived in a house to which numerous captives came and sought counsel from him (8:1; 14:1; 20:1). After five silent years of counseling, he began twenty years of speaking for God. At age thirty, Ezekiel, like our Lord Jesus Christ, began his ministry by a river. In an astounding vision he saw cherubim, angelic hosts, and indescribable sights portraying the very throne room of God. Ezekiel was God's man. He saw God—and it changed his life!

Ezekiel saw God's glorious majesty. All these sights—"awesome gleam of crystal . . . glowing metal . . . like fire [like a] rainbow" (1:22, 27-28 NASB)—were given to Ezekiel to remind him of how awesome, how glorious, and how indescribably majestic God is! "Give unto the LORD the glory due to His name; worship the LORD in the beauty of holiness. [For] the LORD sits as King forever" (Psalm 29:2, 10b).

Ezekiel saw God's final authority. Seeing God's throne taught him that He was in control (1:25a). Ezekiel was a prisoner of war; he was surrounded by numerous enemies who had vandalized his home, dragged him away, and savagely ended the lives of thousands of his people. Yet, in the midst of even that, all the fears of life melted in the radiance of God's sovereign throne. And because God is on His throne, the words of this well-loved song hold true: "When peace like a river, attendeth my way, when sorrows like the sea billows roll; whatever my lot, Thou hast taught me to say, 'It is well with my soul.'"

Ezekiel saw God's absolute supremacy. The term "high up" really spoke to him because the throne of God is atop all else (1:26b). As Ezekiel saw the destruction of his nation he learned that God is not thwarted by man's disobedience. Though God is grieved and saddened, His plan will not fail. Nothing is beyond His throne or above it. God reigns!

Ezekiel saw God's unveiled glory in Christ. The sight of Christ "like a man" (1:26c) reminds us that our Lord Jesus Christ is "the radiance of His glory and the exact representation of His nature, and upholds all things by the word of His power. When He had made purification of sins, He sat down at the right hand of the Majesty on high" (Hebrews 1:3, NASB). Ezekiel got to see Jesus Christ, and now you and I get to see Him in His Book, the Bible.

Ezekiel saw God's unchanging promises. "Like a rainbow" (1:28) is given by God as a sign that He keeps His Word. What He says, He will do.

Did you know that the Word of the Lord can expressly come to you? I don't mean visions; He wants to talk to you through His Word. Will you let Him speak to you today? If you are God's servant, you will be open to God's Word. This means being attuned to His "still small voice" so that you can obey His directives as Elijah did on the mountaintop after the wind, earthquake, and fire of 1 Kings 19:10–12. Otherwise, you might miss a real treasure from the Lord!

Ezekiel waited for the hand of the Lord to lead him—like these angelic beings who followed the Lord's leading exactly, and were in concert with Him: "Wherever the spirit was about to go, they would go in that direction. And the wheels rose close beside them; for the spirit of the living beings was in the wheels" (Ezekiel 1:20 NASB). I would not want to go anywhere if the hand of the Lord was not on me. Would you? That is what God's servants are like.

Ezekiel demonstrated being in concert with the Lord through the loss of his lovely wife (16:2) who died (24:16–18). God in His sovereignty took her life as a preaching illustration for Ezekiel to Judah. Though saddened, Ezekiel followed the God of the new heart's lead to show these people that they needed a new heart. Are you willing to follow His lead regardless of the personal cost?

SATURDAY: Daniel Says to Worship Our God Who Rules

*"This decision is by the decree of the watchers, and the sentence by the word of the holy ones, in order that the living may know that **the Most High rules in the kingdom of men**, gives it to whomever He will, and sets over it the lowest of men."*
—DANIEL 4:17

Some contemporaries of Daniel (605–536 B.C.) were Jeremiah (627–586 B.C.), Habakkuk (612–588 B.C.), and Ezekiel (593–571 B.C.). In God's opinion of history, the kingdom of Babylon was the richest and most glorious of all the kingdoms of the earth. Babylon was the head of gold in the image God revealed to Nebuchadnezzar. As its realm spread across the then-known world, in its wake it left the dust of crushed opponents foolish enough to challenge God's chosen instrument of prophesied judgment. Nobody could stop the Babylonians because God was empowering them. As God is performing His purposes through His Word, we should not fight against Him. We must be in step with Him.

To the helm of that incredible empire rose an incredible young man of God, Daniel. Have you ever considered what it must have been like to be prime minister to the greatest empire in the world in its time? There would be untold streams of decisions, endless meetings, countless conferences, lavish banquets, and clay tablet work (like our paperwork). And don't forget the delays on the freeways in your chariot as well as the everyday needs of life such as going to the sandal shop, stopping to have new wheels put on the chariot, and tending to the needs of the horses.

Daniel was a very responsible man, committed, and most of all *busy*. How did he cope with life at the top? He knelt on his knees three times a day to pray, *just as he always did*. In the midst of his cabinet position in a worldwide empire, and all the pressures that came with such a position, Daniel *faithfully prayed*. Not just at a meal; no, he found a way to stop it all, go to a quiet, private chamber, kneel, and come into the presence of God in thanksgiving. When life is tough, when it seems like the bad guys are winning, remember there is a God in heaven who rules!

Having a God in heaven Who is in charge should cause each of us to live with conviction. Daniel made up his mind that he would not defile himself (1:8). Why? Because God wants His children to have standards of holiness in their lives.

Make a choice to live in hope. Through the testimonies of Isaiah, Jeremiah, Ezekiel, and Daniel, we find living hope to worship our God of salvation, our God of repentance, our God of hope, our God of the new heart, and our God who rules.

As signs of the end of days multiply, never forget that our God rules: "There is a God in heaven who . . . has made known . . . what will be in the latter days" (Daniel 2:28). God is in charge! He cares when you are in the midst of the fires in your life: "Then Shadrach, Meshach, and Abed-Nego came from the midst of the fire" (Daniel 3:26). Just as the Most High God walked beside these three servants in the fire, He will also compassionately walk with you through your fiery trials of faith.

Have confidence in Christ (past and future) because our God moves history along: *"the Most High rules in the kingdom of men"* (Daniel 4:17). Because He reigns, it is better to read His Word than to depend upon the news media to interpret what is happening in the world. Then, when you read or hear the news, you will perceive God's hand in it. For that reason, my interest in the news has been declining. The news is bad and crippling for spiritual lives because we can get addicted to it.

As you have communion (constant prayerfulness) with Christ, you will find enduring hope come what may: *"In the multitude of my anxieties within me, Your comforts delight my soul"* (Psalm 94:19). Like the psalmist, Daniel knew that if he turned to our Sovereign Lord, that he would find help in time of need.

God wants you to bring all your problems and fears to Him: "Daniel went to his house, and made the decision known to . . . his companions: that they might seek mercies from the God of heaven . . . , so that Daniel and his companions might not perish with the rest of the wise men of Babylon" (Daniel 2:17–18). In Daniel's night vision, God revealed the secret of King Nebuchadnezzar's dream. And Daniel responded in praise: "Blessed be the name of God forever and ever, for wisdom and might are His. . . . He gives wisdom to the wise and knowledge to those who have understanding" (Daniel 2:20, 21c).

Once you really see God, nothing else can fully satisfy. Have *you* ever seen Him?

WEEK 23
See Christ in the Old Testament

{ Hosea—Micah }

As the end of days approaches, you can find hope as you see Christ in the Old Testament—from Hosea to Micah![1]

SUNDAY: Hosea Says to Worship Our God of Faithfulness

*Then the LORD said to me, "Go again, love a woman who is loved by a lover and is committing adultery, just **like the love of the LORD** for the children of Israel, who look to other gods and love the raisin cakes of the pagans."*

—Hosea 3:1

Some contemporaries during the time Hosea (753–715 B.C.) prophesied were Jonah (793–753 B.C.), Amos (760–750 B.C.), Micah (742–687 B.C.), and Isaiah (740–681 B.C.). In all twelve minor prophetic books, from Hosea to Malachi, Christ is our "Promised Son of God." Each prophet declares that **God is in control**. Indeed, they do more than merely declare it; the sovereign hand of God is visible everywhere. Overspreading the words of these twelve writers is the reality that God is the sovereign Lord of history. They affirm that nothing happens, either to Israel or to the Gentile nations, that is not the result of His direct determination. The destruction by locusts, in Joel, was God's doing. Nineveh's ups (revival with Jonah) and downs (complete destruction in Nahum) were sent from the Lord. When Assyria decimated Israel, and Babylon wiped out Judah, it was God who did it. Any doubts over the precise purpose of God's actions evaporated the moment they remembered that Almighty God was in control.

All the minor prophets declare that **God is holy**. It was their comprehension of His utter holiness that was the impetus for their scathing indictments of sin. Wherever sin was found among God's people or in foreign lands (Edom, as in Obadiah; Assyria, as in Nahum), it was still an affront to the Lord and had to be dealt with. As nowhere else in the Scriptures, sin is denounced and repentance is ardently and earnestly demanded. These prophets declared that without genuine repentance, the judgment of God is inescapable.

The twelve declared that **God is lovingly just**. His love and justice often appears harsh to some, which simply reveals a basic misunderstanding of the perfections of our Lord. The great love of God for His people (even His love for Nineveh) caused Him to send messengers to warn of coming judgment. At the appointed time, if there was no genuine repentance, judgment fell. Sin is always an affront to God; it always destroys and is always judged. But for His own, the purpose of judgment is to turn the wayward from sin to their rightful Master. These truths must be emphasized as much today as they were 2,800 years ago. Individuals are still sinning and running away from God, just as Israel did. Nations are still offending the righteousness of a holy God, just as Israel did. But, as always, God will restore those who come to Him.

Hosea himself had a life of grief. His only beloved wife, Gomer, was persistently unfaithful. This sorrow gave Hosea a unique perspective to speak about the parallel unfaithfulness of Israel for its Lord. The compassionate heart of God, with no diminishing of His holy standard, is seen in the book of Hosea, which paints a powerful portrait of the coming revelation of the love and holiness of God perfectly revealed in Christ. There is moral and spiritual bankruptcy in the nation; sin is unashamedly practiced, and God is abandoned. Worship of the true and living God is replaced by false and lifeless idols. Hosea depicts the inward decay of a collapsing nation. Ultimately, in 722 B.C., Assyria captured and deported the people of the northern kingdom to the area we would now call modern-day Iraq.

Hope helps us to clearly see God's faithfulness in Hosea. We can learn valuable lessons from how God related to His people, and how they responded. For instance, God faithfully warned His people, but Israel forgot their Maker (8:14). However, He never forgot them; rather, God wanted them to remember Him all through their lives. This teaches the value of listening to God. Because Israel faithlessly lived apart from God by their deeds (Hosea 7:2), we are reminded of the importance of following the Lord. Because Israel faithlessly neglected God's Word and stumbled into sin (4:5; 5:5), but didn't even know it (7:8–9) because she became satisfied and forgot God (8:14; 13:6), we are cautioned to not neglect feeding upon His Word.

Israel faithlessly compromised God's plan by mixing with the nations (7:8), which caused them to wander and rebel (7:13). This ultimately led to their going astray by a spirit of harlotry (4:12; 5:4). Yielding to the enticement of "a little compromise" usually leads to full-blown rebellion. We need to obey the Lord.

God faithfully disciplined His disobedient children when they stumbled into sin (4:1; 5:2). He had to chastise them because they transgressed His covenant (6:6–7; 8:1; 13:4). This is true of nations and people alike, and repentance is the only wise choice of action. Hosea thus urged Israel to acknowledge their guilt (5:15), return to the Lord (6:1), know Him (6:3), and wait for Him (12:6).

With that in mind, we should respond daily to God's Word, and never put off obedience until it is more convenient. Listen to God faithfully, follow Him, feed upon His Word, and then respond in loving obedience. If you do, He will bless you for it!

My Prayer for You This Week: *Thank You, dear Lord, for the privilege of looking at many individual books, and just lightly touching on them, but seeing You, Lord Jesus, operative in each one, guiding, guarding, blessing, and judging those who would not listen. We want to be blessed and we want Your protection because we want to obey You with all our heart. With our whole heart, may we seek You. Oh, let us not wander from Your commandments! We pray in the name of our Lord Jesus Christ. Amen.*

MONDAY: Joel Says to Worship Our God of Wrath

*Alas for the day! For **the day of the LORD is at hand**; it shall come as destruction from the Almighty.*
—JOEL 1:15

Joel (835–796 B.C.) was a contemporary prophet with both Elisha (848–797 B.C.) and Jonah (793–753 B.C.). The book of Joel tells of a great plague of insects that came upon the land of Judah as God's judgment against sin. In the law, God had promised material prosperity to His people for obedience, and adversity for disobedience. The period described in the opening prophecy was one of famine and suffering because an enormous hoard of insects had eaten much of the vegetation. The distress in Judah because of this judgment is seen as a foreshadowing of greater distress in a coming day of greater judgment. That yet-future period is described as "the day of Jehovah," which may be considered as the theme of the book. "The day of Jehovah" is the time of God's judgment on the earth in connection with the Second Coming of Christ.

A simple, basic overview of the book of Joel is as follows:

- **Chapter 1—God seeks repentance.** Joel was commissioned to declare the lesson from the locust plague. So often the scientific explanation neatly blinds the eyes of people to God's hand behind the scenes—His ultimate goal being the repentance of His people, which refers to a "turn about."
- **Chapter 2—God gives revelation.** God alone knows and writes the future in advance. That is one of the exclusive features of the Bible that has set it apart from all other religious books on earth.
- **Chapter 3—God plans restoration.** Verses 1–17 are a portrait of universal judgment, moral declension, and physical disaster. Verses 18–21 are a picture of the eternal age—millennial blessing following the judgment of the day of the Lord, and the land, freed from wickedness, is again blessed of God.

Three benefits of an eschatological study. Eschatological means "related to the end of the world or the events associated with it."

1. **Eschatology points us to Christlike living:** *I fell at his feet to worship him. But he said to me, "See that you do not do that! I am your fellow servant, and of your brethren who have the testimony of Jesus. Worship God! For the testimony of Jesus is the spirit of prophecy." . . . And everyone who has this hope in Him purifies himself, just as He is pure"* (Revelation 19:10; 1 John 3:3).
2. **Eschatology produces hopeful living in us:** *Now may the God of hope fill you with all joy and peace in believing, that you may abound in hope by the power of the Holy Spirit* (Romans 15:13).
3. **Eschatology promotes confident living in us:** *Abide in Him; that when He appears, we may have confidence and not be ashamed before Him at his coming. [For] we know that we are of God, and the whole world lies under the sway of the wicked one. And we know that the*

Son of God has come and has given us an understanding, that we may know Him who is true; and we are in Him who is true, in His Son Jesus Christ. This is the true God and eternal life (1 John 2:28; 5:19–20).

The Lord wants to use disasters and tragedies, such as the locust plague in Joel, to refocus hearts upon Him. As someone once said, "God whispers to us in our joys, but shouts to us in our sorrows." Is there anything in particular in your life today where God is "shouting" to get your attention? In the Scriptures, repentance and forgiveness are always tightly bound together. It is as simple as this: if we repent, we will be forgiven; if we do not repent, we can't be forgiven.

TUESDAY: Amos Says to Worship Our God of Justice

*But **let justice run down like water**, and righteousness like a mighty stream.*
—Amos 5:24

Some contemporaries with the prophet Amos (760–750 B.C.) were Jonah (793–753 B.C.) and Hosea (753–715 B.C.). Amos prophesied during a period of national optimism in Israel. Business was booming and boundaries were bulging. But below the surface, greed and injustice were festering. Hypocritical religious motions had replaced true worship, creating a false sense of security and a growing callousness to God's disciplining hand. Neither famine, drought, plagues, death, nor destruction was forcing the people to their knees. As Amos (the farmer who became a prophet) visualized the nearness of God's judgment, he unflinchingly lashed out at sin in an effort to mobilize the nation to repentance. The nation, like a basket of rotting fruit, stood ripe for judgment because of its hypocrisy and spiritual indifference.

The name *Amos* is derived from the Hebrew root *amas*, which means "to lift a burden, to carry." Thus, his name means "Burden" or "Burden-Bearer." And he lived up to the meaning of his name by bearing up under his divinely given burden of declaring judgment to rebellious Israel.

Amos ministered after the time of Obadiah, Joel, and Jonah—and just before Hosea, Micah, and Isaiah. At this time, Uzziah reigned over a prosperous and militarily successful Judah. He fortified Jerusalem and subdued the Philistines, the Ammonites, and the Edomites. In the north, Israel was ruled by the capable King Jeroboam II. Economic and military circumstances were almost ideal, but prosperity only increased the materialism, immorality, and injustice of the people (2:6–8; 3:10; 4:1; 5:10–12; 8:4–6). During this time period, Assyria, Babylon, Aram, and Egypt were relatively weak. Thus, the people of Israel found it hard to imagine the coming disaster predicted by Amos. However, it was only three decades until the downfall of Israel.

In Amos 1:1–2:16, God explains why He judged the various nations:
- **Damascus** (1:3–5) was judged for **cruelty** (sledges of torture—human rights violations).
- **Gaza** (1:6–8) was judged for **slavery** (slave trafficking—selling people for money).
- **Tyre** (1:9–10) was judged for **dishonesty** (severing a treaty—breaking promises).
- **Edom** (1:11–12) was judged for **vengefulness** (sword of terror—hated her brother).
- **Ammon** (1:13–15) was judged for **violence** (sadistic triumph—cruelty to defenseless).

- **Moab** (2:1–3) was judged for **disrespectfulness** (spoiling tombs—spiteful to the dead).
- **Judah** (2:4–5) was judged for **disobedience** (spurning the Torah—unfaithful to God).
- **Israel** (2:6–16) was judged for **hard-heartedness** (social transgressions—greed-prompted indifference).

In Amos 3:1–6:14 God explains the purpose of the judgment, 7:1–9:10 pictures the judgment, and 9:11–15 predicts the yet-future restoration of Israel and its prosperity. Seven practical lessons can be learned from understanding God's judgment in this prophecy:

1. God patiently gives the nations time to repent before judgment falls. **The lesson:** Be careful to heed God's warnings in your own life.
2. God is no respecter of nations; all will be judged for their sin. **The lesson:** Be patient during personal chastisement. A proper response will yield "the peaceable fruit of righteousness" (see Hebrews 12:3–11).
3. When the cup of sin within a nation is full, judgment will be irrevocable. **The lesson:** Be evangelistic while there is still time; point as many as will listen to Christ's salvation.
4. God is sovereign over all nations, choosing the time of their rise and fall. **The lesson:** Be trusting God for His perfect timing.
5. Nations are held accountable for brutal abuse shown to countries captured in war. **The lesson:** Be praying!
6. God's standards for judging nations are similar, but the results differ. **The lesson:** Be cautious in your responses to world events.
7. God brings judgment on leaders and nations who perpetrate fraud, oppression, and violence against their people. **The lesson:** Be righteous in all your dealings, especially with the poor.

We live in somber times, and must seriously deal with sin lest our usefulness for Christ be hampered. Here is the key to lasting victory: "Rejoice always, pray without ceasing, in everything give thanks; for this is the will of God in Christ Jesus for you. Do not quench the Spirit. Do not despise prophecies. Test all things; hold fast what is good. Abstain from every form of evil" (1 Thessalonians 5:16–22).

WEDNESDAY: Obadiah Says to Worship Our God of Humility

*"The pride of your heart has deceived you . . . ; You who say in your heart, 'Who will bring me down to the ground?' Though you ascend as high as the eagle, and though you set your nest among the stars, from there **I will bring you down**," says the LORD."*
—OBADIAH 3–4

Obadiah (853–840 B.C.) was a contemporary with Elijah (875–848 B.C.), Micah (865–830 B.C.), and Jehu (855–840 B.C.). As A. M. Hodgkin writes,
Between the Gulf of Akaba and the Dead Sea lies a range of precipitous red sandstone heights, known as Mount Seir. Here Esau settled after he had despised his birthright, and his descendants, having driven out the Horites (Gen. 15:6), occupied the whole of the mountain (Deut. 2:12). The

capital city Selah, or Petra, 'Rock,' was a city unique in its kind amid the works of man. Perched like an eagle's nest (ver. 4) amid inaccessible mountain fortresses, the dwellings were mostly caves, hewn out of the soft rock (ver. 3, 6), and placed where you could scarce imagine a human foot could climb.[2]

The story of Esau and Jacob is that of twin brothers, sons of Isaac and Rebekah. They were not identical twins; actually, they were opposites (see Genesis 25:24–34). Esau despised his birthright. The man who had the birthright was in contact with God; he was the priest of his family; he was the man who had a covenant from God; the man who had a relationship with God. In effect Esau said, "I would rather have a bowl of soup than have a relationship with God."

Having seen Esau in the first book of the Old Testament, look now at the last book of the Old Testament and read this strange language: "'I have loved you,' says the LORD. 'Yet you say, "In what way have You loved us?" Was not Esau Jacob's brother?' says the LORD. 'Yet Jacob I have loved; But Esau I have hated'" (Malachi 1:2–3a). This is a strange thing for God to say: "I loved Jacob and I hated Esau." The explanation for that is in the little book of Obadiah where God said to Edom, "The pride of your heart has deceived you" (1:3).

Christ is the model of humility. James Boice points out, "But there is this to add. It is true that the sin of Edom, long indulged, worked itself into the very character of the people and therefore inevitably flowed on in history. But that same flow of history also brought One who lived by an entirely different standard."[3] There was a day in history when two kings confronted one another for the first time. One was an earthly king. He sat that day at the pinnacle of power. His name was Herod Antipas. Herod was a son of Herod the Great, who was an Edomite (or an Idumean, as the New Testament lists it). Herod the Great had slaughtered the babes of Bethlehem in his desire to exterminate Christ. His successor, Antipas, with whom we are concerned, was no better. He had beheaded John the Baptist and had been called "that fox" by Jesus (Luke 13:32). Antipas had everything he wanted. His income, expressed in American money in 2006, would be in excess of six million dollars a year. All the pleasures of life were his. If anyone stood in his way . . . well, the life of that person meant as little to him as the lives of the innocents of Bethlehem had meant to his father. The motto of his reign was: "What will it profit *me*?"

The other king was Jesus. He was the King of Kings, One Who, according to the flesh, was the natural heir to David's throne and who, according to His divine nature, was the Supreme King over all the kings of this earth. But He did not look like a king. He stood in humble clothing. He had been rejected. Within hours He was to die a felon's death. If Jesus had wished, He could have called forth legions of angels who would have vindicated His cause instantly and have swept the usurper Herod from the throne. But Jesus did not want the throne in that way. He did not want the throne until you and I could share it with Him. To make that possible He would die.

Herod said, "What does it profit *me*?" Jesus said, "What can I do that will be the greatest possible benefit to My brethren?" God vindicated Jesus. Jesus went to the cross. He died. But His death was followed by a resurrection, and today He lives to enable those who believe in Him to behave as He did and bring a true, supernatural brotherhood to this world. For his part, Herod went on with his revelry but soon was banished to Lyons, France, where he died in misery.[4]

This is the choice before us: go Herod's way or Jesus' way. We cannot do both. God wants to break us of pride because pride competes with God for control and glory. He therefore offers us actions that promote the growth of humility in our lives. I call these the "Three R's of Spiritual Growth":

- **Refocus:** "Humble yourselves in the sight of the Lord, and He will lift you up" (James 4:10).
- **Remove:** "Denying ungodliness and worldly lusts, we should live soberly, righteously, and godly . . . , looking for the blessed hope and glorious appearing of our Great God and Savior Jesus Christ, who gave Himself for us, that He might redeem us from every lawless deed and purify for Himself His own special people, zealous for good works" (Titus 2:12–14).
- **Request God's humility:** "Younger people, submit yourselves to your elders. Yes, all of you be submissive to one another, and be clothed with humility, for 'God resists the proud, but gives grace to the humble.' Therefore humble yourselves under the mighty hand of God, that He may exalt you in due time" (1 Peter 5:5–6).

Pride is the root of all sin, but humility is the root of all virtue. Pride leads to destruction (Proverbs 16:18), but humility brings blessings and honor from the Lord. Which category most represents your life's present testimony?

THURSDAY: Jonah Says to Worship Our God of Mercy

"**Should I not pity** Nineveh . . . in which are more than one hundred and twenty thousand persons who cannot discern between their right hand and their left—and much livestock?"
—JONAH 4:11

Jonah (793–753 B.C.) was a contemporary with Joel (853–796 B.C.) and Amos (760–750 B.C.). Our Lord God Almighty is both a chastening and a merciful seeking God (Jonah 1:1–2a). Out of the countless lives that have crossed the pages of time, we find two blips on the radar screen of eternity—seemingly insignificant to all but God. Eight centuries before Christ, a great storm swirled around a nameless boat somewhere in the Mediterranean. By all counts, it should have swamped that boat and sent the nameless mariners to the black depth of the sea to await judgment day.

Amazingly, these sinking sailors did not perish. Rather, they were miraculously rescued from harm by the Master of the ocean, earth, and skies. Of all places—sleeping in the dark, creaking, hold was an evangelist. Shaken awake by the terrified captain, questioned by shouted words over the fury of the storm, he spoke. And in Jonah 1:9 the disobedient rebel showed his heart. Asked to go east, he turned west. Told to rescue inland Ninevah, he sought the sea route to the furthermost western city known in his day—Tarshish, in western Spain.

In Jonah 1:3–9, we learn that there is folly in running from God, but power in speaking for God. It is ironic that, in spite of his persistence in disobeying the Lord and the breach of divine fellowship that it produced, Jonah gave a powerful testimony. Though Jonah's actions were wrong, his heart couldn't hide the Word of God for long—it just came out. And in all His power, God spoke to them.

You see, the Scriptures are God speaking. When you share them, the voice of God is unleashed. The Bible is the unsheathed sword of the Spirit. So he said to them, "I am a Hebrew; and I fear the Lord, the God of heaven, who made the sea and the dry land" (v. 9). Those first nine words struck harder than the gale howling about them. It penetrates deeper than the cold sea spraying their faces and stinging their eyes. For you see, the Word can penetrate the very soul of mankind. He may have been endeavoring to resign his commission, but he could not change his heart, which remained that of a true prophet. So he pointed these mariners to the only Lord God.[5]

The God Who will not let go. After Jonah gave his testimony (1:9), the sailors were "exceedingly afraid" (1:10). We have already been told once that the men were frightened of the storm. But why were the men so frightened at this point—apparently more than they were of the storm itself? They knew about Jonah's God. These men had traveled from port to port around the Mediterranean Sea, hearing many stories of other people and their gods. Are we to think they had never heard of the Hebrew people, or of the Hebrew God, Jehovah? Of course, they had heard of Him!

The sailors had probably heard these reports: Jehovah was the God who brought down the plagues on Egypt so that His people might be led out. He parted the waters of the Red Sea to allow the Israelites to escape into the desert, and then closed the waters on the pursuing Egyptian forces. He led the Hebrews in the wilderness for forty years, protecting them by a cloud that spread out over their encampment. By day, that cloud gave them shade, but at night it turned into a pillar of fire to give them light and heat. He provided manna to eat and water to drink. Jehovah parted the waters of the Jordan River to enable the Israelites to cross over into Canaan, and He leveled the walls of Jericho for them. Amazingly, He also caused the sun to stand still at Gibeon so that Joshua would have time to achieve a full victory over the fleeing Amorites. On and on the stories could have gone . . . It is no wonder that these sailors feared Jonah's God!

The great God of the Hebrews. A weak god was not pursuing this boat and its hapless mariners; it was the great God of the Hebrews, and for the sake of Jonah. Oh, how they were terrified! "What shall we do to you that the sea may be calm for us?"—for the sea was growing more tempestuous (1:11). They were unable to escape the fury of the storm, so they cried out to the Lord in fear: "We pray, O LORD, please do not let us perish for this man's life, and do not charge us with innocent blood; for You, O LORD, have done as it pleased You" (1:14). After the men threw Jonah into the sea, they "feared [reverenced] the LORD exceedingly and offered a sacrifice to the LORD and took vows" (1:15-16). The mariners were gloriously converted by our merciful God.

What happened after that? After a whale of a journey (2:1-10), chapter 3 shows Jonah arriving in Nineveh, preaching God's message. Then "the people of Nineveh believed God, proclaimed a fast, and put on sackcloth from the greatest to the least of them" (3:5). The king decreed that everyone was to turn from their evil ways in the hope that God would turn away His fierce anger, and He did (3:7-10). Jonah, however, was displeased with God's mercy, and became angry.

The danger of anger and hasty decisions. When we get angry at God, we often make the same serious mistakes Jonah made. What were they? He quit; he made a private retreat and became a *spectator*. In 4:9-10, God rebuked Jonah for his lack of compassion for the people of Nineveh. Jonah

4:11 reveals the heights of God's mercy when he had pity on that great city because of its 120,000 small children—those "who cannot discern between their right hand and their left."

We need to understand this truth: what God is going to do, He will do. If He has determined to save Mary Jones, God will save Mary Jones. If He has determined to save John Smith, God will save John Smith. Moreover, those whom He saves will never perish; neither will anyone pluck them out of Christ's hand (John 10:28). But note that God can do this through the obedience of His children, as He does later with Nineveh through Jonah, in which case they share in the blessing. Or He can do it through His children's disobedience, as we see here through Jonah's selfishness, in which case they miss the blessing. Either way, God blesses those whom He will bless, but the one case involves happiness for His people while the other involves misery.

Which represents your case? Are you resisting Him? Are you refusing His Great Commission? Or are you obeying Him in this and in all other matters?

Perhaps you are not yet a Christian. If not, learn from God's wonderful grace to the sailors. You have not yet perished in your godless state because God, who made the sea around you and the dry land on which you walk, preserves you. But do not remain indifferent to Him; turn to Him on the basis of the perfect sacrifice for sin made once by His own Son, Jesus Christ. Then follow Him throughout your days.

FRIDAY: Micah Says to Worship Our God of Righteousness

*What does the LORD require of you but to **do justly**, to **love mercy**, and to **walk humbly** with your God?"*
—MICAH 6:8

Micah (742–687 B.C.) was a contemporary with Hosea (753–715 B.C.) and Isaiah (740–681 B.C.). Although Micah was a contemporary with the prophet Isaiah, Isaiah was a court poet, but Micah was from a small village. Isaiah was a statesman, a herald to kings, but Micah was an evangelist and social reformer. He was God's messenger to the misfortunate, oppressed common people. Micah's message, however, like Isaiah's, is one of hope. Both speak of the birth of the coming Messiah and the salvation He would bring. And in two of the most remarkable passages in all Scripture, both speak, almost word for word, of Israel's future and the coming glorious earthly reign of the Messiah (Isaiah 2:2–4; Micah 4:1–3). Only seven chapters long, Micah's message contains some of the most familiar passages in all of Scripture. For example, the prophet announces the place of the Messiah's birth: "But you, Bethlehem Ephrathah, though you are little among the thousands of Judah, yet out of you shall come forth to Me the One to be Ruler in Israel, whose goings forth are from of old, from everlasting" (5:2).

One deeply impactful truth Micah points out is that as the leaders go, so go the people. He says that Jerusalem's leaders "judge for a bribe, her priests teach for pay, and her prophets divine for money" (3:11).

Micah points to Jesus Christ as the only answer to the world's problems. The poor, the oppressed, and the misfortunate have the "One who breaks open [and] will come up before them" (2:13). Christ the Messiah breaks through the obstacles in the path ahead. In the future He will do this for Israel, when the remnant is gathered into the fold. But today He helps us through our perplexing paths, as we trust in Him.

Messiah's kingdom will come (4:1–8), and Jerusalem will be its center (4:1–2). Peace will reign. Nations "shall beat their swords into plowshares, and their spears into pruning hooks; nation shall not lift up sword against nation, neither shall they learn war anymore" (4:3). Prosperity will abound, each will "sit under his vine and . . . fig tree" (4:4). God will be central as "we will walk in the name of the LORD our God forever and ever" (4:5). The same God who brings heaven to earth can bring solutions to our problems today.

What does God want from us in exchange? Micah answers that we are "to do justly, to love mercy, and to walk humbly with [our] God" (6:8). No one is exempt. We are to be clothed with Christ, according to God's expectations of us. We are to live the truth and look to Jesus!

SATURDAY: The Promised Son

> *"But you, Bethlehem Ephrathah, though you are little among the thousands of Judah, yet **out of you shall come** forth to Me **the One to be Ruler** in Israel, whose goings forth are from of old, from everlasting."*
> —MICAH 5:2

Micah's reference to Bethlehem prompts us to reflect upon Isaiah's and Micah's prophecies concerning the Messiah and the salvation He would bring. Almost word for word, they spoke of Israel's future and the coming glorious earthly reign of the Messiah (Isaiah 2:2–4; Micah 4:1–3).

Just as Micah had prophesied around 700 years before Jesus came, the little town of Bethlehem was indeed the birth place of the Messiah—the One who would be *"Ruler in Israel"*—the One *"whose goings forth are from of old, from everlasting"* (Micah 5:2)! At Christmas, we should therefore not only reflect upon the "eternal God's incarnation in the person of Jesus Christ" but also "His millennial reign as King of Kings (cf. Is. 9:6)."[6]

This Jesus Christ, the promised one, was foretold by Isaiah in language that has been heralded as one of the most beloved prophetic Christmas passages ever. In fact, Handel's *Messiah* so captures the beauty and heart of Isaiah 9:6–7 that I would not be surprised to hear this glorious music in the worship center of the universe! As you read through these words once more, worship the One of whom it speaks!

> For unto us a Child is born,
> Unto us a Son is given;
> And the government will be upon His shoulder.
> And His name will be called
> Wonderful, Counselor, Mighty God,
> Everlasting Father, Prince of Peace.
> Of the increase of His government and peace

There will be no end,
Upon the throne of David and over His kingdom,
To order it and establish it with judgment and justice
From that time forward, even forever.
The zeal of the Lord of hosts will perform this.

From this prophetic passage, we can conclude: "The Son will rule the nations of the world (Rev. 2:27; 19:15). . . . The Messiah will be a Father to His people eternally. As Davidic King, He will compassionately care for and discipline them (Isaiah 40:11; 63:16; 64:8; Pss. 68:5,6; 103:13; Prov. 3:12). The government of Immanuel will procure and perpetuate peace among the nations of the world (Isaiah 2:4; 11:6–9; Mic. 4:3)."[7] There is a glorious future in Christ that is yet to come, as our study in Revelation is revealing, but only if you personally grab hold of the eternal God's purpose for His incarnation, which is to "save His people from their sins" (Matthew 1:21).

God had made a promise to David that one of his descendants would have an eternal reign, and God always remembers His oaths. When the perfect time had come, the angel of the Lord appeared to Joseph and announced: "'[Mary] will bring forth a Son, and you shall call His name Jesus, for He will save His people from their sins.' So all this was done that it might be fulfilled which was spoken by the Lord through the prophet [Isaiah], saying: 'Behold, the virgin shall be with child, and bear a Son, and they shall call His name Immanuel,' which is translated 'God with us'" (Matthew 1:21–23).

What was foretold regarding the Messiah was also affirmed through the angel Gabriel, when he told Mary about the Son she was to miraculously bear: "He will be great, and will be called the Son of the Highest; and the Lord God will give Him the throne of His father David. And He will reign over the house of Jacob forever, and of His kingdom there will be no end" (Luke 1:32–33). So when the light of Christ burst forth upon the darkness of this world the night of His birth, a multitude of the heavenly host joyfully sang God's praises: "Glory to God in the highest, and on earth peace, goodwill toward [all] men!" (Luke 2:14). This is the gospel, which is meant for everyone.

Jesus Christ came to earth to bring *"liberty to the captives"* (Luke 4:18), and that was the message He preached at His hometown synagogue. Christ's salvation is offered to all who are in bondage to sin and death. We are powerless to set ourselves free; only Jesus, the Lamb of God, could pay the price necessary for our redemption (Ephesians 1:7; 1 Peter 1:18–21). As Warren Wiersbe has said, "When you trust Jesus as Savior, you are delivered from Satan's power, moved into God's kingdom, redeemed, and forgiven (Col. 1:12–14)."[8]

Make a choice to live in hope. Jesus' birth was the dawning of a new day that knows no night, for our night was ended by His light: "Through the tender mercy of our God, with which the Dayspring from on high has visited us; to give light to those who sit in darkness and the shadow of death, to guide our feet into the way of peace" (Luke 1:78–79).

Dayspring means "sunrise." God's Word sees lost people as those sitting in darkness, death, and distress. However, Christ's birth brought light, life, and peace. Jesus came into a manger one dark night to bear away the sin of the world. If you will ask Him, He will take your penalty, your debt, your stain, your sin. The story of Christmas is that the Sunrise has come! And the story of Revelation is that this same Jesus is coming again, and soon! Are you ready? You can find living hope for the end of days by opening your heart today to Christ!

WEEK 24

See Christ in the Old Testament

{ Nahum — Malachi }

As the end of days approaches, you can find hope as you see Christ in the Old Testament—from Nahum to Malachi![1]

SUNDAY: Nahum Says to Worship Our God of Judgment

The LORD is good, a stronghold in the day of trouble; and He knows those who trust in Him. . . . What do you conspire against the LORD? **He will make an utter end of it.** *Affliction will not rise up a second time.*
—Nahum 1:7, 9

Nahum (663–612 B.C.) was a contemporary with Zephaniah (640–621 B.C.). Two of the Minor Prophets, Jonah and Nahum, wrote their books totally about Nineveh, the capital of Assyria. Over a century before Nahum, Jonah spoke on God's behalf to the Ninevites and, from the king on down, they repented, at least for a season. Initially, they appeared grateful for His mercy. However, not too long afterward they presumptuously began to live in even greater wickedness than before.

The Assyrian monarch may have been checked by God in 701 B.C., but these were still great days for Nineveh. Sennacherib more than doubled the city's size, making it the world's largest city at that time. "A wall surrounded the inner city eight miles in circumference. It was one hundred feet high and so wide that three chariots could race around it abreast. It had twelve hundred towers and fourteen gates. Beyond this was a much longer, outer wall. There was an inner city, an outer city, and what we would call extensive suburbs beyond that. In Jonah this wide expanse was termed a "three days" journey (Jonah 3:3)."[2]

In their tremendous pride, wealth, and power, the Ninevites saw no need of God. They thus made a grave error in thinking of the Lord as being "slow to anger" but failing to recognize that "God is jealous" and "will take vengeance on His adversaries" (Nahum 1:2–3a). As Boice has well said, "There is one inescapable fact of the Universe: the wrath of God may not be evaded. It is so great that it hunted down and sacrificed no less than the Son of God, Christ Jesus! And if God spared not His Son, what will happen to the rebels at the Day of Judgment?"[3]

Nahum's prophecy concerning Nineveh's doom has three main parts. In chapter 1, God's judgment on Nineveh is determined; chapter 2 describes its destruction; chapter 3 reveals that judgment is deserved. Nahum, whose name means *comfort*, found solace in knowing that our sovereign, righteous God of judgment is in absolute control, and that He would right all wrongs in due season. Therefore, He worshiped our perfect God of judgment's character, as reflected in these verses:

- **Nahum worshiped by respecting God's vengeance:** "God is jealous, and the Lord avenges; . . . He reserves wrath for His enemies" (Nahum 1:2).
- **Nahum worshiped by trusting God's patience:** "The LORD is slow to anger and great in power, and will not at all acquit the wicked" (Nahum 1:3).
- **Nahum worshiped by resting in God's omnipotence:** "Who can stand before His indignation? And who can endure the fierceness of His anger?" (Nahum 1:6).
- **Nahum worshiped by waiting for God's good justice:** "The LORD is good, a stronghold in the day of trouble; and He knows those who trust in Him. . . . Behold, . . . the feet of him who brings good tidings, who proclaims peace! . . . For the wicked one shall no more pass through you; he is utterly cut off" (Nahum 1:7, 15).

We know that this prophecy of Nahum actually is a product of Divine inspiration, and not just a vehement thirst for human revenge, because it was fulfilled to the very letter. And in these days when monstrosities of wickedness terrorize the earth, on a scale never known before, when Christian and godly and innocent people in many lands suffer coldly calculated or brutally inflicted cruelties for the sake of upright principles, it is a thoroughly Christian attitude to pray for and to take refuge in the soon-coming final vengeance of God on the wicked, and His vindication of the upright.[4]

> **My Prayer for You This Week:** *Father, we are so thankful that You have chosen to call us Your beloved. As You said through Malachi, "I have loved you." I pray that of all things we would worship You, the God of Love—that You may be pleased to acknowledge Your ownership of us. Help us to be less acquainted with the evil going on around us and more acquainted with Your righteous holiness within us in Your Word. May we be in Your Word regularly, respond to Your Word, speak for You, and see You at all times! May the beauty of the Lord Jesus Christ rest upon us. In His precious name we pray. Amen.*

MONDAY: Habakkuk Says to Worship Our God of Sovereignty

> *Though the fig tree may not blossom, nor fruit be on the vines; though the labor of the olive may fail, and the fields yield no food; though the flock may be cut off from the fold, and there be no herd in the stalls—yet I will rejoice in the LORD,* **I will joy in the God of my salvation.** *The LORD God is my strength; He will make my feet like deer's feet, and He will make me walk on my high hills.*
>
> —HABAKKUK 3:17–19

Habakkuk (612–588 B.C.) was a contemporary with Jeremiah (627–586 B.C.), Daniel (605–536 B.C.), and Ezekiel (593–571 B.C.). God is watching us as we live in a nation suffering the same disease that ancient Israel suffered—a collective societal amnesia about our spiritual heritage. In ancient Israel it had to do with closing the temple down, hiding the Law of God, and neglecting His worship. In America it is found in the growing skepticism about objective truth. It is the dismantling of language, texts, and history to the point that history is eroded; society thus has no tradition and disintegrates! This is the proven lesson of history: when a godly nation turns from its spiritual heritage, judgment is inevitable and inescapable.

Listen to what the mighty prophet Habakkuk had to say:

- Chapter 1—**The burdened prophet talked to his sovereign God.** He asked some tough questions, such as: "Why do You, oh God, allow evil to continue?" Habakkuk concluded: God raises up adversaries to punish the wicked (vv. 5–11). But that raised another difficult question in his mind: "Why do You punish evil by using someone far more wicked?" (vv. 12–17).
- Chapter 2—**The bended prophet listened to his sovereign God.** He took his weighty problem to the Lord and patiently awaited His reply (vv. 1–4). In verses 5–20, he saw the perils of the wicked in which five woes were pronounced against sins. Habakkuk concluded: the righteous live by faith as a way of life, but the wicked have no hiding place.
- Chapter 3—**The blessed prophet praised his sovereign God.** Through prayer, he was comforted as he praised God for His great person (3:1–2), His glorious power (3:3–15), and His gracious plan (3:16–19). Habakkuk concluded: hope in God despite any hopeless situation.

What can we learn from Habakkuk? We should tremble at God's Word: "When I heard, my body trembled; my lips quivered at the voice; rottenness entered my bones; and I trembled in myself, that I might rest in the day of trouble. When he comes up to the people, He will invade them with his troops" (Habakkuk 3:16).

God expects each of His children to praise His holy name. The Scriptures teach that we can do so through echoing His attributes and His actions. One way to do this is by affirming these action truths before the Lord: *When I am burdened, I will talk to You; when I am bended, I will listen to You; when I am blessed, I will praise You!*

TUESDAY: Zephaniah Says to Worship Our God of Hope

> "The LORD your God in your midst, **the Mighty One, will save**; He will rejoice over you with gladness, He will quiet you with His love, He will rejoice over you with singing."
> —Zephaniah 3:17

Zephaniah (640–621 B.C.) was a contemporary with Jeremiah (627–586 B.C.). The Minor Prophets often seem to have a despairing tone. Evil appears to run unchecked. The wicked die, apparently unaccountable for their deeds of cruelty and greed. God's people fail to obey. Death takes them all away. But there is a light in the distance; rays of hope stream from the promise that the Righteous Judge will make all things right some day. And on the horizon is a brand-new world. Impossible? No,

God has already planned the ending. Zephaniah traced a bit of it in his closing words.

Because Zephaniah is a summary of the previous prophets, his content and style are very similar to the other eight. To best learn from Zephaniah, let's focus on the third chapter where we see "the Lord in the midst." Chapter 3 contains a beautiful spiritual lesson. It describes the sinful condition of a soul apart from Christ (vv. 1–2). Those who should have been leaders in righteousness are leaders in iniquity: the princes, judges, prophets, and priests. So the Lord himself takes the place of these leaders, and we see Him "in the midst," fulfilling each office in turn.

Like Zephaniah, we can truly worship our God of hope:

- **Christ is our perfect judge**—Who first comes to our hearts to convict us of all that is sinful there, and to bring His perfect judgment to light (3:5–7).
- **Christ is our perfect prophet**—Who comes to teach us to call upon His name with pure lips. Still "in the midst," He deals with the pride of heart, and brings us low into the place of blessing, in the presence of His holiness (3:8–13).
- **Christ is our perfect King**—Who comes "into our midst" as King, to reign in undisputed sway in the heart that is surrendered to Him. When the Lord fully reigns, the song thus begins (3:14–16).
- **Christ is our perfect High Priest**—Who is "in the midst" as our Great High Priest, bringing us into the place of communion with himself (3:17).

Trusting God in Zephaniah. The third chapter closes with the six beautiful "I wills" of what the Lord will do for us:

1. "**I will** gather those who sorrow over the appointed assembly, who are among you, to whom its reproach is a burden" (v. 18). God looks for genuine contrition over sin!
2. "**I will** deal with all who afflict you" (v. 19a). God deals with our adversaries in His time!
3. "**I will** save the lame, and gather those who were driven out" (v. 19b). God is the defender of the weak!
4. "**I will** appoint them for praise and fame in every land where they were put to shame" (v. 19c). God will give back for all we have lost for Him!
5. "**I will** bring you back, even at the time I gather you" (v. 20a). God has the timing and sequence of His kingdom plans all in order!
6. "**I will** give you fame and praise among all the peoples of the earth, when I return your captives before your eyes," says the LORD (v. 20b). God has chosen to restore Israel to the head of the nations in the Millennium!

Like Zephaniah, worship Christ, our God of hope, with your whole heart. Ask Him daily: "What can I do for *You*, oh Lord?" Then give Him your all.

WEDNESDAY: Haggai Says to Worship Our God of Sacrifice

"Is it time for you yourselves to dwell in your paneled houses, and this temple to lie in ruins?" Now therefore, thus says the LORD of hosts: **"Consider your ways!"**
—HAGGAI 1:4–5

Haggai (520 B.C.) was a contemporary with Zechariah (520-480 B.C.). There are defining moments that have shaped the course of history, and we remember many of them. For example, when Julius Caesar crossed the Rubicon River (taking his legions inside "the line of no return"), he set the stage for the Roman Empire as we know it. Young Martin Luther's hammer on the Wittenburg church doors rang out a message that altered the course of the church to this day. When Hitler invaded Danzig at the end of August, 1939, England's response shaped western history to the present day. Likewise, in redemptive history (the history of God's work in people) the response of the Jews to a message they heard on September 1, 520 B.C. (the modern equivalent of the date Haggai gives in 1:1) shaped the course of biblical history. In twenty-three short days, what had not happened in sixteen long years took place—the second temple was started. The first Temple (Solomon's) was destroyed in 586 B.C. Later, Herod did not build a new temple but expanded and embellished the second (Zerubbabel's Temple). So this was the beginning of the temple of Christ, the apostles, and of A.D. 70's destruction—a great turning point in history!

There are seven timeless truths about God that we can trace from the pages of Haggai:

1. **The Lord we love is powerful.** In this short book, the Lord is called by a name of His power—"the Lord of Hosts"—which was Haggai's favorite name for God. In using this name, our Lord God Almighty reveals the vastness of His control.

2. **The Lord we love is jealous:** " 'Thus speaks the LORD. . . : "This people says, 'The time has not come . . . that the LORD's house should be built.' " ' Then the word of the LORD came by Haggai the prophet, saying, 'Is it time for you yourselves to dwell in your paneled houses, and this temple to lie in ruins?' " (Haggai 1:2–4). The Lord often uses the name Jealous to describe himself. He expects to be given top priority, regardless of what is going on in our lives.

3. **The Lord we love is expecting a response from us:** "'You looked for much, but indeed it came to little; and when you brought it home, I blew it away. Why?' says the LORD of hosts. 'Because of My house that is in ruins, while every one of you runs to his own house'" (Haggai 1:9).

4. **The Lord we love is trustworthy:** "According to the word that I covenanted with you when you came out of Egypt, so My Spirit remains among you; do not fear!" (Haggai 2:5).

5. **The Lord we love is changeless:** "'The glory of this latter Temple shall be greater than the former,' says the LORD of hosts. 'And in this place I will give peace,' says the LORD of hosts" (Haggai 2:9). The Lord is the same "yesterday, today, and forever" (Hebrews 13:8). He is not tied to our museums of past greatness. God wants to live powerfully in and through us today.

6. **The Lord we love is blessing:** "Is the seed still in the barn? As yet the vine, the fig tree, the pomegranate, and the olive tree have not yielded fruit. But from this day I will bless you" (Haggai 2:19). Though He had to judge their past sins, there is blessing on the horizon.

7. **The Lord we love is personal:** "'In that day,' says the LORD of hosts, 'I will take you, Zerubbabel My servant, the son of Shealtiel,' says the LORD , 'and will make you like a signet ring; for I have chosen you,' says the LORD of hosts" (Haggai 2:23). After the word of wrath coming on the nations, the Lord assured an individual named Zerubbabel that he would be specially used of the Lord. God has big plans for each of us. Don't miss His plans for you!

The Lord we love—our great God of sacrifice—is powerful, jealous, trustworthy, changeless, and personal. And this wonderful Lord expects a response from us: worship. When we give Him the honor in our lives that He deserves, He loves to pour out His blessings upon us! Where does He rank in your own priorities?

THURSDAY: Zechariah Says to Worship Our God Who Jealously Seeks Attention

*"Therefore say to them, 'Thus says the LORD of hosts: "**Return to Me**," says the LORD of hosts, "**and I will return to you**," says the LORD of hosts.' "*
—Zechariah 1:3

Zechariah (520 B.C.) was a contemporary with Haggai (520 B.C.). Zechariah is the second of the final three prophets of the Old Testament. His name means "God remembers." Because each word of the Bible is inspired, this offers us a theme of the book. Unlike the thunder of Haggai, his contemporary, Zechariah, gave comforting messages of encouragement. Born as the son of a priest during the Babylonian exile, he seems to have been an orphan. He was called the son of Iddo, who was his grandfather.

Returning with the faithful remnant numbering 42,360 individuals under Zerubbabel, he joined those who came to restore the temple worship of the Lord. His ministry dates to the second year of the King of Persia named Darius Hystapses (521–520 B.C.). This dates his ministry to two months after Haggai stood at the ruins of the temple and preached his first prophetic sermon.

Just like Haggai, God burdened Zechariah for the neglected repair of the temple. However, God extended his prophetic view far beyond the Jews of his day. God sent him on a prophetic voyage that travels to the very end of redemptive history. He was given detailed insights surrounding the events of the coming Messiah, the Tribulation, the golden millennial age of Israel, and the reign of Christ. Because Bible teachers of the magnitude of Martin Luther believed that God was through with the Jews, they concluded that all of this had to be describing the church. Thus, they chose to not write on some parts of Zechariah's book.

Making choices to live in hope. We can choose today to reflect truths from this great Old Testament prophet that can change us.

- **Sin will bring God's judgment:** "Do not be deceived, God is not mocked; for whatever a man sows, that he will also reap" (Galatians 6:7). Pause and examine your heart. Is there a sin that you are trying to hide? Since God sees all things, instead of trying to hide it, turn from it in your heart by seeing sin as primarily against God. Do not blame anyone for your sin; tell God that you have sinned against Him and want to stop. Ask for cleansing grace to start over. Then decide to obey even the little things that God reveals.
- **God's past dealings with sin should cause us to repent:** "The men of Nineveh will rise up in the judgment with this generation and condemn it, because they repented [turned from sin] at the preaching of Jonah; and indeed a greater than Jonah is here" (Matthew 12:41). Since God

has told us that He resists us when we cling to sin in any form, speak to Him and say that you want to love Him and serve Him more than anything else. Remember that there are only two choices we can make in each decision of life—pleasing God or pleasing ourselves. Only what is done for God through Christ will last!

- **Turning from sin brings blessing:** "Therefore say to them, 'Thus says the LORD of hosts: "Return to Me," says the LORD of hosts, "and I will return to you," says the LORD of hosts' " (Zechariah 1:3). Even the most wicked, like Ahab, found mercy in turning. Manasseh, likewise, was forgiven (2 Chronicles 33:9-13). The instant we forsake sin we are blessed, the Spirit of God flows again through our lives, and we experience the new beginning that is our spiritual heritage in Christ. Do not wait, seek Him and find Him right now. Bow and yield, ask and receive.
- **God, like His Word, can never be evaded for long:** "Yet surely My words and My statutes, which I commanded My servants the prophets, did they not overtake your fathers? So they returned and said: 'Just as the LORD of hosts determined to do to us, according to our ways and according to our deeds, so He has dealt with us'" (Zechariah 1:6). God is not mocked and He is full of pardon. He delights in forgiving, cleansing, and giving us a fresh start. He longs to live the best life through us that is possible. Just give the helm to Him, and walk in obedience today.

FRIDAY: Malachi Says to Worship the God of Our First Love

"I have loved you," says the LORD. *"Yet you say, 'In what way have You loved us?' Was not Esau Jacob's brother?" says the LORD. "Yet Jacob I have loved."*

—MALACHI 1:2

Malachi (430 B.C.) was a contemporary with Ezra. In Malachi we find the last words from God in the Old Testament—words of His love! Last words are very important. Christ's last words contained His legacy for us, His body, the church. Our God is a God of love; He has shown that love ever since He came on a search and rescue mission to the Garden of Eden. As soon as Adam and Eve had fallen, God came to their rescue. And He loves with the same depth today.

Malachi is all about loving God, and what He expects from His special people. In just a glance at the book, we can see many problems among those special people, so the Lord points out and questions them about key areas lacking in their lives.

If you read Malachi section by section, you will find powerful spiritual lessons that teach about responding to the love of God (1:1–5), honoring the love of God (1:6–2:9), exposing God's unloving people (2:10–16), trusting the love of God 2:17–3:6), and acknowledging God's loving ownership (3:7–12).

In Malachi 3:7–8, God calls it theft when we disregard His ownership of our lives: "You have gone away from My ordinances and have not kept them. Return to Me, and I will return to you," says the LORD of hosts. "But you said, 'In what way shall we return?' Will a man rob God? Yet you have robbed Me! But you say, 'In what way have we robbed You?' In tithes and offerings." The whole tithe is an expression of God's ownership, or giving of ourselves back to God. Anything less is denying His complete title deed to us. God wants us to see Christ the crucified as the glorious King of Kings, and to rest beneath His wings as we worship our God of first love who owns us.

Because He bought us at such a high price (1 Corinthians 6:19–20), we should give ourselves completely to Him. In Malachi 3:10–12, the Lord is saying that if you give all, and hold nothing back (unlike Ananias and Sapphira of Acts 5), He will "open for you the windows of heaven and pour out for you such blessing that there will not be room enough to receive it."

The Old Testament prophets all spoke of seeing Christ as the One who rules our lives. He is the One whom we can trust to carry out everything. He is our God of hope, the One who will bring everything to pass just as He promised.

We have now come to the end of our study of the last twelve books of the Old Testament—a time when God's people fluctuated between listening, and refusing to listen, to the prophets of God. I pray that you have truly seen Jesus Christ in these books of prophecy and have worshiped Him all through these weeks!

The inter-testamental period. After Malachi came the inter-testamental period, which was the four hundred years between Malachi and Matthew. Many call these years the "silent period" because of the absence of any new inspired scriptures; however, those years are far from silent because God's Word mapped out the events of the entire period in advance.

From studying this period, we learn that the Jews were triumphant as they kept the Word, but were defeated when they lost sight of it. During this time, the four main Jewish religious groups of Christ's day developed: the Essenes, Pharisees, Sadducees, and Zealots. Additionally, the Apocrypha and the conclusion of Nehemiah, Ezra, and Malachi's ministry is clearly recorded. Finally, we see the fulfillment of the most explicit and detailed of all the Old Testament prophecies involving Christ's coming after His herald, John the Baptist, prepares the way. And out of those dark days came some bright saints: Joseph and Mary, Zacharias and Elizabeth, Simeon and Anna.

God always has His servants in every generation who speak for Him, and speaking for God *always* brings great blessings! Are you one of His servants in *this* generation who speaks for Him?

SATURDAY: Finishing Life Fruitfully for Jesus

And behold, there was a man in Jerusalem whose name was Simeon, and this man was just and devout, waiting for the Consolation of Israel, and **the Holy Spirit was upon him**. *And it had been revealed to him by the Holy Spirit that he would not see death before he had seen the Lord's Christ.*
—Luke 2:25–26

Malachi ends with the promise of Elijah who would turn the hearts of the people back to God. We now know that John the Baptist was that Elijah (Luke 1:15–17). Therefore, Dr. Luke, whose writings actually begin the New Testament chronologically, records the bridge to the Old Testament by taking us first to the angel Gabriel's appearance to John's father, Zacharias, as he served in the temple.

Zacharias means "God remembers" and *Elizabeth* (the name of John's mother) means "His oath," so together their names mean "God remembers His oath." Zacharias and Elizabeth are models of how to go on in spite of what others might call extraordinary challenges. (Week 51 will take a more in-depth look at this godly couple.)

Now let us look at two exemplary saints who came out of dark days: Simeon and Anna. They give us one of the clearest examples of how to finish life fruitfully for Jesus.

Simeon was filled with the Spirit. He was Spirit-filled and Spirit-led—a just and devout man who patiently waited for the "Consolation of Israel" because God had promised that he would not die before he had seen the Lord's Christ (Luke 2:25–26). He was Spirit-led, having come to the temple at the precise time Jesus' parents brought Him to fulfill "the custom of the law" (v. 27). Simeon was then Spirit-satisfied: he took Him up in his arms and blessed God and said: "Lord, now You are letting Your servant depart in peace, according to Your word" (Luke 2:28–29).

Warren Wiersbe tells us, "The word *depart* in the Greek has several meanings, and each of them tells us something about the death of a Christian. It means to release a prisoner, to untie a ship and set sail, to take down a tent (see 2 Cor. 5:1–8), and to unyoke a beast of burden (see Matt. 11:28–30). God's people are not afraid of death because it only frees us from the burdens of this life and leads into the blessings of the next life."[5] In the end, because we know he was a genuine believer, Simeon was also Spirit-sealed: "For my eyes have seen Your salvation which You have prepared before the face of all peoples, a light to bring revelation to the Gentiles, and the glory of Your people Israel" (Luke 2:30–32). So Simeon departed from the pages of God's Word—having finished life fruitfully for Jesus.

Anna faithfully waited and worshiped. She, too, finished life fruitfully for Jesus. What do we see in her rare life as a prophetess? She lived out the scriptural pattern for ending life pleasing to God.

In Luke 2:36–37, we see that Anna was what God wanted her to be. She had grown old, but kept on serving right where God had called her to serve—even if it wasn't much by others' estimation. Although she had known pain, she never gave in to despair, disillusionment, and bitterness. She kept on trusting the Lord as a widow, and gave what she had.

Anna fasted and prayed night and day, continually praising the Lord. When she saw an answer to her prayers, she gave thanks immediately (Luke 2:38b). Anna shared Jesus with others by speaking of what God was doing in her life, and telling all about Him to those who looked for redemption (Luke 2:38b).

What guide did Simeon and Anna follow? These two notable lives were the result of believing and following God's Word. Psalm 92:12–15 is a passage they both knew well, and lived: "The righteous shall flourish. . . . Those who are planted in the house of the LORD . . . shall still bear fruit in old age; they shall be fresh and flourishing. To declare that the LORD is upright; He is my rock, and there is no unrighteousness in Him."

Make a choice to live in hope. Simeon and Anna modeled how to finish life fruitfully for Jesus because they lived a life that counted. A fruitful life that pleases God is a chosen path. What pathway are you choosing to live?

I pray that you will decide to let God overflow your life with His grace. Affirm the goodness of God, for He is upright; He is our Rock; He is good! Make the goodness of the Lord your lifelong testimony and you will possess living hope for the end of days.

Remember, what we are going to wear in eternity is what we wore on earth: "Those who are wise shall shine like the brightness of the firmament, and those who turn many to righteousness like the stars forever and ever" (Daniel 12:3).

It is not the length of time we serve that matters most, but the depth of our passion for Him as we finish our race. Plan now how you want to end the race.

WEEK 25
Admire Christ's Perfect Sacrifice

{ Revelation 5 }

As the end of days approaches, you can find hope
as you admire the perfect sacrifice of Christ!

SUNDAY: Admiring Christ at the Throne of Judgment

"**Blessing** and **honor** and **glory** and **power** be to Him who sits on the throne, and **to the Lamb**, forever and ever!"

—REVELATION 5:13

As we look into the final book of the Bible again, remember that it is the revelation of Jesus Christ. The entire Bible is now combined into one majestic picture of Jesus as the Lamb of God. He whom the prophets foretold, the priest portrayed, and to whom John the Baptist pointed, the One who stood unknown in the midst of men, is now shown to be the center of God's plan for the last segment of time prior to when time shall be no more. And at the very center of the universe is His throne—a place of eternal calm, unceasing tranquility, perfect peace, and endless day—like the calm in the eye of a storm.

I had never experienced the calm in the eye of a storm until a hurricane swept through New England in 1989. Hour after hour, the winds increased until mature trees were snapping like little twigs. Then it happened: there was a perfect pool of quiet calm in between the storm's two-pronged devastation. And that is where we are in Revelation 4 and 5—a place of tranquility in between the stormy church age and the tempestuous end of the earth as we know it.

- **Revelation 1–3 reveals His struggling churches.** As Jesus looks at these saints with His laser-like eyes, He takes their pulse and then warns: "I am only finding some of your lives pleasing in My sight. Repent and come back. Do what I commanded you to do at first."
- **Revelation 4 reveals the calm between the two storms.** People who perpetually experience the presence of God can live in the eye of the storm continually, having calmness in the midst of the struggle all around them. Perfect peace always exists in God's presence.
- **Revelation 5–20 reveals the end of the earth.** To fully understand what is going on in these chapters, this week we will admire the perfect sacrifice of Jesus, and remember what He did for us.

In Revelation 5, John transports us from Patmos' prison colony mines to the highest point of heaven to let us gaze at a moment yet future. We are at the throne of judgment, and on the throne is the Judge of all, who is getting ready to take back the control of this earth that is reeling out of control toward destruction.

Chapter 5 is written in two distinct parts: verses 1–5 declare the utter unworthiness of mankind in the sight of God; verses 6–14 magnify the utter worthiness of the Lamb. Admiring the perfect sacrifice of Jesus Christ is all about acknowledging the greatness of what He accomplished at Calvary. You can find peace at the judgment of God by recognizing your unworthiness and guilt before His holy throne, bowing and worshiping the utter worthiness of the Lamb, Who is your perfect substitute!

My Prayer for You This Week: *Thank You, oh Father in Heaven, for the all-together perfect sacrifice of our Lord Jesus Christ, the worthy Lamb. Thank You, Lord Jesus, for being the next of kin to us, our kinsman Redeemer. Thank You for taking upon yourself the form of a servant in the likeness of human flesh. Thank You for humbling yourself and becoming obedient, even to the point of taking our frailty and our weakness and clothing yourself in the veil of Your fallen creatures. Thank You that You are not only next of kin but You were willing and able to redeem us. You wanted to redeem us; You loved us so much that you came to die, and You gave Your blood, Your life. You became sin for us. We admire the perfections of Your sacrifice. As we understand Your Word, may we in the greatest sense of our lives admire Christ's perfect sacrifice. We thank You, worthy Lamb of God, Lord Jesus, Root of David! In Your precious name we pray. Amen.*

MONDAY: The Utter Unworthiness of Mankind

*And I saw in the right hand of Him who sat on the throne a scroll written inside and on the back, sealed with seven seals. Then I saw a strong angel proclaiming with a loud voice, "**Who is worthy to open the scroll and to loose its seals?**" And **no one** in heaven or on the earth or under the earth was able to open the scroll, or to look at it.*

—Revelation 5:1–3

If you were living in the first century, a scroll with "seven seals" had special meaning. In New Testament times, to protect a will from tampering, Roman law required that it had to be sealed seven times. As it was rolled up, the will was sealed every turn or so, for seven times. The seals were not to be broken until after the person who made the will had died. "Seven," the number in Scripture that speaks of "spiritual perfection or completion," reminds us that Revelation 5 represents the perfect time of completion for the scroll to be opened.

These scriptures describe the official document that declares the climax of human history.

- **God has prewritten the future:** "The former things have come to pass, and new things I declare; before they spring forth I tell you of them" (Isaiah 42:9).
- **Ezekiel saw the same scroll:** "Now when I looked, there was a hand stretched out to me; and behold, a scroll of a book was in it. Then He spread it before me; and there was writing on the inside and on the outside, and written on it were lamentations and mourning and woe" (Ezekiel 2:9–10).
- **Daniel did not understand:** "Although I heard, I did not understand. Then I said, 'My lord, what shall be the end of these things?' And he said, 'Go your way, Daniel, for the words are closed up and sealed till the time of the end'" (Daniel 12:8–9).

The scroll before God's throne represents Christ's title deed to all that the Father promised Jesus because of His sacrifice on the cross: "Ask of Me, and I will give You the nations for Your inheritance, and the ends of the earth for Your possession" (Psalm 2:8).

The title deed belongs to the Heir, the only One who has the right to take back the earth: "God, who at various times and in various ways spoke in time past to the fathers by the prophets, has in these last days spoken to us by His Son, whom He has appointed heir of all things" (Hebrews 1:1–2).

No person is worthy to open the scroll. "So I wept much, because no one was found worthy to open and read the scroll, or to look at it" (Revelation 5:4). All humanity falls short of God's glory. No one is worthy among all the pharaohs, Caesars, khans, generals, dictators, and emperors. They, and all their subjects, fail to measure up to God's standard. All have died and have turned to dust.

No one on this sin-cursed earth has ever been born sinless except for One Who did not have an earthly father. He was virgin born, and that is why the virgin birth of Christ is so important. Adam's entire race is fallen. We are sinners by birth and by choice, so God declares every one of us to be sinners except for one—Jesus Christ. No one is good enough to stand beside Jesus and to undo the scroll, for "There is none righteous, no, not one" (Romans 3:10).

Our redemption depends totally on Jesus. For Acts 4:12 says: "Nor is there salvation in any other, for there is no other name under heaven given among men by which we must be saved." Upon whom are you depending?

TUESDAY: The Utter Worthiness of Christ

*But one of the elders said to me, "Do not weep. Behold, **the Lion of the tribe of Judah, the Root of David, has prevailed** to open the scroll and to loose its seven seals."*

—Revelation 5:5

Revelation 5:5 contains two truths: (1) The identity of Jesus is perfect, for He triumphed over sin, death, and the devil; and (2) the location of Jesus is perfect, for He is perfectly positioned. We will discuss the first truth today, and then cover the second in tomorrow's devotional.

"The Lion of Judah" identifies Jesus perfectly. As Jacob was speaking his last words, he prophesied the result of his son's choices: "Judah is a lion's whelp; from the prey, my son, you have gone up. He bows down, he lies down as a lion; and as a lion, who shall rouse him? The scepter shall not depart from Judah, nor a lawgiver from between his feet, until Shiloh comes; and to Him shall be the obedience of the people" (Genesis 49:9–10).

"The Root of David" identifies Jesus perfectly. (See Isaiah 11:1–10 and 61:1.) Christ is called the Son of David, but He is also the source of David because He existed before David. Consider this exchange between Jesus and the Pharisees: "While the Pharisees were gathered together, Jesus asked them, saying, 'What do you think about the Christ? Whose Son is He?' They said to Him, 'The Son of David.' He said to them, 'How then does David in the Spirit call Him "Lord," saying: "The Lord said to my Lord, 'Sit at My right hand, till I make Your enemies Your footstool?'" If David then calls Him "Lord," how is He his Son?' And no one was able to answer Him a word, nor from that day on did anyone dare question Him anymore" (Matthew 22:41–46).

The scribes and Pharisees could not understand what Jesus told them because they did not understand God. Christ is the promised Shiloh, the Root from which David derived his authority, and the son of David from which He got the legal kingly descent to rule over the Jews. And this same Son of David "has prevailed to open the scroll and to loose its seven seals" (5:5).

How did Jesus prevail? He is our beloved kinsman Redeemer in the book of Ruth because He was willing to give His life to set us free from bondage and to restore our lost inheritance. The book of Ruth is one of the most powerful presentations of Jesus Christ as our perfect kinsman Redeemer.

Only Jesus as the "heir of all things" (Hebrews 1:2) meets all the qualifications to become our kinsman Redeemer (see Leviticus 25:23–46): "If one of your brethren becomes poor, and has sold some of his possession, and if his redeeming relative comes to redeem it, then he may redeem what his brother sold" (Leviticus 25:25).

The Old Testament is a huge wealth of background information for understanding the New Testament. The Bible of the apostles and the Lord Jesus Christ was the Old Testament. Jesus showed himself to His disciples in the Old Testament. In Acts 28, Paul was in prison in Rome, but he spent two years convincing people from the Old Testament of the deity of Christ. Can you do that? The kinsman redeemer is someone who takes a helpless, hopeless person and brings them under His wing.

Here is Christ in the book of Ruth: Boaz said to Ruth, "'The LORD repay your work, and a full reward be given you by the LORD God of Israel, under whose wings you have come for refuge.' . . . Then Naomi said to her daughter-in-law, 'Blessed be he [Boaz] of the LORD, who has not forsaken His kindness to the living and the dead!' And Naomi said to her, 'This man is a relation of ours, one of our close relatives'" (Ruth 2:12, 20).

Do you remember the story of Ruth? Naomi and her husband, Elimelech, went to Moab because of famine in Judah. Their sons, Mahlon and Chilion, married Ruth and Orpah, who were Moabite women. After Naomi's sons and husband died, she returned to Judah with her daughter-in-law, Ruth. They were widows who had no one to take care of them, so they went to look for their kinsman redeemer. The first of kin was not willing and able, so he turned over his right to Boaz. Boaz married Ruth, and they became the great-great-grandparents of King David.

Ruth 4:4–6 tells us that a kinsman redeemer had to be three things: (1) closely related to the one in need; (2) willing and able to take the responsibility to redeem; and (3) able to pay the price of redemption.

You and I are like Ruth and Naomi; we are helpless and hopeless. We have lost our inheritance and are living in bondage. Therefore, we need a kinsman Redeemer who is next of kin to us and is able to pay the price of redemption. Jesus became one of us by taking on human flesh, so He is our **close kinsman Redeemer**. Jesus loved us and was willing to lay down His life for us, so He is our **willing Redeemer**. And Jesus paid the price of our sin with His own body and blood, so He is our **abundantly able Redeemer** Who "is also able to save to the uttermost those who come to God through Him" (Hebrews 7:25).

In this manner Jesus Christ prevailed. Thus, when He walked up to the throne of judgment, it could rightfully be said of Him: "the Lion of the tribe of Judah, the Root of David, has prevailed to open the scroll and to loose its seven seals" (Revelation 5:5).

As kinsman Redeemer, Jesus is utterly worthy of praise because He bought all our liabilities and all our sins to the end of our lives! Hallelujah, what a Savior!

WEDNESDAY: Jesus—The Right Person in the Right Place

But He . . . has an unchangeable priesthood. . . . ***He is . . . able to save to the uttermost*** *those who come to God through Him, since He always lives to make intercession for them.*
—Hebrews 7:24–25

Jesus is in heaven as our mediator. God the Son, who has been given "all authority" (Matthew 28:18), stands before the throne of God as omnipotent.

The location of Jesus is perfect. Jesus is perfectly positioned in "the midst of the throne [Jesus is located in heaven] and of the four living creatures, and in the midst of the elders, stood a Lamb as though it had been slain, having seven horns and seven eyes, which are the seven Spirits of God sent out into all the earth" (Revelation 5:6).

In verse 6, "the seven Spirits of God" does not teach that there are seven Holy Spirits. Rather, there is one sevenfold Spirit, described in Isaiah 11:2 as: (1) the Spirit of the Lord; (2) the Spirit of wisdom; (3) the Spirit of understanding; (4) the Spirit of counsel; (5) the Spirit of strength; (6) the Spirit of knowledge; and (7) the Spirit of the fear of the Lord.

The description of the Lamb, if produced literally by an artist, would provide a grotesque picture, but when understood symbolically, it conveys spiritual truth. Since seven is the number of perfection, Jesus is **omnipotent**—He has **perfect power** (seven horns); Jesus is **omniscient**—He has **perfect wisdom** (seven eyes); and Jesus is **omnipresent**—He is **perfectly present** (seven Spirits in all the earth).

Jesus is standing in the right place, as the right person, and is identified to be the Lamb of God. He is not a great angel, or Satan's brother, as the Mormons teach. He is not merely a great created being, as Jehovah's Witnesses claim. Nor is He simply a noble man, as the liberals would have us believe. Neither is He just a great prophet, as Muslims propose. Christ Jesus has all the attributes of Deity: He is the omnipotent, omniscient, omnipresent Son of God!

In Revelation 5:6–8, Jesus was promised as the perfect Lamb. He is called a Lamb (like a little pet lamb in contrast to a big sheep) no less than twenty-eight times in Revelation. A ram was substituted for Isaac (Genesis 22:8, 13), which is a picture of Christ giving His life for the individual (see Galatians 2:20). At Passover, the lamb was slain for each family (Exodus 12:3). Isaiah states that Jesus died for the nation of Israel (Isaiah 53:8; see also John 11:49–52).

John affirms that the Lamb died for the whole world (John 1:29). Peter said, "You were not redeemed with corruptible things, . . . but with the precious blood of Christ, as of a lamb without blemish and without spot" (1 Peter 1:18–19). The more you meditate on the power and scope of Christ's work on the cross, the more humbled and worshipful you should become.

The action of Jesus is perfect. In Revelation 5:7, Jesus takes the title deed as the exalted Lord of glory: "Then He came and took the scroll out of the right hand of Him who sat on the throne." Jesus stepped up to take the scroll, for He had paid the price as the perfect kinsman Redeemer, the heir of all things.

The reception of Jesus is perfect. In Revelation 5:8, Jesus hears and keeps all our prayers: "Now when He had taken the scroll, the four living creatures and the twenty-four elders fell down before the Lamb, each having a harp, and golden bowls full of incense, which are the prayers of the saints."

I love that verse—especially for those of us who are declining in health. Prayers are vital to God, and those of you who have extra time due to health problems can have a dynamic ministry of prayer! God loves to answer prayer, and He blesses churches whose people pray for all aspects of their ministry, and seek to glorify Him in everything. What a perfect love gift you can offer Him in behalf of others!

THURSDAY: The Elements of Christ's Perfection

*And they sang a new song, saying: "**You are worthy** to take the scroll, and to open its seals; for You were slain, and have redeemed us to God by Your blood out of every tribe and tongue and people and nation."*
—Revelation 5:9

In Revelation 5:9, a glorious new song about the plan of Jesus is sung: "You are worthy to take the scroll [worship of Jesus], and to open its seals [authority of Jesus]; for You were slain [substitutionary death of Jesus], and have redeemed us to God by Your blood [redemption of Jesus], out of every tribe and tongue and people and nation [gospel of Jesus], and have made us kings and priests to our God [ministry for Jesus]; and we shall reign on the earth [hope in Jesus]."

WEEK 25: ADMIRE CHRIST'S PERFECT SACRIFICE

In that song we can also see the elements of good Christian music. To truly honor Christ, we must be careful to check the content of what we sing or listen to because there are many new "crossover" songs in modern music that only talk about the Lord but never name Him. We should avoid songs that don't name the name that is above every name—the name of the Lord Jesus Christ! Christ-honoring music will include some or all of the following: worship of Jesus, the authority of Jesus, the substitutionary death of Jesus, the redemption of Jesus, the gospel of Jesus, ministry for Jesus, and the sharing of hope in Jesus.

In Revelation 5:11–12 the perfect sacrifice of Jesus is received. All heaven then breaks forth in celebration of His perfect character: "I heard the voice of many angels around the throne, the living creatures, and the elders; and the number of them was ten thousand times ten thousand, and thousands of thousands, saying with a loud voice: 'Worthy is the Lamb who was slain to receive **power** and **riches** and **wisdom**, and **strength** and **honor** and **glory** and **blessing**!'"

"To receive power!" Jesus came the first time as a weak and helpless baby, and Herod tried to murder Him. But when Jesus comes the second time, He will come as the omnipotent almighty God of the universe!

The Seven Elements of Christ's Perfections:

1. **Power**—Jesus has all power in heaven and in earth.
2. **Riches**—Jesus, Who owns all things, became poor for us. He laid aside all the treasures of heaven to walk on this earth as an itinerant prophet who was supported by gifts, but now He holds the ownership of the entire universe.
3. **Wisdom**—Jesus is the source of true wisdom. He was mocked, scoffed at, derided, and accused of everything evil that His enemies could think of, but now He stands as the wisdom of God.
4. **Strength**—Jesus is the mighty Lion of Judah. He was weary, thirsty, and tired at His first coming, but now He is the Rock, the fountain of the Water of Life, and the source of the power of an indestructible life.
5. **Honor**—Jesus shall be honored and every knee shall bow. At His first coming, He did not have a place to lay His head, but now countless myriads of eternal beings focus their adoration and worship on Him. Countless saints raise their voices in song, and the universe glistens and radiates with His glory.
6. **Glory**—Jesus is the highest of heaven adored. He showed His glory briefly on the Mount of Transfiguration, but now He shines as the brightness of the sun in its strength. All glory and honor is His! Every knee shall bow and every tongue shall confess that He is Lord of all!
7. **Blessing**—He is the One Who produces real and eternal joy.

As you reflect upon the seven elements of Christ's perfections, I encourage you to quietly offer a song of worship to this precious Lamb of God!

FRIDAY: The Lamb Who Overcomes

*"Now salvation, and strength, and the kingdom of our God, and the power of His Christ have come, for the accuser of our brethren . . . has been cast down. And **they overcame him by the blood of the Lamb** and by the word of their testimony, and they did not love their lives to death."*
—REVELATION 12:10–11

Now that we have seen Christ as the perfect sacrifice, consider these other wonderful references to the Lamb of God:

- **Jesus is the wrathful Lamb:** "[They] said to the mountains and rocks, 'Fall on us and hide us from the face of Him who sits on the throne and from the wrath of the Lamb!'" (Revelation 6:16).
- **Jesus is the worshiped Lamb:** "The Lamb who is in the midst of the throne will shepherd them and lead them to living fountains of waters. And God will wipe away every tear from their eyes" (Revelation 7:17).
- **Jesus is the warring Lamb:** "These will make war with the Lamb, and the Lamb will overcome them, for He is Lord of lords and King of kings; and those who are with Him are called, chosen, and faithful" (Revelation 17:14).
- **Jesus—"God with us"—rejoices at the wedding of the Lamb:** "Then he said to me, 'Write: "Blessed are those who are called to the marriage supper of the Lamb!" ' And he said to me, 'These are the true sayings of God'" (Revelation 19:9).

Do you admire the perfect sacrifice of Jesus Christ? Do you admire the worthy Lamb that was slain? From your heart and lips, do you attribute to Him power, riches, wisdom, strength, honor, glory, and blessing?

SATURDAY: Our Triumphant Lamb of Glory

*"Do not be afraid; I am the First and the Last. I am He who lives, and was dead, and behold, **I am alive forevermore**. Amen. And I have the keys of Hades and of Death."*
—REVELATION 1:17–18

Let's now see the Lamb of God in five stations as He brings to completion God's plan of the ages. When you worship, worship this wonderful Lamb of Revelation!

1. **The Lamb walks in the midst of His Church** (Revelation 1:11–18). He reveals himself in these wonderful ways: the Lamb is royal in splendor (1:13); the Lamb is purity and ancient wisdom (1:14); the Lamb is revealed with His power displayed (1:15–16); and the Lamb is revealed with His purpose defined (1:18).
2. **The Lamb waits at the door** (Revelation 3:14–22). Jesus is calling to us: "I stand at the door and knock. If anyone hears My voice and opens the door, I will come in to him and dine with him, and he with Me" (3:20). Remember: Jesus is standing outside the door, knocking.

However, He will not come in without being invited. If we open that door, He promises to dine lingeringly with us, which speaks of a time of sweet communion with Him.

3. **The Lamb is worthy of praise** (Revelation 4:11–5:14). "You are worthy, O Lord, to receive glory and honor and power; for You created all things, and by Your will they exist and were created" (4: 11). His position in the throne room of heaven is that of Creator; all that was done is for His pleasure. He was slain for man's sin, and is the heir to the universe. Because of this we see the rights He receives in Revelation 5:11–12: "power, riches, wisdom, strength, honor, glory, and blessing." This Lion of Judah is mighty, and He shall be honored; every knee shall bow and give Him glory, for He is the highest of heaven adored. And finally there is blessing—He is that which produces real and eternal joy. What is the response of all the universe in Revelation 5:13–14? The same as what ours should be; all creatures praise Him, and the whole universe and "the four beasts" worship Him.

4. **The Lamb wars against sinful men** (Revelation 19:11–20:15). In this scene we worship our Lamb of glory as we see Him triumphing during the Tribulation war. As commander of the armies of heaven, He appears for battle with clothing that is of vestures dipped in blood. He is called the Word of God, and conquers the kings of the earth and chains Satan. In Revelation 20:7–15, we see Him again as He finishes up the final postmillennial war. The key events are: Satan is loosed; the millennial last generation follows his deceptions; they are destroyed, face judgment, then go into eternity without Christ!

5. **The Lamb triumphantly welcomes the redeemed** (Revelation 22:1–21). This final glimpse of Jesus as the Lamb starts at God's throne as the source of the Water of Life, and ends at the seat of the Father and Lamb. Jesus, our Lamb, is the One who offers the tree by the river that brings healing. He declares the eternal triumph, and that there will be no more curse; His servants will now be free to offer unhindered service to Him. Revelation ends with the testimony that He is the Light who was revealed to those who keep His sayings. And because He is a great Savior, His last offer is one of mercy and compassion: "Let him who thirsts come. Whoever desires, let him take the water of life freely" (v. 17).

Make a choice to live in hope. This same Lamb of God walks in the midst of His churches today. He is waiting and watching to see if we are willing to open the door to Him that He may commune with us. All must, and shall, bow before Him in praise of His name above every name. And soon, He, the Lord of glory—the Lamb slain for the sin of the whole world—shall welcome each and every redeemed one to dwell with Him forever. Have you found the living hope that can be yours as you admire Christ's perfect sacrifice at the cross?

WEEK 26
Understand Christ's Wrath

{ Revelation 6 }

As the end of days approaches, you can find hope
as you learn to understand Christ's wrath!

SUNDAY: The Inexplicable Mystery

[He] is able to establish you according to my gospel and the preaching of Jesus Christ, according to **the revelation of the mystery** *kept secret since the world began.*
—Romans 16:25

Revelation 6 opens with the period that is known in the Bible as the Great Tribulation. To some, hearing talk about the impending arrival of Tribulation, such as this world has never known, may seem like just another science fiction story, or simply the delusion of alarmist Christians. Thus, scoffers often mockingly ask: "Where is the promise of His coming? For . . . all things continue as they were from the beginning of creation" (2 Peter 3:4).

Why God delays in reclaiming the kingdom for himself is an inexplicable mystery—the mystery of the presence of evil. For thousands of years, God has allowed Satan to wrap his vicious, slimy, filthy, cruel tentacles around human life and around this earth.

There is no village or town without its seething, and there is no human heart without its insidious darkness. There is no life without its tears and its sorrows. There is no home that ultimately does not get broken by death; there is no family that does not see the circle of the home dissolved by the depths of the grave. The pages of history, from the time of the first murder until this present hour, are written in blood, tears, and death.

Does God know all this? Is He indifferent to it? Is He not able to overcome it? The mystery of how and why God allows sin and suffering to run its deadly course through human history has been one of the most persistent questions that skeptical unbelievers have asked Christians. The infidel, the atheist, the agnostic, and the unbeliever laugh and mock us, and God allows them to laugh and mock.

God seemingly just looks on as our missionaries are slain, our churches are burned to the ground, and countless millions upon millions of people on this earth are oppressed and living in despair. He apparently does not intervene—nor does He say anything, and neither does He move. Sin just develops. It goes on and on. Oh, the mystery of the delay of the Lord God!

But somewhere beyond the starry sky there stands a herald angel with a trumpet in his hand, and by the decree of the Lord God Almighty, there is a day, there is an hour, there is a moment, there is an elected time when the angel shall sound the trumpet and the kingdoms of this world shall become the kingdoms of our God and of His Christ![1] When that trumpet sounds and God intervenes, the entire world will take note of it, and the mystery of God's delay shall be no more. But until then, you and I can find hope in knowing that some day God *will* right all wrongs! For He is the eternal King of Kings and Lord of Lords!

My Prayer for You This Week: *Oh Father, the question You inspired John to write in his rocky exile on Patmos 2,000 years ago is a great one for each of us to ponder: Who is able to stand before Your wrath—the wrath of Jesus, the Creator, the Judge—if You are not our Redeemer? I pray that this will be a sobering thought for any who are not spiritually prepared to stand before Your wrath, oh Christ, the Lamb. May we all realize what You want us to do during the closing hours as this world heads toward a ghastly ending. May we dispense Your antidote with our lips, speaking Your wonderful Words of life! May we not hesitate to do so because people are headed toward the horrors of the pit. I pray that You would touch each Christian's heart, oh Lord, to be Your good and faithful servant. May Your Word be magnified in every life! I pray this all in Your lovely name, Lord Jesus. Amen.*

MONDAY: The Horrors of Christ's Wrath

*"He will . . . say to those on the left hand, '**Depart from Me, you cursed**, into the everlasting fire prepared for the devil and his angels.'"*
—MATTHEW 25:41

Let us now look at that future moment when the trumpet sounds and the Lord opens the Tribulation to begin reclaiming His rights to the earth. One by one Christ will unroll the seals of Revelation 6. As each seal is broken, He will take further possession and control of His inheritance. Listed below are excerpts from the opening of each seal:

- **First Seal (vv. 1–2)—The Conqueror:** "A crown was given to him, and he went out conquering and to conquer" (v. 2b).
- **Second Seal (vv. 3–4)—Conflict on Earth:** "It was granted . . . to take peace from the earth, and that people should kill one another; and there was given to him a great sword" (v. 4b).
- **Third Seal (vv. 5–6)—Scarcity on Earth:** "He who sat on [the black horse] had a pair of scales in his hand. . . . 'A quart of wheat for a denarius, and three quarts of barley for a denarius; and do not harm the oil and the wine'" (vv. 5b, 6b).
- **Fourth Seal (vv. 7–8)—Widespread Death on Earth:** "The name of him who sat on [the pale horse] was Death, and Hades followed with him. And power was given to them over a fourth of the earth, to kill with sword, with hunger, with death, and by the beasts of the earth" (v. 8).
- **Fifth Seal (vv. 9–11)—The Cry of the Martyrs:** "'How long, O Lord, holy and true, until You judge and avenge our blood on those who dwell on the earth?' . . . And it was said to them that they should rest a little while longer, until both the number of their fellow servants and their brethren, who would be killed as they were, was completed" (v. 10b, 11b).
- **Sixth Seal (vv. 12–17)—Cosmic Disturbances:** "There was a great earthquake; and the sun became black as sackcloth of hair, and the moon became as blood. And the stars of heaven fell

to the earth, ... Then the sky receded as a scroll when it is rolled up, and every mountain and island was moved out of its place" (vv. 12–14).

Finally, in Revelation 11:15, when Jesus Christ unrolls the **seventh seal** and the seventh trumpet blows, it will be complete—He will have taken back the rule of His planet: "The seventh angel sounded: And there were loud voices in heaven, saying, 'The kingdoms of this world have become the kingdoms of our Lord and of His Christ, and He shall reign forever and ever!'"

During this terrible time of tribulation, one out of four people will die (6:8)—some through the ravages of war, others by starvation, and many others by the "beasts of the earth." Death may come instantly, without prolonged dread, or it may come slowly and painfully. In 2006, the world's population was 6,491,353,180; that means that at least 1,622,838,295, or more than five times the current population of the United States, will die. Can you imagine that? Because the population of the world doubles every thirty-nine and one-half years, the number of people who will die grows larger every day.

In addition, one-third of all vegetation will be burned up. All grass, every tree, and everything else that is green will be destroyed (8:7). The sun and the moon will be darkened as nature goes into revolt (8:12). The gates of hell will open and hordes of locusts shaped "like horses prepared for battle" will come upon the earth. Those locusts will be permitted to sting men like scorpions, and the pain will last for five months. The Bible says that men will beg God to let them die, but they will not die (9:6).

During the dreaded Battle of Armageddon (14:20), the blood of those killed in battle will flow for two hundred miles, and reach up to the bridle of a horse (about four feet) in the valley of Jezreel. And there will be worldwide famine unlike anything the world has ever seen (18:8).

What has just been described in the last three paragraphs represents only some of the highlights that describe the living hell you will avoid if you are part of the Rapture!

But *before* mankind is destroyed by nations or his own hand, "the Lord Himself shall descend from heaven with a shout, with the voice of the archangel, and with the trumpet of God. And the dead in Christ will rise first. Then we who are alive and remain shall be caught up together with them in the clouds to meet the Lord in the air. And thus we shall always be with the Lord. Therefore comfort one another with these words" (1 Thessalonians 4:16–18).

Do you have the hope of being caught up in the clouds to meet our blessed Lord in the air? Has Christ's forgiveness been applied to your life? If not, it can be today. God still stands with open arms saying: "Look to Me, and be saved, all you ends of the earth! For I am God, and there is no other" (Isaiah 45:22).

Altogether, as many as half the people on earth will be killed during the Great Tribulation. Because the events to come will be so horrible, God has promised that His born-again ones will be taken home to be with Him before His wrath falls upon this planet. Do you now see why God refers to the Rapture as a "blessed hope"? If He were to come today, would you be part of that glorious home going?

TUESDAY: The Chilling Words of God's Warning

*"Of **how much worse punishment**...will he be thought worthy who has trampled the Son of God underfoot, counted the blood of the covenant by which he was sanctified a common thing, and insulted the Spirit of grace?"*

—Hebrews 10:29

Yesterday we saw highlights of some of the dreadful disasters that will occur during the Great Tribulation. We see that same ominous message in Matthew and Mark. Note how Jesus describes the powerful effect of the coming pestilences: "Unless those days were shortened, no flesh would be saved; but for the elect's sake those days will be shortened" (Matthew 24:22; see also Mark 13:20).

Listen to Jesus again as He foretold that one of the signs of His Second Coming would be the onslaught of global pestilences: "There will be . . . famines and pestilences; and there will be fearful sights and great signs from heaven" (Luke 21:11).

There have always been diseases, plagues, and pestilences, but none have been capable of spreading worldwide until the advent of global travel. Until the invention of the steam engine in the nineteenth century, most plague carriers would die before they traveled very far. But beginning with air travel in the twentieth century, it became possible to harbor a plague or pestilence, board a flight, and reach a distant destination before ever exhibiting symptoms. By the time the disease was discovered, all those who had come in contact with that person would have already been exposed to the plague, and perhaps have become carriers themselves.

Consider the magnitude of possibilities from this report in the February 2005 edition of the *New Yorker*:

> The vicious avian flu that has killed dozens of people in Vietnam, Thailand, and elsewhere in the region has caused the deaths of hundreds of millions of animals in nearly a dozen Asian countries in the past two years and could kill millions of people if it becomes capable of spreading efficiently among humans. No such virus has ever spread so quickly over such a wide geographical area, and, unlike most viruses, this one has already affected a more diverse group than any other type of flu, and it has killed many animals previously thought to be resistant. . . .
>
> Robert Webster, a virologist at St. Jude Children's Research Hospital, in Memphis, who has been studying avian influenza for decades, was even more stark: "**This is the worst flu virus** I have ever seen or worked with or read about. We have to prepare as if we were going to war—and the public needs to understand that clearly. This virus is playing its role as a natural bioterrorist. . . . If it does happen, and I fully expect that it will, **there will be no place for any of us to hide**. Not in the United States or in Europe or in a bunker somewhere. The virus is a very promiscuous and effective killer."[2]

Not all politicians have ignored the threat. When Tommy Thompson, the Secretary of Health and Human Services, announced his resignation, he cited an avian-influenza epidemic as one of the greatest dangers the United States faces. The World Health Organization's conservative estimate of the number of deaths that an epidemic would cause is seven million worldwide. Because people transmit flu before they even have symptoms themselves, it would be extremely difficult, if not impossible, to halt the spread of the avian flu virus. And now, even a few years later, scientists around the world are continuing to warn us about the dangers of avian flu.

Amazingly, instead of talking about what *might* happen, current news reports are now talking about what *is* happening. Consider those reports, and others you've heard, in light of the full-blown Tribulation scene in Revelation 6.

Understanding Christ's wrath is exciting because its appearance means that our redemption is drawing near, and He will be reclaiming the earth that is rightfully His. Yet it is also chilling because of what it means to earth's inhabitants—including our unsaved family members, friends, and neighbors. God's people must therefore mobilize and urgently warn as many as possible!

WEDNESDAY: Inescapable Death

*It is **appointed for men to die once**, but after this the judgment.*
—Hebrews 9:27

In yesterday's lesson we saw that there will be nowhere to hide from worldwide pestilences like the avian flu. In a matter of a few weeks, death for millions upon millions would be inescapable. As described in God's inspired Word, that scenario certainly fits with when the Lord is reeling in this rebellious planet at the end of human history: "I looked, and behold, a pale horse. And the name of him who sat on it was Death, and Hades followed with him. And power was given to them over a fourth part of the earth, to kill with sword, with hunger, with death, and by the beasts of the earth" (Revelation 6:8).

The rider on the pale horse begins his deadly ride at some point during the Tribulation, and before his ride is over, a quarter of the population of mankind will be dead from either war, famine, or "the beasts of the earth." The word "beasts" in verse 8 is *therion* in Greek, and means a "venomous beast." The H5N1 avian flu is a viral infection that scientists fear has crossed over from the beasts of the earth to human-to-human transmission. Though the avian flu may not be the instrument of destruction that God uses in the Tribulation, it is plausible that He might use a similar type of disease to execute His wrath.

The existence of a deadly virus, combined with the other signs of the soon return of the Lord, suggests a loose time frame for the end of human history. For 2,000 years, that time frame was "someday" or "eventually." For our generation, however, the ability to kill a quarter of mankind with war, famine, and infectious disease is imminently real. As Dr. Michael Specter observed: "If not this year or the next, the following year, depending on the 'if-then' factor . . .

IF Iran doesn't use its nuclear weapons,

IF the Pakistanis and Indians don't nuke each other,

IF North Korea doesn't use its atomic bombs,

IF a vaccine is discovered for H5N1,

IF terrorists don't get their hands on bio-weapons,

IF no global war arises out of our newly articulated policy of spreading democracy into the Third World, and
IF the ongoing Middle East conflicts don't spark a global thermonuclear war first, THEN, maybe it might take a little longer."[3]
While we wait, we have been gifted, called, and empowered to be His witnesses.

- **The Motivation:** "For God so loved the world that He gave His only begotten Son, that whoever believes in Him should not perish but have everlasting life" (John 3:16). Our marching orders as believers came in Galilee as Jesus invited His disciples to their commissioning (Matthew 28:16–20). We are all to be involved in making disciples. We are to LOVE the lost by going to the lost.
- **The Power:** "No one can come to Me unless the Father who sent Me draws him; and I will raise him up at the last day" (John 6:44). We are to PRAY for the lost.
- **The Method:** "Him we preach, warning every man and teaching every man in all wisdom, that we may present every man perfect in Christ Jesus. To this end I also labor, striving according to His working which works in me mightily" (Colossians 1:28–29). We are to WARN the lost.
- **The Urgency:** "Knowing, therefore, the terror of the Lord, we persuade men" (2 Corinthians 5:11). We are to PERSUADE the lost.

Are you loving, warning, persuading, and praying for the lost? Make whatever time you have left on earth count for Christ—for eternity!

THURSDAY: A Tour of the Grave

*"There **was** a certain rich man who was clothed in purple and fine linen and fared sumptuously every day. But there **was** a certain beggar named Lazarus, full of sores, who was laid at his gate."*
— LUKE 16:19–20

Today we will be taking a tour of the grave—the destination of the vast majority of people whom you live with, work with, and see around you in daily life: "You and I, everybody you meet, from the mailman to the guy next to you at work, has an eternal destiny. That destiny is either a joyful existence in the presence of God, or a Christ-less eternity in the place prepared for the devil and his angels. It is a real place."[4] What I am about to share may change the whole way you look at death, dying, the grave, and the afterlife. The expert witness, the only One Who has ever gone to the grave and returned to report on it, is Jesus. No one has greater reliability or more to say on the afterlife than He. As Revelation 1 says, Jesus Christ alone has the keys to death and to the grave.

In Luke 12:16–20, Jesus told a parable of the rich man who mastered the "eat, drink, and be merry" lifestyle. He was so filled with greedy plans for the future that God said to him, "Fool! This night your soul will be required of you; then whose will those things be which you have provided?" (Luke 12:20).

Now consider what Jesus reports concerning Lazarus and the rich man. It is seen in the very important word "was" in Luke 16:19–20: "There **was** a certain rich man." Unlike Luke 12:16–20, Jesus did not use the word "parable" because He was speaking of a literal event of which He, as God, had knowledge. Jesus continued by saying: "So it was that the beggar died, and was carried by the angels to Abraham's bosom. The rich man also died and was buried. And being in torments in Hades, he lifted up his eyes and saw Abraham afar off, and Lazarus in his bosom. Then he cried and said, 'Father Abraham, have mercy on me, and send Lazarus that he may dip the tip of his finger in water and cool my tongue; for I am tormented in this flame'" (Luke 16:22–24).

Jesus explains another truth in that passage. Before their pardon was secured at the cross of Calvary, the righteous dead (like Abraham, Moses, and so forth) did NOT go directly to heaven as do blood-bought Christians of the church age. Instead, they went to paradise. The grave (Sheol, Hades) was at that time divided into two parts: "Abraham's bosom" was a place of comfort; the other was a place of torment. But both were located physically in the grave, or hell, as it is called in many places.

Note that the rich man could actually see Lazarus, which indicates a literal existence and therefore a literal torment and a literal flame. Abraham explained the division of hell to the rich man, including the fact that Lazarus could not come to him. Now look at the account again as the rich man cried out: "I beg you therefore, father, that you would send him to my father's house, for I have five brothers, that he may testify to them, lest they also come to this place of torment" (Luke 16:27–28).

The rich man remembered his life on earth, as he will for eternity. Thus he remembered his loved ones, and was conscious of their destiny. So he pleaded with Abraham to do something, but Abraham simply told him: "'They have Moses and the prophets; let them hear them.' And he said, 'No, father Abraham; but if one goes to them from the dead, they will repent.' But he said to him, 'If they do not hear Moses and the prophets, neither will they be persuaded though one rise from the dead'" (Luke 16:29–31).

Here is something extremely revealing about their conversation: Abraham is Abraham, and Lazarus, the beggar, is Lazarus; but the rich man had no name. He had his memories; he had awareness of his surroundings; he knew the hopelessness of the situation. The only thing he wanted more than a drink of water was to save his five brothers. But *he has no name*. Why is that so important? Because he does not need one; nobody will ever speak it again. There will be no reprieve, no visitors, no hope, and no need for a name. To all intents and purposes, he is dead, and will be eternally aware of that fact. Eternal, conscious, perpetual, lonely torment—dead forever, yet alive—always remembering the opportunities God had given him to escape such torment!

That is what awaits the mail deliverer, the guy or gal next to you, or friends and relatives of whom you say, "I'll talk to him (or her) when the time is right." Or, when he or she says to you: "I'll think about it. Maybe tomorrow . . . " But at any moment God could unexpectedly say, "Fool! This night your soul will be required of you!"

FRIDAY: The Full-Blown Consequence Engine

> ***Whatever a man sows, that he will also reap.*** *For he who sows to his flesh will of the flesh reap corruption, but he who sows to the Spirit will of the Spirit reap everlasting life. And let us not grow weary while doing good, for in due season we shall reap if we do not lose heart.*
>
> —Galatians 6:7–9

God always rewards good and eventually punishes all evil. No detail, no matter how minute, escapes His attention. But most lost people and many immature believers speculate that God, because He is good, grants some type of general amnesty to people by adding up the good deeds and subtracting the bad. And then, they suppose, He throws in some extra mercy here and there so that just about everybody can make it to heaven one way or another.

In a magazine interview prior to her two-hour special called *Heaven*, which aired on ABC in December 2005, newscaster Barbara Walters reported: "Most of us, regardless of our religious persuasion, do not think that life on earth ends here. We do not believe that this is all there is. There are some 10,000 religions in the world, and nearly all incorporate teachings of an afterlife. In America, nine out of ten people believe that heaven is a real place—and most have faith that they are going there at the end of their lives."[5]

Nothing could be further from Christ's Word in the Bible. Every human choice and action has consequences, whether good or ill. We are all affected by the choices others make as well. This reality of consequences, and God's laws that govern the physical and spiritual universe, I like to call "The Consequence Engine." The concept of the consequence engine is captured in Galatians 6:7–9.

The negative consequence engine operates for everyone in daily life. For example, driving over the speed limit can get us a speeding ticket, and driving under the influence can have more severe consequences. Not paying the rent usually causes a renter to lose his residence. Not showing up for work on time can get one fired. And the slightest disobedience to the drill sergeant in military basic training can prove painfully costly.

"Sensible people" who are law-abiding and "moral" cause less trouble for themselves in this life and are better as long as they live—compared to the person who is irresponsible, promiscuous, or abuses alcohol or drugs, and can't hold a job. Neither type of individual may end up in heaven, but this present life is less painful for people who see the intrinsic order in the world and who follow it as best they can, even if their motives are self-serving, and even if they do not know God.

Always remember that God takes note of everything that is going on. Nothing escapes His notice, especially a person's motives: "Judge nothing before the appointed time; wait till the Lord comes. He will bring to light . . . the motives of men's hearts. At that time each will receive his praise from God" (1 Corinthians 4:5 NIV).

Most people are not interested in knowing the real God; they are actually enemies of God. This general animosity toward the real God is the main cause of the invention of earth's many religions. God gives everyone enough knowledge of His existence and of His attributes so that all men everywhere are without excuse for failing to acknowledge Him (see Romans 1:18–21). When people hear, but reject, the gospel of Jesus Christ, God ordinarily leaves such people alone. They simply live out the rest of their lives, often in relative peace and even prosperity.

The consequence engines of life, inexorable and unavoidable though they may be, do not usually bring immediate consequences in response to our actions. An old proverb says, "The mills of God's justice grind exceeding slow—but they grind exceeding fine."

Because we often do not see the negative consequences of our bad choices right away, we may be persuaded to make bigger and more foolish mistakes. Because God's judgments are usually long delayed in time, many think the Lord never judges anyone at all. But, in the end, they will face not only physical death but also eternal separation from God because they never laid hold of the saving life of Christ.

The record books of life are being kept up daily by recording angels who miss no details. Judgment is totally fair and just, even for the lost. Punishment is appropriately proportional, following the great principle outlined in Romans 2. God weighs the motives of the heart as well as behavior, and He takes into account the individual's actual knowledge of God.

Unbelievers do not cease to exist when they die, nor do they pass into limbo or purgatory. After death they end up intact and conscious at the last judgment, which is the full-blown consequence engine in action for what was done in the flesh on earth: "I saw the dead . . . standing before God, and books were opened. And another book was opened, which is the Book of Life. And the dead were judged according to their works, by the things which were written in the books. The sea . . . and Death and Hades delivered up the dead who were in them. And they were judged, each one according to his works" (Revelation 20:12–13).

For the Christian, however, all sin is forgivable, but all sin *also* has consequences. We will not be judged for our sins, which have been paid in full by Jesus, but, like everyone else, we certainly will be thoroughly evaluated for all our choices in life. We cannot escape this fact: *all choices in life have positive or negative consequences.*

We only have two building materials in life—what will last (positive consequences) and what will not (negative consequences). That is another New Testament description of the consequence engine at work in the believer. What we do (build) will ultimately either endure, or suffer loss (see 1 Corinthians 3:10–15 and 2 Corinthians 5:10–11).

What counts most, actions that lead to positive consequences, are the works Jesus does in and through us when we make ourselves available to God. The basic rule of Christian life is this: "Nothing coming from me; everything coming from Christ!"

SATURDAY: Christ Is the Answer

> "You search the Scriptures, for in them you think you have eternal life. . . . But you are not willing to **come to Me that you may have life**."
>
> —John 5:39–40

I can't say this often enough: these are the last days! The Rapture is coming, and the Tribulation is almost upon us. So look up, for the King is coming! But He isn't here yet . . . and there are plenty of people alive today who won't be here then, either.

In the ten seconds of time it takes me to write this sentence, eighteen human beings awoke in eternity because they died on earth. Every hour, 6,464 more people die. That amounts to 155,131 per day, or 56 million a year. What should those alarming statistics mean to us? Three things:

1. **Life is fragile.** As the Lord has reminded us in His Word, our lives are but a vapor. We can be healthy, strong, and full of life today; yet, a tiny virus can make us sick tomorrow. The next day we can shiver and the following day we can fall over dead—just like the countless birds dying in Asia today. Life is too fragile to be wasted!
2. **Death is inevitable.** Although a few of us will be privileged to be changed in a moment, in the twinkling of an eye, at Christ's coming all lost people and most believers have an appointment with death. Death is unstoppable and inescapable. With the weather growing more violent, people becoming more openly wicked, warfare becoming more globally lethal, and pestilences stalking the planet like never before, life is truly fragile and death is inevitable.
3. **Christ is our only answer**—our only hope. Flu shots cannot help our souls. The United Nations is not able to stop the growth of evil. Our only hope is found in God's Word. The only escape pathway is laid out by Him.

- **God has given us the conclusion to human history**—the Bible. Trust Him completely. Since people are the only investment that lasts eternally, invest heavily in disciple-making.
- **God has given us a job to do while He is away**—soul winning. Therefore, obey Him now. If you have not started to share the gospel, the good news about Jesus Christ, start today.
- **God has given us a way to stay in touch with Him**—time spent in the Word. If you haven't started regular devotions yet, begin now to make reading His Word and praying a priority.
- **God has given us a means to start an investment account in heaven**—sacrificial giving. So then, give sacrificially to support His church. Don't waste the money He's entrusted you with, because God has told us that the earth is doomed. Be a good steward by using His money wisely for Him.

Make a choice to live in hope. As we rapidly approach the end of days, you can find living and abiding hope by choosing to please God and make disciples for Christ. How can you start? Ask the Lord to help you apply what you have learned this week.

WEEK 27
Remember Christ's Love

{ Revelation 7 }

As the end of days approaches, you can find hope as you remember the wondrous love of Jesus!

SUNDAY: The Love of Jesus

*"For **God so loved the world** that He gave His only begotten Son, that whoever believes in Him should not perish but have everlasting life."*
—John 3:16

Who could ever forget the dramatic scene of Revelation 6? Somewhere beyond the starry sky a herald angel stood with a trumpet in his hand, and at an elected time, by the decree of the Lord God Almighty, the trumpet sounded and the kingdoms of this world became the kingdoms of our God and of His Christ! Thus the Tribulation opened, and Christ began taking back the earth, which is rightfully His. One by one Christ will unroll the seals. As each seal is broken, He will gain further possession and control of His inheritance.

Revelation 7 then opens with Jesus sending 144,000 missionaries into this time of Great Tribulation upon the world. This is the most important chapter to help us truly understand the love of Jesus Christ. In no other place in the Bible is it so dramatically etched out as it is in the contrast between the wrath in chapter 6 and the mercy in chapter 7.

Christ's merciful love in Revelation 7 is demonstrated by His sending over four times as many missionaries into the world as are currently serving Him. At the beginning of the twenty-first century, there are only 35,000 missionaries of every persuasion, but during the Tribulation He will provide 144,000 evangelists!

Look at how Jesus shows His love throughout this overview of Revelation 7:

- **Verses 1–3:** Jesus stands with the servants of the Lamb, and prepares them for the bad times ahead. His Spirit signs, seals, and secures them.
- **Verses 4–8:** Jesus knows where His servants are at all times. He directs His servants, and seals 12,000 members of each of the tribes of Israel.
- **Verses 9–10:** Jesus wants His servants with Him.
- **Verses 11–12, 15:** Jesus seeks His servants' worship.
- **Verses 13–14:** Jesus promises His servants a fruitful ministry.
- **Verse 16:** Jesus comforts His servants after all their troubles on earth.
- **Verse 17:** Jesus refreshes His servants by His presence.

What a beautiful chapter! Like Jesus, do you share His loving passion for lost souls? Do you have a burden for the lost? If you haven't up to this point, would you like to get started? You can begin by making a list of unsaved family members, friends, and neighbors, and then start praying for them. Get a supply of gospel tracts at your local church or Christian bookstore, and ask the Lord to give you divine appointments to share those tracts. Then keep praying, and look expectantly for the Lord's direction. Once you begin giving away tracts and loving lost souls, Christ will grant fruit, and you will share in His joy over each person who turns from darkness to the Light.

My Prayer for You This Week: *Oh Lord, we thank You for the magnificence of Your love! It is so comforting to see Your love as the Lamb who shepherds, sustains, and meets every need and fulfills every desire of Your faithful servants. Thank You that before You unleash the horrors of the*

Tribulation on earth, that You put evangelists into every corner of this planet to give the good news of the gospel. Even when You are hated, You still mercifully send Your messengers. Oh, how we pray that we will see the beauty of what messengers of the Master in the Tribulation look like so that we can emulate them! If that is what You honor and love, that is what we want to be. We want to rejoice in the security and the knowledge of how You care for those whom You send out to minister. Open our eyes to behold more wonderful things about You, Lord Jesus, for it is in Your precious name that we pray. Amen.

MONDAY: How Jesus Shows His Love

*After these things I saw four angels standing at the four corners of the earth, holding the four winds of the earth, that the wind should not blow on the earth, on the sea, or on any tree. Then I saw another angel ascending from the east, having the seal of the living God. And he cried with a loud voice to the four angels to whom it was granted to harm the earth and the sea, saying, "**Do not harm the earth**, the sea, or the trees **till we have sealed the servants of our God on their foreheads**."*
—Revelation 7:1–3

We now meet the evangelists our loving God sends to rescue helpless sinners at earth's darkest hour. In the company of the Lamb are those who rest in the absolutely secure safety of the love of Jesus for His servants. Jesus shows His love as He stands with these slaves of the Lamb. How does He do that? Look at the elements of Christ's love in Revelation 7:1–3. Notice that Jesus calls for the angels to hold back the four winds lest the judgment should blow across the earth. Before the judgment sweeps down upon the earth, and these servants who are residing there, Jesus prepares them for bad times. Have you ever thought about that? Have you ever experienced some great and fruitful times of fellowship with the Lord just before bad times hit?

So many times my wife, Bonnie, and I have talked about the challenging and difficult periods we have gone through in our lives, ministry, and family. During such talks, we remembered with gratefulness how the Lord has often given special seasons when our fellowship with Him through the Word and prayer was elongated because He was lovingly preparing us for the hardships ahead.

These Jewish evangelists are also being lovingly prepared for what is ahead by being "sealed" with the mark on their foreheads of Christ's name and the name of His Father. But the term "sealed" is different from anything we know about. In the ancient world, a mark upon a person could stand for at least five different things:

1. **Ownership:** Often a slave was branded with his owner's mark, just as sheep and cattle are branded. In this instance, the 144,000 missionaries belong to the Lamb of God.
2. **Loyalty:** A soldier would sometimes brand his hand with the name of the general whom he loved and would willingly follow into any battle. In the presence of the Lamb stand the veterans who have proved their loyalty.
3. **Security:** Historically, a wax seal pressed with the imprint of an owner would secure that object as owned and belonging to another. Similarly, God's seal upon these witnesses, as

well as upon us (2 Corinthians 1:21–22), shows God's ownership—and the great security that brings!
4. **Dependence:** The great Arab chieftains had some humble clients who were absolutely dependent on them. Often, to outwardly identify that dependence, a sheik would brand his clients with the same mark used to brand his camels. In the company of the Lamb are those who are utterly dependent on His love and the grace of God.
5. **Safety:** "It was common for those who were the devotees of a god to be stamped with his sign. Sometimes that worked very cruelly. Plutarch tells us that after the disastrous defeat of the Athenians under Nicias in Sicily, the Sicilians took the captives and branded them on the forehead with a galloping horse, the emblem of Sicily."[1] So these marked ones in chapter 7 are owned, loyal, secure, dependent, and trusting. They are resting safely in the Lord because they have responded to the love of Jesus. Have you made time to experience Christ's love as you worship Him today?

TUESDAY: The Sealed of Israel

And I heard the number of those who were sealed. **One hundred and forty-four thousand of all the tribes** *of the children of Israel* **were sealed.**"
—Revelation 7:4

In chapter 7, the Lamb's servants are protected; no harm can come to those who are sealed. Who are these people? They are tribes of Israel, the Jews, not the church or anyone else. Many commentators have tried to show that they are not Jews—especially Reformed scholars who believe that God is through with the Jews forever, and is dealing with the church only. They believe that these special missionaries are either denominations or great triumphant Christians of the past. But what do Judah, Rueben, Gad, Asher, Naphtali, Manasseh, Simeon, Levi, Issachar, Zebulun, Joseph, and Benjamin have in common? They are all sons of Jacob.

The servants in this passage are born-again Jewish people. Jesus either confronts each of them personally, just like He did the apostle Paul, or perhaps there is a great outpouring of God in Israel at this time. We do not know for sure how they've come to Christ, but we do know from the Scriptures that these 144,000 are all converted.

In Ephesians 1, we see that when believers come to Christ they are: chosen, sealed, spiritually filled, spiritually led, protected, rewarded, servants, and owned. And, as Romans 8:16 says, the Spirit assures us that we are saved: "The Spirit Himself bears witness with our spirit that we are children of God."

This is exactly what God does for the 144,000 Jews who become Christians. The Holy Spirit of God seals them, so they likewise get to experience the great Shepherd's betrothal gift to His bride, which is the Holy Spirit—"the earnest" or "guarantee of our inheritance" (Ephesians 1:13–14).

The thought behind the word "guarantee" (NKJV) or "earnest" (KJV) is exactly the thought behind the idea of an engagement ring or down payment on something. Just as a bride-to-be delights in showing off her engagement ring, so we are to delight in "showing off" the Holy Spirit before the world to signify that our affections have been engaged to another: "to Him who is raised from the dead" (Romans 7:4). No longer are we to show any allegiance to the decaying and soon-passing world system. That is why it is spiritual adultery to love the world and all that is in it.

If you are truly engaged to Jesus Christ, this will be evident through special spiritual changes in your life. If you can see no such changes, you would do well to question: *Am I really betrothed to Christ? Is He my beloved?*

WEDNESDAY: The Holy Spirit Signs His Servants

*He who establishes us with you in Christ . . . has **sealed us** and **given us the Spirit** in our hearts **as a guarantee**.*
—2 Corinthians 1:21–22

God not only seals and secures His servants, but Jesus also shows His love by always knowing the whereabouts of His servants that He has signed His name upon (Revelation 7:4–8). There is something comforting about this in verse 4: "*One hundred and forty-four thousand of all the tribes of the children of Israel were sealed.*"

If you really want to confound a Jew, ask him, "What tribe are you in?" He won't be able to tell you. In A.D. 70, when the Roman General Titus came and burned the temple, genealogical records that were stored there, and zealously guarded, were destroyed. But God knows which tribe each of His people is in, and Jesus always knows where His servants are.

In Revelation 7:5–8, the tribes are not listed in their right birth order. Not all the tribes are there. Dan is missing, Manasseh is the son of Joseph, and Ephraim is not in this listing. The order according to birth would be: Reuben, Simeon, Levi, Judah, and so on. However, the list as it appears in chapter 7 is God's order. Judah is shown first because that is the royal tribe. The tribe of Dan is not there because they apostatized, and no apostate can be an evangelist. God has His purposes and He sets things in order as He sees fit. (By the way, this is not the same order listed in Revelation 21 and 22.)

Jesus will identify all the members of these tribes, confront them face-to-face, and draw them to himself. Some people have a problem with His chasing after the 144,000 like this because of feeling that in their own lives they had to search for Christ a long time before getting saved. Such persons simply have a wrong view of salvation. No one personally seeks the Lord: "There is none righteous, no, not one; there is none who understands; there is none who seeks after God" (Romans 3:10–11). God is the One who always does the chasing to draw us to himself. We were born dead in our trespasses and sins—we were not born looking for Jesus.

We can clearly see in the 144,000 that there are three elements to what the Holy Spirit does in each believer at salvation: (1) the Spirit signs us; (2) the Spirit seals us; and (3) the Spirit secures us. (We will cover all three elements over the next few days.)

First element of salvation—the Spirit signs us. "He who establishes us with you in Christ and has anointed us is God" (2 Corinthians 1:21). "Anointed" is the signature of God showing that we have security, and authentically belong to God. Many people in Christendom worry a lot about whether or not they are really saved. Usually this is due to having an incorrect view as to how they became a Christian. They forget *who* does the action and *who* is the initiator of salvation. The Bible says that it is always God.

Remember: we don't find Christ; He finds us. We are lost, and He is the seeker: "For the Son of man is come to seek and to save that which was lost" (Luke 19:10). He first finds us, we respond to Him, and then He establishes us. That means He grabs hold of us and anoints us with His Spirit; He signs us so that we are authentically His.

- His gift of salvation is **gracious:** "But as many as received Him, to them He gave the right to become children of God, to those who believe in His name" (John 1:12).
- His supply is **inexhaustible:** "For He whom God has sent speaks the words of God, for God does not give the Spirit by measure" (John 3:34).
- His anointing is **personal:** "But you have an anointing from the Holy One, and you know all things" (1 John 2:20).

It is so wonderful that we don't need a mystical anointing from some teacher. The Holy Spirit signs us so that we are authentically God's. Hallelujah!

THURSDAY: The Holy Spirit Seals His Servants

*After these things I looked, and behold, **a great multitude** which no one could number, of all nations, tribes, peoples, and tongues, standing before the throne and before the Lamb, clothed with white robes, with palm branches in their hands, and crying out with a loud voice, **saying**, "**Salvation belongs to our God** who sits on the throne, and to the Lamb!"*
—Revelation 7:9–10

In the verses above Jesus shows His love by wanting His servants with Him. Christ has a global desire to cry out His message. The 144,000 missionaries will go to the entire world and find the greatest response in history to the gospel—a numberless multitude will come to Christ. Because of His merciful love, Jesus wants lost people on earth to be with Him. Think about this: when you and I witness and share the gospel, we are extending Christ's invitation to people whom He wants to live with Him forever. What a privilege!

Why are the white-robed people there in verse 9? The Beast, the Antichrist, killed them. In fact, the Antichrist and his legions followed them around. Can you imagine being a missionary and having someone with an AK-47 standing behind you, ready to kill the people you lead to salvation? It would be hard to evangelize. Maybe that is why there are not more in the Muslim world coming to Christ because few missionaries are willing to go to them and be killed. But these 144,000 evangelists will boldly go forth to evangelize in spite of Antichrist's agents spying on them, and in spite of seeing those who come to Christ being martyred. They will be so zealous, and God's love in Christ will be so powerful, that as all hell is breaking loose on the planet, countless people will be led to Christ. For they will realize that their true citizenship is in heaven, as Scripture tells us in Hebrews 11:13–16.

Second element of salvation—the Spirit seals his servants. "Who also has sealed us and given us the Spirit in our hearts as a guarantee" (2 Corinthians 1:22a). The ancient world recognized the sealing of goods. People wore signet rings with distinctive markings on them. They would press their signet into soft wax or clay across the opening of a document, tomb, sealed box, and so on; it would bear an exact imprint of that signet ring, which signified that a representation of the owner was going with it.

The Holy Spirit's sealing of us is the believer's security of divine ownership. In other words, we have the image of our owner transferred to us. We bear the image of Christ—our precious possession. As we yield to Him, we will look more and more like Him every day because the Holy Spirit will impress the image of Christ on us.

We can't escape this truth: as we age we will act more like whoever our "god" is. For that reason, it grieves me as a pastor when I see professing Christians who do not look more like Christ every day. Instead, they idolize a current rock star, movie star, or sports figure. Although they may deny it, that person is their "god." Who you admire is who you want to look like. If you admire the Lord Jesus Christ and belong to Him, as you view Him through the picture window of the Bible, you will want to look more like Him every day.

When the Spirit seals us, it assures us of three things:

1. **We are verified**—the image of the owner's signet is transferred to us.
2. **We are signified**—by the presence of the owner. If the owner could not be at a transaction in ancient times, his ring signified that he had been there in spirit at least.
3. **We are certified**—the contents are authentic. We really have God's life and have His image within us!

Who or what do you serve? Is your "god" made in the image of man—or do you serve the authentic Lord God Almighty of the universe? The answer to that question determines your eternal dwelling place.

FRIDAY: The Holy Spirit Secures His Servants

All the angels stood around the throne and the elders and the four living creatures, and fell on their faces before the throne and worshiped God, saying: "Amen! **Blessing** *and* **glory** *and* **wisdom,** **thanksgiving** *and* **honor** *and* **power** *and* **might, be to our God forever** *and ever. Amen." . . . Therefore they are before the throne of God, and serve Him day and night in His temple. And He who sits on the throne will dwell among them.*
—Revelation 7:11–12, 15

Jesus shows His love by seeking His servants' worship. What a great joy it will be for Him to hear this massive outpouring of a sevenfold doxology! How will Christ be worshiped in verses 11 and 12? They will speak to Him. You can speak praises to God, too, and show other people how to prepare for worship. Look again at what He loves to hear: "Amen! Blessing and glory and wisdom, thanksgiving and honor and power and might, be to our God forever and ever. Amen." If you truly love Christ, tell Him: "Oh God, everything that is important I offer to You—my attention, possessions, and pleasure!"

The Old Testament worshipers used to bring their sacrifices in hands that were lifted up. When we enter the Lord's house, we should lift up our overflowing hearts of love in worship as a sweet-smelling sacrifice to God. Jesus longs for us to worship Him through His Word, songs, fasting, and prayer. All this focuses our lives on Him, as He desires.

If you want to enhance your worship experience, I encourage you to arrive early at services; sit down, stop your activity and thoughts, and become still before the Lord. Then open your Bible and get tuned in to the Lord (like you tune in your favorite radio station), for Psalm 46:10 says: "Be still, and know that I am God." We must purposefully open our hearts and let His Word draw us to Him so we can begin to worship Him as He deserves.

Jesus also shows His love by promising His servants a fruitful ministry (Revelation 7:13–14). This is a promise that has been fulfilled. Jesus discussed the Tribulation in the Gospels. In Matthew 10 He spoke to the Jews in particular, and secondarily to us: "You will be hated by all for My name's sake. But he who endures to the end will be saved. When they persecute you in this city, flee to another. For assuredly, I say to you, you will not have gone through the cities of Israel before the Son of Man comes" (vv. 22–23).

In Matthew 10:22–23, Christ is also talking about the 144,000 Tribulation evangelists. They are not only evangelizing the world, but Israel also. He predicted to them that they were going to have a fruitful ministry.

Look at Revelation 7:14 again: "These are the ones who come out of the great tribulation, and washed their robes and made them white in the blood of the Lamb." Jesus promised that His Word would not return void. He promised His servants that if they would give out the Word there would be fruit in response to Christ. Revelation 7:13–14 represents the greatest outflow of missionary evangelism in the history of the world.

As His servants, we ought to cling to His promise that we will be fruitful. All we have to do is go tell people, but sometimes we are unwilling. Perhaps this is due to busyness, fear, thinking they wouldn't be interested, and so forth. If we let him, Satan will happily flood our minds and hearts with excuses to avoid witnessing. It can happen to anyone. For example, someone I led to the Lord always sits in a certain place in our Sunday morning service. When I look in his direction, I am often reminded of how unwilling I was at first to share the gospel with him because I was so busy. Had I not done so, I would have missed the great blessing of seeing that person come to Christ. You and I should never forget that God promises us a fruitful ministry if we will just tell people about Jesus.

Third element of salvation—the Spirit secures his servants. "The Spirit in our hearts [is] as a guarantee" (2 Corinthians 1:22b). I remember so distinctly when I went to the office where my fiancée worked. In my pocket was a little box containing the engagement ring I had finally earned enough money to buy. I had already asked Bonnie to marry me, but she did not know I had a ring with me. We will never forget that diner where we ate lunch that day. After I gave Bonnie the ring, with every bite of food she ate, she displayed it for all to see.

Because I lived 500 miles away from her, I wanted to put a mark of ownership on Bonnie so that no one else could snatch her up. Spiritually, God gives us His pledge by giving us His Holy Spirit who is our "engagement ring" that displays the security of His protection. And He promises to bring us to the wedding day—taking us home to be married to Christ and live with Him forever. That is the threefold cord of our secure salvation: (1) we are signed with the very name of God; (2) we are sealed with the very seal of God; and (3) we are secured by the very presence of God.

Are you being faithful to the One who is to be your beloved Bridegroom?

SATURDAY: Christ Comforts His Servants

*"They shall neither hunger anymore nor thirst anymore; the sun shall not strike them, nor any heat; for **the Lamb** who is in the midst of the throne **will shepherd them** and lead them to living fountains of waters. **And God will wipe away every tear** from their eyes."*
— REVELATION 7:16–17

Jesus shows His love by comforting His servants after all their troubles. In the Great Tribulation, they will be hungry and thirsty, and the sun will scorch them. But in the midst of their suffering, the Spirit of God will draw them, and the Tribulation evangelists will then point them to the Messiah. After Jesus Christ saves them, they will be killed by the Antichrist. What will Jesus do then? He will comfort them. There is nothing like the comforting love of someone who truly cares for us!

Jesus also shows His love by refreshing His servants with His presence. The Lamb who is in the midst of the throne will shepherd them by leading them to living fountains of waters. God will wipe away every tear from their eyes. Can you see all the elements of His loving provision? He is with them, shepherding them, and refreshing them!

The comforting voice of Jesus. It is just like our Lord to speak to us when we need Him the most. His tender *"Fear not!"* can calm the storms in our hearts regardless of the circumstances around us.

- **Abraham heard His comforting voice:** "The word of the LORD came to Abram in a vision, saying, '**Do not be afraid**, Abram. I am your shield, your exceedingly great reward'" (Genesis 15:1).
- **Isaac heard His comforting voice:** "The LORD appeared to him . . . and said, 'I am the God of your father Abraham; **do not fear**, for I am with you. I will bless you and multiply your descendants for My servant Abraham's sake'" (Genesis 26:24).
- **Jacob heard His comforting voice:** "So He said, 'I am God, the God of your father; **do not fear** to go down to Egypt, for I will make of you a great nation there'" (Genesis 46:3).
- **King Jehoshaphat heard His comforting voice:** "**Do not be afraid** nor dismayed because of this great multitude, for the battle is not yours, but God's. . . . Stand still and see the salvation of the LORD . . . ! '**Do not fear** or be dismayed; tomorrow go out against them, for the LORD is with you'" (2 Chronicles 20:15, 17b).
- **Daniel heard His comforting voice:** "'**Do not fear**, Daniel, for from the first day that you set your heart to understand, and to humble yourself before your God, your words were heard;

and I have come because of your words.'... And he said, 'O man greatly beloved, **fear not**! Peace be to you; be strong, yes, be strong!'" (Daniel 10:12, 19).

- **Mary heard His comforting voice:** "The angel said to her, '**Do not be afraid**, Mary, for you have found favor with God'" (Luke 1:30).
- **Peter heard His comforting voice:** "Jesus said to Simon, '**Do not be afraid**. From now on you will catch men'" (Luke 5:10b).
- **Paul heard His comforting voice:** "Now the Lord spoke to Paul in the night by a vision, '**Do not be afraid**, but speak, and do not keep silent; for I am with you, and no one will attack you to hurt you; for I have many people in this city'" (Acts 18:9–10).

Because the Lord prepares His people for troubles, we can see the love of Jesus in all these verses. And you, too, can likewise experience the comfort of God's Son. The next time you feel alone and defeated, meditate on how the Lord ministered to these saints.

Make a choice to live in hope. What are God's servants like? They find hope for living in the fact that the loving Christ wants us to worship Him, wants us to refresh us with His presence, wants us to be still before Him, wants us to trust that He knows where we are all the time, wants to prepare us for bad times, wants to comfort us in all our troubles, wants to give us a fruitful ministry, and wants us to be with Him for all eternity!

These are all marks of Christ's love. We are His servants, and though we are not Jewish evangelists going through the Tribulation, every one of these elements is what God wants to give us today. He wants us to rejoice that we are signed and sealed and that He is going to safely deliver us home through death or the glorious Rapture.

WEEK 28
See Christ's Patience

{ Revelation 8 }

As the end of days approaches, you can find hope as you see the patience of Jesus!

SUNDAY: A Great Mystery of Heaven

When He opened the seventh seal, **there was silence in heaven** *for about half an hour. And I saw the seven angels who stand before God, and to them were given seven trumpets.*

—Revelation 8:1–2

Revelation 8 explains one of the great mysteries of heaven—how God responds to the prayers of His saints. As we gaze into the inner court of the Lord God Almighty, seven archangels are standing in God's presence. Before His throne there is an amazing silence as the voices of myriads of angels, the heavenly creatures, and the saints heard in chapters 4 and 5 are all strangely silent.

It is as if the coming judgments are so dreadfully frightening, so unsettling, that those surrounding God's throne are struck dumb, and all heaven becomes speechless. There, in a holy hush, the Great High Priest, who ever lives to intercede for us, approaches the throne of God and pours out the prayers of His saints.

In this chapter, we will learn how the patience of Jesus and those powerful prayers of His saints work together to fulfill God's purposes and how the vengeance God has promised to His people is poured out upon sinful earth in heaven's perfect time. We will also learn why we need hope and how we can have it.

Revelation 8 is divided into the following topics. In verses 1–2, God waits, giving men time to repent. In verses 3–5, God listens, giving men time to pray. In verses 6-13, God responds, giving us time to flee.

God waits—*time to repent*. Unlike us, God is patient. Before the judgment actually starts in Revelation 8:7, He waits a long time. Because we are a people of action, waiting is something that is hard for most of us. But God says that the greatest action that we can perform is being still before Him and praying. The half hour of total silence before the throne of God reminds us that this chapter is about the power of prayer and silence. As we offer our prayers before His throne, we will see God respond to those prayers, the angel pour out the censer, and the seven angels with the seven trumpets prepare themselves to sound as God begins the Tribulation.

What are some of the lessons ahead in this chapter's study? The coming judgments are dreadfully frightening, terribly unsettling, and the earth dwellers will have a horrifying end. The coming judgments should make us humbly reach out to our God of love and mercy while there is still time. Remember: only you can choose your destination. If you have not already humbled yourself before our merciful almighty God, I urge you to do so today!

My Prayer for You This Week: *Oh Father, how we praise You for being such a patient God! We thank You that there is still time for those who do not yet know You to repent, and to bow and yield themselves to Your great salvation and Lordship over their lives. For You are not willing that any should perish, but that all should come to a knowledge of the truth. May we never forget that prayer is vital and revered by You, our infinite heavenly Father. May we therefore make it a point to pray without ceasing. May our service be prompted by the fact that all around us are dear souls who are going to exist eternally, either in heaven or in hell. So, as we see the horrors coming, help us to be more zealous by laying aside the trifles of life and going out to witness to our family members, friends, and neighbors who do not yet belong to You. In Christ's name we pray. Amen.*

MONDAY: Solar Instabilities Ahead

*"Immediately after the tribulation of those days the sun will be darkened, and the moon will not give its light; the stars will fall from heaven, and **the powers of the heavens will be shaken**."*
—Matthew 24:29

Before continuing on with the next segment of Revelation 8, let us again consider this question: Are we actually close enough to think that we are the final generation?

Jesus said that the generation that sees His plan unfold for the end of days will witness His Second Coming. That promise has kept the church throughout the centuries in the Word, on their knees, and ready to go home to heaven at any moment: "Now learn this parable from the fig tree: When its branch has already become tender and puts forth leaves, you know that summer is near. So you also, **when you see all these things**, know that it is near—at the doors! Assuredly, I say to you, **this generation will by no means pass away till all these things take place**. Heaven and earth will pass away, but My words will by no means pass away" (Matthew 24:32–35).

Based on that passage, are we witnessing the unfolding of His plan for the end of days? Do the following happenings have a bearing upon the answer to that question?

- The global travel Daniel said had to happen is here, as well as the explosion of knowledge.
- The apostle John said that there had to be global commerce that was based on buying and selling with a personal number, and that is also here.
- Jesus said that Israel had to be back in their land, and they are there.

In Matthew 24, Jesus foretold that a series of specific signs would occur to signal the onslaught of birth pangs. Have those pains that signal the end of days started? I am not absolutely sure, but this much is clear: not since the birth of Israel in 1948—and not since the birth of the United Nations (also in 1948), United Europe, the World Council of Churches, and the computer—have we seen so many signs happening contemporaneously.

Just since Christmas 2004, a vast majority of the earth's population witnessed the second largest quake ever recorded; the government has warned that we have been observing the largest solar storm measurable; and now, more than ever, we have become aware that the largest threat to global safety may be hurtling through space toward our world right now.

Does all that mean anything? To sort it out, in Matthew 24:29–32 we find that there are three parts to Christ's warning: (1) the sun will be darkened; (2) the stars will fall; and (3) the powers of the heavens will be shaken. We will look at the first two parts today, and then cover the third one tomorrow.

Part 1 of Christ's warning—"the sun will be darkened." In the Tribulation, the earth will become scorched, and yet the sun will get darker. This could be massive sunspots that lessen visible light and maximize solar radiation. During the past few years, astronomers have witnessed the greatest solar activities ever recorded. The largest and most powerful solar eruptions have dazzled their instruments and made scientists wonder what is in store for the earth in days ahead. For example, on March 6, 2003 the largest sunspot ever seen developed. In October that year, there was "one of the most dramatic periods of solar activity we have seen in modern time."[1] Then, on May 15, 2005, we had one of the highest magnitude solar storms (G-5 in solar terms is like an F-5 tornado) sighted by the NOAA Space Environment Center in Boulder, Colorado.

God says that a day is coming when the sun will scorch the inhabitants of the earth: "Then the fourth angel poured out his bowl on the sun, and power was given to him to scorch men with fire. And men were scorched with great heat, and they blasphemed the name of God who has power over these plagues; and they did not repent and give Him glory" (Revelation 16:8–9).

Though this prophecy is clearly a divine judgment on unrepentant mankind, it is interesting that an event of great enough proportions to alter the earth's atmosphere could also take place due to nuclear war. Were that to occur, there would be "signs in the sun" (Luke 21:25) as the sky became partially darkened from the clouds of dust and debris in the upper atmosphere (which could facilitate God's judgment). However, this could also refer to an increase in sunspots and solar flares.

Part 2 of Christ's warning—"the stars will fall." When Christ returns, there will be global fears of an asteroid or comet strike, and an ensuing devastation. It is interesting that, until more recently, "the ultimate disaster" movie style wasn't common. In previous generations, they were not as aware of the objects hurtling through space faster than bullets and headed our way. Hal Lindsey reports:

> After years of studying the book of Revelation, I am still not sure as to whether the following prophecy is referring to a first-century man's observation of a thermonuclear attack, or if it's about an asteroid hitting the earth. The Apostle John observed:
>
> > *Then the third angel sounded [his trumpet]: And a great star fell from heaven, burning like a torch, and it fell on a third of the rivers and on the springs of water. The name of the star is Wormwood. A third of the waters became wormwood, and many men died from the water, because it was made bitter.*
> >
> > —REVELATION 8:10-11
>
> Whatever this is, it poisons a third of the Earth's fresh water supply, which is the reason it sounds more like the effect of nuclear radiation fallout. But there are some recent discoveries that indicate another possibility.
>
> In February 2004, [Congress introduced a bill which] mandates the allocation of $40 million to survey every near-Earth object 100 meters across or larger.
>
> Three months later, University of Hawaii astronomer David Tholen and a team from Arizona University discovered a new [near-earth object], shooting several photos of it before storm clouds obscured their view. Six months after that, Australian astronomers spotted the asteroid again, naming it 2004 MN4. This time, astronomers were able to calculate the asteroid's trajectory, and announced to the world that it would impact with the Earth on Friday the 13th in April 2029.[2]
>
> On December 28, 2004, astronomers announced they had refined their calculations and said that 2004 MN4 probably wouldn't impact the Earth. They speculated that although MN4 will probably miss the earth in 2029, there are no guarantees. In other words, a collision with 2004 MN4 remains a definite "maybe."[3]

Of course, the original prediction announced that Christmas Eve was overshadowed by holiday events and was soon buried by the event that occurred two days later—the Sumatran-Andaman earthquake.

In spite of the terrifying events to come, God does not want His children to fear—like those who have no hope: "For God has not given us a spirit of fear, but of power and of love and of a sound mind" (2 Timothy 1:7). Trust Him, for He is your safe refuge!

TUESDAY: The Heavens Will Shake!

*"Men's hearts failing them from fear and the expectation of those things which are coming on the earth, for **the powers of the heavens will be shaken**."*

—LUKE 21:26

Not only will the sun be darkened, and the stars fall, but there will also be great earthquakes in various places!

Part 3 of Christ's warning—"the powers of the heavens will be shaken." Both natural and supernatural phenomena in the earth and sky appear to be increasing. And when Christ returns there will be cosmic quakes: "There will be great earthquakes in various places, and famines and pestilences; and there will be fearful sights and great signs from heaven" (Luke 21:11).

On December 26, 2004, two days after that amazing prediction about asteroid 2004 MN4, our planet was struck by the Sumatran-Andaman earthquake. That quake was so massive that scientists are still analyzing what happened. But this we do know: the earthquake lasted about ten minutes; it is the longest quake ever known, and was the most powerful ever recorded. The quake, centered in the Indian Ocean, created the largest gash in the earth's seabed ever observed. It was the second deadliest quake known to history. The quake was also the second largest to hit our planet (that we are aware of) and is only surpassed by the 1960 Chilean quake.

So we have lived through the second biggest, second deadliest, longest, and most powerful quake ever felt and measured by man. We have been warned that a space rock is headed closer than any has ever been and that it will be the first asteroid visible with the naked eye from earth. And, on May 15, 2005, we had the highest-level solar storm sighted by the NOAA.

How can you get ready? Live in the hope of Christ's return. Trust Him with your future. Wait upon Him to guide your daily life. Avoid whatever grieves Him. Resist fearing anything but God!

WEDNESDAY: Prayer—a Sweet-Smelling Sacrifice

*Then another angel, having a golden censer, came and stood at the altar. He was given much incense, that he should offer it with **the prayers of all the saints** upon the golden altar which was before the throne. And the smoke of the incense, with the prayers of the saints, ascended before God from the angel's hand. Then the angel took the censer, filled it with fire from the altar, and threw it to the earth. And there were noises, thunderings, lightnings, and an earthquake.*

—REVELATION 8:3–5

Perhaps the altar spoken of in Revelation 8:3–5 has made you wonder what kind of altar is in heaven. Are there animal sacrifices going on up there? No. Is Jesus offering himself over and over again in heaven? No. So then, what altar is left? If you look at the setting of this passage, you will see that it is right in front of the throne.

The altar noted seven times in heaven (Revelation 6:9; 8:3 twice; 8:5; 9:13; 14:18 and 16:7) is not an altar of burnt offering. Jesus was offered once; therefore, no animal sacrifices in heaven are needed. The only other altar is the altar of incense. This altar is found in the third and fourth books of Moses (Leviticus 16:12; Numbers 16:46). Do you remember the setting? There was a big tent with an outer courtyard housing a brazen altar and a laver. The inner tent was two-chambered. There was a holy place with a table of showbread and the golden candlesticks that lit it. Then, right in front of the doorway into the Holy of Holies, there was an altar of incense. That incense was always to be rising up before the curtain on the other side of the Holy of Holies, the tiny room of God's presence over the ark of the covenant.

In front of that tiny room of God's presence, where God's shekinah (the glory cloud) hovered over the ark of the covenant, was a hollow, rectangular box, covered with gold, standing three feet high and a foot and one-half square. Along the top of this incense altar was a small rail fence to keep burning coals from tumbling off as the priests came and walked past it. As the High Priest annually came with the bowl of the blood of the atoning sacrifice to be sprinkled on top of the mercy seat, he had to walk by this cloud of incense.

What's amazing is that it is almost as if that priest brought his blood sacrifice surrounded by fragrant incense. Because the incense was offered before the first and last sacrifice, it is like the people's offerings were sent to God tied with fragrant ribbons of perfumed incense smoke. What a beautiful picture of how God wants us to offer our prayers to Him! We are to come before Him in the name of Jesus Christ. We are to come because of the sacrifice of Christ and His finished work, but this time of fellowship is to be surrounded by the perfume of our prayers and our devotion to Him.

God listens—time to pray. As we just read in Revelation 8:3–5, although Christ is above time, He shows himself to be God, waiting as He allows the prayers of His saints to arise. Before He acts in vengeance upon the earth, He receives the incense of our prayers as sacrifices rising from the altars of our hearts, a fragrant aroma of perfume from a devoted spirit of worship. This is what the eighth chapter of Revelation is all about: God is waiting for the smoke of the incense of our lives to rise before Him before He will act. How does God, who is sovereign, eternal, and omnipotent, limit himself to wait? That is part of the mystery of God.

Prayer is an awesome privilege. Do you look on prayer that way? What a captivating thought to see God wait for these prayers to rise before Him in Revelation 8. Even now He seeks the same worship, adoration, devotion, and praise from each of us. Is the altar of your soul burning with fragrant incense to God? Are the coals of your soul glowing with fire for Him? Do your prayers fill His presence with your devotion? Those are some remarkable thoughts that should draw you to bow in your soul before your Creator and speak to Him wonderful words of worship.

Jesus Christ asks us to come before Him with our prayers so that He can act on our behalf. How is the smoke of the fire of your heart doing? Are your prayers incense to Him? Right now, you may have nothing more important to give to God than your prayers. If so, rejoice! Jesus is waiting to capture those prayers as they rise and pour them out before His Father, our Lord God Almighty!

THURSDAY: Waiting Hope

*"Those who **wait on the Lord** shall renew their strength; they shall mount up with wings like eagles, they shall run and not be weary, they shall walk and not faint."*
—Isaiah 40:31

Where is your primary citizenship? Is it on earth or in heaven? If your life is tied only to this world, you are an earth dweller. The expression "those who dwell on the earth" is found seven times in Revelation (6:10; 11:10; 13:8, 12, 14; 14:6; 17:8). It is another term for a worldly person—One who is at home here and wants to live for this doomed planet, and does not want to leave it. Such persons will worship Antichrist and take the mark of the Beast, and will have a horrifying end. They will refuse to repent, harden their hearts, and continue to sin. The apostle Paul describes a worldly person like this: "For many . . . are the enemies of the cross of Christ: whose end is destruction, whose god is their belly, and whose glory is in their shame—who set their mind on earthly things" (Philippians 3:18–19). This is someone who lives only for the moment.

God's children, however, are no longer earth dwellers once they come to know Jesus Christ. That is why God hates worldliness in us. Look at how Paul describes the Christian: "For our citizenship is in heaven, from which we also eagerly wait for the Savior, the Lord Jesus Christ, who will transform our lowly body that it may be conformed to His glorious body" (Philippians 3:20–21).

Do you see the contrast? Earth dwellers will have a horrifying end, but God's children will not. On which side do you want to be?

God responds—time to flee. The coming judgments are extremely frightening! In Revelation 8:6–12, the first through fourth angels sound their trumpets and unleash God's judgments: "hail and fire . . . mingled with blood . . . were thrown to the earth" (v. 7); the seas are struck with something "like a great mountain burning with fire" (v.8); "a great star fell from heaven . . . and many men died from the [poisoned] water" (vv. 10–11); and "the sun was struck, a third of the moon, and a third of the stars, so that a third of them were darkened" (v. 12).

Now look at Revelation 8:13: "I heard an angel flying through the midst of heaven, saying with a loud voice, 'Woe, woe, woe to the inhabitants of the earth, because of the remaining blasts of the trumpet of the three angels who are about to sound!'" God reveals what is to come because He wants us to be jolted by the vivid and inescapable sights of future calamities. He always wants us to soberly look at reality. Thus, He has given us the truth that we need to act upon.

If you are not a born-again Christian yet, it is time to flee the wrath to come, and have a true relationship with a holy God. It is not too late. This very moment you, too, can find living hope for the end of days. You can then profit from one of the most fascinating studies I have ever engaged in—the study of biblical hope.

A study of biblical hope. The Hebrew language of the Old Testament is a rich storehouse of words that define hope. It is filled with examples of what the cause and remedy are for periods of hopelessness. There are four Hebrew words that give us valuable insights into the many ways God can help us live in hope. In English, the four are categorized as waiting hope, trusting hope, clinging hope, and sheltering hope. Today through Saturday we will examine all four and see how words written thousands of years ago can leap into our lives in the twenty-first century.

Waiting hope. In Lamentations 3, we find the first of the four Hebrew words for hope—*qavah*[4]: "Through the LORD's mercies we are not consumed, because His compassions fail not. They are new every morning; great is Your faithfulness. 'The LORD is my portion,' says my soul, 'Therefore I hope in Him!' The Lord is good to those **who wait for Him**, to the soul who seeks Him (Lamentations 3:21–25).

The Hebrew word *qavah* describes "waiting hope"—**hope that renews exhausted strength**. The original idea of this verb "wait" was to twist or to stretch something. It was associated with the twisting and stretching of weak strands into a strong rope. From this, the word metaphorically developed into the idea of "enduring under tension." That concept sprung from the fact that even a weak thread twisted together into a rope became strong. The belief grew that as we hope in the Lord's promises, we are woven into His strength and strengthened to withstand the stresses of life.

The most well-known verse in the Bible using this special word *qavah* is Isaiah 40:31: "Those who wait on the LORD shall renew their strength." The major shade of meaning in this verse is "waiting in the expectant *hope* and being strengthened thereby." One margin note renders it "who *hope* in the Lord," which is more accurate. A sure hope in the future enables a person to have superhuman strength: "He gives power to the weak, and to those who have no might He increases strength. Even the youths shall faint and be weary, and the young men shall utterly fall, but those who [hope in] the LORD shall renew their strength; they shall mount up with wings like eagles, they shall run and not be weary, they shall walk and not faint" (Isaiah 40:29–31).

This is exactly the same word and hope that the patriarch Jacob testified about at the end of his 147-year-long life of troubles, stress, and disasters: "**I have waited for** your salvation, O LORD!" (Genesis 49:18).

King David, in writing the Psalms, uses this word for hope more frequently than any other biblical writer. It actually was one of the keys to success in David's life. He recognized that his human strength was never enough to meet the stresses of life.[5] (Emphasis added in the following verses.)

In Psalm 25:3, we see that waiting hope delivers us from being ashamed of hard times: "Indeed, let **no one who waits on You be ashamed**; let those be ashamed who deal treacherously without cause." Waiting hope also makes each day's troubles into a lesson from God just for us: "Lead me in Your truth and teach me, for You are the God of my salvation; **on You I wait** all the day" (Psalm 25:5).

Psalm 27:14 reveals that waiting hope can give us the strength we need so that we do not lose heart: **Wait on the LORD**; be of good courage, and **He shall strengthen your heart**; wait, I say, on the LORD! (Psalm 27:14). And waiting hope promises us that we have victory through the Lord: For evildoers shall be cut off; but **those who wait on the LORD**, they shall inherit the earth. Wait on the LORD, and keep His way, and He shall exalt you to inherit the land; when the wicked are cut off, you shall see it (Psalm 37:9, 34).

In summary, waiting hope focuses our lives upon the Lord (Psalm 39:7), assures us that He is hearing us (Psalm 40:1), and draws us back into God's Word (Psalm 130:5). Are you experiencing waiting hope today? Is your life focused on the Lord and His Word? Wait on the Lord—and He will give you the living hope you need to triumph in the end of days!

FRIDAY: Trusting Hope

> **Trust in the Lord** with all your heart, and lean not on your own understanding; in all your ways acknowledge Him, and **He shall direct your paths.**
> —Proverbs 3:5–6

The coming judgments are terribly unsettling: we are powerless before an angry God. There is nothing that can stop His plan, His judgment, and earth's ultimate dissolution as a planet. For that reason, more than ever we need to find hope that anchors us during these turbulent times.

Trusting hope. The second of the Hebrew words for hope is *yachal*.[6] The Hebrew word *yachal* describes "trusting hope"—**hope that produces great endurance**. The root idea of this word is to wait for something. It came to mean "an expectant waiting under extreme pressure." The scholar R. B. Girdlestone says, "*Yachal* occurs several times in the Book of Job and signifies a long patient waiting."[7] A study of the usage of this word in Job gives the most accurate connotations. He was a man going through extreme tribulation. In rapid succession he lost his great wealth, his children, and his health. Job suffered incredible and constant physical and mental pain. Yet in the most well-known verse using this special word for hope, he said this: *"Though He slay me, **yet will I trust** Him"* (Job 13:15a). From this, we learn that trusting hope guards us from despair. In Job 13:15 "the word *yachal* means to keep on hoping with endurance under extreme pressure. Job's hope in the Lord enabled him to endure and be stabilized even under adverse conditions."[8]

As Hebrews 16:19 says, trusting hope anchors our souls in heaven. Job believed in trusting hope when he said, "If a man dies, shall he live again? All the days of my hard service I **will wait**, till my change comes" (Job 14:14). Trusting hope strengthens us: "Be of good courage, and He shall strengthen your heart, **all you who hope** in the LORD" (Psalm 31:24).

In Psalm 33 we find that trusting hope invites God's blessings: "Behold, the eye of the LORD is on those who fear Him, **on those who hope** in His mercy, let Your mercy, O LORD, **be upon us, just as we hope** in You" (Psalm 33:18, 22). Trusting hope also opens our lives to magnify the Lord: "**But I will hope** continually, and will praise You yet more and more" (Psalm 71:14). And trusting hope points us back to God's Word: "Take not the word of truth utterly out of my mouth, for I have **hoped in** Your ordinances. Remember the word to Your servant, **Upon which You have caused me to hope**" (Psalm 119:43, 49; see also 119:74).

In summary, trusting hope keeps believing even when there is no visible thing in life that points to a possibility of hope, like Noah did in the ark ("So he waited"—Genesis 8:12). Trusting hope gives us a reason to go on, a reason to smile, a reason to bless others with the strength that God alone can give (Psalm 42:5, 11; 43:5). And trusting hope assures us that God hears us (Psalm 38:15). What an anchor!

SATURDAY: Clinging and Sheltering Hope

He will not be afraid of evil tidings; His heart is steadfast, **trusting in the Lord.**
—Psalm 112:7

The coming judgments should make us humbly reach out to our God of love and mercy while there is time. If you listen carefully, the compassionate voice of Jesus is heard all through Revelation, which is a book of woe. He calls John to not be afraid, and He calls the wayward church members to repent and return to Him. It is Jesus who knocks patiently for us, awaiting our fellowship. It is Jesus who sends His witnesses in chapter 7. It is Jesus who sends warnings of doom, the two witnesses of chapter 11, the angel preaching the everlasting gospel in chapter 16, and so on. Jesus is crying out: "While there is time, hear My voice. Do not harden your hearts!" Jesus does not want anyone to perish.

Only you can choose your destination. As the Bible opens, Jesus is seeking His lost ones in the Garden of Eden saying, "Where are you?" (Genesis 3:9); the Bible ends with Jesus calling, "Let him who thirsts come. Whoever desires, let him take the water of life freely" (Revelation 22:17c). Over and over He has extended His invitation. All you need to do is come to Him. You choose your eternal destiny.

One of the most fearful things in the universe is the free will to say yes or no to God. Why? Because you will be eternally held accountable for how you willfully choose to respond to God, who waits silently before He pours out His judgment on this planet. Right now, there is still time to cling to the Lord, but don't delay. Jesus could come back today.

Clinging hope. The third of the Hebrew words for hope is *batach*.[9] The Hebrew word *batach* describes "clinging hope"—**hope that inspires deeper trust**. The most well-known verse using this special word is Proverbs 3:5: "Trust [literally cling to] the Lord with all your heart, and lean not on your own understanding."

Here *batach* is used in the sense of hope that comes from casting one's total future upon God like a little child and trusting Him for everything. This word is most often translated to trust or to have confidence in someone, usually God. But in some contexts it is definitely used to mean hope, as in the great prophetic twenty-second psalm. The Messiah's thoughts while suffering on the cross are predicted here: "But thou [God] art he that took me out of the womb: thou didst make me **hope** [batach] when I was upon my mother's breasts" (Psalm 22:9 KJV).[10]

Clinging hope assures that God is at work: "**Trust in** the LORD, and do good; dwell in the land, and feed on His faithfulness. Delight yourself also in the LORD, and He shall give you the desires of your heart. Commit your way to the LORD, **trust** also in Him, and He shall bring it to pass" (Psalm 37:3–5). In Psalm 40:3 we see that clinging hope can put a song in our hearts that flows out of our lives even in hard times: "He has put a new song in my mouth—praise to our God; many will see it and fear, **and will trust** [cling to] the LORD" (Psalm 40:3).

Clinging hope counteracts and removes our fears: "Whenever I am afraid, **I will trust** [cling to] You. In God (I will praise His word), In God I **have put my trust**; I will not fear. What can flesh do to me?" (Psalm 56:3–4). And clinging hope calms us in whatever trying situation we face: "He will not be afraid of evil tidings, His heart is steadfast, **trusting** [clinging to] the LORD" (Psalm 112:7).

Sheltering hope. The fourth and final of the Hebrew words for hope is *chasah*.[11] The Hebrew word *chasah* describes "sheltering hope"—**hope that offers a secure refuge**. The most well-known verse in the Bible using this special word is Ruth 2:12: "The LORD repay your work, and a full reward be given you by the LORD God of Israel, under whose wings you have come **for refuge**."

This is a beautiful word for hope. Its root meaning is "to seek shelter, refuge, or protection in something or someone."[12] It is used frequently to portray little animals taking refuge in the cleft of a rock, as in Psalm 104:18: "The high hills are for the wild goats; the cliffs are a refuge for the rock badgers."

Figuratively, it came to be used of man's taking refuge in God from the spiritual, emotional, and physical dangers of life. On a few occasions, this concept is translated "hope." In Proverbs 14:32, this is used in a unique way: "The wicked is driven away in his wickedness: but the righteous hath hope in his death" (KJV). When someone who has been declared righteous by believing in Jesus as his Savior faces death, he will have a hope that is a refuge from the uncertainty and fear presented by his own death.[13]

Sheltering hope is a defense and refuge in troublesome times: "The God of my strength, **in whom I will trust**; my shield and the horn of my salvation, my stronghold and my refuge; My Savior, You save me from violence. . . . As for God, His way is perfect; the word of the LORD is proven; He is a shield **to all who trust in Him**" (2 Samuel 22:3, 31). In Psalm 7:1, we find that sheltering hope is also a refuge in times of persecution: "O LORD my God, **in You I put my trust**; save me from all those who persecute me; and deliver me."

Sheltering hope gives confidence and peace to persevere in tough times: "In the LORD **I put my trust**; how can you say to my soul, 'Flee as a bird to your mountain?'" (Psalm 11:1). Psalm 31:1–2 tells us that sheltering hope gives boldness in our prayers: "In You, O LORD, **I put my trust**; let me never be ashamed; deliver me in Your righteousness. Bow down your ear to me, deliver me speedily; be my rock of refuge, a fortress of defense to save me" (Psalm 31:1–2).

Sheltering hope provides security and confidence in calamitous times: "Be merciful to me, O God, be merciful to me! For my soul **trusts** in You; and in the shadow of Your wings **I will make my refuge**, until these calamities have passed by" (Psalm 57:1). And sheltering hope is a safe haven from our enemies: "In You, O LORD, **I put my trust**; let me never be put to shame. Deliver me in Your righteousness, and cause me to escape; incline Your ear to me, and save me" (Psalm 71:1–2).

Make a choice to live in hope. In Revelation 8 we have seen that earth dwellers will experience a horrifying end of dreadfully frightening and unsettling judgments. The coming judgments should make us humbly reach out to our merciful and loving God while there is still time. We can find waiting hope, trusting hope, clinging hope, and sheltering hope in our patient Christ who is a shelter midst the storms of life. He is a solid Rock where we can find safety when we are assailed from without and within!

WEEK 29
Watch Christ's Judgment

{ Revelation 9 }

As the end of days approaches, you can find hope as you watch the judgment of Jesus!

SUNDAY: Enduring Hope in Jesus

*"And you will be hated by all for My name's sake. But **he who endures** to the end will be saved."*
—MATTHEW 10:22

When Jesus commissioned His disciples to go forth in their work for Him, in verse 22b above, He was basically telling them: "He who perseveres under stress and trials by abiding and remaining in Me will be saved." In the last days, Jesus says that this will characterize those who are really His children. Thus, no matter what happens before or during the Great Tribulation—His true children *will* endure.

Jesus also said that the generation who sees His plan unfold for the end of days will witness His Second Coming. How can we best get ready for that momentous event? We need to have *waiting hope* for Christ's return. We need to have *trusting hope* for whatever is to come in our future. We need to have *clinging hope* in Jesus as our all-wise guide for daily life, and avoid whatever grieves Him. And through *sheltering hope*, we must resist fear, for Christ is our safe and secure eternal refuge. In summary, what we need to believe today is what Jesus taught: this world is not our home.

Our real home is the one our master architect, Jesus, went to prepare for us (John 14:2–3), and He says that "moving day" is fast approaching. But until then, we can try to wondrously imagine our brand-new home—a mingling of the familiar and the unfamiliar, the earthly and the more-than-earthly. For heaven is a place, but not exactly like earthly places. It contains recognizable features, but the strangeness and transcendence keep alive our awareness that earthly images do not exist in the ordinary manner in heaven.

I love the way this author expresses his thoughts on heaven: "Oh, the wonders of our promised Haven, the glories of that eternal Home! But nothing will compare with the knowledge that Heaven is just the outflow of Him. In each aspect . . . concerning that heavenly City, we see a character trait of Him, our Savior. Let us seek Him, and in the words of the song–writer so true: 'Tis heaven below, my Redeemer to know, For He is so precious to me.' "

How exciting it is to contemplate these comforting elements of heaven as presented in this excerpt from the Carl F. H. Henry Commencement Address by Harold Lindsell: "The last thing will not be bombs, but blessings; not war, but peace; not uncertainty, but confidence; not sickness, but health; not weakness, but strength; not longing, but satisfaction; not sorrow, but joy; not weariness, but vigor. There's a great time coming, so let us lift up our heads and our hearts, for the day of our redemption draweth nigh."

What should talk about heaven mean to us in the twenty-first century? Simply this: if the simultaneous increase in catastrophic storms, massive earthquakes, deadly pestilences, wars of terror, and looming threats from objects in outer space are indeed some of the "birth pangs" Christ spoke about, then meditating on heaven's glories can be very reassuring. Such thoughts in turn will promote waiting, trusting, clinging, sheltering hope—the hope that anchors—*enduring hope!*

My Prayer for You This Week: *I thank You, dear Father, that You are the God of hope. But I pray for those who do not understand what I am talking about because they have never responded to Your offer, "Come unto Me all You that labor and are heavy laden, and I will give you rest." That was a gracious offer with Your outstretched arms of salvation. I hope in You because I know You, because I know that I have responded to You and that You live within me. I belong to You, but if there are those who do not share that hope, may they flee to You, oh Christ. If they don't know how, may they simply say, "Jesus, I come to You." I pray that no one would hear of Your great salvation and refuse to come. As for we who know You, may You be working in us so that we wait in hope, that we trust in hope that You will see us through the even gloomier days ahead for this planet. May we hold forth the Word of God and shine as a light until the day of Christ, in whose name we pray. Amen.*

MONDAY: Jesus and the Angels of Doom

And I saw a star fallen from heaven to the earth. To him was given the key to the bottomless pit. And **he opened the bottomless pit***, and smoke arose out of the pit like the smoke of a great furnace. So the sun and the air were darkened because of the smoke of the pit.*

—Revelation 9:1–2

In chapter 9, the Apostle John introduces us to the dreadful realm of the fallen spirits and their abode: the abyss. At this point, the fifth angel sounds the fifth trumpet, which is a preview of hell—endless darkness. This bottomless pit is the holding tank of punishment for the fallen angels, demons, the beast, the false prophet, and Satan (Revelation 9:1–2, 11; 11:7; 20:1–3). These spirit-beings of the highest magnitude of evil are left over from Satan's rebellion.

Jude tells us that some of these evil spirit-beings tried to corrupt the human race so that the promised Seed of the woman, Jesus Christ, could never come. Others seem to be key leaders of Satan's forces, while still others have been so vile that they have been held back until Revelation 9. Like Satan, these demonic spirit-beings are filled with a hatred for God and mankind.

The success of Satan's mission "to steal, and to kill, and to destroy" is evident throughout the history of planet Earth. From the time Cain slew his brother, Abel (Genesis 4:8), strife and bloodshed among men has never ceased to exist. But not until Assyria was there a society that conquered in a global way. After the Assyrian conquests, Babylonian, Persian, and Greek armies sowed blood, broken bodies, and death across the face of the earth. In cold, calculated, and cruel efficiency, the Romans then fought and won the world we know.

By the thirteenth century, inhabitants of Asia were mesmerized by the Khans, and the Mongol Empire was carved across the continents, leaving an estimated ten million dead in its path. Five hundred years later, Napoleon ravaged Europe for twenty years, resulting in a death toll of five million as his armies blindly followed him. The most vivid despot, however, is the strange little man who hypnotized some of the most sophisticated and civilized cultures on the planet into becoming barbaric butchers of humanity. Hitler caused upwards of fifty million deaths, six million of them being the gassed and murdered people of promise—the Jews.

Those are dark pages in history—and Satan and his forces have relished every single page so far. But far worse is yet to come. If Revelation 9:1–2 and 11, Revelation 11:7, and Revelation 20:1 and 3 are taken literally, then God has designed an impregnable fortress that holds the most fearsome creatures existing anywhere in the universe. This abyss, or bottomless pit, is only an intermediate step before the final abode of the prince of darkness and all his followers. In Revelation 20, the final place of terror is the lake of fire—the gehenna or hell Jesus spoke of so often in His warnings scattered throughout the Gospels. The fallen Lucifer, Satan himself, will be given permission to open the dungeon of demons and loose the legions of terrors. That is a dreadfully frightening prospect for the earth dwellers!

The apostle Peter warns us to keep alert. "But the day of the Lord will come as a thief in the night, in which the heavens will pass away . . . ; both the earth and the works that are in it will be burned up. Therefore, since all these things will be dissolved, what manner of persons ought you to be in holy conduct and godliness?" (2 Peter 3:10–11).

The coming judgment should motivate you to conduct yourself in the light of eternity, and deploy yourself for God. In these end days, you have the greatest opportunity of all time! Before it is too late, talk to others about Christ and read the Scriptures to them. Be available for divine appointments to lead men, women, and children to the Lord. In other words, I exhort you to be a Christlike example who will draw others to Jesus!

Here are some practical choices you can make for how to live godly every day until the end. Note these five points in 2 Peter 3:10–18:

1. **Keep alert.** Staying alert should encourage you to live a godly life (vv. 10–11).
2. **Build a fireproof life.** Don't fear the day of God, but eagerly look forward to it. Forsake materialism and other worldly interests, and invest in that which lasts forever (vv. 12–13).
3. **Look up.** Live purely by expecting the Lord's return at any moment (v. 14).
4. **Study the Book.** God's Word will help you guard your heart and encourage mature living (v. 17).
5. **Obey Jesus.** If you love Him, you will obey Him. That is essential if you wish to grow spiritually (v. 18).

Suggestion: write the five points above in your Bible, and then refer back to them regularly until you habitually live by each of these truths. If you do, God will greatly bless you for it!

TUESDAY: A Preview of Hell — Relentless Terror

*Then **out of the smoke locusts came upon the earth**. And to them was given power, as the scorpions of the earth have power.*
—Revelation 9:3

As the shaft leading downward is unlocked, the infernal smoke of the pit will billow out of the darkness and unleash the pent-up fury of hell. When that pit is opened, locusts will emerge like the smoke of a furnace. With the most destructive imagery known to man, the Apostle John described the creatures as locusts.

Because locusts were such relentless destroyers, no plague was more fearsome in the ancient world. Truly, the day of the Lord, portrayed in this short prophetic oracle's revelation through God's Spirit, is a day that is to be heeded. God clearly demonstrates the need for repentance and the physical disaster that must follow moral disintegration.

As a vehicle of judgment, three times God uses locusts as a plague of horrific proportions:

1. Moses unleashed an eighth plague on Egypt—locusts that horribly devoured every green thing left after the hail (Exodus 10:4, 12–14, 19).
2. God sent a plague of locusts on Israel that horribly destroyed all that was green and thus caused economic devastation as well (Joel 1–2).
3. The fifth trumpet will sound the release from the abyss of horrible demonic hordes of locusts (Revelation 9:3, 7).

Today, few readers of the book of Joel are likely to experience a locust plague. With current eradication methods, a locust swarm in modern Israel is indeed a rare phenomenon. In ancient times, however, the land of Israel was frequently subject to invasions by the desert locust, *schistocerca gregaria*. Exodus 10:1–20 describes the locust as perhaps nature's most awesome example of the collective destructive power of a species. Adult locusts weigh a maximum of two grams, and yet their combined destructive force can leave thousands of people in famine for years. The locust plagues were very much feared in ancient Egypt. So much so that the peasants were in the habit of praying to the locust god, for Satan likes to keep superstitious peoples enslaved to his demonic horde's evil powers.

John J. Davis reports:

A swarm can contain over a billion creatures that, all together, can weigh more than three million pounds. One locust, with his colleagues, form gregarious marching bands up to ten miles wide and ten miles long. The marching bands move forward at a slow cadence, perhaps no more than 250 feet per hour, and may travel no farther than fifteen miles from their staging area. But within their path the hoppers may consume virtually every tender blade of grass or legume. The extraordinary appearance of this marching band with its mass of tiny pullulating bodies can be unnerving, to say the least. In the words of Joel, "Before them earth trembles, Heaven shakes . . ." (Joel 2:10). The marching bands are oblivious to obstacles: "They rush up the wall, they dash about in the city; They climb into the houses, They enter like thieves by way of the windows" (Joel 2:9).[1]

As we contemplate the horrors ahead, we need to make sure to build our lives upon the Rock, and not upon the sands of life that will sweep us away in the storms. We should live expectantly to hasten the coming of the Lord. How can we hasten the day of God? Jesus will return when the last person to become a part of His church is saved. In light of that, every time I kneel to pray with someone who wants to be born again, I expectantly think: *Maybe this is the last one whom God will save before Jesus calls His church home!*

Do you want to hasten heaven? Lead people to Christ! Build a fireproof life: don't live for what is here on earth, because all this is going to pass away. That is how to best get ready for the end!

WEDNESDAY: The Fearsome Symbol of the Locust

And they were not given authority to kill them [humans], but to torment them for five months. ***Their torment was like the torment of a scorpion*** *when it strikes a man. In those days men will seek death and will not find it; they will desire to die, and death will flee from them.*
—Revelation 9:5–6

The time limit God gives these horrible creatures is the same as the normal life cycle of a physical locust. (It is interesting that this plague lasts the same duration as the flood waters of Genesis 8:1.) After five months, these creatures will be swept back, presumably to where they came from, and God will again close the pit.

Locust plagues were so dreaded in ancient times that even the Hebrew vocabulary used to describe locusts as fearsome. There are six different Hebrew words for locust, and each is sobering:
1. *Gazam*—shearer: This portrays the machine that makes a destructive path of sheared-off living plants left in the wake of these monsters.
2. *Arbel*—swarmer: This is a reference to the innumerable hordes that darken the sky as a black cloud.
3. *Hasil*—finisher: This refers to the devastating aftermath of all green plants finished off by the army that passes.
4. *Solam*—annihilator: This is another glimpse of how those who saw these hordes described their work.

5. *Hargol*—galloper: This notes the incredible speed with which they pour out unstoppable destruction across the face of the earth.
6. *Tzelatzel*—creaker: This reminds us that locusts are ominously heard creaking toward you long before they are seen.

The people who lived in the ancient world dreaded these locusts. They would thus declare that the shearing, swarming, finishing, annihilating, galloping, and creaking army was coming toward them! And that is what God sends in Revelation 9, but He does so by way of the demonic army.

In Revelation 9:7–10, the shape of these creatures is like horses prepared for battle. John was grasping for words to describe monsters that can fly like locusts, gallop around like horses, carry a venomous sting like scorpions, look somewhat human with hair, and bite with sharpness like a lion. These horrible and ghastly creatures will do great damage to humanity!

Revelation 9:11 tells us: "They had as king over them the angel of the bottomless pit, whose name in Hebrew is Abaddon, but in Greek he has the name Apollyon." In Hebrew, *Abaddon* means "Destruction"; in Greek, *Apollyon* means "Destroyer." Thus, leading the most horrible assault ever launched on mankind will be the Destroyer himself—the one who defected from the holy presence of God to decay into the murderous liar and hater of truth—the chief officer of Satan, or perhaps even the old Dragon himself. Most likely this is one of the arch-fallen angels. As Jesus has said, Satan wants to steal God's blessings.

The absolute contrast between Jesus and the Devil is seen in John 10:10: "The thief does not come except to steal, and to kill, and to destroy." When Satan is allowed to do what he wants to do on this planet, he steals the joy of humanity: he destroys life as we know it, and he kills human beings. But Jesus said, "I have come that they may have life, and that they may have it more abundantly."

Jesus says the contrast couldn't be greater: Satan offers to steal everything you have that is worthwhile, destroy anything that is of value, and to kill you. He robs people of true joy and offers them only emptiness. He destroys their virtue and purity. If they follow that path long enough, it leads to death and eternal separation from God in hell. But Jesus said, "If you come to Me, I will give you an abundantly overflowing life that just won't stop." That is what Jesus offers.

Which offer sounds best to you? How foolish it is for anyone to purposefully make any other choice than to receive the eternal hope that is found in Jesus Christ alone. Are you ready to meet Him?

THURSDAY: How to Build a Fireproof Life

> But [those] who were not killed by these plagues, **did not repent of the works of their hands**, that they should not worship demons, and idols of gold, silver, brass, stone, and wood, which can neither see nor hear nor walk. And they did not repent of their **murders** or their **sorceries** or their **sexual immorality** or their **thefts**.
>
> —Revelation 9:20–21

Armies that dwarf all that ever marched are poised, even now, awaiting a moment known only to God. As the sixth angel sounds, the ultimate weapon will be unleashed: angels of doom by the hundreds of millions. These cosmic warriors will be unstoppable and deadly! They will need no weapons, no food, no vehicles, and no rest; and in their wake will fall more than all wars have ever killed. Yet, horribly, the earth dwellers will miss the message and change nothing. They will still turn their backs on God to worship themselves and the demons that have cruelly enslaved them in hatred and lust.

The two-thirds of humanity that Jesus mercifully spares will respond no better than those in hell who gnash their teeth—as Jesus said seven times when He described the horrible place the hard-hearted would go (Matthew 8:12; 13:42, 50; 22:13; 24:51; 25:30; Luke 13:28). Their gnashing implies the hatred of an unrepentant heart poured out at God's judgment. They would not bow their knee when they were alive and breathing; they will not bow their knee other than the forced bowing at the judgment seat; and they will not bow in hell—for even then there will still be gnashing of teeth against God.

What will control the culture at the end of days? Revelation 9:20–21 reveals five striking evils that will grip the souls of humanity in those dark days:

1. **Godlessness:** Mankind will still willfully push the Creator out of their minds. Instead, these terrified earth dwellers will worship demons and the works of their hands: idols of gold, silver, brass, stone, and wood which can neither see, nor hear, nor walk. Wherever idols are worshiped, even in churches today, those are demons. Whenever an idol gives deliverance from whatever is prayed for, it is a demon providing that deliverance. God does not operate through idols. Whether it is Far East or American Indian idols, or idols of religious American churchgoers, those are demons that are being worshiped.
2. **Callousness:** Even when people are dying by the thousands and millions and hundreds of millions, people will still be murdering one another.
3. **Mindlessness:** The word *"sorceries"* in verse 21 is actually *pharmakeia*, which means "druggings, sorceries." Drugs have always been around. There have always been those who have consistently relied on the effects of drugs on their minds. And in this horrible hour, with the message of God calling the world to repentance, people will still be mindlessly following their drug-induced stupors and sorceries.
4. **Licentiousness:** Sexual immorality will abound. During this time of judgment, without the preaching of God's Word that produces righteous influences, evil perversions will run rampant throughout society.
5. **Lawlessness:** While everything is burning, and the demon creatures are killing people, the homes and businesses of those who are killed are looted. Theft abounds!

All the above evils are prompted by a lust for pleasure, a lust for power, a lust for possessions, and a lust to maintain personal pride at the expense of God and others.

If you want to build a fireproof life, humble yourself because "'God resists the proud but gives grace to the humble.' Therefore submit to God. Resist the devil and he will flee from you. Draw near

FRIDAY: When Life Becomes Overwhelming

*Through the LORD's mercies we are not consumed, because His compassions fail not. They are new every morning; Great is Your faithfulness. "The LORD is my portion," says my soul, "**Therefore I hope in Him!**" The LORD is good to **those who wait** for Him, to the soul who seeks Him.*
—LAMENTATIONS 3:22-25

The very anticipation of catastrophic world events on top of everyday personal trials can be so overwhelming that at times it may *feel* like life is just too painful to even go on. Have you ever felt that way? Jeremiah did. In the Old Testament, without all the benefits and blessings we have in this church age, he lived through a life in shambles, friends all dead, and the stench of destruction all around everything he held dear—yet he lived in hope. How can that be?

True children of God endure under affliction. The Greek word for endure, *hupomeno*, is a very interesting word. In fact, I want to give you the privilege of sharing in one of the most spectacular things that I like to do through the Bible: see the *analogia scriptura*—the analogy of the Scripture as one Scripture explains another Scripture, and it all fits together like a beautiful woven tapestry.

Consider this association: The word *meno*, which is used all through John 15, means "to abide." In the Greek language, putting a preposition that amplifies, like *hupo*, in front of a verb like *meno*, gives this meaning: "to abide under something." It means "to abide when you're being squashed, when you're being pressed, to super-abide when things are not the way that you wanted them, or expected, or hoped them to be."

Endure (*hupomeno*) is used only eighteen times in the New Testament, and it is used to describe a genuine believer's response to dreadful and fearsome times, such as when the world is falling apart, as Matthew 24 describes. Some may wonder what "enduring under affliction" means. Let's follow this beautifully illustrated trail through the New Testament to find out:

Mark 13:13: "You will be hated by all for My name's sake. But **he who endures** to the end shall be saved." This verse is a parallel to Matthew 24: it is from the same sermon, the same context, and the same event when Jesus is speaking the Olivet Discourse. The thirteenth verse of both chapters is identical. The verse reflects the response of a true believer, one who endures or abides in Christ under trials.

Romans 12:12: "[Be] rejoicing in hope, **patient in** tribulation, continuing steadfastly in prayer." The bold portion is *hupomeno*, which means "abiding under difficulty." The evidence of a true believer is that he or she patiently and superbly abides in Christ when going through tribulation.

I am often asked: Are Christians going to go through the Great Tribulation? We will not be attacked and stung by all the horrific demon hoards from the pit that opens in Revelation 9. However, we will all experience *thlipsis*, which is the word for tribulation that pictures something being squashed. If you've ever gotten your hand painfully shut in a door, you could say that it was *thlipsised*, or squashed by incredible pressure. That is what tribulation is, and when we are undergoing incredible pressures we are to rejoice in hope, and abide faithfully (*hupomeno*), regardless of the situation (Romans 12:12).

Our American mentality thinks that because we are going to be in the Rapture, we're going to miss all suffering. We will miss the Great Tribulation, but we are not going to miss the tribulation shaping up in our world that is hostile to the gospel. The Muslim faith is committed to opposing everything we believe, and Satan is seeking to erase us from this planet. So we all need to *hupomeno*—to abide faithfully in difficulties with enduring hope as we continue steadfastly in prayer.

First Corinthians 13:7: "[Love] bears all things, believes all things, hopes all things, **endures all things**." This is about the love that Christ implants in our hearts at salvation. When we have Christ and His love shed abroad in our hearts through the Holy Spirit, we will bear all things, believe all things, and have enduring hope in all things

Second Timothy 2:10, 12: "**Therefore I endure** all things for the sake of the elect, that they also may obtain the salvation which is in Christ Jesus with eternal glory. . . . If **we endure**, we shall also reign with Him. If we deny Him, He also will deny us." This is saying: "I will endure or abide faithfully in whatever I am called to go through. I will faithfully hope and trust in the Lord." Christians who are characterized by perseverance will also reign with Christ.

Hebrews 12:2-3, 6-7: "[Be] looking unto Jesus, the author and finisher of our faith, who for the joy that was set before Him **endured** the cross, despising the shame, and has sat down at the right hand of the throne of God. For consider **Him who endured** such hostility from sinners against Himself, lest you become weary and discouraged in your souls. . . . 'For whom the Lord loves He chastens, and scourges every son whom He receives.' If **you endure** chastening, God deals with you as with sons; for what son is there whom a father does not chasten?" This passage is a beautiful picture of Christ's ministry for us. He remained super-faithful under all He was going through, and endured the pain and shame of the cross to the end.

To prevent becoming weary and discouraged in our own trials, we need to consider all that Jesus went through for us. He was both 100 percent God and 100 percent human. In His humanity, God's grace was sufficient for Him, just as it is for us. One of the things we must endure is God's chastening of sin in our lives, which is an evidence of salvation. God hates sin, so He says: "I will punish it. I will not allow you to continue in unrepentant sin. If you endure the chastening by abiding in Me until I've finished what I want to accomplish in you, that is a sign you're My child." If you don't endure God's correction, are never chastened, and habitually choose to run toward sin rather than flee from it, that is a sign you may not belong to Christ.

James 1:12: "Blessed is the **man who endures** temptation; for when he has been approved, he will receive the crown of life which the Lord has promised to those who love Him." James, the brother of Jesus, was the pastor of the first church at Jerusalem. He wrote to his people who were fresh out of Pentecost. If we are faithful under tribulation, under trials, under whatever we have to go through in life to please God, we will receive the crown of life.

So regardless of what you face this week, this month, or this year, grab hold of God's overflowing hope. Let Him weave your weaknesses, like fragile fibers, in with the countless strands of His promises in the Scriptures to stretch and twist you into waiting hope. And then, when troubles increase, let Him bring you a fresh portion of His hope and goodness as you wait, and enduringly find hope in Christ!

SATURDAY: The Hope That Anchors

> *And we know that **all things work together for good** to those who love God, to those who are the called according to His purpose.*
> —Romans 8:28

Do we really believe this assurance? In our testimonies and prayers, and even in some of the songs we sing, we seem to enjoy talking about our little troubles and difficulties, multiplying and magnifying them. This almost sounds like we're *spiritual* hypochondriacs. At such times, perhaps we have simply lost sight of the waiting, trusting, clinging, and sheltering hope that is ours in Christ—the hope that endures and anchors our souls during trials.

In the seventeenth century, a model example of one who possessed the enduring hope that anchors is seen in the life of Martin Rinkart—a pastor at Eilenberg, Saxony, during the Thirty Years' War (1618–1648). Because Eilenberg was a walled city, it became a severely overcrowded refuge for political and military fugitives. As a result, the entire city suffered from famine and disease. In 1637, a great pestilence swept through the area that resulted in the death of around eight thousand persons, including Rinkart's wife. At that time he was forty-one, widowed, and the only minister left in Eilenberg because the others had either died or fled. Rinkart alone conducted the burial services for 4,480 people, sometimes as many as forty or fifty a day!

From that horror came one of the great hymns we possess as Christ's church:

Now Thank We All Our God

Now thank we all our God With hearts and hands and voices,
Who wondrous things hath done, In whom His world rejoices;
Who, from our mothers' arms, Hath blessed us on our way
With countless gifts of love, And still is ours today.
O may this bounteous God Through all our life be near us,
With ever joyful hearts And blessed peace to cheer us;
And keep us in His grace And guide us when perplexed,
And free us from all ills In this world and the next.
All praise and thanks to God The Father now be given,
The Son, and Him who reigns With them in highest heaven,
The one eternal God, Whom earth and heaven adore;
For thus it was, is now, And shall be ever more. Amen.
—Martin Rinkart (1586–1649)

We may well ask why all his dramatic experience and difficulty is not reflected in Rinkart's hymn. Had the good pastor seen so much stark tragedy that he had become insensitive to human needs and problems? Of course not. He simply had come to believe that God's providence is always good, no matter how much we are tempted to doubt it.

Make a choice to live in hope. A favorite and often-quoted Bible verse is Romans 8:28. At the beginning of today's devotional, that reference appears in the New King James Version.

In the unclear world of tomorrow, it is entirely possible that "fitting into His plan" means that we as Christians may experience great difficulty, persecution, and even war and death. We should therefore prepare ourselves and our families for this possibility, so that if such trials come, we might face them with the hope that anchors—in spiritual victory that gives testimony, like Pastor Rinkart's, that ours is a faith that works.

Rinkart's experience and his hymn wonderfully confirm these words of the apostle Paul: "What can separate us from the love of Christ? Can affliction or hardship, Can persecution, hunger, nakedness, peril, or the sword? . . . I am convinced that there is nothing in death or life, in the realm of spirits or superhuman powers, in the world as it is or the world as it shall be, in the forces of the universe, in heights or depths—nothing in all creation that can separate us from the love of God in Christ Jesus our Lord" (Romans 8:35–39 New English Bible).

If you will memorize and meditate upon that passage, God will ground you in this, His living hope that anchors: nothing can separate us from the love of Christ!

WEEK 30
Behold the Mystery of Jesus

{ Revelation 10 }

As the end of days approaches, you can find hope as you behold the mystery of Jesus!

SUNDAY: The Mystery of Jesus

I saw still another mighty angel coming down from heaven, clothed with a cloud. And a rainbow was on his head, his face was like the sun, and his feet like pillars of fire.
—Revelation 10:1

The Revelation of Jesus Christ gives God's record of history from the founding of Christ's church until the end of the earth and the ushering in of heaven. The more you read Revelation the simpler it is.

Chapters 1–3 deal with the church age—God revealing himself to the seven churches through the Lord Jesus Christ in all His Resurrection glory.

In chapters 4–5, God shifts the scene away from earth and takes us heavenward by means of Christ's promised coming to take His bride home. This is a beautiful portrait of the Rapture of the church—the instantaneous removal of all His saints from this planet. The saints will then stand before the glassy sea and the beautiful emerald-surrounded throne as Jesus takes the multi-sealed book, the title deed of the universe, and starts claiming back all that the god of this world, Satan, has usurped.

Chapters 6–19 reveal the horrors of God's wrath upon sin and sinners. Chapters 6–9 show the six seals and the first six trumpets, and then there is an interlude between the sixth and seventh trumpet (Revelation 10:1–11:14). This is so important for understanding God's plan. Chapter 10 is part of a silence where God steps back and shows little parenthetical pictures. It is critical for understanding *the* mystery of God (not *a* mystery).

The chapter we'll be studying this week, Revelation 10, discloses the preparations for the second half of the Tribulation that begins by means of the seventh trumpet. Having taken back His earth, the conqueror and rightful owner, the King of Kings, will plant His feet on land and sea and take possession. This is Jesus the Redeemer Who, in chapter 5, took the title deed to the universe from the majesty on high. He is the One who loosed each seal, and now He prepares for the final assault upon hard-hearted earth dwellers who refuse to bow to Him. With a roar like a lion, He will express His power, and with the sound of thunder He will declare the coming judgment. What is amazing is that verse 7 says, "The mystery of God would be finished, as He declared to His servants the prophets."

There are two parts to Revelation 10:

- **The Mystery—The Vision of the Son of God** (vv. 1–5): These verses focus on Christ and His power. In verse 1, Jesus reflects God's image; in verse 2, Jesus claims His inheritance; in verse 3, Jesus roars His victory; in verse 4, Jesus shows His grace; and, in verse 5, Jesus reveals the image of God.
- **The Vision of the Word of God** (vv. 6–11): This second part focuses on the Word of God and His plan, and what we are supposed to do with it. In verse 6, Jesus shares the plan of God; in verse 7, Jesus explains the mystery of God; and, in verses 8–11, Jesus shows the way of God—to eat His Word.

As Revelation 10 opens, we stare at the mystery of Jesus. It is on the backdrop of an earth that lies in ecological desolation; the land and sea are ravaged. The benumbed survivors have hastily buried billions of corpses in mass graves. The horrible roar of demon locusts is silent for who knows how much longer. That horrific mounted cavalry from hell—the angels of doom by the hundreds of millions—seem to have ceased their murderous campaign. The sun is getting brighter after the strange darkening that caused such weather disasters; the smoke of the grass and forest fires has started to settle; and some specks of light green anticipate that grass should soon be poking up once again from the scorched earth. The bitter waters of the earth are getting clear again, and no stellar debris has fallen to earth lately. It is halftime—the midpoint of the Tribulation.

So then, what about the mystery? What has been the effect of all this unleashed wrath of God on the cosmos? You cannot explain it any other way but God. It has been systematic, unstoppable, and predicted. Everything that has happened has been written down for 2,000 years in exact detail. God has spoken, and the earth has been faced with God's wrath.

At this point, has the cosmic rebellion ceased? Has Satan bowed his knee and confessed that Jesus is Lord? Has the decimated populace of earth seen "the true Light which gives light to every man coming into this world" (John 1:9)? No. That in itself is a mystery to us who know and love the Lord!

My Prayer for You This Week: *Father in heaven, as the end of days fast approaches, we are continually amazed that You would bestow upon us the honor of being able to go home to dwell with You forever. Why You would let Your Son redeem us and then go and prepare a place for us is beyond our wildest imagination! As we look into Your Word this week, we pray that Your Spirit would lead us to comprehend the mystery of our Lord Jesus—our wonderful Jesus! May we see Your glory and may Your glory, as the Apostle Paul says, transform us more and more into the image of Him whom our souls love, our Lord Jesus. Open our eyes that we may behold wonderful things from the wonders of Jesus. In His precious name we come to You, oh Father. Amen.*

MONDAY: See the Mystery

*"It has been given to you to **know the mysteries** of the kingdom of heaven, but to them it has not been given."*
—Matthew 13:11

In the New Testament, a mystery is not something eerie or inscrutable, but rather "a truth that was hidden by God in times past and is now revealed to those who are in His family." This mystery is a sacred secret that is unknown to unbelievers, but understood and treasured by the people of God. When you read the New Testament you will see the word "mystery" often.

- **The Mystery of the Kingdom** (Matthew 13:11). The mystery first appears in Matthew 13 where Jesus presented the truth that the majority rejected the good news. This had not been revealed in the Old Testament. God came down in human flesh, walked on the earth, did all kinds of miracles, but most people still did not believe Him. THIS IS A MYSTERY.
- **The Mystery of Israel's Unbelief** (Romans 11:25). Why would those who were the line through which the Messiah would come—the chosen people whom God so wonderfully protected and provided for—reject Him? Have you ever thought of how much food it took to feed them in the wilderness? There were three million people. If they ate normally, it would take a train with 1,300 boxcars, nine and one-half miles long, to carry enough food supplies for each day. But God provided faithfully, every day, by spreading out manna around their tents! Yet, with all that and so much more, they still did not believe!

- **The Mystery of the Rapture** (1 Corinthians 15:51–52): This is a mystery that God did not reveal until 1 Corinthians 15. That is why so many people who don't understand the Bible don't believe in the Rapture. (It isn't in the Old Testament or the Gospels.)
- **The Mystery of the Unity of Believers** (Ephesians 3:3–6): That all who believe in Christ would be knitted together in Him is a mystery. The mystery of the church as Christ's bride is found nowhere in the Bible until Ephesians 5:24–32. Israel was the wife of Jehovah God (Isaiah 50:1–3; Jeremiah 3:1), but the church is the bride of Jesus Christ.
- **The Mystery of the Indwelling Christ** (Colossians 1:26–27): "The mystery which has been hidden . . . now has been revealed to His saints . . . : which is Christ in you, the hope of glory." The Old Testament saints did not have this privilege.
- **The Mystery of God in the Flesh** (Colossians 2:2–3): The incarnation of the Son of God was a truth not fully revealed in the Old Testament. Isaiah 9:6 declared that God would come, but it did not explain that He would be a person walking around on the earth.
- **The Mystery of Iniquity** (2 Thessalonians 2:7): This refers to sin and how it grows and permeates. Revelation 17 speaks of the mystery of Babylon—the terrible, vile economic and religious system of the end times; and the mystery age will be completed when Christ returns in glory (Revelation 10:7).

The biggest mystery of all human history. Why has God permitted evil? The answer comes in Revelation 10 as the Lord makes a vow that this mystery will be finished—there will be no more delay!

Have you ever read *Robinson Crusoe*? In that classic, Robinson Crusoe teaches English to his servant named Friday, and then tells him about God. Here is basically what Robinson said: "There is a great and mighty God. He is possessor of the entire universe. He is powerful over all." Then he told him that there is a devil, so Friday asked, "If God is so great, why is there a devil?" Robinson did not answer because he said it could not be answered—it is a mystery.

Why *didn't* God do away with the devil in the Garden of Eden or in the wilderness of temptation?

When God flooded the earth and killed everyone but Noah's family, did all the generations that followed believe and follow the Lord? No. Just a few generations after the Flood, they built the Tower of Babel in a group rebellion.

After Moses destroyed the Egyptians in the most public and visible spectacle of divine proportions, did Egypt have a national revival? Did they turn in faith and repentance to the Lord? No.

As Jesus did wonderful miracles and signs that no one could even question, did everyone turn in faith and repentance to Him as the Lord? Did the nation of Israel trust, obey, and follow Him as Messiah? No.

The apostles went out across the world with supernatural power, healing the sick, raising the dead, and speaking with the unquestionable authority of God. Did all the nations they visited turn in faith and repentance to the Lord? No.

Is it any wonder that the descendants of those who survived the Flood—the families of the empire of Egypt, the children of Jesus' day, and the generations born to those who saw and heard the apostles—are any less hard-hearted? They see wonders, hear marvelous things, and experience the indisputable hand of God but turn from it. Oh, the mystery of the human will—so blinded by willful sin!

As you read Revelation 10, it may surprise you to know that in the entire span of time from Creation until now, God has never reigned on earth. Yes, He is the sovereign King over the entire universe, over both heaven and earth, but He has never stood on the planet and been visibly in charge with everyone obeying Him. He has overruled and intervened on earth, and governs all human events, but for now He does so in a way that appears remote and incomplete. Thus, He has never used His absolute power to bring about an end to demonic evil, human rebellion, and global injustice and suffering. So chapter 10 opens with Christ coming down to earth, putting one foot on the sea and one foot on the land, and roaring like a lion!

Jesus Christ does not presently receive the worship and honor that is His due as the sovereign King. He has authority that He chooses not to exercise for now, but when He finally establishes His reign, all sin and all suffering will cease. That is our eternal hope for which we pray whenever we repeat the words: "Your kingdom come. Your will be done on earth as it is in heaven" (Matthew 6:10).

The Mystery: Why does God continue to wait? Why does He warn, offer, and watch for a few more sinners to repent? **The Answer:** The mystery of Jesus is His amazing love for even those who never seem to stop rejecting Him. So He waits, but now, in Revelation 10, it is time for the seventh trumpet to sound.

TUESDAY: Focus on Jesus

*While he was still speaking, behold, a bright cloud overshadowed them; and suddenly a voice came out of the cloud, saying, "**This is My beloved Son**, in whom I am well pleased. **Hear Him!**"*
—MATTHEW 17:5

After the opening of the six seals of Revelation 6, the seventh seal initiates the six trumpets of Revelation 8–9. In Revelation 10, John now sees what lies ahead with the seventh trumpet. This trumpet, which sounds in 11:15, holds the longest of the messages of doom.

Do you remember what has happened to set off this chain of terror? The Lamb who was worthy opened the scroll (5:7). What made Him worthy to be the heir of the universe (Hebrews 1:2)? He was the Lamb slain for sin! In Revelation 10, Jesus is now wrestling the dominion of all things back from the thief, the liar, and the murderer—Satan. He is in the process of judging all that the usurper to the throne has caused in the cosmic rebellion.

At this midpoint in the vision, John records the drama of redemption, and we are reintroduced to the hero—our Lord Jesus. By the inspiration of the Holy Spirit, John paints a beautiful picture of Jesus as the almighty Redeemer and absolute victor. Thus Revelation 10 may well be a snapshot capturing the work of Christ and the grandeur of God's plan of redemption.

Jesus reflects God's image. "I saw still another mighty angel coming down from heaven, **clothed with a cloud**. And a **rainbow was on his head**, his **face was like the sun**, and his **feet like pillars**

of fire" (Revelation 10:1). Jesus was often seen in the Old Testament as a pre-incarnate angel of the Lord. When He appeared it was as a special and mighty angelic messenger from God. In these instances, He would accept and receive worship, which no angel would ever accept, unless it was the usurper himself, Satan. The four descriptions of this mighty angel in verse 1 correspond at each point with previous descriptions of Jesus in Revelation.

This mighty angel comes **"clothed with a cloud"**—the cloud of God's glory. Revelation 1:7 says, "Behold, He is coming with clouds, and every eye will see Him, even they who pierced Him." Jesus was clothed in a cloud like this the last time the apostle John saw Him ascend into heaven in Acts 1:9. And John heard the angels who spoke with the apostles say that Jesus would return "in like manner" (Acts 1:11).

In the Old Testament, God manifested His presence by a visible glowing cloud signifying His glory. Israel was led by a pillar of fire and a cloud (Exodus 13:21). They saw the cloud when God's glory appeared (Exodus 16:10), when the tabernacle was commissioned by God (Exodus 40:38), and over the mercy seat (Leviticus 16:2). In the New Testament, Paul tells us that it was Christ in that cloud who led, watered, and fed them (1 Corinthians 10:1–4). Just as the *shekinah* (the glory cloud) hovered over the Holy of Holies when God's presence was there, so what Matthew describes as a "star" was probably also another of these Old Testament glory clouds that stood over the manger when God was incarnated. Thus the cloud is always associated with Deity.

Revelation 10:1 says that "**a rainbow was on his head.**" The rainbow is a crown. We encountered the rainbow in Revelation 4 as it encircled the throne, reminding us of God's grace from the time of Noah and the Flood (Genesis 9:13). Ezekiel also saw this rainbow around the throne of God (Ezekiel 1:28). Because of the article used in Revelation 10:1, "*the* rainbow," this seems to be God's special crown for His beloved Son, Jesus. It is very interesting that the Hebrew word for "bow" is used for both a rainbow and a weapon that shoots arrows. So this rainbow could speak of God's grace as well as His judgment, which perfectly meet in the person of Jesus (Psalm 85:10). As we have seen so far, the greatest multitude saved in history is coming out of the time of earth's greatest judgment (Revelation 7:14). Jesus loves and seeks sinners at all times and in every place.

John tells us that "**his face was like the sun**" (Revelation 10:1). In Revelation 1, he also saw the face of Jesus with a countenance "shining like the sun" (v.16), so this description matches again. Just like at His Transfiguration (Matthew 17:2) and on the road to Damascus (Acts 9:3), Jesus shines as bright as the sun. This fits what Malachi said when he predicted the coming "Sun of Righteousness" (4:2).

Here is the fourth description of this mighty angel: "**his feet [are] like pillars of fire.**" In Revelation 1:15, the feet of Jesus were like brass glowing from a furnace, which sounds exactly like this mighty angel's description. This being may well be our Lord Jesus Christ appearing to John as a kingly angel. He often appeared in the Old Testament as "the Angel of the LORD" (Exodus 3:2; Judges 2:4; 6:11–12, 21–22; 2 Samuel 24:16). This was a temporary manifestation for a special purpose, not a permanent incarnation. Whenever Jesus appeared that way, the people would be scared to death and fall on their faces to worship Him. And only Jesus accepts worship!

How is your worship of Jesus these days? Are you remembering to worship first—and then serve Him?

WEDNESDAY: Jesus Claims His Inheritance

*He had a little book open in his hand. And he set his right foot on the sea and his left foot on the land, and **cried with a loud voice, as when a lion roars**. When he cried out, seven thunders uttered their voices.*

—Revelation 10:2–3

Revelation 1 tells us that the voice of Jesus is powerful. John describes it as "a loud voice, as of a trumpet" (1:10) and "His voice as the sound of many waters" (1:15). In Revelation 5:5b, we learn that "the Lion of the tribe of Judah . . . has prevailed to open the scroll and to loose its seven seals." And now in Revelation 10:3 we hear the voice of the conquering Lamb roaring as the Lion of Judah in His victory: "When he cried out, seven thunders uttered their voices." Thus we hear the conquering, almighty voice of Jesus declaring His right to possess His possession!

Jesus shows His mighty grace. "Now when the seven thunders uttered their voices, I was about to write; but I heard a voice from heaven saying to me, 'Seal up the things which the seven thunders uttered, and do not write them'" (Revelation 10:4). This is one of the most beautiful verses in Revelation, but most people don't understand it. (I had to read this verse about fifty times before I understood what it was saying.)

When the Lion roared in 10:3, "the seven thunders uttered their voices." That reminds me of a phrase in Psalm 29:3: "the God of glory thunders." Psalm 29 is speaking of the Flood; the last time God conquered the earth was with water. But when the Lion of the tribe of Judah comes, He will roar like a lion and seven thunders will sound. Since seven means "complete" and thunder means "judgment," His roar is the sound of complete judgment.

This sound, however, does not refer to unintelligible noise—the thunders are voices. John was about to write down what they said, but God told him, "Seal up the things which the seven thunders uttered, and do not write them." If God did not want this written down, why did He have John say that he heard something? This is Jesus showing His grace.

Revelation 10:4 is certainly a strange verse without looking at it in light of the whole Bible. John hears and records this event because God wants us to see His loving patience. God, who is not willing that any should perish, halts the annihilation of the human race because there must still be a few more who will be saved. To the end of earth's history, God is still sprinkling His grace. When the seven thunders explode in the decree of final destruction, God seals it up for a bit longer.

God showed grace and mercy in Noah's generation by withholding judgment for all those extra days (Genesis 7:4). As He listened to Abraham's plea to spare Sodom, even if but for a few righteous ones, He was again merciful because God sent the angels to drag Lot out of Sodom and to try to convert his married children. And the earth will be spared once again while God deploys one evangelistic team after another in Revelation 7–14: the 144,000 of chapter 7, the two witnesses of chapter 11, and the angel who goes out in chapter 14.

There may be a similar word in Daniel 12. After the revelation of the coming terrible Tribulation, Daniel is told to seal up the words for three and one-half years as an angel swears by the Almighty (vv. 1–2, 4, 6–7). This may be the same scene John is now seeing. If so, it is a blessed reminder of God's grace in the midst of judgment. Even as the wrath of God intensifies, He continues to offer salvation in spite of the implacable hardness of human hearts that only seems to increase.

Jesus reveals the image of God. "The angel . . . raised up his hand to heaven and swore by Him who lives forever and ever, who created heaven and the things that are in it, the earth and the things that are in it, and the sea and the things that are in it, that there should be delay no longer" (Revelation 10:5–6).

When the Ancient of Days, God the Father, wants to make Himself known, He always does so through His Son. That is why so many Bible teachers through the ages have seen this angel as Jesus. As John 1:18 says: "No one has seen God at any time. The only begotten Son, who is in the bosom of the Father, He has declared Him." In Revelation 10:5–6, this swearing and holding up of the hand reminds us of what the writer of Hebrews says in 1:1–3: "God, . . . has in these last days spoken to us by His Son, . . . heir of all things, through whom also He made the worlds; who being the brightness of His glory and the express image of His person, [upholds] all things by the word of His power."

When God made the covenant with mankind, He said that He could not swear by anybody greater than himself. So God the Son stands there swearing by himself: "and swore by Him who lives forever and ever" (Revelation 10:6a). The One who created heaven and earth is Jesus Christ.

Jesus lays claim to His rightful possession. As portrayed by this mighty angel, Jesus descends and plants His feet on the land and sea. Whether it is Jesus or just an angel representing Him, this is a picture of laying claim to His possession—an exclusive right of Jesus as the One who purchased it by His blood "to reconcile all things to Himself, . . . having made peace through the blood of His cross" (Colossians 1:20).

Jesus is the only One who can reconcile heaven to earth, that which He conquered at the cross. In a special sense, this may show Jesus sharing the right of our redemption, for we are joint heirs with Jesus: "And if children, then heirs—heirs of God and joint heirs with Christ, if indeed we suffer with Him, that we may also be glorified together" (Romans 8:17).

We also see this truth in Hebrews 9:15: "He is the Mediator of the new covenant, by means of death, for the redemption of the transgressions under the first covenant, that those who are called may receive the promise of the eternal inheritance." And in 2 Timothy 2:12, the apostle Paul said, "If we endure, we shall also reign with Him. If we deny Him, He also will deny us."

In Revelation we have already seen some wonderful pictures of Jesus as the Son of Man (1:13); the Creator of the universe (4:2, 11); the slain Lamb (5:6); and the Great High Priest (8:3).

In the Old Testament we find Daniel meeting with a heavenly representative. Let's compare these passages to see if we can identify Daniel's visitor.

Daniel 10:5–6, 18	Revelation 1:13–17
Clothed in linen	Clothed with a garment down to the feet
Girded with fine gold	A golden girdle
Body like beryl	Head and hair white as snow
Face as lightning	Face as the sun
Eyes as lamps of fire	Eyes as a flame of fire
Arms and feet like polished brass	Feet like fine brass
Voice like a multitude	Voice as many waters
At the sight, Daniel retained no strength	John fell at His feet as if dead

There can be no doubt about it—Daniel saw the Lord Jesus in His pre-incarnate glory, and John saw Him as the risen and glorified Son. But both of them are the image of the invisible God. And here in Revelation 10:1–6, we have a vision of what may well be Jesus in all His glory coming to take back His earth and, as He lays claim, He gives a loud cry of victory! Oh, won't that be a glorious day!

THURSDAY: Jesus Explains the Mystery

But in the days of the sounding of the seventh angel, when he is about to sound, ***the mystery of God would be finished****, as He declared to His servants the prophets.*
—REVELATION 10:7

In Revelation 10:7, we again see the term "mystery of God," which is summarized in all the revelation of the Word of God. This m3ystery is God's waiting and watching while the ravages of sin have run seemingly unhindered throughout all history. As the rebellion of humanity and the blindness of His people continue, God patiently waits for any to return to Christ. However, there is a moment when God is going to say, "Enough! I am now turning My attention on My people—My Israel—and I am going to pour out My wrath on the earth, but I am going to save Israel."

As the representative of both the nation of Israel and all of God's servants, John is given the mystery of God's plan. Like Daniel who awaited his part, and all the faithful through the ages, it is sweet to know Jesus and yet bitter to see those destroyed who have by the horrors of their sins fitted themselves for destruction. The amazing fact is that among the most hardened hearts (especially in Israel), there will be some who become softened. As Ezekiel and Paul predicted, God will take the stony hearts of the remnant of Israel and turn them to their Messiah (Ezekiel 36:26; Romans 11).

It is tragic that so many of God's servants who have taught His Word have failed to see all that is promised for Israel. It has become popular to spiritualize promises God made to the Jews and attribute them to His church. But the plan of God focuses on Israel. The apex of that plan is the return of Jesus *to the earth* the second time to save His people as they at last look to Him.

When Jesus comes for His children of faith, He stays in the clouds and we will join Him there. However, we are to return with Him at the climactic moment of history recorded in Revelation

19. The apostle Paul says, "I do not desire, . . . that you should be ignorant of this mystery, . . . that blindness in part has happened to Israel until the fullness of the Gentiles has come in. And so all Israel will be saved, as it is written: 'The Deliverer will come out of Zion, and He will turn away ungodliness from Jacob; for this is My covenant with them, when I take away their sins'" (Romans 11:25–27).

What is God's plan? The apex of His plan is to come back for His people, Israel, and that is what "the little book" in Revelation 10:8–11 is talking about. He is saying that when the fullness of God's plan with the Gentiles is done, He will turn His attention to the hardness of the hearts of His people. This is why chapter 10 is a pivotal chapter. God is not going to delay any longer; He is going to destroy the rebellious of earth and rescue His people Israel.

As we saw in Revelation 8, the momentous time has come for the petition "Your kingdom come" to at last occur. So now, with this seventh trumpet, the delay of God is ended and the time for the end is seen in its final three and one-half years. (In Revelation 11:17, we will then see the declaration of the reign of God commencing.)

Are you getting ready for Christ's appearing? What if He were to come today?

FRIDAY: Focus on the Word

*Then the voice . . . spoke to me again . . . , "Go, take the little book which is open in the hand of the angel who stands on the sea and on the earth." So I went to the angel and said to him, "**Give me the little book**." And he said to me, "Take and eat it; and it will make your stomach bitter, but it will be as sweet as honey in your mouth." Then I . . . ate it, and it was as sweet as honey in my mouth. But when I had eaten it, my stomach became bitter. And he said to me, "You must prophesy again about many peoples, nations, tongues, and kings."*

—Revelation 10:8–11

Revelation 10:8–11 is really the most practical part of the chapter. Jesus shows the way to God—and the way to God is eating His Word. History records an eccentric Ethiopian monarch, Menelik II, who ruled from 1889–1913. This monarch brought Ethiopia out of the dark ages by introducing communication (telephone and telegraph), transportation (railroads), and public education. But he held to a superstition inherited from the ignorance of the past. He believed in a form of self-medication that called for the literal eating of pages from the Bible. Over the years of his reign, it seemed to work quite well. If he felt ill, he ate a page or two. However, at the end of his life, his health was failing in spite of eating one page after another. King Menelik finally ordered the entire book of 1 Kings to be torn out, and he began to eat it page by page. His historians recorded that he died as he was chewing somewhere around the visit of the Queen of Sheba to Solomon.

Old Testament prophets like Jeremiah (15:16) and Ezekiel (2:9–3:4) knew what it was to "eat the Word" before they could share it with others. As Jesus the perfect Word "became flesh" (John 1:14), so we who are His living epistles need to incarnate the written Word in our lives before we can give it to those who need it. Any Christian who merely echoes God's Word, and does not incarnate it by making it a living part of his or her very being, will suffer a great loss of rewards both now and in eternity.

The directions that the angel gave to John in Revelation 10:8–11 should stir us to fulfill our responsibility of assimilating God's Word. He wants us to make it a part of our inner person. It was not enough for John to look at the book or even know its contents and purpose. He had to assimilate it into his inner being. Scripture often compares God's Word to food: (1) bread (Matthew 4:4); (2) milk (1 Peter 2:2); (3) meat (1 Corinthians 3:1–2); (4) wheat (Psalm 81:10); and (5) honey (Psalm 119:103).

Why does God compare His Word to food? God does not force-feed His Word to us. He has provided it, but we are responsible to take in its nourishment. In Revelation 10, John shows that we can never change the effects the Word will have in our lives: sorrow and joy, bitterness and sweetness. God's Word contains sweet promises and assurances, but it also contains bitter warnings and prophecies of judgment. The Christian bears witness of both life and death (2 Corinthians 2:14–17).

The Word of God is a two-edged Sword. His Sword cuts open hearts to the message of salvation, but the gospel also cuts off all who reject Jesus and declares they are facing damnation. Look at what God says in John 3:18: "He who believes in [Jesus Christ] is not condemned; but he who does not believe is condemned already, because he has not believed in the name of the only begotten Son of God."

Unlike the silliness of the Ethiopian monarch, when the apostle John is told to eat the scroll, the imagery is meant for all of God's saints. The Word of God offers such sweetness: ultimate victory on the winning team, God's grace and love, Jesus as our friend and brother, and getting to enjoy the presence of God forever in heaven. But as His Word gets into us, there is also much bitterness. We find out that before we can fully enjoy that bright and glorious future which God has promised, He must reshape our lives from the inside out. The bitter part is not only God's wrath, but also His demand for self-denial: personal change is expected, and we are to take up our cross daily. Suffering and persecution are thus part of our ultimate destiny on earth.

If we eat and assimilate the Word of God, we will be sweetened and then soured until we finally become useful. Like John, through a transformed life we will then be ready to share the message with the world around us. Are you eating? Is the Word of God sweet? Have you felt the bitterness of self-denial? Good! Keep eating—and go in that power to tell the world of Jesus and His great love!

SATURDAY: The Discipline of the Scriptures

> *"It is written, '**Man shall not live by bread alone**, but by every word that proceeds from the mouth of God.'"*
> —Matthew 4:4

As we have just seen in Revelation 10:8–11, Jesus shows the way to God, and the way to God is eating His Word. I pray that you can joyfully identify with Jeremiah in this verse: "Your words were found, and I ate them, and Your word was to me the joy and rejoicing of my heart" (Jeremiah 15:16). His passion for God and His Word was consistently, and relentlessly, demonstrated throughout his life as God's prophet.

Wouldn't you like to capture that same passion in your own life? It all starts by disciplining yourself to spend time listening to God speak to you! To help you start cultivating such a time with the Lord, let's look at three areas of spiritual discipline: (1) reading God's Word; (2) memorizing God's Word; and (3) meditating upon God's Word.

Reading God's Word. The Scriptures are the very voice of God, so we must discipline ourselves to *listen* to Him. If we never inconvenience ourselves enough to be disciplined in our Bible reading, there are truths God has for us that will be missed. Our lives then can't help but be empty.

Dr. Harry Ironside (1876–1951), a well-known Bible commentator and great pastor of Moody Memorial Church of Chicago, was a man with little formal education but great power. He read the Bible fourteen times by age fourteen! His mark is still on Chicago—and, indeed, the entire world.

Another outstanding example of a man who practiced the discipline of the Scriptures is Lt. General William K. Harrison (1895–1987). Except for the Congressional Medal of Honor, he received every other decoration for valor. . . . General Harrison—a soldier's soldier who led a busy, ultra-kinetic life—was also an amazing man of the Word. When he was a twenty-year-old cadet, he began reading the Old Testament once a year, and the New Testament four times. He continued doing so until the end of his life—having read the Old Testament seventy times and the New Testament 280 times by age ninety![1]

Dr. Ironside and General Harrison both lived out the experience of the psalmist, which tells us the attitude we must have if we are going to have this discipline of Scripture: "Oh, how I love Your law! It is my meditation all the day. You . . . make me wiser than my enemies; . . . I have more understanding than all my teachers [and] the ancients, because I keep Your precepts" (Psalm 119:97–100).

Do you see the heartbeat of the man of God? It is God's Word! It only takes fifteen minutes, or three and one-third chapters per day, to read the entire Bible in a year. You can begin to get alone with God when you consider that eating His Word is even more important than your daily meals. You can never have a Christian mind without reading the Scriptures regularly, because you cannot be deeply influenced by that which you do not know.

Memorizing God's Word. Second on the list of how to cultivate a time of getting alone with God is the discipline of *memorizing* the Scriptures. Mrs. Marge Barnhouse said of her famous preacher husband, Donald Grey Barnhouse (1895–1960): "Someone once asked him how long it had taken him to prepare a certain sermon. His answer was 'Thirty years and thirty minutes!' He had immersed himself in the Bible from the time he was fifteen years old, when he memorized the Book of Philippians a verse a day until he knew the entire book by heart, then went on to other passages. He felt it was not enough to learn by rote—it had to be by heart; because you loved and believed it."[2]

Pioneering missionary to Africa, C. T. Studd (1860–1931), is another of God's great disciplined servants. His life was like his grass hut: there were no doors to shut; he lived with, and for, his beloved pygmy tribes. How did he prepare to teach as many as 5,000 at a time? How did he get ready to disciple the scores of church leaders who came to sit at the foot of his cot every morning so that he would awake to what he calls in his journal "a sea of black faces and white teeth" waiting for him to open the Book of God to them? He hid God's Word in his heart beforehand so that he would be ready, at a moment's notice, to minister to all whom the Lord brought to him.

Are you wasting precious time that would have been better spent listening to God? Will you have any regrets when you look back on your life? Why not begin by memorizing at least one verse a week? That is fifty-two verses in one year!

Meditating upon God's Word. Meditation is the spiritual discipline of practicing Christ's words in Matthew 4:4: "Man shall not live by bread alone, but by every word that proceeds from the mouth of God." At salvation, we became a soul that thirsts for God and longs to "drink in" His Word; a soul that longs for the "Water of Life" (the continual flow of eternal life) and "drinks in" freely from God in His Word; a soul that thirsts midst the arid, sun-baked, lifeless deserts of life and finds a beautiful, ever-present oasis through communing with God in His Word. This is the secret of God's great warriors, and a spiritual discipline that we each need to practice.

One outstanding warrior for God is George Mueller (1805–1898), a spiritual giant. His life may be distilled down to these words he wrote in a diary: "It has pleased the Lord to teach me [that] the most important thing I had to do was to give myself to the reading of the Word of God, and to the meditation on it, that thus my heart might be comforted, encouraged, warned, reproved and instructed; and that thus, by means of the Word of God, while meditating on it, my heart might be brought into experimental communion with the Lord."[3]

Meditating upon the Word brings us immediately into the intimate presence of God, but too few are willing to pay the price. However, each of these great men of the Scriptures—Ironside, Harrison, Barnhouse, Studd, and Mueller—responded with joy to Jesus when they understood, through His Word, that He was saying, "If you will listen to Me, and let Me arrange your life for you, and accompany you through life, I want you to live in My power. I want you to have the boldness that comes from knowing that your life has been authorized by Me. I designed it; I am leading it; I am guiding it; and I am praying for and empowering you to live My life here on earth." Wow! What an entirely different and powerful way to look at life! That is exactly what He offers if you will but joyfully pursue the discipline of the Scriptures!

Make a choice to live in hope. To truly discover the enduring hope that anchors, you must discipline yourself to daily spend time alone with God in His Word, for "blessed is the man [whose] delight is in the law of the LORD, and in His law he meditates day and night.... And whatever he does shall prosper" (see Psalm 1:1–3). This is the great necessity of your spiritual life.

E. Stanley Jones once described time spent in the Scriptures as a "time exposure to God." He used the analogy of his life being like a photographic plate which, when exposed to God, progressively bore the image of God in keeping with the length of exposure. You are called by God to intentionally, volitionally, and willfully choose to do those things that will exercise, discipline, and direct your life for godliness (2 Peter 1:5–11).

If you will read, study, meditate on, and internalize the Word of God, you will look like Jesus Christ. And that is exactly what God wants!

WEEK 31
Remember God's Plan of the Ages

{ Revelation 11 }

As the end of days approaches, you can find hope as you remember the plan of the ages!

SUNDAY: The Witness of Jesus

> *Then I was given a reed like a measuring rod. And the angel stood, saying, "Rise and measure the temple of God, the altar, and those who worship there. But leave out the court which is outside the temple, . . . for it has been given to the Gentiles. And they will tread the holy city underfoot for forty-two months."*
> — REVELATION 11:1–2

The verses above help us to understand the eleventh chapter of Revelation. Revelation 11:1–2 takes us to a temple in Jerusalem. Immediately we know that this is an earthly scene, and not in heaven, because there are Jews carrying on Old Testament sacrifices—just as Jesus, Daniel, Paul, and now John predicted would happen.

At this midpoint in the Tribulation, the Lord will send a survey crew to the city of Jerusalem to widen the road and clear the roadblocks the Jews laid because of their unbelief. Jesus will then lay claim to His chosen people.

This chapter confirms what Jesus said in His Sermon on the Mount of Olives—that the temple will be rebuilt and in operation during the Tribulation period. In 2 Thessalonians, Paul wrote about the same thing, and now the apostle John sees it in operation.

The two witnesses (the evangelists) that are introduced are possibly the agents that lead the 144,000 Jews to Jesus in the first three and one-half years. As we learn what is going on, let us not miss the lessons of the four powerful truths in the eleventh chapter of Revelation: (1) God keeps His Word (vv. 1–2); (2) God protects His own (vv. 3–7); (3) God gives endless life (vv. 8–14); and (4) God expects worship (vv. 15–19).

Is the temple the church? Some people believe that verses 1–2 refer to the church, which is one in Christ. But if that were true, why are Jews and Gentiles being segregated? (Ephesians 3 says that the Jews and Gentiles are to be one.) How is it that the worldwide church is localized to Jerusalem? And why are we back to a temple and an altar? Since the middle wall has been broken down, God says that we no longer need temples and altars with Christ. No, as chapter 11 opens in Jerusalem, this is a yet-future event. Something will happen that would have started a world war had it occurred this week. (By the way, although the church has already been raptured by this point, multitudes will become believers throughout the Tribulation period.)

The Book of Daniel, one of the most historically and archaeologically authenticated books of the Old Testament, also says that this is a future event. It is critical to realize that the Book of Daniel existed in documented form almost five centuries *before* Christ was born.

While Daniel (originally deported as a teenager into Babylonian captivity) was in the middle of studying the book of Jeremiah, he understood that the seventy years of Jewish exile were almost up, so he began praying that God would forgive the sins of His people. The angel Gabriel, one of the seven angels that stand before God ready to be sent on His missions, interrupted Daniel's prayer saying, "At the beginning of your supplications the command went out, and I have come to tell you, for you are greatly beloved; therefore consider the matter, and understand the vision" (Daniel 9:23).

The angel Gabriel gave Daniel a four-verse prophecy that is unquestionably the most remarkable prophecy in the entire Bible—Daniel 9:24–27. This prophecy includes the following segments: (1) the scope of the entire prophecy (9:24); (2) the sixty-nine weeks (9:25); (3) the interval between the sixty-ninth and seventieth week (9:26); and (4) the seventieth week (9:27).

To help you better understand Revelation 11, I will cover each of the segments of Daniel's prophecy during this week's devotionals. I hope that you are looking forward to studying this remarkable prophecy!

My Prayer for You This Week: *Oh Father, You who put Your seal of ownership on the temple by measuring it; You who raised up Your special witnesses and sent them throughout the earth with amazing powers; You, the great God who is always in control and never in a hurry, we bow before You. By Your grace and through Your Spirit empower us to understand this most critical chapter in Your Word—that the fullness of all that You have promised You will bring to pass. And that You will bring to pass Your powerful Word in our personal lives as well. May Your will be done in us as it is in heaven, and soon to be done on earth. I pray that death would be a sobering lesson for all of us to live our lives in such a way that we are ready to go home to You at any moment. May we not be fearful and worried, but rather confident and triumphant when that hour comes. Father, speak to us through Your Word. We thank You for the privilege of looking into it again. In the name of Jesus we pray. Amen.*

MONDAY: Daniel's Prophecy Is an End-of-Days Road Map

*"**Seventy weeks are determined** for your people and for your holy city, to finish the transgression, to make an end of sins, to make reconciliation for iniquity, to bring in everlasting righteousness, to seal up vision and prophecy, and to anoint the Most Holy."*

— Daniel 9:24

God's prophetic Word in Daniel 9 is directed at the future of Israel—not the church. In God's Word, more than 75 percent of all prophecies (fulfilled and not yet fulfilled) are about the future of Israel. His Word always has and always will focus on Israel. In his epistle to the Romans, Paul reminded the church of this when he clearly warned them to not forget that they are grafted into the tree, which is Israel (Romans 11:11–36).

Segment one—*the scope of the entire prophecy.* God worked with the Jews 2,200 years before the church and is going to work with them a thousand years after the church. In our little period of time, two thousand years, we are important, but we are not all there is. Israel is critically important. The church is blended together with them now; we are grafted in, but God is going to come and deal with them again. We should therefore diligently lead people to Christ, because as soon as the last one to be saved is saved, we will be raptured out of this planet.

Now let us look at the scope of the whole period. At the beginning of today's devotional, we read Daniel 9:24 in which God said some specific things about the Jews. The idiom of "a week of years" was common in Israel as a "sabbath for the land." You can read about this in Leviticus 25–26 and Deuteronomy 15. These passages talk about a sabbath for the land—about *heptads*, or periods of seven years; the land was to lie fallow every seventh year. It was their failure to obey these and other laws that led to God's sending them into captivity under the Babylonians (2 Chronicles 36). They were to work for six years and take the seventh year off. After forty-eight years, the forty-ninth was the sabbath year—and the fiftieth year was the Jubilee year. It was a wonderful system. God said that they needed that rest and renewal "to anoint the Most Holy. And those who escaped from the sword he carried away to Babylon, where they became servants to him and his sons until the rule of the kingdom of Persia, to fulfill the word of the Lord by the mouth of Jeremiah, until the land had enjoyed her Sabbaths. As long as she lay desolate she kept Sabbath, to fulfill seventy years" (2 Chronicles 36:20–21).

Note that Daniel 9:24 is not directed to the church but focuses upon "your people [Israel] and your holy city [Jerusalem]." The scope of this prophecy includes a broad list of things that clearly are yet to be completed.

Segment two—*the first sixty-nine weeks.* A very specific prediction occurs:

"From the going forth of the command to restore and to build Jerusalem until Messiah the Prince, there shall be seven weeks and sixty-two weeks; the street [open square] shall be built again, and the wall, even in troublesome times. And after the sixty-two weeks Messiah shall be cut off [the Crucifixion], but not for Himself; and the people of the prince who is to come shall destroy [by the Romans, A.D. 70] the city and the sanctuary. The end of it shall be with a flood, and till the end of the war desolations are determined. Then he shall confirm a covenant with many for one week; but in the middle of the week He shall bring an end to sacrifice and offering. And on the wing of abominations shall be One who makes desolate, even until the consummation, which is determined, is poured out on the desolate [the Antichrist, 2 Thessalonians 3]."

—Daniel 9:25–27

This passage encapsulates all of biblical prophecy. It also includes a mathematical prophecy. The Jewish (and Babylonian) calendars used a 360-day year (Genesis 7:24); sixty-nine weeks of 360-day years totals 173,880 days. In effect, the angel Gabriel told Daniel that the interval between the command to rebuild Jerusalem until the presentation of the Messiah as King would be 173,880 days. The "Messiah the Prince" in the King James translation is actually the "Meshiach Nagid"—"The Messiah the King." (Nagid is first used of King Saul.)

This is a prophetic bull's eye: the commandment to restore and build Jerusalem was given by Artaxerxes Longimanus on March 14, 445 B.C.[1] (The emphasis on "the street" and "the wall" in Daniel 9:25 was to avoid confusion with other earlier mandates confined to rebuilding the temple.)

When did the Messiah present himself as King? During the ministry of Jesus Christ there were several occasions in which the people attempted to promote Him as their king, but He carefully avoided it because His time had not yet come (John 6:15).

Then one day Christ meticulously arranged His timely triumphant entry. When He rode into the city of Jerusalem on a donkey, He deliberately fulfilled Zechariah's prophecy (483 years earlier) that the Messiah would present himself as King in just that way: "Rejoice greatly, O daughter of Zion! Shout, O daughter of Jerusalem! Behold, your King is coming to you; He is just and having salvation. Lowly and riding on a donkey" (Zechariah 9:9).

The crowds were thought to be mad when they cried out: "Blessed is the King who comes in the name of the LORD! Peace in heaven and glory in the highest!" (Luke 19:38). Some of the Pharisees in the multitude wanted Jesus to rebuke the people because they felt that the overzealous crowd was blaspheming by proclaiming Jesus as the Messiah, the King (Luke 19:39). However, Jesus did not rebuke the crowd, He endorsed their praise: "I tell you that if these should keep silent, the stones would immediately cry out" (Luke 19:40). This is the only occasion that Jesus presented himself as King. It occurred on April 6, A.D. 32.

The divine precision of prophecy is indisputable. When we examine the period between March 14, 445 B.C. and April 6, A.D. 32, and correct for leap years, we discover that it is 173,880 days exactly—to the very day! How could Daniel have known this in advance? How could anyone have contrived to have this detailed prediction documented over three centuries in advance? But there is even more!

Segment three—the interval between the sixty-ninth and seventieth week. There appears to be a gap between the sixty-ninth week (v. 25) and the seventieth week (v. 27). Look again at Daniel 9:26: "And after the sixty-two weeks Messiah shall be cut off, but not for Himself; and the people of the prince who is to come shall destroy the city and the sanctuary. The end of it shall be with a flood, and till the end of the war desolations are determined."

The sixty-two weeks follow the initial seven, so verse 26 deals with events after the sixty-ninth week, but before the seventieth. These events include the Messiah being killed and the city and sanctuary being destroyed.

As Jesus approached the city on the donkey, He predicted the destruction of Jerusalem: "Your enemies will build an embankment around you, surround . . . and level you . . . to the ground; and they will not leave . . . one stone upon another because you did not know the time of your visitation" (Luke 19:43–44).

The Messiah was, of course, executed at the Crucifixion—"but not for Himself." Christ presented himself, but they did not accept Him, so the Romans killed Him; He was cut off. Thirty-eight years later, in A.D. 70, the Roman legions under Titus Vespasian leveled the city of Jerusalem, precisely as Daniel and Jesus had predicted. Both the city and sanctuary were destroyed. In fact, as one carefully examines Jesus' specific words—"because you did not know the time of your visitation"—it appears that He held the people accountable to know this astonishing prophecy in Daniel 9.

Even as we remember that moment when Christ saw the future desolation of Israel, we also remember that He *wept*. Christ's compassion, even in the face of well-deserved punishment, should move our hearts. He is so aware of our weaknesses; He knows we are dust. He ever lives to intercede for us. And today Jesus wants to be invited to walk through this day, hand in hand with us—guiding us, protecting us, and receiving from us our adoration and love!

TUESDAY: The End of Days Described

"Then he [the Antichrist] shall confirm a covenant with many for one week."
—Daniel 9:27

In yesterday's devotional we saw that Daniel 9:24 says that seven weeks are determined; we have found sixty-nine of them. Daniel 9:27 now references the remaining "one week," or seven-year period yet to be fulfilled, which is the most documented period in the entire Bible. Revelation 6–19 is essentially a detailing of that climactic seventieth week. That is why we say the Tribulation is seven years—there is one week of years still left to be fulfilled.

Segment four—*the seventieth week.* "The interval between the sixty-ninth and seventieth week continues at the present time, but it is increasingly apparent that it may soon be over. The more one is familiar with the numerous climactic themes of end-times prophecy, the more it seems that Daniel's seventieth week is on our horizon. Have you done your homework? Are you and your family prepared?"[2]

Christ said, "When you see the 'abomination of desolation,' spoken of by Daniel the prophet, standing in the holy place . . . , then let those who are in Judea flee to the mountains" (Matthew 24:15–16). And Paul tells us: "That Day will not come unless the falling away comes first, and the man of sin is revealed, the son of perdition, who opposes and exalts himself above all that is called God or that is worshiped, so that he sits as God in the temple of God, showing himself that he is God" (2 Thessalonians 2:3–4).

This temple they spoke of is coming; that is why Jerusalem is such a hot piece of real estate to God and to Satan. Scholars of prophecy do not agree on all the details of future events, but the next two paragraphs are a fair representation of what many prophetic scholars believe concerning the order of events.

WEEK 31: REMEMBER GOD'S PLAN OF THE AGES

First, the church will be raptured (1 Corinthians 15:51–58; 1 Thessalonians 4:13–18), which can occur at any time. Once the true church is gone, the leader of the ten European nations will make a seven-year agreement with Israel (Daniel 9:26–27). After three and one-half years, he will break that agreement (Daniel 9:27). The Antichrist will subsequently begin to control the world and force all people to worship and obey him. At this time God will send Great Tribulation upon the earth (Matthew 24:21). The Antichrist will then set up his image in the temple at Jerusalem (2 Thessalonians 2:3–4; Revelation 13).

Next in the order of events is that the nations will gather at Armageddon to fight both the Antichrist and Israel. (Antichrist will aid Israel at first, but later turn against them.) However, as they all see the sign of Christ's coming, everyone will unite together to fight against Him (Zechariah 12; Revelation 13:13–14; 19:11ff). But Jesus will gloriously return to the earth, defeat His enemies, be received by the Jews, and establish His kingdom (Revelation 19:11ff; Zechariah 12:7–13:1). He will then reign on earth for 1,000 years, which is the period known as the Millennium (Revelation 20:1–5).

What happens to allow this temple to be put in place and not destroy the earth? Ezekiel 37–39 may have the clue. When Ezekiel wrote, he was a captive in exile. Israel was defeated, occupied, and no longer a nation. From the sixth century B.C. until 1948, there has never been a nation called Israel. So this passage *must* be future by every way of consideration. This event may even happen *before* the Tribulation because at the midpoint of the Tribulation the temple is fully functional, and the Antichrist desecrates it. Things will fall apart so greatly in the Tribulation that I don't think there will be much building going on during that time, so the temple will probably be built before the Tribulation starts—or very soon after it begins.

Chapters 37–39 of Ezekiel are so important to God that He repeats himself eight times. Let's start with Ezekiel 37, which is all about the regathering of Israel, and Israel as the "valley of dry bones." In verses 1–6, Israel is going to be regathered, and the dry bones are going to come home. In 37:9 He says, "Come from the four winds, O breath, and breathe on these slain, that they may live." The Jews came back to Israel from every corner of the earth!

In 37:12 we read: "Therefore prophesy and say to them, 'Thus says the Lord GOD: "Behold, O My people, I will open your graves and cause you to come up from your graves, and bring you into the land of Israel." ' " What graves are being referred to? It could be that it is all of those graves including Dachau, Treblinka, Auschwitz, and other concentration camps all around Eastern Europe. I have been to many of these places, and it made me grieve and weep to see what the Jews went through!

In 37:13 He opens the graves: "Then you shall know that I am the LORD, when I have opened your graves, O My people, and brought you up from your graves."

The European Jews (which were the vast majority of all the Jewish population) were so close to extinction that God intervened. The Germans were actually smarter and better soldiers. They had better technology and had the upper hand, but they made some key mistakes. They went to Russia instead of the oil fields in Romania. Hitler could have won. But God says, "You can be the smartest and have the biggest army, but you are not going to win because I am going to let everybody know that I am the Lord!"

Now look at 37:14: "'I will put My Spirit in you, and you shall live, and I will place you in your own land. Then you shall know that I, the LORD, have spoken it and performed it,' says the LORD."

Against the entire United Nations, the whole assembled world, and everyone's better judgment—Israel was allowed to have a land on May 1, 1948—and that was a miracle. We should be really amazed that Israel even exists today. But all this is so we will know that the Lord is God!

As we reflect on how God has kept His Word for Israel, it should thrill us to know that the very same awesome power of an omnipotent God is at work each day in us. Christ's invitation to abide in and live through us (John 15) is the key to living fruitfully. I encourage you to pause right now and renew Paul's prayer and make it your own: "Nevertheless as I live—it becomes less of me and more of Christ who lives in and through me" (Galatians 2:20 author's own translation).

WEDNESDAY: Russia and the End of Days

> *Thus says the Lord GOD: "Behold, I am against you, O Gog, the prince of Rosh, Meshech, and Tubal. I will turn you around, . . . and lead you out, with all your army, horses, and horsemen, all splendidly clothed, a great company with bucklers and shields, all of them handling swords. Persia, Ethiopia, and Libya are with them . . . ; Gomer and all its troops; the house of Togarmah from the far north and all its troops—many people are with you."*
>
> —Ezekiel 38:3–6

In the above passage, Israel is in the land and something is about to happen. Have you ever wondered whether the names in verses 3–6 are connected with Russia? To find a possible answer, one must first identify the areas against which Ezekiel prophesied, and then determine the countries that occupy those land areas today. Ezekiel's prophecy does not point to Russia merely because the words sound similar. Neither should one identify "Meshech" with Moscow or "Tubal" with Tobolsk. Ezekiel had historical rather than modern-day places in mind, so these areas must be located according to Ezekiel's time. This represents the entire Arab confederacy and some great power in the far north. Russia, with the largest landmass on the planet, is the only power that fits. As far back as the Scythians, they have historically been an enemy of Israel.

However, while one must avoid dogmatic assertions, these reasons suggest including Russia within Ezekiel's prophecy. Some of the geographic places named by Ezekiel may have been located in what is now Russia. The armies are said to come "from the far north" (Ezekiel 38:6, 15; 39:2). This probably includes the land bridge between the Black and Caspian Seas, now part of Russia. Ezekiel spoke of a coalition of several nations, many of which are today aligned with or under the influence of Russia. These include Iran (Persia), Sudan and northern Ethiopia (Cush), Libya (Put), and Turkey (Meshech, Tubal, Gomer, and Beth Togarmah). All these nations, possibly led by Russia, will unite to attack Israel (see Ezekiel 38:2–3, 5–6).

Ezekiel was describing a battle that will involve Israel's remotest neighbors. "They will sense their opportunity to attack when Israel feels secure under the false protection of her covenant with the Antichrist sometime at the beginning of the seven-year period. The nations involved in the attack will likely include Russia, Turkey, Iran, Sudan, Ethiopia, and Libya. Ezekiel first pictured the invasion by Gog and his allies (38:1–16), and then described their judgment (38:17–39:29)."[3]

Every time there is a big battle in the Bible, God fights for Israel. Gideon is a classic example of this: with torches, pitchers, horns, and 300 men—180,000 soldiers were routed because God caused the soldiers to turn their swords on each other! And He will display His sovereign intervention again in Ezekiel 38:19–23 by using natural, and possibly even supernatural, means to protect Israel. In His "jealousy" and "the fire of [His] wrath" He will send "a great earthquake in the land of Israel," and "call for a sword against Gog" so that every "man's sword will be against his brother." Furthermore, He will judge them "with pestilence and bloodshed . . . and will rain down . . . great hailstones, fire, and brimstone" (which is a supernatural event). His ultimate purpose is to "magnify" himself so that they shall know that He is the Lord!

In verses 19–23, a coalition of armies is moving toward Israel from the north (all of Israel's invaders usually came from the north—the Assyrians, Babylonians, and Persians). When they get to Israel there is going to be such a severe and devastating earthquake that it will be felt all over the planet.

The word "pestilence" in verse 22 is interesting. Do you remember the "beasties" we saw in Revelation 6? The beasts of the earth are more than lions, tigers, and bears; there are also little beasts of the earth. In laboratories all over the world, terrorists and governments are making anthrax, botulism, typhoid, and all kinds of other lethal organisms.

Although soldiers today don't carry swords, God says that their swords turn on themselves. A normal army today carries enough munitions to destroy the entire army. God turns these weapons against their owners supernaturally. (See also Ezekiel 39:1–9.) It is interesting that God himself will give Israel the victory even though they could use their scores of nuclear weapons. (Israel's stockpile of nuclear weapons is probably what has kept the Arabs at bay.)

When writing in 600 B.C. about this warfare, Ezekiel referred to weapons such as shields and bucklers, bows and arrows, and javelins and spears. Would he have been able to describe modern warfare? No, Ezekiel did not have the necessary vocabulary. But this doesn't mean the armies are going to revert back to chariots and weapons made of wood: "'They will not take wood from the field nor cut down any from the forests, because they will make fires with the weapons; and they will plunder those who plundered them, and pillage those who pillaged them,' says the Lord GOD" (Ezekiel 39:10).

The useable length of life for atomic material is seven years. It is possible that their atomic power plants will have enough plutonium out of those weapons to power the whole nation of Israel for seven years. (Steel or titanium can't be burned.)

How is this possible? They will be following the proper protocol for biological or atomic warfare. If there is an outbreak of atomic warfare the area would have to be isolated. Ezekiel 39:12–16 tells us that "'For seven months the house of Israel will be . . . burying, and they will gain renown for it on the day that I am glorified,' says the Lord GOD. . . . 'At the end of seven months they will . . . pass through the land; and when anyone sees a man's bone, he shall set up a marker by it, till the buriers have buried it in the Valley of Hamon Gog. The name of the city will also be Hamonah Thus they shall cleanse the land.'"

The valley of Hamon Gog is southeast of the Dead Sea, down wind from Israel, on the Arab side. Crews will be going throughout the land to decontaminate the battle area. Even though it would be much easier to dig a big pit where the battle took place and simply push the bodies and weapons into it, they won't want to contaminate the headwaters of the Jordan River. Therefore, all the bodies and weapons will be removed to Hamon Gog.

Now look at 39:17: "And as for you, son of man, thus says the Lord GOD, 'Speak to every sort of bird and to every beast of the field.'" God will send 60 percent of carnivorous scavenger birds to fly their migration routes over Israel every year, and there will be a big feast.

Ezekiel 39:22—"So the house of Israel shall know that I am the LORD their God from that day forward"—is what I think will embolden them to say: "God did this!" Though there is no conversion to Christ, they will be impressed to build the temple once the militant Muslims and possibly the Russians are destroyed: "'Then they shall know that I am the LORD their God, who sent them into captivity among the nations, but also brought them back to their land, and left none of them captive any longer. And I will not hide My face from them anymore; for I shall have poured out My Spirit on the house of Israel,' says the Lord GOD" (Ezekiel 39:28–29).

In conclusion, it is possible that a pre-Tribulation invasion of Israel will spur them on to build the temple with no opposition. But if not, then it will certainly come about because of the false promises of the Antichrist.

Since we don't know when this may occur, we need to keep that same attitude the early church lived—"Perhaps today . . ." If Jesus did come today, what do you wish He would find you doing? That is what you should seek to do. And what would you wish to *not* have Him find you doing? That is what you should avoid. Such choices make life so simple. There are only two options each day: please Jesus, who may come at any moment, or please ourselves, which is so empty.

THURSDAY: The Future Temple in Jerusalem

> *Then I was given a reed like a measuring rod. And the angel stood, saying, "Rise and **measure the temple of God**, the altar, and those who worship there."*
> —REVELATION 11:1

John now begins to weave together one of the longest Old Testament prophecies about Israel's future. Ezekiel devoted nine long chapters to a prophetic description of a massive temple built in Jerusalem. In Revelation 11, John picks up with God surveying for a temple in Jerusalem.

Almost all prophetic writers place the temple of Ezekiel in the millennial times, but the proximity of Ezekiel chapter 39 to chapter 40 is very interesting. The biggest section in which the Bible discusses a future temple is right after this invasion, which reminds us of God's long-term plans for Jerusalem. Therefore, whatever mankind does to oppose Israel only serves to accomplish God's ultimate purposes for them.

In Revelation 11:1 "measuring" speaks of someone setting an area aside to claim it for one's own self. This could be for destruction, preparation for building, restoration, or something else. Now look at the second verse: "But leave out the court which is outside the temple, and do not measure it, for it has been given to the Gentiles. And they will tread the holy city underfoot for forty-two months. And I will give power to my two witnesses, and they will prophesy one thousand two hundred and sixty days, clothed in sackcloth" (Revelation 11:2–3).

There were four courts in the temple—each opening into the other until the Holy of Holies was reached. These courts were:

1. **The Courtyard of the Gentiles:** This was the only place non-Jews could enter without the penalty of death for violation. There was a fence with posted warnings on tablets that spoke of the death penalty for crossing over into the next court by any Gentile.
2. **The Courtyard of the Women:** This was next, and it was the extent of a woman's access to the temple in those days.
3. **The Courtyard of the Israelites:** This was the third courtyard, and it marked the limit of where non-priestly men could enter.
4. **The Courtyard of the Priests:** This was the final area. In this area were the laver, the brass altar of the burnt offering, and the Holy Place. In the temple proper were the two chambers: the Holy Place and the Holy of Holies.

Old Testament worship centered first on the tabernacle, and later the temple; divinely designed liturgy was carried on for 1,500 nearly unbroken years, except when Israel sometimes lapsed into apostasy. The Israelites followed the instructions God gave Moses when he was on Mt. Sinai. The epicenter of that worship was the Holy Place. In the front half of it stood the altar of incense, golden lampstand, and table of showbread. A curtain divided the room; this curtain was actually a finely woven rug four inches thick, sixty feet high and forty feet wide. It was massive and towering; no natural light ever penetrated its dark depths. Even the light of the ever-burning lampstand never reached behind the veil.

In better times, the shekinah glory of the presence of God made the Holiest of Holies behind the veil brighter than noonday. In all Israel's history, probably no more than fifty men had ever gone into the Holy of Holies. Even David, Daniel, and Jeremiah never went in. Only the High Priest could enter, and then only once a year.

Inside that room was a gold-covered box containing the stone tablets of the Law, a pot of manna, and Aaron's rod that had budded. Above the Ark of the Covenant stood two golden cherubim with wings shielding the mercy seat—their faces forever gazing downward, focusing upon the blood to be offered.

When the day came for the High Priest to pass behind that veil, he was garbed carefully in the God-directed robes and priestly garments. He wore bells on the hem of his garment to let the other priests know he was still alive as he was inside. With trembling hands cradling a basin of blood, veiled by a cloud of smoking incense burning in a pot he carried, the High Priest would enter. After sprinkling the blood on that mercy seat on behalf of all the people of God, he hastened out. Why? The only purpose of the veil was to keep people out of the holy presence of God. God was saying: "I AM HOLY. YOU ARE NOT. STAY OUT!"

In Revelation, God's panorama of the end of days has a curious reference to the period of time we call the Tribulation. The Tribulation, and portions of it, are called by many different names such as a "week," "forty-two months," "one thousand two hundred and sixty days," and "a time, times and a half." All these refer to the seventieth week of Daniel 9—a week of years, or seven years. The forty-two months, 1,260 days, and "a time, times and a half" are all references to half of these seven years. But as often happens in prophetic portions of the Scriptures, there are near and far fulfillments.

In Jewish history, a three and one-half year time period is not only a time measurement for the future, but it is also a memory of an event that deeply touched the Jews of the intertestamental period. For three and one-half years, the rebellion against the Syrian King Antiochus Epiphanes' desecration of the temple was waged. The brave soldiers of Judas Maccabaeus fought from June 168 B.C. until December 165 B.C. and, through some amazing victories, drove out the pagan intrusion into the worship of the Lord. Many martyrs fell during this time that was described prophetically four hundred years before it took place (Daniel 7–12).

Regardless of whether God is pouring out great blessings upon His people, or the judgment they deserve, He wants us to know that He is the Lord—and deserves worship. Is that your heart toward Him today?

FRIDAY: God Stakes His Name on Israel

> "At the same time," says the LORD, "I will be the God of all the families of Israel, and they shall be My people." Thus says the LORD: "The people who survived the sword found grace in the wilderness—Israel, when I went to give him rest."
> —JEREMIAH 31:1–2

God has staked His name on one nation—Israel. No city on planet Earth has the history of God's city—Jerusalem! For over 4,000 years Jerusalem has been the city of God. Look with me at this timeline of God's association with Jerusalem.

Well over 4,000 years ago, Jerusalem was the city of Melchizedek (a type of Christ [see Genesis 14]) and Abraham's offering of Isaac; over 3,000 years ago Jerusalem was the city of David, the city of Solomon, and of God's personally designed temple. God calls it "My city" (Hosea 5:15). Two thousand years ago Jerusalem was the place of Christ's Crucifixion—now a place sacred to Jews, Christians, and Muslims. In A.D. 70 the temple (built by Herod) was destroyed. The first temple (Solomon's) was destroyed in 586 B.C. The second temple was built by Zerubbubel, and then greatly enlarged and embellished for over 40 years by Herod. In A.D. 685–691 the Dome of the Rock was built over the same area, and in A.D. 1520–1566 Suleman the Magnificent added the present walls. Today this city of less than a square mile is the focus of most of the nations of the world for one reason: God has chosen Jerusalem to be the focal point for His plan for the end of the world!

God keeps His Word. Now look at Revelation 11:1–2 again where God says that there will be another temple: "Rise and measure the temple of God, the altar, and those who worship there. But leave out the court which is outside the temple, and do not measure it, for it has been given to the Gentiles. And they will tread the holy city underfoot for forty-two months."

Daniel also said that there would be another temple (9:27 and 12:11), as did Christ in Matthew 24:15–16 and Paul in 2 Thessalonians 2:4. Thus, no matter how bleak Israel's situation may become in our fast-darkening world, or how impossible it may seem that they can even survive as a nation, God is in control working out His plan. He has a building project, and all that He has written and promised *will* come to pass.

God protects His own—to the finish. "'And I will give power to my two witnesses, and they will prophesy one thousand two hundred and sixty days, clothed in sackcloth.' These are the two olive trees and the two lampstands standing before the God of the earth. And if anyone wants to harm them, fire proceeds from their mouth and devours their enemies. And if anyone wants to harm them, he must be killed in this manner" (Revelation 11:3–5).

God has always had His witnesses: Enoch, Noah, Abraham, Job, Moses, Samuel, and so on. But who are the two witnesses in verse 3? There are several possibilities. Perhaps they are Joshua and Zerubbabel, as mentioned in Zechariah 3–4. Enoch (Genesis 5:24) and Elijah (2 Kings 2:9–11) are possibilities because neither saw death, and both were fearless prophets during times of apostasy (Jude 14–15).

Moses and Elijah are the most likely choice, however, because of their presence on the Mount of Transfiguration (Matthew 17); their position in God's plan (head of the Law and head of the Prophets); and their God-given power in ministry (Moses' plagues in Egypt and Elijah's fire and drought). Note verse 6: "These have power to shut heaven, so that no rain falls in the days of their prophecy [Elijah]; and they have power over waters to turn them to blood, and to strike the earth with all plagues [Moses], as often as they desire" (Revelation 11:6).

It is intriguing to read that the two at the tomb of Jesus (Luke 24:4, 7) and the two at the ascension of Jesus (Acts 1:9–11) were called "men," and not angels. Malachi 3:3 and 4:5–6 is a very strong prophecy of Elijah's coming. It is very possible that Elijah and Moses witnessed for Christ at the Transfiguration, the Resurrection, and the Ascension. The timing of the ministries of the two witnesses and the 144,000 evangelists is not entirely clear. But if the two witnesses are in the first half of the Tribulation, then the 144,000 could very well be saved and called into duty by the ministry of these particular witnesses.

Now, the first reference to "the beast" (which appears thirty-six times in the book) is in Revelation 11:7: "When they [the two witnesses] finish their testimony, the beast that ascends out of the bottomless pit will make war against them, overcome them, and kill them."

While it is true that God protects His own, the two witnesses will be destroyed by the Antichrist. How can that be explained? God's protection does not preclude disease, death, and martyrdom. However, He protects us from doing anything less than serving Him and fulfilling His will—and His will just might happen to be disease, death, and martyrdom. We don't know what His plan is. We are simply to serve Him by life or death, and trust that He will grant protection for as long as is needed for us to finish His plan.

- **Jacob followed his Shepherd:** "And he blessed Joseph, and said: '... The God who has fed me ... to this day, the Angel who has redeemed me from all evil, bless the lads; let my name be named upon them, and the name of my fathers Abraham and Isaac; and let them grow into a multitude in the midst of the earth'" (Genesis 48:15–16).
- **David finished God's purposes for his life:** "When David had served God's purpose ..., he fell asleep; he was buried with his fathers and his body decayed" (Acts 13:36 NIV).
- **Paul finished the race course God laid out for him:** "I have fought the good fight, ... finished the race, kept the faith. Finally, there is laid up for me the crown of righteousness, which the Lord ... will give to me on that Day, and ... to all who have loved His appearing" (2 Timothy 4:7–8).
- **Jesus confidently cried out in victory:** "So when Jesus had received the sour wine, He said, 'It is finished!' And bowing His head, He gave up His spirit" (John 19:30).

God gives endless life. "And their dead bodies will lie in the street of the great city which spiritually is called Sodom and Egypt, where also our Lord was crucified. Then [all] ... will see their dead bodies three-and-a-half days, and not allow their dead bodies to be put into graves. [All] ... will rejoice over them ... because these two prophets tormented those who dwell on the earth. Now after the three-and-a-half days the breath of life from God entered them, ... and great fear fell on those who saw them. ... And they ascended to heaven in a cloud, and their enemies saw them. In the same hour there was a great earthquake, and ... seven thousand people were killed, and the rest were afraid and gave glory to the God of heaven. The second woe is past. Behold, the third woe is coming quickly" (Revelation 11:8–14).

Imagine the world's immense shock when they see the two witnesses alive again! Raising the dead is certainly nothing new for our omnipotent God—the One "who gives life to the dead and calls those things which do not exist as though they did" (Romans 4:17). He gives this same wonderful promise to us: "He who raised Christ from the dead will also give life to your mortal bodies through His Spirit who dwells in you" (Romans 8:11). Hallelujah!

There will be a quake at the end of each of the series of judgments: the sixth seal, the seventh trumpet, and the seventh bowl. This huge earthquake will kill thousands of people and thereby bring terror to those yet alive. Some will become so afraid that they give "glory to the God of heaven," which may be an indication of the salvation of a Jewish remnant.

We can glean three practical lessons from today's devotional: (1) God keeps His Word; (2) God protects His own; and (3) God gives endless life. Do you trust Him? Do you rest in the confident hope that He will be with you to the finish of the race He's laid out for you? Do you communicate that hope to those around you?

SATURDAY: God Expects Worship

Then the seventh angel sounded: and there were loud voices in heaven, saying, "The kingdoms of this world have become the kingdoms of our Lord and of His Christ, and **He shall reign forever and ever!"** *And the twenty-four elders ... worshiped God, saying: 'We give You thanks, O Lord*

God Almighty, he One who is and who was and who is to come, because You have taken Your great power and reigned. The nations were angry, and Your wrath has come, and the time of the dead, that they should be judged, and that You should reward Your servants the prophets and the saints, and those who fear Your name . . . , and should destroy those who destroy the earth." Then the temple of God was opened in heaven, and the ark of His covenant was seen in His temple. And there were lightnings, noises, thunderings, an earthquake, and great hail.
—Revelation 11:15–19

Heaven is a worship-focused place where God rules and reigns (vv. 15–16). Are you experiencing heaven as you worship Him? Worship flows out of the wonders of God's revelation of himself: He is eternal in character (v. 17a), awesome in power (v. 17b), righteous in judgment (v. 18), and mighty in faithfulness (v. 19)!

The activity in heaven consists almost entirely of worship (Revelation 4; 5; 7:9–12), for there will be no more hunger, thirst, or scorching heat (Revelation 7:16). God will wipe all tears away (Revelation 7:17; 21:4). Death, mourning, and pain will vanish because "the former things have passed away" (Revelation 21:4). Heaven is a wonderfully protected place; all evil is excluded: "There shall by no means enter it anything that defiles, or causes an abomination or a lie" (Revelation 21:27). The sheer freedom from fallen experience is pictured by city gates that "shall not be shut by day (there shall be no night there)" (Revelation 21:25). Oh, how I hope that your heart is filled to overflowing with adoration for the God who loves you so—the One with whom you will dwell *eternally!*

People of faith will "desire a better, that is, a heavenly country"—for the sufferings of this present time are not worthy to be compared with the glory which shall be revealed in us (Hebrews 11:6; Romans 8:18)! God expects worship—do you wholeheartedly adore Him?

Make a choice to live in hope. What is your response to God's plan of the ages? If you want to have living hope for the end of days, reflect upon the glorious afterlife ahead.

WEEK 32
Keep Christ's Perspective

{ Revelation 12 }

As the end of days approaches, you can find hope as you keep Christ's perspective!

SUNDAY: Space Invaders

Be sober, be vigilant; because your adversary **the devil walks about like a roaring lion,** *seeking whom he may devour. Resist him, steadfast in the faith.*

—1 Peter 5:8–9

Above the softness of our blue-green planet there are hostile forces poised! They range across space lurking and flying about at their master's bidding. They are former angels—Satan the dragon's army. They are deadly, vile, malignant, and very intelligent (in Greek, "demon" means "intelligence").

These aliens to our planet are highly skilled, incredibly powerful, and usually invisible warriors. Demons can hear us talk, pass through walls, fly through space, inhabit human and animal bodies, alter human behavior, and afflict humans with disease, anguish, and turmoil. These extra-terrestrial beings can take on various forms that look human, look powerful, and look fearsome. They are watching over the realm of the serpent and his seed. You see, we saints of God are at war.

There is an intense conflict going on that most of us have not fully comprehended. Swirling around us, the unseen beings of the spirit world are locked in mortal combat. Behind the scenes in every boardroom, political planning session, military strategy session, classroom, worship service, and everywhere else—these unseen spirits watch, listen, and whisper their lies. It is the battle for the planet Earth that rages! The god of this world has dispatched his demon warriors with one target: blind the minds of earth's inhabitants until they cannot see and thus will not follow God!

Revelation 12 is one of the more difficult chapters of the Bible because it is so full of pictures and symbols. In no other place in the Word of God is the conflict of the ages more clearly laid out than in Revelation 11:19–12:17 where He names the key players in the battle for planet Earth. And Revelation 12 is His battle plan!

Revelation 11:19–12:7 is divided into three powerful insights for our lives today:

1. **We have victory in Jesus because God is faithful** (11:19–12:6). That is why the passage starts with the temple and the ark of the covenant scene. Faithfulness is one of the attributes of God.
2. **We have victory in Jesus because Satan is vanquished** (12:7–9). God limits everything about Satan. Many of us tremble before Satan. But when Martin Luther wrote his great hymn, "A Mighty Fortress is Our God," he had the right perspective: "We tremble not for him / For lo his doom is sure. / One little word shall fell him."
3. **We have victory in Jesus because saints suffer** (12:10–17). Victory comes through our suffering. Peter tells us in his first epistle that suffering refines us, so we are called to go through various trials. David tells us in the Old Testament that suffering is that which causes us to experience afresh the life-giving and renewing power of God through His Word.

Are you getting the picture that you have victory in Jesus—no matter what is going on in your life? I encourage you to grab hold of that truth and press on with enduring hope for the help that is yours through faith!

WEEK 32: KEEP CHRIST'S PERSPECTIVE

My Prayer for You This Week: *Oh Lord, thank You that we can come before Your Word knowing that we have the precious privilege of having the greatest Bible teacher of all time living within us—the Author. By Your grace and through faith in the Lord Jesus Christ, we have the anointing of Your Holy Spirit. He who dwells within us teaches us Your Word. As we meet with You, we pray that Your precious Holy Spirit will illumine our hearts to Your Word. As we study and ponder and consider it, gently illumine and quiet our hearts to the truth of the response that You wish from us. In this conflict of the ages, in the swirling celestial battlefield that is amassed around Your children, we are the focal point of the dragon who seeks to disarm us from being able to walk in the power of Your Spirit through Your Word. I pray that we would say yes to You, oh God. May we resist the devil so he will flee from us, and may we see many turn from darkness to light around us. I pray that we will learn about the victory of Jesus and be confident that we are more than conquerors through Christ. In His name we pray. Amen.*

MONDAY: Victory in Jesus

Then the temple of God was opened in heaven, and **the ark of His covenant was seen in His temple***. And there were lightnings, noises, thunderings, an earthquake, and great hail.*
—Revelation 11:19

We have victory in Jesus because God is faithful. Think about this for a moment: What makes the earth so important that God and Satan are both so interested in this planet? The answer is simple: God has staked His very name on a person—Jesus Christ; on an event—the cross of Calvary; and on a people—the Jews. God has said that His name is incarnated in Jesus Christ; His power is revealed through the cross; and His plan is centered on the Jews. Those converge on this planet because the center of redemptive history surrounds the earth.

Two lines run through the history of mankind in every event, and they conclude in the culmination of history. To understand the conflict of the ages we need to look at the beginning of Genesis where we are introduced to the two combatants: the line of Christ and the line of Antichrist—the line of the woman's Seed and that of the serpent. In Genesis 3:15 God declared to Satan: "I will put enmity between you and the woman, and between your [the serpent's] seed and her Seed [Jesus Christ]; he [Jesus] shall bruise [crush] your head, and you [Satan] shall bruise His [Jesus'] heel" (Genesis 3:15).

Satan bruised Christ's heel on the cross, but Jesus crushed the serpent's head. The writer of Hebrews says: "Through death He . . . destroy[ed] him who had the power of death, that is, the devil" (Hebrews 2:14). Satan is destroyed—Jesus crushed the serpent!

The serpent's seed has constantly been against the woman. What is meant by that? The whole Bible can be put into perspective with these two statements: (1) The line of Christ begins with Adam, passes via Golgotha, and leads to the heavenly Jerusalem; and (2) The line of Antichrist begins with Cain, passes via Babel, and leads to the lake of fire. There are only two families—God's and Satan's; two destinies—heaven and hell; and two choices—repent or reject. You either belong to one family or the other. You choose your own eternal destiny.

Two programs are at work in the world: God's program of salvation and Satan's program of sin, which is called "the mystery of iniquity" in the Bible. God has a timetable for His program, and nothing Satan does can change that timetable. Just as there was a "fullness of the time" for the coming of Christ (Galatians 4:4), so there is a "fullness of the time" for the appearance of the Antichrist. Nothing will be off schedule. Once the restraining ministry of the Spirit of God has ended, the next event can take place.

These chapters are easier to understand when you look at them up close and then step back in order to see the entire picture. We will start with Revelation 11:19 because the victory of Jesus is based on God's faithfulness.

Although there is a temple in heaven, there won't be one in eternity because God himself will be the temple (Revelation 21). There is a pattern that is a picture of earthly worship in heavenly places. Moses modeled the tabernacle and Solomon modeled the temple after it. The ark of the covenant will be seen in heaven because God wants us to realize how important it is. What is so important about the ark? And why is the temple opened so that through John we can see that it is there? The ark is a symbol of God's abiding presence and promises. Do you remember its contents?

The two stone tablets of the Law. On two stone tablets, with His own finger, God wrote the law that He wanted man to follow—the law declaring that our God is unceasingly holy in the demands of His character. Since the law is so important to God, it should also be important to us. Not that we fulfill it to become righteous, but that the law causes us to realize that God is holy. This is why the law is a schoolmaster that leads us to Christ. Through the law, we realize that we are unable to be as holy as God is, or wants us to be. When we are defeated by sin, we fall before Him and cry out: "We *can't* be holy!" Then God responds: "You can have the righteousness of My Son, Jesus Christ. You can receive the imputed, infused righteousness of Christ."

Aaron's rod that budded. This rod reminds us that only God gives eternal life through His Son, for Jesus said, "I am the resurrection and the life. He who believes in Me, though he may die, he shall live" (John 11:25). In contrast, Satan only gives death and destruction. Jesus said, "The thief does not come except to steal, and to kill, and to destroy. I have come that they may have life, and that they may have it more abundantly" (John 10:10).

The pot of manna. This pot was kept as a picture of Jesus Christ who came as the Bread of Life. On earth, this manna turned to worms if it was kept more than a day, except on the Sabbath weekend. The lesson for us is that we need to gather the Bread of Life daily by reading the Bible. Christ is the only One who can satisfy the hunger of our souls. Just as the manna was good if it was ingested, so Christ is transforming to our lives if we personally receive Him. No one can eat or drink *for* us. Salvation is compared to the bread and water of life because we have to personally partake to have our hunger and thirst satisfied.

When God describes the heavenly pattern, it starts at the ark of His covenant and moves outward. Similarly, the Lord starts in the hearts of those who respond to Him and then He begins the miracle of changing them from the inside out. Salvation is truly of God, and not by self-effort: "Salvation is of the LORD" (Jonah 2:9).

WEEK 32: KEEP CHRIST'S PERSPECTIVE

The tragic error of modern ecumenical evangelism is its reluctance to define who God really is in an effort to not offend other religions and cults. It offends God, though, and ecumenicalism is Satan's church: "There is no other name under heaven given among men by which we must be saved" (Acts 4:12).

Remembering what God revealed about himself by what He called His ark will help us to understand Revelation 12:

- **Ark of the Covenant** (Numbers 10:33): This name spoke of God's **faithfulness**. He makes covenants and does not break them.
- **Ark of the Testimony** (Exodus 25:22): This name spoke of God's **holiness**. Because we are lost, God sent His Son to show us "the Way" of safety. In the Old Testament, the pictures of the sacrifices testified of Jesus; in the New Testament "the Way" was shown through the receiving of the finished work of Christ.
- **Ark of God** (1 Samuel 3:3): This name spoke of God's **uniqueness**; there is no other God, nor any other way to Him but His way.

The ark also spoke of God's mightiness because it was the ark of God's strength, which associated it with God's power and miracles (Psalm 132:8). In addition, the ark spoke of God's approachableness: it was the holy ark where God's throne was set, placed in the center of the camp (except for the period of Israel's sinfulness), with lights never to go out—it was God offering His salvation to all (2 Chronicles 35:3).

Every time we are transported into the throne room, there is a powerful display of God's majesty and omnipotence, and Revelation 11:19 with its "lightnings, noises, thunderings, an earthquake, and great hail" is no exception. We also see similar displays of His awesomeness in Revelation 4:5, 8:5, and 16:18. These demonstrations of God's might are to remind us of what an incredible God we serve! Are you worshiping and adoring the Lord God Almighty as He deserves?

TUESDAY: God's Amazing Plan

> *Now a great sign appeared in heaven:* **a woman clothed with the sun**, *with* **the moon** *under her feet, and on her head a garland of* **twelve stars**. *Then being with child, she cried out in labor and in pain to give birth.*
> —REVELATION 12:1–2

God shares His plan by opening all the end-time events to us through His servants like the Apostle John. Consider these seven openings in heaven:

1. **God opens a door to worship:** "I looked, and behold, a door standing open in heaven. And the first voice . . . was like a trumpet speaking with me, saying, 'Come up here, and I will show you things which must take place after this'" (Revelation 4:1).
2. **God opens the seals of His wrath:** "When the Lamb opened one of the seals . . . I heard one of the four living creatures saying with a voice like thunder, 'Come and see'" (Revelation 6:1).

3. **God opens the pit of doom:** "And he opened the bottomless pit, and smoke arose . . . like the smoke of a great furnace. So the sun and the air were darkened because of the smoke" (Revelation 9:2).
4. **God opens His temple in heaven:** "Then the temple of God was opened in heaven, and the ark of His covenant was seen in His temple. And there were lightnings, noises, thunderings, an earthquake, and great hail" (Revelation 11:19).
5. **God opens the tabernacle of His testimony:** "After these things I looked, and behold, the temple of the tabernacle of the testimony in heaven was opened" (Revelation 15:5).
6. **God opens the gates of heaven:** "Now I saw heaven opened, and behold, a white horse. And He who sat on him was called Faithful and True, and in righteousness He judges and makes war" (Revelation 19:11).
7. **God opens the books of judgment:** "And I saw the dead . . . standing before God, and books were opened. And another book was opened, which is the Book of Life. And the dead were judged according to their works . . . which were written in the books" (Revelation 20:12).

Revelation 12 also contains two signs—the sign of the woman and the dragon. In this highly symbolic section, God continues to show the unfolding of His plan as the world surrounds His nation, Israel.

The first sign—"a woman clothed with the sun, with the moon under her feet." In addition to Revelation 12:1, four other times Revelation mentions women who represent special things. In Revelation 2:20, Jezebel is a picture of Paganism in the church. In Revelation 12:6 the woman is Israel. The scarlet woman described in Revelation 17:1–6 is the apostate church. And in Revelation 19:7, the Lamb's wife is the true church. Now let's look at some ways Bible teachers have identified this woman in Revelation 12:1–2.

The woman's clothing corresponds to Joseph's dream. Genesis 37:9–11 reports that Joseph told his brothers and father about a dream in which "the sun, the moon, and the eleven stars bowed down to [him]." His father "rebuked him" and his brothers "envied him, but his father kept the matter in mind." Joseph is describing Israel—the twelve tribes—the twelve sons in the family of Jacob, or Israel. The clear correspondence here to that truth made Joseph's brothers angry.

The woman cries in labor. This speaks of the nation of Israel as they groan. Ever since they were in Egypt, they have complained, *Why is everyone against us?* When God sent forth His Son to be born in Israel, it was a time of oppression at the hand of Rome. All of Creation groans awaiting redemption, and all women groan in childbirth.

The woman's exalted child can only be Jesus. He is the promised Seed of the woman (Genesis 3:15); He is of the tribe of Judah (Genesis 49:10); He is the Star of Jacob (Numbers 24:17–19); He is God with us (Isaiah 7:14); and He is the Son of Abraham and David (Matthew 1:1).

The woman is cared for by God in the Tribulation hours. Only Israel is promised such care. It can't be the virgin Mary because she is gone. It is not the church because she is never supposed to hide for three and one-half years in the wilderness. It can't be Eve in the Garden of Eden because Eve is gone too. There is only one group of people who are going to be on earth with Satan chasing them during the Tribulation—a people clothed with the sun, moon, and stars—and that is Israel. What is amazing is that they are the only group of people for whom God has prepared a place in the wilderness to hide!

The second sign—"a great, fiery red dragon." Revelation 12:3 reveals that "another sign appeared in heaven: . . . a great, fiery red dragon having seven heads and ten horns, and seven diadems on his heads." This is an easy sign because Satan has been well identified throughout the Scriptures as the serpent, that old dragon, the devil. Satan is the author of the Fall (Genesis 3:14a), the prince of this world (John 12:31; see also 14:30 and 16:11), a murderer and a liar (John 8:44), and an adversary (1 Peter 5:8).

Now that we have identified the "fiery red dragon" as Satan, we must address the "seven heads and ten horns, and seven diadems on his heads." The seven heads are later stated to be seven past kingdoms (Revelation 17:10) and the ten horns to be ten kings of the end times (17:12). This beast is quite similar to the one Daniel saw with one head and ten horns (Daniel 7:7, 20, 24).

As we close today's devotional, I exhort you to remain alert to Satan's mission: he aims "to steal, and to kill, and to destroy" you, so stay vigilant! Remember: that old serpent is a defeated foe, and if you resist him through the power of God's Word and His might, Satan will flee from you!

WEDNESDAY: Satan's Origin and Activity

His tail drew a third of the stars [angels] of heaven and threw them to the earth. And **the dragon stood before the woman** *who was ready to give birth,* **to devour her Child** *as soon as it was born.*
—Revelation 12:4

Where did the devil come from? He was formerly the highest-ranking angel in heaven—Lucifer. Isaiah 14 and Ezekiel 28 tell us that Satan was perfect in his original creation, and that he was the "covering cherub" over the throne of God, reflecting His glory. He walked in the garden of God and then fell into sin. Isaiah describes his fall from heaven through his five "I wills" that culminated in the heart of his iniquity: "I will be like the Most High" (Isaiah 14:12–14). Jesus himself acknowledged this fall when He said: "I saw Satan fall like lightning from heaven" (Luke 10:18). Satan was thrown out of heaven because of pride. Because pride competes with God for control and glory, it is therefore the root of all sin.

When Satan fell from heaven, it appears that he took one-third of the angels to earth with him (Revelation 12:4). What is Satan doing now? His present activity is detailed in 2 Corinthians 4:3: "But even if our gospel is veiled [by Satan], it is veiled to those who are perishing, **whose minds the god of this age has blinded**" (2 Corinthians 4:3). When you share the gospel, and a person looks right at you and says, "I don't get it, and I don't want it," you are seeing the blinding power of Satan in this world.

Many books are being written about "out of body" experiences of people who have died. They commonly report going to a great lighted place where a white-haired man talks to them. This is exactly what Satan is and does today. He does not wear red tights and have a pitchfork tail—he is an angel of light and a deceiver: "**Satan himself transforms himself into an angel of light.** Therefore it is no great thing if his ministers also transform themselves into ministers of righteousness" (2 Corinthians 11:14–15).

What can Satan do? Satan is powerful, but he can do only what God allows (Job 1:12, 2:4–7). However, that is substantial. He tempted Eve and thereby brought sin into the world (Genesis 3); he tempted Christ (Matthew 4); he perverted God's Word (Matthew 4); he hindered God's servant (1 Thessalonians 2); he fought with Michael (Jude 9); he hinders the gospel (2 Corinthians 4); he snares the wicked (1 Timothy 3); he accuses the brethren (Revelation 12:10); he desires the nations (Revelation 16); and he has the world under his controlling influence (1 John 5).

Now look at Revelation 12:5: "She bore a male Child [Christ] who was to rule all nations with a rod of iron. And her Child was caught up to God and to His throne" (v. 5). In this verse, there are three elements unique to Jesus in the entire universe: (1) His incarnation ("bore a male Child"); (2) His ascension ("caught up to God"); and (3) His Second Coming ("His throne").

This "male Child" is to rule all nations with a rod of iron: "Ask of Me, and I will give You the nations for Your inheritance, and the ends of the earth for Your possession. You shall break them with a rod of iron; You shall dash them to pieces like a potter's vessel" (Psalm 2:8).

Biblical scholars differ as to who this "male Child" is, and here are a few of their conclusions: Scott, Newell, Gaebelein, and Alford believe that the "male Child" refers to Christ; Ironside thinks he is Christ and the true church, His body; and Seiss considers him to be the invisible church. Personally, after much study, I am convinced that verse 5 is talking about the incarnated, ascended, and glorified Jesus Christ.

The Greek word for Jesus being "caught up" is *harpadzo*, and is the same word used for both the Rapture of the church (1 Thessalonians 4:17) and Paul being "caught up to the third heaven" (2 Corinthians 12:2).

In Revelation 12:6, we now see a reference to the second half of the Tribulation: "Then the woman fled into the wilderness [to] a place prepared by God, that they should feed her there one thousand two hundred and sixty days." Seven years divided in half is three and one-half years, forty-two months, or 1,260 days—all of which are metaphors for the second half of the Tribulation. That is the time the Antichrist goes into the temple of God in Jerusalem, sets up an image for himself, and starts persecuting the Jews. However, God will protect them again.

Aren't you grateful that as all this is unfolding, you will be safe in your eternal refuge—Jesus Christ? As a child of God, never forget that you are a member of the winning team!

THURSDAY: Satan's Defeat

> And **war broke out in heaven**: Michael and his angels fought with the dragon; [but] the dragon and his angels . . . did not prevail, . . . So **the great dragon was cast out** . . . to the earth, and his angels . . . with him.
>
> —Revelation 12:7–9

WEEK 32: KEEP CHRIST'S PERSPECTIVE

In Revelation 11:19–12:6, we have seen our victory in Jesus because God is faithful. Next we need to consider our victory in Jesus because Satan is vanquished. It is critical that we understand what is going on in the heavenly places around us.

In the whole universe, there is only God and His Creation. The Bible clearly tells us that the entire universe is involved with what is happening on earth because, after God is finished with the Tribulation and the Millennium, He is going to destroy the whole universe and make it brand new. Everything that is happening is happening right here on earth. There are no civilizations on other planets in need of Jesus as Lord and Savior. There are only the humans on earth and the humans under the earth—in Hades; and there are only the angels sealed by God and the fallen angels who joined Satan's army.

If that is all there is—God, humans, and angels—what about UFOs (Unidentified Flying Objects) and science fiction? Why is the world being conditioned for powerful beings that come to earth from somewhere else? The answer is simple: earth dwellers are being prepared for "the beast"—the ultimate extra-terrestrial being who will be released from the pit. It is possible that he could arrive in a space ship, because the world is getting ready for that. But regardless of *how* he comes, he will do so with great powers to control the minds of men.

Can you imagine the effect he will have on this planet? We have terrorists, rogue nations with ballistic missiles and atomic bombs, and biological agents for use in warfare. The world is highly unstable. With all that is going on, it is easy to imagine that someone transported to earth who can perform miracles and control minds will be able to control the world. This is the Antichrist—the one in the place of Christ. So the earth dwellers will conclude: *Who needs Jesus—the lowly One from Bethlehem?*

The advent of "the beast" will be an actual historical event, and Revelation shows us the whole panorama in advance. Up until chapter 12 of Revelation, although God had cast Satan out of his place in heaven, He did not restrict his coming into heaven to accuse believers. Presently, when an individual Christian has sinned and Satan becomes aware of it, it is an opportunity to go before God and accuse that person. Always remember that even though we bear God's image and have His name, we can still "act like the devil" at times. When that happens, Jesus steps forward to remind Satan that He has paid for our sins and we belong to Him now! Charles Wesley's hymn, "Arise My Soul Arise," says, "Five bleeding wounds He bears, / Received on Calvary; / They pour effectual prayers, / They strongly plead for me; / 'Forgive him, O forgive,' they cry, / 'Nor let that ransomed sinner die!'"

Satan is being allowed to interrupt the worship of heaven for a limited time only before God will cast him down forever, bar his access, and restrict him to troubling the earth only.

You might still be wondering: *What is this celestial warfare all about?* Michael the archangel, a warrior, stands in as commander-in-chief for the King of Kings. He first appeared at the burial of Moses. Because of disobedience (Numbers 20:7–11), Moses forfeited his entrance to the Promised Land, but God let him see it from afar before he died (Deuteronomy 34:5–6). Satan wanted to take Moses' body to use as a snare for God's people—like when the brazen serpent used by Moses was transformed into an idol (2 Kings 18:4). The lifeless body of Moses would have been used to start an idolatrous false worship of a messenger in place of the Master. (Miracles associated with dead bones are some of Satan's biggest lies that enslave and destroy multitudes even today.)

Michael also shows up in Daniel 10 in his work of fighting the principalities (leaders of fallen angels): "But the prince of the kingdom of Persia withstood me twenty-one days; and behold, Michael, one of the chief princes, came to help me, for I had been left alone there with the kings of Persia" (Daniel 10:13).

In Ephesians 6:12, Paul warns us: "We do not wrestle against flesh and blood, but against principalities, . . . powers, . . . rulers of the darkness of this age, . . . spiritual hosts of wickedness in the heavenly places." Paul uses the Greek word *arche*, normally translated "principalities," seven other times (Romans 8:38; 1 Corinthians 15:24; Ephesians 1:21, 3:10; Colossians 1:16, 2:15; Titus 3:1). Each time the context is similar to that of Ephesians 6:12, so we can assume that these listings in verse 12 are classes of fallen angels who oversee the hindering of God's work in various nations.

Michael will also figure in the final conflict: "At that time Michael shall stand up, the great prince who stands watch over the sons of your people; and there shall be a time of trouble, such as never was since there was a nation, . . . and at that time your people shall be delivered, every One who is found written in the book" (Daniel 12:1). These words are happening as we open to Revelation 12.

In Revelation 12:7–9, Michael leads God's angels to victory. This becomes significant when we note that Michael is identified with the nation Israel (Daniel 10:10–21; 12:1; see also Jude 9). Another key is that the name Michael may mean "Who is like God?" This could point to Satan when he rebelled against the Lord and said, "I will be like the Most High" (Isaiah 14:14). Michael's very presence fighting Satan is part of the ancient conflict between God and Satan. Satan wanted to be like God, but Michael's name implies that "no one can be like God"—because there is only *one* God. This battle may occur because the devil's unbridled hatred of Israel spurs him to make one final assault against the throne of God. However, as recorded, Michael and the angels of God will defeat him. Amazingly, Revelation 12:9 is the middle verse of the Book of Revelation—and the turning point in eternity!

If you have not yet bowed your knee to Jesus, and embraced Him as your Savior, today can be your "turning point" for eternity. Don't delay! Time is short!

FRIDAY: Saints That Overcome

> "Now salvation, and strength, and the kingdom of our God, and the power of His Christ have come, for the accuser of our brethren . . . has been cast down. And **they overcame him by the blood of the Lamb and by the word of their testimony**, and they did not love their lives to the death. Therefore rejoice, O heavens, and you who dwell in them! Woe to the inhabitants of the earth and the sea! For the devil has come down to you, having great wrath, because he knows that he has a short time."
>
> —REVELATION 12:10–12

We have seen our victory in Jesus because God is faithful (11:19–12:6) and Satan is vanquished (12:7–9). Yet, as verses 10–12 above explain, the saints on earth will suffer. In that passage, many avenues of our powerful victories over Satan are stated. The saints will overcome as more than conquerors through the blessedness of four powerful weapons:

1. **The Word of Testimony:** They will overcome Satan by the reality of their testimony because they have embraced Christ's salvation by faith, and He lives within them. People are saved not by what they say, but by the Word of God which is "living and powerful, and sharper than any two-edged sword, piercing even to the division of soul and spirit, and of joints and marrow, and is a discerner of the thoughts and intents of the heart" (Hebrews 4:12).
2. **The Name of Jesus:** "God . . . has highly exalted Him and given Him the name which is above every name" (Philippians 2:9).
3. **The Blood of the Lamb:** "And they overcame him by the blood of the Lamb and by the word of their testimony, and they did not love their lives to the death" (Revelation 12:11).
4. **The Cross of Calvary:** "And you, being dead in your trespasses . . . , He has made alive together with Him, having forgiven you all trespasses" (Colossians 2:13).

Last of all, our attention is drawn to the triumph factor. John says, "And the dragon was wroth with the woman, and went to make war with the remnant of her seed, which kept the commandments of God, and have the testimony of Jesus Christ" (Revelation 12:17 KJV). Satan cannot win.

What can Satan do with the likes of these godly Jews? Lock them up in prison, and they will convert their jailers; torture them, and they will become partakers of Christ's sufferings and heirs to a great reward; martyr them, and they will go straight to be with Christ; turn them loose, and they will evangelize the world! The more the saints suffer, the more they will draw on Christ; the more they serve Christ, the more they will defeat the devil and have victory in Christ!

Learn from these faithful saints; do not shrink back from the persecution and affliction that is likely to come at work, in your family, and in society. Through the Word of God, the name of Jesus, the blood of the Lamb, and the cross of Calvary—be a saint who overcomes through Christ—like the faithful suffering saints in Revelation 12!

SATURDAY: The Conflict of the Ages

> *The earth opened its mouth and swallowed up the flood, which the dragon had spewed out of his mouth. And the dragon was enraged with the woman, and* **he went to make war** *with the rest of her offspring, who . . . have the testimony of Jesus Christ.*
> —Revelation 12:16–17

God has a place prepared for Israel; it could even be in Petra or Jordan. It does not matter where it is, but God will send the Jews there. When Satan sees them flee, he will cause the beast to send a mighty army that is like a "flood," but it will be "swallowed up" (Revelation 12:16).

We see this same type of judgment in Numbers 16:1–40. Because of the rebellion of Korah, the earth opened up and swallowed those who rebelled against Moses and God—and they went alive

into the pit. (This is another indication that Hades is most likely in the center of the earth.)
- Satan has always tried to destroy his mortal enemy—the Seed of the woman. All of history has been a record of this conflict between the seed of the serpent and the Seed of the woman. Satan has tried to stop God's plan all along the way.
- Satan attempted to destroy God's plan when Cain murdered Abel (Genesis 4).
- Satan attempted to destroy God's plan by demonic intrusion into the human line before the Flood (Genesis 6).
- Satan attempted to destroy God's plan through Goliath, as the serpent's seed sought to destroy the line of the woman's Seed as young David stood before him (1 Samuel 17).
- Satan attempted to destroy God's plan through Haman, a descendent of Agag the Amalekite. At Satan's prompting, Haman nearly succeeded at wiping out the Jews (the book of Esther).
- Satan attempted to destroy God's plan by the decree of Herod to kill all the male infants (Matthew 2:13).

Satan attempted to destroy God's plan by tempting Jesus to take the easy road (Matthew 4).

Satan attempted to destroy God's plan as he entered the infuriated mob that sought to cast Jesus over a cliff (Luke 4:28–29).

Satan hates the Lamb of God and all His followers—whether Jew or Gentile. Therefore, he actively wages war against those who seek to obey God's Word above all else!

Make a choice to live in hope. From Eden onward, there have been two groups on earth: two churches, two congregations, and two directions.

Satan and the Rebels	God and the Saints
Drunken harlot	Chaste bride
Followers of lies	Seekers of Truth
Earth dwellers	Pilgrims
Walkers by sight	Walkers by faith
Hellish	Heavenly

But a collision lies ahead: Satan's kingdom is nearing its final hours on earth—a time when the powers of darkness, demons, and all will rule. The earth will follow the false god, the Antichrist!

There are two competitions—two destinies:
- **Choose Christ:** Follow Adam; pass Golgotha and the substitutionary sacrifice of Christ; trust in Christ and go to heaven.
- **Choose the Antichrist:** Follow Cain; pass Babel and the confusion of religion, and go to the lake of fire.

In this battle for the planet Earth, the victory is in Christ! God's faithfulness to His Word means that Satan is vanquished. If you already know the Lord Jesus, I pray that you will choose to be an overcomer by living in hope through God's Word, the blood of the Lamb, the cross of Calvary, and the name of Jesus that is above all names!

WEEK 33
Marvel at the Genuine Jesus

{ Revelation 13 }

As the end of days approaches, you can find hope as you marvel at the genuine Jesus!

SUNDAY: How to Escape the Mark of the Beast

[He] is able to keep you from stumbling, and to present you faultless before the presence of His glory with exceeding joy.
—JUDE 1:24

As the end of the world approaches, so does earth's darkest hour. Hell will soon open, and the pit will vomit out its demon hordes to run wildly throughout humanity. Other beasts from the abyss will globally wreak death and destruction. Satan himself will invade the earth and seemingly conquer it at last.

At the helm, the visible leader of the world will be the long promised man of sin, the lawless one, the beast, the coming world leader—commonly known as the Antichrist. But behind him, the real power will be the god of this world, the dragon, old Lucifer, the lying serpent of Eden.

Imagine what it would be like if that perfect leader were to step forward tomorrow—a man who appears to seemingly come out of nowhere—almost a person from the past who rolls into one all the great leaders of the world. Imagine one man with the strength of a Caesar, the military genius of an Alexander, the mesmerizing oratory of a Hitler, the warmth of a Ronald Reagan, the ruthless determination of a Ghenghis Khan, and the apparent compassion and tenderness of Jesus Christ!

John Phillips writes: "In 1 Timothy 4:1–3, the Bible clearly teaches that we can expect this invasion from the pit in the last days. During the final days, most people will be led astray by evil spirits and occult teachings. The shadows of these times are already darkening the world. Nothing but the restraining presence of God the Holy Spirit is holding back the floodgates of this time of evil. . . . Advanced demonism was the mark of Noah's day; [and] it is becoming an increasingly evident characteristic of the age in which we live."[1]

Revelation 13 explains (as do other scriptures) what I consider to be one of the saddest doctrines in the Bible—the teaching about the Antichrist, which tells us that the FALSE Christ will be universally embraced by the world after the TRUE Christ has been rejected!

"'Therefore **when you see the "abomination of desolation,"** spoken of by Daniel the prophet, standing in the holy place' (whoever reads, let him understand)" (Matthew 24:15).

"For false christs [pseudo-christs] and false prophets [pseudo-prophets] **will rise and show great signs and wonders to deceive, if possible, even the elect"** (Matthew 24:24).

"I was watching; and the same horn was **making war against the saints, and prevailing against them,** ... He shall speak pompous words against the Most High, **shall persecute the saints** of the Most High, and shall intend to change times and law. **Then the saints shall be given into his hand for a time and times and half a time**" (Daniel 7:21, 25).

"The coming of the lawless one is according to **the working of Satan**, with **all power, signs, and lying wonders**" (2 Thessalonians 2:9).

Far more lethal than rampant viruses, far more poisonous than radioactivity or toxins, a counterfeit Christianity is seeping into our world. Jesus warned of a coming day of deception that was so intoxicating that without His intervention even God's children would succumb. Revelation 13 shows the second flood, which will destroy our world. The first flood in Genesis was with water from God to judge sinful humanity. This second flood is with deception from Satan to seal the doom of humans unwilling to follow the Lord.

Perhaps the Antichrist will step into the world from a battlefield or maybe from the United Nations. Very possibly, a glowing metallic UFO will slowly descend in a globally watched spot and, before the wondering eyes of all the inhabitants of the earth, out will step the ultimate Superman—the first beast! In concise word pictures, John describes the culmination of the lies of Satan. Mankind needs to beware of Satan's counterfeit authority (Revelation 12:17–13:2), counterfeit resurrection (Revelation 13:3–5), counterfeit citizenship (Revelation 13:6–10), counterfeit worship (Revelation 13:11–15), and counterfeit security—the mark of the beast (Revelation 13:16–18).

How can you escape these counterfeits of Satan? The only place of safety is to have the security that the *real* Christ gives. May the wonders of this chapter cause you to seek God's mark—and not the mark of the beast!

My Prayer for You This Week: *Oh Lord, as we read the words in Revelation 13, we are grieved to think of someone who will blaspheme Your name, Your dwelling place—the very God of heaven! We are grieved that he will be allowed to parade and march up and down on this planet for forty-two months, imitating Your three and one-half years of ministry—even imitating Your resurrection from the dead, Lord Jesus—and imitating Your power from heaven. We love You, so our hearts are grieved to think that mankind and humanity would stoop to the depths to be led by this monster from the pit! We want to magnify Your name, for the world is coming to a day when it will seek to obliterate the name of the true and living God—the Creator, the Redeemer, and the righteous Judge from the very consciousness of this planet. We pray that You might be praised through us, and that we might be among those who turn many to righteousness that we might all shine like the stars forever. Give us an insatiable desire to win souls to You, Lord Jesus. We pray all these things in Your precious name. Amen.*

MONDAY: The Ultimate Superman—the Beast

*I was considering the horns, and there was . . . a little one . . . before whom three of the first horns were plucked out by the roots. And there, in this horn, were **eyes like the eyes of a man**, and a mouth speaking pompous words.*

—Daniel 7:8

Impossible? No. He is coming. He may well be walking around today. Ever since Eden, mankind has sought to be "like God" and in this insatiable quest has come the glorification of the "creature more than the Creator." This exaltation of man has allowed men of strong persuasion to be able to rise to extreme heights of power. In history these have been the Ramses, Alexanders, Caesars, and Napoleons. But there is a man on the horizon whose rise shall be as the sun's rays across the earth; he shall be the embodiment of such power and personage that the entire world will be astounded by him. Thus, he will be sought after like no other leader before.

He will be one who seems to stop all threats from weapons of mass destruction. He will take charge and bring an end to the simmering hatred and volatile ethnic conflicts around the planet. The global fear of terrorism, biological warfare, and food shortages will cease through his leadership. He also seems to triumph in a global form of religion that the world can finally agree to. It may even be a counterfeit version of Christianity because "anti" means "in place of" Christ.

Here are some of the attributes that the Antichrist—this Superman of evil—possesses: (Emphasis added in the following verses.)

The Antichrist is super-intelligent. He is portrayed as a Superman of intellect: "In this horn, were **eyes like the eyes of a man**" (Daniel 7:8).

The Antichrist is a super-communicator. He is notable as a Superman of communication: "a mouth speaking **pompous words**" (Daniel 7:8).

The Antichrist is a super-politician. He is a Superman of politics who has unusual abilities to lead and persuade, and seems to conquer in peace: "He shall come in peaceably, and **seize the kingdom by intrigue**" (Daniel 11:21). In Revelation 6:2 he will ride a "white horse" and go out "**conquering and to conquer**."

The Antichrist is a super-businessman. He possesses extraordinary business abilities, and is a Superman of money: "He shall cause deceit to **prosper under his rule; . . . He shall destroy many in their prosperity**" (Daniel 8:25; see also Revelation 18.) He will organize or just use a global digitalization of commerce.

The Antichrist is a super-general. He is the ultimate military strategist, a Superman of the military: "[He] shall **devour the whole earth, trample it and break it in pieces**" (Daniel 7:23). We see the same power revealed in Revelation 13:4 and 7: "So they worshiped the dragon who gave authority to the beast; and they worshiped the beast, saying, 'Who is like the beast? **Who is able to make war with him**?' . . . And authority was given him over every tribe, tongue, and nation." He rules the world!

The Antichrist has a super-ego. He is the Superman of megalomaniacs who lust for great and grandiose performances: "The man of sin . . . opposes and exalts himself above all that is called God or that is worshiped, so that **he sits as God in the temple of God**, showing himself that he is God" (2 Thessalonians 2:3–4). From this, we clearly see his yearning to be "like the Most High God"!

Would it surprise you to know that Americans are actually looking for an ET (extra-terrestrial being) like this "Superman" to come and help? According to pollsters, 72 percent of Americans believe that there is life beyond the earth; 48 percent believe UFOs are real; and 15 percent have seen one, with 3 percent of Americans (that's almost nine million of us) being abducted by aliens into a UFO.

One noted journalist, after studying UFOs and those in contact with them, concluded: "The earth is not inhabited by them, it is infested." What do UFOs do to the Word of God and our faith? I have concluded that UFOs are demonic!

UFOs would support naturalistic evolution to the point of believing that perfection would overcome death, disease, and so forth. When people believe in extra-terrestrial intelligence, that would mean that evolution has gone on for who knows how many billion years and, somewhere out there, life has ascended higher than here on earth.

ETs lessen the incarnation of Jesus. *If there really are many all-powerful aliens out there, this would be the common thinking: What if Jesus did come? What difference does that really make? After all, it may be possible to overcome death and disease because all these beings that can fly around are superior to us, so they have obviously found the answer!*

That erroneous thinking would lead to this conclusion:
- The earth is just an insignificant dot in the universe.
- Man is not the crown of God's creation.
- Sin is just our problem, or not even a problem at all.
- Hope lies in contact with some of these "higher" life forms.
- Christ's death was a local rather than a cosmic event.
- The Word of God is anachronistic, local, and out of touch with the big picture of the cosmos.
- We are not in God's image.

That is what evolution, science fiction, and UFO-ology teaches! And those lies of Satan are deceiving mankind and thus determining their eternal destiny—separated forever from God in the lake of fire with the devil and his angels. We need to spread the Truth to the perishing every chance we get!

TUESDAY: The Person of the Antichrist

And the dragon was enraged with the woman, and he went to make war with the rest of her offspring who... have the testimony of Jesus Christ.... And I saw a beast rising up out of the sea, having seven heads and ten horns, and on his horns ten crowns, and on his heads a blasphemous name. Now **the beast** *which I saw was like a leopard, his feet were like the feet of a bear, and his mouth like the mouth of a lion.* **The dragon gave him his power, his throne, and great authority.**

—Revelation 12:17–13:2

As we examine the person of the Antichrist, drawn in the words of the Apostle John, and see him whose cause is not only to be "anti" (opposed), but also "anti-" (the exact inverse of) Christ Jesus the Lord of glory, there are five horrible lies that this beast (the Antichrist) will foist upon the earth as he carries out his counterfeit operation of imitating Christ.

Lie one: the beast will offer a false authority. In Revelation 12:17–13:2 *"the beast"* is imitating the Kingdom of God, the King of Kings, the Lord of Lords, the Creator. Satan's counterfeit authority is rebellion against God, which actually started in the Garden of Eden when Eve questioned the goodness, authority, and right of God to limit. You can escape his false authority by keeping yourself under the authority of God.

Lie two: the beast will offer a false resurrection. In Revelation 13:3–5, the beast causes the whole world to marvel at his counterfeit resurrection as he imitates the prince of life, the firstborn from the dead, the empty tomb, the way, the truth, and the only hope: "And I saw one of his heads as if it had been mortally wounded, and his deadly wound was healed. . . . So they worshiped the dragon who gave authority to the beast; and they worshiped the beast, saying, 'Who is like the beast? Who is able to make war with him?' And he was . . . given authority to continue for forty-two months."

God allows the beast to be brought back to life after being mortally wounded. In every point, the beast will be mirroring the Lord Jesus Christ. He will be allowed to rule three and one-half years, which is the length of Christ's ministry, and he will counterfeit Old Testament miracles as well.

Lie three: the beast will offer a false citizenship. In Revelation 13:6–10, he offers a counterfeit citizenship to the earth dwellers as he imitates the wonders of our Father's house He's preparing, the heavenly city, the streets of gold, and the Water of Life—making them here on earth and telling those people that they are not to wait for the Son of God from heaven: "Then he opened his mouth in blasphemy against God. . . . It was granted to him to make war with the saints and to overcome them. And authority was given him over . . . All who dwell on the earth . . . whose names have not been written in the Book of Life of the Lamb slain from the foundation of the world. . . . Here is the patience and the faith of the saints."

In this passage, the beast starts a deadly rampage on the earth that causes a counterfeit citizenship. Those whose names are not in the Lamb's Book of Life will worship the beast. But Christians know that "our citizenship is in heaven, from which we also eagerly wait for the Savior, the Lord Jesus Christ" (Philippians 3:20).

Lie four: the beast will offer false worship or religion. In Revelation 13:11–15, the second beast, the false prophet, affirms his false message that imitates the true worship of the living and true God in spirit and in truth, not self-styled but biblical: "Then I saw another beast coming up out of the earth, and he had two horns like a lamb and spoke like a dragon. And he exercises all the authority of the first beast . . . and causes the earth and those who dwell in it to worship the first beast, whose deadly wound was healed. He performs great signs, . . . And he deceives those who dwell on the earth by those signs . . . , telling those who dwell on the earth to make an image to the beast who was wounded by the sword and lived. He was granted power to give breath to the image . . . , that the image of the beast should both speak and cause as many as would not worship the image of the beast to be killed."

The term "another beast coming up out of the earth" is the same term used when Saul got the witch of Endor to conjure up Samuel. I am not sure how much God will allow here, but this second beast is an amazing creature. He will lead false worship. It is hard for us to comprehend right now, but we have become such a globally linked society that we know about things around the world as they are happening. As events happen, it will touch the whole world. This false resurrection will cause everyone in the world to be in wonder, because in the back of everybody's consciousness is the story of Christ. John 1:9 says: "That was the true Light which gives light to every man coming into the world." There is a basic awareness of the true living God. When people see this, most of the world without loving the Truth will start falling for the lie—because they have never known the Word of God.

Lie five: the beast will offer a false security. In Revelation 13:16–18, through the "mark" he is imitating the Holy Spirit's sealing of those in the Book of Life, betrothed to Christ, His very bride, kept and protected by the power of God unto salvation: "He causes all . . . to receive a mark on their right hand or on their foreheads, and that no one may buy or sell except one who has the mark or the name of the beast, or the number of his name. Here is wisdom. Let him who has understanding calculate the number of the beast, for it is the number of a man: His number is 666."

So then, how do we live in hope as we approach these fearsome days?

Examine your address label. Make sure you are addressed to the right destination. Ask yourself: Am I really a citizen of heaven, or just an earth dweller? Philippians 3:20 says that the born-again Christian's "citizenship is in heaven, from which we also eagerly wait for the Savior, the Lord Jesus Christ." In light of that verse, step back and look at your direction. Honestly ask yourself: "Where am I really headed?" For God says: "Examine yourselves as to whether you are in the faith" (2 Corinthians 13:5a).

Turn on your security system. Ask yourself: "Have I really turned on my security system? Am I an authentic, signed original? Am I a sealed and secure container of heavenly treasure?" One way to know if your security system is turned on is to watch what comes out of your life as your body ages and weakens. Is it the treasure of the fruit of the Spirit—love, joy, peace, longsuffering, kindness, goodness, faithfulness, gentleness, self-control—that spills forth from inside? Or is it the works of the flesh that ooze out from within your soul? Second Corinthians 4:7 says, "But we have this treasure in earthen vessels, that the excellence of the power may be of God and not of us." The weaker we get, and the shorter our time on earth, the more the treasure of Christ should spill out of our lives. Oh, how we should allow our weakness to show the righteousness of Christ coming out of us! So the next time you are sick, let the treasure of Christ come out instead of being irritable and angry.

Investigate the real thing. How well do you know Jesus by personal contact? How quickly do you recognize Him in His Book? Have you begun a lifelong pursuit of Jesus Christ in the Bible? Do you know the *real* well enough to recognize the *counterfeit*?

Let me remind you again that, to escape Satan's counterfeits, the *only* place of safety is to have the security that the *real* Christ gives! Have you fled to Him as your eternal refuge? If not, don't delay—He could come back *today*!

WEDNESDAY: The Prince That Shall Come

> *"The prince who is to come . . . shall confirm a covenant with many for one week; but in the middle of the week He shall bring an end to sacrifice and offering."*
>
> —Daniel 9:26a, 27a

The coming world leader, commonly known as the Antichrist, has thirty-three titles in the Old Testament and thirteen in the New Testament. One of these titles, "the prince who is to come," is from Daniel 9:26–27 where it was prophesied that the people of this "prince" would destroy the city and the sanctuary. Its fulfillment occurred in history when the Roman legions under Titus Vespasian destroyed Jerusalem and the temple in A.D. 70. This reflexive reference to the Romans in Daniel 9:26 is one of several reasons why many Bible scholars view the future "prince who is to come" as a Roman or European.

- **The Beast from the Sea—Revelation 13:1-10:** He is the Roman prince of Daniel 9 who will break his covenant with the Jews at the middle of the week. He is the Antichrist, the man of lawlessness (Pentecost, Seiss, Newell). Some think that verse 3 means that he will be raised from the dead (Seiss, Newell).
- **The Beast from the Earth—Revelation 13:11-18:** He is the false prophet—apparently a Jewish religious leader who causes men to worship the first beast. He has the power to do miracles to deceive men (vv. 14–15). Some interpret the Antichrist as "the one instead of Christ" (Scott, Ironside, Gaebelein, Kelly); others see him as the "one opposed to Christ" (Pentecost).

These beasts make war with the saints and overcome them (v. 7). All who are not of the elect will worship the first beast (v. 8). By economic warfare they can starve out those who will not worship the first beast (vv. 16–17).

Point by point, the beast is a poor imitation of Christ. As we examine him in his falseness, gaze at Christ's beauty and see Him more clearly for who He is today! Here are some interesting insights on the beast.

The peacemaker—Revelation 6:1–2. Certainly, this man will be on the scene before the Rapture occurs. He will be a peaceful political leader who unites ten nations of Europe into a strong power bloc (see Revelation 17:12–13). The rider on the white horse will imitate Christ (Revelation 19:11ff). He will go forth to conquer peacefully, and will have a bow, but no arrows. He will bring a brief time of peace to the world (1 Thessalonians 5:1–3) before the storm of the day of the Lord breaks loose.

The protector—Daniel 9:24–27. Although we examined the exciting details of this prophecy in Week 31, it is important to recall certain facts. First, the prophecy applies to Israel, Jerusalem, and the temple, and not to the church. Second, it announces the time when Messiah will come and accomplish certain purposes for the Jewish people. The word "week" refers to a period of seven years; seventy weeks are equal to 490 years. Note that these 490 years are divided into three parts: (1) seven weeks or forty-nine years, during which the city would be rebuilt; (2) sixty-two weeks or 434 years, at the end of which time Messiah would come and be cut off; and (3) one week or seven years, during which a "prince" would have a covenant with Israel. The seventieth week will start with the arrival of Antichrist. He will make a covenant with Israel to protect her and permit her to rebuild her temple. This covenant will be for seven years. He will temporarily solve the Middle East crisis. Israel will rebuild her temple in peaceful times. It is the signing of this covenant, not the Rapture of the church, which signals the start of Daniel's seventieth week, that seven-year period known as the day of the Lord.

The peace-breaker—Daniel 9:27. After three and one-half years, Antichrist will break his covenant with the Jews and take over their temple. This was what Paul termed "the falling away" (2 Thessalonians 2:3b). A better translation would be "the rebellion, the apostasy." Not simply *a* rebellion, but *the* rebellion. Up to this point, Antichrist has been a peacemaking leader of ten European nations, obligated to protect Israel. But now he will reveal his true character by taking over the Jewish temple and demanding that the world worship him (see Revelation 13). Since the Antichrist will be energized by Satan, it is no surprise that he will seek worship; Satan has always wanted the worship of the world. In church history, there have been various apostasies when groups have turned away from God's truth, but this final rebellion will be the greatest of all. The man of sin will oppose everything that belongs to any other religion, true or false. He will organize a world church that will, by worshiping him, actually be worshiping Satan. Our Lord predicted this apostasy: He called it *"the abomination of desolation"* (Matthew 24:15), a clear reference to Daniel 9:27. The world will wonder at this great leader who, with Satan's power, will perform signs and wonders and deceive the nations.

The persecutor—Revelation 13:15–17. Most prophetic students agree that the abomination of desolation will occur three and one-half years after the Antichrist makes his covenant with the Jews (Daniel 9:27—"in the midst of the week," or three and one-half years). This will usher in a period of intense persecution and tribulation. Jesus said, "For then there will be great tribulation" (Matthew 24:21a). Satan will vent his wrath against Israel. He will so control the world's economic system that citizens must bear "the mark of the beast" to be able to buy and sell (Revelation 13:16–17).

The prisoner—Revelation 19:11–21. Keep in mind that God has a timetable. Satan will not be permitted to control the world forever. Jesus Christ will return "in power and great glory" and take the Antichrist, his associates, and Satan prisoner and cast them into the bottomless pit (Revelation 20:1–3). This will be the climax of the great Battle of Armageddon (Revelation 16:16), during which the nations of the world unite with Satan to fight Jesus Christ. This leads to our next event.

What insights can we glean from these interesting statements about the beast? We are reminded of these truths: only Jesus is the Prince of Peace (Isaiah 9:6); only Jesus is omnipotent, omniscient, and omnipresent; only Jesus keeps all His promises; only those who come to Him have peace—the rest are like the restless sea; only Jesus gives true rest for the souls of those who come to Him (Matthew 11:28–30); and only Jesus can set you free (John 8:32–34)! A God like this deserves our *all!*

THURSDAY: Completely Confusing Times Are Coming

> And **the dragon** was enraged with the woman, and he **went to make war with the rest of her offspring, who keep the commandments of God** and have the testimony of Jesus Christ. . . . It was granted to him to make war with the saints and to overcome them. And authority was given him over every tribe, tongue, and nation.
>
> —Revelation 12:17; 13:7

WEEK 33: MARVEL AT THE GENUINE JESUS

When Christ returns there will be powerful, pervasive, and universal lies backed by the most believable signs and wonders ever witnessed on planet Earth. What will life on earth be like during these dark times? Let's look again at the verses from Revelation 12 and 13 above to remind us.

When Jesus came to earth, He was God in human flesh; as the Christ, He was the expression of all the promises of God. To think that **the Christ** in all His grace and beauty came to earth, stayed for thirty-plus years, was rejected as false and fake, and **almost no one followed Him**, is bad enough. But to know that Satan is going to send to earth the expression of all of mankind's desires in the person of **the Antichrist**, and in a very short time **almost all the earth will follow him**, is absolutely heart wrenching!

Imagine a leader as winsome as Reagan, as fearless as Alexander the Great, as mesmerizing as Hitler, as beloved by his people as George Washington, as great a leader as Moses, as unstoppable as Ghenghis Khan, and as spiritually charismatic as David—all in *one* man.

Now imagine that man openly displaying supernatural power in public, and being seen worldwide by way of the electronic media! It will appear that he is from heaven, and he will claim to be God. He will do miracles that everyone can see and believe in, and then offer himself to the world as their Christ.

There is a day coming soon when most people on earth will want to follow this ultimate "Superman." That is the saddest commentary on the fallen heart of humanity there could ever be—always wanting the wrong choice!

We have had several warm-up acts by Satan for this future main event of the final Antichrist. We can see the way Satan works most clearly in the life and accomplishments of Adolph Hitler. Hitler showed the world how just one man can lift a nation from the depths of economic ruin to the heights of power in a very short time (1933–1939)—and then lead the world into the deadliest war of all time (1939–1945). In six years Hitler came uncomfortably close to conquering the world, which is a vivid example of how Satan can indwell and completely harness one man.

Hitler was an Antichrist. Rick Warren writes, "People who had personal contact with Hitler often spoke of the strange hypnotic power he was able to exert. In 1943, one hundred thousand young people in brown shirts filled the Olympic stadium in Munich, Germany, the largest stadium in the world at that time. They formed with their bodies a sign for a fanatical man standing behind the podium. The message read, 'Hitler, we are yours.'"[2]

At the monument to Hitler's evil, the death camp Auschwitz, are the words of Hitler's vision of a generation of young people without a conscience. These words are aptly hung on a wall, grimly reminding the visitor of the hell unleashed when this goal was realized: "I freed Germany from the stupid and degrading fallacies of conscience and morality. . . . We will train young people before whom the world will tremble. I want young people capable of violence—imperious, relentless and cruel."

On display for all to behold are thousands of pounds of women's hair, retrieved and marketed as a commodity by the Nazi exterminators, architects of the final solution that sent multitudes to the gas ovens. The incredible reminders cast an overwhelming pall of somberness upon the visitor.[3]

FRIDAY: Satan Was the Original Antichrist

*"You are of your father **the devil**, and the desires of your father you want to do. He **was a murderer from the beginning**, and does not stand in the truth, because there is no truth in him. When he speaks a lie, he speaks from his own resources, for **he is a liar and the father of it**."*
—JOHN 8:44

Lucifer was the original Antichrist. Isaiah 14 reveals that he wanted the power of God and the worship of God for himself. He demanded equality with the Lord God Almighty. In fact, according to Ezekiel 28, he was "the anointed cherub [angel]." He was "full of wisdom, and perfect in beauty." His response to his endowment by God was one of pride and rebellion.

God rejected his power play and promised his doom in hell in the future. But until that time, Lucifer (Satan) is on the prowl, seeking likely candidates he can lead into occult worship. Rebellion gives Satan an open invitation to establish a stronghold in the rebel's life. Understand this: occult involvement is actually worship of his infernal majesty—Satan!

Satan looks for rebels. Lucifer was the original rebel, and he is looking for rebels to enlist for his own selfish purposes. Rebellion against authority makes a person a prime target for satanic attack.

Hitler is a prime example of the rebellion-occult connection. His early life could be characterized by one word: failure. He had a meager existence while living on his dead mother's limited savings and an orphan's pension which came from his father's service in the Customs Department. His attempt at higher education was thwarted. He wanted to be an artist, so he applied at the Vienna Academy of Fine Arts, but they refused to accept him because his sketches were not up to required standards. Next, he applied to the School of Architecture and was refused. Author Treavor Ravenscroft observes that because Hitler was unable to make friends, he became a more solitary and embittered figure.

To make a long story short, Hitler was angry at God and society because of his plight in life, so he rebelled against both. In his quest for power to change his plight, young Hitler turned to the occult. He began by spending all his free time in the Hofberg Library in Vienna, Austria. He read books on the history of the occult and Eastern religions, but the occult seemed to offer the power for which he was searching.

Demons controlled Hitler. The demons that controlled the demented soul of Adolph Hitler lured him and Germany into World War II, and then abandoned both him and his country to their fate. Hitler and his fellow conspirators came close to succeeding. They failed because the time was not yet ripe in the counsels of God for the forces of Satan to triumph. However, the whole Nazi era was a dress rehearsal for the coming of the beast and the consequent baptism of unregenerate mankind into just such a religion.[4] **Hitler—like Satan—was a destroyer.** He found that Satan lived up to the titles given him in Revelation 9:11: "And they had as king over them the angel of the bottomless pit, whose name in Hebrew is Abaddon, but in Greek he has the name Apollyon." The translation of both words is "destroyer." Hitler was used by Satan to destroy six million plus of God's chosen people. Multiplied thousands more were destroyed in war. Then in mockery of Hitler himself, Satan motivated him to commit suicide, destroying himself.

One of the primary characteristics of those who get involved in the occult, like Hitler, is rebellion against authority. This rebellion is usually evident in one or more of the following three areas: (1) rebellion against parents; (2) rebellion against society; and (3) rebellion against Christianity.

Why do many of those who rebel against parents, society, and Christianity often end up involved in the occult? Those who know the Bible can tell you: rebellion and occult involvement are linked, "For rebellion is as the sin of witchcraft, and stubbornness is as iniquity and idolatry" (1 Samuel 15:23a).

Beware of giving place to the devil. Listen to Paul's stern warning to Christians in Ephesians 4:27, "nor give place to the devil." "Everywhere and always demons have lurked in the dark for the moment when a person becomes weak, when he arbitrarily abandons his human situation in the world order founded by God for him. . . . After the first voluntary downward step he is compelled to the second and third with rapidly increasing speed. . . . Man is unprotected against evil without the living God; he is like a boat without oars, exposed to the tempest, or like a baby without a mother, or like a cloud which dissolves."[5]

Today, thoughtfully and carefully read Ephesians 4:27–5:8 and note each area Paul describes. These are the potential places Satan starts devouring us spiritually. Avoid allowing him to find these "landing spots" in your life.

SATURDAY: The Only Protection from Satan — God's Signature

[You] are kept by the power of God through faith for salvation
ready to be revealed in the last time.
—1 Peter 1:5

When you call upon Christ in repentant faith, God saves you. Salvation is the greatest work of God in the universe. Some years ago a man in a penitentiary studied a Moody correspondence course. He found Christ. In answer to one of the questions, which gave him an opportunity to express where he stood in relation to his newfound faith, he wrote down: "I am a new man in an old body." It was a most perceptive remark. For that is what salvation is. But salvation will go even further than that prisoner realized. One day he will be a new man in a new body. I like to call the work of salvation the signature of God—when God writes himself across our lives. Listen to this summary of what happens to each of us who come by faith to God through Christ:

- **Regeneration—when God changes my heart:** "I will **give you a new heart** and put a new spirit within you; . . . and cause you to walk in My statutes, and you will keep My judgments and do them" (Ezekiel 36:26–27).
- **Conversion—when God changes my life:** "**Unless you are converted** and become as little children, you will by no means enter the kingdom of heaven" (Matthew 18:3).
- **Repentance—when God changes my mind:** "Bear **fruits worthy of repentance**" (Matthew 3:8). When God transforms our minds we change. When we believe right, we begin to behave correctly.

- **Adoption—when God changes my family:** "**You received the Spirit of adoption** by whom we cry out, 'Abba, Father.' The Spirit Himself bears witness with our spirit that we are children of God" (Romans 8:15–16).
- **Sanctification—when God changes my behavior:** "For by one offering He has perfected forever those **who are being sanctified.** But the Holy Spirit also witnesses to us . . . : 'I will put My laws into their hearts, and in their minds I will write them'" (Hebrews 10:14–16).
- **Justification—when God changes my state:** "Having **been justified by faith, we have peace with God** through our Lord Jesus Christ" (Romans 5:1). What does it mean to be "justified"? In popular, everyday language, the word can be paraphrased: "just as if I'd never sinned." It means that God has no record of anything ever having gone wrong in our lives.
- **Glorification—when God changes my place:** "Father, I desire that **they also whom You gave Me may be with Me** where I am, that they may behold My glory which You have given Me; for You loved Me before the foundation of the world" (John 17:24).[6] I encourage you to write these in your Bible, then believe them, live them, and share them as you act on the reality of God's signature across your life!

Make a choice to live in hope. When God writes Himself across your life through faith in Jesus Christ, you have the enduring hope that one day you will behold the brightness of Christ's face for all eternity! No matter how dark it gets in the meantime, Jesus will whisper to your soul: "Fear not, I am with you—peace, be still!" For He has promised to never leave or forsake you; nor will He ever test you beyond what you can bear (1 Corinthians 10:13). And every time you recall that "greater is he that is in you, than he that is in the world" (1 John 4:4 KJV), it gives you cause to keep singing His praises!

WEEK 34
Feel the Compassion of Jesus

{ Revelation 14 }

As the end of days approaches, you can find hope
as you feel the compassion of Jesus!

SUNDAY: The Tide Turns in the War for Planet Earth

*Then I looked, and behold, a Lamb standing on Mount Zion, and with Him **one hundred and forty-four thousand, having His Father's name written on their foreheads**. And I heard a voice from heaven, like the voice of many waters, and like the voice of loud thunder. And I heard the sound of harpists playing their harps.*

—Revelation 14:1–2

WEEK 34: FEEL THE COMPASSION OF JESUS

The tide of the war for planet Earth turns in Revelation 14. In this chapter, Jesus, in His glorified presence, is standing on His holy hill, Zion, and around Him stand His servants. Beneath Zion, the beast from the abyss, empowered by Satan, has crawled ashore. On the earth, death is stalking all who refuse Satan and turn to Jesus.

In Revelation 14, right in the middle of all hell breaking loose across this planet, what do we find? One of the most touching chapters in the Bible—a chapter exposing Christ's great compassion. For those chosen servants, the 144,000 Jewish evangelists, we find that this chapter sets forth the delights of life with Jesus.

In the first half of Revelation 14 we see that Jesus offers: **security** in the face of dangers (vv. 1–2); **joy** in the midst of desolation (v. 3); **purity** in the sea of filth (v. 4a); **truth** in a world of lies (v. 5); and **hope** in the land of doom (vv. 6–7).

In the second half of Revelation 14, we find that there is: **doom** without Jesus (vv. 8–11); **compassion** in the time of judgment (vv. 12–13); and **understanding** in a time of wrath (vv. 14–20).

Although these words in chapter 14 are directed to this special group called the 144,000, the whole book of Revelation was written to encourage the saints of all ages. So today we, too, can enjoy Jesus' security, joy, purity, truth, and hope! But side by side with all the love and compassion of Christ is the result of choosing to ignore and reject His love. Apart from Jesus there is only hopeless and indescribable torment—torment without rest.

In Revelation 14:12–13, the Holy Spirit speaks for the first time, and a note of hope sounds. As He looks down at the multitudes on earth, the Holy Spirit expresses compassion for those saints who patiently endure.

When Jesus walked on earth as a human and a servant, there were only 250 million people on the planet. Presently, there are over six billion people, but by this point in Revelation, many will have died in the Tribulation. However, as He looks at an even greater multitude than those He saw in His earthly ministry, He is moved with sympathy and will encourage His servants before sending them back out. And if they still need help, He will send an angel to preach the gospel. What a compassionate heart!

In the midst of His children's martyrdom and pain, Jesus will offer His patience, obedience, faith, and hope of blessings. God's Word is so precise and inspired that it gives understanding in the time of wrath, for apart from Jesus there is only senseless and immeasurable bloodshed.

Ray Stedman noted that before this book of Revelation is over, we will look beyond these scenes of judgment, beyond the slaughter, beyond the misery that is to come upon the earth. There is a new day of the "winepress." When "Jacob's trouble" is finally over, Israel will blossom and spread its branches throughout the whole earth like a vine; and Israel's Messiah will reign. It will be the long awaited Utopia.[1] But before that morning dawns, the long night of the human race will grow darker, much darker.

My Prayer for You This Week: *Father, as we reflect upon what is coming in this chapter, we feel the sober nature of this passage—that Your judgment falls upon the earth after Your patience and mercy come to an end. It grieves our hearts to realize that so many will reject You and turn their hearts and souls away from Your mercy and grace. You put Your messengers on this planet, and You send an angel to preach the everlasting gospel. You stand among Your servants calling all to come to You.*

Oh Christ, how we thank You for Your love and compassion! Since people are all that can be taken to heaven with us, we want to take some with us. We want to be among those who point many to You, Lord Jesus. Touch our hearts with Your compassion and help us to see the horror of lostness and hardness. As the apostle Paul said, "knowing therefore the terror of the Lord, we persuade men." That is what You have left us to do. Help us to do it with all our hearts. In the name of Jesus we pray. Amen.

MONDAY: Jesus Offers Security and Joy

One hundred and forty-four thousand [have] His Father's name written on their foreheads.... And I heard the sound of harpists playing their harps. **They sang... a new song before the throne** *... and no one could learn that song except the hundred and forty-four thousand who were redeemed from the earth.*

—Revelation 14:1b-3

As the world plunges into desolation and destruction, God gives us living proof of His care! With Jesus are the blameless, unstoppable witnesses—all who have security because their Father's name is written on their foreheads. God is saying, "You are mine." God has named all the stars, which are merely inanimate objects, and He calls them each by name—but God's servants have the *Father's name* written on their foreheads.

Jesus offers security in the face of dangers. Because of His seal, the saints don't have to worry about getting the mark of the beast; they are impervious to it, and will not be tricked into wanting or taking it. As we step back and look at this scene, here is the blessing: all these servants have been deployed like commandos behind enemy lines; they are the ones who are risking their health and lives to give the gospel out during the Tribulation—and Jesus is right there in the middle of them!

Sometimes people quote Matthew 18:20 to me: "For where two or three are gathered together in My name, I am there in the midst of them." But the context of Matthew 18 is church discipline where two or three witnesses are needed to turn someone over to the Lord for discipline. So I tell them that I have something even better—Jesus promised to come for just *one*: "Lo, I am with you always, even to the end of the age" (Matthew 28:20).

Stedman says that heaven, as it is pictured in the Bible, is actually another dimension of existence, just beyond the reach of our five senses. You can be in heaven at the same time that you are on earth. As I read these prophetic passages of Scripture, I am more and more convinced that this is clearly the case: the church will be with the Lord, yet the Lord will be on the earth throughout those seven turbulent years. Amazingly, although the church will be with the Lord ministering to this select group of 144,000 Jews, it will be invisible to the rest of the world.

During this time, Jesus will periodically appear to these living Jews—standing with them and empowering them for their mission. If this is true, then Jesus will be in exactly the same condition with them as He was with the eleven disciples after His Resurrection, when for a period of forty days He appeared to them from time to time. And then He ascended out of sight into heaven in a cloud.

As you examine the gospel accounts of the time between the Lord's Resurrection and Ascension, you find that He was often with them in various times, various places, and then suddenly He would not be with them. It was as if He would step back into the realm of invisibility after appearing for a while in their midst.[2]

In a very real sense, we are sitting in front of God's throne right now. While we are here on earth, we are in the presence of Jesus; He is here in the spiritual realm. When He comes again, He will just step between the dimensions of spiritual heaven and physical earth. In chapter 14, we find Him standing on the earth prior to the Second Coming, for He has not yet come in the clouds of glory to reconquer the earth; He is just with His saints.

Jesus offers joy in the midst of desolation. People sing when they are happy, when they are sad, and sometimes when they are scared—but most often when they have joy. These secure saints, the 144,000 servants of the Lord, have joy in the midst of the desolation of the planet. Everything has gone berserk: the sun is too hot; the waters are polluted; meteorites are crashing onto the earth; demons are running rampant, and yet these saints are singing a beautiful new song that rises above the screams of anguish and hatred.

Like Jeremiah in the smoking ruins of Jerusalem (see the book of Lamentations), God's faithfulness is seen anywhere and at any time. These saints express their intimacy with Jesus by a new song that no one knows but them. This is the second of three new treasures God gives His servants: (1) a new name (v.1); (2) a new song (v. 3a); and (3) a new destination (v. 3b).

When we are redeemed by the substitutionary work of Jesus on our behalf, we receive a *new name* to show that we are His new creations in Christ. We then get to live full of the Holy Spirit and experience that *new song*, which we sing all through life. (The Word of God describes nine new songs: Psalm 33:3; 40:3; 96:1; 98:1; 144:9; 149:1; Isaiah 42:10; Revelation 5:9; 14:3.)

If you get a report that your company is downsizing and you are out of a job, or if your body is sick and is "downsizing" you right into heaven, or if you have a financial crisis or some emotional tragedy, you can still have joy. How is that possible? Joy is a fruit of the Holy Spirit. If you don't have joy in your life, you are quenching the Spirit through coupling your life to your circumstances rather than letting Him produce His fruit of joy in your spirit. Joy is not to be attached to circumstances: joy is produced internally by the welling up of the Holy Spirit within us. So these 144,000 servants have joy in the midst of desolation.

You, too, can have joy today. Ask the Spirit of God to rule in your heart, to help you detach your life from circumstances and to attach to Him.

TUESDAY: Jesus Offers Purity in the Sea of Filth

> *They sang . . . a new song before the throne. . . .* ***These are the ones who were not defiled*** *with women, for they are virgins. These are the ones who follow the Lamb wherever He goes. These were redeemed from among men, being firstfruits to God and to the Lamb.*
>
> —Revelation 14:3a, 4

In the verse above, John further explains who the servants are that sing that new song. At this time the world is intoxicated with fornication, the wine of passion (14:8), for the earth dwellers "did not repent of their murders or their sorceries or their sexual immorality or their thefts" (9:21). So in the midst of such wickedness all over the planet, this group of servants stands out in their purity.

What does "not defiled with women" mean in verse 4? This phrase has been erroneously used to found all kinds of celibate cults throughout the years. It certainly means no fornication, uncleanness, or any other sexual immorality. It can also mean that they are literally like Jesus—unmarried and kept for God's glory alone, and as Paul says in 1 Corinthians 7, "undistracted" by marriage. However, this is a spiritual scene: "For I am jealous for you with godly jealousy. For I have betrothed you to one husband, that I may present you as a chaste virgin to Christ" (2 Corinthians 11:2). Does this mean that none of Paul's converts were married? No. Paul has gone from the physical realm of adultery, fornication, and immorality to the realm of spiritual adultery, fornication, and immorality—just as John does in verse 4.

When we become Christians, we are engaged to Jesus Christ, so we should keep ourselves from other suitors. Who are those suitors? We find the answer in James 4:4–5: "Adulterers and adulteresses! Do you not know that friendship with the world is enmity with God? Whoever therefore wants to be a friend of the world makes himself an enemy of God. Or do you think that the Scripture says in vain, 'The Spirit who dwells in us yearns jealously?'" You and I can commit sin by loving the world.

The world is the earth-dwelling system in which a person lives only for the moment (the pleasure, the thrill, the stuff, the toys, and the entertainment) instead of being a pilgrim and stranger on the earth and looking for heaven. Since you are engaged to Jesus, and He is preparing a home for you to dwell in forever with Him, if another suitor comes to you and says, "He is gone, so spend some time with me," you must firmly say NO. That is what the Christian life is like. Spiritual fornication is loving something that distracts us from our love for Christ. If you are attracted to the world more than to Christ, you are lusting after the world.

Our world is getting so vile: "It is shameful even to speak of those things which are done by them in secret" (Ephesians 5:12). I cannot tell you how many times I have been in the car listening to the news and had to turn it off to keep from hearing about the filth going on in our culture in the highest places of society. In our world there is a constant redefinition of sin. Sodomy has become "gay"; fornication and adultery have become "an affair." But God says fornication is any mental or physical sexual contact with someone who is not your husband or wife. He would thus consider sexual pictures, sensual phone conversations, and fantasy thoughts as adultery and fornication.

Those things destroy spiritual sensitivity, so God tells us clearly: "Do not love the world [all the lust, immorality, godlessness] or the things in the world [toys, trinkets, and distractions]. If anyone loves the world, the love of the Father is not in him. For all that is in the world—the lust of the flesh [desires and pleasure], the lust of the eyes [chasing after stuff we see], and the pride of life [status and power]—is not of the Father but is of the world. And the world is passing away, and the lust of it; but he who does the will of God abides forever" (1 John 2:15–17).

I meet people all the time who want to know the will of God, and I tell them to stay pure. You will not know the will of God if you are living in impurity. You will not know the will of God if you are not a holy, chaste bride seeking out Christ alone. If you love the world and the stuff in the world you will not know the will of God because it is enmity with God to do so. What is the world? It is the whole system that draws us away from a holy walk with God. Television is a classic example: TV has conditioned us to act superficially. The end result is that many of God's children have become only "hearers of the Word" rather than "doers of the Word" (James 1:22–25). This, in turn, causes desensitization to the compassion of Christ. The world's system promotes our pride, assertiveness, and aggressiveness. And our busyness prevents us from having time for people.

In contrast, those who do not defile themselves, who stay pure with Jesus Christ and seek Him, "these are the ones who follow the Lamb wherever He goes" (Revelation 14:4). The Scriptures say that compassion is a universal language that does not require translation. People saw Christ's compassion in His eyes and His life; He did not have to declare it. A true servant of the Lamb will have His spiritual sensitivity; they can follow the Lamb and do His will because they will be pure. So then, if you want to know God's will, stay pure. Deny sin!

WEDNESDAY: Jesus Offers Truth in a World of Lies

*And in their mouth was found no deceit, for **they are without fault** before the throne of God.*
—Revelation 14:5

In the company of the Lamb are those who rest in the absolute delights of His security, joy, purity, and truth. They are like Jesus of whom it was said: "[He] committed no sin, nor was deceit found in His mouth" (1 Peter 2:22).

What is so marvelous is that the Holy Spirit presents these martyrs as the heroes of the book of Revelation. In our world it is popular to lie. People generally believe it is only a lie if you are under oath and there is a transcript, but the God of truth says: "Do not swear, either by heaven or by earth or with any other oath. But let your 'Yes' be 'Yes,' and your 'No,' 'No,' lest you fall into judgment" (James 5:12).

Several years ago, someone wrote a book in which the author speculated as to what would happen if everyone told the truth—the government, the military, salesmen, financial markets, and married couples. What this ungodly writer had to say only points out the fact that worldly people know that they are lying.

These servants of the Lord in Revelation 14:5 have Truth in a world of lies, for they know the Christ who says: "I am the way, the truth, and the life" (John 14:6). The world, however, is so much like their father the devil: "You are of your father the devil, and the desires of your father you want to do. He was a murderer... and does not stand in the truth, because there is no truth in him" (John 8:44).

How will these servants of the Lamb keep from becoming entrapped in the world's web of deceit? They will believe what God has revealed to them: "If you abide in My word, . . . you shall know the truth, and the truth shall make you free" (John 8:31–32).

Modern history testifies to what will happen to those who hear the Truth of the Bible preached. To illustrate, go back with me to 1931—to a living legend named C. T. Studd. After serving fifteen years in China and six in India, he invested his final twenty-one years in the heart of Africa's vast, dark jungles among the fierce, cannibal, head-hunting pygmies.

Once a lean and fit professional athlete, C.T. is now gaunt and emaciated. He is hunched over, halting with each step. But in July 1931 he is surrounded by thousands of glistening black bodies wearing banana leaves. The pygmies of the heart of Africa's jungles have come to hear their beloved Bwana for the last time. He speaks to them only after over two hours of singing the songs he had so lovingly taught them: "Wounded for me, wounded for me, there on the cross He was wounded for me, gone my transgressions and now I can sing, all because Jesus was wounded for me!"[3]

Those saints were converted and transformed by the Lord through the simple passionate preaching of the Truth of God's Word in the Bible—and that Truth had set them free! Why have believers all through the ages seen lives transformed by the preaching of the gospel? Because they simply obeyed what Jesus left them and us to do—and soon the 144,000 Tribulation servants will be doing it as well.

This company around the Lamb are thus secure, joyful, pure, and truthful; they are like Jesus, "Who committed no sin, nor was deceit found in His mouth" (1 Peter 2:22).

On a scale of one to ten, how would you rate your truthfulness? Who are you following—the father of lies or the Father of truth?

THURSDAY: Jesus Offers Hope in the Land of Doom

*Then I saw another angel flying in the midst of heaven, having the everlasting gospel to preach to those who dwell on the earth . . . saying with a loud voice, "**Fear God and give glory to Him**, for the hour of His judgment has come; **and worship Him** who made heaven and earth, the sea and springs of water."*

—Revelation 14:6–7

I do not think we are going to turn the world around. We are not going to save the planet, and the ecology is not going to get better. But I still have great hope, knowing that those I lead to Christ will not be sealed by the Antichrist because they will already be sealed by the Spirit of God. They *will* have a future and a hope! That is why we can have hope in a world of doom; we do not simply hide out, sitting on a mountaintop to wait for the end of the world. No, we rescue as many people as we can by telling them about Jesus.

These servants standing with Jesus in verses 6–7 are witnesses of the endless, unchangeable gospel. Mankind's only hope is to bow to their Creator and reach out to their Redeemer—or face Him as Judge. All who have been saved in any age (law, church, or kingdom) were only saved by the sovereign grace of God, on the basis of the work that was accomplished by our Lord's atoning death. The eternal gospel is a proclamation to all who dwell upon the earth: every nation, tribe, tongue, and people. It is the good news that the judgment of God, so long awaited, is about to be consummated;

and that the groaning earth will be brought back from the reign of the rebel prince, and put under the sway of the Son of God.

The gospel has always been the same: substitutionary atonement. From the Garden of Eden, as soon as Adam and Eve fell into sin, God killed an animal and clothed Adam and Eve with the skins. He could have taken cotton fiber and spun it, but it took a blood sacrifice to atone. This is the first example of being clothed with the righteousness of a blood sacrifice. Right from the beginning it has always been substitutionary atonement. Abel's offering on the altar was a lamb. God said that the Seed of the woman would crush the serpent's head, and that the coming One would sacrifice himself as Isaiah says in chapter 53. The gospel has always been the same: "Fear God and give glory to Him, for the hour of His judgment has come; and worship Him who made heaven and earth" (Revelation 14:7).

There are three elements of the eternal gospel, which are always present.

Conviction—"fear God." If we preach a gospel without conviction, it is not the gospel of God. That is why it bothers me so much today that people can hear the gospel and desire to get saved, but not be convicted of their sinfulness that separates them from God. I thought about that a lot as a little child, and in the fall of 1962, I came to my mother and told her that I did not want to be separated from God. I did not want to go to hell. Like a little child, you should fear God: His wrath, His judgment, and separation from Him eternally!

Conversion—"give glory to Him." The person who truly fears God will turn from his or her old ways and give Him glory; that is conversion. If you have never been saved from sin, you have never been saved from hell. When the Israelites came out of Egypt they wanted a savior, not a Lord. So God destroyed them. There are groups of people in churches across this nation and around the world that want a savior, but not a Lord, and God will destroy them as well. If there is no genuine and lasting repentance, there is no conversion. If there is no conviction of sin, there is no conversion that gives Him glory—that is what the Scriptures teach.

Consecration—"worship Him." Consecration is the fruit of redemption. When we genuinely fear God, we are convicted of our sin, turn to the Savior, and give Him glory. That is the necessary total change of our lives—no longer giving ourselves glory, but Him. Although we will imperfectly do this, and fail at times, this is the longing of the heart of one who fears God. Then, when we consecrate our lives to worshiping Him, out of that worship will flow fruitful service.

God, in His infinite grace, will thus send forth a mighty angel—flying back and forth across the skies during the Tribulation—loudly proclaiming the gospel from one place to another, covering every nation and tribe, speaking in every language, so that no one at the coming judgment would be able to say he or she hadn't heard. What a compassionate Savior!

FRIDAY: Jesus Offers Compassion in the Midst of Judgment

*And another angel followed, saying, "Babylon is fallen, is fallen, that great city, because she has made all nations drink of the wine of the wrath of her fornication." Then a third angel [said] with a loud voice, "**If anyone worships the beast and his image, and receives his mark** on his forehead* *or on his hand,* **he . . . shall also drink of the wine of the wrath of God.** *. . . He shall be tormented with fire and brimstone. . . . And the smoke of their torment ascends forever and ever; and they have no rest day or night."*

—Revelation 14:8–11

The passage above starts the second half of this chapter, in which we are confronted with what happens to those who exist without Jesus—eternal judgment and condemnation. But before I discuss the elements of doom that unbelievers will face, I want to further develop the first half of this fourteenth chapter, in which we see a revelation of Christ's wonderful compassion.

In Revelation 14:1–7, we see Him standing with His servants trying to save those who will come to Him and listen to Him. The most often-noted emotion of Christ's ministry was His compassion. Jesus was shown to be "moved with compassion" no less than thirteen times. (We all need a good dose of His compassion!) A great student of the life and ministry of Christ, the apostle Paul, said his ministry was motivated by Christ's love. What did the compassion of Jesus look like? Let's briefly examine the top ten groups of people who move Him to compassion:

1. **Christ's compassion is for the confused:** "He was moved with compassion for them, because they were weary and scattered, like sheep having no shepherd" (Matthew 9:36; see also Mark 6:34).
2. **Christ's compassion is for the sick and suffering:** "He saw a great multitude; and He was moved with compassion for them, and healed their sick" (Matthew 14:14).
3. **Christ's compassion is for the weak:** "I have compassion on the multitude, because they have now continued with Me three days and have nothing to eat. And I do not want to send them away hungry, lest they faint on the way" (Matthew 15:32).
4. **Christ's compassion is for the desperate:** "Then the master of that servant was moved with compassion, released him, and forgave him the debt" (Matthew 18:27).
5. **Christ's compassion is for the persistent:** "So Jesus had compassion and touched their eyes. And immediately their eyes received sight, and they followed Him" (Matthew 20:34).
6. **Christ's compassion is for the helpless:** "Then Jesus, moved with compassion, stretched out His hand and touched him, and said to him, 'I am willing; be cleansed'" (Mark 1:41; see also Mark 9:22).
7. **Christ's compassion is for the hopeless:** "Jesus did not permit him, but said to him, 'Go home to your friends, and tell them what great things the Lord has done for you, and how He has had compassion on you'" (Mark 5:19).
8. **Christ's compassion is for the bereaved:** "When the Lord saw her, He had compassion on her and said to her, 'Do not weep'" (Luke 7:13).
9. **Christ's compassion is for the misfortunate:** "But a certain Samaritan, as he journeyed, came where he was. And when he saw him, he had compassion" (Luke 10:33).
10. **Christ's compassion is for the repentant:** "But when he was still a great way off, his father saw him and had compassion, and ran and fell on his neck and kissed him" (Luke 15:20).

Jesus was moved with compassion for the confused, the sick and suffering, the weak, the desperate, the persistent, the helpless, the hopeless, the bereaved, the misfortunate, and the repentant!

The doom of life without Jesus. When God speaks of himself as being eternal (which He does eight times in Revelation), He uses the very same word for eternal that is used for the eternal duration of hell (three times in Revelation). So, according to God, it appears that hell lasts as long as He does—forever!

Apart from Jesus there is only hopeless and indescribable torment and judgment. The Word of God describes hell as a place of unending anguish. Jesus talked about hell more than heaven. Revelation 14:11 says that "they have no rest day or night." Remember that Jesus talked about the bottomless pit and a lake of fire in which there is endless falling and no rest. There is no place to stand on to catch your breath—just endless torment.

It is not fashionable to talk about this today. A lot of the mainline denominations disavow hell; they say it is not Christian. It is more Christian than they understand, because Jesus is the One who describes it more than anyone else. The Word of God repeatedly describes hell as unending anguish: "And they shall go forth and look upon the corpses of the men who have transgressed against Me. For their worm does not die, and their fire is not quenched. They shall be an abhorrence to all flesh. . . . His winnowing fan is in His hand, and He will thoroughly clean out His threshing floor, and gather His wheat into the barn; but He will burn up the chaff with unquenchable fire" (Isaiah 66:24; Matthew 3:12; see also Matthew 13:50; Mark 9:43–49; Jude 7).

But a note of hope sounds in verses 12–13 of Revelation 14 as the Holy Spirit speaks for the first time in Revelation (the second and final time is in 22:17, with the last gospel invitation in God's Word): "Here is the patience of the saints; here are those who keep the commandments of God and the faith of Jesus. Then I heard a voice from heaven saying to me, 'Write: "Blessed are the dead who die in the Lord from now on"'" (Revelation 14:12–13).

"The patience of the saints" is a wonderful description of who Christians really are. "The faith of Jesus" means that if you have faith in Jesus Christ and keep His commands through the new birth (the regeneration of God who gives us the heart to obey Him), you are a saint. At the beginning of verse 13, John is commanded for the tenth time to write down the Word of God (see also 1:11, 19; chapters 2–3; 14:13; 19:9; 21:5). We see here the last call to the earth as the angel is saying to preach the gospel. "Blessed are the dead who die in the Lord from now on" is the second of the seven beatitudes in Revelation in which God bestows His blessings. Here is a summary of the Revelation beatitudes:

1. Blessed are readers, hearers, and keepers (1:3)—
   this emphasizes the importance of the Word of God.
2. Blessed are the dead who die in the Lord (14:13)—
   this emphasizes the blessings of eternal life.
3. Blessed are those watching and keeping their garments white (16:15)—
   this emphasizes the Lord's return.
4. Blessed are those invited to the Lamb's supper (19:9)—
   this emphasizes the joy of Christ's presence.

5. Blessed are the participants of the first Resurrection (20:6)—
   this emphasizes deliverance from death.
6. Blessed are those heeding this book (22:7)—
   this emphasizes obedience to the Word of God.
7. Blessed are those with a clean robe and access to the tree of life (22:14)—
   this emphasizes eternal sustenance.

It is sad that so many today are departing from the doctrine of eternal punishment. For if they refuse to accept the gift of His grace, they must remain in their lost condition—eternally deserving, provoking, and receiving the holy wrath of God. I pray that you are among the saints who rest securely in Jesus as their eternal refuge rather than aligning yourself with those who scoff at the horrors to come!

SATURDAY: Jesus Offers Understanding in the Time of Wrath

*Then I looked, and behold, a white cloud, and **on the cloud sat One like the Son of Man**, having on His head a golden crown, and in His hand a sharp sickle. And another angel came out of the temple, crying with a loud voice to Him who sat on the cloud. "Thrust in Your sickle and reap, for the time has come for You to reap, for the harvest of the earth is ripe."*
—Revelation 14:14–15

The impenitent earth dwellers face only doom in their lives. They have told God to leave them alone, and so He will—forever: "These shall be punished with everlasting destruction **from the presence of the Lord** and from the glory of His power" (2 Thessalonians 1:9).

God responds to man's impenitence. The greatest illustration of this is seen in the actions of Judas. He was next to Jesus Christ for three and one-half years, and yet his heart was unmoved to confess his sin and turn to Christ for salvation. Amazingly, Judas saw no beauty in Christ after all he had witnessed in Him. In the end, caring only for gain, dominated only by self, he was ready to sell the Lord for the price of a slave. Judas is a picture of what we see going on in the world in Revelation 14, and God has to do something about it. As Ray Stedman has pointed out, God has three choices in the face of human rebellion:

- **One:** He can indulge it and allow it to go on forever. But in that case all the cruelty, injustice, hatred, pain, and death that now prevail on the earth will go on forever, too. God does not want that—and neither does man.
- **Two:** God can force man to obey and control the human race as if it were a race of robots. But to take away our free will would be to take away our capacity to give our love to God freely. Love cannot be forced.
- **Three:** This is God's only real choice. He must withdraw Himself from those who refuse His love. He must let them have their way forever. Since God is necessary to our existence, the decision to reject God is a decision to plunge ourselves into the most terrible sense of loneliness and isolation a human being can know.[4]

Ultimately, we choose whether God will judge us by deciding either to accept or refuse His grace, love, and forgiveness. As a result, we are choosing everlasting life or everlasting death.

Apart from Jesus there is no other future than verses 14–20 of Revelation 14—senseless and immeasurable warfare and bloodshed. In verse 20b, "the blood came out of the winepress, up to the horses' bridles, for one thousand six hundred furlongs." To have blood for 1,600 furlongs (1 furlong = 607 feet) means 180 miles. From twenty miles beyond Armageddon, that would stretch to twenty miles past Bozrah, an ancient Edomite stronghold, that is twenty miles southeast of the bottom of the Dead Sea.

How to develop compassion as Christ's servants. A good place to start is to follow the areas that John Ruskin, a famous poet and art critic, first pointed out as three keys to being a good artist. Enduring artists must possess: **(1) an eye to see** and appreciate all the beauty they wish to capture on the canvas; **(2) a heart to feel** and register within the picture the atmosphere and the beauty of the scene; and **(3) a hand to perform** by transforming a blank canvas into an image of what the eye has seen and the heart has felt. The skills that an enduring artist must follow are the same three skills a compassionate disciple of Jesus must learn.

This study of Revelation 14 will be meaningless if you don't see the compassion of Jesus. So prayerfully examine your life in light of the following challenges.

Do you have **an eye to see** how helpless our world is? There are six billion sheep, and most of them are without a true knowledge of the Good Shepherd. There were only 250 million in Christ's day. The population of our world is twenty-four times that today! What do *you* see in a crowd? A businessman sees a potential market, an educator sees a potential classroom, and a politician sees potential voters. Nearly everyone thinks in terms of personal benefit. But Jesus was moved with compassion at the sight of a crowd, and that compassion led Him to give His life on a cross of wood, writing a letter of love for the sins of the world.

Do you have **a heart to feel** how much the world needs Jesus? In the Bible, the word for compassion means "to suffer together with." This emotion of compassion constitutes a language that is understood universally. Compassion can be seen and felt by all because it is the language of the heart that needs no translation to be understood. In the twenty-first century, we have lost so much compassion in favor of instant gratification, and have a veneer-thin depth of commitment. The superficiality of emotional expression from TV has seeped into our spiritual lives. We are good actors, but often poor at feeling the pain of others. We need to ask God for a heart of compassion like Christ's—a heart that longs to see people come to Jesus!

Do you have **hands to perform** loving works in the name of Jesus? At the end of Revelation 14:13, it says, "their works follow them." Do you have good works that will follow you to heaven? What ministries are you involved in today that will touch the immortal souls of people for Jesus? Can you name one? Are your hands doing the work of Jesus? Do you share His Word? Do you reach out to point them to Christ? The fruits of such a ministry will follow you to heaven. Your house and car won't; your education and degrees won't; and your accomplishments and money won't. Are you investing your life with the compassion of Christ? If not, by His grace, start today!

Make a choice to live in hope. The most fulfilling and enduring hope you can ever have is to invest your life in others! Make a choice to live in hope by being "a vessel for honor, sanctified and useful for the Master, prepared for every good work" (2 Timothy 2:21).

WEEK 35
Meditate on the Beauty of Jesus

{ Revelation 15 }

As the end of days approaches, you can find hope as you meditate on the beauty of Jesus!

SUNDAY: Slowing Down to See Jesus

Be still, and know that I am God; I will be exalted among the nations, I will be exalted in the earth!

—Psalm 46:10

To worship Him who is worthy of all worship and praise is our duty and purpose of existence. The Father seeks only one thing: worship. True worship is to ascribe to Christ the honor, praise, glory, and majesty that He is worthy of—His true "worthship." Let us now peer through the door of heaven into the chambers of the Most High.

In Revelation 15, John, the heir of the apostolic band, tried to capture with his pen that which, when Paul saw it, was inexpressible. Through the eyes of that faithful and true disciple of love who alone remained, we get to listen to the choirs of angels in numberless circles about the glassy sea and its throne as they sing His worthy praise. We get to listen to those eternal creatures chant "Holy, holy, holy." And by faith's eye we get to see with John that band which no man could number—and listen to their songs of adoration and praise.

In Revelation 15 you will discover: Jesus Christ is patient (v. 1); Jesus Christ's saints are triumphant (vv. 2–4); Jesus Christ is victorious (vv. 5–7); and Jesus Christ is wrathful (v. 8).

Do you know this Christ the Lord who merits such praise as "Worthy is the Lamb that was slain"? I exhort you to meditate on the beauty of Jesus: worship Him in the splendor of His redeeming love through His perfect patience, perfect holiness, perfect redemption, perfect justice (which has no mercy), and perfect wrath.

But to prepare each of our hearts for meditation truly worthy of the Lamb, we need to first slow down and reflect on the paradox of our time in history. For example,

We have taller buildings, but shorter tempers; wider freeways, but narrower viewpoints; we spend more, but have less; we buy more, but enjoy it less.

We have bigger houses and smaller families; more conveniences, but less time; we have more degrees, but less sense; more knowledge, but less judgment; more experts, but more problems; more medicine, but less wellness. We drink too much, smoke too much, spend too recklessly, laugh too little, drive too fast, get too angry too quickly, stay up too late, get up too tired, read too little, watch TV too much, and pray too seldom.

We have multiplied our possessions, but reduced our values. We talk too much, love too seldom, and hate too often. We've learned how to make a living, but not a life; we've added years to life, not life to years.

We've been all the way to the moon and back, but have trouble crossing the street to meet the new neighbor. We've conquered outer space, but not inner space; we've done larger things, but not better things.

We've cleaned up the air, but polluted the soul; we've split the atom, but not our prejudice; we write more, but learn less; we plan more, but accomplish less.

We've learned to rush, but not to wait; we have higher incomes, but lower morals; we have more food, but less appeasement; we build more computers to hold more information to produce more copies than ever, but have less communication; we've become long on quantity, but short on quality.

These are the times of fast foods and slow digestion; tall men, and short character; steep profits, and shallow relationships. These are the times of relative world peace, but increased domestic warfare; more leisure, but less fun; more kinds of food, but less nutrition.

These are days of two incomes, but more divorce; of fancier houses, but broken homes.

These are days of quick trips, disposable diapers, throw-away morality, one-night stands, overweight bodies, and pills that do everything from cheer, to quiet, to kill.

It is a time when there is much in the show window and nothing in the stockroom; a time when technology can bring the universe to our screens but the God of the Universe can't bring us to our knees.[1]

So what is the personal solution to all this? Begin by asking the Lord to help you slow down so that you can truly meditate on the beauty of Jesus as we go through chapter 15 this week.

My Prayer for You This Week: *Oh Father, please reveal areas in my own life where I need to slow down the pace and establish Your priorities instead of my own! As we look into this very special portion of your Word, I ask for Your illuminating power to open our eyes that we might behold wonderful things from Your Word! You have forever settled Your Word in heaven, and this chapter is but a glimpse of the beauty of our Lord Jesus Christ! Thank You for each facet of His beauty and for every word that by Your Spirit You inspired Your servants to write. Your Word is so profitable and meant to guide us in the way of Christlikeness as we, Your servants, seek to follow You wherever You go and serve You all our days. May this chapter encourage us to that end as we bow before You now. In the name of Jesus we pray. Amen.*

MONDAY: Jesus Christ Is Patient

*Then I saw another sign in heaven, great and marvelous: seven angels having the seven last plagues, for **in them the wrath of God is complete**.*

—Revelation 15:1

Learning how to slow down the pace of your life to establish God's priorities instead of your own is what patience is all about. Revelation 15 is a wonderful portion of God's Word to teach us about the patience we can have in Christ.

If you recall, the sixth seal commenced the Day of the Lord: "For the great day of His wrath has come, and who is able to stand?" (Revelation 6:17). If you know anything about the Bible, you know that the Lord is dragging the final judgment out for as long as He can because of His patience and mercy. He has been withholding the final blow when He will melt all His enemies: "The LORD will strike all the people who fought against Jerusalem: Their flesh shall dissolve while they stand on their feet, their eyes shall dissolve in their sockets, and their tongues shall dissolve in their mouths" (Zechariah 14:12).

God's patience goes way back, for Jesus has been patient for a very long time. Look at Jude 14–15: "Now Enoch, the seventh from Adam, prophesied about these men also, saying, 'Behold, the Lord comes with ten thousands of His saints, to execute judgment on all, [for] their ungodly deeds . . . against Him.'" The Lord has been waiting since the time of Enoch to execute His judgment, but His patience will come to an end in Revelation 15:8.

Do you have genuine patience? Patience is the absence of personal irritation at the actions of others. Amazingly, Jesus never evidences personal irritations at ignominy and wickedness during the Tribulation hour. Instead, He patiently waits while sending wave after wave of witnesses and wave after wave of good news to the earth.

Patience is the "bearing long" with people that Paul spoke of in 1 Corinthians 13. Patience is also one of the supreme attributes of God. Revelation 15:1 is so critical because it talks about how Jesus is waiting. He is waiting with the plagues, and His wrath is going to be complete. But He has waited since Enoch, since Noah, since He came and walked this earth and was rejected; He has waited through all of the trumpets and the seals, and now He is waiting before He pours out those bowls—the final outflow of His wrath.

It is Christ's character to be gracious and longsuffering, and we should try to be like Him. Since Jesus can wait through all these terrible responses of humanity and keep pouring out His mercy on the earth, we ought to work on being patient in our own lives.

The supreme characteristic of God is His patience: "The LORD, the LORD God, merciful and gracious, longsuffering, and abounding in goodness and truth." (Exodus 34:6). Although God is patient, He does not forget unless we come and plead beneath the shadow of the blood of Christ: "The LORD is longsuffering and abundant in mercy, forgiving iniquity and transgression; but He by no means clears the guilty" (Numbers 14:18).

Remember: through the pleadings of Abraham, God withheld the destruction of Sodom until a few people were rescued; God withheld the death angel's hand when David sacrificed and stopped the plague of God; and when Moses and Aaron interceded, and ran out with the censers, it stopped the plague that was going through Israel. God is so patient that He withholds His wrath in response.

God is patient, so He gives patience: "Now may the God of patience and comfort grant you to be like-minded toward one another, according to Christ Jesus" (Romans 15:5). To get along with fellow Christians pray: "God of patience and comfort, make me patient! I need Your comfort so that I will not respond adversely to frustrating situations." Do you know how powerful a church is when its members are patient with one another? One of the great marks of maturity is patience.

Throughout the Tribulation, Jesus Christ patiently offers His salvation: "The Lord is not slack concerning His promise, . . . but is longsuffering toward us, not willing that any should perish but that all should come to repentance" (2 Peter 3:9).

Ask yourself: *Am I more patient than I was three months ago, or less?* Patience is a fruit of the Holy Spirit. Are you letting the Holy Spirit bear that fruit in your life? Or are you spraying the fruit killer of impatience on it? If we are not increasing in patience, it is because we are not yielding and submitting to the Holy Spirit.

William Barclay has this to say about the meaning of patience, as used in 2 Peter 1:6: "The word never means the spirit which sits with folded hands and simply bears things. It is victorious endurance, masculine constancy under trial. It is Christian steadfastness, the brave and courageous acceptance of everything life can do to us, and the transmuting of even the worst into another step on the upward way. It is the courageous and triumphant ability to bear things, which enables a man to pass the breaking point and not to break, and always to greet the unseen with a cheer."[2]

Patience is a learned art, and sometimes we need to learn a lot in certain situations. We have to learn to allow the Spirit of God to bring this forth in our lives. The opposite of patience can be seen in the signs of anger: irritability, impatience, glaring eyes, raised voice, hurtful words, explosive actions, silent treatment, argumentative words, clenched teeth, and heavy breathing. This is not what God wants in us.

How can you stop impatient anger? Note these steps to resolving anger: Accept responsibility for anger and its symptoms. See your anger through the eyes of others. View anger as an alarm for unresolved guilt. Act quickly to resolve past guilt, offenses, failures, and bless the one making you impatient. Acknowledge the anger of forefathers. Regain the ground of past anger. Fully forgive the offender. Learn to see the benefits in tragedy. Exchange all personal rights to God. Establish daily accountability.

A word of caution: holding on to your anger overnight gives place to the devil (Ephesians 4:27). The tormentors are the destructive emotions of fear, guilt, depression, anger, and anxiety. The way out is to confess specific sins (1 John 1:9); claim the blood of Christ (Revelation 12:11; Colossians 2:14–15); and ask God to restore the place surrendered to Satan. God promises that you can tear down Satan's strongholds with His truth (2 Corinthians 10:4–5).

The patience of Jesus is amazing—He waits so long. If it were up to us, we might have resorted to dealing with the world's rebellion with a few H-bombs! But Jesus just waits on the prayers of the saints, and then He waits still further for more prayers of the saints. Next, He allows the Devil to start a shuttle service to heaven by killing so many people in the Tribulation that the martyrs will pile up in heaven. But that is really the beauty of this chapter as Jesus continues to shows us His patience.

The lesson: We should act quickly to resolve our impatience and be wrapped in the beauty of Jesus!

TUESDAY: Jesus Christ's Saints Are Triumphant

> *And I saw something like a sea of glass mingled with fire, and those who* **have the victory over the beast***, over his image and over his mark and over the number of his name, standing on the sea of glass, having harps of God.*
> —Revelation 15:2

Now I want to show you the triumph that the patience of Christ produces. "I saw something like a sea of glass" is not an actual sea of glass; it is like a sea of glass. I don't know what it is, and we shouldn't try to figure it out. But it is crystal clear, which is indicative of the holiness of God—nothing is hidden.

"Mingled with fire" (also seen in the river of fire flowing out from the throne) speaks of the fire of persecution and refinement through which these saints have gone. They "have the victory over the beast" and are now "standing on the sea of glass, having harps of God." From a human perspective, all the people standing on the sea were simply killed, and that is the end of them. But Jesus said in Mark 8:35: "Whoever desires to save his life will lose it, but whoever loses his life for My sake and the gospel's will save it."

Satan will lose because these people will gain the triumph for Christ through martyrdom. Look at how many people Revelation 7:9–12 says are here: "*I looked, and behold, a great multitude which no one could number . . . standing before the throne and before the Lamb, clothed with white robes, with palm branches in their hands, and crying out with a loud voice, saying, 'Salvation belongs to our God who sits on the throne, and to the Lamb!' All the angels . . . and the elders and the four living creatures . . . fell on their faces before the throne and worshiped God, saying: 'Amen! Blessing and glory and wisdom, thanksgiving and honor and power and might, be to our God forever and ever. Amen.'*"

This is the same group that we see in chapter 15—the martyrs of the Tribulation. Someone once asked me, "If a person takes the mark of the beast, can they go to heaven?" No, they cannot. But there will be a great number who will not take that mark. Do you know what the triumph of God is? Through the darkest hour of the earth, there will be the greatest revival the planet has ever known! An innumerable number of people will be saved in a very short period of time. Why? Jesus is patient. And when Jesus is patient, the saints will be triumphant as He conquers through them.

These martyrs will sing the song of Moses, the servant of God, and the glorious song of the Lamb (Revelation 15:3a). Don't you think it fascinating that the first song mentioned in the Bible is in Exodus 15— and the final song of the Scriptures is in Revelation 15? Those two songs come together in this chapter because Exodus gives us "the song of Moses" and Revelation gives us "the song of the Lamb." These two songs converge in Revelation 15:3–4.

WEEK 35: MEDITATE ON THE BEAUTY OF JESUS

The first song is a song of deliverance after the safe crossing of the Red Sea. Moses, through his sister Miriam, marvelously leads the nation of Israel in singing this song of triumph. Let's look at some of its verses from Exodus 15:1–21 to see how greatly this song glorifies the Lord: "*Then Moses and the children of Israel sang this song to the Lord, and spoke, saying: 'I will sing to the Lord, for He has triumphed gloriously! The horse and its rider He has thrown into the sea! The Lord is my strength and song, and He has become my salvation; He is my God, and I will praise Him; My father's God, and I will exalt Him'*" (vv. 1–2).

Note that the Israelites gave the Lord alone the glory for the triumph over their enemies. The strength that leads to ultimate victory is in God, and not in ourselves: "Who is like You, O LORD, among the gods? Who is like You, glorious in holiness, fearful in praises, doing wonders?" (v. 11). In verse 21 we see Miriam then leading the women to echo what the men sang in verse 1: "And Miriam answered them: 'Sing to the Lord, for He has triumphed gloriously! The horse and its rider He has thrown into the sea!'"

Songs of worship are to be about the Lord. The song of Moses and the song in Revelation 15 do not point at all to the singers. This is a good principle of what God expects in our worship. Today, many of our contemporary songs draw attention to the singers and to everything else but the Lord. I believe that points to one reason why the church is so weak globally—our worship is focused inwardly instead of outwardly on the Lord.

This song of Moses was stamped upon the memory of the Jews. It was sung at every Sabbath evening service in the synagogue. At every Jewish service the recital of the *Shema*, the creed of Israel, was (and still is) followed by two prayers, and one of these prayers refers to this song: "True it is that thou art Jehovah our God, and the God of our fathers, our King, and the King of our fathers, our Savior, and the Savior of our fathers, our Creator, the Rock of our Salvation, our Help and our Deliverer. Thy name is from everlasting, and there is no God beside thee. A new song did they that were delivered sing to thy name by the seashore; together did all praise and own thee King, and say, Jehovah shall reign, World without end! Blessed be the LORD who saveth Israel."[3] I find it noteworthy that the lives of Moses and Christ parallel in these areas:

- Both were delivered in infancy from great danger.
- Both were named by God.
- Both were able to meet with God on the mountain—Moses on Mount Sinai and Christ on the Mount of Transfiguration.
- Both of them gave out the Word of God.
- Both were prophets to the people of God.
- Both were rejected by God's people.
- Moses brought redemption from a temporary oppression in Egypt; Jesus brings redemption from the eternal penalty of sin.

It is no wonder then that the song in Revelation 15:3b-4, which is a lovely picture of Christ's beautiful attributes, is very similar to the song of Moses. (We will go over this song in depth in tomorrow's devotional.)

There is always a majestic backdrop to remind us of God's unfailing purpose! What do I mean? There are eleven songs in Revelation that make up the background music to the story. They are songs of worship and triumph:

Revelation	Worship Theme	Worshipers
4:8	Holy, Holy, Holy	Living creatures
4:11	Worthy is the Creator	24 elders
5:8–10	Worthy is the Redeemer	Living creatures, 24 elders
5:11–12	Worthy is the Lamb	Creatures, elders, angels
5:13	Blessing and honor to the One on the throne	Every created being
7:9–10	Salvation belongs to God	A great multitude
7:11–12	Amen! Blessing and glory to our God forever	Angels
11:15	World's kingdoms are now the Lord's kingdoms	Loud voices
11:16–18	Thanksgiving to God	Elders
15:2–4	Great and marvelous God	Victors over the beast
19:1–8	Alleluias (4) for the marriage of the Lamb!	Great multitude, 24 elders, living creatures, great voices

The majestic declarations of God's glory and greatness in praise by the angels, Creation, the redeemed, and all of these together, show the constant backdrop for the shifting scenes in Revelation 15—worship.

Behind the shifting scenes of man's changing world of human history, portrayed by the symbols of Revelation, is an unchanging and vivid reality. In God's eternal world: God's purposes don't fail; God's plan doesn't change; God's Christ is always victorious!

WEDNESDAY: The Song of Jesus

> **"Great and marvelous are Your works, Lord God Almighty!** *Just and true are Your ways, O King of the saints! Who shall not fear You, O Lord, and glorify Your name? For You alone are holy. For all nations shall come and worship before You, for Your judgments have been manifested."*
> —Revelation 15:3b-4

Revelation 15 contains the final song of the Scriptures. Both the song of Moses and the song of the Lamb, which are very similar in content, capture well the beauty of Jesus.

Although these victorious martyrs will sing two songs, the song of the Lamb is a song which only they could learn: "They sang as it were a new song . . . ; and no one could learn that song except the hundred and forty-four thousand who were redeemed from the earth" (Revelation 14:3).

These 144,000 who are with Christ will probably also know this song, will go out and share this message, and then their converts will sing it as well. We don't know what it is, but through the eyes of John we see them singing this song and then breaking forth into this beautifully combined song of Moses and the song of the Lamb.

So here they are, these converts of the 144,000 Jewish missionaries, blessing the Lord! The song of Moses commemorated the greatest deliverance in the history of God's people, Israel; and the victorious martyrs, brought through the sea of persecution to the promised land of heaven, will sing that song of Moses. But the martyrs will also have their own special song. Their song is drawn from the Old Testament. Note the lines of the song and the Old Testament foundations:

"Great and marvelous are Your works, Lord God Almighty!" (from Psalm 92, 111, 98 and 139). This very unique title of God is only used in Revelation, and it appears five times. Because saints praise God's works, we are to worship His power, for God is omnipotent!

"Just and true are Your ways, O King of the saints!" (from Psalm 145:17). Because saints praise God's ways, we are to worship His plan, and the way that plan unfolds. That is why we should be so thankful in our lives even for the unchangeable features: the family God put us in, the body He put us in, and the place in life He gave us. We should not chafe against that.

Are you following God's plan? Look at Revelation 14:4: "These are the ones who follow the Lamb wherever He goes." That includes the plan of God—they will follow God's plan; they will go the way God tells them to go. That is part of our worship; we are to worship God for His great hand leading us in our lives.

"Who shall not fear You, O Lord, and glorify Your name? For You alone are holy" (from Psalm 86:9; 1 Samuel 2:2; Psalm 99:3; and Psalm 111:9). Because saints praise God's wonders, we are to worship His perfections. God is perfect, but we are not. We should thus say to Him: "God, You are perfect in Your knowledge, perfect in Your ways, perfect in Your Word that You have revealed to us—and I worship You!"

We can cultivate our worship as we look at the power of God, the ways of God, and the wonders of His plan. You will never be disappointed if you wait for God's perfect plan. God wants you to know His will more than you want to know it. It takes a long time to know His will because God is patient, and we are not. So God lets us chafe, fight, and struggle. Then when we don't know where to turn, we turn to Him and He shows us His plan as we let His Word dwell in us.

"For all nations shall come and worship before You, For Your judgments have been manifested" (from Psalm 86:9; Psalm 98). Because saints praise God, we are to worship not only His plan but also His purposes. We are not going to be on earth when all this happens, but God is letting us know ahead of time what will occur. Why? So that we can marvel at how wonderful God is, and how He planned all this—and then tell others!

THURSDAY: Jesus Christ Is Victorious

I looked, and behold, **the temple of the tabernacle of the testimony in heaven was opened.** *And out of the temple came the seven angels having the seven plagues, clothed in pure bright linen, and*

having their chests girded with golden bands. Then one of the four living creatures gave to the seven angels seven golden bowls full of the wrath of God who lives forever and ever.
—Revelation 15:5–7

This passage in Revelation 15 speaks of Jesus Christ's coming triumph. What does "the temple of the tabernacle of the testimony" in verse 5 signify? The Old Testament states seven elements of the tabernacle.

Element one—the way to the presence of God. This is seen in the shekinah—God's sign of His glorious presence from Eden onward. (It is mentioned 100 times in Revelation.) Every time God came, there was the glory cloud: in the burning bush when Moses saw Him; in the flaming cherubim as they kept Adam and Eve out of the Garden of Eden; over the completed tabernacle; over the completed temple; and leaving the temple in Ezekiel after the apostasy of Israel. That cloud is the sign of God's presence. The way into God's presence is through the tabernacle of the testimony.

Jesus is our Emmanuel, God with us: "The virgin shall be with child, and bear a Son, and they shall call His name 'Immanuel,' which is translated, 'God with us' " (Matthew 1:23).

Element two—the way of access to God. The purpose is to not just get into His presence, for God spoke in the tabernacle. Do you remember that in the Old Testament there would be a voice over the mercy seat speaking? God was accessible to the high priest and Moses: "Moses took his tent and pitched it . . . far from the camp, and called it the tabernacle of meeting. . . . Everyone who sought the Lord went out to the tabernacle of meeting, which was outside the camp" (Exodus 33:7).

Jesus is the image of the invisible God: "No one has seen God at any time. The only begotten Son, who is in the bosom of the Father, He has declared Him" (John 1:18). Jesus declares God. When the tabernacle of the testimony is open it is a testimony of God's presence and His accessibility.

Element three—the way of forgiveness with God. "And it shall be, when he is guilty in any of these matters, that he shall confess that he has sinned in that thing" (Leviticus 5:5).

Jesus is our cleansing: "But if we walk in the light as He is in the light, we have fellowship with one another, and the blood of Jesus Christ His Son cleanses us from all sin" (1 John 1:7). The tabernacle is *open*. Do you understand what is going on? We are at the high point of the Tribulation in Revelation 15—ready for the sickle to cut the grapes down and squash them. What does God do just before He does that? He opens the tabernacle and says, "I am accessible; My presence is open; My forgiveness is available." What a God of mercy we have!

Element four—the way of guidance by God. "Then the cloud covered the tabernacle of meeting, and the glory of the LORD filled the tabernacle. And Moses was not able to enter the tabernacle of meeting, because the cloud rested above it, and the glory of the LORD filled the tabernacle. Whenever the cloud was taken up from above the tabernacle, the children of Israel would go onward in all their journeys. But if the cloud was not taken up, then they did not journey till the day that it was taken up. For the cloud of the LORD was above the tabernacle by day, and fire was over it by night, in the sight of all the house of Israel, throughout all their journeys" (Exodus 40:34–38).

Jesus wants to guide us. The tabernacle of the testimony opens in heaven and God is saying, "This is the way! Do you want out of this mess? Look up! Follow Me!" Of course, people won't, even though He continues to offer: "I am the light of the world. He who follows Me shall not walk in darkness, but have the light of life" (John 8:12).

Element five—the way of protection from God. "Then the Philistines took the ark of God and brought it from Ebenezer to Ashdod.... They brought it into the house of Dagon and set it by Dagon. And when the people ... arose ..., there was Dagon, fallen on its face ... before the ark of the LORD. So they took Dagon and set it in its place again. And ... the next morning, there was Dagon, fallen on its face ... before the ark of the Lord. The head of Dagon and both the palms of its hands were broken off on the threshold; only Dagon's torso was left of it" (1 Samuel 5:1–4). The Philistines got the message that God's ark was the sign of God's protection of His people because He started smiting the Philistines wherever they took the ark.

Jesus promised us His care: "And I give them eternal life, and they shall never perish; neither shall anyone snatch them out of My hand" (John 10:28). That is why we need to tell people how to get God's mark—the seal of the Holy Spirit—so that they are not eternally separated from God's presence.

Element six—the way of cleansing with God. "And he shall bring his trespass offering to the LORD.... The priest shall make atonement for him with the ram of the trespass offering before the LORD for his sin.... And the sin which he has committed shall be forgiven him" (Leviticus 19:21–22).

Jesus has opened the way for us: "Let us draw near with a true heart in full assurance of faith, having our hearts sprinkled from an evil conscience and our bodies washed with pure water" (Hebrews 10:22).

Element seven—the way of blessings from God. "Delight yourself in the LORD; and I will cause you to ride on the high hills of the earth, and feed you with the heritage of Jacob your father" (Isaiah 58:14).

Jesus alone offers the overflowing life: "I have come that they may have life, and that they may have it more abundantly" (John 10:10). God says, "As long as you will come and worship Me at My tabernacle, I will rain My blessings on you—for I came to give you an abundant life. If you won't come, however, I will withhold those blessings" (see Zechariah 14:17).

The next verse, Revelation 15:6, can be summarized in three words—*Jesus is holy*: "And out of the temple came the seven angels having the seven plagues, clothed in pure bright linen, and having their chests girded with golden bands." These angels are dressed like Old Testament priests, symbolizing the holiness of Jesus.

The final verse of this passage, Revelation 15:7, can also be summarized in just three words—*Jesus is eternal*: "Then one of the four living creatures gave to the seven angels seven golden bowls full of the wrath of God who lives forever and ever." Jesus is God the Son—and He is eternal.

Do you know this holy, eternal Jesus? Are you worshiping Him in the beauty of holiness?

FRIDAY: Jesus Christ is Wrathful

The temple was filled with smoke *from the glory of God and from His power, and no one was able to enter the temple till the seven plagues of the seven angels were completed.*

—Revelation 15:8

This is one of the saddest points in Scripture! At the end of Revelation 15, Christ has run out of patience. Thus, there is something new in verse 8. There has always been a glory cloud, but never smoke. Smoke showed up on Mount Sinai because the law speaks of judgment, but never in the tabernacle or temple—except here, because God's mercy has ended. The smoke indicates that the way to the presence of God is now closed: the way of forgiveness, guidance, cleansing, and blessing is over, and no one henceforth can enter.

Some day soon it will be too late, just as it was in the days of Noah: "Then the LORD saw that the wickedness of man was great in the earth . . . and He was grieved in His heart. So the LORD said, 'I will destroy man whom I have created . . . , both man and beast, creeping thing and birds of the air, for I am sorry that I have made them'" (Genesis 6:5–7).

The smoke in Revelation 15:8 portrays God's judgment. He is basically saying, as He did in Luke 12:20: "Fool! This night your soul will be required of you; then whose will those things be which you have provided?" I pray that you will not be among those who hear Christ exclaim: "Fool!"—and face eternal separation from the One who created you, died for you, and yearns for you to be with Him forever!

For Christians, the greatest day of our lives will be the day when we stand alone in front of Jesus Christ and look up at Him, the One who will forever bear in His body the marks of the price of our redemption, and have Him assess our life publicly. Then we will await what we long for—His looking at us and saying: "Well done, good and faithful servant!"

Martin Luther, the great reformer, made a statement that I just can't get out of my mind: "I have but two dates on my calendar: today and the day of the judgment seat of Christ!" He said that was what kept him going on translating the Bible into the vernacular and the language of his people. And that is what inspired him to continue as he stood all alone against the whole religious world. Oh, how God has used him to actually alter the course of history from a human perspective. And all because he had just two dates on his calendar!

Is your life any more complicated than that? Do you want to accomplish something? Do you want to have a life like Martin Luther's that is still powerful after many years? Then live the simple life of two dates on your calendar: today, living for Jesus because you have a second date on your calendar—the day you are going to stand in front of Him.

Are you getting ready to appear at Christ's throne? When we take pilgrims to Greece, the most moving spot of all is in the city of ancient Corinth. I have seen travelers who were just "tourists" for the whole trip until they reached that spot. But there beneath the raised stone platform, called in Greek the *bema*, suddenly the awesomeness of the moment overtakes them and they see themselves at a future day standing before Christ's throne. Often tears, even deep silence, and always reverence, fill each one as the scene unfolds before their eyes.

Jesus said: "Whoever desires to save his life will lose it, but whoever loses his life for My sake will find it" (Matthew 16:25). The real victory is not to prudently preserve our life as long as possible. Rather, as martyred Jim Elliott once said, we ought to "give what we cannot keep, to gain what we cannot lose."

SATURDAY: Resting in the Beauty of Jesus

For we are the circumcision, who worship God in the Spirit, rejoice in Christ Jesus, and have no confidence in the flesh.

—Philippians 3:3

To worship is to change. Because heaven is the worship center of the universe, to get ready to appear before Christ's throne you need to learn to worship Jesus as He deserves. For worship and praise are our duty and purpose of existence. The Father therefore seeks that we ascribe to Christ the honor, praise, glory, and majesty of which He is worthy—His true "worthship." Just as worship begins in holy expectancy, true worship ends in holy obedience. If worship does not propel us into greater obedience, it has not been worship. To stand before the Holy One of eternity is to change.

Understanding the nature of worship leads to very practical applications in our lives. For example, resentments cannot be held with the same tenacity when we enter into Christ's gracious light. As Jesus says, we need to leave our gift at the altar and go set the matter straight (Matthew 5:23–24). In worship an increased power steals its way into the heart sanctuary and an increased compassion grows in the soul.

Holy obedience saves worship from becoming an opiate, an escape from the pressing needs of modern life. Worship enables us to hear the call to serve clearly so that we respond, "Here am I! Send me" (see Isaiah 6:1–8).

Make a choice to live in hope. As you meditate on the beauty of Jesus—the splendor of His redeeming love shown through His perfect patience, holiness, redemption, justice, and wrath—you will find living hope that spills over into the worship that He longs for! In doing so, you can rest in His beauty that will fill your soul to overflowing and transform you by His power so that earth's dark shadows flee as you steadily gaze on Jesus, the brightness of the Father's glory!

WEEK 36
Rejoice That You Have Christ

{ Revelation 16 }

As the end of days approaches, you can find hope as you rejoice that you have Christ!

SUNDAY: Life Without Jesus

*"Then He will also say to those on the left hand, '**Depart from Me, you cursed**, into the everlasting fire prepared for the devil and his angels.'"*
—Matthew 25:41

Have you ever wondered what the world would be like without Jesus? Perhaps you yourself are seeking, but haven't found. You are considering, but haven't decided. You are looking, but haven't placed your heart's desire on Jesus Christ and willfully chosen to follow Him. If that is your situation, pay close attention to the sixteenth chapter of Revelation, which shows what life without Jesus Christ would be like. It is the most graphic, vivid, powerful description in the Scriptures of what hell will be like. Life apart from Jesus Christ is nothing less than a living hell.

In the twenty-one dramatic verses of Revelation 16, John sees and records what happens when mankind joins the fallen angels in living without God. He wants us to see that the seven bowls of His wrath are the coming results for a world that rejects what Jesus alone can give them. These seven bowls will be described in the devotionals this week.

In the final days, mankind's unending fight with God will at last bring them the freedom they have always wanted—life without God. What does life become without God? That is what we will see as we go through the sixteenth chapter of Revelation. By this point in the Tribulation, the end has come. In a very brief span of time, the long-awaited moment has arrived. In seven swift strokes the desire of a world wanting no part of Jesus is granted. These seven bowls of plagues are for the lost; Revelation 16 is no less than a foretaste of hell. Think of how the earth dwellers will feel as they begin their inescapable plunge toward hell!

For the redeemed, however, the glory of Jesus shines from each plague. Jesus offers the ultimate security in contrast to the utter insecurity of the earth dwellers. Revelation 16 is an art gallery with seven divinely inspired portraits of Christ. Against the darkened screen of His wrath poured out upon sin are seven glowing pictures of Jesus:

1. **Jesus has sanctifying power (vv. 1–2).** He is the One who cleanses and keeps (Jude 23–24). Have you let Him sanctify and clean you from the inside out? I am not talking about just

turning over a new leaf, making promises you can't keep, but letting Him thoroughly change you from the inside out. That is Christianity.

2. **Jesus has life-giving power (v. 3).** He is the One who gives abundant life (John 10:10).
3. **Jesus has satisfying power (vv. 4–7).** He is the One who promises that we will never thirst (John 7:37–39). Are you thirsting because of sin?
4. **Jesus has liberating power (vv. 8–9).** He is the One who sets us free (John 8:31–36).
5. **Jesus has enlightening power (vv. 10–11).** He is the One who gives us daily light and true spiritual sight (John 8:12; Acts 26:18).
6. **Jesus has conquering power (vv. 12–16).** He is the One who will always lead you into triumph (2 Corinthians 2:14).
7. **Jesus has securing power (vv. 17–21).** He is the One who gives you your ultimate eternal security (Romans 8:31–39; Hebrews 7).

Are you worshiping Jesus for His sanctifying and life-giving power? Have you been set free from sin? Do you let Jesus give you daily light in His Word? Are you following Him? Have you received His security through faith? I hope that you can answer each of these probing questions with a resounding "Yes!"

My Prayer for You This Week: *Dear Father, as we think about the last moments of human history, we are amazed to see repeated blasphemy and hardened hearts. It is blatant during the Tribulation, but more subdued in our present world. But those who have heard the good news of Jesus, and yet have rejected and hardened their hearts, are actually blaspheming You in the same way as these at the end of the Tribulation will do. We thank You that You so loved that You gave, and You gave so much that You emptied the very treasure of heaven—the Lord Jesus Christ sent to earth for sinful mankind. Lord, we pray that we will see Your power and draw upon You by allowing Your Spirit to minister the power of Jesus in our lives. In the name of Jesus we pray. Amen.*

MONDAY: Jesus Has Sanctifying and Life-Giving Power

*Then I heard a loud voice from the temple saying to the seven angels, "Go and pour out the bowls of the wrath of God on the earth." So **the first** went and **poured out his bowl** upon the earth, and a foul and loathsome sore came upon the men who had the mark of the beast and those who worshiped his image. Then **the second** angel **poured out his bowl** on the sea, and it became blood as of a dead man; and every living creature in the sea died.*

—REVELATION 16:1–3

In this passage, we find that the world without Jesus is decaying and corrupting. Since Jesus is the One who cleanses and keeps, corruption and decay do not have to occur, for He *is able to keep you from stumbling, and to present you faultless before the presence of His glory with exceeding joy* (Jude 24). As the first bowl is released, look at what happens to those who have spurned Christ.

The First Bowl—Malignant Sores. This judgment reveals the horrors of locked hearts. As someone once said, "Perhaps the most terrible situation in life, is when Almighty God is powerless to gain an entry into the citadel of the human heart . . . for God has given men the terrible responsibility of being able to lock their hearts against Him."[1]

In the first bowl, malignant sores will thus ooze out the unmitigated corruption, the filth of unrepentant souls (see also Exodus 15:26; 23:25; Deuteronomy 32:39). God will let everyone see on the outside what they are really like on the inside. This is the fulfillment of Moses' prophecy of Deuteronomy 28:27, 35: *"The LORD will strike you with the boils of Egypt, with tumors, with the scab, and with the itch, from which you cannot be healed. . . . The LORD will strike you . . . from the sole of your foot to the top of your head"*

Einstein once said, "It is easier to denature plutonium than to denature the evil spirit of man." Judgment will not produce repentance because only God's kindness does: "Do you despise the riches of His goodness, forbearance, and longsuffering, not knowing that the goodness of God leads you to repentance?" (Romans 2:4).

Jesus has sanctifying power. What is the lesson in Revelation 16:1–2 for the Christian ? Only Jesus has the power to cleanse us on the inside and keep us. At the end of verse two, those who have the mark of the beast will ooze corruption. In contrast, out of those who have the seal of the Holy Spirit will flow love, joy, peace, longsuffering, kindness, goodness, faithfulness, gentleness, and self-control (Galatians 5:22–23).

The Second Bowl—the Sea of Death. This sea of death in Revelation 6:3 will affect the world's food chains and hydrological cycle. From time to time, off the coast of California and elsewhere, a phenomenon known as "the red tide" occurs. These red tides kill millions of fish and poison those who eat contaminated shellfish. In 1998, one of these red tides hit Hong Kong. First the water turned yellow, but by midsummer it was thick and viscous with countless billions of dinoflagellates, tiny one-celled organisms. Miles of stinking fish fouled the beaches. Much marine life was wiped out, even bait used by fishermen died on the hooks. Eventually the red tide subsided, only to appear again the following year. Eating fish contaminated by the tide produced severe symptoms caused by a potent nerve poison. An unchecked population explosion of toxic dinoflagellates would kill all the fish in the sea. The phenomenon is well known, but scientists do not know what causes the proliferation of these creatures or what normally limits it. This may not fully explain what will happen when the second vial is outpoured, but it certainly illustrates it.[2]

Jesus has life-giving power. As the Creator, He is the One who has the power to say, "Fear not!" Jesus, as the Good Shepherd, says in John 10:10: "I have come that they may have life, and that they may have it more abundantly." Christianity (being born again and receiving Jesus Christ) is no less than abundant life. It is an utter internal transformation from the inside out and produces life "more abundantly"— it just overflows.

In Revelation 16:3 we see that without Jesus there is death and hopelessness, but with Jesus we have life-giving power from the One who gives abundant life. Those who come to Christ live according to the power of an endless life: no death, no decay, no destruction, no lifelessness.

TUESDAY: Jesus Has Satisfying Power

*Then **the third angel poured out his bowl** on the rivers and springs of water, and they became blood. And I heard the angel of the waters saying: "You are righteous, O Lord, the One who is and who was and who is to be, because You have judged these things. For they have shed the blood of saints and prophets, and You have given them blood to drink. For it is their just due." And I heard another from the altar saying, "Even so, Lord God Almighty, true and righteous are Your judgments."*
—Revelation 16:4–7

Have you ever given thought to how important water is, and what will happen when every drop of water on the planet turns to blood?

Water is the wonder fluid; for a liquid that is colorless, tasteless, odorless, and calorie free, water packs a punch. It is the only substance necessary to all life. Many organisms can live without oxygen, but none we know of can live without water. Life, and life to come, can both be reduced to a simple common denominator: no known life-form on earth can exist without water. And no life-form will ever be able to exist in eternity without Jesus, the Water of Life.

Water comes closest to being the universal solvent. While you drink from a tumbler, the water is busily dissolving molecules from your glass. It travels upward in defiance of gravity. So strongly do water molecules adhere to one another that when one evaporates from the leaf of a tree, it pulls up those behind, like links of a chain. This molecular attraction forms the surface film on which water bugs race without wetting their feet, and which permits you to float a darning needle atop a glass of water. The average American uses eighty-seven gallons a day to drink, cook, bathe, and wash. One hundred twenty gallons are needed to produce one hen's egg, and thirty-five hundred gallons are needed for a steak. With these indirect uses, our daily need soars to some two thousand gallons each. Four trillion gallons of precipitation falls on the United States each day, yet we use a mere tenth of it. None is lost: the water that John used for baptizing Jesus still exists—its billions of molecules are now dispersed around the world.

God gives an unbelieving world a graphic picture. No water—no life. Why? To portray the spiritual truth that only Jesus satisfies; only He can give the Water of Life! To not thirst can only mean that we come to Him. For that reason, Revelation ends with a call—the last gospel invitation. The Bible begins with God seeking us and it ends the same way: "Let him who thirsts come. Whoever desires, let him take the water of life freely" (Revelation 22:17).

The Third Bowl—Poisoned Waters. God is saying to a world that is plunging toward destruction: "Have you in your heart experienced the thirst that comes without Christ? Have you come to the place where you desire to have Him? Then take Christ, the Water of Life, freely!" And to the very end of the Scriptures God offers salvation. Yet, even in churches today, there are some who have never said yes to Jesus Christ and submitted to Him. They have not acknowledged that they are lost apart from Him and are thus without hope.

Hell is a place where people will have eternally unsatisfied desires for drugs, alcohol, and sex. However, those desires will be multiplied without the means to satisfy them. They will live forever in the blackness of darkness, in a bottomless pit, suffering fire with those desires just eating them up from the inside out. This is the unending consuming worm of hell— the lusts accumulated over a lifetime.

Only Jesus Christ can satisfy your righteous desires or take away the wrong ones to replace them with a spring of fresh water so that you no longer desire the saltwater of this world: "My soul thirsts for God, for the living God" (Psalm 42:2). Only Jesus can satisfy your soul; only God can quench your thirst.

Jesus has satisfying power. In Revelation 16:4–7 we see that life without Jesus is endless thirst, but Jesus has the power to satisfy us so that we will never thirst: *"If anyone thirsts, let him come to Me and drink. He who believes in Me, . . . out of his heart will flow rivers of living water"* (John 7:37–38).

I am reminded of the fastest-growing segment of cyberspace: the thirst-inducing segment. Did you know that lust and all the accompanying products that develop lust in human beings (as in pornography and all its deviances) is like a thirsting person in the desert drinking saltwater, hoping to stop his thirst? The more he drinks, the thirstier he becomes. It is a self-destructive pattern. Jesus says, "If you are not in Me, you will have nothing but endless thirst." In Christ, we will be constantly satisfied by Jesus and never experience such endless thirst.

WEDNESDAY: Jesus Has Liberating Power

*Then **the fourth angel poured out his bowl** on the sun, and power was given to him to scorch men with fire. And men were scorched with great heat, and they blasphemed the name of God who has power over these plagues; and they did not repent and give Him glory.*
—Revelation 16:8–9

The last words of the Old Testament pronounce a doom upon those who won't allow Jesus to be their Sun of Righteousness: *"'For behold, the day is coming, . . . and all the proud, yes, all who do wickedly will be stubble. And the day which is coming shall burn them up,' says the LORD of hosts, 'that will leave them neither root nor branch. But to you who fear My name the Sun of Righteousness shall arise with healing in His wings'"* (Malachi 4:1–2).

Jesus is either the Sun of Righteousness who heals you or the One who will burn you to stubble. The choice is yours. What is your response to Jesus Christ? Have you come to Him to heal your sin-sick soul and to give you eternal life? Or are you turning away from Him and willingly hardening your heart by locking its door to keep Jesus out (Revelation 3:20)? He will consume you if you do, and you will experience a foretaste of it in the emptiness of life right now.

The Fourth Bowl—The Ultimate Sunburn. Every year, around a million people are diagnosed with skin cancer in America, most of which is caused from an overexposure to the sun's rays. Yet people still lay out in the sun. Similarly, when God causes a solar fire to scorch all the earth dwellers, they will stubbornly face the sun's heat rather than repent. So they will curse Almighty God instead.

Listen to what John Phillips has to say in *Exploring Revelation* about Revelation 16:8–9:

The sun, in its normal state, pours out a continuous stream of high-energy particles which race toward the Earth at a peak speed of three million miles an hour. The earth is surrounded by a field of radiation, the magnetosphere, which protects it from full exposure to this deadly assault.

God who created the sun and the Lord Jesus who lit that solar furnace will turn the thermostat up during this time of the Tribulation. Everyone will find that the earth is a prison house and they are going to be trapped. This will be much like when irresponsible parents leave their child locked in the car and the heat inside builds up and incapacitates or even kills the child. God is going to let this planet become a locked prison house and it is going to get hotter and hotter until people are scorched.[3]

So Jesus, who can free men from doom and liberate them from damnation, will *still* be rejected. What a contrast of choices—to be burned up or blessed beyond description! Have you made your choice?

Jesus has liberating power. Without Jesus, life on earth is a burning prison house (Revelation 16:8–9). But He has the power to set the prisoner free, and "if the Son makes you free, you shall be free indeed" (John 8:36; see also 8:31–35). This is what is wonderful about Christ—He liberates us and breaks the power of sin. However, the world doesn't want Jesus, and so they are imprisoned.

To all who look to Him, Jesus is liberator in three powerful ways: (1) He leads us in triumph (2 Corinthians 2:14); (2) He crucifies our flesh so that we can die daily to self (Galatians 2:20; 1 Corinthians 15:31); and (3) He washes (KJV) and releases (NASB) us from our sins (Revelation 1:5). Are you in the triumphal procession? Are you dying daily to your flesh? When you fall, do you let Him wash you?

THURSDAY: Jesus Has Enlightening Power

> Then **the fifth angel poured out his bowl** on the throne of the beast, and his kingdom became full of darkness; and they gnawed their tongues because of the pain. They blasphemed the God of heaven because of their pains and their sores, and did not repent of their deeds.
> —Revelation 16:10–11

The next plague is strikingly similar to the ninth plague upon Egypt in Exodus 10:21–29. They will taste the blackness of hell forever. There is one thing that people don't realize about hell: it is not only fire but also dark fire—it is blackness of darkness. Many times when I preached in the bar districts of southern mill towns, those men would tell me that they would be with their friends in hell. I told them that they would not see their friends there. It will be blackness of darkness: the ultimate loneliness, forever falling in the bottomless pit, with black fire consuming you on the inside and outside.

The Fifth Bowl—Utter Darkness. The bowls will be poured out over a very quick period of time, maybe a month or less. Here, people will still have their sores from the first bowl, and they can smell the dead fish and sea creatures from the oceans and waterways. When they run water to wash off their sores, they will find blood coming out of their faucets. And while they deal with that, the blazing heat will come. And now they will experience absolute darkness and pain.

According to Ray Stedman, the scope of this bowl of judgment is limited to the realm of the beast—or the revived Roman Empire of Western Europe. This judgment involves a great part of the earth, causing a sudden and unexplainable darkness to fall. Steadman writes:

> This is not the first time such a phenomenon has occurred. In the middle of the day on May 19, 1780, the entire region of New England was covered by darkness—a day which has become fixed in New England history as The Dark Day. The mysterious blackout lasted for several hours.
>
> In the early afternoon of March 19, 1886, a similar zone of darkness moved across central Wisconsin, causing the sky to turn from a bright cloud-dappled blue to midnight black in the space of about a minute. This darkness blanketed several villages and towns to the west of Lake Winnebago and lasted about ten minutes. Similar unexplained occurrences of sudden darkness have occurred in Memphis, Tennessee (December 1904), Louisville, Kentucky (March 1911), and other places and times in the United States and around the world. All of these events have two things in common: (1) no one was ever able to explain these events in terms of a known phenomenon such as an eclipse, and (2) most of the people who experienced these events were filled with terror, believing the end of the world had come.
>
> The events in the sky or beyond the sky, which caused these midday nightfall's, might have been the same as that which caused three hours of darkness during the crucifixion of Christ.[4]

In all these earlier events of unexplained darkness, most of the people believed that the end of the world was upon them. They soon discovered that was not true, but when the fifth bowl is poured out, there will be no doubt in the minds of the earth dwellers that the end has indeed come—and yet they still will not repent. Note three penetrating truths:

1. **Closed hearts face judgment.** Those who would not embrace the true Light of the World will now face the horrors of absolute darkness. But those who would embrace the true Light of the World—trusting, embracing, and receiving Christ as the Light of Salvation—will never be in impenetrable darkness!
2. **The most horrible judgment is the blackness of darkness in hell.** Jesus stands in the way and only you can turn Him down or take Him in.
3. **Jesus is light and salvation.** Do you seek His light? Do you walk in His light?

I can't emphasize this enough: the most horrible judgment of all is associated with the hopelessness that the blackness of darkness brings. Egypt's plagues parallel the final judgment of God: the death angel came after the blackness (Exodus 10:21–29; see also Joel 2:2, 10; Amos 5:18, 20; Zephaniah 1:15). Jesus warned of the ultimate judgment, and that the plagues on Egypt (Exodus) and the day of the Lord (Revelation 6–19) were only a foretaste of the horrors to come (see Matthew 8:12; 13:42, 50; 22:15; 24:29, 50; 25:30; 2 Peter 2:4; Jude 13). Where is the hope in all this?

Jesus has enlightening power. Since closed hearts face judgment, hope is found by opening your heart to Christ. In Revelation 16:10–11, we see that Jesus has the power to give daily light and true spiritual sight (John 8:12; Acts 26:18). Because judgment in hell is blackest darkness, you can choose to avoid it by meeting and embracing Jesus, who is light and salvation.

Without Jesus there is impenetrable darkness. Because *"men loved darkness rather than light, because their deeds were evil,"* God now lets the world experience what they want. The impenetrable darkness causes them to chew and gnaw on their own tongues. They are in such pain that they can do nothing but inflict more pain on themselves because of the horror.

With Jesus, there is endless enlightening power from the One Who gives us daily light and true spiritual sight. In Acts 26:17-18, Jesus said in His appearance to Saul (Paul): "I will deliver you from the Jewish people, as well as from the Gentiles, to whom I now send you, to open their eyes, in order to turn them from darkness to light, and from the power of Satan to God, that they may receive forgiveness of sins and an inheritance among those who are sanctified by faith in Me." That is the power of Jesus!

In light of all this, and the terrifying results if you make the wrong choice, I exhort you to prayerfully examine yourself to see if you have really opened your heart's door to Christ!

FRIDAY: Jesus Has Conquering Power

*Then **the sixth angel poured out his bowl** on the great river Euphrates, and its water was dried up, so that the way of the kings from the east might be prepared. And I saw three unclean spirits like frogs coming out of the mouth of the dragon, out of the mouth of the beast, and out of the mouth of the false prophet. For they are spirits of demons, performing signs, which go out to the kings of the earth and of the whole world, to gather them to the battle of that great day of God Almighty. "Behold, I am coming as a thief. Blessed is he who watches, and keeps his garments, lest he walk naked and they see his shame." And they gathered them together to the place called in Hebrew, Armageddon.*
—Revelation 16:12-16

The Sixth Bowl—Called to Armageddon. The time has come for the fighting of that final war of the age, the name of which has become a byword among men since John first wrote it down—Armageddon! God has chosen the Holy Land as the stage upon which two crucial events take place, one on a mountain, and one on a plain. Mount Calvary and the Plain of Megiddo are the two altars of sacrifice that dominate the history of the world.[5]

What will draw all the nations of the world into the area of Armageddon? They will gather themselves there for perhaps various reasons. It would seem that the following are of the more important reasons.

The Sovereignty of God: In at least five distinct passages, we are told that God Himself will gather the nations here: Isaiah 34:2; Joel 3:2; Zechariah 14:2; Zephaniah 3:8; and Revelation 16:16 (because of the deception of Satan [Revelation 16:13-14]).

Three special unclean spirits will trick the nations into gathering at Armageddon because of their devilish hatred of Christ (Psalm 2:1-3; Revelation 11:18). The nations, led by Antichrist, will doubtless realize the imminent return of Christ (Revelation 11:15; 12:12). They will also be aware of

His touching down on the Mount of Olives (Zechariah 14:4; Acts 1:9–12). Thus, it is not unreasonable to assume that they will gather in that area to destroy Him at the moment of His return to earth!

The Destruction of Jerusalem: Their end is **inescapable**. Their defeat is **ultimate**. Our King is **unconquerable**. Perhaps the saddest event during the Tribulation will be the siege and destruction of the Holy City. This will be the forty-seventh and last takeover of the beloved city of David. Consider what Jesus said in Luke 21:20: "But when you see Jerusalem surrounded by armies, then know that its desolation is near" (see also Zechariah 12:2 and 14:2). Christ saw a near and far fulfillment in this verse. In A.D. 70 the early church remembered this verse and fled to Pella so that none were trapped in the city. But Matthew 24 shows that Christ's words stretch far beyond this to the final siege and attack of God's chosen people of promise—the Jews. When these two events transpire, both the angels in paradise and the demons in perdition will surely hold their breath.

Jesus has conquering power. In Revelation 16:12–16, we see that without Jesus there is only enslavement to demon masters because these demons trick and lure people. The Scriptures say that all idols are demons. I find it very interesting that there are not many world religions—only many facets of Satan's kingdom. Every false religion in the world has demons behind it. There is only ONE revelation of the truth of Jesus Christ: everything else (even the ones who smile on TV and are family friendly) are inspired by demons. Only Jesus has the conquering power to always lead us into triumph (2 Corinthians. 2:14). The way for someone to keep from getting the mark of the beast is to be sealed by the Holy Spirit.

Are you experiencing the triumph of Christ? When I take groups to the Holy Land and we go to the Plain of Megiddo, I always say the same thing: "Most of you who are here will probably never come back again on a bus. But all of you are going to come back on a horse." The Scriptures say that the whole world will converge there. The earth dwellers, following their demon masters, will surround Jerusalem from Megiddo all the way past Jerusalem down into the region below the Dead Sea. Those hundreds of millions of people will try to fight against God; and at that climactic moment the sky will split and the King of Kings—Jesus Christ—will come on a white horse! And all of us will be coming behind Him flying through the air! You and I will have an aerial view, coming in behind the greatest leader of all time, the great tour guide, Jesus Christ himself, as He comes down to speak a word and incinerate that army of hundreds of millions.

Zechariah 12:10 tells us exactly what will happen: "And I will pour on the house of David and on the inhabitants of Jerusalem the Spirit of grace and supplication; then they will look on Me whom they pierced. Yes, they will mourn for Him as one mourns for his only son, and grieve for Him as one grieves for a firstborn."

Zechariah 14:12–13 says that He is coming though the air and, as He comes, He will stand on the Mount of Olives, which is the Second Coming proper. The mount then splits in two: "And this shall be the plague with which the LORD will strike all the people who fought against Jerusalem: Their flesh shall dissolve while they stand on their feet [they start melting], their eyes shall dissolve in their sockets, and their tongues [speaking blasphemous things against God] shall dissolve in their mouths. It shall come to pass in that day that a great panic from the LORD will be among them."

Christians, however, are more than conquerors! Remember: we are assured of victory in Jesus "who always leads us in triumph in Christ" (2 Corinthians 2:14). So in verses 12–16 of Revelation 16, Jesus has conquering power as the One who always leads us into triumph.

What kind of response should we have to this truth? We need to establish the right priorities—God's! For God offers us an unshakable kingdom (Hebrews 12:25–29). So don't put your treasures where they are going to be destroyed, because Jesus has called us to have an unwavering focus (2 Peter 3:10–18).

The end is coming. The world is going to fall apart. Mankind and life as we now know it will soon cease to exist. So what does God want now that we are listening to His Revelation? He wants us to worship His Son!

SATURDAY: Jesus Has Securing Power

*Then **the seventh angel poured out his bowl** into the air, and a loud voice came out of the temple of heaven, from the throne, saying, "It is done!" And there were noises and thunderings and lightnings; and there was a great earthquake, such a mighty and great earthquake as had not occurred since men were on the earth. Now the great city was divided into three parts, and the cities of the nations fell. And great Babylon was remembered before God, to give her the cup of the wine of the fierceness of His wrath. Then every island fled away, and the mountains were not found. And great hail from heaven fell upon men, each hailstone about the weight of a talent. Men blasphemed God because of the plague of the hail, since that plague was exceedingly great.*

—REVELATION 16:17–21

Against the rumble of the seventh bowl's massive quake comes the final glorious portrait of Christ!

The Seventh Bowl—A Massive Earthquake. As we study this mega-quake, the "Big One" that has long been feared, allow yourself to hold on to the immense and powerful security we have in Christ.

The judgments of Revelation 16:17–21 I take to be literal. What is described here is very possible with today's weapons. Other than the hail and lightning, the same effects would result from both hydrogen and plutonium bombs.

Have you ever looked at a map of the fault lines of the earth? Like an egg, God has cracked the earth just right for this moment. Note where they run: from Alaska to Chile, from Siberia to New Zealand, from the southern Mediterranean fanning out across the Mideast and then across Asia and south to the heart of Africa. When those tectonic plates move in one quake, the power of 20,000 nuclear bombs is unleashed. On December 26, 2004, the resultant tsunami from just one quake killed 150,000-plus souls. And in Pakistan and India, over 70,000 lost their lives in a quake in the fall of 2005. With more far-reaching devastation than that ahead, our ultimate security can only be found in Jesus.

Jesus has securing power. In verses 17–21 of Revelation 16, we see that without Jesus there can only be hopeless destruction. As the world converges on Jerusalem in Satan's last effort to destroy the Jews, God will convulse the earth and obliterate them with hailstones. But with

Jesus there is securing power from the One who gives us our ultimate eternal security (Romans 8:31–39; Hebrews 7).

On Mount Calvary, grace redeemed the world by the sacrifice of God's Son. On the plains of Megiddo vengeance offers up the armies of the world in a sacrifice of doom. Both are blood baths; both are the descent of wrath upon sin. And both are brought about by God's bitterest foes who, in spite of themselves, work out God's perfect and sovereign will. Across both Mount Calvary and the plains of Megiddo can be written the words of Peter: "The Gentiles and the people of Israel, were gathered together to do whatever Your hand and Your purpose determined before to be done" (Acts 4:27–28). From each of these bloodbaths proceeds a supper: one a feast of remembrance for the people of God, and the other a feast of retribution for the carrion.

Make a choice to live in hope. At Calvary there rang up to the gates of heaven a victorious cry, "It is finished!" And at Armageddon there rings down to earth an answering cry from the temple gates in glory, "It is done!"

Both events shake the earth—the quake of Matthew 27:51–54 at Christ's Resurrection and here in Revelation 16:18, the greatest quake of all time. Both events attack and conquer Satan's domain. At Christ's death the graves opened and saints were raised from death (contrary to Satan's power); in Revelation 16 the seven bowls will be poured out on the air—the present headquarters of Satan.

Both events represent a path: which are you on? One leads to the enduring hope of eternal bliss in the presence of your glorious Savior, Jesus Christ. The other leads to utter hopelessness and devastation with the ultimate destiny of eternal suffering in hell with the devil and his fallen angels—forever separated from the God who loved you and gave himself for you.

WEEK 37
Understand the True Bride of Jesus

{ Revelation 17 }

As the end of days approaches, you can find hope as you understand the true bride of Jesus!

SUNDAY: The True Bride of Jesus

*I am jealous for you with godly jealousy. For **I have betrothed you to one husband**, that I may present you as a chaste virgin to Christ.*

—2 CORINTHIANS 11:2

WEEK 37: UNDERSTAND THE TRUE BRIDE OF JESUS

In Revelation 17 we find the collapse of the apostate world's church. In the process we see Satan's harlot bride: the delusion of religion. From Eden onward, Satan has been building his church. Although Eve was tempted and fell into sin, she never joined the old serpent's assembly. Cain was Satan's first member (1 John 3:12), and that church has flourished ever since.

Today the church of Satan has many congregations. Whenever the God of Scripture is left out, there is only one other source of authority—Satan. Some followers meet in the ivory towers of academia where God is banished from education. Other congregations include those masses who ignore God altogether, and some even worship Satan directly. But the most insidious congregations meet in churches, synagogues, mosques, cathedrals, and temples where organized religion stresses the achievements of humans working their way to God. This "church of good works" promotes self-righteousness: "I will do it my way." When you join such a church, you are required to "follow the rules"—and hope that the good outweighs the bad in the balance of religions. This religion deceives mankind into thinking that there are many ways to God, and many gods to seek. Refusing to acknowledge that they were created in God's image, these followers create their god in their *own* image instead.

In the seventeenth chapter we see Satan's ongoing system of counterfeiting the true church, the true worship, and the true seeking of God. Revelation 17 can therefore be divided into these sections: Satan's plan **exposed** (vv.1–6); Satan's plan **explained** (vv. 7–15); and Satan's plan **extinguished** (vv. 16–18).

To pass off counterfeit money, I would not show you a blue twenty-dollar bill, because right away you could tell it is a fake. The best way to fool someone is to choose currency that looks as much like the genuine article as possible. Most who talk and think about Satan's church think of warlocks, witches, and human sacrifices. But I don't think he spends much time on that. His goal is not to make a "blue twenty-dollar bill" but to make one that looks exactly like the real thing. Therefore, Satan slyly represents the real thing as closely as possible while still having a deadly difference that is damnable. So when you think of Satan's church, don't be tricked into assuming that it simply involves Buddha, animists, and stone gods in the jungle. No, his church will also have Christ, the Bible, and words that are familiar to Christians. The deadly difference that is damnable is that the reality of the substitutionary work of Christ, and the essence of the gospel of grace, will be missing. That is Satan's counterfeit church.

Jesus came to seek and save the lost and make them His bride. He gave himself to purchase her from sin and damnation. Jesus ever lives as a Great High Priest to purify and cleanse His bride from all defilement. The true bride of Jesus is a pure and chaste virgin, washed in the blood of the Lamb, sealed by the Holy Spirit, and awaiting the day of marriage to Jesus.

Satan also has a bride. We meet her in Revelation 17. She is a drunken, licentious harlot. She is the full-grown woman of the Tower of Babel. She is the queen of heaven of the Old Testament. She is the mystery religion in the cults of the Near and Far East. She is the one-world church of the World Council of Churches and National Council of Churches of America. Nothing is more satanic and deceptive in the entire world than the ecumenical (one united) church movement. God hates religious deception! She is also the embodiment of a false Christianity, led by a false Christ and embodied in the image of the very mother of Jesus. That is why John was so shocked. No other beast in sixteen chapters of death, demonism, and destruction shocked him until he saw this false harlot bride.

My Prayer for You This Week: *Dear heavenly Father, bless us with Your enlightening power. Open our eyes to behold wonderful truths from Your Word. May the humility of Christ, the insights of Your Spirit, and Your blessed plan be present in our lives. As we increase in knowledge, may we not become puffed up with pride, but rather humbly receive Your engrafted Word that we may grow in Christlikeness. We pray that in Jesus' name and love we will go out to reach the world around us—the world that is dying without hope of the Savior. Help us to be constantly ready to step heavenward, and to know less of this world as our home and be more expectant of heaven. We pray all this in Jesus' precious name. Amen.*

MONDAY: Satan's Plan Exposed

And no wonder! For **Satan . . . transforms himself** *into an angel of light.*
— 2 Corinthians 11:14

The seventeenth chapter of Revelation describes the doom of the Babylonian system. This system is seen as a woman portrayed as a harlot. She seems to be a symbol of Satan's world religion. This chapter records the demise of the counterfeit church Satan founded at Eden—the one he has worked on ceaselessly ever since. The beast (Satan's incarnation as a false Jesus) finally destroys the apostate church and sets up unhindered satanic worship (via the beast and false prophet's work). To make this happen, Satan's ultimate goals in the world today are to forge global unity politically, religiously, and financially.

In Revelation 17, as God's Word unmasks the apostasy of false religions, we discover the true bride of Jesus. God reveals that the true bride is made up of His own saints who are *"called, chosen, and faithful"* (17:14). They are Christians who are called by God to salvation, chosen by God because He placed His love on us, and faithful to the One who called us. What a beautiful description of the church!

There is a very significant contrast between the two women of Revelation: God's saints are seen in Revelation 12 and Satan's church is revealed in Revelation 17. God's way is a narrow path, but Satan's way is a broad path. Yet both are seemingly headed in the same direction. God's way is narrow and straight—it is a hard path and few find it (Matthew 7:13–14). However, Satan's way is broad, and the path is easy and level. In fact, the devil gives you a nice little slant so you can coast along. In contrast, God's path is slanted upward, and it is difficult to climb.

God's way is exclusive, which is what bothers people so much. In fact, in a United Nations forum on global religion, the members discussed the bothersome exclusiveness of Christianity. In San Francisco there is now a group seeking to unite all the religions of the world. As they see it, a hindrance to such unity is the small part of religion in Christianity that they call "exclusive"—those who are devoutly committed to following God and His Word. The Bible, God, and His church with its so-called exclusiveness are thus continually attacked; satanic inclusiveness—where anybody can believe anything and go Satan's way—is lauded.

God's way is the true church; Satan's way is the false church. God has a true bride; Satan has a false bride. God says there is no other name under heaven whereby you must be saved. Satan says the way is ecumenical: Muslims, Mormons, and Jehovah's Witnesses believe in one god, so that is good; Hindus, down deep, don't believe in one god, but they believe in truth, so they are also good. They find a way for every belief to fit in, and that is called ecumenical inclusivism.

God says there is one way; Satan says there are many ways. God says that we are to look for a heavenly destination; most satanic, ecumenical religions put their focus on the earth. It is an earthly way, and most of the people in these religions are involved in preserving and worshiping the planet Earth.

God's way is Jerusalem; Satan's way is Babylon. God's way is the city of peace; Satan's way is the city of confusion.

God speaks in spiritual terms; Satan speaks in fleshly terms. God talks about an internal transformation; Satan talks about an external reformation. God is the God of Creation since He initiates; Satan is the god of evolution as things just somehow happen. God is a God of love; Satan is a god of hate.

In God we have spiritual worship that is invisible; no images are involved. Satan is always associated with idolatry. Look at even the self-professed, not-idolatrous Muslims: how do they worship? At the Kabala they worship massed around a black stone in Mecca. Spiritual worship is at the heart of God's true church; idolatry is at the heart of all earthly religions.

God's way is divine; Satan's way is humanistic. God's way leads to contentment; Satan's way always leads to covetousness. God's way is appropriated by faith; Satan's way is merely intellectually appropriated.

God's way is through the Spirit; Satan's way is through religious rituals and works. God's way put Christ on a cross of shame; Satan's way puts a crown of pride on men. God's way is a pure bride; Satan's way is a wicked, unfaithful, impure harlot.

Which way have you been following?

TUESDAY: Satan's Plan Explained

Now the Spirit expressly says that in latter times some will depart from the faith, giving heed to deceiving spirits and doctrines of demons.

—1 Timothy 4:1

Revelation 17 records the demise of Satan's church. He began building his church in the Garden of Eden in anticipation of the moment when he can install his false Christ at the head of it. At that time he will destroy the scaffolding that built the church. That is why there is going to be a complete break with organized religion sometime in the Tribulation. The most likely time is when the image is placed in the temple of the Jews. All the earth dwellers who were never converted (those never born again) are going to be shocked when the woman portrayed as a harlot is destroyed and the beast installs himself as Christ and demands to be worshiped. Basically, *the beast is Satan's incarnation as the false Jesus.*

Satan's ultimate goals in the world today are to forge global unity politically, religiously and financially. He doesn't care whether Antichrist is called Christ or Satan—just that he is worshiped instead of God. He is content to be called Buddha, Confucius, Mohammad, or any name at all as long as you are not worshiping the true God.

Satan is orchestrating a worldwide political unity (the seven heads of Revelation 17 speak of totality of rule). It is not the world that thought up the concept of the United Nations; Satan is behind the scenes working in men's minds and hearts to establish a one-world political unity: "All who dwell on the earth will worship him, whose names have not been written in the Book of Life of the Lamb slain from the foundation of the world [Satan is interested in a united earth]. . . . He causes all . . , to receive a mark on their right hand or on their foreheads, and that no one may buy or sell except one who has the mark or the name of the beast, or the number of his name" (Revelation 13:8, 16–17).

Satan desires worldwide financial and business unity. He is also looking for a worldwide financial organization (Revelation 13:17). Why is that so critical? Because the one who controls the purse strings is really in charge. This is very interesting: the more you study prophecy the more you realize that it won't be long before we will know who is really committed in the church. As soon as the government moves a little bit further, perhaps through an economic downturn or a non-linearity in the global economy, there are going to be some changes. When that happens, I am sure that church giving and similar kinds of donations will no longer be tax deductible. It will then be very unprofitable to be a Christian. Right now, it is very profitable for a lot of people; it will get you votes, and you are looked upon as good. But as soon as there is a financial, social, and political step back from Christianity, there will be fallout. Whenever it becomes politically incorrect to be a Christian, like it was for so many years in Eastern Europe, you will be denied privileges. Just as there have been racial barriers in this country, there will be religious barriers.

Satan desires worldwide spiritual and religious unity. This will be achieved as the beast is worshiped (Revelation 13:8, 11–12; 14:9; 16:2), the beast is beloved (Revelation 13:3), the beast is honored (Revelation 13:8), and the beast is confidently followed (Revelation 13:4).

Because Satan has to control the purse strings, there has to be a global financial system. When that happens, a political control will follow right behind, and then a worldwide religion to pull together this worship. That is what it says in Revelation 13:8a, 11–12: "All who dwell on the earth will worship him, . . . Then I saw another beast . . . And he exercises all the authority of the first beast . . . , and causes the earth and those who dwell in it to worship the first beast, whose deadly wound was healed."

The same concept of global worship appears in Revelation 14:9–10a: "If anyone worships the beast and his image, and receives his mark . . . , he himself shall also drink of the wine of the wrath of God." In Revelation 16:2 we see God's wrath being poured out on the First Church of Antichrist when "a foul and loathsome sore came upon the men who had the mark of the beast and those who worshiped his image."

This reminds me of a book by Peter Kreeft—*Ecumenical Jihad*, which I read in part. On the back cover, two well-known Christians recommend its reading. Do you know what the book is about?

Briefly stated, the author, a Dutch theologian, was out surfing, got hit on the head, and had an out-of-body experience and stepped into heaven. The first to supposedly greet him and shake his hand in heaven was Confucius. The theologian asked him, "What are you doing here?" Confucius explained that he believed in one God, too, and assured him that it was the same god. Then he met Buddha and was really shocked. Buddha told him that the four laws of Buddhism are exactly what he, the theologian, believed. After thinking about it, he answered Buddha saying, "Yes, I guess I do." Next, he met Mohammed and asked, "Mohammed, you are in heaven?" He said, "Yes, I believe in Mary, too." And I thought: *Okay, this must be a joke.* Then the theologian met Moses in this out-of-body experience in heaven. Moses reportedly informed him, "Yes, Buddha, Confucius, Mohammed, and a lot of other people are here because we all are seeking the same thing. We are seeking to worship Jesus and his mother."[1]

I shut the book right then. But as I shut it, on the back cover I noticed this recommendation by J. I. Packer: *"Catholics, Protestants, and Orthodox alike need to ponder Peter Kreeft's vision of things—preferably in discussion.* **What if he is right?**"[2]

To question whether something that God says is wrong—is *wrong*, and it is dangerous. For example, if parents tell their child no, that child shouldn't ask a question that directly controverts what they said because that is a rebellious response. So then, as God's children, we shouldn't ask if what Kreeft says is true because we already know it is not.

What Jesus promised is that this coming global church is not going to be a church of snake handlers and demon worshipers. It is going to be a church of purported Christ worshipers. Satan will form his First Church of Antichrist *in place of* Christ—not *against* Christ. Members will worship a convenient Christ—a Christ that anyone can believe in because he doesn't offend them.

Jesus said, "He who is not with Me is against Me" (Matthew 12:30a). There can be no neutrality in this conflict of the ages: you are either an earth dweller who will worship the Antichrist, or a pilgrim who will be raptured before the Tribulation to worship and enjoy the Lord God Almighty forever!

WEDNESDAY: Who Is the Woman on the Beast?

Then one of the seven angels who had the seven bowls came and talked with me, saying to me, "Come, I will show you **the judgment of the great harlot** *who sits on many waters."*
— REVELATION 17:1

The woman of chapter 17 is in great contrast to the woman of chapter 12, who is of God. There are several clear identifying marks of the harlot bride of Satan in Revelation 17. If you think with me, you will understand what the apostle John is talking about. As we compare current events to the Scriptures, it gives us a good illustration of what may be the Revelation 17 scenario.[3]

The harlot is the apostate church. I personally believe that the apostate church will be the Roman Catholic Church merged with all the world religions. You may not believe that they would ever do that, but they already are. That is the horror of this. Most Americans don't pay any attention to this fact, but everyone else in the world knows.

The woman is a harlot. "Then one of the seven angels who had the seven bowls came and talked with me, saying to me, 'Come, I will show you the judgment of the great harlot who sits on many waters'" (Revelation 17:1). A harlot (prostitute) is a woman who has promised, but not kept her promise. It is a woman without faithfulness in spiritual worship. She is a spiritual fornicator—the great whore "with whom the kings of the earth have committed fornication" (17:2).

In verse 3 we see that the woman of chapter 17 is ungodly: "I saw a woman sitting on a scarlet beast which was full of names of blasphemy, having seven heads and ten horns." The only thing that conspicuously qualifies here is the Vatican and the Roman Catholic Church. A newspaper article reported that in 1986 the leaders of the world's major religions gathered together with Pope John Paul II in Assisi, Italy.[4] In addition to an immense group of Protestant religious leaders, those present with all their objects of worship included snake worshipers, fire worshipers, spiritists, animists, Buddhists, Muslims, Hindus, and North American Indian witch doctors. They all came to pray for peace. The Buddhists were allowed to place a drape over the altar of the Catholic church, add their little idols of Buddha, and worship. After the Buddhists took that down, the witch doctors were permitted to come in and dance around in their trance as they called out to their great spirit god. Next were the fire worshipers, the animists, and then all the pagan worshipers with the Dali Lama. The gathering allowed every religious group to come and worship as they saw fit because they said, "We are all seeking the same god."

This is the only thing that was true in the whole article: they are all seeking the same god—and that is the problem. The god of this world is not sought on an altar that is given over to snakes, fire, images, great spirit gods, and occult trances. There is only one entity that has continuously sought and conspicuously promoted spiritual fornication, and that is the ecumenical movement that shows up in many world religions, including the Roman Catholic Church. After 1986, Pope John Paul II sought to gather every religious leader of the world, and he found them all willing to make a pilgrimage to his doorstep.

The harlot wears purple and scarlet. This woman is not only a harlot and a woman, she "was arrayed in purple and scarlet" (17:4a). If you have ever watched any of these religious enclaves on the news, purple and scarlet is another identifier pointing to Rome whose external precious treasures of spiritual trappings are to make her beautiful. Purple and scarlet are the colors of the cardinals and the Roman religious system; they are also the two colors of the Roman Empire.

In the ancient world, purple was the most valuable and exquisite material for making clothing. Because it was so costly, only the Caesars and the very wealthy could afford it. That is why they threw a purple robe on Jesus—to make fun of Him; they hit Him with a stick because they knew He could never afford such a robe. It was all a big joke to them. The Roman Catholic Church is conspicuous in the external precious treasures—the spiritual trappings. The first floor's artwork in St. Peter's Cathedral is incalculable in its value. Some of those sculptures are forty feet high and twenty feet wide. They are worth hundreds of millions of dollars, and St. Peter's Cathedral is just one of thousands of buildings and businesses owned by the Roman Catholic Church around the world.

The harlot is wealthy beyond calculation. She is "adorned with gold and precious stones and pearls" (17:4b). No religious institution, past or present, even comes close to possessing the incalculable wealth of the Roman Catholic Church, which is estimated in the trillions of dollars by some Italian newspapers. Do you remember what Peter said? "Silver and gold I do not have, but what I do have I give you: In the name of Jesus . . . ." (Acts 3:6). In contrast, the Roman Church says, "Silver and gold? I have lots of it! And you can't come in the name of Jesus anymore!" See how things have changed? This woman, the harlot, is wearing purple and scarlet and has wealth beyond description.

The harlot is a city that sits on seven hills. "The seven heads are seven mountains on which the woman sits" (17:9). John was shocked at this. Perhaps it was because he saw it was a form of the church. (Or maybe that he also recognized Mary. It is interesting that Jesus commissioned John to take care of Mary until she died, which he did.) It really doesn't matter what shocked John, but rather that nothing else in Revelation had shocked him until now. Rome, often called the Eternal City, has always been known as "the city on Seven Hills" (the Palatine, Aventine, Caelian, Capitoline, Esquiline, Quirinal, and Viminal Hills). This city is the home of a church that is intolerant of biblical truth, gives birth to much religious error, is the center of a mystery, is guilty of spiritual adultery, and has a golden cup. It is wealthy, clothed in purple and scarlet, and is a woman and a harlot.

The harlot rules over the kings of the earth. "The waters which you saw, where the harlot sits, are peoples, multitudes, nations, and tongues" (17:15). In verse 3 she is first seated on the beast, which means for a time that she directs the beast. This global political influence where she "sits on waters" stands for all peoples, which has often been wielded by the Roman Catholic Church in both European and present world history. There is only one religion that has ruled over the kings of the earth. Yes, the Muslim religion enslaved a lot of people. Yes, there are different religions that have political connotations, but there is only one church that has "sat" to raise up and put down kings. There is only one church that has determined the fate of the nations. If you read history, you will know that church—the Roman Catholic Church. She is sitting on the beast when we first meet her, and then the beast will consume her.

But what does that mean for our lives today? This truth prompts me to want to follow the disciplines that Paul charged Timothy to follow in 1 Timothy 4: nourish my soul in the Word of God daily (v. 4:6b), meditate on God's Word (v. 15), plus take heed to doctrine and hold on to it (v. 16). When we live in the end times, and the world is filled with deceiving spirits (v. 1), our only hope is in God, through His Word, and by His Spirit!

THURSDAY: What Is the Mass?

__Not that He should offer Himself often__, as the high priest enters the Most Holy Place every year with blood of another—He then would have had to suffer often since the foundation of the world; but now, once at the end of the ages, He has appeared to put away sin by the sacrifice of Himself.
—Hebrews 9:25–26

The harlot is a woman wearing purple and scarlet with wealth beyond calculation, but the most graphic telltale mark is that this woman, this harlot, is wicked in spiritual adultery.

If we apply the first law of interpretation of the Bible, we will reason: What did the *Apostle John* think about when he heard those words? (Not: What do those words mean to us today? And not: How can we somehow shoehorn somebody to fit into this standard?) All the way through Revelation 17, you have to remember that this is the Apostle John who is on a sun-baked island out in the middle of the Aegean Sea as a prisoner of Rome. When he saw purple and scarlet, he saw the Roman Caesars and Legionnaires. When he saw inestimable wealth, he saw the city of Rome. When he saw the city that ruled over the nations of the world, he was looking at the city of Rome.

I find it interesting that the Assyrian Empire, the Babylonian Empire, the Egyptians, and the Greeks came and went. However, the Romans came and they have never gone. Did you know that the Roman Empire was never defeated or destroyed? It just broke up and dissipated. But there have been efforts to regather it: Napoleon, Bismarck, and Hitler all have tried. When John saw it, he saw a kingdom that had not been destroyed and is going to come back. But when he thought of this *"golden cup"* with the *"abominations and the filthiness of her fornication,"* he was not talking about peep shows and pornography shops. From God's perspective, he was speaking of spiritual abominations, spiritual adultery, and spiritual fornication.

The harlot is wicked (17:4). "The woman was arrayed in purple and scarlet, and adorned with gold and precious stones and pearls, having in her hand a golden cup full of abominations and the filthiness of her fornication." This woman in purple and scarlet has a golden cup in her hand. This is the holiest instrument in Roman Catholicism: the golden chalice of the Eucharist. No doctrine in the world is more damnable than the doctrine of transubstantiation (re-crucifying Jesus at every Mass in every church around the world every day). This cup is a picture of a false and vile counterfeit of true communion with God. The golden chalice is filled with the filthiness of her abominations. Did you know that this is what they teach? They transform the "host" into the real body of Jesus; then they symbolically crucify it again. They pour out His blood again because they do not believe that His blood was sufficient when He shed it on behalf of the sins of the world—past, present, and future. Thus, they have to repeatedly re-offer Him.

The biblical view of the sacrifice of the Mass, the very heart of Roman Catholicism, is a denial of the completed work of the cross, which states that "Christ was offered once to bear the sins of many" (Hebrews 9:28a). Verse 28a does away with Romanism: not once an hour in the big cathedrals; not once a day at all the other ones; not all day long at those chapels surrounding St. Peter's Cathedral, the largest Roman Catholic Church in the world, but ONCE FOR ALL. This is the stake in the heart of Romanism. To those who trust in that once-for-all sacrifice, and eagerly wait for Him, He is going to appear—but not to those who are looking to be saved by crucifying Him over and over again. Do you see why this teaching is so important?

Please do not misunderstand what I am saying. I am not against catholicism: I am against Romanism—the Mass, purgatory, confessions, sacraments, Mary, penance, extreme unction, beads, robes, cathedrals, and Popes. True catholicism is Peter, Paul, Jesus, John, and the New Testament.

I love born-again Catholics, and all Catholics everywhere, but I hate any false teaching that denies salvation, as does Romanism.

Most people don't realize the dominant role the Roman Catholic Church has had. Did you know that the calendar of the world (except for the Muslims, Hindus, and Jews) was instituted by the Pope? The reason why there is a French Canada and a Catholic South America is a result of Papal edicts. The reason we are here in Protestant North America is due to a miscalculation of the Pope. So many things in the culture of the world have been decided by the Roman Catholic Church, which has exerted incredible control over civilization for 2,000 years. However, they are not the only culprit.

The harlot is a system (17:17). "For God has put it into their hearts to fulfill His purpose, to be of one mind, and to give their kingdom to the beast, until the words of God are fulfilled." This will occur when false world religions are united. As we saw in Revelation 13, the beast will change all religions into the worship of Antichrist. What is amazing is that the Roman Catholic Church is just a part of this whole system Satan has built. This is the system that substitutes God and His way for Satan's way, and God's truth for Satan's lies. The whole system evolved into a religion and, as we saw in Pergamos, when Rome conquered the world, they moved the center of the Babylonian's worship, including all the altars in Babylon, and brought them to Rome.

The problem is not just that they utilize those little temples, but that they worship the same way. Until the Roman Church began its domination under Constantine, there were no robes, no beads, no rosaries, no venerated images, no scapulas, no holy artifacts, no feast days, no confessions, no penances, no indulgences, no sacraments, no candles, no saints, and no Lent. Those things were assumed or developed after they took over the Babylonian traditions.

The harlot is a city (17:18). "And the woman whom you saw is that great city which reigns over the kings of the earth." The "great city" is Rome. No other existing city in the world has a three-thousand-year history of continuous inhabitation, once ruled the world, and once headed a worldwide empire that has never been destroyed—only Rome. So John was shocked because he saw the church he loved, and had given his life spreading the gospel for, merge into one with the Roman Empire.

Should this city of rebellion that is to come discourage us? No, we must always remember what city we are to be looking for. We should not spend our lives looking for the city that will be destroyed, rather, as Hebrews 11 instructs us, we are to look for "the city which has foundations, whose builder and maker is God" (v. 10). We ought to live each day seeing it "afar off" (v. 13), and be trusting our great and faithful God who has "prepared a city" (v. 16) for all who believe in Him and seek Him here on earth (v. 6).

FRIDAY: The Origin of Paganism in Romanism

"But we will certainly do whatever has gone out of our own mouth, to burn incense to **the queen of heaven** *and pour out drink offerings to her, as we have done, we and our fathers, our kings and our princes, in the cities of Judah and in the streets of Jerusalem. For then we had plenty of food, were well-off, and saw no trouble."*

—Jeremiah 44:17

How did Rome inherit such wickedness? Here is a brief overview of world history.

Pagan origin. It is shocking for Roman Catholics to learn that the proposal of the Lord's Supper as a sacrifice was first made in the ninth century by a Benedictine monk, Radbertus, who was the subject of many fierce verbal battles by the bishops until Pope Innocent III declared it an official Roman doctrine in A.D. 1215. The very principles found in the bloodless sacrifice of the Mass, as it is in the church of Rome today, can be traced back through the labyrinth of paganism to the fountain of idolatry—ancient Babylon. Rome's most blasphemous and massive religious fraud originated in Chaldean idol worship and will continue until the time of the end when, according to Revelation 17 and 18, amid the wonder and admiration of the world, Rome will be judged with violence and be thrown down and shall be found no more at all, for strong is the Lord God who judges her. This brutal, bloody, and blasphemous harlot is none other than the universal false church, the wicked wife of Satan!

"God had no sooner begun the blessed work in preparing for himself a people than the devil did likewise. In fact, the first baby to be born on this Earth later became Satan's original convert!"[5] See Genesis 4:8; this is where religion starts. As 1 John 3:12 explains, Cain was the tool of Satan. We shall now consider the historical, current, and future activities of this perverted prostitute.

The Harlot Viewed Historically: Satan's church began officially at the Tower of Babel in Genesis 11:1–9. This is the beginning of organized religion, nearly twenty-four centuries before Christ. Here, in the fertile plain of Shinar, probably very close to the original Garden of Eden, the first spade of dirt was turned for the purpose of devil-worship.

The first full-time minister of Satan was Nimrod, Noah's wicked and apostate grandson (Genesis 10:8–10). Secular history and tradition tell us that Nimrod married a woman who was as evil and demonic as himself. Her name was Semiramis. Knowing God's promise of a future Savior (Genesis 3:15), Semiramis brazenly claimed that Tammuz, her first son, fulfilled this prophecy.

Semiramis thereupon instituted a religious system that made both her and her son the objects of divine worship. She became the first high priestess. Thus began the mother-child cult which later spread all over the world. From Babylon it spread to Phoenicia under the name of Ashteroth and Tammuz. From Phoenicia it traveled to Pergamos in Asia Minor. This is the reason for John's admonition to the church of Pergamos in the book of Revelation: "I know your works, and where you dwell, where Satan's throne is" (Revelation 2:13). In Egypt the mother-child cult was known as Isis and Horus. In Greece it became Aphrodite and Eros. In Rome this pair was worshiped as Venus and Cupid.

What was the teaching of Semiramis' false church? That Semiramis herself was the way to God. She actually adopted the title "Queen of Heaven." She alone could administer salvation to the sinner through various sacraments, such as the sprinkling of holy water. Her son, Tammuz, was tragically slain by a wild boar during a hunting trip. He was, however, supposedly resurrected from the dead forty days later. Thus, each year afterward, the temple virgins of this cult would enter a forty-day fast as a memorial to Tammuz' death and resurrection. After the forty-day fast, a joyful feast (Easter) called Ishtar took place. At this feast colored eggs were exchanged and eaten as a symbol of the resurrection. An evergreen tree was displayed and a Yule log was burned. Finally, hotcakes marked with the letter "T" (to remind everybody of Tammuz) were baked and eaten! This is similar to the practice of using wafers in the Mass today that are stamped with a symbol to make it a bloodless sacrifice of Christ's body.

In light of this history, it should be easy to understand the need to be discerning. Most of what is called "Christian" today is engineered by Satan, who masquerades as "an angel of light" (2 Corinthians 11:14). Ask the Lord daily to lead you in Truth so that you may be alert to "the wiles of the devil" (Ephesians 6:11).

SATURDAY: Satan's Plan Extinguished

*Inasmuch then as the children have partaken of flesh and blood, He Himself likewise shared in the same, that **through death He might destroy him who had the power of death**, that is, the devil.*
—HEBREWS 2:14

How will Satan's masterful plan be extinguished? This is how. When the true church exits, the wheat and the chaff will be separated—the true bride of Jesus will be with Him in heaven while the false church remains on earth!

What is our hope as believers in Christ? We, like those converted during the Tribulation's horrors, are those whose names are written in the Lamb's Book of Life. Revelation 13:8 sums it up: "All who dwell on the earth will worship him, whose names have not been written in the Book of Life of the Lamb slain from the foundation of the world."

You see, those who are in the Lamb's Book of Life will never worship the beast. Instead, we will joyfully witness of our faith in Christ. Look at Revelation 17:8: "The beast that you saw was, and is not, and will ascend out of the bottomless pit and go to perdition. And those who dwell on the earth will marvel, whose names are not written in the Book of Life from the foundation of the world, when they see the beast that was, and is not, and yet is."

There are six glorious elements describing those whose names are written in the Lamb's Book of Life:

1. **They are victorious ones because they are overcomers:** "He who overcomes shall be clothed in white garments, and . . . I will confess his name before My Father and before His angels" (Revelation 3:5).
2. **They are joyful witnesses because they are secure:** "Help these women who labored with me in the gospel . . . and the rest of my fellow workers, whose names are in the Book of Life" (Philippians 4:3).
3. **They are newborn ones because it is the Book of Life:** "Anyone not found written in the Book of Life was cast into the lake of fire" (Revelation 20:15).
4. **They are blood-bought ones because it is the Book of the Lamb that was slain:** "There shall by no means enter in anything that defiles, or causes an abomination or a lie, but only those who are written in the Lamb's Book of Life" (Revelation 21:27).

5. **They are glorified ones because they can enter the heavenly city:** "Those who are written in the Lamb's Book of Life" (Revelation 21:27).
6. **They are the before-known ones because the Book of Life was written before the foundation of the world:** "In the Book of Life of the Lamb slain from the foundation of the world" (Revelation 13:8).

Are you worshiping our Lord who has called you—and chosen you—the One to whom you should be faithful all your days?

Make a choice to live in hope. If you are a member of the true bride of Jesus, God has loved you with an everlasting love! With loving kindness He has drawn you to himself. He chose you in Christ before the foundation of the world that you should be holy and blameless before Him. Because you have been called and chosen, be faithful to Him—as a pure bride for her husband. You can choose to live in hope in these end times by rejoicing that your name is written in the Lamb's Book of Life. Rejoice that you will never be plucked out of your Father's hand! Rejoice that you have been sealed by the Holy Spirit and will never be deceived from your faith and hope and joy in Christ! Rejoice that you are thus eternally secure!

WEEK 38
Live for What Is Eternal

{ Revelation 18 }

As the end of days approaches, you can find hope as you live for what is eternal!

SUNDAY: The Coming Global Financial Collapse

"No man can serve two masters; for either he will hate the one and love the other, or else he will be loyal to the one and despise the other. ***You cannot serve God and mammon*** *[earthly treasures]."*
—MATTHEW 6:24

A cataclysmic day is on the horizon of the future that will launch a series of events arresting everyday life on planet Earth! In a single moment—on a single day all over the world—the food supply will end; the transportation system will grind to a halt; the banking system will freeze and default; the luxuries, precious metals, gems, art, and all other hoarded wealth in every country will become worthless; the communications industry will be cut off, and there will be no radio, no TV, no telephone, no Internet; the supply of power will fade and blink off, and darkness will rule in the homes and businesses of the world. In short: there is a day when the lights are going off all over planet Earth—and they won't be coming on any time soon!

The eighteenth chapter of Revelation gives us a road map for the coming economic collapse of the world. By learning the lessons God has laid down in His Word, we can see what response He desires from His servants not only in the ultimate collapse but also in any other financial reversals or crises that may prompt widespread panic before the big and final crash.

Now let's look at an overview of Revelation 18, which is a twin to Revelation 17. In Revelation 17 we find the collapse of the apostate world church—Satan's harlot bride, the delusion of religion. Revelation 18 now reveals the other member of Satan's family—materialism, worldliness, and covetousness. From the Garden of Eden onward, Satan has been offering the elusive "greener grass" to humans. According to each person's own vulnerability, Satan thus whispers his lies: "If only you eat this 'fruit,' you will have it all! If only you earn this income, you will be happy! If only you reach this level of popularity, power, or success, you will be fulfilled!"

Hand in hand with Satan's fall is the insatiable desire for more. Lucifer himself was discontented with the highest position in heaven—he wanted still more. Humans are born with a thirst for more of whatever they desire. This is the **idolatry of covetousness**.

The Bible clearly describes covetousness—this concept of the idolatrous worship of things: "to long for, be preoccupied with having what God has not given us." Possessiveness (which is a cousin of covetousness) is "to be selfish and un-sharing with what God has given us."[1] The Book of Proverbs is full of illustrations of such idolatry. The Old Testament prophets have provided many examples of people who were preoccupied with and longed for what God had not given to them: they wanted something else—someone else's wife or land. Worldliness either makes us covetous (we want what we do not have) or possessive (we want to hold on to what we have). Both are evil.

The most visible sign of covetousness is materialism. A sure sign of the covetous nature of materialism is its *insatiability*. Legitimate desires (such as food, drink, and companionship) can be satisfied. Illegitimate desires (such as pride, envy, greed, and lust), by their very nature, can't be satisfied.

Materialism is the desire for "things" as opposed to spiritual worship, which is the desire for God. Materialism is seen in a passion for money, possessions, and endless pursuits of physical pleasures and recreations. But all that is going to end. In Revelation 18, the music stops, money fails, and possessions are worthless. In other words, the party is going to be over the moment the lights go out!

Revelation 18 describes the coming global financial collapse. Jesus condemns worldliness (vv. 1–3); Jesus calls saints to come out of worldliness (vv. 4–8); Jesus describes the worthlessness of worldliness (vv. 9–19); and Jesus celebrates the end of worldliness (vv. 20–24).

Why would John have such a vision on a prison island? When we come to Revelation 18 we are looking at the fully-grown evils of this world. As we saw in our study of Revelation 17, Babylon is at the same time an ancient city, a kingdom of the past, as well as a system of religion and a present way of life—worldliness, materialism, and covetousness. Babylonian materialism in Revelation 18 may be distilled down to one word in the Bible: covetousness, which is idolatry. It is the worship of *"mammon"* (money, possessions, and so on) instead of God.

In John's day, Rome had gone to the limits in extravagance. The Caesars would spend fortunes on a single meal by demanding the most exotic and rarest dishes for their personal consumption. Nero decorated his banquets with roses from Egypt that cost $70,000; he wore an outfit costing $40,000—which he only wore once, as was his custom. Caligula demanded such meals as hummingbird and flamingo tongues, pearls costing $200,000 dissolved in wine, the livers of pike fish, and the brains of peacocks. Because the commoners only earned a penny a day at this time, that gives you a better idea of the extreme lavishness of the Roman hierarchy.[2]

In the fifth century, St. Augustine noted the message of Revelation 18: the central problem of mankind is idolatry. Idolatry is when we use what we are supposed to worship—and worship what we are supposed to use.

If you put all the evils of our world into that grid you will come up with this conclusion: Idolatry is using God for our own purposes, such as when we're in danger (in a foxhole, a hospital, a storm cellar, a plane shaking, and so forth) and worshiping anything else (by our devotion to money, sex, and pleasure). In other words, idolatry is using God, whom we are supposed to *worship*, and worshiping the things of earth that we are supposed to *use*.

So then, what does God want us to learn from Revelation 18? Many things, but primarily this: there is life beyond money. Life is more important than possessions; all you can take with you to heaven is people.

My Prayer for You This Week: *Oh Father, we think about how often our beloved Lord Jesus talked about money. He told us that money is the monitor of our heart—that our money and the pathway of our money show where our true treasures are invested. And by our use of money we prove to You where our allegiance and worship are directed. We pray that we will, in a very sobering and sincere way before You, ponder what it would be like in this world if we did not have money—if all our possessions and material things were stripped away from us either temporarily or permanently. What is left after we have no finances is really important for eternity. We pray that we would start rethinking life—about how to live in a way that counts, whether we have possessions or not. May we truly start thinking eternally, planning strategically, and talking prophetically so that our life's testimony points to the fact that this world is not our home—we are just parked here temporarily. We pray that You will open our hearts to these truths. For Jesus' sake, Amen.*

MONDAY: Jesus Condemns Worldliness

*"I saw another angel . . . having great authority, and the earth was illuminated with his glory. And he cried . . . with a loud voice, saying, '**Babylon the great is fallen . . . and has become a dwelling place of demons, a prison for every foul spirit**, and a cage for every unclean and hated bird! For all the nations have drunk of the wine of the wrath of her fornication . . . and the merchants of the earth have become rich through the abundance of her luxury.'"*

—Revelation 18:1–3

WEEK 38: LIVE FOR WHAT IS ETERNAL

The first lesson of Revelation 18 is that worldly possessions can't buy spiritual life, but they *can* buy spiritual death. What we see in the first three verses is the drunkenness of the nations, their fornication, and their living for everything that God will not give them.

In these verses, I can see the rich and powerful families of the world—from Rockefeller to Rothschild, from Getty to Gates—who will stand and watch their billions go up in smoke from the wrath of God. This scene depicts graphically what Jesus said in Matthew 16:26. And I believe it is what the "loud voice" of Revelation 18:2 will be booming throughout the earth at this global collapse: "For what profit is it to a man if he gains the whole world and loses his own soul? Or what will a man give in exchange for his soul?"

In the 1930s, William Randolph Hearst controlled many of the world's newspapers. He was so wealthy that he did not even know what he owned. He bought castles in Europe, had pieces of them taken apart and shipped to California, and then reassembled on his estate. At one time his desire for art was so insatiable that he wanted to have every painting by a particular great master. He vowed to pay any price to get them all. In fact, he gave a blank check to a man he commissioned to travel throughout the world looking for the last painting. After two years, he finally found it. It was crated up in a storage facility in Long Beach, California, in a high security area. When he finally tracked down the owner—it was Hearst himself!

If you possessed all the paintings, money, stock, and comforts of life, but lost your own soul—what would you give back in exchange for your soul? That is what Revelation 18 is about. You can have it all on earth, but miss it all in heaven. What a sobering warning! God therefore says, "You rich, weep and howl for your miseries that are coming upon you! Your riches are corrupted, and your garments are moth-eaten. Your gold and silver are corroded, and their corrosion will be a witness against you. . . . You have heaped up treasure in the last days. . . . You have lived on the earth in pleasure and luxury" (James 5:1–6).

From the Old Testament in the Garden of Eden through today, and to the end of time, God says to all peoples: "Get away from the worship of this world!" Don't lay up treasures that when you leave home you are afraid something might happen to them. Don't have so many possessions that you cannot sleep if you forget to turn on the burglar alarm. Don't have so much stuff that you cut your vacation short because you have to get back to protect it. The care of riches is covetousness and idolatry. So the Lord says, "Give it to Me!"

The Bible has many grim markers that show where an illegitimate desire has given birth to immense disaster.

- **Achan's** lust for more led to his death by stoning, and a similar death for all his family. (See Joshua 7.)
- **Balaam's** greed made him fail to hear his own message. He wanted to die the death of the righteous, but he did not want to live the life of the righteous. (See Numbers 22:4–35.)
- **Delilah** betrayed a man who trusted her, for a payoff. (See Judges 16.)
- **Solomon's** insatiable desire for more of everything led him away from God. He was warned not to multiply gold, women, and horses. However, he multiplied all three. (See Deut. 17:16–17.)

- **Gehazi** was not content with serving God; he lied to get more and paid dearly for it. (See 2 Kings 5:20–27.)
- **Judas** measured the inestimable value of Jesus in pieces of silver. (See Matthew 26:15.)
- **Annanias and Sapphira** could not let go of the money they possessed, nor the applause they coveted, so God killed them. (See Acts 5:1–11.)

Anything can be worshiped. Worship, simply stated, is "anything which captivates and draws us toward itself." Here are the most common examples plus questions to help you evaluate whether or not you worship something other than God.

- **Work Worshipers:** These are workaholics who are so captivated by work that they are irresistibly drawn to work all the time. Can you give up your career and your goals in your field to the Lord if He calls you to change directions for Him?
- **Escape Worshipers:** These persons want to escape reality by worshiping the effects of alcohol or drugs, and thus they become alcoholics or drug addicts. Can you completely stop taking whatever substances help you escape reality, and give your life to the Lord? If not, you worship the effects that substance gives you. The Lord says, "You cannot worship both that and Me."
- **Pleasure Worshipers:** These may worship pleasure in the sensual realm, and thus become sex addicts, perverts, or burn with adulterous lust. Can you completely end all selfish sensual pleasure pursuits—pornography, fornication, sodomy, and adultery—and repentantly give those desires to the Lord to deal with in His perfect time and way?
- **Wealth Worshipers:** These persons are drawn by the allurements of wealth and possessions. They may become like the materialistic, greedy, and selfish rich fool Jesus spoke of —one who only planned for prosperity, eating, drinking, and enjoying life. Can you completely give up your money, security, and power into the Lord's control? We cannot keep anything that we grasp onto—only what we give away will last forever.
- **Self Worshipers:** These are drawn to the praise of man, and thus they are proud, inward-seeking, calloused, and unfeeling self-centered persons. Can you give up your pride, self-seeking, self-absorption, and self-focus to humble yourself, deny yourself, and take up your cross to follow Jesus?

The ultimate test of whether or not you worship something other than God is quite simple: *Can you give it up today?* When nothing satisfies you—you are on dangerous ground!

TUESDAY: Jesus Calls Saints to Come Out of Worldliness

*"And I heard another voice from heaven saying, '**Come out of her, my people, lest you share in her sins, and . . . receive of her plagues**. For . . . God has remembered her iniquities. Render to her just as she rendered to you, and repay her double according to her works. . . . In the measure that she glorified herself and lived luxuriously, . . . give her torment and sorrow; for she says in her heart, "I sit as queen, and am no widow, and will not see sorrow." Therefore her plagues will come in one day—death and mourning and famine. And she will be utterly burned with fire, for strong is the Lord God who judges her.'"*

—Revelation 18:4–8

Revelation 18:4–8 is a repetition of the continually repeated warning. God wants us, His saints, to live out our high calling. We are called to be holy in all parts of our lives. To "separate from" and "get out of Babylon" is called for seven times in the Word of God. (See Isaiah 48:20; 52:11; Jeremiah 50:8–9; 51:6, 8; Zechariah 2:6–7; Revelation 18:4.) Some of the key calls of God have been for men to get out of worldliness. You may be thinking: *Wait a minute, this is the Tribulation, the end of the world. So what is this?* There are still going to be Christians on the planet. There will always be Christians on this planet because we have the two witnesses (Revelation 11), the 144,000 (Revelation 7 and 14), and the angel preaching the everlasting gospel (Revelation 14). The gospel is continually going out, and people will be responding throughout the Tribulation.

From the Garden of Eden to the end of time, God has the same call to His saints: "Come out of worldliness! Get away from the worship of this world!" Look at what He has to say about this in the following verses.

God called Abraham out of his world to follow His way: " 'Get out of your country, from your family And from your father's house, to a land that I will show you' " (Genesis 12:1).

God called Lot to totally abandon the sinfulness of Sodom: "Then the men said to Lot, 'Have you anyone else here? Son-in-law, your sons, your daughters, and whomever you have in the city—take them out of this place!' " (Genesis 19:12).

God called Moses to stay out of the very presence of those rebelling against the Lord: " 'Speak to the congregation, saying, "Get away from the tents of Korah, Dathan, and Abiram" ' " (Numbers 16:23–24).

God promises great blessing for living a life that avoids the ungodliness around us: "Blessed is the man who walks not in the counsel of the ungodly, nor stands in the path of sinners, nor sits in the seat of the scornful; But his delight is in the law of the LORD, and in His law he meditates day and night" (Psalm 1:1–3).

Jesus prayed for our realization that this world is not our home: "I have given them Your word; and the world has hated them because they are not of the world, just as I am not of the world. I do not pray that You should take them out of the world, but that You should keep them from the evil one" (John 17:14–16).

God expects His children to come out—and stay out—of worldliness: "Do not be unequally yoked together with unbelievers. For what fellowship has righteousness with lawlessness? . . . For you are the temple of the living God. As God has said: 'I will dwell in them and walk among them. I will be their God, and they shall be My people.' Therefore 'Come out from among them and be separate, says the Lord. Do not touch what is unclean, and I will receive you' " (2 Corinthians 6:14–17).

God calls us to be careful to not associate with sin: "Do not lay hands on anyone hastily, nor share in other people's sins; keep yourself pure" (1 Timothy 5:22).

Are you obeying God's call to come out of worldliness? Are you worshiping God—and God alone? If you are struggling with worldliness, the key to victory and freedom is yielding to and obeying the Lord! For Jesus says, "He who abides in Me, and I in him, bears much fruit; for without

Me you can do nothing. . . . If you abide in Me, and My words abide in you, you will ask what you desire, and it shall be done for you. . . . If you keep My commandments, you will abide in My love" (John 15:5, 7, 10a).

WEDNESDAY: The Worthlessness of Worldliness

> "**The kings of the earth** who committed fornication [they knit their lives to the things of this world] and lived luxuriously with her **will weep and lament** for her, when they see the smoke of her burning."
> —REVELATION 18:9

The possessions of this world are not worth coveting or worshiping. The words "weep and lament" speak of an uncontrollable sobbing and beating of the breast in anguish. Worldly possessions won't last forever—they are insecure and will not endure in the end. Everything you see around you is going to be destroyed. Therefore, "since all these things will be dissolved, what manner of persons ought you to be in holy conduct and godliness?" (2 Peter 3:11).

Worldly possessions can't meet our deepest needs. Look at what happens in these verses: " ' "Alas, alas, that great city Babylon, that mighty city! For in one hour your judgment has come." And the merchants of the earth will weep and mourn over her, for no one buys their merchandise anymore. . . . The fruit that your soul longed for has gone from you, and all the things which are rich and splendid have gone from you, and you shall find them no more at all' " (Revelation 18:10–14).

That passage lists eight categories of possessions that are going to be destroyed:

1. **Possessions of security:** In the entire world's history, the wealth of the rich has been protected against inflation, warfare, and decline because of their investments in gold, silver, and precious stones.
2. **Possessions of external beauty:** These are the fine materials of clothing, decorating, and fashion.
3. **Possessions of exquisite furnishings:** This refers to rare woods and other expensive building materials like ivory and marble.
4. **Possessions of personal luxury:** These are the fragrances of perfumes and incenses, the oils of ointments and beautifiers, the spices of exotic cuisine.
5. **Possessions of personal indulgence:** The inclusion of wine would cover all the personal intoxicants, including distilled spirits (not known in the ancient world) and drugs (known and used back then). The oil named may be the olive oil of the ancient world or a prophetic look ahead to the vast petroleum industry.
6. **Possessions of life:** The list also has foodstuffs for daily life; this would be all agricultural products plus the named fine meats.
7. **Possessions of transportation:** The word for chariot is not the normal two-wheeler that we might picture from movies like *Ben Hur*; it is the four-wheeled wagon (Greek, *rheda*) of travel. This may be a prophetic look at the vast automotive industry.

8. **Possessions of Slavery:** The inclusion of slaves ("souls of men") may indicate a resurgence of slavery which, though outlawed by Christian nations in the nineteenth century, continues in Asia and Africa. This could also be a spiritual reference to the sale of indulgences. All these things will be gone.

Worldly possessions can blind the soul to eternal concerns. Look at the depth of these verses in Revelation 18:15–19:

> " 'The merchants . . . will stand at a distance . . . , weeping and wailing, and saying, "Alas, alas, that great city that was clothed in fine linen, purple, and scarlet, and adorned with gold and precious stones and pearls! For in one hour such great riches came to nothing." Every shipmaster, all who travel by ship, sailors, and as many as trade on the sea, . . . cried out when they saw the smoke of her burning, saying, "What is like this great city?" They threw dust on their heads and cried out, weeping and wailing, and saying, "Alas, alas, that great city, in which all who had ships on the sea became rich by her wealth! For in one hour she is made desolate." ' "

Remember what the prophet Zephaniah said: "Neither their silver nor their gold Shall be able to deliver them In the day of the LORD's wrath; but the whole land shall be devoured By the fire of His jealousy, For He will make speedy riddance of all those who dwell in the land" (Zephaniah 1:18).

In four verses in Revelation 18 the earth dwellers lament their loss of luxuries, money, and things (vv. 9, 11, 15, 19) as well as the lightning-like speed of their loss (vv. 10, 17, 19). The "weeping and wailing" is the sound of the uncontainable bawling of someone who has lost something irreplaceable. But in all the weeping and wailing, they fail to even notice that the greatest loss is of their own souls! What a tragic scene!

THURSDAY: The End of Worldliness

> " 'Rejoice over her, O heaven, and you holy apostles and prophets, for God has avenged you on her!' Then a mighty angel took up a stone like a great millstone and threw it into the sea, saying, 'Thus with violence the great city Babylon shall be thrown down, and shall not be found anymore. . . . For **your merchants were the great men of the earth, for by your sorcery all the nations were deceived**. And in her was found the blood of prophets and saints, and of all who were slain on the earth.' "
> —REVELATION 18:20–24

The people refused to listen to God's servants—His holy apostles and prophets. Thus they lost their opportunity to live forever; instead, they will die forever.

Worldliness uses the deafening spell of entertainment. Gone will be the diversions. There will be no more music and tunes to drown out God and their problems. Music and entertainment will be shut down. The work that has captivated so many, keeping them from spiritual things, will cease. The regular grind (millstone) of life will stop. There will be nothing left to distract the earth dwellers from thoughts of God. This is just another of the endings of chapter 18: the profits of commerce end in verse 11; the enjoyment of exotic commodities end in verse 14; the whole system of materialism burns up in verse 21; and the very sounds of life—music, industry, and home—cease in verse 22. Finally, even light and social life stop in verse 23.

Why? Because of their sorceries "all the nations were deceived" (18:23). The Greek word for "sorcery" is *pharmakeia*, which refers to the drug-induced stupors of addiction, the demonic-induced bondage of the astrology industry, the godless and mindless following of evolution, and the dehumanization of mankind by philosophy and secular education.

Drugs and substances will be very prevalent during the end of days, and this trend is present even now. A friend of mine, who was recently in London, said that 200,000 marched there for the legalization of marijuana. People want their drugs and their escape. So God will say, "You were intoxicated, and did not hear My voice, so there is now no hope for you." All these evils are facing Judgment Day.

Is there any diversion in your life that is distracting you from giving your all to God?

FRIDAY: Are You a Worldly Person?

*"Do you not know that friendship with the world is enmity with God? Whoever . . . wants to be **a friend of the world makes himself an enemy of God.**"*

—JAMES 4:4

In Revelation 18 we also find that there are seven elements of the worldly system that Jesus will bring to an end. This is a cause for rejoicing, as they will no longer cause earth dwellers to ignore Him. The Lord will remove everything that has distracted people from looking at Him. To identify current dangers, traps, and snares, we will examine what the Lord will end. Here are the elements that worldliness is built upon, and thus what disrupts our fellowship with the Lord.

A worldly person's identity is found in this world, and not in heaven. "Thus with violence the great city Babylon shall be thrown down, and shall not be found anymore" (18:21b). Such a person's identity is found in what they do, have, and hold onto here. They dress like the world, act like the world, and are drawn toward the world. But God will destroy any and all identities that are established apart from Him.

A worldly person finds escape through amusements, entertainments, and pleasure-seeking. "The sound of harpists, musicians, flutists, and trumpeters shall not be heard in you anymore" (18:22a). A worldly person has to be amused. Do you know what amusement means? "Muse" means to meditate, so "amuse" means "without meditation." One of the fastest growing sectors of our economy and our culture is amusement: parks, games, arcades, and movies. People no longer want to think, they just want to be carried along by the action and excitement. Society has become so captivated by movies, music, and all else in the entertainment field that they never engage with the living and abiding Word of God. But God is going to turn it all off, and there will be no more distractions.

A worldly person uses work, career accomplishments, and even daily life as a way out of spiritual responsibilities. "No craftsman of any craft shall be found in you anymore" (18:22b). Christians act the same worldly way when they say, "I don't have time for that because I have to work" or "I don't have time to lead my family or read the Bible." By the sweat of our brow, and diligent labor, we are supposed to earn money to support our family. If we don't, the Scriptures say that we are worse than an infidel—an unbeliever. Yet, we must not be so wound up in our work that we are inconsistent in worship, and miss the joys of fellowship. It is a sign of worldliness when our career, plans, finances, work schedule, recreation, and entertainment make us so busy that we infrequently engage with the people of God. Even the needs of daily life, such as food and housing, can keep some people away from heavenly living. But God will stop the cycle of life for all earth dwellers.

A worldly person is tied to the technology, science, and knowledge of this world—and not the next. "The light of a lamp shall not shine on you anymore" (18:23a). Such a person constantly looks at the Bible through science rather than looking at science through the Bible. The Bible has always communicated the basic principles of hydrology, astrophysics, the rotation of the earth, and the balancing of the continents, but the sciences are just now catching up with the Bible. In the industrialized world there has been a blind acceptance and intoxication of humanity by technological convenience. But God will soon cut short that technology.

A worldly person is tied to social life, party life, the calendar, and holidays. "The voice of bridegroom and bride shall not be heard in you anymore" (18:23b). This is the person who lives for the weekend. He or she goes from one social event to another because life represents an endless party. Life is more than identifying with this culture and its amusements and entertainment. There is so much more God wants us to know. That is why He lets us see that when He strips away these things, the socialites and partygoers will have nothing left. So they will weep and howl and cry out. But God will stop their partying, and that is all they had to live for.

A worldly person is tied to finances, wealth, and possessions. "Your merchants were the great men of the earth" (18:23c). Our society makes gods of the millionaires and billionaires of this world. These earth dwellers find their greatness in money and belongings. They live to acquire and hold and enjoy things. But God is going to erase all the worldly person's assets.

If your assets were erased, what would you have left that really mattered? You would have the results of what you have invested in finances and time for Christ. You would have the opportunity, without the baggage of things, to go forward in His kingdom.

A worldly person is intoxicated by the world. "By your sorcery all the nations were deceived" (18:23d). The end of this verse speaks of drugs and sorcery, which can include alcohol as well as drug-induced witchcraft. But there are also people who are intoxicated by the world itself. They can't understand, and don't care, about the gospel. But God is going to bring an end to this familiar world.

What will the earth really be like when God pulls the plug? In Revelation 18:23a, we find some amazing words: "The light of a lamp shall not shine in you anymore." In twenty-first century terms, this verse says the power grid will be shut down. It says that no power, no electricity, and no technology that uses electricity will be running. Revelation 18 marks the end of the world as we know it. According to the Word of God, that will not happen for at least seven years from now. The world that ends in this chapter is a highly technological world that has some type of cashless society.

This would require well-functioning computers, or something beyond computers that we don't even know about yet.

Although there is much more that I could say on this, I don't want you to miss the point of today's lesson. And that is to examine yourself in the light of Scripture to see whether any of these descriptions of a worldly person are common in your own life. If you feel convicted by the Holy Spirit, you need to know this truth: "You are slaves to the one whom you obey" (Romans 6:16). But you are not without hope.

Through Christ's empowerment, you can break any bondage that manifests itself in a love for the world and all that is in it! The cure begins with the antidote of *contentment*, which we'll administer in tomorrow's lesson. So take heart, for relief is on the way!

SATURDAY: Seven Keys to Contentment

*"I have learned in whatever state I am, **to be content**."*
—PHILIPPIANS 4:11

Contentment is a byproduct of following the Shepherd. It is experiencing the inner-peace that only He can provide. It is knowing that He will promote you at the right time. Contentment is the sense of satisfaction that comes to a husband and wife as they emulate the provision and care of the Shepherd to their own children. Contentment comes from serving Christ instead of money, and from providing not only financially for your family, but also emotionally, morally, and spiritually.[3]

How can such contentment be cultivated in our life? First Timothy 6:6–17 describes seven principles that promote contentment.

Principle 1—Remember that things are only temporary. "Godliness with contentment is great gain. For we brought nothing into this world, and . . . we can carry nothing out" (1 Timothy 6:6–7). You cannot take it with you. There are no U-Haul trailers behind hearses.

Principle 2—Only seek necessities, and wait for the rest. "Having food and clothing, with these we shall be content" (1 Timothy 6:8). We need shelter and the basic provisions of life, but everything beyond that is simply a great blessing. Whether it comes or goes is okay. God has said that all we are supposed to expect in life is food and clothing, so we should be happy with that.

Principle 3—Avoid a consuming desire for prosperity. "Those who desire to be rich fall into temptation and . . . many foolish and harmful lusts. . . . For the love of money is a root of all kinds of evil, for which some have strayed from the faith . . . and pierced themselves through with many sorrows" (1 Timothy 6:9–10).

America has been fed a prosperity diet. You might say, "That is not me—I am not rich." If you own a car, you are rich. Ninety-five percent of the people in the world can't afford a car. Your watch and the clothes you have on are worth more than what hundreds of millions of people on earth have. Tens of thousands even starve to death around the world each year, but Americans regularly throw away super-sized leftovers.

Principle 4—Flee materialism. "Pursue righteousness, godliness, faith, love, patience, gentleness" (1 Timothy 6:11). Do you seek to accumulate possessions—or to grow in Christlikeness? Value what will count for eternity!

Principle 5—Cling to eternal life. "Fight the good fight of faith, lay hold on eternal life, to which you were also called. . . . Keep this commandment without spot, blameless until our Lord Jesus Christ's appearing" (1 Timothy 6:12-14). We need a whole generation of people who are holding tighter to eternal life than they are to this world.

The writer of Hebrews says, "You had compassion on me in my chains, and joyfully accepted the plundering of your goods, knowing that you have a better and an enduring possession for yourselves in heaven" (Hebrews 10:34). When those Christians were persecuted and their jobs and possessions taken away, they still rejoiced because their focus was on Christ.

If we're not careful, before long our possessions can possess *us*. They then become an anchor that holds us back. The care of riches clouds our mind from seeking the purity of Christ.

Principle 6—Fix your hope on God. "Command those who are rich . . . not to be haughty, nor to trust in uncertain riches but in the living God" (1 Timothy 6:17). There is nothing wrong with wealth, but we are to recognize the danger of relying upon it. All that we own can evaporate as quickly as a blip on a computer screen. There are few things that are real possessions in this world. Through money, stocks, and bonds you are trusting that a company, a bank, or a government won't fail. But the living God, who gives us richly all things to enjoy, can never fail us—and our trust in Him is certain!

Principle 7—Give until it hurts. "Let them do good, . . . ready to give, willing to share, storing up for themselves a good foundation for the time to come, that they may lay hold on eternal life" (1 Timothy 6:18). The real cure for materialism is to give until it hurts! Giving "until it hurts" means giving at the cost of personal sacrifice. For example, the widow gave both of her mites, or all that she had (Mark 12:42-44). The woman who anointed Jesus broke the flask of fragrant oil and irrecoverably gave all she had to Him (Luke 7:37-47). Sacrificial gifts are especially important to Jesus.

Make a choice to live in hope. The advantages of contentment are many: freedom, gratitude, rest, peace—all of which are also components of good health. Those who are content do not have to worry about the latest styles or what to wear tomorrow. Those who are content can rejoice in their neighbor's good fortune without having to feel inferior. Those who are content do not fret about wrinkles or graying because they accept what comes. Those who are content do not have to worry how they might buy this or that because they have no desire for this or that. Those who are content are not consumed with how to get out of debt because they have no debt. They thus have time for gratitude even in small things, and they have time for relationships because their possessions and the bank do not own them.

If what was just described seems beyond you right now, I encourage you to ask the Lord to help you move in that direction. In doing so, you will be choosing to live for what is eternal. Be content—willingly surrender all that you are and have to the Lord. Then faithfully fight the good fight of faith by laying hold on the eternal life to which you were also called.

WEEK 39
Give All to God

{ Revelation 18; 2 Corinthians 8:5 }

As the end of days approaches, you can find hope as you give your all to God!

SUNDAY: Giving God Your All

*"**What do you have that you did not receive?** Now if you did indeed receive it, why do you boast as if you had not received it?"*

—1 Corinthians 4:7

Last week, we learned that Revelation 18 spelled out the end of the political and economic system of our world. In one brief chapter all the ages of man's greed comes to a halt. That chapter is about God disrupting everyday life. It defines the judgment of God upon a society which worships the creation—technology, pleasures, comforts, and all other allurements of this world—instead of the Creator.

God wants us to give Him everything, which starts by first giving ourselves to the Lord (2 Corinthians 8:5). If Christians aren't careful to remain alert to the deceptions of the Devil, they, too, can become ensnared with a love for this world and all that is in it—often without realizing that they have been taken captive.

Becoming gradually attached to the world can happen to anyone (1 Corinthians 10:12). Have you ever heard the frog story? It is simply this: If you place a frog into boiling water, it immediately senses the danger and will hop back out. However, if you place that same frog into tepid water, and then slowly turn up the heat, the frog is deceived into thinking everything is fine—until it is too late! Satan works his wiles in the same manner, so we must remain alert in order to escape being ensnared in his "worldliness trap."

So, before moving on to Revelation 19, we will do a three-week "Life Stewardship Series" on how to conquer worldliness. We will learn how to give our all to God; how to give to God what is His in this life; and how to live contentedly and victoriously for Christ, which is our Great Physician's antidote for worldliness. It all starts with discerning whether you are a pilgrim sojourning here for a short time—or an earth dweller with roots.

Have you read John Bunyan's (1628–1688) classic book entitled *Pilgrim's Progress*? (If you haven't, I hope you will.) He wrote from an English prison cell to which he was condemned for unlicensed preaching of the gospel. This is how he interpreted the words of Christ and Paul: "Whatever good thing you do for Him, if done according to the Word, is laid up for you as treasure in chests and coffers, to be brought out to be rewarded before both men and angels, to your eternal comfort."

If you are a pilgrim in the biblical sense, you have the opportunity to send ahead building materials for the home you are going to live in. God's children are not going to be walking in the clouds wearing halos and strumming our harps all the time. We are actually going to have a place where we eat, and most likely to which we can invite people. Jesus said, "In my Father's house are many mansions" (John 14:2a). That means rooms in a great house. We will have an address some day, and we are going to go live there eternally. Isn't that fantastic?

But there is one catch. God says that there are only two types of building materials: wood, hay, and stubble—or gold, silver, and precious stones. I believe that for all eternity the evidence of our stewardship on this planet will be displayed by the place in which we dwell in our Father's house. That is why God is going to have to wipe away all the tears when we get there, for some of us have been sending wood, hay, and stubble that will turn to soot and ashes! But that need not be your case; learn from what these godly saints sent ahead.

- **John Wesley:** "I value all things only by the price they shall gain in eternity."
- **David Livingstone:** "I place no value on anything I possess except in relation to the Kingdom of God." (That is why he lived out his last days in Africa.)
- **Martin Luther:** "I have held many things in my hands and I have lost them all. But whatever I have placed in God's hands, that I still possess."

God's kingdom was the reference point for these men. They viewed everything in light of the kingdom. They were compelled to live as they did because they treasured the right things.

To which world are you attached? Do you have the pilgrim mentality that recognizes that this world is not your real home—or are you clinging to this old world for the duration of your life? I believe that God will show you the truth as you move through the next few weeks of lessons. And you will be blessed because of it!

My Prayer for You This Week: *Father, I pray that Your Spirit will touch our hearts with the reality that You own the universe and are sitting at the finish line. May we live this life acknowledging that You own "me and mine." I pray that we would hold our unclenched hands toward You and say, "All I am, and all I have, I give to You." Father, I pray that You who inhabit our thoughts and hear our words before they are on our tongues would have heard from Your people the most transforming word we could give You from our salvation onward—"We relinquish the care of all that we are and have so that we can be free to live and walk by faith as Your servants." Lord, we want to be good stewards; help us to invest time in Your Word getting our marching orders. Help us to spend time talking to You to find out how You want us to manage our time, treasures, and talents. Help us to desire to do things that draw us to You, oh Christ, in whose name we pray, Amen.*

MONDAY: Are You a Pilgrim or an Earth Dweller?

*"**These all died in faith**, not having received the promises, but . . . were assured of them, embraced them and confessed that they were **strangers and pilgrims on the earth**."*

—Hebrews 11:13

When it comes to money, possessions, and eternity, if someone were to assess your life, would they say that more of you is here on earth—or more of you is in heaven? Tertullian (ca.155–230), a lawyer who became a Christian in the early years of the church, once said: "And so it is that when a man walks along a road, the lighter he travels, the happier he is; equally, on this journey of life, a man is more blessed if he does not pant beneath a burden of riches."

As we look through the Scriptures at what the Spirit of God inspired the Old Testament writers to say, what Jesus said, and what the apostles said, realize that I will never give any disclaimers. In other words, I will never tell you: "That is what the Bible says, but it doesn't mean that." If you really look at what the Bible says to Christians about money, it is very uncomfortable. It is not my job to make you feel comfortable; my job is to share what the Bible says.

Thomas a Kempis (c. 1380–1471), who authored the classic book entitled *Imitation of Christ*, had this advice: "Let temporal things serve your use, but the eternal be the object of your desire."

J. H. Jowett once said, "The true measure of our wealth is how much we would be worth if we lost all our money."

The great prophet Hosea, who wrote several hundred years before Christ, tells us: "When they had pasture, they were filled . . . and their heart was exalted; therefore they forgot Me" (Hosea 13:6). Every time our pastures get green and our fields get full, we run the risk of forgetting who made them green, and who filled them. God owns it all! Have you ever given back the title deed of whatever He has entrusted to you?

When I bought my first car as a young man, I purchased it from a white-haired lady about eighty years old. She had this "boat"—an old Caprice that was so big that you could put a couch in the back seat. This lady told me that she wanted to sell her car to me for a good price. I knew she was serious when she pulled out the title and signed it over to me. Many of us have told God that we would like to give Him our life and everything we have, but He knows we are actually serious about such a commitment when we pull out the title deed to our life and say: "All I am, all I have, and all I will ever be—I now sign over to You!"

Have you signed over the title deed of your life to Christ? Prayerfully consider 2 Corinthians 8:5: "They first gave themselves to the Lord, and then to us by the will of God."

Are you rich toward God, or just yourself? The parable in Luke 12:13–21 portrays the futility of wanting more and more possessions. Jesus called the rich man, "Fool!" (v. 20). Prayerfully consider what Jesus said next, "So is he who lays up treasure for himself, and is not rich toward God" (v. 21).

Do you live for yourself each day, or for Him? Prayerfully consider 2 Corinthians 5:15: "He died for all, that those who live should live no longer for themselves, but for Him who died for them and rose again."

Does God have the proper place in your life? Prayerfully consider Romans 14:12: "Each of us shall give account of himself to God."

If you have signed over the title deed of your life to God, and are rich toward Him by living for Christ every day, and are giving the Lord His proper place in your life, then you are a pilgrim. If you were not able to honestly affirm that you've given your all to Him, then you are most likely living with the attitude of an earth dweller.

TUESDAY: Jesus, Money, and the Believer

*"So is he who lays up **treasure for himself**, and is not rich toward God."*
—Luke 12:21

While I was pastoring in the South, I heard this story about a new pastor. His first sermon had three points. The first was: "Make all the money you can make." The people said, "Amen." The second was: "Save all the money you can save." And the people then said, "Amen!" The last point was: "Give all you can to God." It suddenly got very quiet in the church. After the sermon, the elderly head of the deacons commented: "That was a great sermon till you ruined it on the last point." In other words, we like to make all we can make, and save all we can save, but as soon as people start talking about our money and giving, we get offended—and call that "meddling."

Why talk about money at all? One out of every seven words Christ spoke was about money and possessions. If you do the math, the emphasis is there, no matter how you analyze Christ's words. Sixteen of His thirty-eight parables focus upon the handling of money. Of the nearly 2,800 verses in the four Gospels, 288 direct our use and possession of money. Fifteen percent of the teachings of Christ are about proper and improper handling of our stewardship: "For where your treasure is, there your heart will be also" (Matthew 6:21).

There are over 500 references to prayer in the New Testament, just under 500 references to faith, but over 1,000 references to money and possessions, and where God fits in all that. That amounts to twice as many references to money as there are to prayer. Isn't that interesting? The conclusion: Christ accorded to money an astounding prominence in His teaching.

Why did He give it such prominence? Money is one of the central realities of life, and it affects us all from the cradle to the grave. Jesus would have been unrealistic had He not given it due prominence. So what place does money have in your daily plans for your life?

Money is an acid test of character. Whether a person is rich or poor, if you discover his attitude about money, you will gain a deep insight into his character. One cannot be neutral where money is concerned. Do you love money or God most?

Money has potential for good or evil. This fact is obvious, and thus needs no elaboration. Are your money-making and spending choices causing you to be more godly—or less?

Jesus teaches that some people hold on to things with grasping, clenched fists, and end up losing them. He advises that the way to keep things longer is to open our hands, hold those treasures in upturned palms, and say: "You are the Giver of all that I have. You alone are the Owner of all things. I am Your servant forever. I will be a steward for You of all these possessions. When You want anything back, just tell me, and it is Yours!"

The Jews used to do this. If you could be transported back in time to the tabernacle or the temple, you would see Jewish people walking in. The father would be at the head of the family procession, and he would hand their wave offering to the priest. They were saying to Him: "It is in my hands and it belongs to You. Everything I have comes from You. Everything I have belongs to You." It was a visible representation of God's ownership.

Such an attitude changes us from thinking "How much of *my* money should I give?" to "How much of *God's* money should I keep?" So then, stewardship is giving of ourselves, without reservation, to the Lord.

WEDNESDAY: God Owns You and Me

> *"Your body is the temple of the Holy Spirit . . . and **you are not your own** . . . For you were bought at a price; therefore glorify God in your body and in your spirit, which are God's."*
> —1 Corinthians 6:19–20

God owns you and He owns me. God owns the universe, and the finish line that we are all going to cross, whether we die or He comes for us. In the verses above, Paul is saying, "No, it's not your life. You own nothing, not even yourself. When you came to Christ you surrendered the title to your life. So you belong to God, and not yourself. He is the only One who has the right to do what He wants with your life—your body, sexual behavior, money, possessions, everything. If you belong to Him, you owe God your full obedience."

Look at the problems the Corinthian believers suffered because they did not grasp Paul's point:
- Chapter 1: They were puffed up with their wisdom.
- Chapter 2: They discussed who was enlightened and who was not.
- Chapter 3: They built on the wrong foundation.
- Chapter 4: They argued over the stewardship of things.
- Chapter 5: They had problems morally.
- Chapter 6: They took each other to court.
- Chapter 7: They had problems with their marriages.
- Chapter 8: They did things with demons.

They had one problem after another. Do you know what these people were doing wrong? By their lifestyle, they were saying what we often say about our own life: "I can do what I want with it."

The point is this: God is not just the Owner of the Universe in general, but the Owner of each of His saints in particular. In fact, we are twice God's—first by creation, and second by redemption. Recognizing His ownership means living in the light of this overriding truth. It is living life with the acute awareness that we are managers, not owners. We are caretakers of God's assets, which He has entrusted to us while we are on earth. I have many friends who manage companies. They do not own them; they manage them, and are answerable to the owners or stockholders. Owners are answerable to the marketplace and the government, and they have more power.

How we handle our money and possessions will be determined by whom we really believe to be their true owner—and ours: "He died for all, that they which live should not . . . live unto themselves, **but unto Him** which died for them, and rose again" (2 Corinthians 5:15 KJV).

When I first memorized 2 Corinthians 5:15, it was a class assignment at college. Those three words "but unto Him" really gripped me. I remember taking a marker and writing on the face of my watch "but unto Him." Because we look at our watches frequently, I would see those words and think:

Is the way I am living right now acknowledging the fact that He died for me that I should no longer live for myself but unto Him? When will we be measured for how we did at living for Jesus? Second Corinthians 5:10a gives the answer: "We must all appear before the judgment seat of Christ."

We are all going to stand individually before Him "that each one may receive the things done in his body, according to what he has done, whether good or bad" (2 Corinthians 5:10b). The conclusive proof of spiritual change will be seen in an altered perspective on handling money and possessions.

Note the words of John the Baptist's message of a changed heart's response: "Then he said to the multitudes that came out to be baptized by him, '. . . Who warned you to flee from the wrath to come? Therefore **bear fruits worthy of repentance** [for] every tree which does not bear good fruit is cut down and thrown into the fire.' So **the people asked** him, saying, 'What shall we do then?' He . . . said to them, 'He who has two tunics, let him give to him who has none; and he who has food, let him do likewise.' **Then tax collectors** also came to be baptized, and said to him, 'Teacher, what shall we do?' And he said . . . , 'Collect no more than what is appointed for you.' **Likewise the soldiers asked** him, saying, 'And what shall we do?' So he said . . . , 'Do not intimidate anyone or accuse falsely, and be content with your wages' " (Luke 3:7–14).

Our life will be judged according to whether or not it was lived "unto Him" or "unto self." The first step to grasping Christian stewardship is acknowledging that God is the Owner of all—you included. Do you have this mindset: "I don't own *anything*. My life is to be lived 'unto Him'!"?

THURSDAY: God Owns It All!

*"Indeed heaven and the highest heavens **belong to the LORD your God**, also the earth with all that is in it."*
—DEUTERONOMY 10:14

We need to let God's Truth impact us today. As you read through the verses below you will see that God really does own everything!

- "All that is in heaven and in earth is Yours; . . . And You are exalted as head over all. Both **riches and honor come from You**, . . . In Your hand it is to make great and to give strength to all" (1 Chronicles 29:11–12).
- "**Everything** under heaven is Mine" (Job 41:11).
- "The earth is **the Lord's**, and all its fullness, the world and those who dwell therein" (Psalm 24:1–2).
- "**The world is Mine**, and all its fullness" (Psalm 50:12).
- " 'The silver is **Mine**, and the gold is **Mine**,' says the LORD of hosts" (Haggai 2:8).
- "If I . . . said to fine gold, 'You are my confidence'; If I have rejoiced because my wealth was great . . . ; If I have observed the sun when it shines, Or the moon moving in brightness, So that my heart has been secretly enticed, . . . This also would be an iniquity deserving of judgment, For I should have **denied God** who is above" (Job 31:24–28).

Job was saying, "If I am counting on anything or anyone but God to help me to the end of my life, then I have offended God." That does not mean that you should get rid of all your money, because God's Word clearly says that you are supposed to prepare for the future by wise financial stewardship. In fact, Proverbs says a lot about saving money. The problem is that in our humanness we have trouble knowing when to save, and when to make a new investment in God's work.

Since money is one of the essentials of the work of the kingdom, it is not surprising that God's great adversary, Satan, does all in his power to prevent money from finding its way into the Lord's treasury—and for that Satan has many tricks in his bag to deceive His saints.

Spending. Satan encourages us to over-commit by purchasing more than we can afford, so that there is little left over to give to God. Is your spending under control?

Upgrading. Satan plays on our competitive instincts and incites us to constantly upgrade our standard of living so that any increases in income are already committed. When John Wesley was earning thirty dollars a year, he lived on twenty-six dollars and gave the rest to God. When his salary was raised to sixty dollars, he lived on twenty-six and gave the rest to God (the dollar amounts equal British pounds). That would be viewed as ridiculous in our society.

Waiting. Satan dries up the fountains of generosity in the heart by suggesting postponement of giving to some future time. The stifling of a generous impulse today makes it easier for us to do the same tomorrow. You hear an appeal, and are touched to help with a mission project or other investment in the kingdom of God, but you wait. Delay dries up the grace of giving.

Leveraging. Satan so arranges things that the assets of the generous man become frozen or over-committed so that he cannot give what he genuinely wishes to give. Expanding business too rapidly often demands reinvestment on a scale that leaves little for giving. (Luke 12 and the parable of the rich fool come to mind here.)

Keeping it to the end. Satan takes advantage of our uncertain times by promoting fear in many elderly that their savings will be exhausted before they expire. Others, he motivates to hoard to pass the wealth on to their children.

Satan thus encourages people to short-circuit current giving to God's work through what Dr. A. J. Gordon called "extra corpus benevolence"—that is the postponement of generosity until after death. This is an interesting concept. We should be sure to invest in God's work before we die.

Why is it that so many Christians make "death" their executor, leaving thousands and millions to be dispensed by his bony fingers? There is no doubt that it is wise to make modest provision for our dependents, as we are able, but surely it cannot be termed Christian generosity when a man waits until death to shake his wealth out of his pockets.

Let us give all we can in our lifetime, and have the joy of seeing our money work for God. He promises a reward for "deeds done in the body," not out of it. To be generous with God from right motives brings its reward here as well as hereafter.

FRIDAY: Seeing the Finish Line

*"I have fought the good fight, I have finished the race, **I have kept the faith**."*
—2 Timothy 4:7

God is the One waiting at the end of life to assess our lives. He is the One who is going to determine our eternal habitation: eternal bliss or doom. He inhabits all of time—the past, present, and future. In fact, He Himself is beyond time. How can that be?

If you were on the star Alpha Centauri, 4.2 light years away, the light reaching you would be from four years ago. We don't have any trouble thinking about that. If you were on some distant galaxy that is hundreds of light years away, looking back at planet Earth through a telescope, you would be looking at events that happened hundreds of years ago.

In a real sense, everything that has happened here is still traveling out into the cosmos. I don't know how that can be, I just know that God said all the events (past, present, and future) are in front of Him at all times. Did you know that every word we have said, everything we have done, is radiating up in front of God right now? He sees it all equally, and He is standing at the finish line of our lives. The only thing that gets rid of the bad we have done is the blood of Jesus Christ. That is why it is so wonderful being a Christian. Although unbelievers have to face all their sins at Judgment Day, we get to "delete files" that we know are bad.

Jesus is standing at the finish line—and He controls all things: " 'I am the First and the Last. I am He who lives, and was dead, and behold, I am alive forevermore. Amen. And I have the keys of Hades and of Death' " (Revelation 1:17–18). And Psalm 103:12 tells us that "As far as the east is from the west, so far has **He removed our transgressions from us**."

Remember: "We must all appear before the judgment seat of Christ, that each one may receive the things done in the body, according to what he has done, whether good or bad" (2 Corinthians 5:10). When I talk to people about Christ, I like to show them these verses. We need to know that all of us are going to stand alone before God.

We are going to individually answer His questions to account for our life, for God owns both the universe and the finish line: "For none of us lives to himself, and no one dies to himself. For if we live, we live to the Lord; and if we die, we die to the Lord. Therefore, whether we live or die, we are the Lord's. . . . We shall all stand before the judgment seat of Christ. For it is written: '. . . Every knee shall bow to Me, and every tongue shall confess to God.' So then each of us shall give account of himself to God" (Romans 14:7–12).

Stop for a moment and think about what you expect to have in heaven. Remember: all that you can take with you are those you've influenced with the Word of God. And, the only thing that you can send ahead is money and time invested in the Lord. In the space provided below, you may wish to list some of your accountings as of today.

1. Here is a list of those I have seen come to Christ through my witnessing and prayers:
2. I have invested time for the Lord in the following ways:
3. I have invested money sacrificially by giving to these areas Jesus approves of:

How are you doing in your getting ready to stand before Jesus to give an account of how you invested your life?

SATURDAY: Transferring the Title Deed to God

> "***Present your bodies a living sacrifice***, *holy, acceptable to God, which is your reasonable service. And do not be conformed to this world, but be transformed by the renewing of your mind, that you may prove what is that good and acceptable and perfect will of God."*
>
> —Romans 12:1–2

God owns all things, whether we recognize it or not. But life becomes much clearer, and in some respects much easier, when we consciously and continuously choose to acknowledge that Truth. The question is not whether we theoretically affirm God's ownership. The question is whether we have deliberately transferred the ownership of our assets and ourselves to Him—like that sweet little white-haired lady who wanted to sell me her car when I was a teenager. It was hers, and no matter how much she told me she wanted me to have it, it was not mine until she relinquished the title deed to it; then it became mine. We can talk about God, and sing numerous songs of commitment, but until we actually give our all to Him, it is not real.

Have you invited Him to be what Scripture says He is—the Creator, Owner, and Controller of your family, your possessions, your money, and yourself? And have you extended the invitation again after you have taken things back into your own hands? Such self-surrender to God is the beginning of true stewardship.

When we come to grasp that we are stewards, not owners of our money, it totally changes our perspective. Suddenly we are no longer asking, "How much of *my* money shall I, out of the goodness of *my* heart, give to God?" Rather, we are asking, "Since all of my money is really *Yours*, Lord, how would *You* like me to invest it today?"

Commonly, most Christians reverse this. Instead, they think that it is really magnanimous of them to give God something. But in reality, it is all His anyway, so how much are you keeping of His money? His time? His talents?

It was revolutionary when I truly realized that God has a claim on *100 percent* of "my money"— not just a few dollars to throw in an offering plate, or whatever percentage I was willing to give Him. Suddenly I was God's steward, God's money manager. I am not God. Money is not God. God is God. He is in His place, and I am in mine.

Not only does God own everything, but He also controls everything. Again, the implications of this are enormous. I don't have to own everything. I don't have to control everything. It is better in His hands than mine. And when catastrophe strikes, I can honestly adopt the posture of John Wesley when someone told him that his house had just burned down while he was away from home preaching. He said, "No, the Lord's house burned down. That means one less responsibility for me."

As Wesley did, we must remind ourselves of both God's role and ours to gain perspective in the face of loss or turmoil. What a life-changing and freeing perspective is God's ownership and sovereignty when the house is robbed, the car is totaled, the bike is stolen, and even when the diagnosis is cancer. We thus can think: *It is not my life; it is not my body; my possessions are not mine. They belong to God.* Accordingly, we have two choices:

1. **We can give ourselves to God:** "They gave themselves first to the Lord and then to us in keeping with God's will" (2 Corinthians 8:5 NIV). It is easier to staff the material needs and ministry positions of a church if this is obeyed absolutely and positively.
2. **We can neglect to give ourselves to God and live for our own pleasure:** "This is how it will be with anyone who stores up things for himself but is not rich toward God" (Luke 12:21 NIV).

Do you believe that God owns you? Have you acknowledged that to Him? Will you relinquish the anxious care of stuff and the continuous calculating of whether you will have enough? Will you trust God to tell you when He wants some of it, and how to be a steward of it?

If you send your treasures ahead to be with Christ, you will never have to worry about which way the markets go. And you won't have to fret about lightning strikes, tornadoes, or floods—because He is the Master of the winds and the waves. You can safely entrust all that you have to the care and control of your Almighty God.

Make a choice to live in hope. When we come to Christ, God puts all His resources at our disposal. He also expects us to put all our resources at *His* disposal. This is what stewardship and life in Christ is all about.

If God has deeply touched your heart through this week's devotionals, to reinforce this vital concept of stewardship in your mind, I suggest you sit down and actually draw up a title deed to your life. (You may wish to use the one below from Randy Alcorn's incredible book: *Money, Possessions, and Eternity.*[1])

Date:

I hereby grant to the Lord my God myself, all of my money, possessions and all else I've ever thought of as mine, even my family.

From this point forward I will think of them as His to do with as He wishes. I will do my utmost to prayerfully consider how He wishes me to invest His assets to further His Kingdom.

In doing so I realize I will surrender certain temporary earthly treasures and gain in exchange eternal treasures, as well as increased perspective and decreased anxiety.

Signed:

In light of all He's done for you, what are you willing to do for Jesus? I exhort you to make a choice to live in hope!

WEEK 40
Giving God What Is His

{ Revelation 18; 2 Peter 3:10–18 }

As the end of days approaches, you can find hope as you learn to avoid materialism and give God what is His in this life!

SUNDAY: First I Give Myself

"They first gave themselves to the Lord, and then to us by the will of God."
—2 Corinthians 8:5

Last week we learned how to give our all to God. This week, we will focus on how to give God what is already His in this life. Some of this material may overlap a bit concerning principles discussed previously, but please bear with me. A subject this critical to building a fireproof life often needs to be said in different ways so that every reader can more fully grasp the importance of the message.

What I am about to share contains some principles that my Christian parents began to instill in me when I was yet a young boy. The earliest memory I have of growing up in a Christian home is that of separating out the Lord's part from whatever I earned each week. Until I was older, my parents said that I could give the Lord's portion to our church or send it to missionaries. Thus, I started supporting missionaries when I was eight years old—at an age when I could write just legibly enough to be read.

When I was twelve years old, a missionary visited our church in search of Mr. Barnett, thinking that my dad was the one who had been supporting him. Dad corrected that missionary's misconception and referred him to the chubby kid in tennis shoes. The missionary then asked me, "You are Mr. Barnett?" I said, "That's me, and I have been supporting you for four years." I had sent my ten dollars every month to that missionary in Thailand. Why? Because my parents taught me that God would always bless and honor sacrificial giving. My parents said that I should start by giving at least ten percent to the Lord. They told me that that is not the rule, but where you should start. So I used to experiment with ten, twenty, and thirty percent to see if I had anything left at the end of the month.

When Bonnie and I were preparing to be married, we decided that starting with our first paycheck we were going to give not ten percent, but eleven percent (not wanting to be legalistic about our giving). The next month we gave twelve percent, then thirteen, fourteen, and so on. We kept increasing the percentage until it was in the twenties, and then our first child was born. Expenses were much higher, so we dropped percentage points until we could balance our budget. As we were able, we started giving even more, until our second child was born, and then we had to go back down again.

In this process, we learned that if we were going to give to God, we could not live at the same level as the people around us who were earning the same amount of money. Although you may not have the same conveniences, comfort, and freedom that those people do, when you choose to honor God with what is rightfully His, you have chosen the better way—the fireproof way!

What you are going to see in the Scriptures in this week's devotionals is very true—God cannot be outdone when it comes to His blessings. That does not mean that if you give everything to the Lord you are going to be rich. But among His people there is to be a sacrificial, systematic, proportionate giving out of the blessings He has given. In eternity, such giving will be of inestimable value; on earth, it is an act of obedience.

If you can maintain the same standard of living as the person living next door who earns the same amount of money, then I would suggest that you have not learned to honor God with your possessions. It costs something to honor the Lord.

It is critical for your spiritual life that you learn, as Martin Luther said, "The last part of a human being to get saved is their money." God wants to *own you*—not just touch your life!

My Prayer for You This Week: *Father, we know that Christ died for all, that we should henceforth no longer live unto ourselves, but unto You. Therefore, we freely give to You that which is already Yours. May we dispense it for Your glory, and in Your name, that we might have eternal treasures. We pray that You will make us Your good and faithful stewards. We pray that we will give as Your Word instructs, and that we will limit our lifestyle so that we are able to give systematically. We do not want to go one step ahead or behind Your plan. We bow to You now, for Christ's sake, Amen.*

MONDAY: What Is Materialism?

"**Put to death** your members which are on the earth: fornication, uncleanness, passion, evil desire, and **covetousness, which is idolatry.**"

—Colossians 3:5

God has given us stern warnings about materialism. Materialism is when we make our sources of security, hope, trust, and pleasure in some material thing instead of the Lord. It grows into an insatiable desire for us to have things as our security, pleasure, and for the building up of our lives.

Greed is demonstrated in possessiveness (selfishness with *what we have*) and covetousness (longing for *what we don't have*). Just as hate amounts to murder in 1 John 3:15 and lust amounts to adultery in Matthew 5:28, so greed amounts to idolatry.

The Bible has given believers insider information. As Revelation 18 records, on the horizon is a major upheaval in the worldwide social and economic situation. All the currency of the world—its money, possessions, fashions, and whims—will be worthless at our death or Christ's return, both of which could be imminent. This should utterly change our investment strategy.

For us to expend our precious time and energies building up more and more wealth and possessions is foolish. In light of the inevitable future, storing vast sums of money for some day in the distance is equivalent to rushing out to hoard Confederate money on the day before Sherman took the South.

To place our hope in money, despite an awareness of its worthlessness, portrays a basic ignorance or unbelief in the Scriptures. Kingdom currency, backed by the eternal treasury, is the only medium of exchange recognized by the Son of God, whose government will last forever. The currency of His kingdom is our present faithful service and sacrificial use of our resources for Him. The payoff in eternity will be "a sure foundation," consisting of treasures beyond our wildest dreams.

Christ has told us to keep alert (Ephesians 6:10–13). This ought to encourage Christlike living. Look at 2 Peter 3:10: "But the day of the Lord will come as a thief in the night; in which the heavens shall pass away with a great noise, and the elements will melt with fervent heat; both the earth and the works that are in it will be burned up."

Everything that people have spent all their time investing in will be gone. Many months ago when we were driving across the Adirondack Mountains in New York, I looked out the window and saw an old run-down house. In the front yard were three piles of stuff plus a U-Haul. I imagined that an older couple had lived there and passed on, so their children had descended on the house to decide what to do with the things. They were carefully carrying out the antique furniture; putting things on tables for an estate sale; and the rest was put in a huge pile of trash. That elderly couple's life had been reduced to three things: trash, yard sale stuff, and things their children wanted to keep. They did not get to take any of it with them. The only thing they got to take with them is what they sent on ahead (if they sent anything at all, that is).

Although I have mentioned this previously, I want to remind you of this vital truth again: Christ said that He was going to prepare a place for us—He is building a room for each of us in His Father's house. The Apostle Paul added to that by saying that we only have two categories of building materials from which our room will be built in heaven. Our room will be built out of wood, hay, and stubble—or gold, silver, and precious stones. What you and I do on earth for Christ will determine which will be used. You see, Christ is going to put all that we've done through the fire, and what is left is what we will have for eternity. Therefore, Christ said, "Don't cloud your mind with earthly interests—loving the world and all that is in it!"

Now look at 2 Peter 3:11: "Since all these things will be dissolved [the world, the beauty of it, our possessions, all that we've labored for and built], what manner of persons ought you to be in holy conduct and godliness?" That question needs to be answered in each of our lives. We must decide that, above all else, we want to be characterized as pilgrims and strangers on this earth. Consider the Apostle Paul, who took the gospel to the Gentiles, and wrote half of the New Testament: "For I am already being poured out as a drink offering, and the time of my departure is at hand" (2 Timothy 4:6).

That verse uses the same term as a boat shoving off. When we lived in Rhode Island, people used to take our family out on the ocean in their sailboats. There was a science to how the ropes were wrapped around the mooring. They did not want to secure it permanently, but just enough so the boat would not come loose and drift away. Paul said that he was ready to let the rope loose and sail away.

The other way verse 6 is described is breaking camp. The Roman legionnaires who conquered the world lived in tents. Before a campaign, they would methodically set up their perimeter with their tents; soldiers would then go fight the battles. But they never drove their tent stakes too deeply in case they needed to break camp quickly. Paul did not pound his tent stakes in too deeply, so he was ready to pull them out at any moment. Materialism, however, makes us bury our tent stakes and put concrete on top. Materialism ties the mooring rope in knots. So Christ is saying, "Since the Day of the Lord is coming, and everything is going to be dissolved, be careful how you live—because how you live is going to determine what your 'forever life' is like."

TUESDAY: Materialism Clutters Our Lives

"Looking for and hastening the coming of the day of God, because of which the heavens will be dissolved, being on fire, and the elements will melt with fervent heat? Nevertheless we, according to His promise, **look for new heavens and a new earth** *in which righteousness dwells."*

—2 Peter 3:12–13

Because materialism clutters our lives, we are so covered over with the things of life that bog us down that we fail to realize nothing here is going to last forever. That fact ought to discourage materialism and encourage us to live expectantly, as Peter said above.

Committing everything we have to Christ will make us build with fireproof materials. While we lived in California, we saw that grass fires would throw sparks on wood roofs and burn houses down. The residents there soon learned that they could not use wood shingle roofs, so they switched to tile shingles that look similar but are made of fireproof material. They are heavier, last longer, and they won't burn. Scripture says that we are living on the edge of a swift fire that is racing toward us. Therefore we ought to be conscientiously building our life with fireproof materials. All that is solely for use on earth is temporary, but anything elevated from its earthly use and given to Christ will last forever. And that is exciting!

Some people get discouraged if they can't find a parking place, the TV isn't working, or if they are picked on at school or at work. Now compare those small inconveniences with living every day in the dark, by torch light, in a sewer. That is what the Christians did during the great persecutions in Rome. When I take a tour group to Rome, we visit one of the most incredible spots in the city. Next to the Coliseum, about forty feet underground, are the catacombs—the garbage and sewer system of the Coliseum. Those drainage systems provided a safe haven for the Christians because no one wanted to come after them there. At night, after their loved ones had been martyred in the games, these believers would climb up the storm sewers, push off the lid, gather up any remains, and carry them back to the catacombs to be buried in niches in the rocks.

What would keep a person going during such great tribulation? The only way to endure adversity of that nature is to not look down, but up for Christ. Now apply that to today's ominous times: I am not looking for the Antichrist or the mark of the beast—I am looking for Jesus! That is the only way you can really live abundantly in this present life.

There are those who believe that Bible prophecy is simply trying to figure out what the mark of the beast is, and who is going to get it. But the Bible says that we should not be concerned with that. The whole purpose of Bible prophecy is not to sell books and make charts, but to make us expectant of Christ's return. Materialism, however, clouds our eyes so that we can't see clearly enough to look up expectantly. We must therefore learn to develop an enduringly hopeful life—and live purely: "Therefore, beloved, looking forward to these things, be diligent to be found by Him in peace, without spot and blameless" (2 Peter 3:14).

Keep looking up because your redemption is near! That hope is why the Apostle Paul said that our citizenship is in heaven, and that is why the early Christians made it through such horrific persecution.

WEDNESDAY: Materialism Clouds Our Minds and Wills

> *"Beware lest you . . . fall from your own steadfastness,*
> *being led away with the error of the wicked."*
> —2 Peter 3:17

What happens when our minds are clouded with materialism? Our Bibles become closed! This ought to warn us to be more alert to guard our heart and live more maturely.

Materialism clouds our minds. If you are not careful, you won't make time for God's Word. One classic example is the impact of a television set on your stewardship of time and resources. After wasting time watching TV for hours, you must then deprogram your mind because it deadens you to God's Word. Have you ever had precious fellowship in prayer and communing with God after watching TV for three or four hours? Inviting the world into our living rooms via TV night after night simply will not enhance that type of worship. What I find in my own life is that after I spend time watching TV, I have to read the Bible to warm up my heart again.

What did Christ teach? He told us to be content. And Paul said that godliness with contentment is great gain. So be careful to not invest in the mammon of unrighteousness. Jesus warned of this happening in the Laodicean church age: "Because you say, 'I am rich, have become wealthy, and have need of nothing'—and do not know that you are wretched, miserable, poor, blind, and naked" (Revelation 3:17). That church represents the age in which we now live. Churches have every piece of equipment, gadgets, investment programs, online services, programs—and *closed* Bibles.

Materialism clouds our wills. Instead of collecting and holding on to things here on earth, Peter says that we are to "grow in the grace and knowledge of our Lord and Savior Jesus Christ" (2 Peter 3:18). This ought to encourage us to grow spiritually and to live growingly.

So then, why should we avoid possessiveness and covetousness? Because that way of life will cloud our minds, clutter our lives, and keep our eyes from looking for Jesus' return. It will close the Book and distract our will from obeying Christ! Look at what a pastor from Chicago, A. W. Tozer, wrote about fifty years ago: "The man of pseudo-faith will fight for his verbal creed but refuse flatly to allow himself to get into a predicament where his future must depend upon that creed being true. He always provides himself with secondary ways of escape so he will have a way out if the roof caves in. What we need very badly these days is a company of Christians who are prepared to trust God as completely now as they know they must do at the last day."[1]

As Tozer has just pointed out, most of us recognize that God says that He—the One who faithfully clothes the lilies of the field and feeds the birds—is to be trusted. We even say that we believe that, but, "just in case," we have a backup plan of our own. There needs to be a balance here: we are supposed to be prudent, and care for our family, but if we are trusting in material things to care for our family, then we are not trusting God.

I once met an elderly farmer in South Carolina who lived at the time when the Emergency Banking Act of 1933 led to confiscating gold above a certain value from American citizens. He had a beautiful farm with six hundred acres. He sold it, received payment in gold, and deposited the gold in the bank—on the very day the law was passed! That law allowed the government to wipe out gold accounts. And every time he drove by that farm, he thought about the moment that everything his family had accumulated for years was turned from gold into paper.

That day is going to come again. The Scriptures say that there is going to be a cataclysmic change. So don't put all of your treasures on earth; invest in heaven instead. Christ is looking for a group of people who are willing to trust Him as much today as they are going to have to at the end! Are you a member of that group?

THURSDAY: Giving to God What Is His

*"Or do you not know that your body is the temple of the Holy Spirit who is in you, whom you have from God, and you are not your own? For you were bought at a price; therefore **glorify God in your body and in your spirit**, which are God's."*

—1 Corinthians 6:19–20

As we learned last week, God owns all things whether we recognize it or not. But life becomes much clearer, and in some respects much easier, when we consciously and continuously choose to recognize it. Have you invited Him to be what Scripture says He is—the Creator, Owner, and Controller of your family, your possessions, your money, and you? And have you extended the invitation again after you have taken things back into your own hands? This self-surrender to God is the beginning of true stewardship and thus the end of being ensnared by materialism.

True Biblical Stewardship. From a proper view of God's *ownership* comes true biblical *stewardship*. If we belong to God, then we recognize that we are not owners, but stewards. Unless you travel on cruise ships you probably don't see many stewards. The term is not a common one used in our vocabulary. A steward was someone that a wealthy person had in their household who took care of their goods for them. There was never a thought that the steward was the owner or master. A steward was a slave or servant who was responsible for oversight of his master's possessions. Believers are stewards, slaves of their Master, the Lord Jesus Christ, which is wonderful to be.

Stewardship is the giving of ourselves without reservation to the Lord. In fact, one of the conditions of discipleship is that we be a steward of Jesus for life. Early in my ministry I met a ninety-year-old pastor who was a true steward of God. After I got to know him I discovered the secret of his long and fruitful ministry—he had distilled life down to three points: 1) unrivaled love for Jesus, 2) unceasing cross-bearing, and 3) unreserved surrender. Let's go over each of these points so that you will better understand the heart of a steward.

Stewardship is unrivaled love for Christ. In Luke 14:25–26, large crowds were traveling with Jesus. These people were there for every reason: some had been healed, a few were raised from the dead, some had been fed by Jesus, and others just liked the show. So He turned to them and said, "If anyone comes to Me and does not hate his father and mother, wife and children, brothers and sisters, yes, and his own life also, he cannot be My disciple" (v. 26).

That seems like a contradiction; we are not to hate, are we? No, Jesus meant this: "If you compare the love you have for Me to the love for your family and relatives, the two cannot stand side by side. Your love for Me should be so great that the difference between the two is like love and hate." He would never tell us to hate our family, but that our love for Him is to be so great that it appears that we do. The first part of being His steward and His disciple is that we have unrivaled love for Him. Nothing else can be on the same shelf. Many Christians claim, "Christ is first in my life," and then put Him up there on a shelf along with everything else.

Jesus warned that our relationship with people, the world, and possessions can rival our love for Him. So He said, "He who loves father or mother more than Me is not worthy of Me. And he who loves son or daughter more than Me is not worthy of Me" (Matthew 10:37). If what your mother and father think causes you to disobey Christ, you are not worthy of Him. I am glad Jesus said that; those may be "fighting words" to some, but that is the unrivaled love that Christ demands from us as His disciples.

All this deals with the **affections of our heart**. Jesus said, "If you claim to love Me, but the love you have for Me is not unrivaled, you can't be My disciple." Do the affections of your heart reflect Jesus Christ in this manner?

Stewardship is unceasing cross-bearing for Christ. Jesus has already made the standard so high that it is out of reach of everybody except by the power of God. Yet, He doesn't stop with unrivaled love. He continued by saying, "Whoever does not bear his cross and come after Me cannot be My disciple. . . . And he who does not take his cross and follow after Me is not worthy of Me" (Luke 14:27; Matthew 10:38). In other words, Jesus did not stop with the affections of our hearts—He said there must also be unceasing cross bearing, which deals with our **conduct in life**.

Frances Ridley Havergal wrote the lines to a song we so often sing without due seriousness and commitment. It is a matter of record that this hymn was autobiographical, and I believe it well expresses the nature of cross-bearing. In the third stanza she wrote: "Take my will, and make it Thine; / It shall be no longer mine. / Take my heart, it is Thine own; / It shall be Thy royal throne. / Take my love, my Lord, I pour / At Thy feet its treasure store. / Take myself, and I will be / Ever, only, all for Thee."

Jesus wants us to give Him our all! Are you unceasingly bearing your own cross? Discipleship doesn't stop there, however. In Luke 14:33 Christ is still laying down the ground rules.

Stewardship is unreserved surrender to Christ. "Whoever of you does not forsake all that he has cannot be My disciple" (Luke 14:33). Christ is in the same breath, the same setting, talking to the same people. He already told them they had to love Him more than anything else, and then He told them they had to take up a cross, which meant death to self. His next qualification for a disciple is the requirement to forsake all for Him. This deals with **personal possessions**.

Jesus has the right of disposal. It is not *our* money or *our* life, because both belong to God. Discipleship is not about thinking: *I'll give God His ten percent, and then the rest is mine.* If you keep the rest for yourself, you are keeping ninety percent of *God's* money—because He owns it all. Instead, you are to be a steward of the Lord's money, which should always be at His disposal.

Henry Parsons Crowell, the founder of the Quaker Oats Company, gave away ninety-six percent of his income and lived on just four percent. It doesn't matter which percentage is involved, however, as all of it is God's. You don't get a ribbon if you give more because Jesus says it is all His anyway. He is the Owner, and we are only employees. Christ therefore asks that He be above all our treasures on earth, whether money or possessions. For Jesus has said, "If you want to be perfect, go, sell what you have and give to the poor, and you will have treasure in heaven; and come, follow Me" (Matthew 19:21). The man He spoke to went away sadly. Why? Because he said what so many people say today: "God, You can have my voice, my body sometimes, my time now and then, but you are not going to have everything." But Jesus says, "If I can't have everything—I don't want anything."

A true disciple humbly acknowledges this truth: "Everything I have comes from You—and belongs to You." Such an attitude changes us from thinking in terms of how much of *my* money should I give to how much of *His* money should I keep!

FRIDAY: Stewardship—Giving to God Without Reservation

*"For they all put in out of their abundance, but **she out of her poverty put in all that she had**, her whole livelihood."*

—Mark 12:44

In *Enjoying Intimacy with God*, noted author J. Oswald Sanders has this to say about giving to God without reservation:

Whether we tithe or not tithe, our Lord's life on Earth as a man set the standard for His disciples, and this principle applies equally to living for God and giving to God. Paul holds Him up as the supreme Example. "You know the grace of our Lord Jesus Christ, that though He was rich, yet for your sake He became poor, that you through His poverty might become rich" (2 Cor. 8:9).

Judaism was an expensive religion, and as a devout Jew, who fulfilled the whole Law, our Lord was meticulous in fulfilling its financial obligations. What would He pay into the Temple treasury from what He earned as a carpenter?

A Jew was first required to give one-tenth to God. Then at harvest time, the farmer must give the firstfruits to God, and that consisted of one-sixth of his increase. Then every three years a second tenth was given for the poor—social security tax. In addition were the special offerings of cleansing and consecration. That means that his total contributions to religion would be nearer a fourth of his income than a tenth—and that does not include voluntary support to the local synagogues. It is not difficult to imagine the temptation in times of stringency to withhold the tithe. So here we have our answer as to how much of His income Jesus gave to God. We know that Christ fulfilled all righteousness so we know that He gave all He could.

If we object that the Jews were under law and we Christians are under grace, and that for us the law of the tithe has been abrogated, another question arises. Will a Christian who is experiencing intimacy with his Lord wish to take advantage of grace so that he can give less to God's work than the less privileged Jew who knew nothing of Calvary's sacrifice and the inestimable blessings it has brought? Do you think God expects less from us? Was our Lord's matchless generosity in becoming poor for us intended to beget stinginess in His children? Paul cited it rather as an incentive to sacrificial giving. Grace is the super abundant overflowing—Not "I have to give this." That is the Law. Grace is "all I am, all I have, all I'll ever be."[2]

The people closest to Christ gave up all they had and followed Him. One might say, "That is the apostles, not us." Such thinking is why the church is not conquering the world anymore. When has it ever done that? In the nineteenth century, through the ministry of the Cambridge Seven (C. T. Studd and friends), many students chose to give up careers in England and move to mission fields at the farthest corners of the world. They gave up their ownership of things. Through their sacrifices, the gospel went to every corner of the planet in about thirty years because England was touched with such dedicated stewardship.

A biblical view of tithing. "Woe to you, teachers of the law and Pharisees, you hypocrites! You give a tenth of your spices—mint, dill, and cumin. But you have neglected the more important matters of the law—justice, mercy, and faithfulness. You should have practiced the latter, without neglecting the former" (Matthew 23:23 NIV). Jesus said tithing was proper, and thus relevant to us. Admittedly, tithing is nowhere specifically commanded in the New Testament, since that is not the genius of God's method under grace. Instead of legislating regulations, Jesus enunciated principles by which His disciples were to regulate their conduct. "I am not commanding you" were Paul's words. He knew that a lavish hand without a loving heart was valueless.

The patriarchs practiced tithing four hundred years before the Law was given (Genesis 14:20; 28:22). The usage of consecrated tithes prevailed among Romans, Greeks, and Arabians as well as with the Jews; so tithing seems to rest on the common law of God's kingdom rather than on special Hebrew legislation. Jesus Himself gave tithes and offerings. Is the servant greater than his Lord?

W. A. Criswell (1909–2002), the great expository teacher for many years at First Baptist Dallas, tells the story about the pastor who was asked, "How many church members do you have?" The answer was, "One hundred fifty." The pastor was further asked, "How many of them are tithers?" The pastor replied, "One hundred fifty." In astonishment the inquirer exclaimed, "What! All one hundred fifty, the entire church, are tithers?" "Yes indeed," said the pastor. "About fifty of them bring the tithe to the storehouse, and God collects it from the rest." In the end "we do not cheat God," concludes Dr. Criswell. "I can either give it to Him in a deeply spiritual act of worship, or He can collect it. In either case, God gets His own."[3]

What does God truly want from us? Since no one has ever seen the Father, we need to listen to Jesus, who said: "You shall love the LORD your God with all your heart, with all your soul, and with all your mind. This is the first and great commandment" (Matthew 22:37–38).

And Jesus has said that if we love Him, we will obey Him—and that includes how we handle His money, His possessions, and His time!

SATURDAY: Building a Fireproof Life

*"If anyone's work is burned, he will suffer loss; but **he himself will be saved**, yet so **as through fire**."*

—1 Corinthians 3:15

What we have been studying in Revelation is only a foretaste of what is to come. But God has not left us without instructions. In Revelation we have seen Truth to live by for a safe future. So, how do we survive in the early twenty-first century? We need to build a fireproof life. Thus, there are three truths that I want you to remember from this week so that you can truly give God what is His.

Truth 1: Jesus compares your earthly life to a building, so you must watch what you build with—and where. Jesus says to build your life with what won't burn up: *"As a wise master builder I have laid the foundation, and another builds on it. But let each one take heed how he builds on it. For no other foundation can anyone lay than that which is laid, which is Jesus Christ. Now if anyone builds on this foundation with gold, silver, precious stones, wood, hay, straw, each one's work will become clear; for the Day will declare it, because it will be revealed by fire; and the fire will test each one's work, of what sort it is. If anyone's work which he has built on it endures, he will receive a reward. If anyone's work is burned, he will suffer loss; but he himself will be saved, yet so as through fire."* (1 Corinthians 3:10–16).

With what are you building your life? Are you building it with wood, hay, and stubble that will burn up—or are you building your life with gold, silver, and precious stones? The gold speaks of seeking God first; the silver and precious stones speak of sacrificing your time, talents, and resources to God before they dissipate and burned up here.

Truth 2: Jesus says your life is a stewardship, so watch where you invest it. As a faithful steward, beware of investing your life—and His money—in the pursuit of so-called "Make it rich quick!" schemes. Such scams bilk people out of millions, fold companies, and cause stock market crashes.

God is going to let everyone know once and for all whom we really lived for—ourselves or for Him. He says that "we must all appear before the judgment seat of Christ, that each one may receive the things done in the body, . . . whether good or bad" (2 Corinthians 5:10). That is decided one moment, one day, one week, one month at a time through living in the light of eternity.

Truth 3: Jesus says your life is like a race, so watch out for the rules. Know the boundaries, and keep the "baggage" at a minimum. Stay within the lines, follow the rules, and be careful to not get tripped up in the race. Paul says, "Since we are surrounded by so great a cloud of witnesses, let us lay aside every weight, and the sin which so easily ensnares us, and let us run with endurance the race that is set before us, looking unto Jesus, the author and finisher of our faith" (Hebrews 12:1–2).

If anything trips you up in life, get rid of it—everything that holds you back and keeps getting caught so that it drags you down (like the long robes men wore in that day that they would tie up and tuck into their belt so they could run without getting tripped up). Check your life to see if you have piled up too much baggage that will prevent you from saying "YES, LORD"—yes to His will and His way. Can you really pull up stakes at any time to do God's will, or will it interrupt your plans? God says to keep the baggage to a minimum so that you can follow Him.

In 2 Corinthians, Paul said that the Macedonians excelled in their giving because they gave of themselves first. If you have never surrendered yourself, you need to do it now. There is no substitute for giving yourself to the Lord. You will never know the joy of the grace of giving (or any other grace) until you do!

WEEK 41
Living Contentedly for Christ

{ Matthew 11:28–30 }

As the end of days approaches, you can find hope
as you learn to live contentedly for Christ!

SUNDAY: A Lifelong Refuge for the Weary

*"**I have learned** in whatever state I am, **to be content**: I know how to be abased, and I know how to abound. . . . I can do all things through Christ who strengthens me."*
—Philippians 4:11–13

This is the last of my three-part "Life Stewardship Series." The first week of the series (Week 39) we learned how to give our all to God. Last week, we focused on how to give God what is His in this life. Now we will learn how to live contentedly and victoriously for Christ—our Great Physician's antidote for worldliness.

Worldliness itself can be a symptom of being totally stressed out, weary with the continual "drip, drip, drip" of the demands of living in a fast-paced society that is spinning out of control. As a result, many Christians look to distractions that will give even a moment's reprieve from their problems. But that is not a long term solution, and it certainly does not contribute to building a fireproof life.

If anyone should have been stressed out and weary, it was Jesus. He lived the perfect human life, yet He lived in a whirlwind of activity. He was constantly eating, walking, talking, and sleeping with twelve men who never seemed to leave Him alone. His life was so full of people and ministry that He often didn't have a chance to stop to eat because vast crowds and desperate individuals sought him out. He was even chided, rebuked, and scoffed at by His own family.

Jesus was also the personal target of Satan, who tempted Him, tried to derail Him, and entered people to drive them to destroy Him. He was thus attacked by every demon that could be rounded up to scream at Him, thrash around in front of Him, and seek to bother Him. And through Satan's influence, civil and religious authorities hounded him, always plotting to catch Him and take Him off for punishment and execution.

Yet, in the midst of all that, Jesus was peaceful, calm, focused, and confidently following God's will. How did He do that? If we follow Christ, we can find His secret. Though we can never be sinless, we can learn to let the Holy Spirit empower us to imitate Jesus' pattern for the perfect life in step with God's will. Although He lived an extremely full, busy, and demanding life, every time Jesus is seen in the Scriptures He is composed, and led by the Spirit.

Jesus was God, yet He lived the perfect human life as a man. What kept that perfect life on earth so strong? It was time alone with God that rested His soul. He had cultivated the discipline of resting in His Father by being alone with Him. Jesus had learned the secret of waiting on God. His whole life reveals that intimate communion with God is needed to live a godly life full of power, under the control of God's Spirit. And He calls each of us to do the same. So you must learn to seek and find a solitary place in your life to be alone with God regularly. If you do, this is what you will find:

- Christ is your "holy place" and your "righteousness." He is the only Refuge when you feel unclean, defiled, or guilty.
- Christ is your safe and strong "shoulder." He is the only Refuge when you feel weary, exhausted, or stressed.
- Christ is your "fellowship." He is the only Refuge when you are lonely, and feel left out, left behind, homeless, or forsaken.
- Christ is your "stronghold" or "fortress." He is the only Refuge when you feel helpless, fearful, and powerless.
- Christ is "exalted" and He is in the "heights." He is the only Refuge when your heart darkens and you feel hopeless.
- Christ is "separated" and holy, made higher than the heavens. He is the only Refuge when you struggle and feel so weak when you are tempted.

You will find so much more in Christ if you spend time alone with Him regularly. Instead of fleeing to the world and its enticements, flee to Jesus as your Refuge from weariness!

My Prayer for You This Week: *Father, our hope is in You. You are our Refuge. Although You do not remove the difficulties of life, You just make it so much sweeter in those times when we flee to You. For there in Your embrace we find hope and joy and peace and strength to go on—and to go* back and to endure until You come or call. May we do that in Your glorious name, that name that is above every name. We pray in the name of Jesus, Amen.

MONDAY: Finding Christ

*"Come to Me, all you who labor and are heavy laden, and I will **give you rest**."*
—MATTHEW 11:28

Jesus promises that If we to come to Him, we will find a resting place in a Friend on whom we can lay our burdens. A new believer typically asks, "Can I hold out?" God compassionately replies, "I will hold you, My child!" The Lord Jesus is our strong and loving Savior.

Because most Christians can find no rest trying to live life their way instead of God's, they become weary of the daily grind. What are some common roots for weariness?

First, we are weary because of the **change and stress** which derail us from seeking God's promised rest: " 'In returning and rest you shall be saved; in quietness and confidence shall be your strength' " (Isaiah 30:15).

Secondly, we are weary because of the **ceaseless pressures of debt** that prevent us from taking advantage of God's promised rest.[1] God says, "Oh, that you had heeded My commandments! Then your peace would have been like a river, and your righteousness like the waves of the sea" (Isaiah 48:18).

Today, our lives are addictively intertwined in the economic system, and the credit-debt mentality has been fully normalized. Someone has described a modern American as a person "who drives a credit union-financed car over a bond-financed highway on credit-card gas to open a charge account at a department store so he can fill his bank-financed home with installment-purchased furniture."[2]

Thirdly, we are weary because the **hurry and rush** surrounding us always displaces God's time for us to rest. Even our sentences are peppered with such words as *time crunch, fast food, rush hour, frequent flyer, expressway, overnight delivery, and rapid transit.* The products and services we use further attest to our hurry: We pull in our speeding cars for gas and snacks at QuikTrip, send packages overnight by Federal Express, talk while we do other things on a cell phone service called Sprint, manage our personal finances on Quicken, schedule our appointments on a DayRunner, diet with SlimFast, and even buy swimming gear made by Speedo.

Rest for our souls is the great necessity of our spiritual lives! We need to be alone with God daily. We need to find times to get away alone. We need to get up early if necessary. Few of us are called to spend many hours in daily prayer, but *all* of us must spend *some* time. If it is impossible when the family is awake, pray before they get up. If you have no place you can do this at home, find a place to park your car on the way to work and pray in the anonymity of the passing traffic. However you do this is up to you, but you need to make time to find Christ who is the Refuge for the weary!

TUESDAY: Respond to Christ

*"**Come** to Me, all you who labor and are heavy laden, and I will give you rest. **Take** My yoke upon you and **learn** from Me, for I am gentle and lowly in heart, and you will find rest for your souls."*
—Matthew 11:28–29

From these verses, we can easily see how Jesus is the Refuge for the weary. Note the three imperatives: come, take, and learn. There is no sheep of Jesus' pasture that He doesn't invite to find rest in Him. He seeks us, finds us, and offers His perfect rest to us. Jesus said, "I am the answer. Come to Me!" This is salvation. Rest for the weary starts with salvation because the lost (and disobedient believers) have no rest in their sin. Restlessness is their lifestyle: "But the wicked are like the troubled sea, When it cannot rest. . . . 'There is no peace,' says my God, 'for the wicked' " (Isaiah 57:20–21).

In God's Word, listening to Christ is listening to the Holy Spirit and that means obeying the Word of God. Jesus called for us to completely turn unto Him as the way to live life. Now look at the bold second half of verse 28: "Come to Me, **all you who labor and are heavy laden,** and I will give you rest." This sounds so beautiful in the word-for-word rendering of the Greek. Here is each word in order of the text: "Come toward Me all the ones laboring and the ones having been packed, and I will rest you." This calls for us to admit that something is wrong. We have to acknowledge our need. Therefore, Jesus calls for those who are overloaded—"all the ones laboring and the ones having been packed"—to come to Him.

Is life itself laborious for you? Do you feel packed in, and piled so high, that you can't take another step? Then Jesus says, "You need to listen to Me." How can you best do that? By getting to the root of the problem.

Dr. Robert Swenson has expressed modern society's problem as OVERLOAD. Today, we will cover the first part of a diagnostic test that can help you discern whether you are suffering from this deadly condition called "overload." As you read, carefully think about whether or not you have any of these symptoms (most people do!).[3]

We allow our lives to have activity overload. We book our lives weeks into the future, and often in the desire to be more efficient, we book several things into the same time period. "Activity overload takes away the pleasure of anticipation and the delight of reminiscence." God says: "Stop! Hold still so that you can know Me." (See Psalm 46:10.)

We allow our lives to have change overload. "Nothing defines our age more than the furious and relentless increase in the rate of change," summarizes historian Arthur M. Schlesinger Jr. For thousands of years of recorded history change came in a slow, controlled, and understandable rate, but now we are brutally jerked forward at warp speed—whether we like it or not. God says, "Seek out the old paths where you can find rest for your soul!" (See Jeremiah 6:16.)

We allow our lives to have commitment overload. Most of us make more commitments than we have time to give them. In his great book, *Balancing Life's Demands*, Dr. J. Grant Howard says, "Some people can't say no. They take on too many relationships and too many responsibilities. They enroll in too many courses, hold down too many jobs, volunteer for too many tasks, make too many appointments, serve on too many committees, have too many friends. They are trying to be all things to all men all at once all by themselves!"[4] God says, "Seek Me most—seek me with all your heart." (See Psalm 27:4.)

We allow our lives to have choice overload. In the 1970s there were 11,767 items in the average supermarket. In the early twenty-first century, that number has risen to near 30,000. This includes over 186 different choices of breakfast cereal alone! And for entertainment, you can get a satellite dish that offers 1,500 movie choices per month! Futurist Allan Toffler warns, "We are in fact, racing toward 'over-choice.'"[5] God says, "Choose whom and what you will serve with all your heart." (See Joshua 24:15; James 1:8.)

We allow our lives to have competition overload. It is part of the American dream. To compete is American and it is therefore constantly emphasized in school, business, and athletics—but is it spiritually healthy? God says, "Jesus taught a non-aggressive, non-self-asserting, non-self-promoting lifestyle for His followers in the Sermon on the Mount." (Read His Beatitudes in Matthew 5:1–8.)

What different counsel we get from man! J. B. Phillips (1906–1982) illustrates this when he alters the Beatitudes to read as follows:

1. Happy are the "pushers": for they get on in the world.
2. Happy are the hard-boiled: for they never let life hurt them.
3. Happy are they who complain: for they get their own way in the end.
4. Happy are the blasé: for they never worry over their sins.
5. Happy are the slave drivers: for they get results.
6. Happy are the knowledgeable men of the world: for they know their way around.
7. Happy are the troublemakers: for they make people take notice of them.[6]

We allow our lives to have debt overload. From the White House to the bungalow on your street, most of America is awash in red ink. It is debilitating and unbiblical! God says, "Do not steal, nor hold on to another's possessions more than love would allow." Look at Romans 13:8: "Owe no one anything except to love one another, for he who loves another has fulfilled the law" (Romans 13:8). Does "owe no one anything" refer primarily to the Christian's financial practices? Some people believe that it does, and that it is a sin to have a debt.

J. Hudson Taylor, the godly missionary to China, would never incur a debt, basing his conviction on this verse. Charles Spurgeon, the great Baptist preacher, had the same conviction. However, the Bible does not forbid borrowing or legal financial transactions that involve interest. What the Bible does forbid is the charging of high interest, robbing the brethren, and failing to pay honest debts (see Ex. 22:25–27; Neh. 5:1–11). Matthew 25:27 and Luke 19:23 indicate that banking and investing for gain are not wrong. Certainly no one should get into unnecessary debt, or sign contracts he cannot maintain. "Thou shalt not steal." But to make Romans 13:8 apply to all kinds of legal obligations involving money is, to me, stretching a point.[7]

We allow our lives to have decision overload. "Every day we have more tough decisions to make and less time to do it in. The trivial ones are objectionable just because of how many there are [what flavor, which topping, mint or tartar control, low fat, low sodium, diet or regular ...] But we also are facing new choices generations past never dreamed of: whether or not to wait to have children; whether to move and change jobs; whether both dad and mom should work outside the home; whether we should put grandma in the home or not. Too many decisions trivial or not in too short a time is vintage overload."[8] God says, "Bring each decision in life to Me. Wait for Me to lead, and don't be in a hurry to just go on through life your own way—and thus miss My blessing and My leading." (See Proverbs 3:5–6.)

We allow our lives to have hurry overload. "Haste is a modern ailment. It is also fashionably American. Our lives are nonstop, lived at a breathless pace. We walk fast, talk fast, eat fast and then excuse our selves by saying, 'I must run.' "[9] Alexander Solzhenitsyn once said that hastiness and superficiality were the psychic diseases of the twentieth century. God says, "Wait patiently for Me. Don't run ahead and don't lag behind. Walk in step with My Spirit." (See Psalm 37:7–9; Galatians 5:16, 24.)

Have you spotted any symptoms so far of this deadly condition called overload? If so, I encourage you to pray about each of them, asking the Lord to continue to open your eyes to areas in your life that need His gentle touch.

WEDNESDAY: How to Unload Your Life

"Do not lay up for yourselves treasures on earth . . . ; but **lay up . . . treasures in heaven**. *. . . For where your treasure is, there your heart will be also."*
—Matthew 6:19–21

Yesterday was the first part of a diagnostic test that can help us detect the symptoms of overload. Two remain, which I'll cover today, and then share God's simple solution for getting out from under such a deadly burden. So then, what are some other ways that we have let ourselves become entrapped in the overload syndrome?

We allow our lives to have possession overload. We have more "things per person" than any other nation in history. Closets are full, storage space is used up, and cars can't fit into garages. Having first imprisoned us with debt, possessions then take over our houses and occupy our time. This begins to sound like an invasion. Everything I own owns me in return as I become responsible to care for it, maintain it, clean it, insure it, store it, update it, and so forth. So why would I want more? God says, "Beware of having so much in life that the care of things makes your heart grow cold toward Me." (See Matthew 13:22; Luke 12:21; 1Timothy 6:8–10; Hebrews 13:5.)

We allow our lives to have media overload. Did you know that a single edition of the Sunday *New York Times* has more information than the average seventeenth-century Briton would have encountered in a lifetime? We live in an era of information overload! Solomon, who God says is the wisest man who ever lived, had this to say at the end of his life: "Of making many books there is no end, and much study is wearisome to the flesh" (Ecclesiastes 12:12). I like John MacArthur's comment on that verse: "Books written on any other subject than God's revealed wisdom will only proliferate the uselessness of man's thinking."[10]

But an even more damaging effect than being constantly bombarded with information in books is the power of TV, movies, and games. Ninety-nine percent of Americans have TV in their homes; the average U.S. home has two, and both are blaring seven hours a day. Such distraction robs us of depth, neutralizes the benefits of meditation, and encourages restlessness.

In contrast to time spent on the information-overload treadmill, how well do you know God? How much depth is there in your personal relationship with Him? For instance, do you know His Word as well as you know your favorite hobby or sport? That is the danger of information overload—our minds become full of so much that does not matter to God or for eternity. God says, "To know Me, you must guard your heart." (See Isaiah 33:14b-17.)

Spending regular time alone with God is the only way that you will ever get to see "the King in His beauty." You will never find God's best for your life while drowning in the overload syndrome. Remember what wise old Solomon concluded after his quest to find the meaning of life: "Fear God and keep His commandments, for this is man's all. For God will bring every work into judgment, Including every secret thing, whether good or evil" (Ecclesiastes 12:13–14).

Submit to Christ's rule. It would be the rare person who did not spot any symptoms of the "overload syndrome" in his or her own life. But the good news is this: you can find relief and rest for your soul by obedience to Christ's command: "Take My yoke upon you" (Matthew 11:29). The yoke is a universal sign of submission. The Bible begins and ends with the call to submit to Christ. From Adam and Eve in Genesis to the end of the age in Revelation, Scripture tells us that we are to obey God—or face the consequences along with those who rebel and come under God's endless wrath forever.

Have you given obedience to God the highest place in your life, as the inspiration for every action and motivation? If you yield to the searching of the Holy Spirit, you may find that you have never given Him total submission, or that you have somehow, over time, taken it back. I exhort you therefore to go before the Spirit in prayer and ask Him to show you: how defective the Christian life is where obedience doesn't rule all; how that life can be exchanged for one of full surrender to absolute obedience; and how sure it is that God in Christ will enable us to live it out![11] So ask yourself: *Does submitting to God take the highest place in my life?*

Become Christ's lifelong disciple. "Take My yoke upon you and **learn from Me** . . . and you will find rest for your souls" (Matthew 11:29). Cling to Jesus that you may obey His admonition to "learn from Me." Surround yourself with His true Word. Meekness toward God is that disposition of spirit in which we accept His dealings with us as good, and therefore without disputing or resisting. In the Old Testament, the meek are those wholly relying on God, rather than their own strength, to defend them against injustice. Thus, meekness toward evil people means knowing God is permitting the injuries they inflict, that He is using them to purify His elect, and that He will deliver His elect in His time. (See Isaiah 41:17; Luke 18:1–8.)

Gentleness, or meekness, is the opposite of self-assertiveness and self-interest. It stems from trust in God's goodness and control over any situation. The gentle person is not occupied with self at all. This is a work of the Holy Spirit, not of the human will (Galatians 5:23). Are you a gentle spirit—or one who is wrapped up in self?

THURSDAY: Christ's Promised Refuge for the Weary

"I am gentle and lowly in heart, and **you will find rest for your souls***. For My yoke is easy and My burden is light."*
—Matthew 11:29–30

As we continue our study of how to apply Matthew 11:28–30 to learning to live contentedly and victoriously for Christ, we have come to the part where we get to find out how to enjoy Christ's promised refuge for the weary. What a blessing!

Everything that Jesus did was in submission to knowing and doing the will of God. This included:

Jesus' purpose in life: "Behold, I have come—In the volume of the book it is written of Me—To do Your will, O God" (Hebrews 10:7). Do you want God's will more than your own plans?

Jesus' delight in life: "My food is to do the will of Him who sent Me, and to finish His work" (John 4:34). Are the things of earth more delightful to you than the Truth of God?

Jesus' patience in life: "Sacrifice and offering You did not desire; My ears You have opened. Burnt offering and sin offering you did not require" (Psalm 40:6). Are you patient enough to let God choose what is best? Remember: God gives the very best to those who leave the choice to Him!

Jesus' priority in life: "I have come down from heaven, not to do My own will, but the will of Him who sent Me" (John 6:38). Are you dying to self daily so that you are alive unto Christ in the Spirit?

Jesus' attitude in life: "Father, if it is Your will, take this cup away from Me; nevertheless not My will, but Yours, be done" (Luke 22:42). Are you humbly whispering daily to Jesus: "Not my will, but Yours, be done"?

Again, I remind you: Jesus is the Refuge for the weary. There is no sheep of His pasture that He doesn't invite to find rest in Him. He seeks us, finds us, and offers His perfect rest to us. As the world around us accelerates, our energies wane. But we are not defenseless victims. Fleeing to Jesus as your Refuge will replace frenzy with peace and rest!

Find stillness as you bow before God. "Be still and know that I am God" (Psalm 46:10). Before hurrying past that profound command, stop and consider it in your mind. The scene is one of stillness and quietness, listening and waiting before Him. That is largely a foreign experience in these busy times. Nevertheless, knowing God deeply and intimately requires such discipline. Silence before Him is indispensable if we hope to add depth to our spiritual life.

Offer yourself in surrender to God. This is done by trusting the Lord completely as you exercise the discipline of surrender. There is a wonderfully challenging book by the founder of Wheaton College, Raymond Edman.[12] Nothing better describes the give-and-take struggle of our early years as a Christian. They are words from a collection of Puritan prayers and devotions:

When thou wouldst guide me
I control myself.
When thou wouldst be sovereign
I rule myself.
When thou wouldst take care of me

I suffice myself.
When I should depend on thy providing
I supply myself.
When I should submit to thy providence
I follow my will.
When I should study, honor, trust thee,
I serve myself;
I fault and correct thy laws
to suit myself,
Instead of thee I look to
Man's approbation,
And am by nature an idolater.
Lord, it is my chief design to bring my
Heart back to thee.

Prepare for true worship.[13] The answer to the problem begins with Saturday preparation. (Any men who interpret the following as women's work are wrong. Both husband and wife should share responsibility for the practical and spiritual preparations for the Lord's Day.) It is advisable that young families have their clothing clean and laid out on Saturday night, and even that the breakfast be decided upon. The whereabouts of Bibles and lessons should be known, and even better, ought to be collected and ready. There should be an agreed-upon time to get up which leaves plenty of time to get ready for church. Going to bed at a reasonable hour is also a good idea. Spiritually, prayer about the Lord's Day is essential—prayer for the service, the music, the pastors, one's family, and oneself.[14]

Cultivate the discipline of simplicity in your life. You can do this by reordering your private world.[15]

The Decision:	The Discipline:
To reorder one's private world	Simplicity
To be still	Silence
To cultivate serenity	Solitude
To trust the Lord completely	Surrender

FRIDAY: Enjoying Jesus—Your Refuge From Weariness

> "Truly my soul silently waits for God; From Him comes my salvation. He only is my rock and my salvation; He is my defense; I shall not be greatly moved."
>
> —Psalm 62:1–2

Fleeing to Jesus as your Refuge will help you have the genuine expectancy of God's presence. A knowledge of God through His Word ought to heighten your expectations and instill healthy fear and reverence. As Annie Dillard wrote: "On the whole, I do not find Christians, outside of the Catacombs, sufficiently sensible of conditions. Does anyone have the foggiest idea what sort of power we so blithely invoke? Or as I suspect, does no one believe a word of it? . . . It is madness to wear ladies' straw hats and velvet hats to church; we should all be wearing crash helmets. Ushers should issue life preservers and signal flares; they should lash us to our pews. For the sleeping god may wake someday and take offense, or the waking god may draw us out to where we can never return."[16]

Fleeing to Jesus as your Refuge will help you preserve your experience of the depths of God in your life. How can you preserve your heart for the Lord's Day? Edith Schaeffer tells how, when living in Villars, Switzerland, the church bells would toll every Saturday at 4:30 P.M. as a reminder to prepare for the Lord's Day. The bells were ignored by most but were a poignant reminder of a more enlightened day.[17]

Is Christ like a "city of refuge" to you? Do you find Him easy to reach? Are His arms open to you? Do you see His entrance as never locked, and that He is a completely sufficient Refuge? Do you see that there is no other hope but Him? Then He is *your* blessed Refuge! (If you would like to study the wonderful truths of this facet of Jesus, see the description of the "Christ Our Refuge" resource on the DTBM website.)

How can you start cultivating the practice of fleeing to Christ's promised refuge for the weary? Jesus demonstrated that as being our priority, but where do we start? We simply begin by making it a precious habit to read God's Word every day. Remember to faithfully follow the adage I mentioned earlier in this book: no Bible—no breakfast; no Bible—no bed.

Rest for your soul comes most readily by reading God's Word. This is the voice of God, and we must listen. No Christian can lead a Spirit-filled life full of power without regularly reading the Bible. Our minds are such that we do not retain what we need to know. They need to be refreshed again and again—which includes memorizing and meditating upon God's Word regularly!

SATURDAY: Rest at Last!

"Blessed is the man [whose] . . . delight is in the law of the Lord, And in His law **he meditates day and night***. . . . And whatever he does shall prosper."*
—PSALM 1:1–3.

Why is meditating upon the Word so very important? Meditation brings us immediately into the intimate presence of God. Few are willing to pay the price, but for those who do, the rewards are great!

I believe Mrs. Nguyen Thi An (name changed) learned the art of fleeing to Jesus as her Refuge in weariness. She is a glorious example of how to live contentedly and victoriously for Christ—regardless of the circumstances. Though she has lost everything, she has all things in One. Her husband, her home, and her belongings were all taken away, yet the Vietnamese could not take her contentment.

Mrs. An's husband was a pastor in Vietnam. When police closed their church, he was thrown into prison. Without official papers, she and her children were evicted from their apartment, but her faith forged a sanctuary out of her surroundings, from which she greets us:

My Dear Friends,

. . . You know around here we are experiencing hardships, but we thank the Lord He is comforting us and caring for us in every way. When we experience misfortune, adversity, distress and hardship, only then do we see the real blessing of the Lord poured down on us in such a way that we cannot contain it.

We have been obliged recently to leave our modest apartment and for over two months have been living on a balcony. The rain has been beating down and soaking us. Sometimes in the middle of the night we are forced to gather our blankets and run to seek refuge in a stairwell.

Do you know what I do then? I laugh and I praise the Lord, because we can still take shelter in the stairwell. I think of how many people are experiencing much worse hardships than I am. Then I remember the words of the Lord, "To the poor, O Lord, You are a refuge from the storm, a shadow from the heat" (cp. Isaiah 25:4), and I am greatly comforted. . . .

Our Father . . . is the One who according to the Scriptures does not break the bruised reed nor put out the flickering lamp. He is the One who looks after the orphan and the widow. He is the One who brings blessings and peace to numberless people.

I do not know what words to use in order to describe the love that the Lord has shown our family. I only can bow my knee and my heart and offer to the Lord words of deepest thanks and praise. Although we have lost our house and our possessions, we have not lost the Lord, and He is enough. With the Lord I have everything. The only thing I would fear losing is His blessing!

Could I ask you and our friends in the churches abroad to continue to pray for me that I will faithfully follow the Lord and serve Him regardless of what the circumstances may be? As far as my husband is concerned, I was able to visit him this past summer. We had a 20-minute conversation that brought us great joy. . . .

I greet you with my love.

Mrs. Nguyen Thi An[18]

Learn from Mrs. An's wonderful example of how to live contentedly and victoriously in Christ. And then flee on your own to Jesus as your eternal and secure Refuge!

Make a choice to live in hope. I pray that over the past three weeks you have made the choice to live in hope by giving your all to God, giving God what is His in this life, and committing to learn how to live contentedly and victoriously for Christ! May God, through the Holy Spirit, grant the empowerment to embrace as a lifestyle 1 Timothy 6's seven keys to biblical contentment:

1. Remember that things are only temporary (vv. 6–7).
2. Only seek necessities—wait for the rest (v. 8).
3. Avoid a consuming desire for prosperity (vv. 9–10).
4. Flee materialism (v. 11).
5. Cling to eternal life (vv. 12–16).
6. Fix your hope on God (v. 17).
7. Give until it hurts (v. 18).

WEEK 42
Look for the Returning Jesus

{ Revelation 19:1–10 }

As the end of days approaches, you can find hope as you look for the returning Jesus!

SUNDAY: Home At Last

*"Many will come from east and west, **and sit down with Abraham, Isaac, and Jacob** in the kingdom of heaven."*
—Matthew 8:11

Are you getting ready for the ultimate banquet? The King of Kings, the Lord of the Universe, is preparing a wedding feast like none other! In the most breathtaking location imaginable, He is spreading an immense table. The greatest names of all times will be present and seated. At dinner the invited guests will be rubbing shoulders with Adam and his lovely wife, Eve. One of their twin sons, Abel, will be sitting with them as well as Seth and his wife. Noah and family will be nearby. On down the long table lavishly set will be the likes of Job and clan, Abraham, Isaac, Jacob, and Joseph. What a reunion as Moses and Elijah walk around talking with guests and visiting with old friends! Further on, Jeremiah sits in rapt attention with Daniel and Isaiah as Ezekiel points out again the wonders they see about the Banquet Hall. Interspersed with all these Old Testament saints will be multitudes of beaming faces well known to us. Matthew and the rest of the twelve will be at the entrances to the twelve gates that the guests will stream through on their way to be seated at the banquet. Paul, at one gate, is weeping for joy as he finally sees so many of his spiritual children and grandchildren. At another gate, John also weeps for joy as he returns to this place he saw from Patmos.

And then the party begins. The hallelujahs begin to echo down the aisles of the Marriage Supper of the Lamb. Expectantly, each guest personally invited by Jesus looks up. And then they see Jesus, the glorious and majestic Savior, as He comes to each and all, calling them by name, extending His nail-scarred hands, and touching them with His love. We have come to the culmination of what all saints desire. It is the wedding banquet, the Marriage Supper of the Lamb, and it is the scene of Revelation 19 when those who have loved Him, and waited all their life for Him, honor Jesus. It is the assembly of those who have and love the testimony of Jesus.

The first ten verses of Revelation 19, which we will cover this week, have these very glorious themes: the **Celebration** (vv. 1–6) and the **Consummation** (vv. 7–10). There are four hallelujahs in the first six verses, and in verse 7 a calling to the celebration starts. If verses 1–6 are the celebration *preparation*, then verses 7–10 are the *consummation* of all that God has promised.

It is hard to put these things on a time line chart, however. God knows the end from the beginning. What that means is that when you are God, and you are outside and above time, the beginning of Creation, the present time, and the consummation of all things are all equally happening at the same time. We are linear: when we try to illustrate time, we draw a straight line and mark events on it. But to God, past, present, and future occur all at the same time—the end and the beginning are all equally before Him. If you think about it, in a very real sense, that means that at this banquet Enoch, Paul, and the people at the end of the Tribulation will all get there at the same time we do. Chronologically, it is different times; but in eternity it is all happening at the same time. Thus, John was actually seeing these events because everything is unfolding before God simultaneously. Amazing!

I believe that everyone is going to get to the banquet table at the same time. That is why I don't believe that the bride of Christ refers to only the church; I believe it encompasses all the saints of all time. The Bible never specifically says that the bride is the church, only that the church is an espoused virgin and is going to be married (1 Corinthians 11:2; Ephesians 5). Israel is His wife, but the saints are all collectively coming to the marriage supper and will be married to the Lord in Christ. What these verses picture is a marvelous event!

God does not distinguish between pre-Flood saints, pre-Abrahamic saints, pre-Mosaic saints, pre-New Testament saints, pre-Tribulation saints, pre-millennial saints, and pre-eternity saints. In heaven, there is one great merger of them all.

As you reflect upon the prayer below, imagine that you are at that banquet even now and think of the delights you shall soon experience with Jesus.

My Prayer for You This Week: *Father, the love that sent Your Son to die the most cruel and humiliating death imaginable to pay the penalty for our sin is beyond comprehension! Now, not only are we going to be able to get to heaven, but also You are preparing a banquet for all Your saints to celebrate with the One who loved us and gave Himself for us. You are going to allow us to be married to our Savior forever! Oh, Father, we do not understand the concept of spiritual union with You. But what we can understand is that it is going to be glorious, and that there is something we need to do here to get ready for that wedding—to make sure that we have the appropriate attire. We pray that Your Spirit would help us prepare for this marriage celebration as it draws closer. We ask that You would bless our hearts through Your Word this week, and may we respond in a pleasing manner to You. In the name of Jesus we pray, Amen.*

MONDAY: A Celebration of Jesus' Salvation and Judgment

*"I heard a loud voice of a great multitude in heaven, saying, '****Alleluia! Salvation and glory and honor and power belong to the Lord our God!*** *For true and righteous are His judgments, because He has judged the great harlot who corrupted the earth with her fornication; and He has avenged on her the blood of His servants shed by her.'"*

—Revelation 19:1–2

What we are going to see in Revelation 19:1–6 is God's greatest celebration of all the ages. Verse 1 starts off with "Alleluia!"—which is the same word as "hallelujah." There are 144 mentions of this word in the Bible; four of these are in verses 1–6. Seventy-six are in the Psalms where it says "may God be praised"; sixty-four occur in the rest of the Bible. "Alleluia"—meaning "Praise God"—is an imperative.

Each *"alleluia"* in these celebration verses is related to one of these themes: a celebration of Jesus our **salvation** (v. 1); a celebration of Jesus the **judgment** (vv. 2–3); a celebration of the Jesus we **worship** (vv. 4–5); and a celebration of Jesus our **sovereign** (v. 6).

A celebration of Jesus our salvation. "I heard a loud voice of a great multitude in heaven, saying, 'Alleluia! Salvation and glory and honor, and power belong to the Lord our God!'" (Revelation 19:1). This is the first celebration of salvation because Babylon, the false worship of God in world religions, has been overthrown; materialism and Satan's kingdom have also been overthrown. Finally, as God is gathering all to the banquet table, salvation is celebrated.

We should recognize that, all through the ages, each saint has been saved the same way. I am saved because I personally looked back and believed that Jesus Christ was the Lamb of God—who bore the pain and paid the price of my sins with His own blood on the cross. Adam, Enoch, Job, and Abraham all looked forward to that same Lamb of God—the One who would come as a sin offering. All of us who are redeemed believe in a substitutionary atonement. They looked forward to the cross, and we look back. The people in the Tribulation and Millennium will look even further back to the Substitute. All who are saved say, "I cannot save myself; Someone paid the price in my place, and that was God in human flesh, the Lamb, Jesus Christ." That is what is complete here: He has brought His redeemed to be with Him, and He is now there in their presence.

Here is why it is so hard to make a time line chart of this: do the events in Revelation 19:1–10 (heaven exalts over Babylon) have to happen before verse 11 (Christ on a white horse)? What is absolutely remarkable is that John is seeing these events from God's perspective. We know that they are going to happen precisely as God wants them to happen, but Revelation cannot be charted well. Why is that? As soon as my chart doesn't match your chart, you won't listen anymore due to human nature. As 19:10 tells us, this book was written to draw us to worship Christ, and this banquet does, too. This is a celebration of His salvation completed, and at this point we will forever be in the presence of God and the saints of all times!

How can all that take place before the Millennium is over? From God's perspective, no one is going to be late; that is why I believe that everyone gets to the banquet at the same time. Yes, those who are already dead are absent from the body and present with the Lord. How does that work? I don't know. But I do know that Scripture assures us that those who die are immediately in the presence of Christ. I also know from Scripture that the Old Testament saints before the cross went to a place of waiting for the presence of Christ. When Jesus finished His work on the cross, He went and got them, and took them to live in His presence. And I know that all the people in the future, who have not yet trusted in Christ, are going to have to do that. God is not going to let anybody be late and miss this great event. He will work it out, so you needn't worry, just file the matter in your "too hard to understand" folder—and trust Him!

A celebration of Jesus the judgment. "For true and righteous are His judgments, because He has judged the great harlot who corrupted the earth with her fornication; and He has avenged on her the blood of His servants shed by her.' Again they said, 'Alleluia! Her smoke rises up forever and ever!'" (Revelation 19:2–3).

Praise God! Jesus has judged the harlot—the false religions of the world that corrupted the church. Is this celebration proper? Isn't it fascinating that hell is talked about at this banquet? To God, it is not distasteful to talk about hell. You can praise God that the same One who promises that our life will be endless also promises that the judgment of the unrighteous will be eternal. To us, it is hard to understand the two at the same time. It is too awful to contemplate. But God is just and righteous, and He says, "I have so freely offered this salvation that if some reject the offer, it is righteous that I judge them forever." If you struggle with that, as I think all of us do, look at these verses: Psalm 104:35; Romans 12:19; 2 Thessalonians 1:8; Hebrews 10:30.

As Psalm 104:35 reveals, when you worship God, part of the worship should thank God for His sacrifice; the other part should thank Him that He is going to condemn sinners to eternal destruction who refuse His free gift of salvation. Romans 3:5 asks, "Is God unjust who inflicts wrath?" No—God is just.

So then, the answer to whether it is proper to celebrate God's judgment is repeatedly yes. As He said at the overthrow of Sodom: "Far be it from You to do such a thing as this, to slay the righteous with the wicked, so that the righteous should be as the wicked; far be it from You! Shall not the Judge of all the earth do right?" (Genesis 18:25).

TUESDAY: A Celebration to Worship Our Sovereign Jesus

"And the twenty-four elders and the four living creatures fell down and worshiped God who sat on the throne, saying, 'Amen! **Alleluia!***' Then a voice came from the throne, saying, '***Praise our God***, all you His servants and those who fear Him, both small and great!' "*

—Revelation 19:4–5

A celebration of the Jesus we worship. The twenty-four elders may represent the twelve tribes of Israel and the twelve apostles. The twelve foundations of heaven are the apostles, and the twelve gates are the twelve tribes. All of the Scriptures were written through the Jews, and the apostles were the foundation writers of Jesus Christ's gospel of the church; these two groups of twelve merged together. The four living creatures represent all the angels that worship God. They are the ones saying, "Amen! Alleluia!" That is a celebration of worship. But the number twenty-four is only used in Scripture when it relates to priests; so the church plus Israel's twelve plus the apostle's twelve may speak of all of us as Christ's priests in worship.

The "voice came from the throne" could be God speaking, or a voice He creates out of the throne. "His servants and those who fear him, both small and great" are bondservants—those who will be in heaven, at the Marriage Supper, and those who will enjoy God forever. These are His servants, and His servants worship Him. Worship and bowing before Him acknowledges that God is Who He said He is, and thus obedience is His due. A bondservant is someone who does what the Master says. Those who are going to be in heaven are those who have given themselves up to do the will of God.

What is a servant? The Greek word for "servant" is *doulos*, which means "a slave, bondman, man of servile condition; one who gives himself up to another's will; devoted to another to the disregard of one's own interests." In Philippians 2:7 we see that Christ's servants have His mind; in Colossians 4:12 they are prayerfully minded servants; and in 2 Timothy 2:24 they are gently minded servants—God's servants who don't strive and fight to get their way.

The transformed slaves of God will be there to celebrate worshiping Him. He longs for servants whose hearts well up and say, "God, You are who You say You are! I believe that, bow my life before You, and joyfully want to do whatever You say!" Sometimes we all struggle with obedience, but the direction of our life should be toward greater service to Jesus Christ—because this is what we are going to do forever.

Do you recall the parable of the ten virgins? They were waiting for the groom to come for them. While he was delayed, they all slumbered and slept. At midnight they heard the announcement that he had arrived. The five wise virgins arose and took oil in their vessels with their lamps; the five foolish virgins were not prepared, and their lamps went out. As a result, the foolish ones were not allowed into the wedding because they didn't have any oil for their lamps.

Bible scholars often say "oil" is the Holy Spirit. But oil here does not mean the Holy Spirit because the oil is to be purchased, and the Holy Spirit cannot be purchased. What may fit here is that the burning oil represents their Spirit-energized lives—being and living in righteousness as visible saints of God. They could put on an act for a while, but they eventually ran out of oil and never purchased more. (They never were actually living in righteousness and doing good works.) So when they came to the door, their lamps were out; there were no good works in their lives and they are excluded from heaven even though they thought they were going there. If you are saved, you will do good works, which prove that you are going to heaven. There are a lot of foolish people in the church today whose lamps are out. They are not consumed with the desire to be righteous, and to live out Christ's righteousness. When the Bridegroom comes, they are going to be locked out.

Jesus spent all of His ministry warning people who think they are going to heaven but are not, because they are not doing what He said (see Matthew 7:21–23). These people believe that He is Lord by their words, but their works do not flow from a personal relationship with Christ. Who will get in and spend eternity with Christ and God the Father and the Holy Spirit and all the redeemed of all times? Those who do His will. The person Jesus was speaking of most clearly was Judas. He is the prime example. Judas prophesied and preached in Jesus' name; he cast out demons and did other wonders. But Jesus will look at him, and all the other Judases that have filled the church since, and He will say, "I never knew you" (Matthew 7:21–28). How do you know if you know Him? Your works will determine your destiny. They won't get you into heaven, but the nature of your works, if driven by the Spirit, will show that you are going to heaven. That is the catastrophic problem now—people perceive that they can be saved without having a transformed life. Jesus said that those at the Marriage Supper have a transformed life. That is the message of Revelation.

A celebration of Jesus our sovereign. "Alleluia! For the Lord God Omnipotent reigns!" (Revelation 19:6). Jesus is above all: all things are through Him, and to Him, and for His glory! What is this attribute of our God? Isaiah 40 clearly develops His absolute sovereignty. What is His name? The Old Testament name *Shaddai* means "the all-sufficient God, the God who is enough." In the New Testament, God is called "the Almighty" ten times (nine times in Revelation and once in 2 Corinthians 6:14). It is the key word for God in the Book of Job as he discovers in all his struggles that "God is the God who is enough."

As you contemplate His glorious sovereignty, doesn't it just make you want to burst forth and sing: "All hail the pow'r of Jesus' name! / Let angels prostrate fall; / Bring forth the royal diadem, / And crown Him Lord of all"! I hope that is your spirit because, if it isn't, you will feel out of place at the ultimate wedding banquet.

WEDNESDAY: The Consummation—The Wedding Banquet

> "'Let us be glad and rejoice and give Him glory, for the marriage of the Lamb has come, and His wife has made herself ready.' And to her it was granted to be arrayed in fine linen, clean and bright, for the fine linen is the righteous acts of the saints. Then he said to me, 'Write: **Blessed are those who are called to the marriage supper of the Lamb!**" And he said to me, 'These are the true sayings of God.' And I fell at his feet to worship him. But he said to me, 'See that you do not do that! I am your fellow servant, and of your brethren who have the testimony of Jesus. Worship God! For the testimony of Jesus is the spirit of prophecy.'"
>
> —REVELATION 19:7–10

Look at verse seven above. The result of the elements we have looked at is this: we should be glad and rejoice and give Him glory because the marriage of the Lamb has come! His wife has made herself ready. You cannot get ready for heaven in heaven. We are talking about your time on earth—choices you have made and are going to make. If you are the wife-to-be of Jesus Christ, at that moment you are going to be shown for what you did to get ready.

We can learn how to get ready for that great day by understanding how royal weddings were celebrated in the ancient Near East. In that culture, a wedding feast was inseparable from the wedding which involved a weeklong series of meals and festivities, and was the highlight of all social life. For a royal wedding such as the one Jesus mentions here, the celebration often lasted for several weeks. Guests were invited to stay at the house of the groom's parents for the entire occasion, and the father would make as elaborate provisions as he could afford. A royal wedding, of course, would be held in the palace, and a king would be able to afford whatever he desired.

A wedding feast that a king prepared for his son would be a feast of all feasts, and Jesus was therefore picturing the most elaborate celebration imaginable. The fact that it was a wedding celebration was incidental to the purpose of the parable in Matthew 22, the only mention of the groom being that of identifying him as the king's son. No mention at all is made of the bride or of any other aspect of a wedding. The point is that because the feast represents the greatest festivity imaginable, given by the greatest monarch imaginable, for the most-honored guests imaginable, a royal wedding feast was chosen as the illustration of the ultimate celebration.[1]

As we discover in the testimony of Jesus in Revelation 19:1-10, we are with Jesus as He celebrates His union with His wife and bride. Why did Jesus never marry while on earth? He was waiting for His perfect bride in heaven. As His perfect bride, on your way to the table at that heavenly banquet, what gift are you going to have with you? What is your offering of love to the One Who loves you with an everlasting love?

Marriage is a biblical symbol for the relationship between God and His people. Note these excerpts from Old Testament verses where God is speaking to Israel: "For your Maker is your husband" (Isaiah 54:5); "I am married to you" (Jeremiah 3:14); and "I will betroth you to Me" (Hosea 2:19-20).

Salvation—knowing God and being a child of God—is the highest relationship we can know on this planet. God said, "I want you to have the closest human relationship with Me that you will ever know on this planet, only more glorious." But because of Israel's continued unfaithfulness, God divorced them: "I had put her away and given her a certificate of divorce" (Jeremiah 3:8).

In the New Testament we have the symbolism of the church as Christ's bride: "The kingdom of heaven is like a certain king who arranged a marriage for his son [and] the wedding hall was filled with guests" (Matthew 22:2, 10). In Matthew 25:1, Jesus told the parable of the virgins who took their lamps and "went out to meet the bridegroom" (Matthew 25:1). In Mark 2:19, He said, " 'Can the friends of the bridegroom fast while the bridegroom is with them?" In John 3:29, Jesus said that the friend of "the bridegroom" rejoices when hearing "the bridegroom's voice." In 2 Corinthians 11:2 we see His godly jealousy when He says, "I have betrothed you to one husband." And in Ephesians 5:23, Paul states that "the husband is head of the wife, as also Christ is head of the church" (Ephesians 5:23).

As a godly marriage grows in its love, so a relationship with Jesus grows in its love. As the intimate relationship of a husband and wife is meant to be the closest and deepest sharing known on earth, so the relationship we have with the Lord is to be the deepest, closest, and most intimate—and that begins now, while we are still here on earth. As a loving marriage is meant to bring our truest joys, so is a genuine relationship with Jesus. Marriage demands loyalty and faithfulness, so we must offer absolute loyalty to our Lord Jesus.

THURSDAY: Whom Do You Love?

*"He who has My commandments and keeps them, **it is he who loves Me**. And he who loves Me will be loved by My Father, and I will love him and manifest Myself to him."*
—JOHN 14:21

When I was engaged to my wife, Bonnie, I was not in America most of those months. I spent ninety-six days touring forty-two countries. Everywhere I checked into a hotel, I went to the manager's desk and gave them my name. They would look me over, and then pull out a letter for me; Bonnie had found me in the most remote parts of the world. I dropped my baggage to the floor, and sat down wherever I was to read her letter. It did not matter to me whether I found my room or not—I read the letter from the one I loved.

Do you know that you have a letter waiting for you every day from your Beloved One? Have you dropped your "baggage" lately because you long for the One you love? As a godly marriage brings the most precious joys we can know on this planet, so does a genuine relationship with Jesus. It gets sweeter as the years go by! That is why I love to get to know saints who have been in love with Jesus for a long, long time. They have discovered the great joys of living by Matthew 22:37: "Jesus said to him, 'You shall love the Lord your God with all your heart, with all your soul, and with all your mind.'"

Now we come to the wedding banquet in Revelation 19—the Marriage Supper of the Lamb. But what can we bring to the Lamb as a wedding gift? What gift is worthy of giving to our Beloved at our wedding celebration? How can we express our love to the One Who loved us so much that He gave His very life for us?

When I am out shopping with Bonnie, we often meet people who are shopping for baby showers, bridal showers, weddings, and so forth. Most people are very particular about what they buy for those they love. And the greater the love, the more particular they are in the choice of their gift. They want it to be special, useful, and needed, and even want to wrap it to show how important it is. Have you ever thought that you are going to get to give something to Jesus? Do you know what He wants? He has completed His wedding registry in His Word.

Have you been listening to what He says He loves and wants so much? There are at least ten elements of daily life that He will reward whenever He sees them in us. Do you know what they are? Are you practicing these reward-getters at every opportunity?

First let me sketch them; and then we can ponder ways to seek for Christ's "Well done!" Most importantly, Jesus loves to see His character reflected in us. How? Here are the first three of the ten elements that represent the gift He desires from each of us.

Element 1—Christlike disposition in adversity. "Blessed are you when they revile and persecute you, and say all kinds of evil against you falsely for My sake. Rejoice and be exceedingly glad, for great is your reward in heaven, for so they persecuted the prophets who were before you" (Matthew 5:11–12). When you are attacked, maligned, or defrauded in any way, remember Stephen. Where did he look for an example? He looked at and followed the example of Jesus!

Element 2—Christlike secrecy in spiritual disciplines. "But when you do a charitable deed, do not let your left hand know what your right hand is doing, that your charitable deed may be in secret; and your Father who sees in secret will Himself reward you openly. And when you pray, . . . go into your room, and when you have shut your door, pray to your Father who is in the secret place; and your Father who sees in secret will reward you openly. . . . Moreover, when you fast, . . . anoint your head and wash your face, so that you do not appear to men to be fasting, but to your Father who is in the secret place; and your Father who sees in secret will reward you openly" (Matthew 6:3, 16–18).

Jesus loves for us to do secret and sacrificial things—and to be excited to do them even though no one finds out. Start acting like Jesus did. He went out to commune before day sometimes. He stayed up all night in prayer other times. The key to success is to have an unbelievable longing for God!

Element 3—Christlike attitude toward possessions. "Do not lay up for yourselves treasures on earth . . . ; but lay up for yourselves treasures in heaven. . . . For where your treasure is, there your heart will be also" (Matthew 6:19–21). Take some of your stacked possessions and overnight them to the Bank of Heaven. Jesus says, "*Give* and you will *have* forever. *Keep* and you *lose* forever!"

FRIDAY: Loving Like Jesus!

" 'And I have declared to them Your name, . . . that the love with which You loved Me may be in them, and I in them.' "
—John 17:26

Remember: Jesus loves to see His character reflected in us. Now here are the seven remaining elements of daily life that we can give to our Beloved Bridegroom. He desires the following from each of us.

Element 4—Christlike loving of the unlovely. "Love your enemies, do good, and lend, hoping for nothing in return; and your reward will be great, and you will be sons of the Most High. For He is kind to the unthankful and evil" (Luke 6:35). Do you have a neighbor, co-worker, or relative who is unpleasant to you? Show them love and offer kindnesses in the name of Jesus!

Element 5—Christlike serving of the unfortunate. "When you give a feast, invite the poor, the maimed, the lame, the blind. And you will be blessed, because they cannot repay you; for you shall be repaid at the resurrection of the just" (Luke 14:13–14). Now look at this verse: "Inasmuch as you did it to one of the least of these My brethren, you did it to Me" (Matthew 25:40). Pick new social companions. Befriend the handicapped, the poor, the informally educated, the lonely, the shut-ins, the dying, the prisoners, and any others God puts in your path. That is the body of Christ—accepting, color blind, unable to be shocked, incredibly generous. Make plans right now to use your house, your car, and your money to minister His love unto the least of persons, those who cannot do anything in return. And Jesus will reward you in heaven!

Element 6—Christlike investment in people over things. "Now he who plants and he who waters are one, and each one will receive his own reward according to his own labor" (1 Corinthians 3:8). Jesus counts souls invited in. He counts lives touched by the gospel, by prayer, by deeds of kindness. What have you done this week that He has counted? Have you prayed for people and given out the gospel? Investments in people last forever; investments in things don't!

Element 7—Christlike devotion to God's will. "And whatever you do, do it heartily, as to the Lord and not to men, knowing that from the Lord you will receive the reward of the inheritance; for you serve the Lord Christ" (Colossians 3:23–24). What are you called to do this week? Go to school? Then act like you are a Rhodes Scholar for Jesus. Go to work for your company? Be as productive as if it were your own. Are you home rearing children? Raise them like you were Mary raising Jesus! Elevate whatever you do as if you were doing it for Christ.

Element 8—Christlike loving expectancy. "There is laid up for me the crown of righteousness, which the Lord, the righteous Judge, will give to me on that Day, and not to me only but also to all who have loved His appearing" (2 Timothy 4:8). Does a newlywed husband need to be told to look forward to seeing his beloved after work? Does a new mom need to be prodded into loving that sweet little bundle of joy? Long for Jesus the way He loves to be loved! He wants us to have the fervor of a newlywed with Him.

Element 9—Christlike endurance in trials. "That the genuineness of your faith, being much more precious than gold that perishes, though it is tested by fire, may be found to praise, honor, and glory at the revelation of Jesus Christ" (1 Peter 1:7). What are you struggling with? If it is health, you can be rewarded for having a good attitude. If it is adversaries, you can be rewarded for how you treat them. Regardless of the type of trial, you can be rewarded for how you respond to adversities if your responses are Christlike!

Element 10—Christlike focus on the Word. "Love one another. This is love, that we walk according to His commandments . . . that we do not lose those things we worked for, but that we may receive a full reward" (2 John 5–8). Jesus rewards those who love Him so much that they get His Word into their lives.

Are you overflowing with the world—or the Word? Do you long for His Word more than anything else?

SATURDAY: Clothed With Christ

"Put on the Lord Jesus Christ, and make no provision for the flesh, to fulfill its lusts."
—ROMANS 13:14

In Revelation 19:8 John sees saints clothed in their "righteous acts." What is this? Isn't salvation by grace alone? Are these works that He is speaking of? Yes, and yes! God has paid the full and final price in Christ for our salvation. However, we were saved for a purpose. Look at Ephesians 2:8–10: "For by grace you have been saved through faith . . . ; it is the gift of God, not of works, lest anyone should boast. For we are His workmanship, created in Christ Jesus for good works, which God prepared beforehand that we should walk in them."

The "righteous acts" in Revelation 19:8 are not to be confused with the righteousness of God imputed to us at conversion (see Romans 3:21–22). We can only *receive* this gracious gift since it can never be earned. All the good deeds of an unsaved person amount to dirty bandages full of filth (see Isaiah 64:6). Apart from Christ we can do nothing, so any righteous deeds we wear are the result of yielding to the Holy Spirit, "for it is God who works in you both to will and to do for His good pleasure" (see Philippians 2:13). Oh, what a blessing to be such channels in His hands!

WEEK 42: LOOK FOR THE RETURNING JESUS

Revelation 19:8, therefore, is referring to the righteous acts of believers during their earthly lives. When will these acts of righteousness be revealed? At the Judgment Seat of Christ. Here are the main portions that deal with this event.

It is a **reflection** of our sanctification in our body: "But why do you judge your brother? Or why do you show contempt for your brother? For we shall all [be presented] before the judgment seat of Christ" (Romans 14:10).

It is a **revelation** of our selection of our building materials: "For no other foundation can anyone lay than that which is laid, which is Jesus Christ. . . . If anyone's work which he has built on it endures, he will receive a reward. If anyone's work is burned, he will suffer loss; but he himself will be saved, yet so as through fire" (1 Corinthians 3:11–16).

It is a **reception** sponsored by our Savior: "For we must all appear before the judgment seat of Christ, that each one may receive the things done in the body, . . . whether good or bad" (2 Corinthians 5:10).

Now then, here are some probing questions that might make you squirm a bit. Has it ever occurred to you, Christian, that you are making your own outfit to wear at this Marriage Supper of the Lamb—the greatest of all events? What are you putting into this special wedding garment? In the Old World a father spent years building the bride's hope chest, and spent years selecting items to lovingly fill it. Are you giving your preparation for heaven that much care? Are you being sanctified by continual washing by the Word? What good are you doing for God that will be spared by the flames of His refining fire? (All self-glorification will burn up and all self-gratification will go—everything done in the energy of the flesh will turn to soot.) What building materials have you provided that will survive?

Finally, will you be wearing the fruits of a good and godly life? The pure white linen of a self-sacrificed life lived in dedication to Christ is a stark contrast to the purple and scarlet of the harlot of Revelation that lived for self alone. Think about it!

Make a choice to live in hope. You cannot get ready for heaven in heaven. Choices you have made and are going to make will determine both your wedding garment at the Marriage Supper of the Lamb and the type of room in the mansion He's building for His bride. And that determines what rewards you will receive in heaven.

What are these rewards, and how are they described in Scripture? What we know about rewards is given in terms that are more general than specific. The following are those Christ has promised.

The promise of His crowns: This seems to be used as a symbol of victory, authority, and responsibility. On display at the Bema seat will be five great crowns for loyal and trustworthy servants of Christ. To steadfast believers tested by prison and persecution even to the point of death, God will give a crown of life (Revelation 2:10). A never-fading, never-tarnishing diadem awaits the self-sacrificing pastor-shepherds of the flock (1 Peter 5:2–4). Everyone who ran life's race with patient endurance and perseverance will receive a crown of righteousness (2 Timothy 4:8). Evangelists and soul winners can eagerly anticipate receiving the crown of rejoicing (1 Thessalonians 2:19–20). Finally, all who overcome will be handed a wonderful victor's crown (1 Corinthians 9:25).

The promise of His treasure: This reward stresses their eternal value and security (see Matthew 6:20; 1 Peter 1:4).

The promise of His commendations: This is seen in those passages where a reward is administered in the form of acknowledgements such as *"Well done, good and faithful servant"* (cf. Matthew 25:21; Luke 19:17; 1 Corinthians 4:5b).

The promises to His overcomers: Rather than a general promise to all believers, these rewards could refer to a special blessing of those believers who overcome unique trials and tests. (See Revelation 2:7, 11, 17, 26, and others.)

The Promise of special responsibilities and authority for Him (cf. Matthew 19:28; 24:45–47; 25:21, 23; Luke 19:17–19; 22:29–30; Revelation 2:26).

I encourage you to ask the Lord to work in you whatever is necessary to give Him the greatest gift possible at the Marriage Supper of the Lamb. Get excited about this time of great praise and rejoicing! Just think: the King of Kings and the Lord of the Universe is preparing a wedding feast like none other, and, if you are a Christian, you are invited! So make the choice today to live in hope by lovingly preparing yourself for His return!

WEEK 43
Rest in the Vengeance of Jesus

{ Revelation 19:11–21 }

As the end of days approaches, you can find hope as you rest in the vengeance of Jesus.

SUNDAY: The Vengeance of Jesus

"O Lord God, to whom vengeance belongs . . . **Render punishment to the proud.** Lord, how long will the wicked . . . triumph? They . . . speak insolent things; All the workers of iniquity boast in themselves. They break in pieces Your people, O Lord, And afflict Your heritage. They slay the widow and the stranger, And murder the fatherless. Yet they say, 'The Lord does not see, Nor does the God of Jacob understand.' "

—Psalm 94:1–7

We usually don't think of Jesus as being vengeful. That is why Revelation 19 is so astounding! Since time began, His saints have pondered the wonder of Jesus' waiting to avenge evil upon the earth. This passage is representative of the heart's cry of God's people for thousands of years.

For all of human history since Eden, Satan has seemingly triumphed. Sin and death have run riotously around the globe. Un-avenged evils, from the time of the first murder until this present hour, are still pending. Human history has been written in blood, tears, and death. Yet Jesus still waits—and we, His children, continue to persevere in the hope of Him that endures and anchors our souls. For we know that somewhere beyond the starry sky is a herald angel standing ready, by the decree of the Lord God Almighty, to sound his trumpet, and the kingdoms of this world shall then become the kingdoms of our God and of His Christ. In that moment Jesus will return in all His glory to His world!

The climax of all human history unfolds in this week's text, Revelation 19:11–21. The purposes of God long hidden in His eternal counsels are now made clear. When Jesus steps back into history, He will no longer be the Suffering Servant—He will be Lord of All! Hallelujah!

Read that passage now to see exactly how the Lord Jesus' victory will unfold What an awesome event! And in that passage we see two remarkably vivid truths: 1) the absolute security of trusting the timing of Jesus (vv. 11–16), and 2) the absolute futility of resisting the offers of Jesus (vv. 17–21).

Contemplate the significance of this majestic scene as you reflect upon the content of the prayer below.

My Prayer for You This Week: *Glorious Lord Jesus, we, with the Apostle John and the saints of all times, say, "Even so, come quickly, Lord Jesus." Come to wreak Your vengeance upon this world; come to right all wrongs; come to settle all debts—for vengeance is Yours. You who are a consuming fire in Your holiness, oh Father, have committed all judgment to Your Son. How we await His coming! We know that He will come for us, Your beloved ones in Your church, to take us from this world before the hour of the Great Tribulation comes upon the earth. We know that we shall return, as Your Word says, clothed in white, riding on a white horse as a member of Your army at Your return. As we look into this very beautiful passage, may we see the wonderful truth of Your character revealed. Help us to be expectant of Your coming, or Your calling of us home. May we be found looking and living in a way that pleases You! We thank You in Your precious name, Lord Jesus, Amen.*

MONDAY: The Absolute Security of Trusting Jesus' Timing

"Now to Him who is able to keep you from stumbling, And to present you faultless Before the presence of His glory with exceeding joy, **To God our Savior, Who alone is wise, Be glory and majesty, Dominion and power***, Both now and forever. Amen."*

—Jude 24–25

No book is more tied to the rest of the Bible than Revelation, for Revelation is not only the conclusion but also the summation of the entire Scriptures. Everything that began in Genesis, and has woven its way through all the other books of the Bible, comes to a conclusion here.

Now let us look closely at Revelation 19 as God pulls back the veil and reveals the awesome majesty of the King of Kings and Lord of Lords in all His glory! Remember that this is the vivid, eyewitness account of John. He briefly saw this whole revelation from God's perspective—almost at once. Imagine what it would have been like for John to actually *see* the Second Coming of Christ: "I saw heaven standing open and there before me was a white horse, whose rider is called Faithful and True. With justice he judges and makes war" (Revelation 19:11 NIV).

The One who ascended to heaven (Acts 1:9–11) and had been seated at the Father's right hand (Hebrews 8:1; 10:12; 1 Peter 3:22) will return to take back the earth from the usurper and establish His kingdom (Revelation 5:1–10). The nature of Christ's Second Coming shows how it differs from the Rapture. At the Rapture, Christ meets His own in the air; in Revelation 19 He comes with them to earth. At the Rapture, there is no judgment; the Second Coming is all about judgment. The Day of the Lord (as the Second Coming is called in the Old Testament) is preceded by blackness—a darkened sun, a moon turned blood red, stars seemingly falling from the sky, thick smoke like from a furnace—then lightning and blinding light as Jesus comes. These details are not recorded in Rapture passages (John 14:1–3; 1 Thessalonians 4:13–18).

In verse 11 are also two of the wonderful titles of Jesus Christ—Faithful and True. These titles remind us that we can fully trust Him. Not one word He spoke will ever be false. Not one promise He made will ever fail. Christ came for His saints, as He promised (Revelation 4:1), and now He will return with them. During all of human history, He has been watching and waiting. Nothing has missed His eyes. Now He will begin to bring Truth to bear upon all lies, falsehoods, and deception.

In the broad scope of God's plan for the ages, we know that His timing can be nothing other than perfect. He is never too early and never too late; His timing is always precise. Every genuine prophecy ever made will be fulfilled—exactly as predicted.

On a personal level, the same holds true. We can trust Jesus to hear every prayer that is according to His will, and if He hears us, we have the petition requested (1 John 5:14–15)—at just the right and sometimes absolutely incredible moment.

We can always rest in the absolute security of His perfect timing, whether it is that of fulfilling prophecy or meeting individual needs, for He is the God who does all things well (Mark 7:37)!

As you meditate on the wondrous character of Jesus, let your heart feel sweetly secure in the One who is called *"Faithful and True"*—the lover of your soul! No one but Jesus is always faithful and true, and very few are regularly that way. You can expect to be let down at some point by others, but Jesus will never let you down!

TUESDAY: Jesus Will Right All Wrongs

> *"Do not avenge yourselves, but . . . give place to wrath; for . . . 'Vengeance is Mine, I will repay,' says the Lord. . . . The Lord knows how to deliver the godly out of temptations and to reserve the unjust under punishment for the day of judgment."*
> —Romans 12:19; 2 Peter 2:9

Did you know that the earliest prophecy in the Bible was from the first known prophet in the Bible, one who lived *before* the Flood? There were three categories of people involved in the Flood: 1) the one who was taken out *before* the Flood came—Enoch; 2) Noah's family which was preserved *through* the Flood; and 3) the earth dwellers who perished *in* the Flood.

The earliest recorded prophecy in the Bible was by Enoch, who was seven generations from Adam. He had a son, Methuselah, who lived the longest of anyone; he was the one whose very name in Hebrew means "when he dies the judgment will come." And so it seems to have happened at the very same year that Methusaleh died—the Flood began! Methuselah's son was Lamech, and he fathered Noah. In Noah's six hundredth year, the Flood came.

Have you ever thought about how many people perished in the Flood? If the families were the same size as biblical families, and they kept having children as long as was usual back then, there may have been a billion people on this planet when the Flood came. One creationist, Henry Morris, believes that there were four to six billion. If you want to know about God and His justice, how many people survived the Flood? Only nine—one was taken out just before, and eight went through it. If you think that the majority of the world is going to get to heaven, then you are not thinking like God does. God offers salvation to all, but so few come to Him.

Methuselah, according to Jewish tradition, lived until one week before the rain started. Look at what his father prophesied while he lived here: "Enoch . . . prophesied about these men also, saying, 'Behold, the Lord comes with ten thousands [hundreds of millions] of His saints [His army of the church saints, pre-church saints, pre-Flood saints], to execute judgment on all, to convict . . . of all the harsh things which ungodly sinners have spoken against Him' " (Jude 14–15). This is a prophecy of Christ's Second Coming. God's analysis of this planet apart from His intervening grace and hearts responsive to Him is "ungodly, ungodly, ungodly." There is a moment in the future when God will say, "That is it!" He will then execute judgment on all.

Just as it was at the time of the Flood, in the Tribulation we see the same type categories of people: the saints of the church age who will be pulled out just *before* the Tribulation; the Tribulation witnesses—the 144,000 and the two witnesses—who will be preserved *through* it; and the world that will perish under all the horrors of God's wrath *in* the Tribulation.

To His saints, He offers assurance that He is faithful and true. That is important to grasp, especially when it comes to the matter of executing vengeance. If someone harms you or despitefully uses you, God promises that Jesus will execute vengeance, so He says, "Wait for Me to handle it." The ungodly are punished in this life through never experiencing Christ, but they will also be punished in the life to come. Therefore, we don't need to personally add to their punishment.

Jesus will repay every evil—He asks us to trust Him. "'Vengeance is Mine, I will repay,' says the Lord. And again, 'the Lord will judge His people'" (Hebrews 10:30). Jesus has promised that He will repay every evil, so trust Him. Getting out of sorts spiritually through anger and bitterness expends vital energies that are better spent elsewhere. So the Lord says, "Trust Me. I will repay every evil if you will just give them to Me instead of trying to handle them yourself."

Jesus will vindicate all who have been oppressed—He asks us to hope in Him. "The Lord executes righteousness And justice for all who are oppressed. . . . The Lord also will be a refuge for the oppressed, A refuge in times of trouble" (Psalm 103:6; Psalm 9:9).

Jesus will reward the righteous—He asks us to work for Him. "So that men will say, 'Surely there is a reward for the righteous; Surely He is God who judges in the earth'" (Psalm 58:11). God asks us to work for Him, hope in Him, trust in Him, and wait for Him. If someone oppresses you because you are a Christian, the most powerful thing you can do is leave vengeance up to the Lord. That will free you up to serve Him: "Rejoice . . . , for great is your reward in heaven, for so they persecuted the prophets who were before you" (Matthew 5:12).

Are you assured that Jesus is really the Truth? Are you daily pouring out all your sadness, anxieties, and woes on Him? Only Jesus can give you the rest and peace that all will be well in Him (Matthew 11:28–30). Let Jesus be your pattern for how to respond to offenses. When He was reviled, He never retaliated. Revelation 19:11–16 bears witness that we can go through our earthly days trusting in the timing of Jesus to right all wrongs.

WEDNESDAY: The Absolute Futility of Resisting Jesus' Power

*"Then I saw an angel standing in the sun; and he cried with a loud voice, saying to **all the birds** that fly in the midst of heaven, 'Come and **gather together for the supper of the great God**.'"*
—REVELATION 19:17

In Revelation 19:17–21, we see the folly of the world as they finally begin to reap the justice they deserve. What does the Lord reveal as the elements of this futile resistance against God? The earth dwellers will find that God's plan and His programs are inescapable. Remember Ahab and the bowshot in 1 Kings 22:34? Ahab was the wicked king of Israel. He thought he was smart, so he disguised himself and went into battle with the righteous king of Judah. The king of Judah wore his kingly robes, but he was God's man. In warfare, the opposing forces always tried to attack the king. If they killed him, his army would scatter. The Syrians started shooting their arrows at the king of Judah, but God protected him. But, when a soldier of the Syrian army decided to shoot an arrow at random, God directed that arrow between a joint in Ahab's armor and killed him. God had said that Ahab would face His judgment because of his grievous sins, so Ahab could not escape the plan of God. Though a person may run, he or she can never hide from God!

Now look at these elements that further reveal the absolute futility of trying to resist God's power.

The inescapable humiliation of pride by God. "'[The birds] may eat the flesh of kings, the flesh of captains, the flesh of mighty men, the flesh of horses and of those who sit on them, and the flesh of all people, free and slave, both small and great'" (19:18). Do you remember Satan's five "I wills" in Isaiah 14? You can try, but you will never succeed in exalting yourself. That is why the Lord says in James 4:6b: "God resists the proud, but gives grace to the humble."

The inescapable power of God. "And I saw the beast, the kings of the earth, and their armies, gathered together to make war against Him who sat on the horse and against His army" (19:19). All the powerful of the planet will come to fight God. Doesn't that make you wonder how anyone can fight God? What will they fight with?

The inescapable judgment of God. "Then the beast was captured, and with him the false prophet who worked signs in his presence, by which he deceived those who received the mark of the beast and those who worshiped his image" (19:20). The beast will be captured—the one who led the whole world astray. He and the false prophet will then be the first to be cast alive into the Lake of Fire burning with brimstone.

The inescapable execution by God. "And the rest were killed with the sword which proceeded from the mouth of Him who sat on the horse. And all the birds were filled with their flesh" (19:21). All the Lord will have to do is speak and there will be a 180-mile-long river of blood draining from human bodies! Their blood will flow to the horse's bridles! At one point near the end of World War II, so many had been killed at Okinawa (150,000 Japanese troops and 15,000 American troops) that survivors tell of walking for miles through pools of blood as they carried away the wounded.

Why does the Lord give such a horribly graphic view of these, His enemies? To remind us of the absolute futility of resisting the power of Jesus! Are you "spinning your wheels" trying to resist Him? Or have you submitted and are now basking in His love?

THURSDAY: Jesus Offers Intimacy

"And this is eternal life, **that they may know You***, the only true God, and Jesus Christ whom You have sent."*

—John 17:3

Not many experience intimacy with Jesus because they often don't seek Him deeply. When we read some of the old hymns like the eleventh-century song by Bernard Clairvaux—"Jesus the very thought of Thee, with sweetness fills my breast"—the wording seems foreign because we are not customarily prone to thinking in such a manner. Why is that? The old saints intimately spent hours with the Lord. Martin Luther translated the whole Bible from Hebrew and Greek to German, and yet he found time to pray three to four hours a day. Most of today's Christians can finish prayer in five minutes or less. Men like Luther weren't "asking" the Lord for things—they were "basking" in the delights of Him! "Basking" is resting and nourishing ourselves in the presence of the Lord, getting to know Him personally. Have you ever thought about what a precious, blessed privilege that is?

Jesus said in John 14:21: "He who has My commandments and keeps them, it is he who loves Me. And he who loves Me will be loved by My Father, and I will love him and manifest Myself to him." Think about it! The Lord is waiting to unveil more of Himself to you. Do you want to experience the God of the Universe intimately? Then spend both quality and quantity time with Him.

Do you know why I love astronomy, oceanography, and science in general? What intrigues me so much about all that is getting to learn more about God in nature because I want to know as much as possible about my Lord. If you want to know God, will you accept the greatest offer of all? A personal, always-present relationship with the Majesty on High? The One who is the very center of all-that-ever-will-be wants to show you more of Himself every day.

Jesus wants us to remember what salvation is: "My sheep hear My voice, and I know them, and they follow Me" (John 10:27). That is the Christian life in one short statement: we are His sheep because we can hear His voice—He knows us, and we follow Him. If you struggle with assurance of your salvation, are you hearing the voice of the Lord? Is He revealing Himself to You? Are you following Him?

Jesus offers us the enjoyment of intimacy. Are you enjoying an intimate relationship with Him today? Are you enjoying the personal revelation of Him? Do you enjoy talking to Him? Are you reading His letters to you—the Bible's books? Are they at the top of your pile? When the mail comes, I usually sort through it very quickly. Half of it normally goes into the trash, and half can be read any time. But there is usually a letter or two that I just can't wait to open because I can tell by the handwriting or some other sign that they are of personal interest to me.

Most people anticipate the delivery of the mail. But far greater is the fresh letter the Lord Jesus mails to us through His Word every day, and He wants us to put it at the top of our pile. I recently met with someone who told me that they were having a bad week and, in fact, a bad summer. I asked, "What is so bad about it?" They admitted that they had not been reading the Bible much. My diagnosis was that they were spiritually sick. At times when we have called the pediatrician about one of our children, their doctor always asks if there is a loss of appetite or lethargy. When that happens, the child is actually sick. As God's child, if you have lost your appetite for God's Word, and have become spiritually lethargic, you are likewise sick. The cure: Do not expose yourself to things that grieve and quench the Holy Spirit of God. Someone has aptly said this about the Bible: "This Book will keep you from sin—or sin will keep you from this Book."

What do you know of Jesus that only comes by long hours shared with Him? I'm not talking about learning from what some great writer has written, but what you personally know from seeing Jesus reflected in His Word until your heart can't help but rise in intimate worship of God. Now do you see how the old saints could pray for hours? Such prayer is a reflection of a heart panting after Christ: "As the deer pants for the water brooks, So pants my soul for You, O God" (Psalm 42:1).

FRIDAY: Resting in His Redemption

> "*In Him we have redemption through His blood*, . . . *and the blood of Jesus His Son cleanses us from all sin. [He is] the faithful witness, the firstborn from the dead, and the ruler over the kings of the earth . . . who loved us and washed us from our sins in His own blood.*"
> —Ephesians 1:7; 1 John 1:7; Revelation 1:5

The blood of Christ is the scarlet thread that ties all of the Word into one. It is in His shed blood that we hope. Are you resting in Christ's perfect redemption and in the hope you have? Romans 8:1 says, *"There is . . . no condemnation to those who are in Christ Jesus."* Our sins are gone, and God will never condemn us for them. We will never have to stand in judgment for our sins because Jesus paid it all.

What are you holding onto to get you to God? Do you trust only in the sacrifice of Jesus for you? Do you trust in all that He did, and His redeeming blood—or is it "Jesus' blood plus my baptism" or "Jesus' blood plus 'I'm a good guy'"? It ought to be as hymn writer Count Nicholaus Ludwig von Zinzendorf wrote in 1739: "Jesus, thy blood and righteousness my beauty are, my glorious dress; 'midst flaming worlds, in these arrayed, with joy shall I lift up my head."

Jesus asks us to trust in His faithfulness. "The armies of heaven, clothed in fine linen, white and clean, followed Him on white horses" (Revelation 19:14). This is wonderful! Not one of the members of His armies is lost, missing, or AWOL. He has faithfully cared for them (and always will) through sickness, health, adversity, prosperity, loneliness, and joy. He is thus called Faithful. The very character of God is that of faithfulness: "God is faithful, by whom you were called into the fellowship of His Son, Jesus Christ our Lord" (1 Corinthians 1:9; see also 1 Thessalonians 5:24; 2 Thessalonians 3:3; 1 Peter 4:19).

Jesus reminds us to wait for His judgment. "Now out of His mouth goes a sharp sword, that with it He should strike the nations. And He Himself will rule them with a rod of iron. He Himself treads the winepress of the fierceness and wrath of Almighty God" (Revelation 19:15). At last it comes, the wrath of God falls. This judgment of Christ's Second Coming is a "compression into a sudden flash, all the inevitable results of wrong doing."[1] Just as the crashing down of the Red Sea upon Pharaoh was the demonstration of the danger to any human power that defies the supreme power of God, and the inescapable fiery brimstone God used in the judgment on Sodom was about those who trifle with sexual promiscuity, so the fierce wrath of God here at Christ's return is the clear judgment of God upon sin.

Jesus asks us to submit to His authority. "And He has on His robe and on His thigh a name written: KING OF KINGS AND LORD OF LORDS" (Revelation 19:16). Like Job and Jeremiah, we must trust God even when we can't understand Him: " 'Let not the wise man glory in his wisdom, Let not the mighty man glory in his might, Nor let the rich man glory in his riches, But let him, who glories, glory in this, That he understands and knows Me, That I am the LORD, exercising lovingkindness, judgment, and righteousness in the earth. For in these I delight,' says the LORD" (Jeremiah 9:23–24).

Are you worshiping the Lord, your faithful God? One of the doctrines that some people hold to is the idea of losing your salvation. It attacks the very nature of God because you did not get saved on your own, and you can't lose salvation on your own. It is a free, gracious gift from God—and He is faithful to keep all that you have committed to Him.

Are you resting in His faithful provision for your needs right now? Are you confident in any adversity that God is above all, and is working His glory through it? How about your health? Is it in His faithful hands? Your children, marital hopes, childbearing desires, or college dreams—are they all given to the Faithful One? God will bring them to fruition according to His perfect plan and timing. Trust in His faithfulness!

So then, what does the Second Coming of Christ teach us? Jesus offers us the assurance that He is faithful and true; Jesus offers us the enjoyment of intimacy with Him; Jesus offers us the rest of His redemption; Jesus asks us to trust in His faithfulness; and Jesus asks us to submit to His authority.

Say "Yes, Lord, yes!" to His will and to His way. Trust and obey Him. And when the Spirit speaks to you, with your whole heart agree with Him.

SATURDAY: Great Is God's Faithfulness

"Through the Lord's mercies we are not consumed, Because His compassions fail not. They are new every morning; **Great is Your faithfulness***."*

—Lamentations 3:22–23

What should be our response to what we've learned through Revelation 19 this week and last? Look at verse 19:10 again: "I fell at his feet to worship him. But he said to me, 'See that you do not do that! I am your fellow servant, and of your brethren who have the testimony of Jesus. Worship God! For the testimony of Jesus is the spirit of prophecy.'" There are two gems in this verse: 1) worship God, and 2) see Jesus.

Worship God by giving Jesus your consecration. Focus on the reverent presentation of all you have to God, which is your spiritual worship: "Present your bodies a living sacrifice, holy, acceptable to God, which is your reasonable service. And do not be conformed to this world, but be transformed by the renewing of your mind, that you may prove what is that good and acceptable and perfect will of God" (Romans 12:1–2).

Worship God by giving Jesus your devotion. Let Jesus reveal Himself to you in every page of His Book. Learn to pause and often pray Psalm 119:18 before you study God's Word: "Open my eyes, that I may see wondrous things from Your law." Yield to Him as He opens the Word; earnestly seek Him, and prayerfully allow Him to open your eyes. Give Him the devotion of your spirit in worship, and your body as a living sacrifice.

Worship God by yielding to Jesus. "Beginning at Moses and all the Prophets, He expounded to them in all the Scriptures the things concerning Himself. . . . It came to pass, as He sat at the table with them, that He took bread, blessed and broke it, and gave it to them. Then their eyes were opened and they knew Him; and He vanished from their sight" (Luke 24:27–31).

Worship God by earnestly living for Jesus. "Of this salvation the prophets have inquired and searched carefully, who prophesied of the grace that would come to you, searching what, or what manner of time, the Spirit of Christ who was in them was indicating when He testified beforehand the sufferings of Christ and the glories that would follow" (1 Peter 1:10–11).

Worship God by prayerfulness. "Rejoice always, pray without ceasing, in everything give thanks; for this is the will of God in Christ Jesus for you" (1 Thessalonians 5:16–18). In these few verses, God gives the prerequisites for living the kind of life that truly honors Him: rejoice, pray, and give thanks!

Make a choice to live in hope. To live in enduring hope, reaffirm today that you will not let anything interfere with consecrating your body and your life to Him. Ask the Lord to empower you to not walk in pride, to not walk undisciplined in lust, to not let anything wicked be before your eyes, and to not let your hands be used for things that defile and thus grieve and quench the Holy Spirit.

Make this commitment to Jesus: *By Your grace, I will not let myself be any less than a consecrated sacrifice to You.* That is how you can worship the Lord as He deserves.

So then, I exhort you to choose to see Jesus as Faithful and True. See Him as the faithful One Who always speaks Truth. See Him as the One Who will never break a promise. See Him as the One you can always trust!

WEEK 44
Look for Paradise on Earth

{ Revelation 20:1–10 }

As the end of days approaches, you can find hope as you look for Paradise on earth!

SUNDAY: The Real Utopia

> " 'The wolf and the lamb shall feed together, The lion shall eat straw like the ox, And dust shall be the serpent's food. **They shall not hurt nor destroy in all My holy mountain**,' Says the LORD."
> —Isaiah 65:25

We now come to the incredible part of the Book of Revelation! So much of what we think about this book will now be covered—heaven and the perfections of a restored earth.

I grew up in a church where we often recited the Lord's Prayer. Part of it says, "Your kingdom come. Your will be done on earth as it is in heaven" (Matthew 6:10). Recitation of that prayer is not common today. Yet, from God's perspective, everything related to the coming of His kingdom is right on schedule, and in this week's devotionals we will see what is going to happen.

It is time to focus our attentions on the new world God has planned, because this old one is dying. Although this old world is doomed, He has some great plans for the future of this planet. God has planned for a whole new world—far beyond anything we could ever plan or do. The Lord is preparing to restore an Eden-like paradise on earth again! There are dozens of promised changes until the world blossoms like a rose garden—yet with no blight and no bugs! When will all that happen? It will occur in the Millennium.

Revelation 20 is the step between Earth, as we know it, and Heaven for Eternity. It declares that the golden age will arrive. The armies of the nations have been disbanded, and the great military academies have fallen into ruin and decay. The machinery of war has all been smelted down and converted to the implements of peace. Jerusalem has become the world's capital. The throne of David is there, and the twelve apostles are there judging the twelve tribes of Israel, for Israel rules the World. The millennial Temple has been built to crown Moriah's brow, and the nations of the Earth come there to worship the living God. Prosperity is evident from pole to pole. Poverty is unknown. Every man has all that his heart can desire. There are no prisons, no hospitals, no mental institutions, no barracks, no saloons, no houses of ill repute, no gambling dens, and no homes for the aged and infirm. Such things belong to a past and lesser age. The bloom of youth is on everyone's cheek, for a man is a stripling at a hundred years of age. Cemeteries are crumbling relics of the past, and tears are rare. The wolf and the lamb, the calf and the lion, the cow and the bear, the child and the scorpion, all are at peace. Jesus has come, and the millennium is here. The golden age, so frequently heralded by the prophets of Israel's past, has dawned at last, and the Earth is filled with the knowledge of God. Jesus is Lord, and He rules the nations with a rod of iron. His reign is righteous, and the nations obey. The principles of the Sermon on the Mount are the laws of the Kingdom, and men obey them because infractions are not allowed. Sin is visited with swift and certain judgment. The era lasts for a thousand years.[1]

As you read that description of what it will be like in the Millennium, didn't your heart respond with joy at the very thought of what God has planned?

My Prayer for You This Week: *Oh Lord, as we think about Revalation 20, we are reminded of what so many in our world are longing for—to preserve the beauty of Your Creation. But it is so sad because they do not know the Creator! They want to preserve the wonder of life that You breathed into this planet, but they have never met the Lord of Life. They want to see Paradise restored, but they do not understand why Paradise was lost in the first place. Help us to better comprehend Your plan for bringing about the temporary abatement of the curse on this earth. And yet, it will only further reveal that human hearts are not influenced by their environment. Oh God, only the blood of Jesus can deal with and cleanse away the deep dark stain of sin that all of us were born with! Oh, how we want to be numbered among those who say YES to You, Lord, and be among those who want to do Your will every day. Thank You for this glorious chapter! In Jesus' name, Amen.*

MONDAY: The Return of Christ—the King of Kings

"Now I saw heaven opened, and behold, a white horse. And He who sat on him was called Faithful and True, and in righteousness He judges and makes war. His eyes were like a flame of fire, and **on His head were many crowns***. He had a name written that no one knew except Himself. He was clothed with a robe dipped in blood, and* **His name is called The Word of God***."*
    —Revelation 19:11–13

To best understand chapter 20, we need to first look at Revelation 19:11–20:10 where we see God's mighty plan in three distinct strokes: 1) the **return** of Christ—the King of Kings (19:11–21); 2) the judgment of Satan—his **restraint** (20:1–3); and 3) the Millennium—the **rule** of the Messiah

(20:4–10). Those are the three general divisions of this Scripture passage that we will be learning about this week.

The Apostle John and others vividly show us Christ's re-entry. Here are the biblical elements that burst forth in this moment as Christ returns.

Christ returns in judgment—seen by everyone on the planet. As heaven opens, Jesus enters the sky, and the sign of the Son of man appears (Matthew 24:30). He rides on a white horse, accompanied by the armies of heaven. Out of His mouth goes forth a sharp two-edged sword, and He Himself treads the winepress of the wrath of God Almighty (Revelation 19:11–16). Jesus wears blood-dipped garments (Revelation 19:13), and holds a ruling rod of iron (Revelation 19:15, which is a response to Psalm 2:9).

Jesus pours out His wrath on sin as One who treads the winepress (Revelation 19:15, which refers back to Isaiah 63:1–6). The "robe dipped in blood" makes us think primarily of Jesus and His sacrifice on the cross. Isaiah says that He is the One who is trampling the earth in His wrath, and the grapes squirt up on His white robe. The blood of Him trampling out the winepress of His wrath is why His garment is spoken of as "dipped in blood."

Jesus gathers all the rebels as One who threshes the harvest floor (Micah 4:12–13; Matthew 3:12). He reaps the earth with the sickle of Divine Judgment (Joel 3:13; Revelation 14:17–18).

Christ returns in judgment—feared by all rebels. No one can escape, even though some will have displaced the bats out of caves during the Tribulation in an effort to hide from God (Isaiah 2:19). Jesus is recognized by the earth dwellers when the despised Jesus of Nazareth appears on earth again, and all the families of the earth will wail (Matthew 24:30)! The Day of the Lord that was spoken of by Joel and Amos will have arrived (Joel 1:15, 3:14; Amos 5:20). Jesus is visibly angry: this is the "day of His fierce anger" (Isaiah 13:13) and the "great and terrible" day (Malachi 4:5).

Jesus' return is like the worst storm imaginable. This will be a "day of darkness and of gloominess, a day of clouds and thick darkness" (Joel 2:2; Zechariah 14:6). Jesus terrifies the earth: in horror, the earth dwellers will creep into the clefts and ravines (Revelation 6:15) or hide in the caverns of the rocks and the holes of the earth (Isaiah 2:19). They will cry out to the mountains, "Fall on us! And to the hills, cover us!" (Luke 23:30; Revelation 6:16; 9:6). But, it will be impossible to escape from God's judgment.

Christ returns in judgment—poured on all rebels. His arrival will be like the swift and blinding flash of lightning (Matthew 24:27). All the chariots of His army will sweep the earth as a tempest (Isaiah 66:15). His eyes are as flames of fire (Revelation 19:12). His voice is as the voice of a lion (Joel 3:16; Isaiah 30:30), and the slain of the Lord will be many (Isaiah 66:15–16; Psalm 110:6).

Jesus' vengeance is as a flaming fire (2 Thessalonians 1:8; Isaiah 66:15–16). His day is as a fiery oven (Malachi 4:1; Matthew 13:41–42) and is an inescapable snare (Luke 21:35). His fear is a sudden destruction that will *"seize all"* (1 Thessalonians 5:3). Jesus' wrath is as inescapable as the Flood in the days of Noah (Matthew 24:38–39), and as the fiery judgment that overtook Sodom and Gomorrah (Luke 17:28–32).

Christ returns in judgment—glorified by all rebels. The Lord will first appear on the Mount of Olives (Zechariah 14:4), where He formerly ascended (Acts 1:9, 12). Every eye will see Him (Revelation 1:7; Matthew 24:30). All the people will be so terrified and transfixed that they can't hide. Every contradiction will be silenced (Matthew 22:12; Job 9:3)—everything they have ever spoken against God. Every tongue will confess that Jesus Christ is the Lord, to the honor of God the Father (Philippians 2:11). This will include everyone who has ever lived! The KING OF KINGS AND LORD OF LORDS has returned! Hallelujah!

TUESDAY: The Judgment of Satan—His Restraint

> "Then I saw an angel coming down from heaven, having the key to the bottomless pit and a great chain in his hand. **He laid hold of the dragon,** that serpent of old, who is the Devil and Satan, **and bound him for a thousand years**; and he cast him into the bottomless pit, and shut him up, and set a seal on him, so that he should deceive the nations no more till the thousand years were finished. But after these things he must be released for a little while."
>
> —Revelation 20:1–3

In this passage, the King of Kings and Lord of Lords has now returned. He has squelched the rebellion, terrified the inhabitants of the earth, and He has slain the rebels.

What the Apostle John started seeing in chapter 19 takes us from the earth to the end of the earth, into the Millennium to the end of the Millennium, and then into the eternal state. These events happened in chronological sequence to show that the Millennium is actually a literal 1,000 years. Up until St. Augustine (A.D. 354–430), everyone believed that the return of Christ was to be followed by a literal 1,000 year reign. But when he wrote The City of God, confusion entered in. St. Augustine viewed the city of God as the church on earth; thus the 1,000 years was merely figurative. That would mean that we would be fulfilling God's kingdom here on earth, and thus people ought to invest all they have on earth—and not in heaven. But St. Augustine's interpretation was mistaken, and it has confused people ever since.

Some people have felt that the twentieth chapter of Revelation isn't actually going to happen— even though Scripture specifically says "thousand years" five times in verses 2 through 7 of chapter 20. According to Scripture, the Millennium is a literal event, and this is a chronological sequence. The only way that God can fulfill all the millennial passages is through this literal event. Not only is there a sequence that shows the literal event, verse 3 states that Satan is placed in the bottomless pit. If you recall, this bottomless pit (or abyss) was last opened by Satan in chapter 9. He had a key, so he let out all those monsters! But now the angel has the key, opens the pit, and throws Satan in.

In Revelation 20:2, notice the names that are given in this biography of the devil: "the dragon, that serpent of old, who is the Devil and Satan." That is basically the history of Satan's career. He is the dragon that took the heavenly hosts with him; he is the serpent that tempted Eve who then led Adam into the rebellion; he is the devil who has been seeking to tempt and pervert humanity; he is Satan, the adversary, who has always stood against God's plan and God's people.

Satan gets true justice when he is bound and placed in the bottomless pit. John says that the angel "cast him into the bottomless pit, and shut him up, and set a seal upon him." There is a poetic justice in God's dealings with Satan. Centuries ago, the evil one saw to it that the mortal remains of God's beloved Son were shut up in a tomb and sealed. So it is interesting that God has Satan put in a tomb and sealed just like the Son of God. But that is where the similarity ends: the Son of God rose triumphantly, and Satan is held captive.

Tomorrow, we will see the millennial blessings ahead for those who love the Lord!

WEDNESDAY: The Millennium—The Rule of the Messiah

"And I saw thrones, and they sat on them, and judgment was committed to them. Then I saw the souls of those who had been beheaded for their witness to Jesus and for the word of God, who had not worshiped the beast or his image, and had not received his mark. . . . And **they lived and reigned with Christ for a thousand years***. But the rest of the dead did not live again until the thousand years were finished. This is the first resurrection. Blessed and holy is he who has part in the first resurrection. Over such the second death has no power, but they shall be priests of God and of Christ, and shall reign with Him a thousand years."*

—Revelation 20:4–6

But what is the final state of earthly history? It is the rule of Christ. Let us now note these views on the Millennium.

The Millennium is God establishing what He promised in Daniel 2:35, 44:

The image—all earthly government—is crushed by the Rock—Dan. 2:44, "And in the days of these kings the God of heaven will set up a kingdom which shall never be destroyed; and the kingdom shall not be left to other people; it shall break in pieces and consume all these kingdoms, and it shall stand forever. Inasmuch as you saw that the stone was cut out of the mountain without hands, and that it broke in pieces the iron, the bronze, the clay, the silver, and the gold—the great God has made known to the king what will come to pass after this. The dream is certain, and its interpretation is sure." What we are seeing here is the Millennium—Rev. 20—the establishment of this kingdom that God cut without hands out of the rock and crushes all the kingdoms of the earth and this rock grows into a Kingdom that will never cease.[2]

The Millennium is God confirming the kingdom of the Son of Man which prepares an end for the bloodthirsty beasts of Daniel's world empire. For the first time, it exalts to the throne of international history true humanity in the sense of Holy Scripture—humanity in the image and likeness of God (Genesis 1:27; Daniel 7:13, comp. 2–7; Matthew 26:64).

The Millennium is God revealing the kingdom of heaven, which comes down from heaven, and therefore brings into this earthly world heavenly nature and heavenly happiness (comp. Daniel 4:23). Don't confuse the Millennium with heaven. Sin is only held back; it is not removed. That is why people can still sin during the 1,000 years. Much of Isaiah is about the Millennium, and he says that if someone dies at the age of 100 they are considered a mere child. People live the whole 1,000 years—unless they are in rebellion, and then God cuts them off. We will be here on earth reigning and ruling with Christ. And Jesus will be here literally. There will be a massive temple in Jerusalem which is so big that all the inhabitants of the earth will come through regularly to observe what is going on in there. Literal sacrifices will even be offered. Just as the Lord's Supper looks forward until Jesus comes, the sacrifices will be reinstituted to atone for people, but they will look back on the sacrifice of Christ. Like the Old Testament covenant that pictured Christ for the Jews, so in the Millennium they are going to have the same thing pointing back to His sacrifice on the cross. No one was saved in the Old Testament by killing a lamb, and no one will be saved in the Millennium by killing a lamb. No one is saved by taking part in the Lord's Table either. They are all pictures to illustrate a biblical truth. It will be a very fascinating time when God reveals His kingdom and brings such heavenly joys!

The Millennium is God fulfilling the kingdom of God, which was planned from the very beginning—*"Then the King will say to those on His right hand, 'Come, you blessed of My Father, inherit the kingdom prepared for you from the foundation of the world' "* (Matthew 25:34). This kingdom was striven for through the ages (Matthew 6:10); founded by Christ (John 18:36–37); preached by His followers (Acts 20:25; 28:31); expected by mankind (Romans 8:19); and set up on the old earth (Revelation 11:15; 19:6), after the final catastrophe of the hitherto existing world (Revelation 20:7–15), to run on into the new eternal creation (Revelation 21 and 22).

What will planet Earth be like during the Millennium? The sky will change (Isaiah 4:5–6; 30:26; 60:19). The earth will apparently be surrounded by a new kind of atmospheric light that will accelerate productivity. It will be like living in a greenhouse again. Harmful solar radiation will be gone, and there will be a global tropical climate.

The world of nature will change during the kingdom—the curse will be removed! The animal kingdom will find compatibility with human life. There will be no more predators or scavengers. (Isaiah 11:6–9; 65:25). Agricultural production will be abundant (Isaiah 30:23–25; 35:1–2; 55:12–13). The threat of disease will change as there will be no sickness or deformity of any kind (Isaiah 29:17–19; 33:24; 35:3–6). There will be exceptionally long life (Isaiah 65:19–23).

The political climate will change as Jesus brings real peace and justice to the earth during His reign (Isaiah 2:4; 42:6–7; 54:14–15). Christ will be the perfect ruler: no lawsuits, no crime, no political machinations, and no unfulfilled promises.

The spiritual climate will change as earth will be filled with the knowledge of the Lord and His Word (Isaiah 2:3; 11:9; 12:4–5; 52:6–10). Everyone will go to Jerusalem to see the King on His throne, the temple, and all that points to God. In fact, if you don't come to the temple, it won't rain on your part of the world. God will rule and show His power!

THURSDAY: The Release and Doom of Satan

> *"**The devil**, who deceived them, **was cast into the lake of fire** and brimstone where the beast and the false prophet are. And they will be tormented day and night forever and ever."*
>
> —Revelation 20:10

WEEK 44: LOOK FOR PARADISE ON EARTH

Now that we have seen that the King of Kings will return, Satan will be restrained, and Christ will rule in the Millennium, what is next? Look at Revelation 20:7: "Now when the thousand years have expired, Satan will be released from his prison."

When will that happen? Satan's release will occur immediately at the end of the thousand-year reign of Christ. It is almost like a meter: God puts in a thousand-year quarter, turns the knob, and the timer starts. Satan will have been raging, and thinking about everything, but then he gets one more chance to afflict the earth: "[Satan] will go out to deceive the nations which are in the four corners of the earth, Gog and Magog, to gather them together to battle, whose number is as the sand of the sea" (Revelation 20:8).

It is mind boggling to think that people could sink so low as to listen to Satan after 1,000 years of seeing Jesus and what the world was like under His rule! There was perfect justice, perfect peace, perfect health, and perfect agricultural production. But then the old dragon gets out—and he has a huge following once again. "Gog and Magog" is just another way of saying "all the peoples of the world." There will still be nations, but this is not identifying Russia as the evil ones. "Gog and Magog" is a euphemism for the people who are in rebellion against God.

So then, Satan gathers them to do battle. He gets the whole planet to rebel and try to attack the Beloved City. Look at verse 9: "They went up on the breadth of the earth and surrounded the camp of the saints and the beloved city. And fire came down from God out of heaven and devoured them." God didn't say a word. Remember the rebellion of Korah in the Old Testament where Nadab and Abihu disobeyed and fire came? Satan gets the same fate in Revelation 20:10: "The devil, who deceived them, was cast into the lake of fire and brimstone where the beast and the false prophet are. And they will be tormented day and night forever and ever."

Let's go back to Revelation 19:20 because I want you to be aware of a terrible theological error called "annihilationism." That view says that God is too good to keep anyone burning in hell, so He simply evaporates them and they cease to exist. Here is what really happens to people who are in the Lake of Fire: *"Then the beast was captured, and with him the false prophet who worked signs in his presence, by which he deceived those who received the mark of the beast and those who worshiped his image. These two were cast alive into the lake of fire burning with brimstone."*

Now look at the end of 20:10: "They will be tormented day and night forever and ever." Those two characters were thrown alive into the Lake of Fire—the first ones in there. What are they like after 1,000 years in the fire? Are they consumed? No, they are still alive and conscious and experiencing the horrors of hell.

Why is Satan being released again? He will be released to demonstrate once and for all that a perfect environment does not change man's sin problem. This will illustrate the incurable wickedness of Satan who returns immediately to his deceptive ministry. It will justify eternal punishment and show that man, even though exposed to righteousness for an extended period of time, when given the opportunity to accept Christ, will still reject Him.

Where will Satan go after his release is over? He will be cast into the Lake of Fire where he will be tormented day and night forever.

Mankind was tried—and found guilty on every count. In this brief moment, as all of history flashes before us, man is found to be absolutely guilty! In the Millennium his sin is absolutely inexcusable. Mankind was tested in the Garden of Delight, but he broke the only prohibition laid upon him, and sinned. He was tested under conscience (pre-Flood); corruption and violence filled the earth, which had to be cleared by the deluge. He was tested again under the restraining influence of divinely appointed (post-Flood) government, but man went into idolatry, thus turning his back upon his Creator.

Mankind was tested under Israel's law, but he cast off all restraint and crucified the Lord of Glory. Mankind was also tested under grace (the church). In this present dispensation of the Holy Spirit, he has shown himself utterly unable to appreciate such mercy, has rejected the gospel, and gone ever deeper into sin.

Mankind was tested under the personal reign (the Millennium) of the Lord Jesus Christ for a thousand years. While He is here on earth in all His glory and power, personally meting out judgment and revealing Himself, He will stand in the millennial temple and say, "This points to Me." Yet the whole world refuses to hear Him. So Satan will lead the whole world astray moments after his release. In conclusion, mankind will have been tested and found guilty at every level!

God cares. (See Hebrews 4:14–16.) He is genuinely interested in this world, its needs, and its inhabitants—now as well as in the future. God cares so much that He has warned us that all of this is coming. That is why President Johnson's Great Society programs in the 1960s did not work. If you clean up every city and slum, and remove every bad influence, the problem still exists because it is inside of us. Therefore, God says, "You don't need a new city, house, job, or clothes. You need a new heart." Even the perfect world with no sin and rebellion, and a perfect Paradise, is polluted by the sin of man's heart, the sin nature that man is born with. By nature, by choice, by God's divine decree we are cursed, but Jesus Christ can remove it.

God controls. (See Daniel 4:35.) He has not lost control. Satan is on a time schedule and he can only go so far before God will shut him up in the pit. God is sovereign, and He is working all things together for good now as well as in the future. All the way through the millennial time, He sovereignly offers the temple to the people. You can read about it in Ezekiel chapters 40–48. It describes the temple in detail (how big it is, the rooms, the courtyard). There is a life-giving river flowing out from under the altar that goes to the Dead Sea, and makes that area one of the most fertile areas in the world. Everybody can see it. God is in total control, yet people still reject Him.

God communicates His Way to us. The God we serve is not a God of silence. He does not want to leave us in the dark. He lets us know what is going to happen—right down to some very minute details. We can have great confidence from knowing what is going to happen. Are you obeying Him? As Christians, we shouldn't spend our time trying to save the earth; we need to focus on saving souls. Give people the good news that God offers a new heart and a new spirit—that He will take away their stony heart and replace it with a soft heart.

It is interesting to live in a world where the enemies of God are getting the most powerful technology. That will lead so fast to Israel being surrounded, and without hope, until they look up.

But until that moment happens, we are supposed to be opening people's eyes to God's Word. Are you faithfully sharing the Word with those who so desperately need to hear it?

FRIDAY: A Summary of Old Testament Millennial Promises

> " 'Simon has declared how God at the first visited the Gentiles to take out of them a people for His name. And with this **the words of the prophets agree**, just as it is written: "After this I will return And will rebuild the tabernacle of David, which has fallen down; I will rebuild its ruins, And I will set it up; So that the rest of mankind may seek the Lord, Even all the Gentiles who are called by My name, Says the Lord who does all these things." 'Known to God from eternity are all His works.' "
> —Acts 15:14–18

How does what we've been learning so far in Revelation 20 compare with Old Testament millennial promises? Various prophetic commentators have traced it like this.

Isaiah describes the kingdom in such glowing terms. Throughout his entire prophecy Isaiah sees, through faith's telescope, the glorious time when Israel and Judah shall be one people in their own land, restored in soul to God, dwelling in peace every man under his own vine and fig tree, and the glory of the Lord covering the earth as the waters cover the sea. He tells how even nature itself shall respond to Messiah's rule, and the wilderness and the solitary place shall be glad for them, and the desert shall rejoice and blossom as the rose. The brute Creation too shall be delivered from the curse. They shall not hurt nor destroy in all God's holy mountain. The lion shall eat straw like the ox. The lamb shall lie down with the wolf, and *"a little child shall lead them."* All nations will then ask the way to Zion; and Jerusalem shall become the metropolis, not only of a rejuvenated Palestine, but also of the whole earth.

Jeremiah takes up the same happy strain, and foresees the God of Israel sending *"fishers"* out into the sea of the nations, fishing out His people no matter where they may be hidden, and bringing them back to the land of their fathers. He sees the city built again and inhabited by a peaceful, happy nation under the reign of the righteous Branch whom God has promised to raise up unto David, and "in his days, Judah shall be saved, and Israel shall dwell safely; and this is His name whereby He shall be called, THE LORD OUR RIGHTEOUSNESS." Then they shall no longer need to "teach every man his neighbor, and every man his brother, saying, Know the Lord, for they shall all know Him, from the least to the greatest of them."

Ezekiel adds to the wondrous story, and tells of the Spirit being poured out from on high, and describes the services of the regenerated Israel, a priestly nation, through whom the law of God goes forth to all the lands of the nations. He depicts the millennial temple, and even tells us how the land is to be divided among the tribes, and does not close his remarkable book until he can say, "The name of the city from that day shall be Jehovah—Shammah—THE LORD IS THERE."

Daniel's companion-apocalypse visions conclude with the bringing in of the fifth universal kingdom, and this he tells us is the Kingdom of the Son of Man, which is to displace every other, and is to stand forever. This is the Stone cut out without hands that falls upon the feet of the Gentile image and grinds it to powder, and then becomes a great mountain and fills the whole earth. This is the Kingdom conferred upon the Son of Man by the Ancient of Days, when the bodies of the beasts (symbolizing the four great empires that have borne rule over all the civilized earth) shall be cast into the burning flame.

Hosea shows that Messiah would come in lowly grace, be rejected by Israel, and return to His place until they acknowledge their sin and seek His face. Then He would come back to restore their souls and to ransom them from the power of the grave, bringing in everlasting righteousness, and making them a blessing to all nations.

Joel sees the Great Tribulation in all its intensity, but beholds the glory that shall follow, and predicts the outpouring of the Spirit, not on Israel only, but on all flesh.

Amos bears witness to the gathering again of the outcasts of Israel, and their re-settlement in their land under Jehovah's perfect rule.

Obadiah wrote the shortest of all the prophecies, and he speaks chiefly of judgment upon Edom, declaring triumphantly, *"The Kingdom shall be the Lord's."*

Jonah alone, of all the prophetic brotherhood, seems to have no reference to that day of Jehovah's power; yet, we may learn through him how wonderfully God will empower the testimony of Hebrew missionaries in the beginning of the Kingdom Age, as they go forth to spread the gospel among those who have not heard His fame, nor seen His glory.

Micah joins with Isaiah in describing the time when "the mountain of the Lord's house shall be established in the top of the mountains, and all nations shall flow to it," when "the law shall go forth from Zion, and the word of the Lord from Jerusalem." Then "the nations shall beat their swords into plowshares and their spears into pruning-hooks, and shall learn war no more."

Nahum predicts the judgments that shall befall the enemies of Jehovah in the day of His preparation; while **Habakkuk**, standing on his watch-tower, sees the coming King bringing in the glory.

Zephaniah and **Haggai** point onward to the restoration of Israel, and through them the blessing of the whole world, when the Lord their God is enthroned in the midst of them, and they serve Him with one consent.

Zechariah, the prophet of glory, gives minute details that no others have touched upon, and even tells of the provision to be made for children's playgrounds in the restored capital of Palestine, for he says, "The broad places of the city shall be full of boys and girls, playing in the broad places thereof" (literal rendering). He sees every spot in Jerusalem holy to the Lord, and all Nations wending their way thitherward from year to year to keep the feast of tabernacles.

Malachi completes the series and announces the soon-coming of the King, heralded by the prophet Elijah, to tread down the wicked and sit as a refiner of silver to purify the sons of Levi, and to make His name great from the rising of the sun to the going down of the same.

Thus "to Him give all the prophets witness," not only that through His name remission of sins is now to be proclaimed among all nations, but that He is to reign in righteousness over all the world, when He comes the second time to claim the inheritance which is His by divine fiat, as Son and Heir of all things. Then all the earth will rejoice for the eyes of the blind shall be opened, the tongue of the dumb shall sing, the lame man shall leap as the deer, sorrow and sighing shall flee away, and the Lord alone shall be exalted for a thousand glorious years!

SATURDAY: Truths That Bring Hope

*"Inasmuch then as the children have partaken of flesh and blood, He Himself likewise shared in the same, **that through death He might destroy him who had the power of death**, that is, the devil."*
—Hebrews 2:14

The following are truths that you are not likely to ever hear, except from the Book that only tells the Truth—the Word of God!

Satan is stoppable and vulnerable (Revelation 20:1–3). We can overcome him by: the way of goodness—a fruit of the Spirit (Romans 12:21); the Word of God (1 John 2:14); the walk of faith (1 John 5:4); and the blood of Jesus and the word of our testimony (Revelation 12:11).

Suffering is valuable (Revelation 20:4–6). Suffering for Jesus partners us with the Holy Spirit (Romans 8:17–24), and suffering for Jesus is God's plan: "For to you it has been granted on behalf of Christ, not only to believe in Him, but also to suffer for His sake" (Philippians 1:29). Suffering for Jesus allows us an intimate sharing with Christ's sufferings that we "may know Him and the power of His resurrection and the fellowship of His sufferings, being conformed to His death" (Philippians 3:10).

Suffering for Jesus strengthens our walk in the Lord: "We ourselves boast of you among the churches of God for your patience and faith in all your persecutions and tribulations that you endure" (2 Thessalonians 1:4). Suffering for Jesus prepares us for future service for the Lord in heaven: "If we endure, we shall also reign with Him. If we deny Him, He also will deny us" (2 Timothy 2:12). We can share in His sufferings (1 Peter 4:13), and be strengthened by persevering through the trials (1 Peter 5:10).

People are so deceivable and gullible (Revelation 20:7–9). Christ has therefore warned us to beware of deceptions, especially in the last days: " 'Take heed that no one deceives you. For many will come in My name, saying, "I am the Christ," and will deceive many' " (Matthew 24:4–5; see also Matthew 24:11, 24).

May Christ's kingdom come! Now let us turn our focus to Christ's coming and the Lord's Prayer. Although I touched on this verse a little earlier, I'd like to develop it a bit more: "Your kingdom come. Your will be done On earth as it is in heaven" (Matthew 6:10). These are familiar words in our Lord's giving of a model prayer to His disciples. What kingdom is He talking about? We know that it is not the universal, providential, sovereign rule of God because that is occurring right now.

David had this to say about God's kingdom in this present age: "The Lord has established His throne in heaven, And His kingdom rules over all" (Psalm 103:19). Paul affirmed God's rule in Ephesians 1:11: "In Him also we have obtained an inheritance, being predestined according to the purpose of Him who works all things according to the counsel of His will."

We do not pray for that which already exists. No, the key is in the clause that qualifies all three petitions: "On earth as it is in heaven." So then, what is the petition Christ desired to ever be on the hearts and lips of His own people—we Christians? He wants us to earnestly pray: *Your kingdom come, Your will be done on earth just like it is in heaven*. Therefore, Christ must come to put this rebellion down—and for that, we are to pray!

Make a choice to live in hope. Since God will keep His Word about the kingdom, we can count on Him to also keep His Word about today. Perhaps your life presently seems miserable and difficult, and you long to escape whatever is weighing you down. Sometimes people think that if they could only change their circumstances that they would be happier or better off in some other way. But did you know that external change is powerless?

A change in outer circumstances can effect no real inner transformation. Christ's visible presence on earth during the Millennium proves that even an outward Paradise does not produce godliness within. No, the solution to living in enduring hope is to choose to let Him reign within your life.

God therefore wants you to believe: "My presence is always with you, and I will give you rest!" He wants you to cling to Him in hope because He has promised to bring you victoriously through whatever trial(s) you may be experiencing. For God works in all things for the good of those who love Him (Romans 8:28)!

WEEK 45
Fear the Holiness of Jesus

{ Revelation 20:11–15 }

As the end of days approaches, you can find hope as you learn to fear the holiness of Jesus!

SUNDAY: The Holiness of Jesus

"*Then He will also say to those on the left hand, '**Depart from Me, you cursed**, into the everlasting fire prepared for the devil and his angels.'*"

—Matthew 25:41

Perhaps no scene in the entire Bible grips our minds and stirs our souls as much as the last verses of Revelation 20. Imagine the scene: in one moment all the angels and all the humans who have ever lived on this planet—perhaps as many as forty-five billion souls will be assembled.[1] In utter silence the scene opens. In the glow of God's glory surrounding His throne stand the redeemed of all the ages. Behind them, in countless ranks, are all the angelic hosts. The four angelic creatures hover about God's presence while our representatives, the twenty-four elders, stand, and then kneel before the throne.

All the dead, small and great, are in this assembly. Every single person who has ever lived is there: not one soul will escape this summons to the court of God Almighty—His last and greatest and final roll call.

All the wicked rulers of this world are present. Those evil emissaries of Satan that gassed women and children hide no more in disguise to escape penalty; they each stand exposed. All the "Genghis Khans" of this world who flayed their enemies alive now have no armies to protect them; they, too, stand alone before the Judge.

The Scythians, the murderous horsemen who killed their foes and used their skulls as cups to drink blood, stand silent. The ashes of countless cremated warlords and ruthless business executives cast to the winds and seas, hopeful of escaping God, are now reassembled into bodies. Souls imprisoned in Hades now regain habitation in the bodies in which they sinned and turned from God.

All God-haters, from Voltaire to Hitler, now face the One they despised. The God-resisters who denied God and said no to Him are now assembled, from Pharaoh to the priests of Molech, and they, too, are quaking in dread. They are all present—no one can escape this, the final hour. Before this silent multitude, speechless in the sight of the God they never wanted to know, nor ever wanted to meet, is the eerie flicker of the cauldron of God's holy wrath, the Lake of Fire.

It is a lake; it is on fire. It is already filled with the Devil, his two apostles (the beast and the false prophet), and all the malignant hordes of evil angels. They have already sunk into utter blackness to begin their eternal plunge to the never-ending depths of the blackened pit of darkness. Eternally tormented with the very desire that gripped them—to be away from the Light, the Truth, and the Life—they plunge downward.

As for the billions who stand frozen with the dreadful fear of inescapable doom, the last word of the final judgment begins. This section of Revelation divides into five sobering truths which I will state now, and we will examine later in the week: 1) the Judge is great (v. 11); 2) the judgment is inescapable (v. 12); 3) the standard is exact (v. 13); 4) the sentence is final (v. 14); and 5) blessed is the Book of Life (v. 15).

Before you end up in the congregation of the doomed at that Great White Throne, bow to the Lord Jesus Christ. And if you know Him, as His child by grace, bow your heart before Him in worship. Cry out to Him for insights that will impact your life from His Word!

My Prayer for You This Week: *Father, we know that You are not desiring that any should perish, but that all should come to the knowledge of the Truth, to repentance, and to life eternal. You have told us that those who go to hell have fitted themselves for destruction by their refusal, either actively or passively, to say yes to Jesus. We pray that the horror of eternity apart from Your grace, and facing Your wrath, will motivate us to be like the Apostle Paul who confessed as his testimony: "Knowing,* therefore, the terror of the Lord, we persuade men." May we go out to a dying world and point them to You as their only hope for the resurrection and the life. May we soberly, knowing Your terror, persuade lost souls to receive the free gift of eternal life, to repent, and to follow and obey You. Open our hearts to this challenging portion of Your Word so that Christ will be exalted in our lives! We ask all these things in the precious name of the Lord Jesus, Amen.

MONDAY: Jesus Spoke of Hell More Than Heaven

*"And do not fear those who kill the body but cannot kill the soul. But rather **fear Him who is able to destroy both soul and body in hell**."*

—MATTHEW 10:28

We are examining the most horrifying doctrine in God's Word for humans to talk or think about. The fact is that God Himself talks more about hell than He does about heaven. Therefore, I want to remind you of the reality of an eternal hell that has been prepared for those Jesus said did not receive Him.

In Christian circles we speak more of *heaven* than hell. Yet, Jesus warned of hell from the very start to the end of His ministry. For example, in the Gospel of Matthew, from chapter 3 through chapter 26, you will find this common theme: eternal judgment. Jesus preached continually about the horrors awaiting the unsaved lost ones—in public, in private, with saints, and with sinners. Jesus spoke much of it; we speak little of it.

Over twenty years ago I began an intense study of every verse in the Bible. As I read through the Scriptures, I looked for verses on the doctrine of the eternal punishment of the lost. Later this week we will examine some key passages. But for now, I want to give you a summary: "That hideous doctrine of hell is fading. How often have you thought of it in the past month, for instance? Does it make a difference in your concern for others, in your witness? Is it a constant and proper burden? Our Lord's words on the subject are unnerving. In Luke 16, He tells us of a rich man who died and went to Hades (the abode of the unsaved dead between death and final judgment)."[2]

Hades is the place where all who reject Jesus Christ, from the time of Adam and Eve through the time of the end of this planet, go. All of those who die without Christ go to the same place—Hades. From that story and a few other revelatory facts, we can infer several characteristics of hell.

Hell is a place of great physical pain. The rich man in Luke 16 is a living immortal soul in the vestibule of the Lake of Fire. This is not hell proper. The Bible describes hell in the last book of the Bible, and it is called Gehenna. Jesus talked about that, too, but Hades is "the waiting room" before the final judgment. In other words, Hades is the abode of the dead, and the rich man was there.

Do you realize why Jesus spoke about hell so often? He wants us to be like Paul, "Knowing, therefore, the terror of the Lord, we persuade men" (2 Corinthians 5:11a). "God does not leave us with simply the mute fact of hell's physical pain. He tells us how real people will respond to that pain. Our Lord is not being macabre; He is simply telling us the truth."

Hell is a place of "weeping" and "wailing." "There will also be 'weeping' (Luke 13:28). Weeping is not something we get a grip on; it is something that grips us. Recall how you were affected when you last heard someone weep. Remember how you were moved with compassion to want to protect and restore that person? The Lord wants us to know and consider what an upsetting experience it is for the person in hell.

"Another response will be 'wailing' (Matthew 13:42). While weeping attracts our sympathy, wailing frightens and offends us. It is the pitiable bawl of a soul seeking escape, hurt beyond repair, eternally damaged. A wail is sound gone grotesque because of conclusions we can't live with."

Hell is a place of "gnashing of teeth" (Luke 13:28). "Why? Perhaps because of anger or frustration. It may be a defense against crying out or an intense pause when one is too weary to cry any longer."

More than heaven, Christ spoke of hell. More than love, Christ spoke of eternal destruction. More than the church to come, Christ Jesus warned of God's wrath and judgment and hell.

Every year, about fifty-six million people enter eternity—the vast majority of them without Christ. I believe that it is imperative for us to pause and reflect on the destination of all those travelers who are leaving the earth to experience eternal suffering. Why? Because Jesus did. And what is important to Jesus should be important to us!

TUESDAY: The Horrors of Eternal Darkness

*"Are set forth as an example, **suffering the vengeance of eternal fire**."*
—Jude 7b

What I am about to share in today's devotional is a continued summary of what an insightful person once wrote of all the verses on the doctrine of hell.[3] If you synthesized them together, and put them in a flowing passage, this is how it would read.

"Hell has two . . . aspects, rarely considered, which are both curious and frightening. On earth we take for granted two physical properties that help keep us physically, mentally, and emotionally stable. The first is light; the second is solid, fixed surfaces. Oddly, these two dependables will not accommodate those in hell."

Hell is a place of darkness (Matthew 8:12). Imagine the person who has just entered hell—a neighbor, relative, co-worker, or friend. After a roar of physical pain blasts him, he spends his first moments wailing and gnashing his teeth. But after a season, he grows accustomed to the pain, not that it's become tolerable, but that his capacity for it has enlarged to comprehend it, yet not be consumed by it. Though he hurts, he is now able to think, and he instinctively looks about him. But as he looks, he sees only blackness.

In his past life he learned that if he looked long enough, a glow of light somewhere would yield definition to his surroundings. So he blinks and strains to focus his eyes, but his efforts yield only blackness. He turns and strains his eyes in another direction. He waits. He sees nothing but unyielding black ink. It clings to him, smothering and oppressing him.

Realizing that the darkness is not going to give way, he nervously begins to feel for something solid to get his bearings. He reaches for walls or rocks or trees or chairs; he stretches his legs to feel the ground and touches nothing.

Hell is a *"bottomless pit"* (Rev. 20:1–2 KJV). The new occupant is slow to learn. In growing panic, he kicks his feet and waves his arms. He stretches and he lunges. But he finds nothing. After more feverish tries, he pauses from exhaustion, suspended in black. Suddenly, with a scream he kicks, twists, and lunges until he is again too dizzy to move, too nauseous to think, and too exhausted to even continue.

He tumbles onward, alone with his pain. Unable to touch a solid object or see a solitary thing, he begins to weep. His sobs choke through the darkness. Those sobs become weak, then lost in hell's roar.

As time passes, he begins to do what the rich man did—he again starts to think. His first thoughts are of hope. You see, he still thinks as he did on earth, where he kept himself alive with hope. When things got bad, he always found a way out. If he felt pain, he took medicine. If hungry, he ate food. If he lost love, there was more love to be found.

So he casts about in his mind for a plan to apply to the hope building in his chest. Of course, he thinks, Jesus, the God of love, can get me out of this. He cries out with a surge, "Jesus, Jesus! You were right! Help me! Get me out of this!" He waits, breathing hard with desperation. The sound of his voice slips into the darkness and is lost. He tries again, "I believe, Jesus! I believe now! Save me from this!" Again the darkness smothers his words.

Our sinner is not unique. Everyone in hell believes. When he wearies of appeals, he does next what anyone would do—assesses his situation and attempts to adapt. But then it hits him—this is forever.

Jesus had made it very clear. He had used the same words for *"forever"* to describe both heaven and hell. Forever, he thinks, and his mind labors through the blackness until he aches. "Forever!" he whispers in wonder. The idea deepens, widens, and towers over him. The awful truth spreads before him like endless, overlapping slats. When I put in ten thousand centuries of time here, I will not have accomplished one thing. I will not have one second less to spend here.

As the rich man pleaded for a drop of water, so, too, our new occupant entertains a similar ambition. In life he learned that even bad things could be tolerated if one could find temporary relief. Perhaps even hell, if one could rest from time to time, would be more tolerable. He learns, though, that "The smoke of [his] torment goes up forever and ever; and [he has] no rest day and night" (Revelation 14:11 NASB).

No rest day and night—think of that. Thoughts of this happening to people we know, people like us, are too terrifying to entertain for long. The idea of allowing someone to endure such torture for eternity violates the sensibilities of even the most severe judge among us. We simply cannot bear it.

But our thoughts of hell will never be as unmanageable as its reality. We must take this doctrine of hell, therefore, and make sure we are practically affected by it. A hard look at this doctrine should first **change our view of sin**. Most believers do not take sin as seriously as God does. We need to realize that in God's eyes and in His actual plan, sin deserves eternal punishment in hell.

WEEK 45: FEAR THE HOLINESS OF JESUS

We can actually learn, by comparison, to hate sin as God hates it. As the reality of hell violates and offends us, for example, so sin violates and offends God. As we cannot bear to look upon the horrors of hell, so God cannot bear to look upon the horrors of sin. As hell revolts us to the point of hatred for it, so also God finds sin revolting. The comparison is not perfect, but it offers a start.

Second, the truth of hell should **encourage our witness**. Can we ever hear a sigh of weariness, see a moment of doubt, or feel pain without being reminded of that place? In all honesty, can we see any unbeliever, watch his petty human activities, realize what he has in store, and not be moved with compassion? It encourages us to witness in word and in deed. That hideous doctrine may grip our souls in dark terror and make us weep, but let us be sure it also prompts us to holiness and compassion.

WEDNESDAY: God's Last Word

> "**Man is destined to die once** and after that to face judgment."
> —Hebrews 9:27 NIV

Two thousand years ago, God spoke these words to His church as a warning to be shared. We need to grasp the implications of this incredible spiritual law from God. It is man's destiny to die. From Eden onward, anyone who sins dies. Without Christ, no one can escape death's penalty. Every person born on planet Earth is destined to die once: no reincarnation, no second chance, no intermediate step. God says that life is a one-way street: no returns. Literally, it is a dead-end street. At God's final appointment with all who ever lived, without Christ, they face *judgment*. They will be lost, forever lost, and they didn't have to be—they *chose* to be! Meditate on the immensity of that thought! Let's now look at Revelation 20:11–15, which divides into five sobering truths.

Truth 1: The Judge is great. "Then I saw a great white throne and Him who sat on it, from whose face the earth and the heaven fled away. And there was found no place for them" (v. 11). God is great because of His majesty—He is the Creator, Sustainer, God of Gods, Lord of Lords, King of Kings, the Rock, and the Endless of Days! The throne is white because of His holiness; He has revealed Himself as the Light, life everlasting, and the consuming fire.

Truth 2: The judgment is inescapable. "And I saw the dead, small and great, standing before God, and books were opened. And another book was opened, which is the Book of Life. And the dead were judged according to their works, by the things which were written in the books" (v. 12). We know from Paul that at death believers are instantly transported to the presence of Jesus in heaven (2 Corinthians 5:6–8). As most scholars believe, the Bema Seat of Christ (2 Corinthians 5:10) takes place then; as believers we are analyzed by Jesus for our degree of obedience to Him in this life, and then rewarded. John seems to imply that this event is all complete by Revelation 19:8, when the saints are at the great banquet of Christ's redeemed.

In Revelation 20:12, however, we now see the last, the greatest, and the final roll call. No one will go to hell because they didn't know about Jesus; it doesn't say that in the Bible. The only thing that will send someone to hell is sin, not failure to hear of Jesus. He is the only remedy, but the cause of hell is sin. Jesus said, "You will die in your sins." That is the most horrible thing He could say. Anyone who dies in their sins instead of being in Christ is condemned at that moment eternally, and will be banished forever from the presence of God. Why? Because God said, "No sin will be allowed to exist eternally with Me in My holy presence. Only those whose sin is dealt with, who have Jesus as their covering, are allowed in My presence." So the works of every dead person are to be exposed: every act, thought, word, and intent of the heart is revealed one by one.

Truth 3: The standard is exact. "The sea gave up the dead who were in it, and Death and Hades delivered up the dead who were in them. And they were judged, each one according to his works" (v. 13). They will be judged both by Christ's words and by their works: "He who rejects Me, and does not receive My words, has that which judges him—the word that I have spoken will judge him in the last day" (John 12:48). Jesus has spoken, and He has revealed Himself. Psalm 19 says that His voice has gone throughout the whole world.

All unbelievers will give an account as to why they rejected "the true Light which gives light to every man coming into the world" (John 1:9). The Light has come to all who have been born into this world "so that they should seek the Lord, in the hope that they might grope for Him and find Him, though He is not far from each one of us" (Acts 17:27). Those who reject that Light cannot escape His judgment, which is a very exacting standard.

Truth 4: The sentence is final. "Then Death and Hades were cast into the lake of fire. This is the second death" (v. 14). Each personal account will be finalized. The self-righteous will see that they are wearing filthy rags (Isaiah 64:6). The vain babblers will be dumb before Him (Matthew 22:12). The greats of earth will be pitiful in wretchedness that day (Psalm 2:1–5). Each will get their sentencing, but don't think that everyone will receive the same degree of punishment. There will be individual portions (Matthew 24:51). It will be better for Sodom and Gomorrah than for those who were alive during Jesus' ministry and heard His words (Matthew 10:15). It will be easier for Tyre and Sidon than for the city and people of Bethsaida (Matthew 11:21–22). There are different levels of punishment within the horrors of hell. Matthew 12:42 says that the Queen of Sheba will rise up in the judgment and condemn the generation that lived through Christ's ministry. And "then He will also say to those on the left hand, 'Depart from Me, you cursed, into the everlasting fire prepared for the devil and his angels'" (Matthew 25:41). God prepared the Lake of Fire for Satan and his angels, not for humans, but those who follow the devil and his rebellion will follow him into the lake.

Truth 5: Blessed is the Book of Life. "And anyone not found written in the Book of Life was cast into the lake of fire" (v. 15). The names of all souls who experience the saving process of Jesus' blood are recorded in the Lamb's Book of Life. What is our hope as those who believe in Christ? Revelation 17:8 sums it up: "The beast that you saw was, and is not, and will ascend out of the bottomless pit [where Satan was kept for 1,000 years] and go to perdition. And those who dwell on the earth will marvel, whose names are not written in the Book of Life from the foundation of the world, when they see the beast that was, and is not, and yet is."

Do you know whose names are in the Lamb's Book of Life? The ones whom Jesus will bring one at a time before the Father, confessing: "This is My blood-bought child" (see Revelation 3:5). Imagine your joy when you hear the Father saying, "Bring the best robe and put it on My child!" Jesus will say that to all who will come by faith and trust in His finished work.

THURSDAY: Jesus Describes Hell

*"Their worm does not die And the **fire is not quenched**."*
—Mark 9:44

In the Gospel of Matthew Jesus explains that life has:
- Two **entrance gates**—the wide and the narrow.
- Two **roads**—broad and difficult.
- Two **destinations**—destruction and life.
- Two **groups of travelers**—many and few.
- Two **lifestyles**—the sayers and the doers.
- Two **inevitable ends**—being thrown in the Lake of Fire and entering the kingdom of heaven.

After the Sermon on the Mount, Jesus specifically warns everyone to flee—to avoid the Lake of Fire at all costs by doing whatever it takes to not end up there. He warns us over forty times in the Gospel of Matthew alone. Since Jesus preached on hell so much, we need to give this doctrine, tough as it may be, the attention He wants it to have. Therefore, today and tomorrow we will look at many references in the Gospel of Matthew where Jesus warned about hell. Because the doctrine of hell is being lost by our generation as a true doctrine, it would be a good idea to mark these in your Bible. (Emphasis added to the verses.)

Jesus describes hell. The Pharisees and Sadducees who came to Jesus' baptism were vehemently asked, "Who warned you to **flee from the wrath to come**?" (3:7). Following that rebuke was an illustration of a tree that does not bear good fruit being **"thrown into the fire"** (3:10) and worthless chaff that is burned up **"with unquenchable fire"** (3:12).

In one of Christ's most well-attended sermons (probably over 30,000 people), Jesus said that whoever is angry with his brother without a cause **"shall be in danger of hell fire"** (5:22). In verses 29–30, He went on to warn that if one part of your body causes you to practice sin, it is better to get rid of it than have **"your whole body to be cast into hell."** He was convinced that there is a judgment coming for those who never turn from their sin, repent of their iniquity, and embrace Christ as their only hope. And so it was very loving to warn them of such consequences ahead.

Jesus warned to choose His narrow path because the broad one **"leads to destruction"** (7:13). The person who does not bear good fruit is to be **"thrown into the fire"** (7:19) and will hear His **"I never knew you; depart from Me, you who practice lawlessness!"** (7:23). Jesus pointed out that what matters is not merely saying the right thing—it is what you do in life that counts. Everything Jesus said about salvation in all four Gospels, and the need to bear good fruit, is summarized right here in these verses where He is basically saying: "Salvation is not based on whether or not you said and did great things; it is whether or not *God* did something inside of you. That is what the gospel is all about. When the gospel takes root in the heart, it brings forth good fruit."

Jesus said that the "sons of the kingdom" would be **"cast out into outer darkness"** (a place of inky black, impenetrable darkness) where there will be **"weeping and gnashing of teeth"** (8:12). In verses 28–29 we see a testimony from the other side—from a demon, an immortal intelligence, a living spirit that has phenomenal powers that are thousands of years old, and has been in the very presence of God. Look at what this demon says: "Have You come here **to torment us before the time**?" The demons know that Jesus is the Judge, and that there is a time of torment and inescapable judgment coming. For them, however, there is no hope, no opportunity for salvation; they chose instead to go in rebellion with the devil, thereby denying God and going against Him. But we are the ones that the angels look at in wonder. Why? Because we have the Son of God who became a Son of Man so that the sons of men could become sons of God!

In Matthew 10:15 Jesus warned that "it will be **more tolerable** for the land of Sodom and Gomorrah in the day of judgment than for that city!" Even in hell there are levels of tolerability. For those who have grown up hearing the gospel and seeing it lived before them, it will be excruciating to have that awareness of how close they came to knowing Him, but never embracing Him, than for the person who is in hell because of being a sinner rather than rejecting Jesus. And so it will be more tolerable for the land of Sodom and Gomorrah (the land characterized by homosexuality, bestiality, and sinful, grotesque licentiousness) than for the people who have had the light of the gospel upon them. Therefore, in verse 28 Jesus says to "fear Him who is able to **destroy both soul and body in hell**" (10:28).

Jesus warned that it would be **"more tolerable"** (Matthew 11:22–24) in the day of judgment for Tyre and Sidon and the land of Sodom than for those who dwelled in cities where He'd done mighty works. Why? Because Jesus lived there; it was His hometown, and His ministry headquarters. Those people actually lived with God and chose to reject Him. Although they lived with the miracles of heaven around them, they told Jesus: "All that You do is great, but we really don't care about that. We want our sins more than You."

Whoever speaks against the Holy Spirit, Jesus said, would **"not be forgiven . . . , either in this age or in the age to come"** (12:32). Hell is all about unforgiven, unatoned for, and uncleansed sins. In verse 36, Jesus said that for every idle word that man speaks, he will **"give account of it in the day of judgment."** No one goes to hell; the condemned are cast into hell. The initial place called Hades is where people go before the judgment, and it will only be emptied momentarily at judgment time. At the end, as it says in Revelation 20, whoever does not have his name written in the Book of Life will stand before God speechless, and acknowledge that He is just and right to send him to hell.

FRIDAY: More of What Jesus Says About Hell

> "[Apostates are] wandering stars for whom is reserved the **blackness of darkness forever.**"
> —Jude 13b

In the following verses, Jesus gets even more graphic in His description: "Let both grow together until the harvest, and I will say to the reapers, 'First gather together the tares and bind them in bundles **to burn them**, but gather the wheat into my barn' " (13:30). "Therefore as the tares are gathered and **burned in the fire**, so it will be at the end of this age" (13:40). "And [the angels] will **cast them into the furnace of fire**. There will be **wailing and gnashing of teeth**" (13:42). In verse 48 we see that when the dragnet "was full, they drew to shore; and they sat down and gathered the good into vessels, but **threw the bad away**."

Jesus said to let the true and the false, the fruit bearers and the non-fruit bearers, grow together. In the church, there are some who merely appear to be Christians. They can "talk the talk" and even seem to "walk the walk" so well that it is difficult to sort out the real Christians from the fake. It is like wheat and tares, all growing up in the same field. Jesus was saying, "Don't clear out the church. There will always be believers and unbelievers, but let them be together. At the time of the harvest, I will sort them out." Notice that all of Jesus' stories are clear-cut choices: good and bad; righteous and evil; fruit bearing and not fruit bearing; heaven and fire. There is no middle ground here—either you make it or you don't. In verses 49–50 Jesus therefore warns: "So it will be at the end of the age. The angels will come forth, **separate the wicked from among the just**, and cast them into **the furnace of fire**. There will be **wailing and gnashing of teeth**."

Jesus said, "Every plant which My heavenly Father has not planted **will be uprooted**. Let them alone. They are blind leaders of the blind. And if the blind leads the blind, **both will fall into a ditch**" (15:13–14).

Now look at these verses: "You are Peter, and on this rock I will build My church, and the **gates of Hades** shall not prevail against it. For whoever desires to save his life **will lose it**, but whoever loses his life for My sake will find it. For what profit is it to a man if he gains the whole world, and **loses his own soul**? Or what will a man give in exchange for his soul? For the Son of Man will come in the glory of His Father with His angels, and then He will **reward each according to his works**" (16:18, 25, 27).

Jesus also told a lot of parables and stories that don't have what we would call a happy ending. In Matthew 18:34 Jesus speaks about the agony in life of having bitterness and anger: "His master was angry, and **delivered him to the torturers** until he should pay all that was due to him." These "torturers of life" that we don't deal with—emotional pain, depression, and anger—are merely a tiny foretaste of the horrors of hell.

The judgment of the Jewish leaders against the wicked vinedressers turned out to be Christ's judgment against them: "He will **destroy those wicked men miserably**, and lease his vineyard to other vinedressers who will render to him the fruits in their seasons. . . . And whoever falls on this stone will be broken; but on whomever it falls, it **will grind him to powder**" (21:41, 44). This is speaking again of the intensity of the eternal judgment.

In Matthew 22:7 we see another picture of what judgment will be like: "When the king heard about it, he was furious. And he sent out his armies, **destroyed** those murderers, **and burned up their city**." Jesus continued in verse 13: "Then the king said to the servants, 'Bind him hand and foot, take him away, and cast him **into outer darkness**; there will be **weeping and gnashing of teeth**.'"

Jesus sternly rebuked the scribes and Pharisees: "Hypocrites! For you devour widows' houses, and for a pretense make long prayers. Therefore you will receive **greater condemnation**. . . . For you travel land and sea to win one proselyte, and when he is won, you make him twice as much a **son of hell** as yourselves" (23:14–15). Now look at verse 33: "Serpents, brood of vipers! **How can you escape the condemnation of hell?**"

Jesus said that the master of an unfaithful evil servant will come, when he least expects him, to "**cut him in two** and appoint him his portion with the hypocrites. There shall be **weeping and gnashing of teeth**" (24:51). The weeping is because of the pain, and the gnashing of the teeth and wailing is due to the inescapable punishment.

Matthew 25:30 speaks of the unprofitable servant who will be cast "**into the outer darkness**. There will be **weeping and gnashing of teeth**." Have you heard this enough to catch your attention? In verse 41 are Christ's last words about hell; this is the judgment, and Jesus is sitting on the throne: "Then He will also say to those on the left hand, 'Depart from Me, you **cursed**, into **the everlasting fire** prepared for the devil and his angels.'"

Hell was not made for humans. God did not plan for, and want to deliver, the lost to the place of everlasting judgment. Therefore, He is not willing that any should perish. Now tie that with John 3:16: "that they should not perish but have everlasting life." God does not want you to go to the everlasting fire. It was prepared for the devil and his angels. But look at verse 46: "And these [the cursed who practice iniquity—who reject Christ, and refuse to believe and repent] will go away into everlasting punishment, but the righteous into eternal life."

Life in heaven will be endless, but so will life in hell. The only reason hell even exists for mankind is because they love their sins instead of the living and written Word of God. Have you embraced God and His Word? Are you sharing His gospel with others so that they do not become cursed and be cast into the everlasting fire?

SATURDAY: The Apostles Add Their Warnings of Hell

> *"Knowing, therefore, **the terror of the Lord**, we persuade men; but we are well known to God, and I also trust are well known in your consciences."*
>
> —2 Corinthians 5:11a

Now that we have seen what Jesus spoke about hell, let us finish up this subject with what Paul, Peter, Jude, John, and the writer of Hebrews had to say on this subject.

Paul wrote: **"tribulation and anguish, on every soul of man who does evil."** (Romans 2:9). In 2 Thessalonians 1:9 he said, "These shall be **punished with everlasting destruction** from the presence of the Lord and from the glory of His power." The writer of Hebrews warned, "It is a **fearful thing to fall into the hands of the living God**" (Hebrews 10:31). And Peter had this to say: "God did not spare the angels who sinned, but **cast them down to hell** and delivered them into **chains of darkness**, to be **reserved for judgment**." (2 Peter 2:4).

In Jude we learn that "the angels who did not keep their proper domain, . . . He has **reserved in everlasting chains under darkness for the judgment** of the great day." The apostates will be "**suffering the vengeance of eternal fire.**" They are like "wandering stars **for whom is reserved the blackness of darkness forever.**" (See Jude 6–13 for a complete description of this judgment.)

In Revelation 14:11 we are told: "And **the smoke of their torment ascends forever and ever**; and **they have no rest day or night**, who worship the beast and his image, and whoever receives the mark of his name."

Now look at Revelation 19:20: "Then the beast was captured, and with him the false prophet who worked signs in his presence, by which he deceived those who received the mark of the beast and those who worshiped his image. These **two were cast alive into the lake of fire burning with brimstone.**"

Finally, in Revelation 20:10–15, we see: "The devil, who deceived them, was **cast into the lake of fire and brimstone** where the beast and the false prophet are. And they will be tormented day and night forever and ever. Then I saw a great white throne and Him who sat on it, from whose face the earth and the heaven fled away. And there was found no place for them. And I saw the dead, small and great, standing before God, and books were opened. And another book was opened, which is the Book of Life. And the dead were judged according to their works, by the things which were written in the books. . . . Then Death and Hades were **cast into the lake of fire**. This is the **second death**. And anyone not found written in the Book of Life was **cast into the lake of fire.**"

What happens when we receive the Word of God? Why did the rich man of Luke 16 go to hell? What happened to him? He refused to let the Word of God change him; it never pierced his heart. When God's Word is received by faith, our life begins to change: self-centeredness begins to die; self-indulgence begins to be disciplined away; self-sacrifice begins to be pursued; and compassion, kindness, caring, and love take root and grow.

Make a choice to live in hope. This has been a hard week's reading, hasn't it? Although it is painful to have your eyes opened to the realities of the horrors of hell, it is absolutely essential that you not be "in the dark" regarding the truth about this doctrine.

What is the most important point that I want to drive home in this week's devotionals? This amazing Truth—Jesus Christ died for sinners. All who receive Him are forgiven of their sins—past, present, and future. All who are forgiven receive eternal life!

Have you received Jesus Christ? Do you know, beyond a shadow of a doubt, that your sins have been removed? If they have not been, I exhort you, with all that is within me, to delay no longer! No one knows how long they will live, and you could be ushered into eternity at any moment. Oh, dear reader, make a choice to live in hope. Choose to bow your knee to Jesus Christ, who loves you and gave Himself for you!

WEEK 46
Taste the Joys of Heaven

{ Revelation 21–22 }

As the end of days approaches, you can find hope as you taste the joys of heaven!

SUNDAY: Thoughts on Heaven

*"In My Father's house are many mansions; if it were not so, I would have told you. **I go to prepare a place for you**."*

—John 14:2

When you think of heaven, what comes to mind? As for me, thoughts of heaven always lead back to sweet memories of my being a little boy in Sunday school and singing this song: "I'm going to Heaven, can't wait; / Going to see Jesus, can't wait; / Heaven is wonderful, bright and fair, / Praise the Lord, I'm going there!"

A childlike wonder permeates the minds and hearts of the very young—especially when it comes to things of the Lord. Thus, little lambs can joyfully think: *Can't wait to get to heaven!* But as lambs grow into sheep, the manifold distractions of this world can crowd out that joy, childlike wonder begins to fade, and that sweet song of a soft heart changes to: *I'm going to Heaven, but it can wait; going to see Jesus, but He can wait; Heaven is wonderful, bright and fair, praise the Lord—but it can wait!* In other words: *Heaven with Jesus sounds wonderful, but let's hold it off for a little while!*

Isn't that how we become as we age? Usually, not until we are approaching the end of our life do our thoughts go back to: *Can't wait to get to heaven!* It is that in-between time when we are at the greatest risk of heaven losing its wonder in our minds and hearts. If we're honest, most of us would say that we are hoping for heaven, but not just yet. Why is that? Dave Hunt comments,

> For most Christians heaven is a place they desire to reach eventually, but not until they have lived out their full days on earth. Their hopes, ambitions, and interests, contrary to what Christ taught and the early Church lived, are really bound up in the life they aspire to live in this world. Heaven is a distant and unreal destination they reluctantly expect to reach at the end of life, but it is not desired before then. To be suddenly raptured to heaven would be, for most Christians, an unwelcome interruption of their earthy plans and ambitions.[1]

Most of us have thus forgotten how to embrace the awe of being in our Father's house! Restoring that childlike wonder is my goal for this week's devotionals. And it is my heartfelt prayer that when you have finished on Saturday that you will, with joy, be singing, "This world is not my home / I'm just a passing through."

Would the Rapture be an unwelcome interruption of the plans you have for this life, or your greatest joy? Are you an earth dweller at heart, or a pilgrim who longs for "heaven's open door"?

My Prayer for You This Week: *Oh Father, we do thank You for heaven! We thank You that the writer of Hebrews says this hope we have is an anchor of our souls. Oh Lord, we pray that You will make sure that we are believing the Truth about You, and following the way that You would have us to go. Open our minds and hearts to embrace the Truth as we detach ourselves from this place and choose to attach our affections upon heaven—to look forward to our Father's house. We thank You for what You will teach us! In the name of Jesus we pray, Amen.*

MONDAY: In My Father's House

*"**In My Father's house** are many mansions."*

—John 14:2a

Christ's promise to us in John 14:1-6 comes in the language of the Bible, and it is bound by culture and time. Therefore, understanding the Scriptures involves more than knowing what the words mean. We need to understand those words from the perspective of the people that God chose both to write them and to have those words communicated to them in the New Testament world. Therefore the people God chose as His instruments, the people to whom He revealed Himself, were Hebrews living in the Near East. We can't divorce ourselves from that context or we won't fully understand God's Word. Remember the world is divided into Oriental and Occidental—we're Occidental, a western culture. They are Oriental—an eastern culture—so they think in terms of concrete reality. The western world thinks more in ideas and an abstract mode rather than the concrete mode, which the Hebrew and Greek languages use. Their language was one of pictures, metaphors, and examples rather than ideas, definitions, and abstractions.[2]

If we were to have a little concert of worship in today's church vernacular, someone might say, "Oh, God, I praise Your mighty omniscience!" Or another might say, "I am so grateful for Your omnipotence!" But you wouldn't hear those kinds of words in a Hebrew prayer meeting. A Hebrew preferred to pray: "The Lord is my Shepherd." Do you know what that means to the Hebrew? "The Lord is all-knowing; He never slumbers or sleeps; He is all-providing; He watches over us night and day, and leads us." They are saying that God is the One who is not only with them but also provides for them.

Now look at the concrete imagery of John 14:1-6 as we go through this passage:

- "Let not your heart be troubled; you believe in God, believe also in Me."—Jesus is speaking to His disciples, who don't know what's ahead.
- "In My Father's house"—That is a description of heaven!
- "are many mansions"—These are dwelling places, nests, places of rest—an innumerable amount of rooms are there.
- "if it were not so, I would have told you. I go to prepare a place for you"—Heaven isn't an idea, or merely another dimension; it is a place. Jesus is saying, "I am going away to prepare

a special place for you, so be sure that you have your room reserved!" He is preparing a place for all those who make prior reservations before they leave this earth (that is what salvation is about).

- "And if I go and prepare a place for you"—"A place" speaks of an individual room for each of His children.
- "I will come again and receive you to Myself; that where I am, there you may be also. And where I go you know, and the way you know."—If you search the Scriptures, you know all about this because heaven covers the Scriptures from Genesis to Revelation. And what beautiful pictures they are!
- "Thomas said to Him, 'Lord, we do not know where You are going, and how can we know the way?' "—Thomas is speaking here for all of us!
- "Jesus said to him, 'I am the way, the truth, and the life.' "—Jesus told them, "I am the Way to heaven, the Truth about heaven, and the Life that you long for because you will have My unbroken presence!"
- "No one comes to the Father except through Me."—Coming to the Father is the same as going to live in the Father's house, and Jesus is the Door through which we must enter.

Heaven is the unbroken presence of God forever, the unsoiled shores of Paradise, the unending enjoyment of the Living and True Almighty Lord of Heaven and Earth. Thus heaven has always been the source of comfort, hope, and focus of God's servants.

When Christ's disciples felt extremely distressed in their hearts because He told them He was going to die, and not be with them anymore, Jesus comforted them with heaven. Heaven is what those in the Coliseum clung to as they went to their death in the arena. Thoughts of heaven gave enduring hope to those in the dungeons, going through the fires of persecution, and dying for their faith. They all clung to heaven as their secure hope for the future. We, too, should cling to heaven because Jesus intended that heaven be our comfort as we walk His path on earth.

The early church lived in such a way that they looked every day for Christ. When they saw the sun rising their thoughts became like those in this song: "When morning gilds the sky / My heart awaking cries, / May Jesus Christ be praised." They thought, *Perhaps today He will come . . .* That is what those early believers lived, which is so often remote from our culture. We plan our lives so far in advance that if the Rapture happened this week it would ruin our plans. We should be planning according to *His* plans! Yes, we need to prepare wisely for the future, but the real need we have is to long for heaven. That should take precedence over any personal agendas. Long for your Father's house, but most of all, long for Jesus!

TUESDAY: Heaven Is a Dwelling Place

*"In My Father's house are **many mansions**; if it were not so, I would have told you. I go to prepare **a place** for you."*

—John 14:2

Heaven is the eternal and very distant world that is the abode of God, the angels, and glorified believers. But to help us grasp some of its wonder, join me in a look at what heaven is.[3]

Heaven is a dwelling place. Jesus has told us that there are many dwelling places in His Father's house. The most frequent association with heaven is that it is the place where God dwells. Although God is the central inhabitant of heaven, He is not its only resident. The angels live there as well, as more than a dozen verses tell us. The company of the redeemed also lives in heaven; at the end of Elijah's earthly life, God took him up to heaven by a whirlwind (2 Kings 2:1), and Revelation repeatedly portrays glorified saints as inhabiting heaven. A preponderance of the Bible's pictures of heaven show it to be a crowded place.

When you think about heaven, though, don't consider it to be an endlessly huge place. Think about it in Bible terms. Let me show you one that just makes me chuckle—a reference to heaven in the Old Testament. I love this one because it reminds me of our family of ten! (You might say that our home is "a little bit like heaven" in this sense.) Right in the middle of warning King Ahab about the consequences of his sin, there is this little note in 1 Kings 22:19: "Then Micaiah said, 'Therefore hear the word of the LORD: I saw the LORD sitting on his throne, and all the host of heaven standing by, on His right hand and on His left.' "

What is that all about? Well, heaven might be huge, but the idea is that everybody will be crowded right around the throne—as close as they can get to God! Do you see what it is? Heaven is shown to be a massive place that could house 100 billion people—each having a room with space that would equal the size of a whole palace of their own. Yet, in spite of that, the descriptions of heaven almost remind me of what my beehives look like: the queen bee is right there, and all the bees are gathered together as close to her as they can get. That is what heaven is like: we will all be gathered together around our heavenly Father's throne just to be near Him!

What does that have to do with my home? When Bonnie and I are brushing our teeth, I'd say that 90 percent of our family is standing right there by us brushing their teeth as well. And, if Bonnie is in our kitchen, everybody is right around her in the kitchen. Why does my family stay so close by? Because we love to be together! Do you know what heaven is? A dwelling place of those who want, more than anything else, to be where God is. They want to adore Him, worship Him, magnify Him, see Him, know Him, and be with Him! For that reason, Jesus was named Emmanuel, "God with us," so that we could get to be with God!

Being with God forever is the fulfillment of everything about which the Scriptures speak. God created Adam and Eve for fellowship with Him, and to walk with Him, but they fell into sin and broke that bond of fellowship. So, through Jesus, He came back to redeem them—to bring them to Himself by offering a means of escape from the curse of sin—from the penalty they incurred because of their transgression. In the New Testament, Jesus Christ became the fulfillment of those promises (Matthew 1:21, 23).

God came to be with us so that we can go to be with Him. The ultimate description of heaven is the dwelling place where we get to be with God. We get to know Him, to be like Him, to see Him as He is. We get to spend forever with the One who loved us and gave Himself for us! If we die in our sleep, as David said, "When I awake, I will awake in Your likeness because I want to be like You, and I want to be with You" (see Psalm 17:15).

WEDNESDAY: Heaven Is a Real Place

> *"In My Father's house are many mansions; if it were not so, I would have told you. I go to prepare* **a place** *for you."*
>
> —John 14:2

I want to underline in your mind that heaven is not an idea alone. In the Bible, heaven is emphatically a definite locale. To enter it is to enter a definite space. In the verse above, note that Jesus specifically said that He was going to prepare "a place." If we ask where this heavenly place is, the answer overwhelmingly is that it is above the planet Earth. Vertical imagery dominates in the placing of it.

Heaven is a place from which God looks down to the earth. "The LORD looks down from heaven on the sons of men to see if there are any who understand, any who seek God" (Psalm 14:2 NIV). Psalm 80:14 says, "O God Almighty! Look down from heaven and see!" (NIV). And in Psalm 102:19, "the LORD looked down from his sanctuary on high, from heaven he viewed the earth" (Psalm 102:19 NIV).

So what is heaven? Not only the dwelling place of God, but it has an incredible vertical imagery. It is the place, first of all, from which God looks down upon us.

Heaven is the place from which Christ came down. "For the bread of God is He who comes down from heaven and gives life to the world" (John 6:33). The Bible describes heaven not only as the place from which God looks down upon the earth but also the place from which Christ came down to the earth.

Jesus said, "For I have come down from heaven not to do My own will, but the will of Him who sent Me . . . I am the bread which came down from heaven" (John 6:38, 41). So where is heaven? God says, "I am above you—looking down at you!" That is where heaven is, and that is where Jesus came from. For that reason the Jews grumbled at Him saying, "Is this not Jesus, the son of Joseph, whose father and mother we know? How is it then that He says, 'I came down from heaven'?" (John 6:42).

Heaven is the place to which people look up from earth. "It [the Truth] is not up in heaven, so that you have to ask, 'Who will ascend into heaven to get it and proclaim it to us so we may obey it?'" (Deuteronomy 30:12 NIV). When Elijah and Elisha were on their way from Gilgal, "the LORD was about to take Elijah up to heaven in a whirlwind" (2 Kings 2:1 NIV).

In Luke 18:13, the repentant tax collector "would not even look up to heaven, but beat his breast and said, 'God, have mercy on me, a sinner'" (NIV). Jesus said that when you raise your eyes toward the sky, you are looking toward heaven.

Heaven is the place to which Christ ascended after His earthly life. As He was ascending, "they were looking intently up into the sky as he was going, when suddenly two men dressed in white stood beside them. 'Men of Galilee,' they said, 'why do you stand here looking into the sky? This same Jesus, who has been taken from you into heaven, will come back in the same way you have seen him go into heaven' " (Acts 1:10–11 NIV). Did you catch the vertical imagery of heaven in these verses? Amazing! Heaven is the place to which Christ ascended after His earthly life; the place to which people look up from earth; the place from which Christ came down; and the place from which God looks down upon us!

Heaven is a literal dwelling place—a place of absolute security. Heaven is always described as being "up" from our perspective of living on earth. Heaven is remote from earth, a higher and superior mode of existence, and a regal place of supreme authority. It is the command center; it is the place where we can be secure. This is indicated by nearly a dozen references to God's throne being situated in heaven. This royal quality indicates both the splendor of heaven and the authority of the God who rules the universe from heaven.

Heaven is sometimes the regal palace of the King of the Universe. It has many rooms, specifically prepared by Christ for His followers, leading us to view it as a place where people live (John 14:1–3).

Heaven sometimes has the features of a celestial temple. This is in keeping with the worship that occurs there: "I saw the LORD seated on a throne, high and exalted, and the train of His robe filled the temple" (Isaiah 6:1 NIV). Now look at Revelation 3:12: "He who overcomes, I will make him a pillar in the temple of My God, and he shall go out no more. I will write on him the name of My God and the name of the city of My God, the New Jerusalem, which comes down out of heaven from My God. And I will write on him My new name."

The one who "overcomes" is every born-again believer. And every true child of God will become "a pillar in the temple of God," never again to leave God's presence; we will forever be His servants. This is a command center in heaven, and God will write His name on each believer, and the name of the city of God, the New Jerusalem, which is coming down out of heaven from God.

I could take a piece of paper and write just three lines on it—and that one piece of paper would find its way to one person out of six billion if I included the name, address, city, state, and country. Just three lines can separate one person from six billion! Do you want to have some security? In Revelation 3:12, God is saying, "When you are born again, I am addressing you for heaven, so you can be sure to arrive safely. I identify you as Mine, one out of billions, and you are going to go to the place I've prepared for you, a place of ultimate security."

More than anything else—heaven is a city. In Revelation 20–22, we see that this city is replete with walls, gates, and streets. This testifies to us as believers being united in one place in the worship of God. We are all going to be delivered securely to a city in heaven that is perfect and eternal. But though a city, it is unlike any city we know here on earth, for this city also possesses the features of an earthly paradise. We will have the right to eat from the tree of life, which is in the Paradise of God (Revelation 2:7). There is also the crystal-clear river of life that flows from the throne of God. On each side of the river is the tree of life, that bears twelve crops of fruit every year, and its leaves are for healing the nations (Revelation 22:1–2).

Just think: in heaven, we will also be with all our brothers and sisters in Christ! And the great blessing is that we won't be together for just a visit now and then—but for eternity!

THURSDAY: Heaven Is a Permanent Place

*"He waited for **the city which has foundations**, whose builder and maker is God."*
—Hebrews 11:10

Poets have always depended on artistic imagery when portraying heaven. Such images combine hardness of texture and brilliance of light to suggest a realm of superior permanence, value and splendor, when compared with the cyclic, vegetative world in which we live. Jewel imagery is the most prevalent type of artistic imagery.

Ezekiel's vision of a heavenly level of reality is replete with such imagery: flashing fire and lightning, burnished bronze that sparkles, gleaming chrysolite, and sapphire (see Ezekiel 1). To this we can add the memorable pictures in Revelation of a sea of glass, like crystal; the appearance of God in splendor like that of jasper and carnelian; golden crowns, gates of pearl, and a city of pure gold. In addition to jeweled imagery, physical light and its equivalent—glory—are recurrent in biblical images of heaven. In the heaven portrayed in Revelation, the light of the sun and moon are no longer needed "for the glory of God is its light, and its lamp is the Lamb," and by the light of heaven "shall the nations walk" (Revelation 21:23-24). There will be no more night. They will not need the light of a lamp or the light of the sun, for the Lord God will give them light, and they will reign with Him forever and ever (Revelation 22:5).

Heaven is a holy place. The purity of existence in heaven and the spiritual perfection of those who are "enrolled in heaven" (Hebrews 12:23) are expressed by imagery of washed robes (Revelation 7:14), white garments (Revelation 3:5, 18; 4:4; 6:11; 7:9, 13), clothing of "fine linen, bright and pure" (Revelation 19:8), and chaste people who are "spotless" (Revelation 14:4-5).

Daniel pictures the people as shining "like the stars forever and ever" (Daniel 12:3)—symbolic of permanence and glory. Revelation also pictures the redeemed receiving such things as the morning star (Revelation 2:28), a white stone with a secret name written on it (Revelation 2:17), and water from a fountain of life (Revelation 21:6). Similarly, those who enter heaven will become pillars in the temple of God (Revelation 3:12).

Heaven is an unimaginable place. While not a major part of the images of heaven, beings that have never existed in human experience are included in the visions of Ezekiel and Revelation. Examples from Ezekiel's vision include living creatures with four faces, four wings, and soles like those of a calf's foot (Ezekiel 1:6-7). These creatures move about in a riot of motion, and something that looks like torches of fire moves among them (Ezekiel 1:13). There is a celestial chariot replete with gleaming wheels which have rims full of eyes (Ezekiel 1:15-18). "The spirit of the living creatures was in the wheels" (Ezekiel 1:21)—which mystifies us still further. Revelation's pictures of creatures with six wings "full of eyes in front and behind" (Revelation 4:6-8) likewise contain the motif of strangeness.

The effect of all this is to reinforce the difference between heaven and earth and to underscore the sense of mystery surrounding heaven. The far reaches of incomprehensibility enter when we read: "Eye has not seen, nor ear heard, Nor have entered into the heart of man The things which God has prepared for those who love Him" (1 Corinthians 2:9).

Heaven is a worship-focused place. Compared to the relatively plentiful descriptions of heaven as a place, the Bible gives little information about the activity that transpires there. Activity in heaven consists almost entirely of worship (see Revelation 4; 5; 7:9–12). Revelation 14:4 adds the picture of the redeemed following the Lamb wherever He goes. We also read that God will "dwell" with his people and "be with them" (Revelation 21:3). In addition, there is also the transformation of our earthly experience into a different mode.

Half of the equation is the negation or canceling out of fallen earthly experience. There will be no more hunger or thirst, no more scorching heat (Revelation 7:16). God will wipe tears away and death shall be no more (Revelation 7:17; 21:4); mourning and pain will vanish, "for the former things have passed away" (Revelation 21:4). As part of this exclusion of evil, heaven is a protected place: nothing unclean shall enter it or anything "that defiles, or causes an abomination or a lie" (Revelation 21:27). The sheer freedom from fallen experience is pictured by city gates that "shall not be shut at all by day (there shall be no night there)" (Revelation 21:25).

The other half of the equation is the creation of earthly categories into something "new." The main example is the new heaven and new earth that fills the last two chapters of the Bible, as well as the image of New Jerusalem, with its suggestion of earthly reality raised to a higher level of perfection. The writer of Hebrews claims that people of faith "desire a better country, that is, a heavenly one" (Hebrews 11:16 NASB).

Heaven is a joyously satisfying place. The two dominant human responses to new life in heaven are joy and satisfaction. The joy of heaven's inhabitants is pictured by the scenes of praise in Revelation, the white-robed conquerors waving palm branches (Revelation 7:9), and the guests at the wedding supper (Revelation 19:1–9). This is buttressed by the imagery of some of Jesus' parables, where attaining heaven is compared to attending a banquet (Luke 14:15–24) or entering into the joy of one's master (Matthew 25:21, 23).

From the perspective of life in this world, heaven is the object of human longing and the goal of human existence. Hebrews 11:13–14 employs the imagery of quest to express this reality: "These all died in faith, not having received the promises, . . . for . . . they seek a homeland."

In addition to being the goal of a quest, heaven is the reward for earthly toil, as in Paul's picture of himself as having "finished the race" and looking forward to "the crown of righteousness" (2 Timothy 4:7–8). We see this, too, in Peter's vision of "the Chief Shepherd" conferring "the crown of glory" on those who have served faithfully (1 Peter 5:4).

There is also the glorious picture of believers having come to "Mount Zion, to the heavenly Jerusalem, the city of the living God . . . to thousands upon thousands of angels in joyful assembly" (Hebrews 12:22 NIV). Images of satisfaction emerge from the pictures in Revelation of saints being guided by a divine Shepherd to springs of living water (Revelation 7:17) and having access to "the tree of life with its twelve kinds of fruit, yielding its fruit each month" (Revelation 22:2 RSV).

Heaven is a rest after labor. Those who die in the Lord "rest from their labors, and their works follow them" (Revelation 14:13). Similarly, "there remains a sabbath rest for the people of God," which believers "strive to enter" (Hebrews 4:9–11 RSV).

Author and pastor John Piper once said,

The radical pursuit of joy in God may cost you your life. . . . But it will be worth it. The world has an inconsolable longing, which it tries to satisfy with anything but God. Scenic vacations. Sexual exploits. Ascetic rigors. Managerial excellence. Sports extravaganzas. We have turned our back on the breathtaking beauty of God and fallen in love with our shadow. To delight in the Light is a dangerous duty indeed. It may cost you your friends. It may cost you your reputation. It may cost you your life. But it will be worth it. Because the steadfast love of the Lord is better than life (Psalm 63:3)![4]

FRIDAY: Entering Heaven

*"And Jesus said to him, '. . . Today **you will be with Me in Paradise**.'"*
—Luke 23:43

If the Lord tarries, each of us will cross through the valley of the shadow of death to enter heaven. Erwin Lutzer tells a wonderful story about dying grace. He writes:

When Corrie ten Boom was a girl, her first experience with death came after visiting the home of a neighbor who had just died. When she thought of the fact that her parents would die someday, her father comforted her by asking, "When I go to Amsterdam, when do I give you your ticket?" "Just before we get on the train." "Exactly. Just so your heavenly Father will give you exactly what you need when we die—He'll give it to you just when you need it."[5]

To have dying grace does not mean that we will be free from sorrow, whether at our own impending death or the death of someone we love. Some Christians have mistakenly thought that grief demonstrates a lack of faith. Thus they have felt it necessary to maintain strength rather than deal honestly with a painful loss (Hebrews 5:7).

As Christians, we live with the tension between what is "already ours" and the "not yet" of our experience. Paul said believers should look forward to Christ's return "that you may not grieve, as do the rest who have no hope" (1 Thessalonians 4:13 NASB). Grief was expected, but it is different from the grief of the world. There is a difference between tears of hope and tears of hopelessness.

Donald Grey Barnhouse, on the way home from the funeral of his first wife, was trying to think of some way of comforting his children. Just then a huge moving van passed by their car and its shadow swept over them. Instantly, Barnhouse asked, "Children, would you rather be run over by a truck or by its shadow?" The children replied, "Of course we'd prefer the shadow!" To which Barnhouse replied, "Two thousand years ago the truck of death ran over the Lord Jesus . . . now only the shadow of death can run over us!" (see Psalm 23:4). Death is the chariot our heavenly Father sends to bring us to Himself.[6]

We are accustomed to talking about the differences there will be when we make our transition from earth to heaven, but there are also some similarities. Given the fact that *our personalities continue*, we can expect continuity. Heaven is the continuation of the glorified and perfected earthly life of the believer.

Personal knowledge continues in heaven. (See Matthew 8:11.) Jesus said at the banquet in heaven we will sit and fellowship with people we know about—Abraham, Isaac, and Jacob.

Personal love continues in heaven. I like what a news article once attributed to Chet Bitterman after his missionary son was killed by guerrillas: "We have eight children. And they all are living: one's in heaven and seven are on earth." (See Romans 8:18.)

Personal feelings continue in heaven. (See Psalm 16:11; Revelation 6:9–10; 7:17; 21:4.) David was promised that when he was at last in the presence of God he would experience the emotion of "fullness of joy"!

Personal activities continue in heaven. "We are," says Maclaren, "saplings here, but we shall be transported into our heavenly soil to grow in God's light. Here our abilities are in blossom; there they shall burst forth with fruits of greater beauty. Our death is but the passing from one degree of loving service to another; the difference is like that of the unborn child and the one who has entered into the experiences of a new life. Our love for God will continue, but awakened with new purity and purposefulness."[7]

There is no intermediate state. (See 2 Corinthians 5:1 and Revelation 6:9–10.) Believers go directly into the presence of Christ at their moment of death or at His gathering of the church at the Rapture. They are conscious and in command of all of their faculties.

We will each have a resurrection body (1 Corinthians 15:42–44). We are sown a perishable body, but we will be raised imperishable. Like a seed sown in the ground, there is continuity between the acorn and the tree, between the kernel and the stalk. Not every particle that ever was a part of you has to be raised, and God just might add additional material to make up the deficiencies. In heaven, no one will comment on your age or notice that the years are beginning to take their toll. You will look as young a billion years from now as you will a thousand years from now. As Dr. Hinson wrote: "The stars shall live for a million years / A million years and a day. / But God and I will live and love / When the stars have passed away."[8]

We are sown in dishonor, but raised in power. When a body is transported to a funeral home it is always covered by a sheet to shield gaping eyes from the ignominy of looking upon the corpse. Every dead body is a reminder of our dishonor, a reminder that we are but frail. However, we shall be raised in power.

We are sown in weakness, but raised in strength. The resurrection body is not subject to material forces. Remember how Christ came through closed doors after the resurrection. Keep in mind that the reason the angel rolled the stone from the tomb was not to let Christ out, but to let the disciples in!

We are sown a natural body, but we are raised a spiritual body. To say that we will have a spiritual body does not mean that we will just be spirits. Christ's glorified body was so human that He invited the disciples to touch Him and affirmed, "See My hands and My feet, that it is I Myself; touch Me and see, for a spirit does not have flesh and bones as you see that I have" (Luke 24:39). There will be continuity with a difference. Our future body will be like Christ's resurrection body: "We know that, when He appears, we shall be like Him, because we shall see Him just as He is" (1 John 3:2). Just think of the implications. See Revelation 19:7![9]

SATURDAY: Heaven—The Place to Be

*"In my Father's house are many rooms; . . . I am going there to prepare a place for you. And . . . I will come back and take you to be with me **that you also may be where I am**."*
—John 14:2–3 NIV

What we need to believe today is what Jesus taught us—this world is not our home. Our real home is the one He went to prepare for us. All that we see, use, and have here on earth is only temporary. That is the key to a pilgrim view of life.

In John 14:2–3, Jesus assures us that death for His children is only a transfer to permanent housing. Paul declares: "As long as we are at home in the body we are away from the Lord. We live by faith, not by sight. We are confident, I say, and would prefer to be away from the body and at home with the Lord" (2 Corinthians 5:6–8 NIV).

The great English Bible commentator, Matthew Henry, might reflect our feelings best:

Would you like to know where I am? I am at home in my father's house, in the mansion prepared for me here. I am where I want to be—no longer on the stormy sea, but in God's safe, quiet harbor. My sowing time is done and I am reaping; my joy is the joy of the harvest.

Would you like to know how it is with me? I am made perfect in holiness. Grace is swallowed up in glory. Would you like to know what I am doing? I see God, not as through a glass darkly, but face to face. I am engaged in the sweet enjoyment of my precious redeemer. I am singing hallelujahs to him who sits upon the throne, and I am constantly praising him.

Would you like to know what blessed company I keep? It is better than the best of earth. Here are the holy angels and the spirits of just men made perfect. I am with many of my old acquaintances with whom I worked and prayed and have come here before me.

Lastly, would you like to know how long this will continue? It is a dawn that never fades. After millions and millions of ages, it will be as fresh as it is now. Therefore, weep not for me![10]

Oh, the wonders of our promised haven, the glories of that eternal home! But nothing will compare with the knowledge that heaven is the outflow of Jesus Christ. Let us seek Him, like the words of this song so true: " 'Tis heaven below, / My Redeemer to know, / For He is so precious to me." That is heaven.

"My Redeemer to know" is what God created us for; that is what Jesus is preparing for us; and that is what He's coming again for, either in a personal rapture through the valley of the shadow of death or in a corporate rapture when He comes to take His church home—but He *will* come again to take us to that place!

Make a choice to live in hope. As Christians, we look forward to an event that will pale all others. It will happen the second we pass through death's shadow into heaven's splendor and see our Lord face-to-face: "Think of—Stepping on shore, and finding it Heaven! Of taking hold of a hand, and finding it God's hand. Of breathing a new air, and finding it celestial air. Of feeling invigorated, and finding it immortality. Of passing from storm to tempest to an unbroken calm. Of waking up, and finding it Home."[11]

What a thrilling moment! Thinking about it can make our hearts beat faster! So rejoice in heaven! Rejoice in what your Father has done— and is doing for you even now: "You received the Spirit of adoption by whom we cry out, 'Abba, Father.' The Spirit Himself bears witness with our spirit that we are children of God . . . —heirs of God and joint heirs with Christ. . . . The sufferings of this present time are not worthy to be compared with the glory which shall be revealed in us" (Romans 8:15–18).

Make a choice to live securely in hope because you have a relationship with God that allows you to cry out to Him, "Abba, Father" (a term of endearment meaning "Daddy" or "Papa")! As His child, heaven means "going home to Daddy"—to enjoy His presence forever! Whatever you go through before your home-going will only make your time in heaven that much more precious because of remembering His Son's sacrifice of love and His faithful companionship during your sojourn on earth. You are a joint heir with Jesus—to be glorified together with Him! What a joyous privilege!

Isn't it hard to live in a tiny two-room apartment when you know that you will soon get a mansion and gardens—and will live forever with the Lord in Paradise?

WEEK 47
Discover Our Marriage to Jesus

(Revelation 21:1–8)

As the end of days approaches, you can find hope as you discover our marriage to Jesus!

SUNDAY: The Bride's Perfect Home

> "I, John, saw the holy city, New Jerusalem, coming down out of heaven from God, **prepared as a bride adorned for her husband.**"
> —Revelation 21:2

Last week, you got to have a taste of the joys of heaven! I hope that you will now savor learning even more about the glories of heaven—just as an amazingly brilliant scientist, Dr. Harry Rimmer, did in his lifetime. In 1953, only a week before his death, he shared his unique perspective of the City of Gold in a letter to the great radio Bible teacher, Dr. Charles Fuller, who was just starting a series on heaven. As you read Dr. Rimmer's letter, ask yourself: *Is my confidence as firm as his?*

Next Sunday you are to talk about Heaven. I am interested in that land, because I have held a clear title to a bit of property there for more than fifty-five years. I did not buy it. It was given to me "without money and without price." But the donor purchased it for me at a tremendous sacrifice. I am not holding it for speculation, since the title is not transferable. It is not a vacant lot.

For more than half a century I have been sending materials, out of which the Great Architect and Builder of the Universe has been building a home for me, a home which will never be remodeled nor repaired, because it will suit me perfectly, individually, and will never grow old. Termites can never undermine its foundations, for they rest upon the Rock of Ages. Fire cannot destroy it. Floods cannot wash it away. No locks nor bolts will ever be placed on its doors, for no vicious person can ever enter that Land where my dwelling stands, now almost completed and almost ready for me to enter in and abide in peace eternally, without fear of being ejected.

In Revelation 21 we find Jesus taking His bride home to a world that is perfect—just as God wants it to be. What will heaven be like? It certainly won't be that of sitting around on clouds playing harps for eternity, as some would have us think. No, God paints an entirely different picture in His Word:

"Now I saw a new heaven and a new earth, for the first heaven and the first earth had passed away. Also there was no more sea. Then I, John, saw the holy city, New Jerusalem, coming down out of heaven from God, prepared as a bride adorned for her husband. And I heard a loud voice from heaven saying, 'Behold, the tabernacle of God is with men, and He will dwell with them, and they shall be His people. God Himself will be with them and be their God. And God will wipe away every tear from their eyes; there shall be no more death, nor sorrow, nor crying. There shall be no more pain, for the former things have passed away.' Then He who sat on the throne said, 'Behold, I make all things new.' And He said to me, 'Write, for these words are true and faithful.' And He said to me, 'It is done! I am the Alpha and the Omega, the Beginning and the End. I will give of the fountain of the water of life freely to him who thirsts. He who overcomes shall inherit all things, and I will be his God and he shall be My son. But the cowardly, unbelieving, abominable, murderers, sexually immoral, sorcerers, idolaters, and all liars shall have their part in the lake which burns with fire and brimstone, which is the second death' "

—Revelation 21:1–8

Didn't God paint a beautiful picture of heaven for us? Are you longing for the time when we will all be together with Him *forever*?

My Prayer for You This Week: *Oh Lord God, our Father, Creator, and Builder of that glorious home You are preparing for us, we love You! Thank You that You are going to make all things new so that we need not despair about our body getting old or our world decaying. Nothing is enduring here because our pilgrimage is heading us to the Celestial City, to a building not made with hands, to a place that has foundations that shall never be moved. We praise You, Lord Jesus, for purchasing our place of abode forever with Your own blood! We pray that by Your grace we will enjoy discovering* more of the wonders of heaven—the mansions of Jesus to which we are headed, and where we long to be. Even so, come quickly, Lord Jesus. As we wait, may we not be ashamed before You when You come. Thank You for what great things You will do in our lives today as we bow before You. In the name of Jesus we pray, Amen.

MONDAY: What Will the New Heaven Be Like?

" *'Eye has not seen, nor ear heard, Nor have entered into the heart of man* **the things which God has prepared for those who love Him.**"

—1 Corinthians 2:9

In Revelation 21, I want you to understand these points in particular: heaven is made of new materials; heaven includes the New Jerusalem; and heaven is inhabited by new people. So then, let us look at these aspects of the new heaven.

The heavens and the earth will be made of new materials (21:1). In verse 1, God says that there will be "no more sea." To the ancients, the seas were dangerous, unpredictable, and caused separation. So it is a glorious thought that God is going to make everything new—including us! Everything will be affected right down to the atomic level. There is a dissonance in the core of every atom—an atomic flux. Paul said that the whole universe is groaning, waiting for the redemption, because Satan, his rebellion, and evil have infected the universe.

Look at what Peter says in 2 Peter 3:10–13: "But the day of the Lord will come as a thief in the night, in which the heavens will pass away with a great noise, and the elements [at an atomic level] will melt with fervent heat; both the earth and the works that are in it will be burned up. Therefore, since all these things will be dissolved, what manner of persons ought you to be in holy conduct and godliness, looking for and hastening the coming of the day of God . . . ? Nevertheless we, according to His promise, **look for new heavens and a new earth** in which righteousness dwells" (2 Peter 3:10–13).

This passage is not describing the Rapture, because the Rapture does not come as a thief in the night. That has a negative connotation, but the coming of Christ to take His own to be with Him is a positive thing. The "day of the Lord" (the major theme of Old Testament prophetic writings) speaks of His return in glory and judgment at the Second Coming. Peter (who wrote after Paul explained the two-part Second Coming of Christ to the Thessalonians and Corinthians) merely lumps all the Old Testament and New Testament prophetic events together; he truncates the whole thing into the "day of the Lord."

Peter envisioned what we see in Revelation 21:1a: "I saw a new heaven and a new earth." That which Peter and all the Old Testament prophets longed for is what finally comes about in Revelation 21—the heavens and the earth will be made new. The original was not a failure; rather, God is going to correct and triumph over His initial creation where He allowed man to go into sin and then redeemed him. The place where God intersected with time, winning the victory and paying the price for man's salvation, will be redeemed and made brand new.

Heaven includes a New Jerusalem (21:2, 10): "Then I, John, saw the holy city, New Jerusalem, coming down out of heaven from God . . . And he carried me away in the Spirit to a great and high mountain, and showed me the great city." The concept here is like that of a John Wayne western movie in which the hero conquers all the bad guys, and then takes his bride up to the top of the hill to show her his ranch. We are the bride on the honeymoon, and our glorious Husband, who paid a great price for us, will take us to a mountain top to show off the gorgeous lay of His land. The One crucified in the old Jerusalem will now be crowned in the New Jerusalem.

The gospel message is that the Lamb is the Foundation "having been built on the foundation of the apostles and prophets [the church], Jesus Christ Himself being the Chief Cornerstone " (Ephesians 2:20). The foundation of the New Jerusalem is the Lamb.

Heaven is founded on the Lamb and His sacrifice. The New Jerusalem is the city that all saints of all time have been waiting and longing for: "[Abraham] waited for the city which has foundations, whose builder and maker is God. . . . These all [the heroes of the faith] died in faith, not having received the promises, but having seen them afar off were assured of them, embraced them [the promises of God] and confessed that they were strangers and pilgrims on the earth. . . . They desire a better, that is, a heavenly country. Therefore God is not ashamed to be called their God, for He has prepared a city for them" (Hebrews 11:10, 13–16).

Born in 2166 B.C., Abraham was looking for this city. He knew what it was because God had revealed it to him. All of the heroes of faith listed in Hebrews 11 lived their lives with it being "very far off." Isaiah said, "Your eyes will see the King in His beauty; They will see the land that is very far off" (Isaiah 33:17). In spite of that, they embraced the promises of God and confessed that they were strangers and pilgrims on the earth (a rare attitude today).

When we desire a better country, a heavenly one, God is pleased to be called our God, and He has prepared a city for us: it is a holy city (Revelation 21:27); it is a prepared city (John 14:1–6); and it is a gorgeous city (Revelation 21:10–21).

Heaven is inhabited by new people (21:3–8). At last, Christ's High Priestly *prayer "that they may be as one" will be fulfilled (John 17:11). His prayer was not only for His twelve disciples but also for those in the future who would believe. Until this point in Revelation, the church will never have been truly united. Some in the Old* Testament were in "the waiting room" of Abraham's bosom, but after His resurrection Jesus took them to be with Him. However, they presently are still waiting for all the redeemed to come home too. The people yet to be redeemed will be gathered together in Revelation 21. John 17 will then be fulfilled when we are all finally united as one—from Eden's first redeemed to the last of every kindred, nation, and tribe. All repentant sinners, transformed by grace, will live together in this new heaven. Will you be among them?

TUESDAY: What Will and Will Not Be in Heaven

*"But there shall by no means enter it anything that defiles, . . . but **only those** who are written **in the Lamb's Book of Life**."*

—Revelation 21:27

What will be in heaven? **Fellowship**: visible, face-to-face communion with Christ for we *"shall see His face, and His name shall be on* [our] *foreheads"* (Revelation 22:4). That is what I long for! First Corinthians 13:12 says that *"for now we see in a mirror, dimly, but then face to face."*

Now look at this great passage: "Behold what manner of love the Father has bestowed on us, that we should be called children of God! . . . It has not yet been revealed what we shall be, but we know that when He is revealed, we shall be like Him, for we shall see Him as He is" (1 John 3:1–2).

That is what we are waiting for. All that God has when we see Him face to face will then come into fruition. At that time, we will have full and complete **knowledge**: *"Now I know in part, but then I shall know just as I also am known"* (1 Corinthians 13:12b).

We will have **abundance** without charge, restrictions, or restraint: "I am the Alpha and the Omega, the Beginning and the End" (Revelation 21:6). Christ said that He is the Initiator and the Satisfier. We will possess all that God has promised us, and no longer be limited by our frailties and flesh.

We will have meaningful **service**: "And there shall be no more curse, but the throne of God and of the Lamb shall be in it, and His servants shall serve Him" (Revelation 22:3). We'll be able to do what we have always wanted to do, with no restraints. We can totally serve God the way we long to!

We will have **worship**—the main activity in heaven: "The tabernacle of God is with men, and He will dwell with them, and they shall be His people" (Revelation 21:3). The redeemed will follow the Lamb wherever He goes (Revelation 14:4). We will experience the completion of our worship. In fact, our entire service for Him will be one of worship!

All of these possessions will be joyously treasured as we live together in the Celestial City—a place of unbelievable, shining, brilliant beauty (Revelation 21:10–21)!

What will not be in heaven? To begin with, there will be no time in the sense of yesterday, tomorrow, early, or late. But in Revelation 22:2, there seems to be an allusion to time: "each tree yielding its fruit every month." And now comes a great part! Look at all that God will be doing for us! There will be no seas (21:1); no tears (21:4); no death (21:4); no crying (21:4); no pain (21:4); no temple or church building (21:22); no sun, moon, or night (21:23); no sin, unbelievers, or evil forces (21:27); no sickness (22:2); and no curse (22:3). Hallelujah! Praise God!

WEDNESDAY: Heaven Will Fulfill Us Forever

*"**I will dwell** in the house of the Lord **forever**."*
—Psalm 23:6b

God says that we *"shall reign forever and ever"* (Revelation 22:5). How long will we be in heaven? Forever—all because of faith in the Lamb who sacrificed Himself for us (Revelation 7:4; 22:14)!

In Revelation 21:1–8 we discover the husbandly love of Jesus unveiling Paradise for His bride. Picture it: standing on the hill, with the rising sun, Jesus says, "Here it is, My beloved!" Let us look to the fair land of our pilgrimage and see that city which has foundations, whose Builder and Maker is God! And in the wonders that we shall behold, let us see *Him* who has made it our home-to-be, for the Lamb *is* the glory of Emmanuel's land. God *Himself* should be our greatest desire for reaching heaven!

The founder of the Christian and Missionary Alliance, A. B. Simpson wrote this poem:

Himself

Once it was the blessing, now it is the Lord;
Once it was the feeling, now it is His Word;
Once His gifts I wanted, now the giver own;
Once I sought for healing, now Himself alone.
Once 'twas painful trying, now 'tis perfect trust;
Once a half salvation, now the uttermost;
Once 'twas ceaseless holding, now He holds me fast;
Once 'twas constant drifting, now my anchor's cast.
Once 'twas busy planning, now 'tis trustful prayers,
Once 'twas anxious caring, now He has the care;
Once 'twas what I wanted, now what Jesus says;
Once 'twas constant asking, now 'tis ceaseless praise.
Once it was my working, His it hence shall be,
Once I tried to use Him, now He uses me;
Once the power I wanted, now the Mighty One;
Once for self I labored, now for Him alone.
—A. B. SIMPSON (1843–1919)

Modern advertisements mesmerize us into thinking we are to be amused, comforted, and secure in this world. But God says that true satisfaction and fulfillment can only be obtained through *Him!*

THURSDAY: The Best Part of Heaven

*"I will come again and receive you to Myself; **that where I am, there you may be also**."*
—JOHN 14:3

Although I can't wait to see the gates made of pearl, the precious stones of heaven, and the city's numerous other glories, that is not what I am looking forward to most. I can't wait to see Christ face to face! Jesus is the best part of heaven!

The Seven Perfections of Jesus. The subject of heaven is often spoken of as "the sweet by and by," and images of harps, clouds, angel wings, and a seemingly ethereal world of misty spirit form in the mind. But, in reality, heaven is a glorious place of wonder and beauty. Of all its indescribable beauties and unending glories, there is, above all else, Jesus, who is the most beautiful aspect of heaven. And there are seven wonderful facets of the love of Jesus for all the saints, His bride.

Facet 1—Jesus will be with us. "God Himself will be with them and be their God" (Revelation 21:3 NASB). First, there will be the unbroken presence of Emmanuel, "God with us." Secondly, there will be the fulfillment of all that He has promised. The Bible contains all the promises of God, but one day we will get to experience the Person behind the promises.

Facet 2—Jesus will comfort us. "God will wipe away every tear from their eyes; there shall be no more death, nor sorrow, nor crying . . . nor pain" (Revelation 21:4 NASB). Even though we know Jesus and His promises are with us, this present life is hard. However, the sadness of current disappointments will end with the security of divine appointment; the dread of death will end with the Lord of Life; the frailties of the flesh will end when entering our heavenly habitation. The future, like the past, is kept securely by Him with whom our anchor is cast.

Facet 3—Jesus will refresh us. "I will give of the fountain of the water of life freely to him who thirsts" (Revelation 21:6 NASB). A life of dryness will be gone; the refreshing Spring of Life will be ever with us. Although He can comfort and be with us in this present life, heaven is the ultimate comfort: "He who believes in Me, . . . out of his heart will flow rivers of living water" (John 7:38). This is an endless supply, for He within us shall be that Fountain.

Facet 4—Jesus will captivate us. "I saw no temple in it, for the Lord God, the Almighty, and the Lamb are its temple" (21:22 NASB). This is the culmination of all the types from which they were fashioned: the True One showing facets of His image by His holiness, His character, and His redemption. We are to not make images of Him, but we are to see Him through the types of the tabernacle and the temple. Which satisfies you most—the picture or the Person? The figures have been there for time, but the fullness will be for all eternity. Worship will be unbounded by location or proximity; it will be unending and all-present because our worship will be focused on Him as He captivates us.

Facet 5—Jesus will keep us secure. "And nothing unclean . . . shall ever come into it, but only those whose names are written in the Lamb's Book of Life" (21:27 NASB). The wonder of heaven is that He will keep us secure, just as He has here on earth. There will now be an exclusion of all evil forever. At last, our freedom will be completed! At Calvary, we were freed from both the penalty and power of sin; at the Celestial City, we will forever be removed from the presence of sin. All the washed ones, those washed in the Lamb's blood and written in the Lamb's Book of Life, will be welcomed there.

Facet 6—Jesus will lead us. "The throne of God and of the Lamb shall be in it, and His bondservants shall serve Him" (22:3 NASB). He is the Master; we are the servants who will follow Him. The return of Christ's rule as King of the kingdom will be unhindered—and He wants complete dedication, not mere compliments. He never simply said, "Accept Me!" Rather, He declared: "Leave all and follow Me, or you can't be My disciple." Jesus wants glad and unhindered service forever. After the complete destruction of the curse's doom, we will no longer struggle with the weeds of sin so that we can fully follow the Lamb's wishes.

Facet 7—Jesus will light us. "There shall be no night there: . . . for the Lord God gives them light. And they shall reign forever and ever" (Revelation 22:5 NASB). The Source of light in the new heaven will be the Savior, the Lamb, who is the Light. And in that glow we shall walk in unbroken communion. The denial of dark deeds will be consigned to the blackness of darkness forever, but we shall rule by submission to Him forever. The despair of darkness will be ended; there will be no more unfinished plans, for He is the completion of all. This is the fulfillment of Christ's First Coming: "The Dayspring from on high has visited us; To give light to those who sit in darkness and the shadow of death, To guide our feet into the way of peace" (Luke 1:78–79).

FRIDAY: Three Worms That Spoil the Fruit

> "Because you say, 'I am rich, have become wealthy, and have need of nothing'—and do not know that **you are . . . blind**, and naked—I counsel you to buy from Me gold refined in the fire, that you may be rich; and white garments . . . that the shame of your nakedness may not be revealed; and **anoint your eyes with eye salve, that you may see**."
>
> —REVELATION 3:17–18

Jesus promised that He would get all His children home safely, and we will live with Him forever. Although that is exciting news, what we often forget is the need to be sending treasures on ahead because there are only pre-paid treasures in heaven. Our mission on earth therefore is to be transmuting earthly treasures into heavenly currency.

When we take that final trip with Jesus—through the valley of the shadow of death or in the skies through the clouds at the voice of the archangel and the trump of God—no baggage left here can accompany us. Only what we have sent on ahead will make it to heaven. Transmuted wealth is all that will be worth anything in heaven.

Pastor Jan Hettinga wrote a book on this subject that is so good that I just have to share a portion of it with you. Except for the Bible, Hettinga's *Follow Me* is one of the few books I've read more than once. What struck me most when I read it is this: there are three terrible dangers that can rob anyone of finishing well and earning Christ's "Well done!" Afterward, I thought: *Wow! I don't want to be robbed of Christ's "Well done—good and faithful servant!"*

Here are the three dangers that should concern all who seek Christ's full rewards in heaven:[1]

Danger 1—Beware of the sins of old age. These sins (which can occur at any age) can erase Christ's "Well done!" Remember Solomon: he began by sacrificing thousands of animals and building the most beautiful worship place for the Lord, but he failed to finish well. He got to heaven "yet so as by fire." (In today's language, we'd say that Solomon got into heaven "by the skin of his teeth.") What are these sins of old age?

The lust for comfort and convenience: This sin is epidemic. We continually lust for comfort. People read magazines on how to make their home or car even more comfortable. We are guilty of lust, which is to have a strong desire for comfort and convenience. Do you know how I know that occurs even in the church? Every time it rains or snows heavily, attendance is down. And excuses like this are common: "It's just too inconvenient in bad weather to load everybody into the car, slosh through puddles and mud in the parking lot, and then have to deal with all the wet coats once we get into the building." A life consumed with a lust for comfort and convenience like that won't finish well.

Greed for recognition: Older people usually want to receive recognition of some sort. In fact, it seems that almost everyone lusts for the applause of others. We must beware of seeking approval from people and instead seek approval only from God.

Covetousness for security: Our whole country has become security-obsessed. People want to know how to best secure retirement funds, how to secure college education funds, how to get job security, and how to secure their homes and other possessions. We are caught up in the pursuit of security and are wasting valuable time and energy to protect things we cannot keep.

These sins of old age—the lust for comfort, greed for recognition, and covetousness for security—can erase Christ's "Well done!"

Danger 2—Beware of the problem of "exceptionism." What is exceptionism? It is thinking that your life is an exception to God's Word. Thus you excuse yourself from doing anything for heaven because of things like your past, pain, poverty, or poor self-image. The reason exceptionism can erase Christ's "Well done!" is because when we hear an exhortation to "Go into all the world, speak to every creature, and live your life looking for Christ"—many excuse themselves saying, "Oh, I can't do that just now. At this time in my life I can't spare a minute—not even for reading the Word, ministering, praying, or evangelizing."

Think carefully on this: *you will never be in the future what you are not becoming today.* If you are not responding to and obeying God's Word now, and you feel like you're always an exception, that attitude will stay with you till the end. Consider Annanias and Sapphira, who thought they were exceptions to the rule. Since everybody else was sacrificing, and they felt that they couldn't, they decided to at least *look* like they did. That bad decision not only cost them their lives but also erased Christ's "Well done!"

Danger 3—Beware of unmortified pockets of pride. "Unmortified pockets of pride" sounds like abscesses in the body, but that is really what he is talking about. Allowing such pockets of pride to grow can make you secretly, inwardly proud of your intellect (thinking you are smarter than others), or proud of your achievements, or proud of your giftedness (even in the church), or proud of your goodness ("I'm not as bad as they are"). Sin, in the light of sin, never does look bad, but sin in the light of God's holiness always looks bad. Pockets of pride in your life can erase Christ's "Well done!" The cure is to allow the power of God's Word through the Holy Spirit to deal with even the slightest prideful "abscess" at the moment it begins to erupt.

To avoid these dangers and to help you get ready for Christ's "Well done!" in heaven, you must listen carefully to what Jesus has to say about what He expects when He comes back for us. What does He want to see cultivated in our lives? I have located twelve expectations, and we will go over them in tomorrow's devotional.

SATURDAY: Will You Hear Christ's Well Done?

*"**Well done, good and faithful servant**; you were faithful over a few things, I will make you ruler over many things. Enter into the joy of your lord."*

—Matthew 25:21, 23

Don't you long to hear Christ say, "Well done, My good and faithful servant, enter into the joy of your Master's home!"? A "Well done!" from Him will make this life on earth all worthwhile. What does God expect from us so that we can faithfully earn His "Well done!"?

Expectation 1—Dream about winning the ultimate prize. (See Matthew 25:14-30.) When people have something on their mind, it shapes the whole direction of their life. Jesus has told us that when He returns for us He expects to find us doing what He asked us to do. Keeping that utmost in your mind is a strong motivator. It will shape your life if you dream about winning the ultimate prize—Christ's "Well done!" You must want it, and long for it. In fact, that is one of the marks of salvation.

Expectation 2—Seek to be the greatest Christlike servant. (See Matthew 20:28-30.) Imitation is one of the highest forms of compliments. The Apostle Paul said, "Imitate me, just as I also imitate Christ" (1 Corinthians 11:1). Is your life worth imitating? Do you reflect your Lord in all that you do? Those who are most Christlike in their servanthood are the greatest in His kingdom and will hear His "Well done!"

Expectation 3—Love to sacrifice for Him through financial generosity. (See Luke 21:1-4.) Jesus said that "where your treasure is, there your heart will be also." The key to sacrifice is to do it now. Don't wait. Be sure that while you do have something and can sacrifice, do it! Some day, every dollar, every piece of gold, and every jewel will be devalued, wiped out forever (2 Peter 3:10).

You are sending ahead either "wood, hay, and stubble" or "gold, silver, and precious stones" for building your mansion. What are you sending? Those who are financially generous for Christ will reap an everlasting treasure Jesus says will never be lost.

Expectation 4—Love trials by joyfully accepting injustice. (See Matthew 5:11-12.) When you are mistreated for Christ's sake, and accept it graciously "because of conscience toward God," Jesus says that you will be rewarded in heaven with His "Well done!"

Expectation 5—Love strangers through biblical hospitality. (See Matthew 10:40-41; 18:27; 25:40-45.) There is a wonderful insight from an outsider named Aristeides who looked at the early church. He wrote this note to the Roman Emperor in A.D. 155: "Now the Christians, O King . . . if there is among them a man that is poor and needy, and they have not an abundance of necessities, they fast two or three days that they may supply the needy with their necessary food. For Christ's sake they are ready to lay down their lives." How does that spirit line up with your own life? If you minister Christ's love to those in need, you will hear His "Well done!"

Expectation 6—Restrain your flesh by seeking spiritual disciplines. (See Matthew 6:5.) In his book *Intimacy with the Almighty*, Charles Swindoll writes: "We have reared a generation of strong-willed, belligerent, independent young men and women. Surrender is not a word in their vocabulary. Too bad since it is the key that unlocks the vault of God's best and deepest treasures. He patiently waits for us to yield, to quit fighting Him, to allow His plan to run its course, to turn to Him for our security and significance. As He witnesses our doing that, He begins to reveal Himself and His will in greater depth."[2]

Swindoll also sets forth the need to cultivate these spiritual disciplines: "The decision to reorder one's private world is the spiritual discipline of simplicity. The decision to be still is the spiritual discipline of silence. The decision to cultivate serenity is the spiritual discipline of solitude. The decision to trust the Lord completely is the spiritual discipline of surrender."[3] Pursuing these spiritual disciplines will earn Christ's "Well done!"

Expectation 7—Love your lot in life through vocational faithfulness. (See Colossians 3:22–24; Philippians 2:8–9; 1 Peter 5:6.) You should serve your masters (authorities) in the same manner that you serve Christ, for God has promised that if you humble yourself under His mighty hand that He will exalt you in due time. Being faithful in your vocation or service for His sake will earn His "Well done!"

Expectation 8—Love the hard to love. (See Luke 6:27–28.) When others have revealed themselves to be enemies, Jesus expects you to do good to them, and to bless rather than curse them—for His sake. Loving the hard to love will earn Christ's "Well done!"

Expectation 9—Love God's Truth. (See 2 John 1–2, 4, 8; Colossians 3:16.) Jesus wants you to love His Word so much that you are literally filled to overflowing with it! Living the Word-filled life will earn Christ's "Well done!"

Expectation 10—Love to take people to heaven with you. (See 1 Thessalonians 2:19; 1 Corinthians 3:6–8.) Paul says that your hope, joy, and crown of rejoicing should be to see others to whom you've witnessed be in the presence of our Lord Jesus at His coming. Loving to be a soul winner will earn Christ's "Well done!"

Expectation 11—Love Jesus' return. (See Luke 12:35–38; 2 Timothy 4:8.) God says that you are a blessed servant if you faithfully watch for His return! In fact, He will give you the crown of righteousness if you love His appearing. This spirit will earn Christ's "Well done!"

Expectation 12—Love Jesus' refinement of you through trials. (See 1 Peter 1:7; Hebrews 6:10.) God is greatly pleased when He sees you loving Jesus so much that when He leads you through further refinement, you view it as a blessing. He will not forget your work and labor of love, for you will hear His "Well done!"

Make a choice to live in hope. Are you dreaming about winning the ultimate prize? Are you Christlike? Are you investing in heaven now? Are you suffering joyfully for Him? Are you welcoming strangers? Are you saying no to sin? Are you living contentedly? Are you loving others with Christ's love? Do you love God's Word? Are you taking others to heaven with you? Are you waiting and watching for Christ's return? Are you letting Him prune you?

If your heart's longing is to be able to positively affirm each of these questions, even though you can't do so perfectly, then you are choosing to live in hope—and you will taste of the joys of heaven and discover the ecstasies of being with Jesus!

WEEK 48
Behold the Wonders of Jesus

{ Revelation 21:9–27 }

As the end of days approaches, you can find hope as you behold the wonders of Jesus!

SUNDAY: The First and the Last Books

*"Blessed is he who **reads** and those who **hear the words** of this prophecy, and **keep those things** which are written in it; for the time is near."*
—REVELATION 1:1–2

Graham Scroggie wrote this wonderful exposition of why the early Christians studied the book of Revelation, and why we should do the same today:

> Not without reason did the early Church study this Book. Practically the whole of it is reproducible from the Christian writers of the first three centuries. . . . As no other Book, the Revelation stands in certain relations to all other parts of the Bible, a fact that gives the seal of finality to it. Take two illustrations only. It is interesting that those who were closest to Christ spoke most often from this Book.
>
> The Book of the Revelation completes the whole Bible. In Genesis is the Foundation of God's redeeming purpose; in Exodus to Jude, the Superstructure of it; and in Revelation, the Completion of it. . . . Revelation completes the Book of Genesis. The first and last Books of the Bible present most striking comparisons and contrasts. By way of comparison: In Genesis are the First Heaven and Earth, and in Revelation, the Last. In Genesis is the First Rest, and in Revelation, the Final Rest. In Genesis Paradise is Lost, and in Revelation it is Regained. In Genesis God makes Husband and Wife, and in Revelation, the Lamb and the Bride.
>
> But the contrasts between these two Books are even more striking: In the first, Satan is victorious; in the last, he is defeated.
>
> In the first, judgment is pronounced; and in the last it is executed.
>
> In the first, the divine face is hidden; and in the last, we see His face forever more. In the first, the gates are shut against us; and in the last, they are never shut. In the first, Adam and Eve were banished from the Tree of Life; and in the last, we have a right to it. In the first, we were exiles from the earthly Garden; and in the last, we are inheritors of the heavenly City.[1]

It is truly sin that made the earth bad.[2] Before the sin of Adam and Eve in the Garden of Eden, there could be no death, disease, famine, war, natural catastrophe, cancer, weakness, rust, pollution, hatred, murder, rape, lying, corrupt government, wife beating, child molesting, greed, and a thousand other ills that have plagued man for six thousand years of history. Every broken body, every disturbed mind, every hurting heart—the collective tears of the human race—can trace their origin back to the sin of Adam and Eve in the Garden of Eden. As a consequence of sin, man has polluted the ocean, raped the earth, and poisoned the heavens—the very sphere which God committed to man's authority. Is there any wonder, then, that the present heaven and earth must be dissolved—purged by fire to loose it from the consequences of sin—to make way for a new heaven and earth?

In the new heaven and earth there will be no more twisted wrecks of car and plane accidents; no more lifeless forms that have been shocked, poisoned, drowned, or suffocated; no more crippled bodies; no more torturous therapy and throbbing pain; no more arthritis, insomnia, and bodily dysfunction; no more merciless onslaught of age and its accompanying aches and disintegration.

In heaven we see the wonders of Jesus. In Revelation 21:9–27 we find the wonders of Jesus. I hope you are rejoicing in all that your heavenly Father has in store for you!

My Prayer for You This Week: *Oh, Father in Heaven, why You would let Your Son redeem us, and then go and prepare a place for us, is beyond our wildest imaginations! As we look into Your Word, we pray that Your Spirit would lead us to comprehend the wonders of our Lord Jesus who has prepared this place in which every part radiates Your glory. May we see Your glory, and may Your glory, as the Apostle Paul says, transform us more and more into the image of Him whom our souls love. Open our eyes, and let us behold magnificent things from the wonders of Jesus. In His precious name we come to You, oh Father, Amen.*

MONDAY: New Things in the New Heaven and Earth

"Now I saw a **new heaven and a new earth**, for the first heaven and the first earth had passed away. Also there was no more sea."
—Revelation 21:1

Over the next few days we will be looking at seven new things in the new heaven and the new earth.

The first new thing is the new heaven (21:1): "A new heaven and a new earth" does not necessitate the annihilation of the present heaven. However, it will be at least a thorough and basic transformation (2 Peter 3:10–13). As you know, the law of the conservation of matter which God built into this universe means that matter is never created or destroyed in the world that we know; it is only transferred back and forth. It is very possible that God just transfers the matter of this universe to energy and in a creative act puts it back like it was. All of that is necessary because there can't be even a trace of sin remaining.

The second new thing is the new earth (21:1): The earth will not be written off as a corrected failure of God's rule, but as an eternal triumph of His rule. There will be sweeping transformations on earth as well as in heaven, for there will be "no more sea" in the new earth.

The third new thing is the new peoples (21:3–4). Israel will certainly be one of them (Isaiah 66:22). But all the peoples on the new earth will be God's people (v. 3). Death, sorrow, crying, and pain will be unknown (v. 4). Righteousness will be its great characteristic (2 Peter 3:13).

The fourth new thing is the New Jerusalem (21:9–22:7). This is either a literal city (according to authors Seiss, Newell, Gaebelein, Pentecost); a symbolical city (Scott); or it is both literal and symbolical. It seems to be suspended over the planet Earth during the Millennium (v. 10). What do I mean by "seems to be"? Once we get into eschatological things (things related to the end of the world or the events associated with it), we are in the realm of the Bible in which we should not be dogmatic. Rather, it should cause us to study even further, and be very forbearing of differing opinions. The greatest Christian minds of all time have studied the future. The more I read their commentaries, the less I see of total agreement and the more I see of wondrous diversity. With that said, it therefore seems to me that this heavenly Jerusalem will be suspended out in space during the Millennium because we will be with Christ, and the millennial saints can still see us. However, we will get to come down to the earth even though we won't actually live here any more—working, marrying, and giving in marriage. We will be celestial, yet still be able to come and go from heaven, the New Jerusalem.

In verse 16, the New Jerusalem appears to be in the shape of a cube (Seiss, Newell, Gaebelein, Pentecost); however, Ironside views it as a pyramid, with the reminder that the shape of the most holy place in both the tabernacle and the temple was a cube. Because there is always a trinity in everything God does, the city will have three dimensions: length, breadth, and height. From the description God gives, that is why I think it will be a beautiful crystal cube.

The inhabitants of the New Jerusalem—the resurrected and glorified New Testament church who sought the coming city (Hebrews 13:14)—are clearly indicated as being there with God the Father, the Son, and the Holy Spirit (v. 22). The names of the twelve apostles will be on the foundations of the city (21:14). The resurrected and glorified Old Testament saints will also be there because they likewise looked forward to this heavenly dwelling place. Thus, God is preparing a city for them (Hebrews 11:16), and on the city's twelve gates will be the names of the twelve tribes of Israel (21:12). This is an amazing correlation: the new people of God will be identified with the city's foundations, and the old people of God will be identified with its gates.

There is a lot of speculation on the height of the walls and the size of the gates. If you read Revelation 21 without trying to make it like something on earth, it appears that the walls will be as high as the city. The only measurement given is 144 cubits, which is 216 feet (probably the thickness of the wall), and it most likely reaches to the top. Why would we need any walls at all? I don't really know, but God will put them there and He says they look like jasper. To us, jasper is a reddish stone. However, jasper is also the word used for diamonds in Scripture. It could be that the outer wall will glisten like a polished diamond, with its light emanating inside-out through the walls. If after visiting some distant place you were to come to heaven to see God's glory, you would see something like the largest diamond in the universe spraying light out in every direction. Nothing that defiles can ever enter (v. 27), and its amazing splendor will be absolutely astonishing (vv. 18–21)!

Will anything that defiles still exist? Yes, the last few verses of Isaiah tell us that we will be able to look down, off in the distance, and see the horrors of hell. In the biblical sense, hell never ends just as heaven never ends. We will therefore be aware of God's wrath, but those in hell will never be able to leave.

TUESDAY: The Pearly Gates of Heaven

*"Also she had a great and high wall with **twelve gates**, and twelve angels at the gates, and names written on them, which are the names of the twelve tribes of the children of Israel: . . . The twelve gates were **twelve pearls**: each individual gate was of one pearl. And the street of the city was pure gold, like transparent glass."*
—Revelation 21:12, 21

In Revelation 21:12–21, we notice the twelve gates, each a single pearl. Since God designs twelve gates to enter His city, the focus of today's devotional will be the wonderful ways that God's Word has offered us entrance into His fellowship and partaking in ministry for Him. As we look at heaven consider these things.

Our occupation will be the worship of God. "Then a voice came from the throne, saying, 'Praise our God, all you His servants and those who fear Him, both small and great!' And I heard . . . the sound of mighty thunderings, saying, 'Alleluia! For the Lord God Omnipotent reigns!' " (Revelation 19:5–6; see also Revelation 4:5 and 1 Kings 8:27). If we want to prepare well for our final destination, we should faithfully worship God here on earth. Our arrival in heaven will only be a continuation of what we have already begun. Praise is both the language of heaven and the language of the faithful on earth. Thus, we will be occupied with worshipful service to the Lord (Revelation 22:3–4; Matthew 4:10; Luke 2:37; Acts 24:14).

Our family will be all our brothers and sisters in Christ. "Whoever does the will of God is My brother and My sister and mother" (Mark 3:35). Jesus said that if we love Him, we will keep His commandments (John 14:15). All those who have kept His commandments, just as He kept the Father's, will abide in His love (John 15:10) and get to live together with Him forever!

Our faith that saves will be an assurance of Truth. "Now faith is the substance of things hoped for, the evidence of things not seen" (Hebrews 11:1). Faith is a conviction, a sense of assurance or confidence that something is true. If we are convinced of the Truth of Scripture, we will be saved (1 John 5:9–13).

This faith is directed to Christ alone (Romans 10:9–10). If you are persuaded that Christ did all that is necessary, and all that ever will be necessary to bring you to God, you not only will be saved but also will know it (1 Timothy 1:12; Romans 10:17). This faith is confirmed by the Holy Spirit (Romans 8:16–17). This faith bears spiritual fruit (Ephesians 2:10). This faith grows (Ephesians 4:11–16).[3]

Revelation 21:21 tells us that "the twelve gates were twelve pearls." The **pearls** represent the **doors to rewards** gained by pursuing what Christ is looking for in His beloved children—His expectations of us. Listed below is a summary of His twelve expectations (one for each gate) that were covered on Saturday of Week 47:

- Love the ultimate prize—seek Christ's "Well done!"
- Love service—seek to be the greatest servant.
- Love sacrifice—give generously.

- Love trials—joyfully accept injustice.
- Love strangers—show biblical hospitality.
- Love to restrain your flesh—seek the spiritual disciplines.
- Love your lot in life—be faithful in your vocation.
- Love the unlovable—model Christlikeness.
- Love God's Truth—pursue doctrinal integrity.
- Love ministry—take people to heaven with you.
- Love Jesus—watch for Christ's return.
- Love refinement—accept suffering.[4]

Upon hearing of the assassination of John and Betty Stam in China in 1934, Will Houghton, former president of Moody Bible Institute, wrote these words:

So this is life. This world with its pleasures, struggles and tears, a smile, a frown, a sigh, friendship so true and love of kin and neighbor? Sometimes it is hard to live—always to die! The world moves on so rapidly for the living; the forms of those who disappear are replaced, and each one dreams that he will be enduring. How soon that one becomes the missing face! Help me to know the value of these hours. Help me the folly of all waste to see. Help me to trust the Christ who bore my sorrows and thus to yield for life or death to Thee.[5]

WEDNESDAY: The New Temple of Worship

*"**True worshipers will worship the Father in spirit and truth**; for the Father is seeking such to worship Him. God is Spirit, and those who worship Him must worship in spirit and truth."*
—JOHN 4:23–24

In Monday's devotional, we learned about four of the seven new things that will be in the new heaven and earth. Today and tomorrow, we will cover the remaining three.

The fifth new thing is the new temple (21:22). "I saw no temple in it, for the Lord God Almighty and the Lamb are its temple." The entire universe will become a place of worship! God will be the focus of everything; He will no longer be detached from His children any more. Heaven will be full of new worship—we are going be totally enraptured in worshiping God! Revelation 21 mentions seven new ways that we will worship Jesus.

First New Way to Worship—Jesus the Lamb as our Beloved. "Then one of the seven angels . . . came to me . . . saying, 'Come, I will show you the bride, the Lamb's wife' " (Revelation 21:9). The first time these angels are mentioned in Scripture it says: "one of the angels having one of the seven bowls." This is now the seventh, and the last time, they appear. It seems that these seven angels that surround God's throne each unleash a bowl of His wrath during the Tribulation.

The emphasis is that we will be worshiping Jesus the Lamb as our Beloved One. That is what Anne R. Cousin wrote in "Immanuel's Land": "The Bride eyes not her garment but her dear bridegroom's face. / I will not gaze at glory but on my King of grace. / Not at the crown He giveth but on His pierced hand; / The Lamb is all the glory of Immanuel's land."

That is what we will do—worship Jesus because He is our Beloved Husband. It is not the splendors of the city that will captivate us. God doesn't want us to get caught up in the glory of His riches. He wants us to focus on Jesus, His Son, and worship the Lamb as our Beloved.

Second New Way to Worship—Jesus the Lamb as our Foundation. "Now the wall of the city had twelve foundations, and on them were the names of the twelve apostles of the Lamb" (Revelation 21:14). Our hope for all eternity rests in Jesus the Lamb, and we will worship Him as our Foundation upon whom we as His church have been built, as Peter says in 1 Peter 2:4.

Third New Way to Worship—Jesus the Lamb as our Temple. "But I saw no temple in it, for the Lord God Almighty and the Lamb are its temple" (Revelation 21:22). He will be the focus of our worship. Why am I emphasizing all this? After all, we are not in heaven yet. The scriptural principle is this: anything that God is going to like in the future, He likes right now; anything that God is going to do in the future, He would appreciate it if we would get in step with it right now. That is why it is so interesting to read what God does in the future. He wants us to honor Him now to prepare us to later worship Jesus the Lamb as our Temple.

Fourth New Way to Worship—Jesus the Lamb as our Light. "The city had no need of the sun or of the moon to shine in it, for the glory of God illuminated it. The Lamb is its light" (Revelation 21:23). He is the One who provides all the light we will ever need. In fact, when the Apostle Paul gave his testimony he said, "This is salvation to open our eyes and to turn us from darkness to light" (see Acts 26:18). When Jesus was promised to us in Luke 1:78b-79a, it says that "the Dayspring from on high has visited us . . . who sit in darkness." He is our Light, and we will worship Him in heaven as our Light. Therefore, the city will have no need of the sun or the moon to shine in it. It doesn't mean there aren't going to be stars or moons, because there will be. We just won't need them anymore—the glory of God, the Lamb, illuminates the city. So in heaven, this new worship is that we worship Jesus the Lamb as our Light. What a wonder that will be!

Fifth New Way to Worship—Jesus the Lamb as our Guardian. "There shall by no means enter it anything that defiles, . . . but only those who are written in the Lamb's Book of Life" (Revelation 21:27). We will worship Him who guarded, secured, and kept us. The Lamb is our Guardian; He is the One who writes in the Lamb's Book of Life; He is the One who keeps all who come to Him from falling, and will present them faultless before His presence. We will therefore worship Jesus the Lamb as our Security, our eternal Guardian.

Sixth New Way to Worship—Jesus the Lamb as our Spring of Life. "And he showed me a pure river of water of life . . . proceeding from the throne of God and of the Lamb" (Revelation 22:1). It is interesting that there will no longer be any seas or oceans, but there is going to be a springing up of the water of life. Why won't there be any oceans? Probably the same reason there isn't any blood in heaven. Jesus has said that flesh and blood shall not inherit the kingdom of God. After His resurrection body, Jesus stated that He had a body and bones, but He did not mention anything about blood (Luke 24:39). Why? Blood has to do with corruption; it is the disinfecting system; it is actually the garbage system of our body. Blood takes out all the dead cells and the poisons and filters them out of our bodies.

Do you know how the oceans function on our planet? They act as a giant cleaning system. Rains catch all the impurities and put them into the rivers and streams to run them out into the ocean. After that, only pure water is evaporated, like distilled water, which then goes up into the clouds, comes back down, cleans the air and the ground, and then flushes everything right back into the septic tank of the planet—the oceans.

Just as God doesn't need oceans, we won't need blood. There won't be any waste by-products (we can't conceive of this because we are in a fallen universe). The Lamb Himself will be our Spring of Life. The "water of life" no longer carries trash out because it proceeds from the throne of God and of the Lamb. The millennial temple will have water coming out from underneath the altar, which is a symbol of God's throne. But here, when the temple is done away with, the water will flow out from underneath the throne. No longer will we need to have the altar as a symbol, because we will be gathered around God's throne itself. And the Water of Life flowing from under His throne is symbolic of true endless life flowing from God. We will thus worship Jesus the Lamb as our Spring of Life!

Seventh New Way to Worship—Jesus the Lamb as our King. "And there shall be no more curse, ...and His servants shall serve Him" (Revelation 22:3). Remember: in Genesis, God cursed the earth and the universe because of the transgression of Adam as he followed Eve in her transgression. But here it says there will be no more curse—God removes and destroys it—the curse is annihilated. Jesus is our King whom we worship by serving. And that makes me want to burst forth singing: "King of my life I crown Thee now; Thine shall the glory be!" It is no wonder then that we worship Jesus the Lamb as our King!

THURSDAY: The New Paradise of God

> *"And he showed me a pure river of water of life, . . . proceeding from the throne of God and of the Lamb. In the middle of its street, and on either side of the river, was the tree of life, which bore twelve fruits . . . every month. The leaves . . . were for the healing of the nations. And there shall be no more curse, but the throne of God and of the Lamb shall be in it, and His servants shall serve Him. They shall see His face, and His name shall be on their foreheads. There shall be no night there: They need no lamp nor light of the sun, for the Lord God gives them light. And they shall reign forever and ever."*

—Revelation 22:1–5

The sixth new thing is the new Paradise (22:1–5). We will be living in the new Paradise, the beautiful Garden of God! What a thrill to see again the Tree of Life, a river of the Water of Life! And, most of all, that which makes heaven to be heaven: unhindered access to God. We will experience Emmanuel *at last*—God with us and we with God!

The seventh new thing is the new Light (21:23). "The city had no need of the sun or of the moon to shine on it, for the glory of God illuminated it. The Lamb is its light." The Garden of God will be lit with a different kind of light. This is hard for us to understand because we can't conceive of life apart from the sun.

The ancients used to worship the sun because it sustains all life. Most fossil fuels are a product of sunlight being captured through the wonders of photosynthesis and converted into energy stored in plants and trees. Most fossil fuels are compressed and decomposed plants and trees. Here we see that we no longer will be dependent on the sun for the heat, light, and energy it gives because the glory of God lights the city. The Lamb becomes the lamp of the city; His light will illuminate the nations of the earth and day will be supreme. There will be no more darkness, and in the absence of darkness there will be no more fear, death, or evil associated with it.

In James 1:17 we are told that "with [God] there is no variation or shadow of turning." Those are two astronomical terms meaning that there is no eclipsing of God. In other words, nothing will come between Him to cut off His light as an eclipse does on the earth. With God there will be no eclipsing—no variations as when the stars pulsate. Individual stars differ in their light and electromagnetic radiation output, but no longer will we have such variation. There will be no burning out, and no eclipsing. Thus, we will worship Him who is the Light, and who has lighted our souls forever by His Truth.

FRIDAY: The Perfections of the New Heaven

"Behold, I make all things new."
—Revelation 21:5

What other priceless lessons can we learn from Revelation 21? Now that we've seen seven new things in heaven, and seven new ways we will joyously worship the Lamb of God, let us look at ten perfections of the new heaven.

Perfection one—fellowship. "And . . . there was no more sea" (Revelation 21:1 KJV). Vanquished are the depths of the seas that often gave storms and caused separations! The idea of no more seas may take us back to the idea of never being separated by the distance of a sea from those we love, and thus pointing to God as ever near.

Perfection two—consolation. "And God shall wipe away all tears from their eyes" (Revelation 21:4 KJV). The Comforter will give everlasting comfort for any tears over our own failures, the hurts caused by others, and the sorrow over the loss and hurt of loved ones. All the ravages of sin will be gone forever.

Perfection three—living. "And there shall be no more death" (Revelation 21:4, KJV). Never again will we have to watch the life drain from a beloved spouse, parent, or friend. There will be no more death vigils in Intensive Care Units and waiting rooms. The Prince of Terrors will be gone and the Prince of Peace will reign.

Perfection four—joy. "And there shall be no more . . . sorrow, nor crying" (Revelation 21:4 KJV). Yes, Christians feel sorrow and they cry when parents pass away. They grieve the loss of a marriage partner who goes ahead of them to the presence of Christ. The depth of such losses is fully experienced, but Jesus has promised that we will have abundant life (John 10:10)—and in this world we have only tasted of the Spirit's fruit called joy. But oh, the joy of our future reunion!

Perfection five—health. "And there shall be no more . . . pain" (Revelation 21:4 KJV). There will be no more colds, flu bugs, arthritis, painfully incapacitating diseases, or any other physical ailments!

Perfection six—sustenance and resources. "'I will give unto him that is athirst of the fountain of the water of life freely'" (Revelation 21:6 KJV). For the millions who have agonized in hunger and thirst on earth, that will be no more. Gone will be the pressures of securing daily provisions because the Provider will have come (Revelation 7:16). Jesus came that we might never hunger nor thirst (John 6:35)!

Perfection seven—worship. "The Lord God Almighty and the Lamb are the temple of it" (Revelation 21:22 KJV). The mere representation or symbols of God will be replaced by the immediate and actual presence of God. There will be no more cold hearts and fainting prayers; no more wandering minds in song, study, and prayer. The personal God who promised to be with us will be there. And we will forever be with Him who loved us and sent His Son to give Himself for us! That is why we will break into worship and song so often in Revelation. It will be absolutely perfect there!

Perfection eight—illumination. "The Lamb is the light thereof" (Revelation 21:23 KJV). No more brownouts, blackouts, power surges, or power failures. No more gloomy days. No more dark days. The Light of the World has come and we will at last walk in the light as He is in the Light!

Perfection nine—security. "And the gates of it shall not be shut at all by day" (Revelation 21:25 KJV). All the fears and phobias of the old world are gone. The dangers of robber and stalker are past. The constant awareness of imminent loss is gone. The need to protect ourselves from intruders and assailants has passed with the arrival of our Protector and Fortress. We will be under the wings of the One we can wholly trust: no more fear of defilement or pollution; no need to purify air, water, and food; no screens, locks, combinations, doors, or guns. We will be free at last!

Perfection ten—refreshment. "There shall be no night there" (Revelation 21:25 KJV). There will be no end to activity; no exhaustion; no place for evil men and their evil plans (John 3:19). All that will be is the enjoyment of a day that knows no end. At last we'll have glorious bodies fashioned like our Savior's (Philippians 3.21). Oh, that will be glory for me! How about you?

SATURDAY: The Wonder of Entering Heaven

> "**Precious** *in the sight of the LORD* **is the death of His saints.**"
> —PSALM 116:15

When your appointment with death arrives, the Lord Jesus Himself will wondrously take you by the hand and usher you instantly into heaven. At the moment you are absent from the body you will forever be in His presence! Jesus Christ, who has guided you through the valley of the shadow of death, will continue to guide you as He takes you by the hand and leads you up past the marshaled ranks of the angels!

The Scriptures talk about what God's throne looks like. It is raised up, and sits in the sides of the north; in front of it is a glassy sea; surrounding it in concentric circles are the angels. When

Daniel saw them, he said there were myriads of myriads—ten thousands of ten thousands. What does "ten thousand times ten thousand" equal? Hundreds of millions of standing angelic beings! How powerful are angels? Just one angel slew 185,000 Assyrian soldiers in one night! They are very powerful—and hundreds of millions of these super powerful angelic creations stand by God's throne.

So then, you will walk by the marshaled hosts, the ranks of the angels, up through the golden boulevards of glory, up past the cherubim. When you get closer to God's throne, you will see creatures with four faces and six wings surrounding His throne. Hovering, they constantly say, "Holy, Holy, Holy is the Lord." The seraphim, which means "burning ones," join them. So these burning, holy creatures are speaking about God. Finally, Christ will lead you up to the throne of God Himself.

What happens next? Having passed from this life, which is physical, into real life, which is supernatural and spiritual, Jesus will then hold your hand and walk you up past all the angels, cherubim, and seraphim to the very throne of God. Jesus will then confess your name before His Father and the angels (Revelation 3:5). He will introduce you saying, "Father, I would like You to meet one for whom I died—one whom I bring to You as My beloved, as one whom I purchased. I now present My child to You . . . " Then you will hear Jesus, the King of Kings and Lord of Lords, actually say *your* name! Talk about the most unbelievable moment of your existence!

Do you remember how you will be clothed? In a white robe! If you will recall, when Jesus was transfigured, He pulled back the veil of His flesh to let us see what He's really like as God in His eternal divine state. Scripture tells us that His clothing began to glow so white that it was whiter than anything ever seen on earth. His face also began to shine. In fact, when John saw Him He was shining like the sun! And you, too, will have a glowing white robe because you will no longer be terrestrial, but celestial!

Psalm 104:2 tells us that Jesus is clothed "with light as with a garment." Because you will see Him as He is, you will look like Jesus— as white and bright as the day, and pure as light. What a reward it will be to have that robe draped around your shoulders and be invited to walk the shining paths of glory! But the greatest and richest part will be to hear Jesus Christ confess that you are His good and faithful servant! What a wondrous entrance into heaven!

Make a choice to live in hope. G. Campbell Morgan, a great Bible teacher in Britain a hundred years or so ago, wrote of this moment also, and he said:

> You are to remember with the passion burning within you that you are not the child of today. You are not of the Earth, you are more than dust; you are the child of tomorrow, you are of the eternities, you are the offspring of Deity.
>
> The measurement of your lives cannot be circumscribed by the point where blue sky kisses green earth. All the facts of your life cannot be encompassed in the one small sphere upon which you live. You belong to the infinite. If you only make your fortune on the Earth—poor, sorry, silly soul—you have made a fortune, and stored it in a place where you cannot hold it. Make your fortune, but store it where it will greet you in the dawning of the new morning.[6]

Since Jesus is going to usher you into heaven and take you to meet your Father sitting on the throne, think about what you want to send ahead. All that you did on earth is going to follow you to heaven!

I once ordered a small technical gadget over the Internet and received an e-mail asking me to track it. I had never done this sort of thing, so I hit the proper key and got this message: "Your package was put in a truck in Philadelphia and headed for the airport at 7:31." I thought: *Oh, that's great!* I checked later in the day, and this time it said: "Your package has now arrived at the Philadelphia airport." I tracked that package's whereabouts every day until finally, as I checked it for the last time, the doorbell rang and the delivery man was actually dropping it at the door. I then thought to myself: *We think nothing of tracking packages, but God says, "I'm tracking everything you've done on earth, and the part that is eternal is going to follow you—it's going to arrive with you in heaven."* The question is this: Is anything following you to heaven? When you come face to face with Jesus, what will you bring with you to offer the Lamb of God?

WEEK 49
Fall in Love with Jesus All Over Again

{ Revelation 22:1–21 }

As the end of days approaches, you can find hope as you fall in love with Jesus all over again!

SUNDAY: Jesus Is Extravagant

"And I, if I am lifted up from the earth, **will draw all peoples to Myself.***"*
—John 12:32

When the Bible opens in Genesis, we find ourselves transported into the Garden of Eden, a paradise of perfection and beauty. When the Bible closes in Revelation 22, we are transported forward to the fringes of eternity to step out into the Garden of God, that final Paradise which far exceeds anything man could ever envision. And its perfection is absolutely breathtaking!

To realize how glorious heaven will be, we need to go back and meet the first two humans on earth. We need to once again listen to the inspired, accurate, and divine recounting of their experience in the Garden of Eden.

WEEK 49: FALL IN LOVE WITH JESUS ALL OVER AGAIN

Imagine what it was like in the dawn of Creation. Think about life as a perfect human: Your first memory is that of waking up in God's garden, Eden. You are in a comfortable world with no extremes of hot and cold, no storms, no disasters to fear. It is a secure home with no pestering bugs, no poisonous snakes, and no deadly spiders. You are surrounded with the continual beauty of fragrant and color-filled flowering orchids on the verdant green trees. Blooms never fall off, yellow, or wilt. Full, juicy fruit hangs ripe on the branches, but none falls off and rots.

Even more, you have a body that never aches, a digestive system that never rebels, eyesight that never needs correction, and your ears can hear the sweet sounds of life all around. There are no pains, never a sorrow, not even a fear. There is no weariness—only peace-filled living.

In God's perfect Garden of Eden, it is paradise living. Every day is an adventure of new colors, new fragrances, and new symmetry in flowers, butterflies, and all the wonders of a perfect animal world. There are no predators, no scavengers, and no carnivores. There are only placid and magnificent creatures reflecting the majesty of God. Around every corner of towering and graceful trees, which were each perfectly planted by God, are flocks, herds, and gatherings of exquisite animals.

Best of all is the sweet sound of the voice of the Lord. About suppertime each day, a gentle breeze whispers by, and then you hear the voice of God. The Gardener and Planner of the Universe is walking among His creatures in the cool of the day. He desires fellowship with you, His best friends, whom He made to look just like Himself. Your ears, that He created, hear the sweetest sound of all—the voice of Jesus who created them.

And then the bad guy enter Paradise—the dragon serpent, Satan! And all of Creation is turned upside down . . .

By Revelation 22, however, Satan will no longer be a threat. God will seal him in the Lake of Fire along with those who have refused to stop following him. But we who have listened to Jesus and followed Him will be in the new Garden of God—our eternal and glorious Paradise.

All of God's children, those who have placed their faith in the Lamb's shed blood on the cross, will be dwelling in the city He has prepared for us. And it is described beautifully in Revelation 22: the Celestial City is comforting (vv. 1–5), and the Celestial City is calling us to come home (vv. 6–21).

As you experience the extravagance of Jesus, who saved and washed you from your sins, you will understand just how much He is going to lavish on you in the future Garden of God!

My Prayer for You This Week: *We worship You, oh mighty King, for there is none like You! It is truly extravagant of You to have taken us from the pit, out of the miry clay, to wash and robe us with Your righteousness; to set our feet upon the Rock; to give us a new name, and a personal intimate relationship with You—and to promise to us all the rights of being a joint heir with You, oh Jesus! We are overwhelmed with unspeakable gratitude! At the conclusion of Your Revelation, we pray that we will understand how You are truly pouring out Your grace, mercy, and love in abundance—our inheritance in Christ. And we thank You in advance for that! Bless us as we study this week; fill our hearts with the wonders of who You are, Lord Jesus. Then help us to choose to live in such a way that we, too, will reflect Your wonders. In Your precious name we pray, Amen.*

MONDAY: All Things New

*"Then He who sat on the throne said, 'Behold, **I make all things new.'** And He said to me, 'Write, for these words are true and faithful.'"*

—REVELATION 21:5

As we come to the twenty-second chapter of Revelation, consider how unlike the first Adam is to this last Adam: Satan challenged the first man, Adam. The Last Adam, Jesus, challenged Satan by resisting him with God's Word. Satan ruined the first Adam. The Last Adam crushed Satan. The First Adam involved the human race in his defeat. The Last Adam included the human race in His victory. The First Adam stood as the head of the race, and falling, dragged the whole race down with him. The Last Adam stood as the Head of the new race, and being victorious, lifted that race with Him.

The Celestial City is comforting. In Revelation 22:1–5, we discover that our heavenly home, the Celestial City, is like a beautiful garden. As we saw a few moments ago, the Garden of God seems much like the Garden of Eden. However, there are also some differences. There were four rivers in Eden (Genesis 2:10–14), but God has only one river in His Celestial City. When Ezekiel saw a river for cleansing and life, it was flowing from under the altar of the millennial temple (Ezekiel 47), but this river of life flows from God's throne because the Lord God Almighty is the source of all true purity.

In Eden humans were prohibited from eating of "the tree of the knowledge of good and evil" and of "the tree of life" (Genesis 2:15–17; 3:22–24). But in the Garden of God we will have unhindered access to the Tree of Life. As we ponder this heavenly scene, we realize that the river and the tree are not only literal but also symbolic of the abundant life we inherit in this glorious Celestial City.

When John wrote in Revelation in 22:3 that there is "no more curse," he was reminding us of the dark days of Genesis 3:14–19, when the curse began. It is also remarkable that even the Old Testament closes with the warning: "Lest I come and smite the earth with a curse" (Malachi 4:6). But with Jesus came hope, life, and liberation from the Curse. Because of Calvary, God can announce: "There shall be no more curse!" For the Prince of Death, Satan, will be consigned to hell; the Prince of Life, our Lord Jesus, has liberated all of creation, and made it new; and in heaven we will see that the curse of sin will be gone forever.[1]

Note the contrasts between the old and the new in the chart below.[2]

PROBATIONARY WORLD (Genesis)	ETERNAL WORLD (Revelation)
Division of light and darkness (1:4)	No night there (21:25)
Division of land and sea (1:10)	No more sea (21:1)
Rule of sun and moon (1:6)	No need of sun or moon (21:23)
First heavens and earth finished (2:1–3)	New heaven and earth forever (21:1)
Man in a prepared Garden (2:8, 9)	Man in a prepared city (21:2)

WEEK 49: FALL IN LOVE WITH JESUS ALL OVER AGAIN

River flowing out of Eden (2:10)	River flowing from God's throne (22:1)
Tree of Life in the midst of the Garden (2:9)	Tree of Life throughout the city (22:2)
Gold in the land (2:12)	Gold in the city (21:21)
God walking in the Garden (3:8)	God dwelling with His people (21:3), no longer coming in the cool of the day as in Genesis; we are with Him forever.
The Spirit is energizing (1:2)	The Spirit is inviting (22:17)
Garden accessible to the liar, Satan (3:1–5)	City closed to all liars (21:27)
Man in God's image (1:27)	Man in God's presence (21:3)
Man the probationer (2:17)	Man the heir (21:7)
CURSED WORLD (Genesis)	**REDEEMED WORLD (Revelation)**
Cursed ground (3:17)	No more curse (22:3)
Daily sorrow (3:17)	No more sorrow (21:4)
Sweat on the face (3:19)	No more tears (21:4)
Thorns and thistles (3:18)	No more pain (21:4)
Eating herbs of the field (3:18)	Twelve manner of fruits (22:2)
Death and returning to the dust (3:19)	No more death (21:4)
Coats of skins (3:21)	Fine linen, white and clean (19:14)
Satan opposing (3:15)	Satan banished (20:10)
Driven from the Garden; kept from the tree of life (3:24)	Eternal access to the Tree of Life (22:14)
Banished from the Garden (3:23)	Free entry to the Garden of God (22:14)
Redeemer promised (3:15)	Redemption accomplished (5:9–10)
Evil continually (6:5)	Nothing that defiles (21:27)
Seed of the woman (3:15)	Root and offspring of David (22:16)
Cherubim guarding (3:24)	Angels inviting (21:9)

So then, the end of history and the beginning of history belong together. The last leaf of the Bible corresponds with the first. Holy Scripture begins with Paradise (Genesis 1:2), and with Paradise it ends (Revelation 22).

TUESDAY: The Celestial City Is Calling — Come!

*"And the Spirit and the bride say, 'Come!' . . . And let him who thirsts come. **Whoever desires, let him take the water of life freely."***

—REVELATION 22:17

The conclusion is greater than the beginning! The future Paradise is not only that which was lost and regained, but also, above all, it is the heavenly and eternally glorified Paradise.

- **In the lost Paradise** there was danger: "On the day in which you eat thereof you will die the death" (Genesis 2:17); **in the glorified Paradise** full security reigns, and "there shall be no more curse" (Revelation 22:3).
- **In the lost Paradise**, the serpent said: "You will become as God" (Genesis 3:5); **in the glorified Paradise** Scripture says: "His name [His nature] shall be on their foreheads" (Revelation 22:4).
- **In the lost Paradise** stood a tree of knowledge (Genesis 2:9); **in the glorified Paradise** it is no longer required (Revelation 22:1–5)—for we behold with direct vision the face of God (Revelation 22:4) and thus have the true and personal knowledge of Him forever as our heritage.
- **The lost Paradise** had an end through the defeat of man (Genesis 3:24); **the glorified Paradise** abides eternally for the overcomers (Revelation 2:7), and "they shall reign for ever and ever" (Revelation 22:5).

Thoughts of the Celestial City are comforting and glorious as we await that day, but the city is also calling to us. I believe that the message of Chapter 22 starts in verse 6: "Then he said to me, 'These words are faithful and true.' " The saints of old lived their lives looking for, longing for, and seeking a heavenly city (Hebrews 11:13). And that heavenly city is likewise calling each of us to come—to long to be there.

Revelation 22:6–21 provides these practical applications for us even in today's age:

- **Keep the Word**—God's Word is to be our priority (vv. 6–11, 18–19).
- **Serve God**—God's work is to be our focus (vv. 12–14).
- **Stay pure**—godly purity is to be our goal (vv. 15–16).
- **Watch for Jesus**—Christ's return is to be our hope (vv. 17, 20–21).

Heaven is more than a destination; it is God's deeply moving call to action to us who are on earth. Our heavenly destiny ought to make a difference in our present lives. When the Old Testament saints learned that they had a heavenly city, it challenged them to walk with God, and to serve Him better. When Jesus needed encouragement in the Garden of Gethsemane as He faced death on the cross, it was the hope of returning to His Father in heaven that strengthened Him (Hebrews 12:2). Our heavenly home should be the anchor of our soul that pulls us upward, heavenward, homeward, and Godward.

What is the first call from heaven? We need to keep His Word: "These words are faithful and true. . . . 'Behold, I am coming quickly! Blessed is he who keeps the words of the prophecy of this book' " (Revelation 22:6–7). This is the sixth of the seven beatitudes in which God promises a blessing.

What does "keeps the words of the prophecy of this book" mean? Jesus told us that if you obey His Word, you love Him. To love Him entails hungering for His Word, interacting diligently with His Truth, and yielding to His Holy Spirit that you may be increasingly conformed to the image of Christ.

Have you presented your body to Christ as a living sacrifice? Are you being continually transformed by "the renewing of your mind to prove what is that good and acceptable and perfect will of God" (see Romans 12:1–2)? I pray so!

WEDNESDAY: The Revelation Beatitudes

"**Blessed** is he who reads."
—Revelation 1:3a

Do you recall that there are seven beatitudes—seven blessings in Revelation? Because these have application for how to prepare for heaven even now, we will go over these blessings today and tomorrow.

The first beatitude—Christ's Word. "Blessed is he who reads and those who hear the words of this prophecy, and keep those things which are written in it; for the time is near" (Revelation 1:3). Those who read, hear, and keep His Word are blessed!

The second beatitude—Christ's gift of eternal life. "Blessed are the dead who die in the Lord from now on" (Revelation 14:13). This speaks of the happiness of those who die in the Lord, emphasizing that eternal life is a blessing. What we were, what we did, what through God's power we accomplished in Jesus' name while on earth, will go with us. Unbelievers must leave everything behind; but God's children are blessed because works done in the energy of the Holy Spirit will follow us. Christ's gift of eternal life is a blessing because we get to enjoy Jesus and offer Him our service forever.

The third beatitude—Christ's coming. "Blessed is he who watches, and keeps his garments, lest he walk naked and they see his shame" (Revelation 16:15). This is an emphasis on the Lord's return. Of course, this is for Tribulation saints because Jesus will not come for us as a thief in the night, but as our blessed and loving Bridegroom. However, His coming will be a blessing for us as well as those in the Tribulation. We should therefore all be watching for Him—keeping our garments clean, lest they become soiled with the filth of this world. For the Christian, Christ's coming is not something to be dreaded, but a glorious blessing!

The fourth beatitude—Christ's presence. "Blessed are those who are called to the marriage supper of the Lamb!" (Revelation 19:9). To be invited to the Marriage Supper of the Lamb is a blessed delight because Christ will be there!

The fifth beatitude—Christ's assurance. "Blessed and holy is he who has part in the first resurrection" (Revelation 20:6). This verse emphasizes deliverance from death. It is an assurance to those who are not raptured, those awaiting the resurrection (sleeping in the dust, as Daniel puts it), that there is a great blessing in that they, too, will reign with Christ during the Millennium. If we have believed Christ's Word, received His gift of eternal life, and have looked for Christ's coming and longed for His presence, then we have the blessed assurance of Jesus Christ.

THURSDAY: More of Revelation's Beatitudes

"**Blessed** is he who keeps the words of the prophecy of this book."

—Revelation 22:7

Yesterday, we looked at the first five of seven beatitudes—the blessings in Revelation. Today, we will see the remaining two.

The sixth beatitude—Christ's service. "Blessed is he who keeps the words of the prophecy of this book" (Revelation 22:7). There is great blessing and joy for those who heed God's Word because obedience to Him is what Jesus longs for: "He who has My commandments and keeps them, it is he who loves Me. And he who loves Me will be loved by My Father, and I will love him and manifest Myself to him" (John 14:21). Never forget this point: you will find joy as you not only read and hear God's Word but also keep it! As we keep His Word by the energy and power of the Holy Spirit, to the grace of Jesus Christ, we will have the blessing of Christ's service. Serving Christ by obeying Him is both a joy and a blessing! As the song by Oswald J. Smith expresses, "There is joy in serving Jesus, / As I journey on my way; / Joy that fills the heart with praises / Ev'ry hour and ev'ry day."

The seventh beatitude—Christ's home. "Blessed are those who do His commandments, that they may have the right to the tree of life, and may enter through the gates into the city" (Revelation 22:14). This verse emphasizes the fact that He will eternally sustain us. The home He has prepared for us is the happy result of getting that clean robe and having eternal access to the Tree of Life.

Now look at 22:11: "He who is unjust, let him be unjust still; he who is filthy, let him be filthy still; he who is righteous, let him be righteous still; he who is holy, let him be holy still." Some people struggle with this verse because they think it means: "If you are a sinner, stay a sinner." But God is actually saying that in the eternal state there is no possibility of change.

Consider Warren Wiersbe's comments on this verse:

Does Revelation 22:11 suggest that God does not want men to repent and change their ways? No, because that would be contrary to the message of Revelation and of the gospel itself. The angel's words must be understood in light of the repeated statement, "Behold, I come quickly" (Rev. 22:7, 12), as well as His statement, "For the time is at hand" (Rev. 22:10). Jesus Christ's coming will occur so quickly that men will not have time to change their characters. Revelation 22:11, therefore, is **a solemn warning that decision determines character, and character determines destiny.** Suffering believers might ask, "Is it worth it to live a godly life?" John's reply is, "Yes! Jesus is returning, and He will reward you!" It is worth it to be righteous, [and] it is worth it to be holy but you won't be able to wait till the last minute. When you see the Lord coming, it will be too late to say yes. You must choose Him now.[3]

FRIDAY: Worthy Is the Lamb!

" '**Worthy is the Lamb** who was slain to receive power and riches and wisdom, And strength and honor and glory and blessing!' "

—Revelation 5:12

WEEK 49: FALL IN LOVE WITH JESUS ALL OVER AGAIN

Today, I exhort you to step into the worship center of the universe! Through the eyes of the Apostle John, picture yourself standing in the vestibule and peering through the door into the chambers of the Most High. Gaze at the One who is seated on the eternal throne. As you watch, exalt God in your spirit as the endless praise ascends around His throne. Be still and know who it is before whom you stand. And then fall in love with Jesus all over again as He is at the center and focus of your worship!

Through the Apostle John's descriptions, listen to the choirs of angels in numberless circles about the glassy sea and heaven's throne as they say His worthy praise. By faith's eyes and ears, listen to those eternal creatures chant, "holy, holy, holy." For "the four living creatures . . . do not rest day or night, saying: "Holy, holy, holy, Lord God Almighty, Who was and is and is to come!" (Revelation 4:8).

Listen to the twenty-four elders as they fall down before He who sits on the throne, and cast their crowns before Him, saying: "You are worthy, O Lord, To receive glory and honor and power; For You created all things, And by Your will they exist and were created" (Revelation 4:11).

Now see that band which no man can number singing their songs of adoration and praise: "And they sang a new song, saying: 'You are worthy to take the scroll, and to open its seals; For You were slain, and have redeemed us to God by Your blood out of every tribe and tongue and people and nation, And have made us kings and priests to our God; and we shall reign on the earth.' Then I looked, and I heard the voice of many angels around the throne, the living creatures, and the elders; and the number of them was ten thousand times ten thousand, and thousands of thousands, saying with a loud voice: 'Worthy is the Lamb who was slain To receive power and riches and wisdom, And strength and honor and glory and blessing!' And every creature which is in heaven and on the earth and under the earth and such as are in the sea, and all that are in them, I heard saying: 'Blessing and honor and glory and power Be to Him who sits on the throne, And to the Lamb, forever and ever!' Then the four living creatures said, 'Amen!' And the twenty-four elders fell down and worshiped Him who lives forever and ever" (Revelation 5:9–14).

To worship the Lord God Almighty—who is worthy of all worship and praise—is your duty and purpose of existence. The Father seeks only one thing, and that is that you might worship Him. To truly worship Him is to acknowledge His "worthship" by ascribing to Him the honor, praise, glory, and majesty of which He is worthy. Do you really know Him, this Christ the Lord, who alone merits such praise?

Oh, may God enable you to see Him, the Lamb that was slain, who alone is worthy to be praised by us who owe Him our all! In quiet reverence of this moment, I encourage you to worshipfully sing this song to our worthy Lamb.

SATURDAY: Experiencing Jesus

*"And this is eternal life, **that they may know You**, the only true God, and Jesus Christ whom You have sent."*

—JOHN 17:3

The mission that flows out of our loving fellowship, our spiritual growth, and our praise is that of being God's faithful and obedient instruments in His divine plan to redeem the world. That plan began in eternity past, before the foundation of the world. But it did not go into effect until Adam chose to sin, fell from fellowship with God, and was spiritually separated from Him.

Since that fateful day in the Garden of Eden, fallen, natural man has been trying to hide from God, and God has been redeeming men back to Himself. From that first time of sin, it has always been God who, solely out of His own gracious love, has taken the initiative to restore men to righteousness. God has always taken the initiative for man's salvation and restoration, from His first call to Adam, "Where are you?" (Gen. 3:9), to His last call in Revelation: "The Spirit and the bride say, 'Come.' And let the one who hears say, 'Come.' And let the one who is thirsty come; let the one who wishes take the Water of Life without cost" (Revelation 22:17).[4]

Revelation 22 ends the Word of God with the same themes of practical Christian living that have wound their way across most of God's Holy Scriptures: keep the Word (vv. 6–11); serve God (vv. 12–14); avoid sin (vv. 15- 16); and watch for Jesus (vv. 17–21).

The same Jesus that bids us come calls us to keep on the same path He starts us on, the path of grace through faith: "As you have therefore received Christ Jesus the Lord, so walk in Him" (Colossians 2:6).

Make a choice to live in hope. If you have not yet partaken of the Water of Life, choose to live in hope by drinking of Him, and you will find the first true satisfaction you have ever known in your life. I pray that if your garments are soiled with sins not atoned for that you would turn to the Savior today and say, "Your blood avails for me! Save me Jesus, and forgive me!"

If you already have a personal relationship with Christ Jesus the Lord, may you keep His Word, and serve Him faithfully from now throughout all eternity. Be careful to turn from any sin that weighs you down so that you may live watching for Christ's return. Ask God to continually fill your mind and heart with the wonders of who He is and to choose to live in such a way that you reflect His wonders in your life. When all is said and done, may He enable you to say, with all your heart, "Even so, come quickly, Lord Jesus!"

It is my deep prayer that you will fall in love with Jesus all over again as you reflect upon what He has in store for you—both in this age, and in the age to come. If we learn to live in hope by falling in love with Jesus over and over again we will be able to go through all the hardships, pains, and trials that life will bring.

WEEK 50
Experience Jesus Often

{ Revelation 1–22 }

As the end of days approaches, you can find hope as you experience Jesus often!

SUNDAY: The Greatest Event of All Time

*"**The Revelation** of Jesus Christ, **which God gave Him** to show His servants."*
—Revelation 1:1a

God has invited us to the greatest event of all time! The ultimate communication from God has arrived, and it is a beautiful work of art, a picture of vivid color and radiance. It is a full-color portrait of His Son, Jesus. God presents this photograph as His precious gift to us. We can do with it as we please, but He promises an unusual blessing to all those who take the time to look hard and close at this picture.

What is the picture? It is the unveiled Jesus of Revelation—the uncovered glory of the image of God in Christ Jesus. It is God's great gift of Hope for us to share in and with a sin weary world *looking* for hope!

Have you been captivated by the irresistible attraction and the incomparable satisfaction of experiencing God? To all who have such a desire, our Lord proposes that experiencing His Son Jesus is the highest pleasure and greatest treasure to be found. Worshiping God is the highest calling we can have as His creation!

We were created to worship God. Yet, I find more resistance in my life to worship than anything else. Distractions pour in, doubts arise, and the constant downward tug of the world, the flesh, and the devil all make it hard to focus on Jesus as He deserves. On the positive side, however, we can all agree that the most precious moments in our life are those few that we know were spent standing consciously in the very presence of God. May I ask you to now rise to such a moment in your heart?

This week's devotionals represent an invitation to worship Christ, who died in our place, as well as to rejoice in God the Father's perfect plan for the ages. So I ask you to discipline yourself to lay aside all the plans, imaginations, and distracting thoughts of other things so that you can give the gift of your total attention to God each day. I exhort you to meditate on the Scriptures and, in a spirit of continual prayerfulness, ask the Lord to open your heart more and more to Him! This is the hardest and yet most rewarding exercise I can think of!

For today's text, I am sharing a verse from every chapter of the Revelation so that you can experience the entire book in three minutes. I encourage you to read these twenty-two references aloud right now, and hear the wonder of this powerful book.

"The Revelation of Jesus Christ, which God gave Him to show His servants—things which must shortly take place. And He sent and signified it by His angel to His servant John" (1:1).

"To the angel of the church of Ephesus write, 'These things says He who holds the seven stars in His right hand, who walks in the midst of the seven golden lampstands' " (2:1).

"He who has an ear, let him hear what the Spirit says to the churches" (3:6).

"After these things I looked, and behold, a door standing open in heaven. And the first voice which I heard was like a trumpet speaking with me, saying, 'Come up here, and I will show you things which must take place after this' " (4:1).

"And I saw in the right hand of Him who sat on the throne a scroll written inside and on the back, sealed with seven seals" (5:1).

"Now I saw when the Lamb opened one of the seals; and I heard one of the four living creatures saying with a voice like thunder, 'Come and see' " (6:1).

"After these things I saw four angels standing at the four corners of the earth, holding the four winds of the earth, that the wind should not blow on the earth, on the sea, or on any tree" (7:1).

"When He opened the seventh seal, there was silence in heaven for about half an hour" (8:1).

"Then the fifth angel sounded: And I saw a star fallen from heaven to the earth. To him was given the key to the bottomless pit" (9:1).

"I saw still another mighty angel coming down from heaven, clothed with a cloud. And a rainbow was on his head, his face was like the sun, and his feet like pillars of fire" (10:1).

"Then I was given a reed like a measuring rod. And the angel stood, saying, 'Rise and measure the temple of God, the altar, and those who worship there' " (11:1).

"Now a great sign appeared in heaven: a woman clothed with the sun, with the moon under her feet, and on her head a garland of twelve stars" (12:1).

"Then I stood on the sand of the sea. And I saw a beast rising up out of the sea, having seven heads and ten horns, and on his horns ten crowns, and on his heads a blasphemous name" (13:1).

"Then I looked, and behold, a Lamb standing on Mount Zion, and with Him one hundred and forty-four thousand, having His Father's name written on their foreheads" (14:1).

"Then I saw another sign in heaven, great and marvelous: seven angels having the seven last plagues, for in them the wrath of God is complete" (15:1).

"Then I heard a loud voice from the temple saying to the seven angels, 'Go and pour out the bowls of the wrath of God on the earth' " (16:1).

"Then one of the seven angels who had the seven bowls came and talked with me, saying to me, 'Come, I will show you the judgment of the great harlot who sits on many waters.' " (17:1).

"After these things I saw another angel coming down from heaven, having great authority, and the earth was illuminated with his glory" (18:1).

"After these things I heard a loud voice of a great multitude in heaven, saying, 'Alleluia! Salvation and glory and honor and power belong to the Lord our God!' " (19:1).

"Then I saw an angel coming down from heaven, having the key to the bottomless pit and a great chain in his hand" (20:1).

"Now I saw a new heaven and a new earth, for the first heaven and the first earth had passed away. Also there was no more sea" (21:1).

"And he showed me a pure river of water of life, clear as crystal, proceeding from the throne of God and of the Lamb. . . . The grace of our Lord Jesus Christ be with you all. Amen" (22:1, 21).

My Prayer for You This Week: *Father, we thank You for letting us traverse these wonderful verses in Revelation that You have given as a gift to Your people. We can think of no higher honor, no greater privilege, no more solemn responsibility than to come before Your presence throughout today and every day. We come humbly, asking You to clothe us with humility. We come reverently, asking You to cleanse and purge us from any of the leaven of sin that always seeks to attach itself to us. We thank You for Christ's cleansing blood shed on our behalf. We come worshipfully and overflowing with joy, asking that You would accept the upraised hearts we are offering to You. We pray that every part of our upcoming last glimpse through Revelation will have Your favor upon it. Meet with us in an unusual way—in a very special and transforming and glorifying way in our lives—so we will know that surely we have been with Jesus, in whose name we ask all this, Amen.*

MONDAY: Your Beloved Bridegroom

"For I am jealous for you with godly jealousy. For I have betrothed you to one husband, **that I may present you as a chaste virgin to Christ.***"*

—2 Corinthians 11:2

As you worship Jesus you will discover what it means to experience Him, for He is wonderful, glorious, and He is your Beloved Bridegroom! As you start in the process of worshiping Him, I encourage you to sit still before Him in front of His awesome majesty, for He says to you: "Be still, and know that I am God; I will be exalted among the nations, I will be exalted in the earth" (Psalm 46:10 NIV).

Start your worship silently before the majesty of our Lord on high: "The Lord is in his holy temple; let all the earth be silent before him" (Habakkuk 2:20 NIV).

As you comprehend even a fraction of who He is, and how utterly magnificent He is, stop again in awe, with wondrous reverence and sheer delight. Think of the magnitude of His power, might, and infinitude. Agree with the psalmist who said, "Let all the earth fear the Lord; let all the people of the world revere him" (Psalm 33:8 NIV). Honor the Lord for who He is, for how greatly He is to be praised, and how He is infinitely above all that is mundane—and yet He condescends to us of low degree to meet with us. Hallelujah!

As you linger in the glow of His presence, your lack of holiness should become painfully revealed: "For this is what the high and lofty One says—he who lives forever, whose name is holy: 'I live in a high and holy place, but also with him who is contrite and lowly in spirit, to revive the spirit of the lowly and to revive the heart of the contrite' " (Isaiah 57:15 NIV).

Are you experiencing a pang of hunger for Christ yet? Do you desire to know Him, love Him, and adore Him more and more? Your heart should be filling up with wonder and gratitude for even the chance to have this moment. And your heart, like the psalmist's, should echo: "O God, you are my God, earnestly I seek you; my soul thirsts for you, my body longs for you, in a dry and weary land where there is no water" (Psalm 63:1 NIV).

Awash with wonder by now, you should be feeling the sheer delight of a new hope as He begins to flood your soul with His response of bearing away the deadening load of your sin. If you feel the burden lifted, the stains removed, the coldness warmed, and the emptiness filled, you are experiencing your God. So go ahead and boldly ask Him: "One thing I ask of the LORD . . . : that I may dwell in the house of the LORD all the days of my life, to gaze upon the beauty of the LORD and to seek him in his temple" (Psalm 27:4 NIV).

The whole Book of Revelation expounds upon that temple in which you can worship the Lord. In His Revelation you will discover that you can: worship Jesus for His majesty (Revelation 1); worship Jesus for His message (Revelation 2–3); worship Jesus for His mission (Revelation 4–19); and worship Jesus for His mansions (Revelation 20–22).

So worship Jesus throughout Revelation by experiencing your wonderful, glorious, and Beloved Bridegroom!

TUESDAY: Worship Jesus for His Majesty

"When I saw Him, I fell at His feet as dead. But He laid His right hand on me, saying to me, 'Do not be afraid; I am the First and the Last.'"
—REVELATION 1:17

Let us now look at how you can worship every facet of Jesus Christ in Revelation 1.

Worship the ministry of Jesus. In Revelation 1:1–3, Jesus desires to reveal Himself to His bondservants who will pay attention. For "the eyes of the LORD run to and fro throughout the whole earth, to show Himself strong on behalf of those whose heart is loyal to Him" (2 Chronicles 16:9). He is always looking for those whose hearts will be focused on Him so that He can reveal Himself to them. The Spirit of Christ speaking through Moses said, "[If] you will seek the LORD your God, . . . you will find Him if you seek Him with all your heart and with all your soul" (Deuteronomy 4:29). Worship Jesus for His ministry of revealing Himself to His children!

Worship the peace of Jesus. Revelation 1:4 reveals that He offers "Grace to you and peace from Him who is and who was and who is to come." This reveals the rest that is yours in Christ; so worship Jesus for the peace that He so freely gives!

Worship the blood of Jesus. In Revelation 1:5 we see that Jesus is "the firstborn from the dead." The blood He shed on the cross is your Source of Eternal Life. Because He sacrificed His life for you, worship Jesus for the blood He shed—give your life back to Him!

Worship the plan of Jesus. Revelation 1:7–8 and 9–20 reveal His heart when He said, "I am coming" and "I am the Alpha and Omega." He is the One who began, and is going to finish,

WEEK 50: EXPERIENCE JESUS OFTEN

all things. Worship Jesus for His plan to reveal His heart because He wants you to know and trust Him!

Worship the eyes of Jesus. Revelation 1:14 reveals Jesus' omniscience: "His eyes were as a flame of fire." He reveals His all-seeing omniscience as He looks into your life and sees what no one else can see. He sees the fears and deepest needs of your heart. As He sees what you don't want anyone else to see, He will remove those things if you ask Him. So worship Jesus for His eyes that search your soul to see if there is any wicked way in you!

Worship the voice of Jesus. Revelation 1:15 reveals His omnipotence. His voice can be so sweet and yet it can also be like "the sound of many waters." Jesus has the power to accomplish all things in your life as you yield to Him. So worship Jesus for His voice that reveals His almighty omnipotence!

Worship the touch of Jesus. Revelation 1:16–18 reveals His humanity: "When I saw Him I fell at His feet as dead, but He laid His right hand on me." He identifies with you and is able to meet you where you are. Worship Jesus for His gentle and loving touch!

Worship the glory of Jesus. Revelation 1:9–20 reveals His character. When John was on Patmos, he heard the sound of the Spirit raising him up and opening his mind to God and the trumpet sound. As he turned to hear the voice, he saw a man standing there. It was then that Jesus unveiled that He is the glorious Son of Man. Worship this Jesus for His glory!

Imagine what it must have been like for John to hear a voice like a trumpet and then to see these **seven perfections of Jesus' divinity**.

1. **The Perfect Man:** Jesus can identify with us, "for we do not have a High Priest who cannot sympathize with our weaknesses, but was in all points tempted as we are, yet without sin" (Hebrews 4:15). As the Perfect Man in His divinity, He now comes to us as "Son of Man" (eighty-four times He calls Himself this, but no one else does). He came to seek and to save the lost of Adam's fallen race—as the Son of Man, He is the Conqueror of Adam's fallen race.

2. **The Perfect Priest:** He is robed to the feet as the Perfect Priest. All other priests carried around sacrifices, but this Priest was Himself the Perfect Sacrifice who died for us. As Hebrews pictures Him, He is ever living to intercede for us.

3. **The Perfect Judge:** As the Judge, He was girded around His breast with a gold band, which was an ancient symbol of restrained emotions. He judges rightly because He is sinless, and full of love and wisdom. No one but He can make decisions perfectly!

4. **The Perfect Image of God:** He is white-haired as the Ancient of Days. His white hair is a sign of maturity, and absolute holiness. (In Daniel 7:9 we see this same description.) Hebrews 1:3 tells us, "Being the brightness of His glory and the express image of His person, and upholding all things by the word of His power, when He had by Himself purged our sins, sat down at the right hand of the Majesty on high."

5. **The Perfect Truth:** With His eyes of fire, Jesus is the Seer of All Secrets. He is a penetrating Scrutinizer that can discover and, with consuming light, reveal secrets. As Psalm 19:6 reminds us, "nothing is hidden" from the eyes of the One Who is Truth, sees clearly, and will leave no sin unpunished but those hidden beneath His blood.

6. **The Perfect Defender:** He is a trampler of foes! Those feet of military bronze will crush His enemies—even those who cry out: "Lord, Lord!" But Scripture says "He never knew them." With His brazen feet, the Ultimate Judge will crush all foes!
7. **The Perfect Communicator:** With the voice of God as thunderous as the twelve million cubic feet of water crashing at Niagara's base every hour, commanding all to pay attention, the deaf and the dead can hear it—and so should we!

Jesus is the Christ. Christ is the One who fulfills all the promises of God perfectly. In everything He is perfect, complete, and our all in all.

WEDNESDAY: Worship Jesus for His Message

*"I was in the Spirit on the Lord's Day, and I heard behind me **a loud voice, as of a trumpet**."*
—Revelation 1:10

Yesterday, we saw that we should worship Jesus for His majesty. Today we will see that we should worship Jesus for His message. Here is the start of a study of all the promises Jesus gave to His seven churches, who represented all of us in His church.

True believers have an abundant life. "To him who overcomes I will give to eat from the tree of life, which is in the midst of the Paradise of God" (Revelation 2:7). He is revealed as the Infinite One, and He begins giving His message that true believers will have an abundant life! As Jesus has promised, "He who believes in Me, . . . out of his heart will flow rivers of living water" (John 7:38). This means that believers will have infinite life in Paradise Regained (John 3:16).

Jesus offers an overflowing life. "Whoever believes in me, . . . streams of living water will flow from within him" (John 7:38 NIV). He also offers an extraordinary life: "I have come that they may have life, and that they may have it more abundantly" (John 10:10).

True believers have an indestructible life. "He who overcomes shall not be hurt by the second death" (Revelation 2:11). Jesus' message also says that true believers will be overcomers. We will not be hurt by anything Satan can throw at us because we are indestructible. We live, as the writer of Hebrews says, after the power of an endless life.

Believers are secure from any physical adversary. "And I give them eternal life, and they shall never perish; neither shall anyone snatch them out of My hand. My Father, who has given them to Me, is greater than all; and no one is able to snatch them out of My Father's hand" (John 10:28–29). They are also secure from any spiritual adversary: "For I am persuaded that neither death nor life, nor angels nor principalities nor powers, nor things present nor things to come, nor height nor depth, nor any other created thing, shall be able to separate us from the love of God which is in Christ Jesus our Lord" (Romans 8:38–39).

True believers have an inexhaustible supply. "To him who overcomes, I will give some of the hidden manna to eat. And I will give him a white stone, and on the stone a new name written which no one knows except him who receives it" (Revelation 2:17). Jesus said, "I came to give you an inexhaustible supply. I will nourish you, and intimately reveal myself to you; I will give you all things good!" If we just come to Him, His supply will never run out.

Believers have all their spiritual needs met: " 'I am the bread of life. He who comes to Me shall never hunger, and he who believes in Me shall never thirst' " (John 6:35). They also have all their spiritual desires fulfilled: "And I will do whatever you ask in my name, so that the Son may bring glory to the Father. You may ask me for anything in my name, and I will do it" (John 14:13 NIV).

True believers have an inexpressible future. "He who overcomes, and keeps My works until the end, to him I will give power over the nations" (Revelation 2:26).

Believers will be rewarded with immeasurable treasures: "There is no one who has left house or brothers or sisters or father or mother or wife or children or lands, for My sake and the gospel's, who shall not receive a hundredfold now in this time— . . . and in the age to come, eternal life" (Mark 10:29–30). Believers will also be overwhelmed by God with unbelievable pleasures: "He was caught up into Paradise and heard inexpressible words, which it is not lawful for a man to utter" (2 Corinthians 12:4).

The more you experience Jesus here on earth, the more you can talk about the unbelievable glory of God seen in the face of Jesus Christ. Oh, how I pray that you long to see that place He is preparing for you!

THURSDAY: Overcomers Will Be Blessed!

*"He who **overcomes**. . . "*
—Revelation 3:5a

Today's devotional is a continuation of worshiping Jesus for His message!

True believers have incredible coverage. "He who overcomes shall be clothed in white garments, and I will not blot out his name from the Book of Life; but I will confess his name before My father and before His angels" (Revelation 3:5). The white garments speak of holiness, joy, and honor bestowed upon us by Jesus.

Believers have Christ as their Garment: "Put on the Lord Jesus Christ, and make no provision for the flesh, to fulfill its lusts" (Romans 13:14). Believers have Christ as their Advocate: "But He . . . has an unchangeable priesthood. . . . He is also able to save to the uttermost those who come to God through Him, since He always lives to make intercession for them" (Hebrews 7:24–25). Believers also have Christ as their Relative: "And if children, then heirs—heirs of God and joint heirs with Christ, if indeed we suffer with Him, that we may also be glorified together" (Romans 8:17).

True believers have an inescapable destination. "He who overcomes, I will make him a pillar in the temple of My God, and he shall go out no more. I will write on him the name of My God and the name of the city of My God, the New Jerusalem, which comes down out of heaven from My God. And I will write on him My new name" (Revelation 3:12).

Believers will be a pillar because we are secure: "Let not your heart be troubled. . . . In My Father's house are many mansions; if it were not so, I would have told you. I go to prepare a place for you.

And . . . I will come again and receive you to Myself; that where I am, there you may be also" (John 14:1–3). We will never have to fear for our future!

Believers will also have a special name—because we are a love gift from the Father to the Son: "Father, I desire that they also whom You gave Me may be with Me where I am, that they may behold My glory which You have given Me; for You loved Me before the foundation of the world" (John 17:24).

True believers have intimacy with God. "To him who overcomes I will grant to sit with Me on My throne, as I also overcame and sat down with My Father on His throne" (Revelation 3:21). Intimacy is a promise: "He who has My commandments and keeps them, it is he who loves Me. And he who loves Me will be loved by My Father, and I will love him and manifest Myself to him" (John 14:21). Intimacy is a Person: "And this is eternal life, that they may know You, the only true God, and Jesus Christ whom You have sent" (John 17:3). And intimacy is permanent: "He who overcomes shall inherit all things, and I will be his God and he shall be My son" (Revelation 21:7).

Jesus came to give, and to give more abundantly! Have you received what He offers? Are you worshiping Him as He deserves? Worship the message of Jesus because it challenges you to listen to Him. Look again at what He has to say to the seven churches in Revelation 2–3:

1. **Ephesus:** Worship the **jealousy of Jesus** because He challenges you to exalt Him to be all that you really love.
2. **Smyrna:** Worship the **hope of Jesus** because He challenges you to exalt Him to be all that you truly possess.
3. **Pergamos:** Worship the **security of Jesus** because He challenges you to exalt Him to be all that you cling to.
4. **Thyatira:** Worship the **chastisement of Jesus** because He challenges you to exalt Him to be all that you fear.
5. **Sardis:** Worship the **riches of Jesus** because He challenges you to exalt Him to be all that you value.
6. **Philadelphia:** Worship the **approval of Jesus** because He challenges you to exalt Him to be all that you enjoy.
7. **Laodicea:** Worship the **request of Jesus** as He tells us to repent of anything that keeps us from Him; He challenges you to exalt Him to be all that you need.

FRIDAY: Worship Jesus for His Mission

*"Now I saw heaven opened, and behold, a white horse. And He who sat on him was called Faithful and True, and **in righteousness He judges and makes war**."*
—Revelation 19:11

Worship Jesus not only for His majesty and His message, but also for His mission, which is clearly seen in Revelation 4–19.

- **Worship the loveliness of Jesus** as He is at the center and focus of your worship, saying: "You are worthy, O Lord!" (Revelation 4)

- **Worship the sacrifice of Jesus** at the throne of the universe as the Lamb of God. For worthy is the Lamb who was slain! (Revelation 5)
- **Worship the wrath of Jesus** as He unleashes the seals that display His holy wrath against sin. (Revelation 6)
- **Worship the love of Jesus** as He, in the midst of the destruction of the planet, sends His witnesses to rescue more lost and helpless sinners by giving them the gospel message. (Revelation 7)
- **Worship the patience of Jesus** as He controls His wrath to listen and respond to prayer while He awaits His perfect timing and continues to freely offer salvation. (Revelation 8)
- **Worship the judgment of Jesus** as He judges hardened and unrepentant sinners. (Revelation 9)
- **Worship the mystery of Jesus** as Judge, for *"the little book"* given to John to eat, and that the mystery of His plan will be finished—just as He declared through His servants, the prophets. (Revelation 10)
- **Worship the witness of Jesus** by trusting His Word through the two witnesses that all things that God has promised will be fulfilled. (Revelation 11)
- **Worship the victory of Jesus** as He shows His people His ultimate triumph. God's saints are seen overcoming the devil by the blood of the Lamb, the word of their testimony—and by not loving their lives unto death. (Revelation 12)
- **Worship the genuineness of Jesus** as He exposes the *lies* of Antichrist—the counterfeit Christ who so poorly represents the infinite eternal Jesus. (Revelation 13)
- **Worship the compassion of Jesus** in sending the everlasting gospel even when the earth is falling apart and the nations are under the wrath of God. (Revelation 14)
- **Worship the beauty of Jesus** in the splendor of His redeeming love while the redeemed sing the song of Moses and the song of the Lamb as they worship His works, His power, His ways, and His plan. (Revelation 15)
- **Worship the power of Jesus** as He judges the horror of locked hearts to show people the atrocities of their sin. (Revelation 16)
- **Worship Jesus as the bride of Jesus** when this chapter unmasks the apostasy of the last days and reveals the true bride (born-again believers) who will sit at the feet of her Beloved Bridegroom. (Revelation 17)
- **Worship the authority of Jesus** judging materialism and acclaiming true values as He keys in to humanity's great lack of real values. (Revelation 18)
- **Worship at the banquet for the marriage of Jesus** as He celebrates union with His bride—the saints of all the ages. Join in the hallelujahs they offer for His salvation and the judgment of the lost and the wicked. (Revelation 19:1–10)
- **Worship the re-entry of Jesus** as He conquers the rebellion, He who is called Faithful and True in righteousness, He whose name is King of Kings and Lord of Lords! (Revelation 19:11–21)

SATURDAY: Worship Jesus for His Mansions

*"Let not your heart be troubled. . . . In My Father's house are many mansions. . . . **I go to prepare a place for you.**"*

—JOHN 14:1–2

Worship Jesus not only for His majesty, His message, and His mission, but also for His beautiful mansions that are so clearly seen in Revelation 20–22. Now we see what He promised to go and prepare for us.

- **Worship the triumph of Jesus** as He vanquishes the devil into the bottomless pit, and renews the earth. (Revelation 20:1–10)
- **Worship the last word of Jesus** damning the rebels to the Lake of Fire—those whose names are not found written in the Lamb's Book of Life. (Revelation 20:11–15)
- **Worship the honeymoon of Jesus** as He unveils Paradise to His bride, and leads us prepared as a bride adorned for her husband. (Revelation 21:1–8)
- **Worship the wonders of Jesus** as from a high mountain He shows His bride all the beauty of the Holy Jerusalem radiating His glory as it descends out of heaven from God. (Revelation 21:9–27)
- **Worship the extravagance of Jesus** who, like Boaz of old, has freely offered overflowing handfuls of His blessings of salvation to all who will come to Him. (Revelation 22:1–21)
- **Worship the entire experience of Jesus** as He opens and closes the Revelation of Himself! (Revelation 1–22)

Make a choice to live in hope. As you worship the Jesus of Revelation, you are choosing to live in hope by discovering what it means to experience the Son of God for who He is—your Beloved Bridegroom. Whether in this life or the next, what He wants from you most, as His bride, is your worship and your love!

WEEK 51
The First Coming of Jesus

{ Luke 1 and Matthew 2 }

As the end of days approaches, you can find hope as you ponder the First Coming of Jesus!

SUNDAY: God Uses Ordinary People

"There was in the days of Herod, the king of Judea, a certain priest named Zacharias, of the division of Abijah. His wife was of the daughters of Aaron, and her name was Elizabeth."
—Luke 1:5

For the past fifty weeks, the Second Coming of Jesus has been uppermost in our minds and hearts. For the remaining two weeks, since those who began reading this book on January 1st are now celebrating the First Coming of Jesus, we will reflect upon the glorious Christ of Christmas, the Promised One—the Savior who came to a manger one dark night to bear away the sin of the world. For without His loving sacrifice on Calvary, none of us could have living hope for the end of days!

The characters that God chose to put into the Christmas story are what we would call ordinary, like the couple we are introduced to in Luke 1:5, Zacharias and Elizabeth. They were ordinary people, who lived with all the ordinary troubles, stresses, and pains of life. They even had an ordinary response to God—mixed belief and unbelief.

Zacharias and Elizabeth also had an ordinary occupation in Jerusalem in the first century; we would call them religious professionals. They were a priest and his wife who lived and worked in the shadow of the temple of God. Being from the priestly family, they could trace their family tree back to Aaron and the tribal genealogy of Levi.

From their earliest days, Zacharias and Elizabeth had known about the Lord. They had grown up much like many Americans of past generations—surrounded by the Truth, seeing and hearing it in many ways and places. So, in that sense, we all are ordinary people. We all share the same struggles, trials, and pains of life.

But one thing about Zacharias and Elizabeth was extraordinary—*they actually believed all that Truth about God.* Because He was real to them, they loved and served Him as best they could. As with each of the other godly members of the Christmas story—Joseph and Mary, the shepherds and the Magi, Simeon and Anna—their lives are examples to us of how to see Christ clearly this Christmas. For how these ordinary persons lived stands in direct contrast to another similar group that we will study this week—the religious professionals who did not internalize the Truth.

Even to this day, it is amazing how the true story of Christmas can polarize a family, a church, a nation, and a world. All around us nearly everyone is comfortable with this "holiday season." But press the issue of Christ, and Him being at the center of Christmas, then things change immediately. For example, try to display a representation of Christ's birth on public land, or try to call a Christmas tree by that name, and the entire government goes into overdrive. Sadly, we live in a post-Christian era. However, that only makes the message of Christmas even more precious and distinct!

In today's devotional, we will examine the contrast between Zacharias and Elizabeth and the ungodly religious professionals identified in the Christmas story. The differences are so stark and distinct that I consider them to be like continental divides—junctures of monumental and eternal proportions. Here is an illustration of that point. On a family trip, as we glided along the interstate highways crossing the Appalachian Mountains, I noticed this sign:

Continental Divide:
A raindrop falling on this side will flow to the Gulf of Mexico;
one falling on the other side will flow to the Atlantic.

Afterward, that sign made me think of the Christmas story and the junctures and choices of monumental eternal proportions that God's people made. Zacharias and Elizabeth's little acts of obedience, choices, affirmations of consecration, and cries to their great God made completely divergent endings to their lives in contrast to that of the other religious professionals. They all did the same work in the same place; they even wore the same clothes and lived in the same houses. The main difference between the two groups was that Zacharias and Elizabeth were looking forward to the First Coming of Jesus; the other group was not looking for Him at all. That difference is what I liken to a continental divide.

As I gave some more thought to continental divides, separators that determine destinations, a very sobering feeling settled over my heart and mind: two raindrops can fall just inches apart—yet arrive at two vastly different destinations. The Christmas story itself contains just such a picture of two "raindrops": two sets of people—so close in every way—yet so far apart in destiny.

That is what America has become. We have an entire nation of almost 300 million people listening to the same songs, seeing the same nativity scenes, and going to the same holiday events. But one group is blessed beyond words while the other group heads to a different destination. The lesson for us at Christmas is therefore this: beware of being *acquainted with Christ* but never *knowing Him*. Zacharias and Elizabeth were not only acquainted with Him, but also believed.

Are you seeing Jesus this Christmas? Or are you missing out on all that God offers you? Everyone who was looking for Jesus to come welcomed His arrival. Who are you going to be like this Christmas—Zacharias and Elizabeth or the religious professionals?

> **My Prayer for You This Week:** *Father, we thank You for the lessons we can learn from the lives of Your faithful servants, Zacharias and Elizabeth. For these ordinary people had an extraordinary relationship with You! May we see You through their eyes, who by faith saw You. I praise you for Zacharias' extraordinary song—his beautiful psalm of praise to You—because it reminds us of our precious salvation. Through his words, may we want to worship You, and affirm those little choices that make our "raindrop" flow a different direction. We pray that this week's devotionals will be a "continental divide" in our lives so that we stop and reaffirm what is true about You. May we not let this Christmas season go by without being among those who see Your coming, and talk about Your coming, and experience the joy of "God with us"—redeeming us, cleansing us, forgiving us, and keeping us from all our fears. In the name of Jesus we pray, Amen.*

MONDAY: A Christmas Blessing for Ordinary People

> *"They were both righteous before God, walking in all the commandments and ordinances of the Lord blameless."*
>
> —Luke 1:6.

WEEK 51: THE FIRST COMING OF JESUS

The names of this righteous couple have special significance related to the First Coming of Christ. Zacharias means "God remembers" and Elizabeth means "His oath"; together their names mean "God remembers His oath." What was that oath? In Psalm 89 God made a promise to David that one of his descendants would have an eternal reign. When God broke through human history after four hundred years of silence, Luke set the stage for us to see that Christ is that promised One. And in Luke 1, we see that God chose Zacharias to witness His speaking for the first time in centuries.

God uses people who are busily doing what He has called them to do. He didn't ask Zacharias and Elizabeth to alter their lives. God used them right where they were, and that is common in the Scriptures. When we are busy doing what He has called us to do, God will direct us into further and wider fields of ministry.

Zacharias was just one of 24,000 priests serving at the temple two weeks per year. While placing fresh incense upon the altar (a once in a lifetime service) before the great curtain within the Holy of Holies, the angel Gabriel appeared to Zacharias with a message from God. When he announced John's coming birth, disbelief set in. Because Zacharias doubted, Gabriel told him he would be mute until the child was born. Now he, instead of God, was the one who would be silent for a season.

God often uses struggling people. "But they had no child, because Elizabeth was barren, and they were both well advanced in years" (Luke 1:7). Zacharias and Elizabeth were good models of how to persevere in spite of what others might call extraordinary challenges. You see, their world measured God's blessing and personal worth by whether or not you had a son. In the Jewish culture, the passing on of the name, the tradition, the heritage, and the family right was so very important. Thus, every woman who wasn't able to have children bore a stigma, and this caused very deep pain. So Zacharias and Elizabeth spent their entire married life hoping for a child, a son in particular. But they didn't let that cripple them. They just kept on faithfully doing what God called them to do, and that is the kind of people that He uses.

God loves to use ordinary people. Elizabeth may have been an ordinary woman by all outward signs, but inwardly she was anything but ordinary because she chose to respond to God with amazing obedience. Although Zacharias wrestled with doubt, Elizabeth believed the Lord. She was rewarded by His taking away her "reproach among people" (Luke 1:24–25). She became the first example of a New Testament woman of faith—one who endured her difficulties and enjoyed the blessing and favor of God. Either way, whether struggling or blessed, she was determined to serve the Lord.

There is something else unique about Elizabeth: she was the first recorded New Testament person filled with the Spirit (1:41). I love that about her. Isn't it amazing that God picked an ordinary woman for that honor? What a model of having a responsive heart to the Lord! Of course, John the Baptist (1:15) and Zacharias (1:67) were also filled with the Spirit. This family is actually what we would call the first Spirit-filled family of the New Testament.

Elizabeth was the first recorded "Titus 2 woman" as she encouraged Mary (1:45). Think of what a ministry Elizabeth had to Mary, a young woman with so many challenges as an unwed mother in the Jewish culture. As an older woman who had herself borne reproach, Elizabeth had walked with God for many years. Thus, she could confidently assure Mary that God would bring to pass all that He had revealed to her. Elizabeth was ordinary by man's standards, but extraordinary by God's because she let Him do whatever He wanted to in her life.

Elizabeth told God, "I want to do what You want me to do. If you want me to go through life barren, and looked down upon, then that is fine with me. I will trust your grace." But when God later announced, "I want to make you the mother of My last great Old Testament prophet and the herald of the New Testament," she quickly responded, "Then that is what I want to do." In whatever God asked of her, Elizabeth humbly chose to serve the Lord!

Perhaps you yourself feel ordinary, like you are "just a number" on a crowded planet. But it doesn't have to be that way. By faith, the Lord can work wonders in your life. You were created for a purpose; there is no one quite like you. In that sense, you are a spiritual snowflake. God blended you together with a certain mix of His gifts and abilities. Thus, He has a calling for your life that no one else can accomplish but you!

TUESDAY: Christmas Put a Song in Our Hearts

"Glory to God in the highest, and on earth peace, goodwill toward men!"
—LUKE 2:14

Did you realize that at that first Christmas God introduced New Testament believers to the songs of heaven? Christ's birth was surrounded by the songs of the saints. Since Luke continued with the record of the early church in Acts, and Paul told us that Spirit-filled saints sing, we can be sure that the early church sang much and often.

Luke recorded a series of five Spirit-prompted songs:
1. Elizabeth broke into song at Mary's arrival. This was the first song of the New Testament, which is known from the first words of the Latin Vulgate as the "Exclamavit" (1:42–45).
2. Mary followed with her marvelous "Magnificat" (1:46–55) in which she quotes over twenty different Scriptures!
3. Zacharias broke forth into his famous "Benedictus" (1:68–79), which means "good saying."
4. Angels broke into the night sky over the shepherds' fields of Bethlehem with "Gloria" (2:14).
5. While holding the infant Jesus in his arms, Simeon lifted his eyes to God and sang his "Nunc Dimittis" (2:29–32).

And some day, when we at last enter into Christ's presence, Revelation says that we will forever be singing that He alone is worthy!

The song Zacharias sang summarized John's ministry of pointing to Jesus. It introduced the Coming One, and explained why Jesus came. But it also reflected notes from Zacharias' forty-plus weeks of Bible study as he waited in mute silence for his son's birth.

By the act of faith naming his son "John," as Gabriel had instructed (Luke 1:63), God loosed Zacharias' tongue and, filled with the Holy Spirit, he burst forth into this hymn:

WEEK 51: THE FIRST COMING OF JESUS

> " 'Blessed is the Lord God of Israel, For He has visited and redeemed His people, And has raised up a horn of salvation for us In the house of His servant David, As He spoke by the mouth of His holy prophets, Who have been since the world began, That we should be saved from our enemies And from the hand of all who hate us, To perform the mercy promised to our fathers And to remember His holy covenant, The oath which He swore to our father Abraham: To grant us that we, Being delivered from the hand of our enemies, Might serve Him without fear, In holiness and righteousness before Him all the days of our life. 'And you, child, will be called the prophet of the Highest; For you will go before the face of the Lord to prepare His ways, To give knowledge of salvation to His people By the remission of their sins, Through the tender mercy of our God, With which the Dayspring from on high has visited us; To give light to those who sit in darkness and the shadow of death, To guide our feet into the way of peace.' "
> —LUKE 1:68–79

If you examine Zacharias' song closely, you will see beautiful pictures of what the First Coming of Jesus really means.

Jesus came to open our prison door—our lives are redeemed (v. 68). The first thing Zacharias points out is that Jesus redeems: He buys us out of slavery. There is great power in the word "redeem," which means "to set free by paying a price." It referred to the ancient custom of releasing a prisoner, or liberating a slave, by purchasing them. Jesus Christ came to earth to bring "deliverance to the captives" (Luke 4:18).

There is NO BONDAGE that Christ's power cannot break. There is no secret or public sin from which Jesus cannot liberate us: no bondage too costly, no bondage too powerful, and no bondage too gripping. Simply say to Him, "Jesus, open the prison door of my bondage—I want to be set free!" John 8:36 says, "If the Son makes you free, you shall be free indeed."

There is NO FEAR that Christ's presence cannot banish. Jesus says to us, "My Presence is with you at all times!" (Matthew 28:20b). Are you chained to fear about the past, the present, or the future? Simply say to Him, "Jesus, redeem me from my fears!"

There is NO STAIN that Christ's precious blood cannot cleanse. There is no stain too deep for the blood of Jesus Christ to cleanse (Revelation 1:5b). Simply say to Him: "Lord Jesus, cleanse me now" and hear Him say, "I am willing—be clean."

There is NO PAST that Christ's Words cannot make new. When the woman caught in adultery stood alone before the Lord, Jesus said, "Is there no one left to condemn you?" And she replied, " 'No one, Lord.' And Jesus said to her, 'Neither do I condemn you; go and sin no more' " (John 8:11). You, too, can have a fresh start. Simply say to Him: "Jesus, let me start over again in You. Give me Your new beginning!"

Christ's power can set you free from any bondage; His presence can dispel any fear; His blood can cleanse any sin; and His forgiveness and compassion can give you a new beginning. All you have to do is ask. What a Savior!

WEDNESDAY: Christmas Means Victory in Jesus

"And she will bring forth a Son, and you shall call His name Jesus, for **He will save His people from their sins**.*"*
—Matthew 1:21

Let us now continue our look at the song of Zacharias, his "Benedictus"—a beautiful psalm of praise to God.

Jesus came to defeat our enemies—our enemy was defeated (vv. 69–75). In the Old Testament a horn symbolizes power and victory (1 Kings 22:11; Psalm 89:17, 24). As Zacharias studied the Scriptures, he reflected upon God as He is often pictured in the Old Testament—delivering the army of His people as they were about to be taken captive. When the Lord arises, the enemy is defeated. In the first word picture, we as captives are set free. In the second word picture our enemy is defeated *so that he cannot capture us as prisoners any more.* God offers total victory to us, His people.

No enemy can stand before Christ: not death, darkness, despair, defeat, or defilement. In John 8:31–36, Jesus promises to those who believe in Him: "If you abide in My word, you are My disciples indeed. And you shall know the truth, and the truth shall make you free. . . . Therefore if the Son makes you free, you shall be free indeed."

Jesus came to pay our debts—our debt was cancelled by His death (vv. 76–77). All of us are in debt to God because we have broken His law and failed to live up to His standards (Luke 7:40–50). Furthermore, all of us are spiritually bankrupt, unable to pay our debt. But Jesus came and paid the debt for us (Psalm 103:12; John 1:29). This is the glorious Truth of our great salvation through Christ.

- When Jesus **justified** us, we as sinners stood before God as accused and were declared righteous by His imputed righteousness.
- When Jesus **redeemed** us, we as sinners stood before God as slaves and were granted freedom by His ransom.
- When Jesus **forgave** us, we as sinners stood before God as debtors and our debt was cancelled by His payment.
- When Jesus **reconciled** us, we as sinners stood before God as enemies and were made friends by His peace.
- When Jesus **adopted** us, we as sinners stood before God as strangers and were called sons and daughters by His choice.

Jesus, the "Dayspring from on high," came to bring the dawning of a new day that knows no night—our night was ended by His Light (Luke 1:78–79). "Dayspring" means "sunrise." God's Word sees lost people as those sitting in darkness, death, and distress. But Christ's birth brought light, life, and peace. His birth was the dawn of a new day because of the tender mercies of God.

Jesus is the only key to the day that knows no night. He came into a manger one dark night to bear away the sin of the world. And He will take your penalty, your debt, your stain, and your sin if you ask Him to.

The story of Christmas is that the Sunrise has come—He is here. If you haven't already done so, I pray that you will open your heart to Him!

THURSDAY: The Other Side of the Continental Divide

*"Choose . . . this day whom **you** will serve."*
—Joshua 24:15a

As we saw earlier this week, there are continental divides—separators that determine destinations. A raindrop falling on one side will flow to the Gulf of Mexico; one falling on the other side will flow to the Atlantic. Two raindrops can fall just inches apart, and yet arrive at two vastly different destinations.

Two people can live side-by-side, walk through life so similarly, yet in the end go to opposite destinations. One chooses eternal life in the new Paradise; the other chooses eternal separation from God in the Lake of Fire. Zacharias and Elizabeth made the right choice; the chief priests and scribes made the wrong one—they were close to God in every way but in their hearts.

How close can you get to Jesus and still be too far away? That is what the religious leaders of Christ's day demonstrate to us this Christmas. So close they were, and yet so far away they remained. It is possible to be as close as them, and yet miss all that Christ and Christmas have to offer.

In Matthew 2:1–6, the chief priests and scribes were summoned by King Herod. When he inquired of them where the Christ was to be born, they instantly responded "in Bethlehem." But the story stopped there for them. No delegation was chosen to go find the Christ child; there was no serious inquiry, no personal seeking, and no investigation by the Bible scholars. They knew the Truth, but didn't believe it in their hearts. Oh, the danger of being so close to God in every way, except in our hearts!

Who were these priests and scribes in Matthew 2:4? Most likely the priests were descendents of Aaron and Zadok, who were designated to watch over the temple sacrifices. The scribes were descendents of Ezra, the great Old Testament scholar. Because language had changed over the centuries, Ezra took the Scriptures from the Mosaic and Davidic times and copied and unified them into a Hebrew that the people could read.

The lack of character in these men was in direct contrast to Ezra's. In Ezra 7:10, we find that he prepared his heart, did as God directed, and then taught the Law. But by Christ's time, Ezra's descendents were only teaching the Law. They weren't preparing their hearts or following God's commands.

Zacharias, however, was so moved by what the Lord told him that he entered into an even more intense study to prepare himself to know about the birth of John. While he was mute, he followed the tradition of Ezra and studied God's Word. In Zacharias' Benedictus (Luke 1:68–79), he used promises of Christ's coming from Psalms 18, 23, 32, 34, 83, 106, and 132 in addition to quotations from Genesis, Exodus, Leviticus, Isaiah, Jeremiah, and Malachi.

Zacharias' life modeled Ezra's devotion to God's Word, but this type of personal devotion in a religious professional was rare. Out of thousands, only four got to see Jesus Christ, and two of them were women who weren't even in the count: Anna and Elizabeth. Today, with all the songs about Christmas, if you feel all alone in your worship of God when you hear the sacred music, it is understandable. That is how it has been from the beginning. The indifferent and Christ-neglecting religious leaders are a warning to us today. Think of all the opportunities these religious professionals had to get close to God.

They daily lived in the presence of God. Old Testament worship centered around the tabernacle and then the temple—in the building where His presence dwelt in better days. When the Shekinah glory had been there, they did not even need light inside the Holy of Holies. For nearly 1,500 years, divinely designed liturgy was carried on in the way Moses was directed by God on Mount Sinai.

They daily saw the symbols and pictures of salvation. Exodus 25–40 describes the tabernacle the priests entered to go into the presence of God. They understood that the altar of incense typified the intercessory work of Christ; the table of showbread was a picture of the fellowship—the Bread of Life, Jesus Christ; and that the ever-lit lampstand represented the illumination of the Spirit of God. These men were surrounded by the symbols and got to work in the very presence of God!

They daily held the holy revelation of God's Word. Most people could not afford a personal copy of God's Word, but these men were surrounded by mountains of scrolls. They were read, discussed, copied, and stored everywhere around them. The scribes even wore ink pots tied to their belts because it was a very revered thing to copy God's Word.

They daily sang from the Psalms. Each day the temple rituals included public readings, Levitical singing, and chanting of God's Word. Most of these men would have read these regular portions so frequently that they would know long passages and even many chapters by memory.

They wore clothing daily that reminded them in every way of God. As prescribed by Moses, to set them apart and help them realize that things were extraordinary when they came before God, upon arrival in the temple area, priests changed into white robes and special sashes. Those who were involved in the sacrifices would have had blood splashed upon them every day as an innocent and spotless animal was slain. The offerer would place his hands on its head, confess his sins and those of his family, and then the priest would kill the animal, catch its blood, pour it around the altar, and burn the sacrifice. This was a complete picture of the sinless Lamb of God, who spotlessly offered Himself on the cross of Calvary to shed His blood for the sin of the world.

What was wrong with their performing this liturgy? The priests only held God's Word in their hands, but not in their hearts. God was only near in their mouths, but not in their hearts. And that is exactly what is going on in so many churches around the world today. Countless people are close in every way to God: they go to church, hold the Holy Bible, recite the holy Words, sing the holy songs, view the holy ongoing events on the calendar, and see all the Bible stories captured in the stained-glass windows. They, too, are close in every way to God—except in their hearts.

FRIDAY: Head Knowledge vs. Heart Knowledge

" 'These people draw near to Me with their mouth, And honor Me with their lips, But **their heart is far from Me**. And in vain they worship Me, teaching as doctrines the commandments of men.' "
—Matthew 15:8

Jesus had a lot to say about religious professionals. In the verse above, Jesus is saying about them, "In vain they get dressed in their outfits; in vain they splash blood on themselves; in vain they put the incense in; in vain they stand there as the offering animal is brought; in vain they worship Me." And then Jesus addresses the scribes whom He indicts for their "teaching as doctrines the commandments of men."

All that exposure to God ended up only in their heads, not in their hearts. The spiritual skin of their lives, overexposed to the Light of God's Truth, had developed the deadliest cancer of all—spiritual indifference.

It was only one small point that made the two raindrops fall so close and end up so distant—these religious professionals were indifferent to God's Word. They were not looking for Jesus. The sad lesson of Christmas comes from those who were on the other side of the continental divide from Zacharias and Elizabeth.

Again, think of the dangerous place these religious leaders were in when summoned before King Herod (Matthew 2:4–5). The immediate reaction of the theologians of Herod's court who knew the Scriptures well was *"in Bethlehem."* They knew about the texts and this event, but didn't care enough to go five miles south of town and experience it. They pointed others to seek out the Savior, but never went to worship themselves. They knew the prophets, but did not believe the prophecies. They knew the Scriptures, but failed to take the words to heart. What a sobering warning that is for us this Christmas season.

They missed the Word. They dealt with God's Word, but God's Word was never allowed to deal with them: "These people draw near with their mouths And honor Me with their lips, But have removed their hearts far from Me, And their fear toward Me is taught by the commandment of men" (Isaiah 29:13). They sang the songs at the festivals and feasts, and they quoted all the passages that they were supposed to quote, but yet they were more worried about what others thought of them than fearing God who could see their hearts.

They missed the worship. The religious leaders were religious, but not worshipful. The religious leaders were acquainted with God, but they had never experienced Him. They had only learned to externally rend their clothes and go through the rituals: "So rend your heart, and not your garments; Return to the Lord your God, For He is gracious and merciful, Slow to anger, and of great kindness; And He relents from doing harm" (Joel 2:13). They were good at the outward emotions but lacked the inward worship. Although God actively seeks worship (John 4:24), He is very selective about who can worship Him—only those who have new hearts.

They missed the walk. The religious leaders were hearers, not doers; they were talkers, not walkers: "While they promise them liberty, they themselves are slaves of corruption; for by whom a person is overcome, by him also he is brought into bondage" (2 Peter 2:19).

They missed the witness. The religious leaders were self-righteous. They felt they were good enough for God. Consequently, they thought: God's Word isn't for me here and now. It is something out there in the future—or for someone else. They knew about the texts, but failed to notice the significance of Christ's birth, so Jesus said to them: "Woe to you, scribes and Pharisees, hypocrites! For you are like whitewashed tombs which indeed appear beautiful outwardly, but inside are full of dead men's bones and all uncleanness" (Matthew 23:27).

They missed it all! These men possessed only head knowledge. They lacked the heart knowledge that led to saving faith, for saving faith always changes a person from the inside out.

The chief priests and scribes are a lesson to us this Christmas to be vigilant so that we don't miss out on all God has for us!

SATURDAY: Is There Room in Your Heart for Jesus?

> "Behold, **I stand at the door and knock**. If anyone hears My voice and opens the door, I will come in to him and dine with him, and he with Me."
> —Revelation 3:20

Zacharias and Elizabeth were looking for the First Coming of Jesus, but the religious professionals weren't looking for Him at all. Zacharias and Elizabeth were ordinary people who faced the ordinary troubles, stresses, and pains of life that we do, but they made room in their hearts for Jesus. They kept their focus on His First Coming.

That same continental divide, separators that determine destinations, still exists today. There are still two groups: one looking for the Second Coming of Jesus and the other that could not care less about Him. The ultimate outcome for each has monumental and eternal proportions: one is headed for God's new Paradise and the other for the Lake of Fire.

So much superficial religious activity and externalism goes on at Christmas because people are close to God in every way but in their hearts, because that is a supernatural event associated with the new birth—being born again. For that reason, the whole world can have the Christmas symbols around them, and the songs and great doctrine in the hymns, but still not get it.

God continues to seek those who will worship Him—those who are circumcised in their heart. That is the New Covenant: "I will give you a new heart and put a new spirit within you; . . . and cause you to walk in My statutes" (Ezekiel 36:26–27). Only those to whom God gives a new heart can truly worship Him this Christmas season.

Make a choice to live in hope. Zacharias and Elizabeth embraced the Christ of Christmas, the Promised One, in their hearts. In faith, they believed that Jesus came to that manger one dark night to bear away the sin of the world—its penalty, debt, and stain. That sacrifice for sin is the only reason you and I can have enduring hope for the end of days.

So choose to live in that hope this Christmas because the Sunrise has come—He is here! Open your heart wide to Him. Jesus is the only key to the day that knows no night. As a possessor of the Light of the World, you no longer walk in darkness; you no longer need to fear the dark because you have the Sunrise from on High. What a joy to have that confidence and comfort this Christmas season!

WEEK 52
Wise Men Still Seek the King!

{ Matthew 2:1–11 and Luke 2:8–20 }

As the end of days approaches, you can find hope as you become one of the King's seekers!

SUNDAY: When Life Is a Blur — Focus!

*"**Be still**, and **know that I am God**; I will be exalted among the nations, I will be exalted in the earth!"*
—Psalm 46:10

Sometimes our lives fly by so fast that the days begin to blur. That is especially true at the holiday season. When that happens we can often miss the beauty around us. For example, as we drove back from taking our children to college we went by the Great Smoky Mountain National Park on Interstate 40 in Tennessee. As we sped along we saw a sign that said, "Scenic Parkway." Looking at Bonnie, I said, "Let's try that!" Suddenly we were off the seventy-mile-per-hour river of cars and trucks jockeying for one car length over each other, and on a quiet winding road through the mist-covered Smoky Mountains.

Soon, even the children were crowded at the windows pointing out barns, fields, colored leaves, and waterfalls. *It is amazing what you can see when you slow down and look!*

How about it? Have you been looking for Jesus during this Christmas season? Or has Christmas already flown by the windows of your life so fast that you missed what God was offering you? Everyone who *looks* for Jesus to come will enjoy His arrival!

My prayer is that you will pull off the "rat race highways" and take the scenic route to enjoy Jesus Christ the Lord! One way to do that is to take a lingering look at the First Coming of Christ, which is the greatest event since Creation. Therefore, we will spend another week on that all-important event.

When God came from heaven, wrapped in baby clothes, and laid in a stone feeding trough called a manger, He was only welcomed and worshiped by two groups of people outside of His own family. Those two groups, the wise men and the shepherds, were poles apart socially, economically, culturally, ethnically, and in every other way but spiritually. However, when the wise men and the shepherds knelt at the feet of Jesus, they worshiped on common ground.

The wise men and the shepherds stand out at the First Coming of Christ because, of all the creatures on earth created in His image, they were the only ones who came seeking the newborn King! Thus, I call them "the King's seekers."

What does Matthew 2 record as the reaction of these seekers of the King? Worship. Shortly after the birth of the Messiah, Judean shepherds bowed at His feet, singing His praises. Then later, Babylonian Magi from the East arrived in Jerusalem asking King Herod where the *real* king of the Jews was born. As we discussed last week, the response of the Bible scholars of Herod's court was "in Bethlehem." The still startling fact is this: although they could recite the right answer, their hearts were indifferent to the Truth of God's Word. Their reaction revealed the terrible condition of indifference to God. They knew the Scriptures—they just did not believe them. What a tragic indictment upon these servants of God! They did not want to travel the five or so miles to Bethlehem to see their Messiah!

How far will you go to see the King? What is it costing you to serve Him?

My Prayer for You This Week: *Father in heaven, I thank You for the blessing of these wise men. I pray that we would each exhibit faith like the Magi. They were drawn by You, oh God. They were most likely instructed by Your Word, but it was a heart-felt response. It wasn't academic like the religious leaders. It wasn't hatred or indifference. It was love. For that is what You have told us—no one who loves You will ever miss out on seeing You. And that is true this Christmas season. I pray that we would pull off the highway onto the scenic parkway and in our hearts love You, come to You, see You, fall before You, and worship You. For then You will draw from us as we open to You what we have and give it to You. Oh, make this the most precious, worship-filled, Christ-exalting celebration of the Christmas season of our lives! We pray in the name of Jesus and for His glory, Amen.*

MONDAY: Wise Men Believe Christ — Sight Unseen

" '*Where is He* who has been born King of the Jews? For we have seen His star in the East and have come to worship Him.' "

—MATTHEW 2:2

What does Matthew record as the first response of those who found Jesus? Worship. As the Holy Scriptures pull back the cloak of time, with vibrant freshness, let us further consider this hallowed moment—the moment God entered time and space as an infant!

In Matthew 2:1-11, Scripture records three responses to Christ which are still present today: Herod hated Him, the leaders ignored Him, and the Magi loved Him. Because the Magi "came from far away" (v. 1), it shows that they had a single-minded devotion because they kept asking everyone where King Jesus was (v. 2). In verses 3–8 Matthew paints the drama of all the possible detractors and how the wise men were not daunted in their mission by false seekers like Herod or the religious professionals. In verse 9, Matthew shows how they just kept following God's leading until they found what they were seeking—Jesus—the King of their worship. Their emotions in finding Jesus at last were revealed by their great anticipation (v. 10). Finally, the Magi fulfilled their purpose in coming so long and so far: they came to see Jesus, to worship Him, and to give to Him. When they "had come . . . they saw, . . . fell down, . . . worshiped, . . . opened [and] presented gifts to Him: gold, frankincense, and myrrh" (v. 11). The significance of these gifts is beautiful.

Gold speaks of Christ as the King of Heaven, or His Deity, as a study of the tabernacle makes plain. **Frankincense** speaks of Christ's role as both our Great High Priest and the Perfect Lamb of God, just as it gives forth its *perfume* only as it is brought into contact with fire. **Myrrh** speaks of Christ's sacrificial death as myrrh is only harvested after the tree is bruised with stripes cut into the bark. Resin that flows as a healing balm to the damaged bark of the tree's *suffering*, has always associated myrrh with the death and burial of our Lord.

Thus these wise men, by the gifts they presented to Him, expressed first, their faith in His Deity; second, their adoration of His sinless life; and third, their anticipation of His sacrifice of Himself for the sin of the world by His death.[1]

What simple lessons can we draw from the wise men? God has servants in unexpected places; He gets glory from unexpected people; He is found only by hearts and not heads; finding God is costly; and true faith is unstoppable.

The Magi were willing to follow God's way anywhere in order to find the promised King and Savior. Are you seeking the King? If you want to seek and find Him, here is God's pattern for how to do that.

Come to Jesus personally. Do you see the lesson in the way these wise men gave? They did not send their gifts by another's hand; they brought them personally to Jesus. God wants you, in person, to come to Him. Undaunted by the long and arduous journey, they must have been astonished to find a mere Baby in a stable. After the magnificence of King Herod's palace, and his overpowering presence, it is incredible that they fell down to worship Jesus as they did. Choosing to disobey Herod's demand that they reveal the location of Jesus indicates their faith. That choice could have cost them their lives. So, in every way, their lives were marked by a personal coming to Jesus.

Have you come personally to Jesus in prayer, worship, and adoration? Have you given *yourself* to Jesus this Christmas season? That is the first gift He wants (2 Corinthians 8:5)!

Give sacrificially of your time, freedom, and comfort for Jesus. From the two year calculation of Herod's death-warrant on the babies of the region, we can infer that it took many months for the Magi to travel to Jerusalem. Herod added some months on each end to cover any potential birth near that time. Back then, it was difficult traveling 1,100 to 1,200 miles. From the regions of Babylon, Persia, or Media, they would have had to walk and ride across hot and arid deserts, through rivers, and cross over cold and dangerous mountain passes to get to Christ's birthplace. Even today, that journey would be very difficult and dangerous. What are you giving to Jesus that really costs you something?

Immediately present what you have to Jesus. The wise men brought prophetic gifts that pictured what Christ's earthly work was all about. They brought what they had in their lives as wealthy rulers. And that is what God wanted; that is why He chose them. When God chose you it was not to bring their kind of gifts, but yours. Remember how the Lord accepts the gifts of each individual. None are the same; all are precious to Him.

Present what you have to Him today. Give Him your mind, and let Him fill it. Give Him your hands, and let Him guide and use them. Give Him your future, and let Him plan and direct your life. Give Him your treasures—He can store them and invest them in safe places that bring everlasting rewards!

Reverently offer your worship to Jesus. More than the coming and presentation of gifts is the greatest moment of all: they fell down and worshiped Him! Worship is a rare and easily lost atmosphere of devotion, adoration, sacrifice, and communion. Those wise men were overwhelmed at the sight of the One they had come so far to see, had waited so long to honor, and had paid so much to sacrifice their gifts upon. When at last they saw Him, they could do nothing less than fall down and worship Him!

As you end this year and start a new one, measure your personal worship temperature. To help you do that, consider William Temple's definition of worship: "[Worship is] to quicken the conscience by the holiness of God, to feed the mind with the truth of God, to purge the imagination by the beauty of God, to open up the heart to the love of God, to devote the will to the purpose of God."[2]

TUESDAY: The Shepherds Were Wise Men

"***Humble yourselves*** *in the sight of the Lord, and He will lift you up.*"

—JAMES 4:10

Before the Magi ever arrived, who came first to the birthplace of the King? The first to arrive were men who were wise in the eyes of God, but in man's eyes they were the humblest, lowliest, and most unworthy of all who lived around Bethlehem—the shepherds. These humble men were of the least likely profession to see a King, and yet the shepherds were the most honored of all Christ's greeters and seekers. You see, God really loves and responds to humility! (That Truth has shaped my whole outlook on life, on worship, on Bible study and, most of all, prayer.)

Shepherds of the first century lived in a world that made it hard to make a living. They struggled and scraped along on minimum wages. In fact someone has described the first century like this: "Taxes were high; wages were low, hypocrisy was rampant; honesty was rare. Freedom was gone; Roman occupation was hard. The rich were getting richer; the poor were always struggling. Morality was ebbing; rebellion was brewing; cruelty was reigning."

Life for shepherds was difficult at best. They experienced cold nights, long days, distant family, and rare friends. Also, sheep stank, and shepherds had to continually search for them because they wandered. Life was never restful and work was never done. But that was all part of what could be expected in a shepherd's life.

In the community at large, shepherds were at the low end of Jewish society. Away from the synagogue, absent from the temple, and defiled by dead animals, they were outcasts to the Jerusalem crowd. Unable to even be a witness to special events they seemed to almost be outside of the culture. But then everything changed.

God captivated the humble shepherds. On the hillsides of Bethlehem, under the stars, the angel's glorious announcement of Christ's birth left one band of shepherds stunned: "Do not be afraid, for behold, I bring you good tidings of great joy which will be to all people. For there is born to you this day in the city of David a Savior, who is Christ the Lord. . . . You will find a Babe wrapped in swaddling cloths, lying in a manger.' And suddenly there was with the angel a multitude of the heavenly host praising God and saying: 'Glory to God in the highest, And on earth peace, goodwill toward men!'" (Luke 2:9–14).

That was an awesome, fearful moment! The first angel's glorious words would always echo in their hearts. And that blazing light of heaven, accompanied by the praises of those angelic multitudes, was captured forever in their minds. The shepherds rushed from the glowing skies over the fields and searched diligently until they found Jesus. I wonder this Christmas season: *Will you allow God to captivate you?*

God changed the humble shepherds. The scene they witnessed in the stable would forever change their lives—they had found Jesus, and they would never be the same again. In just a moment, everything they had ever heard about the Scriptures came alive: God, angels, heaven, Messiah, promises, and prophecies suddenly became real. I wonder this Christmas season: *Will you allow God to forever change you?*

God became near to the humble shepherds. Those endless sacrifices, countless lambs, myriads of offerings, innumerable sins, and promises of forgiveness became intensely personal. The ordinary sheep they watched and sold became the extraordinary pictures of God's mercy and grace. The temple they supplied now became the place where sacrifices for their sins were offered. At last all those mysteries, rites, and ceremonies made sense: they had found the promised Lamb of God! I wonder this Christmas season: *Will you allow God to become personal, real, and near to you?*

God started the humble shepherds down a new path. Up until that night of nights, their lives as shepherds had been monotonous and predictable. They were used to sheep which varied little in their habits. They had walked so often down the same path that it soon became a rutted canyon. But now, with the advent of Christ, life took on a whole new meaning! Nothing would ever be the same again—even though sheep would still be helpless, dumb, and dirty! Because of Jesus, the shepherds' whole perspective on life had changed, and they had fresh hope. I wonder this Christmas season: *Will you allow God to start you down a new path, His pathway for your life?*

So then, a group of wise and patient men, who sat on the same hills their grandfathers had sat upon, were watching the stars and talking that night—and then God came down to earth. Wow!

WEDNESDAY: The Wise Humbly Seek the King

*"Seek the Lord your God, and you will find Him if you **seek Him with all your heart** and with all your soul."*

—Deuteronomy 4:29

The shepherds remind us of how God comes to mankind. God is the seeker; He is the initiator; and He responds to those who humble themselves before Him. Humbly, and wisely, the shepherds responded, willing to listen and obey, proving once more that God can use the most distant, defiled, and outcast. For *"God has chosen . . . the base things of the world and the things which are despised . . . that no flesh should glory in His presence. . . . As it is written, 'He who glories, let him glory in the LORD'"* (see 1 Corinthians 1:27–31).

The shepherds humbly came to God—just as they were. Instead of backing away with the excuse of lack of education, lack of clothing, or lack of standing, they welcomed God's message in wonder, in fear, in uncertainty, and in hope. There was no time to become someone else; God called them just as they were (Luke 2:8).

The shepherds humbly responded to God at once. When God spoke, they listened! They received the message and acted upon it immediately (Luke 2:15a). They did not doubt; they did not disagree; they did not question; and they did not hesitate. They just heard and responded, so they were thus the first to see Jesus. The shepherds had little knowledge, but great faith. Since Jesus would soon be moved by His parents, had they hesitated they would have missed Him. But their simple faith was richly rewarded. The journey that began in faith would end in joy!

The shepherds went against the tide of the crowd. In their day and time, they were not welcomed by others. They often heard, "Stay where you came from! Go away! We don't like you! You smell!" They were outcasts, and were unwelcome in public. Yet, they ignored public opinion and earnestly sought for Jesus: "They came with haste and found Mary and Joseph, and the Babe lying in a manger" (Luke 2:16). They kept searching and never gave up, and when they found Him, they believed in Jesus.

The shepherds humbly told everyone the Good News. "They made widely known the saying which was told them concerning this Child. . . . Then the shepherds returned, glorifying and praising God for all the things that they had heard and seen, as it was told them" (Luke 2:17–20). Just like the rest of the New Testament would record, these shepherds went back to their old jobs—but *as new men.* If anyone is in Christ Jesus, he or she is a new creation; old things pass away, and all things become new (2 Corinthians 5:17)!

So how can we, like the shepherds, see Christ this Christmas season? By humbling ourselves just as they did!

The greatest plague on earth—pride. Most people have missed grasping the significance of the First Coming of Christ because of pride. Wanting our own way instead of God's is how He described our pitiful condition as lost ones: "All we like sheep have gone astray; We have turned, every one, to his own way; And the LORD has laid on Him the iniquity of us all" (Isaiah 53:6).

Just as humility is the root of all virtue, so pride is the root of all sin. John MacArthur comments, "Pride is the sin of competing with God, and humility is the virtue of submitting to His supreme glory. We all tend to exaggerate our own good qualities and minimize the good qualities of others. Humility takes off our rose-colored glasses and allows us to see ourselves as we really are."[3]

Pride is the ultimate sin. Pride is the supreme temptation from Satan, because pride is at the heart of his own evil nature. It was pride that caused Lucifer to challenge God and be cast out of heaven and ultimately into the Lake of Fire. Our only protection against pride, and our only source of humility, is a proper view of God.

James 4:6 tells us that "God resists the proud, But gives grace to the humble." In verses 7–10, He then gives us the pathway to genuine humility: "Submit to God. Resist the devil and he will flee from you. Draw near to God and He will draw near to you. Cleanse your hands . . . and purify your hearts."

Humble yourself in the sight of God. Pride comes in many forms. We may be tempted to be proud of our abilities, possessions, education, social status, appearance, power, and even our biblical knowledge or religious accomplishments. All conflicts and troubles are rooted in pride. The source of every gossip, hurt feeling, church division, and departed "sheep" is pride. At the heart of every fight is pride. But throughout Scripture the Lord calls His people to humility. God therefore says, "Let another praise you, and not your own mouth; a stranger, and not your own lips" (Proverbs 27:2; see also Proverbs 15:33; 22:4).

Humility begins with proper self-awareness—"the virtue," said Bernard of Clairvaux, "by which a man becomes conscious of his own unworthiness." It begins with an honest, unadorned, un-retouched view of oneself.

Humility produces spiritual blessing. Just as every sin starts in pride, every virtue begins in humility. And just as pride is behind every conflict we have with other people and every problem of fellowship we have with the Lord, so humility is behind every harmonious human relationship, every spiritual success, and every moment of joyous fellowship with the Lord. Humility allows us to see ourselves as we are, because it shows us before God as He is.

What we all need today is to cultivate godly humility: "As the elect of God, holy and beloved, **put on** tender mercies, kindness, humility, meekness, longsuffering" (Colossians 3:12; see also 1 Peter 5:5).

What are you wearing today? The righteous garment of humility—or the filthy rags of the proud?

THURSDAY: The Wise Humbly Serve the King

*"And Samuel answered, 'Speak, for **Your servant hears**.'"*
—1 Samuel 3:10b

Have you decided to be among those who are seeking the King this Christmas season? You can if you will come humbly like the shepherds. The shepherds were truly wise men! They represent the best of all God's Word about the rewards that come to those who seek and find the Lord. Will you experience the glad tidings of the gospel? Will you experience great joy? You can if you humbly choose to follow the pathway they followed!

Decide to listen to God when He speaks. Like the shepherds, tune your heart to listen and look for God while you are at work, at school, or at home. Remember that the eyes of the Lord are looking down for someone looking up and seeking God: "For the eyes of the LORD run to and fro throughout the whole earth, to show Himself strong on behalf of those whose heart is loyal to Him" (2 Chronicles 16:9a).

Decide to come to God just as you are. Recognize the doctrinal Truth of the third stanza of this classic song: Just as I am, Thou wilt receive, Wilt welcome, pardon, cleanse, relieve; Because Thy promise I believe, O Lamb of God, I come, I come! Ask Him to change you, melt you, mold you, fill you, and use you! Tell Him, "O Lamb of God I come just as I am—for you to fix." There is no time, no reason, and no ability to become someone else; God calls you just as you are so He Himself can make you anew!

Decide to seek Jesus until you find Him—don't delay. Just as the shepherds would have missed that precious moment if they had waited, so the Lord says, "While you hear My voice—don't wait!" So respond to Him: "O God, You are my God; Early will I seek You; My soul thirsts for You; My flesh longs for You!" (Psalm 63:1). Seek Him with your whole heart while He may still be found!

Like Peter, Andrew, James, and John, drop your net and follow Him. Like Peter say, "I have left all behind to follow You!" Like Paul, say, "I count everything else as trash so I can have You." Like David, say, "One thing have I desired above all others, and that is *You*, O Lord."

Jesus tells us that the gate is narrow, and the road is hard. We must press into His Kingdom. We must draw near to Him. We can't serve two masters—only One. As Joshua declared: "Choose . . . this day whom you will serve . . . But as for me and my house, we will serve the LORD!" (Joshua 24:15). For as Paul confessed, "for me, life is Christ—and death is only better because I am with Him" (Philippians 1:21).

Decide to tell everyone the Good News. Be like those at Christ's resurrection and at Pentecost—they couldn't stop telling the great news. They went everywhere and told everyone what He had done in their lives. In His power, you can do the same in our generation: "Go, stand in the temple and speak to the people all the words of this life" (Acts 5:20).

As this year is fast coming to an end, will you be among the wise who still seek the King? Will you serve Him like the humble but wise shepherds? Will you experience and share the glad tidings of the gospel with others? Will you experience great joy?

FRIDAY: The Wise Still Seek the King!

> "He . . . is the blessed and only Potentate, **the King of kings and Lord of lords**, who alone has immortality, dwelling in unapproachable light, . . . to whom be honor and everlasting power. Amen."
>
> —1 TIMOTHY 6:15–16

The First Coming of Christ is all about a holy God, Jesus, coming into the world to die for sinners. Holman Hunt, a famous artist, painted what has been called "Jesus at the Door of the Carpenter's

WEEK 52: WISE MEN STILL SEEK THE KING!

Shop in Nazareth." In that painting, Jesus is depicted as a boy. Coming out of His dad's shop He is shown as going to the door to stretch.

His limbs . . . had grown cramped over the bench. He stands there in the doorway with arms outstretched, and behind him, on the wall, the setting sun throws His shadow, and it is the shadow of a cross. In the background stands Mary; as she sees that shadow there is the fear of coming tragedy in her eyes. Jesus came into the world to live for men, and, in the end, to die for men. He came to give for men his life and his death. Gold for a king, frankincense for a priest, myrrh for the One who was to die—these were the gifts of the wise men, and, even at the cradle of Christ, they foretold that He was to be *the true King, the perfect High Priest,* and in the end *the only Savior of mankind.*[4]

As we rejoice these days in the First Coming of Christ, may we not be neglectful of rejoicing in the anticipation of His Second Coming as well. For this true King, this perfect High Priest, the only Savior of mankind, will return soon to take us home—and so shall we forever be with the Lord!

But if you are only *acquainted* with Him, and do not yet really *know* Him, you need to be mindful that the days of promised terror loom on the horizon. Christ's description of these days includes people dying of heart failure because they witness such inescapable horrors. Thus, now is the time for the wise to seek the King—to flee to the safest spot in the universe—Jesus Christ!

Are you wisely learning to seek and find Him with all your heart? Are you learning to worship Him in the power of the Spirit and in the truth of His Word?

Make a choice to live in hope. Martin Luther, who experienced more intense and ongoing trials than most of us will ever experience, chose to live, come what may, in the enduring hope of our eternal Refuge, Jesus Christ. Luther's life testimony ended up impacting the world to this very day.

From what Luther said about the power of music, I believe that God ministered comfort and strength to his tried soul through music as well, for he said: "I am strongly persuaded that after theology there is no art than can be placed on a level with music; for besides theology, music is the only art capable of affording peace and joy of the heart . . . the devil flees before the sound of music almost as much as before the Word of God."[5]

As these end times become increasingly more difficult and painful, remember Luther's testimony. Like Luther, choose to live in enduring hope through basking in both the power of God's Word and biblically-based music that exalts the King of Kings and Lord of Lords as you eagerly look forward to Christ's soon return!

May you be strengthened, comforted, and encouraged by these excerpts of devotional comments by John MacArthur on Horatio Spafford's lyrics to the timeless song, "It Is Well With My Soul." I believe they embody what it means to possess living hope for the end of days.

The . . . songwriter's focus was on an objective spiritual reality that anchored him at all times—whether he was experiencing "peace, like a river" or whether billowing sorrow overwhelmed him [as when his four daughters drowned at sea]. In the midst of both emotional extremes, his heart and mind returned to the truth that kept him spiritually anchored—the promise that his soul was eternally safe from God's judgment. . . .

Spafford's hope was in Christ, who 'shed his own blood' on the believer's behalf. So when Spafford tasted the anguish of human sorrow, his mind turned to the infinite suffering that Christ had already borne on his behalf. That is why in circumstances when most men's minds would have been consumed with self-pity and bitter emotions, Spafford wrote a gospel song of gratitude for Christ's vicarious atonement.

This song is a potent reminder of how every Christian should respond to the vicissitudes of life—particularly life's heartaches. Whatever the source of our sorrows ("Though Satan should buffet, though trials should come"), we can find a powerful comfort in knowing that Christ literally shed His own precious lifeblood for us [see Romans 8:31–32]. . . .

Although Spafford's earthly sorrows were an excruciating burden for him, he knew those sorrows were temporary. And that temporal burden served as a poignant reminder that an even greater, eternal burden had been lifted from him by Christ, who took the full guilt of sin and carried that guilt to the cross. Thereby paying the full penalty for our sins, He canceled forever every claim that the law of God had against us. It was as if He took all the divine ordinances that demanded our condemnation and nailed them to the cross (Colossians 2:14). "O the bliss of this glorious thought!"

The closing verse looks forward to the day when the Lord will consummate our redemption. Even our bodies will be redeemed, and everything good we have hoped for will be realized ("the faith shall be sight"—cf. Romans 8:22–25). In the meantime—and even while we're suffering unspeakable earthly grief—true believers in Christ can find sufficient comfort in knowing that all is eternally well with their souls.[6]

It Is Well With My Soul

When peace, like a river, attendeth my way,
When sorrows like sea billows roll;
Whatever my lot, Thou hast taught me to say,
It is well, it is well with my soul.

Though Satan should buffet, though trials should come,
Let this blest assurance control,
That Christ has regarded my helpless estate,
And has shed his own blood for my soul.

My sin—oh, the bliss of this glorious thought;
My sin not in part, but the whole
Is nailed to the cross and I bear it no more,
Praise the Lord, praise the Lord, O my soul!

And Lord, haste the day when the faith shall be sight,
The clouds be rolled back as a scroll,
The trump shall resound and the Lord shall descend,
"Even so," it is well with my soul.

—Horatio G. Spafford (1828–1888)

SATURDAY: Come, Lord Jesus!

"Let us run with endurance the race that is set before us, looking unto Jesus, the author and finisher of our faith."
—Hebrews 12:1b-2a

To us who love and serve God, the goal of the Book of Revelation was to show His Son, Jesus Christ. I hope that is what you have seen in this year long devotional contemplation of the Revelation of Jesus Christ.

God the Father gave the Revelation of Jesus Christ—which shows Jesus in all His beauty—to be shared with us, His servants. In its pages God reveals that we shall forever be satisfied as we behold Him whom we love.

- Christ is **the key** to Living Hope.
- His Word is **the food** for Living Hope.
- His Spirit is **the power** for Living Hope.
- His presence is **the guard** for Living Hope.

Living hope comes down to you through Christ—who has done it all—so believe what He has said and receive His hope!

When we get to the end of everything--what is left? In other words, what will last forever? Revelation 22 ends with God, Heaven and one more element—***servants serving God***.

Who are those surrounding God's Throne?

*And there shall be no more curse, but the throne of God and of the Lamb shall be in it, and **His servants shall serve Him**.*
—Revelation 22:3

*Then he said to me, "These words are faithful and true." And the Lord God of the holy prophets sent His angel to **show His servants** the things which must shortly take place. . . . Then he said to me, "See that you do not do that. For I am **your fellow servant**, and of your brethren the prophets, and of those who keep the words of this book. Worship God."*
—Revelation 22:6, 9,

All who love and serve God long to hear Christ say, "Well done, My good and faithful servant, enter into the joy of your Master's home!" A "Well done!" from Him will make this life on earth all worthwhile!

Through this book, *Living Hope for the End of Days*, we have had fifty-two weeks to learn how to live in hope, strength, joy, purpose, and peace! As you read through this entire book, you discovered the precious topics contained in Revelation, each of them rich in hope. And, as you read every word of God's final book of the Bible, you reaped a harvest of promised blessings!

Hope for the end of days.

    Strength for when we are weak with fear.

        Joy when surrounded by dread.

            Purpose in the midst of an aimless culture.

                Peace when storms of anxiety roll across our horizons.

So how do we have this Living Hope for the End of Days? Only in Christ! Jesus offers to each of us to be our Living Hope when we are unclean, when we are weary, when we are homeless, when we are helpless, when we are hopeless, and when we are tempted.

Christ is the closest, safest, and only Living Hope for us through all of life—to the very end!

Have you fled to the safest spot in the universe, the open arms of Jesus? If not, do so today. If you have, look around—Christ wants to be your moment by moment Living Hope for the End of Days!

" *'Surely I am coming quickly,' Amen. Even so,* **come, Lord Jesus!** *The grace of our Lord Jesus Christ be with you all. Amen*"

—Revelation 22:20–21

ENDNOTES

Week 1
1 William Temple, *Readings in St. John's Gospel, First Series* (London: Macmillan and Company, 1940), 68.
2 Richard Foster, *Celebration of Discipline* (San Francisco: Harper Books, 1998), 170.

Week 2
1 Adapted from James Montgomery Boice, *John: Those Who Received Him, John 9–12* (Grand Rapids: Baker Books, 1999), 3:785ff.
2 Ravi Zacharias, *A Shattered Visage: The Real Face of Atheism* (Grand Rapids: Baker Books, 1990), 167.
3 Adapted from John Phillips, *100 New Testament Sermon Outlines* (Grand Rapids: Kregel, 2002), 100.
4 John Phillips, *100 Sermon Outlines from the New Testament* (Chicago: Moody Press, 1997), 100.
5 Erwin Lutzer, *One Minute After You Die* (Chicago: Moody Press, 1997), 143.

Week 3
1 J. Barton Payne, *Encyclopedia of Biblical Prophecy* (Grand Rapids: Baker Books, 1980), 631–75.
2 Sherrie Gossett, "Paying for Drinks with a Wave of the Hand," *WorldNetDaily*, April 14, 2004, http://www.wnd.com/index.php?pageId=24179.3

Week 4
1 Jack Kinsella, "The Explosion of Knowledge," *Omega Letter Intelligence Digest* 14, no. 1 (2002), http://www.omegaletter.com.
2 Jack Kinsella, "Confessions of a Techno-Junkie," *Omega Letter Intelligence Digest* 20, no. 23 (2003), http://www.omegaletter.com.

Week 5
1 Matthew Henry, *Matthew Henry's Commentary on the Bible* (Peabody, MA: Hendrickson Publishers, 1997), in loc.
2 *IVP Bible Background Commentary: New Testament* (Downers Grove, IL: InterVarsity Press, 1994), in loc.
3 Francis Schaeffer, *The Complete Works of Francis Schaeffer, Hebrews 7* (Westchester, IL: Crossway Books, 1985), in loc.
4 Harry A. Ironside, "The Way of Peace" (Garland, TX: American Tract Society, 1940).

Week 6
1 Warren W. Wiersbe, *The Bible Exposition Commentary: Leviticus* (Wheaton, IL: Victor Books, 1997), in loc.
2 Charles Swindoll, *Shedding the Light on Our Darker Side* (Fullerton, CA: IFL, 1998), 100–01.
3 J. I. Packer, *Knowing God* (Downers Grove, IL: InterVarsity Press, 1973), 162–64, 170.
4 Robert Coleman, *Master Plan of Discipleship* (Grand Rapids: Revell, 1987), 160–76.

Week 7
1 D. Martyn Lloyd-Jones, *Spiritual Depression: Its Causes and Cures* (Grand Rapids: Eerdmans, 1965).
2 James Montgomery Boice, *Psalms: An Expositional Commentary* (Grand Rapids: Baker Books, 1998), 1:1–6.
3 J. J. Steward Perowne, *Commentary on the Psalms* (Grand Rapids: Kregel, 1989), 1:181.
4 Lloyd-Jones, 14.
5 Boice, 109.
6 Boice, 110.
7 Lloyd-Jones, 19.
8 Boice, 111.

Week 8
1 "Lasers," *National Geographic*, March, 1984, 335–363. Emphasis added.
2 Kent Hughes, *Disciplines of a Godly Man* (Wheaton, IL: Crossway Books, 1991), 121.

Week 9
1 *Our Amazing World of Nature* (Pleasantville, NY: Reader's Digest Books, 1969), 229–31.
2 *National Geographic*, July, 1993, 83–103.
3 *National Geographic*, June, 1950, 809–28.

Week 10
1 *Our Amazing World of Nature* (Pleasantville, NY: Reader's Digest Books, 1969), 261–63.
2 Catherine Marshall, *A Man Called Peter: The Story of Peter Marshall* (New York: McGraw-Hill, 1951), 310–19. Emphasis added.
3 See Preserved Smith, *Luther's Table Talk* (New York: Ames Press, 1907) for a critical study of the table talks.
4 Dwight L. Carlson, "Exposing the Myth that Christians Should Not Have Emotional Problems," *Christianity Today*, February 9, 1998.

Week 11
1 Lee Siegel, "A Major Flare Shot Off the Sun Friday July 14, Pummeling Earth with the Biggest Solar-R Radiation Storm in Almost Six Years," *Space.com*, July 14, 2000, accessed online at http://www.space.com/scienceastronomy/solarsystem/solar_storm_000713.html.
2 John MacArthur Jr., *The MacArthur Study Bible* (Nashville: Thomas Nelson, 1997), at Joshua 1:2.

Week 12
1 Robert Boyd Munger, *My Heart—Christ's Home* (Downers Grove, IL: InterVarsity Press, 1986).

Week 13
1 *San Diego Tribune*, November 5, 1993. Emphasis added.
2 Drawn from J. A. Seiss, *The Apocalypse: Lectures on the Book of Revelation* (Grand Rapids: Zondervan, 1983).

Week 14
1 John MacArthur Jr., *The MacArthur Study Bible* (Nashville: Thomas Nelson, 1997), 1994.

Week 15
1 John MacArthur Jr., *The Church in Prophetic Perspective: Bible Study on Revelation 2-3* (Panorama City, CA: Word of Grace, 1985).
2 William Barclay, *The Revelation of John* (Philadelphia: Westminster Press, 1976), 1:76-77.

Week 16
1 C. H. Spurgeon, "Samson Conquered" (1858), http://www.ccel.org/ccel/spurgeon/sermons04.lx.html.
2. Lawrence O. Richards, *The Teacher's Commentary* (Wheaton: Victor Books, 1987).

Week 17
1 John F. MacArthur, *The MacArthur New Testament Commentary* (Chicago: Moody Press, 1983).

Week 18
1 Drawn from Warren W. Wiersbe, *The Bible Exposition Commentary* (Wheaton: Victor Books, 1997).
2 John Phillips, *Exploring Revelation* (Chicago: Moody Press, 1974), electronic edition, in loc.

Week 19
1 James Strong, *The New Strong's Expanded Exhaustive Concordance of the Bible* (Nashville: Thomas Nelson Publishers, 2001), words 227 and 228.

Week 21
1 Robert Boyd Munger, *My Heart—Christ's Home* (Downers Grove, IL: InterVarsity Press, 1986).
2 William Temple, *Readings in St. John's Gospel, First Series*. (London: Macmillan and Company, 1940), 68.
3 R. Kent Hughes, *Acts: The Church Afire* (Wheaton: Crossway Books, 1996), 50.
4 Adam Clarke, *Clarke's Commentary: John* (Albany, OR: Ages Software, 1999), electronic edition, in loc.
5 John MacArthur Jr., *The Ultimate Priority* (Chicago: Moody Press, 1998), electronic edition, in loc.

Week 22
1 For further reading, see *Wilmington's Visualized Study Bible* (Wheaton: Tyndale House, 1984); J. Sidlow Baxter, *Baxter's Explore the Book* (Grand Rapids: Zondervan, 1987); W. Graham Scroggi, *The Unfolding Drama of Redemption* (Grand Rapids: Kregel, 1995); W. A. Criswell, ed., *The Criswell Study Bible* (Nashville: Thomas Nelson Publishers, 1979); A. M. Hodgkin, *Christ in All the Scriptures* (London: Pickering & Inglis, 1943); C. H. Mackintosh, "Notes on the Pentateuch," *Genesis to Deuteronomy* (Neptune, NJ: Loizeaux Brothers, 1989); John MacArthur, *Ashamed of the Gospel* (Wheaton: Crossway Books, 2001), 76-77; J. Oswald Sanders, *Spiritual Discipleship* (Chicago: Moody Publishers, 2007), 129-36.

Week 23
1 For further reading, see Week 22, endnote 1.
2 A. M. Hodgkin, *Christ in All the Scriptures* (London: Pickering & Inglis, 1943), 17-41.
3 James Montgomery Boice, *The Minor Prophets: An Expositional Commentary* (Grand Rapids: Zondervan, 1986), 2:201.
4 I am indebted for this comparison to a small tract written years ago by Joseph Hoffman Cohn for the American Board of Missions to the Jews entitled "The Man from Petra," No. 65 in the series, "What Every Christian Should Know About the Jews" (1961).
5 Drawn from Frank E. Gaebelein, *Four Minor Prophets: Obadiah, Jonah, Habakkuk, and Haggai* (Chicago: Moody Press, 1970), 78.
6 John MacArthur Jr., *The MacArthur Study Bible* (Nashville: Thomas Nelson, 1997), 1304.
7 MacArthur, 968.
8 Warren W. Wiersbe, *The Bible Exposition Commentary* (Wheaton: Victor Books, 1989), electronic edition, in loc.

Week 24
1 For further reading, see Week 22, footnote 1.
2 James Montgomery Boice, *The Minor Prophets: An Expositional Commentary* (Grand Rapids: Zondervan, 1986), 2:59.
3 Boice, 2:59.
4 J. Sidlow Baxter, *Baxter's Explore the Book* (Grand Rapids: Zondervan, 1960), 204.
5 Warren W. Wiersbe, *The Bible Exposition Commentary* (Wheaton: Victor Books, 1989), electronic edition, in loc.

Week 26
1 Drawn from W. A. Criswell, *Expository Sermons on Revelation* (Grand Rapids: Zondervan, 1966), 190.
2 Michael Spector, "Nature's Bioterrorist," *New Yorker*, February 28, 2005, 50. Emphasis added.

3 Drawn from Jack Kinsella, "Plain Text, the Beasts of the Earth," *The Omega Letter Intelligence Digest* 40, no. 25 (January 25, 2005), http://www.omegaletter.com.
4 Jack Kinsella, "Like a Vapour," *The Omega Letter Intelligence Digest* 6, no. 21 (February 21, 2003), http://www.omegaletter.com.
5 Gail Cameron Westcott, "In Search of Heaven," *Reader's Digest*, December 2005, 64.

Week 27

1 William Barclay, *The Revelation of John: Chapters 6–22* (Louisville, KY: Westminster John Knox Press, 2004), 117.

Week 28

1 Paal Brekke, quoted in Robert Roy Britt, "Sun on Fire, Releases 3 More Major Flares," *Space.com*, November 3, 2003, http://www.space.com/scienceastronomy/solar_flares_031103.html.
2 Hal Lindsey, "Doomsday 2029?" *WorldNet Daily*, April 15, 2005, http://www.wnd.com/index.php?pageId=29851.
3 Guy Gugliotta, "Asteroid Identified as a Threatening Object," *San Francisco Chronicle*, April 17, 2005, http://www.sfgate.com/cgi-bin/article.cgi?f=/c/a/2005/04/17/MNGONC93DQ1.DTL.
4 James Strong, *The New Strong's Expanded Exhaustive Concordance of the Bible* (Nashville: Thomas Nelson Publishers, 2001), #6960.
5 Hal Lindsey, *The Terminal Generation* (Old Tappan, NJ: Fleming H. Revell Company, 1976), 92–93.
6 Strong, #3176.
7 Robert Baker Girdlestone, *Synonyms of the Old Testament* (Grand Rapids: Eerdmans, 1948), 104.
8 Lindsey, *Terminal Generation*, 92–93.
9 Strong, #982.
10 Lindsey, *Terminal Generation*, 95.
11 Strong, #2620.
12 F. Brown, et al., *A Hebrew and English Lexicon of the Old Testament* (London: Oxford Press, 1907), 875.
13 Lindsey, *Terminal Generation*, 97–98.

Week 29

1 John J. Davis, *Moses and the Gods of Egypt: Studies in Exodus* (Grand Rapids: Baker Book House, 1986), 128–30.

Week 30

1 Kent Hughes, *Disciplines of a Godly Man* (Wheaton: Crossway Books, 1991), 76–77.
2 Hughes, 76–77.
3 W. Graham Scroggie, *Method in Prayer* (London: Pickering, 1955), 17–18.

Week 31

1 Drawn from Robert Alexander, *The Coming Prince* (Grand Rapids: Kregel Classics, 1957). Alexander's original work on these astonishing figures first appeared in 1894.
2 Chuck Missler, "Daniel's 70 Weeks," Koinonia House Online, November, 2004, http://www.khouse.org/articles/2004/552/.
3 Drawn from John F. Walvoord and Roy B. Zuck, *The Bible Knowledge Commentary* (Wheaton: Scripture Press, 1985), in loc.

Week 33

1 John Phillips, *Exploring the Future: A Comprehensive Guide to Bible Prophecy* (Neptune, NJ: Loizeaux Brothers, 1992), 227–28.
2 Rick Warren, *The Purpose Driven Church: Growth Without Compromising Your Message and Mission* (Grand Rapids: Zondervan, 1995), 357.
3 Ravi Zacharias, *Can Man Live Without God?* (Dallas: Word, 1994), 23.
4 Drawn from Phillips, 227–28.
5 Quoted in Merrill F. Unger, *Biblical Demonology* (Grand Rapids: Kregel, 1994), 197–98.
6 John Phillips, *100 New Testament Sermon Outlines* (Grand Rapids: Kregel, 2002), 100.

Week 34

1 Ray C. Stedman, *God's Final Word: Understanding Revelation* (Grand Rapids: Discovery House Publishers, 1991), in loc.
2 Drawn from Stedman, 264.
3 Norman Grubb, *With C. T. Studd in Congo Forests* (Grand Rapids: Zondervan, 1954), 216–17.
4 Stedman, 266.

Week 35

1 Bob Moorehead, "The Paradox of Our Age," *Words Aptly Spoken* (Kirkland, WA: Overlake Christian Bookstore, 1995).
2 William Barclay, *Daily Study Bible Series: The Letters of James and Peter* (Louisville, KY: Westminster John Knox Press, 2000), in loc.
3 Alfred Edersheim, *Sketches of Jewish Social Life* (Montville, NJ: Hendrickson Publishers, 1994), electronic edition, chapter 17.

Week 36

1 William Barclay, *The Revelation of John: Chapters 6–22* (Louisville, KY: Westminster John Knox Press, 2004), 151–52.
2 More information can be accessed online at http://www.hku.hk/civil/envhydraulics/home.htm.
3 John Phillips, *Exploring Revelation* (Chicago: Moody Press, 1974), 202.

4 Ray Stedman, *God's Final Word* (Grand Rapids: Discovery House, 1991), 280.
5 Drawn from Herman Hoyt, *The End Times* (Chicago: Moody Press, 1969), 163.

Week 37

1 Paul Kreeft, *Ecumenical Jihad* (San Francisco: Ignatius Press, 1996), 100.
2 Kreeft, 100. Emphasis added.
3 Dave Hunt, *A Woman Rides the Beast* (Eugene, OR: Harvest House, 1994); Ray Stedman believes this chapter gives ten clues about the identity of the woman, see *God's Final Word* (Grand Rapids: Discovery House, 1991), 287–97.
4 Peter Gould, "Pope Lights Beacon of Hope," *BBC News*, January 24, 2002, http://www.news.bbc.co.uk/1/hi/world/europe/1780792.stm.
5 Harold Wilmington, *Wilmington's Guide to the Bible* (Chicago: Tyndale House, 1981), 536.

Week 38

1 Randy Alcorn, *Money, Possessions, and Eternity* (Wheaton: Tyndale, 1989), 55.
2 William Barclay, *Revelation* (Louisville, KY: Westminster John Knox Press, 2000), 2:157.
3 Farrar, *Better Homes and Jungles* (Portland, OR: Multnomah, 1977), 189–90.

Week 39

1 Randy Alcorn, *Money, Possessions, and Eternity* (Wheaton: Tyndale, 1989), 185–86.

Week 40

1 A. W. Tozer, *The Root of the Righteous*, vol. 2 of *The Best of A. W. Tozer*, ed. Warren W. Wiersbe (Grand Rapids: Baker Book House Company, 1980).
2 J. Oswald Sanders, *Enjoying Intimacy with God* (Chicago: Moody Press, 1980), 151–158.
3 R. T. Kendall, *Tithing* (Grand Rapids: Zondervan, 1982), 103.

Week 41

1 Richard A. Swenson, *The Overload Syndrome* (Colorado Springs: NavPress, 1998), 97–98.
2 Paul E. Billheimer, *Destined for the Throne: A New Look at the Bride of Christ* (Fort Washington, PA: Christian Literature Crusade, 1975), 53.
3 This section on the symptoms of overload was adapted and quotations were taken from Richard A. Swenson, 83–87.
4 J. Grant Howard, *Balancing Life's Demands* (Portland, OR: Multnomah, 1983), 144.
5 Alvin Toffler, *Future Shock* (New York: Bantam, 1984), 269.

6 John Bertram Phillips, *The New Testament in Modern English* (London: G. Bles, 1958), at Matthew 5:1–8.
7 Warren W. Wiersbe, *The Bible Exposition Commentary* (Wheaton: Victor books, 1997), in loc.
8 Robert Kanigel, "Too Much of a Good Thing?" *Washington Post*, January 12, 1998, 25.
9 Swenson, 126–133.
10 John MacArthur Jr., *The MacArthur Study Bible* (Nashville: Thomas Nelson, 1997), 939.
11 Andrew Murray, *Absolute Surrender* (Chicago: Moody Press, 1897), 24.
12 V. Raymond Edman, *The Disciplines of Life* (Wheaton: Scripture Press, 1948), 83.
13 The following pamphlets are available from Chapel of the Air: #7245, *Getting Ready for Sunday* by David and Karen Mains; #7451, *Rules for the Sunday Search* by David R. Mains; #7462, T*he Sunday Search: A Guide to Better Church Experiences* by Steve Bell.
14 R. Kent Hughes, *Disciplines of a Godly Man* (Wheaton: Crossway Books, 1991), 109–15.
15 Charles Swindoll, *Intimacy with the Almighty* (Dallas: Word Publishing, 1996), 28.
16 Annie Dillard, *Teaching a Stone to Talk* (New York: Harper & Row, 1982), 40–41.
17 R. Kent Hughes, *Disciplines of Grace* (Wheaton: Crossway Books, 1993), 82–84.
18 Quoted in Steve Farrar, *Better Homes and Jungles* (Portland, OR: Multnomah, 1977), 189–90.

Week 42

1 Adapted from John MacArthur Jr., *MacArthur New Testament Commentary* (Chicago: Moody Press, 1983), at Matthew 22.

Week 43

1 F. B. Meyer, *Exodus* (Grand Rapids: Kregel, 1978), 133.

Week 44

1 These are the headlines of Revelation 20 through the eyes of noted Bible teacher John Phillips, *Exploring Revelation* (Grand Rapids: Kregel Publishing, 2005), 251.
2 Erich Sauer, *The Triumph of the Crucified* (Grand Rapids: Eerdmans, 1966), 154–65.

Week 45

1 How many people are we talking about? Some have calculated that there have been up to 40 billion souls who have lived on earth. In a one-hour judgment per person, 40+ billion people would take over 5 million years! After the Flood until Christ's day, Noah and his family (eight people) produced a population of just over 100 million people. From the time of Christ to George Washington's

ENDNOTES | 523

death (1,800 years later) the population rose to 1 billion; by 1930, which was 130 years later, we arrived at 2 billion; 45 years after that (1975) we doubled to 4 billion. Today (2006) we have over 6 ½ billion souls. At the present rate of growth, in less than 25 years we will be at 10 billion. (According to an article in *Time*, Jan. 2, 1989, 26, 48). This growth is despite 4,000 children dying of starvation daily, plus 1,000 each day lost in various wars, plus the death factor of all who die of natural causes each day.

2 During the next two days, the text has been adapted, paraphrased, and quoted from John Thomas, "That Hideous Doctrine," *Moody Magazine*, September 1985.

3 Thomas.

Week 46

1 Dave Hunt, *How Close Are We?* (Eugene, OR: Harvest House, 1993), 320.

2 Ray Vander Laan, *That The World May Know: Set 4, Leaders Guide for Faith, Lessons 19–27* (Colorado Springs: Focus on the Family, 1997), 2.

3 The following is adapted, drawn, and quoted from Leland Ryken et al., *Dictionary of Biblical Imagery* (Downers Grove, IL: InterVarsity Press, 2000).

4 John Piper, *The Dangerous Duty of Delight: The Glorified God and the Satisfied Soul* (Sisters, OR: Multnomah Publishers, 2001), 21.

5 Erwin W. Lutzer, *One Minute After You Die* (Chicago: Moody Press, 1997), 46.

6 Ray C. Stedman, "The Cure for Troubled Hearts," *Secrets of the Spirit* (1973), http://www.pbc.org/dp/stedman/secrets/3123.html.

7 Lutzer, 62.

8 Lutzer, 67.

9 Lutzer, adapted slightly from 62–67.

10 Quoted in C. T. Quintard, *Balm for the Weary and Wounded* (Columbia: Evans & Cogswell, 1864), 35–37.

11 "Heaven," in *Poems That Live Forever*, ed. Hazel Felleman (New York: Doubleday, 1965), 331. A version of this poem has also appeared under the title "The Homeland," attributed to Myrtle Erickson in *Knight's Master Book of New Illustrations*, ed. Walter B. Knight (Grand Rapids: Eerdmans, 1987). 279.

Week 47

1 Adapted from Jan David Hettinga, *Follow Me* (Colorado Springs: NavPress, 1996), 83, 189, 190–194.

2 Charles Swindoll, *Intimacy with the Almighty* (Dallas: Word Publishing, 1996), 66–71.

3 Ibid, 28. ??

Week 48

1 W. Graham Scroggie, *Know Your Bible* (Old Tappan, NJ: Fleming H. Revell Company, 1965), 362–75.

2 On the second of the six days during which God created the universe, He created the heavens (Gen. 1:6–8),

and on the third day He created the earth (Gen. 1:9–10). The divine commentary on all that God created is this: "And God saw everything that He made, and, behold, it was very good" (Gen. 1:31). But soon Adam and Eve disobeyed God, and because of that disobedience, a curse was placed on man and that domain of heaven, earth, and the sea over which he was authorized to reign (Gen. 1:28). The heaven and earth which were created "very good" now became very bad.

3 Adapted from Erwin W. Lutzer, *How You Can Be Sure That You Will Spend Eternity With God* (Chicago: Moody Press, 1996), 112–21.

4 This list was adapted from Erwin W. Lutzer, *Your Eternal Reward* (Chicago: Moody Press, 1998), 87–100.

5 Ibid., 100. ??

6 G. Campbell Morgan, *The Gospel According to Matthew* (New York: Revell, 1929), 64–65.

Week 49

1 Adapted from Warren W. Wiersbe, *The Bible Exposition Commentary* (Wheaton: Victor Books, 1997), Revelation 22.

2 Henry M. Morris, *The Revelation Record* (Wheaton: Tyndale House, 1983), electronic edition, in loc.

3 Wiersbe, emphasis added.

4 John MacArthur. *The MacArthur New Testament Commentary* (Chicago: Moody Press, 1983), electronic edition, in loc.

Week 52

1 A. Gibbs, *Worship* (Kansas City, MO: Walterick Publishing, 1950), 45.

2 William Temple, *Readings in St. John's Gospel, First Series* (London: Macmillan and Company, 1940), 68.

3 John F. MacArthur, *The MacArthur New Testament Commentary, Ephesians 4* (Chicago: Moody Press, 1983), electronic edition, in loc.

4 Paraphrased and quoted from William Barclay, *Daily Study Bible Series: The Gospel of Matthew*, rev. ed. (Louisville: Westminster Press; 2000, 1975), electronic edition, in loc. Emphasis added.

5 Quoted in *Hymns for the Family of God* (Nashville: Paragon Associates, 1976).

6 Quoted in Joni Eareckson Tada, et al., *O Worship the King* (Wheaton: Crossway, 2000), 27–29.

Discover the Book
Everyday
at DTBM.ORG

You are invited to visit the online home of Discover The Book Ministries. Learn more about Dr. John Barnett and the global mission of DTBM. Immerse yourself in a wealth of Biblical studies, ministry resources and practical daily direction for real life. From podcasts to videos, hundreds of Dr. Barnett's best sermons and teachings are offered in a variety of formats—one to fit every need.

- Radio Broadcasts
- Podcasts
- Holy Land Video Tours
- Audio, Print, and Video Sermons
- Multi-Lingual PDF Library
- MP3 and Book Library
- Online Shopping
- E-newsletter

Whether you choose to expand your spiritual horizons from home, while you're at work, or in quick moments spread throughout your busy day, our interactive website is here to serve you in your Christian walk.

Visit Us Today

Discover The Book Ministries
A Nonprofit 501(c)3 Bible Teaching Ministry